NOTABLE AMERICAN NOVELISTS

NOTABLE AMERICAN NOVELISTS

Volume 3
Tim O'Brien — Richard Wright
811 – 1196
Index

edited by
CARL ROLLYSON

SALEM PRESS, INC.
Pasadena, California   Hackensack, New Jersey

Some of these essays originally appeared in *Critical Survey of Long Fiction, English Language Series: Revised Edition*,
1991. New material has been added.

∞ The paper used in these volumes conforms to the
American National Standard for Permanence of Paper
for Printed Library Materials, Z39.48-1992 (R1997).

Library of Congress Cataloging-in-Publication Data
Notable American novelists / editor, Carl Rollyson
      p.   cm. — (Magill's choice)
  Includes bibliographical references and index.
  ISBN 0-89356-161-4 (set : alk. paper). — ISBN
0-89356-162-2 (v. 1 : alk. paper). — ISBN 0-89356-163-0
(v. 2 : alk. paper). — ISBN 0-89356-164-9 (v. 3 : alk.
paper)
    1. American fiction—Bio-bibliography Dictionaries.
2. Novelists, American—Biography Dictionaries. 3. American fiction Dictionaries I. Rollyson, Carl. II. Series.
PS371.N68   2000
813.009′03—dc21
[B]   99-34407
                                           CIP

Second Printing

PRINTED IN THE UNITED STATES OF AMERICA

Contents – Volume 3

O'Brien, Tim 811
O'Connor, Flannery 816
O'Hara, John 824

Percy, Walker 837
Porter, Katherine Anne 850
Potok, Chaim 858
Price, Reynolds 867
Pynchon, Thomas 878

Rand, Ayn 889
Reed, Ishmael 894
Rice, Anne 904
Roth, Philip 909

Salinger, J. D. 920
Saroyan, William 929
Silko, Leslie Marmon 940
Sinclair, Upton 945
Stegner, Wallace 955
Stein, Gertrude 963
Steinbeck, John 975
Stowe, Harriet Beecher 985
Sturgeon, Theodore 997
Styron, William 1006

Tan, Amy 1020
Theroux, Paul 1025
Twain, Mark 1033
Tyler, Anne 1043

Updike, John 1059

Vidal, Gore 1072
Vonnegut, Kurt, Jr. 1082

Walker, Alice 1092
Welty, Eudora 1103
West, Nathanael 1114
Wharton, Edith 1121

Wilder, Thornton 1132
Woiwode, Larry 1140
Wolfe, Thomas 1148
Wouk, Herman 1159
Wright, Richard 1173

Terms and Techniques 1183
Time Line 1193
Index 1199

Complete List of Contents

Contents—Volume 1

Alcott, Louisa May, 1
Anaya, Rudolfo A., 8
Anderson, Sherwood, 13
Asimov, Isaac, 22
Auchincloss, Louis, 28
Baldwin, James, 39
Barth, John, 54
Beattie, Ann, 68
Bellow, Saul, 74
Bowles, Paul, 88
Boyle, T. Coraghessan, 97
Bradbury, Ray, 104
Brautigan, Richard, 115
Buck, Pearl S., 121
Burroughs, William S., 129
Cable, George Washington, 139
Capote, Truman, 147
Cather, Willa, 157
Chandler, Raymond, 168
Cheever, John, 180

Chopin, Kate, 193
Cooper, James Fenimore, 202
Coover, Robert, 215
Crane, Stephen, 225
Delany, Samuel R., 234
DeLillo, Don, 247
Dick, Philip K., 256
Dickey, James, 264
Didion, Joan, 270
Doctorow, E. L., 282
Donleavy, J. P., 291
Dos Passos, John, 299
Dreiser, Theodore, 308
Ellison, Ralph, 319
Erdrich, Louise, 330
Farrell, James T., 338
Faulkner, William, 345
Fitzgerald, F. Scott, 365
Gaddis, William, 378
Gardner, John, 388

Contents—Volume 2

Glasgow, Ellen, 403
Hammett, Dashiell, 411
Hawthorne, Nathaniel, 420
Heller, Joseph, 434
Hemingway, Ernest, 444
Hersey, John, 455
Hijuelos, Oscar, 462
Howells, William Dean, 467
Hurston, Zora Neale, 477
Irving, John, 485
James, Henry, 500
Jewett, Sarah Orne, 515
Jones, James, 526
Kennedy, William, 535
Kerouac, Jack, 543

Kesey, Ken, 553
Kincaid, Jamaica, 564
King, Stephen, 569
Kosinski, Jerzy, 583
Lee, Harper, 592
Le Guin, Ursula K., 597
Leonard, Elmore, 608
Lewis, Sinclair, 615
London, Jack, 627
Lurie, Alison, 635
McCarthy, Cormac, 644
McCarthy, Mary, 650
McCullers, Carson, 658
Macdonald, Ross, 668
McGuane, Thomas, 677

McMurtry, Larry, 686
Mailer, Norman, 697
Malamud, Bernard, 716
Melville, Herman, 727
Michener, James A., 736
Miller, Henry, 745

Morris, Wright, 754
Morrison, Toni, 765
Nabokov, Vladimir, 776
Naylor, Gloria, 785
Norris, Frank, 793
Oates, Joyce Carol, 801

Contents—Volume 3

O'Brien, Tim, 811
O'Connor, Flannery, 816
O'Hara, John, 824
Percy, Walker, 837
Porter, Katherine Anne, 850
Potok, Chaim, 858
Price, Reynolds, 867
Pynchon, Thomas, 878
Rand, Ayn, 889
Reed, Ishmael, 894
Rice, Anne, 904
Roth, Philip, 909
Salinger, J. D., 920
Saroyan, William, 929
Silko, Leslie Marmon, 940
Sinclair, Upton, 945
Stegner, Wallace, 955
Stein, Gertrude, 963
Steinbeck, John, 975

Stowe, Harriet Beecher, 985
Sturgeon, Theodore, 997
Styron, William, 1006
Tan, Amy, 1020
Theroux, Paul, 1025
Twain, Mark, 1033
Tyler, Anne, 1043
Updike, John, 1059
Vidal, Gore, 1072
Vonnegut, Kurt, Jr., 1082
Walker, Alice, 1092
Welty, Eudora, 1103
West, Nathanael, 1114
Wharton, Edith, 1121
Wilder, Thornton, 1132
Woiwode, Larry, 1140
Wolfe, Thomas, 1148
Wouk, Herman, 1159
Wright, Richard, 1173

TIM O'BRIEN

Born: Austin, Minnesota; October 1, 1946

Principal long fiction · *Northern Lights*, 1975; *Going After Cacciato*, 1978; *The Nuclear Age*, 1985; *In the Lake of the Woods*, 1994; *Tomcat in Love*, 1998.

Other literary forms · Tim O'Brien wrote magazine and newspaper articles about the Vietnam War while he was a soldier. He published articles on American politics as a reporter for the *Washington Post* in the mid-1970's. Popular magazines and literary quarterlies also published his short stories and essays. *If I Die in a Combat Zone, Box Me Up and Ship Me Home* (1973, revised 1989) contains partially fictionalized memoirs, and *The Things They Carried* (1990) collects short stories that are also closely based upon his tour of duty in Vietnam. Some critics consider these books loosely organized, episodic novels.

Achievements · O'Brien won accolades from war veterans and literary critics for his fiction and memoirs concerning the Vietnam War. In 1976 and 1978 he received the O. Henry Memorial Award for chapters of *Going After Cacciato*, which also earned for him the National Book Award in 1979. He won the Vietnam Veterans of America Award in 1987 and, the same year, the National Magazine Award in Fiction for the short story "The Things They Carried." In 1990, he was awarded the Heartland Prize from the *Chicago Tribune*, and in 1991 he was nominated for both the National Book Critics Circle's Melcher Book Award and the Pulitzer Prize for *The Things They Carried*. He also received France's Prix du Meilleur Livre Étranger for that book and the James Fenimore Cooper Prize of the Society of American Historians for *In the Lake of the Woods*. O'Brien held fellowships from the National Academy of Arts, Breadloaf Writers' Conference, the American Academy of Arts and Letters, and the Guggenheim Foundation.

Biography · William Timothy O'Brien, Jr., was born in Austin, Minnesota, in 1946, placing him among the baby-boom generation, which would become eligible for the draft during the Vietnam War (1964-1973). His father was an insurance salesman and a World War II combat veteran; his mother, Ava Schultz O'Brien, was an elementary school teacher. When O'Brien was nine years old, the family, which included a younger sister and brother, moved to Worthington, near the Minnesota-Iowa border, and he grew up there. His childhood, by his own account, was lonely. He played baseball and golf but occupied himself mainly with magic and reading.

After high school, O'Brien attended Macalester College and majored in political science. He participated in protests against the Vietnam War, wrote antiwar editorials for the college newspaper, and canvassed in support of Senator Eugene McCarthy's presidential campaign in 1968. He was elected student-body president his senior year. Immediately after graduating with a bachelor's degree, summa cum laude, he was drafted into the army. Despite his hatred for the war, he quelled the urge to flee to Canada and was trained as an infantryman.

In February, 1969, he arrived at an advanced firebase in Quang Ngai Province,

Republic of Vietnam. Nearby was My Lai, a hamlet where troops from O'Brien's division had murdered as many as five hundred civilians in one day. O'Brien, like most Americans, did not learn about the massacre there until one year later. For most of every month his company patrolled a deadly combat zone, battling the Viet Cong and constantly terrified of land mines, disease, and the prospect of appearing cowardly. He saw many wounds and deaths. In fact, he was wounded by shrapnel from a grenade, and his best friend died in a skirmish, two events that deeply affected him. Even before leaving the country, he published accounts of his experience in Minnesota newspapers and *Playboy* magazine.

After his discharge in 1970, O'Brien studied at the Harvard School of Government. In 1973 he published *If I Die in a Combat Zone, Box Me Up and Ship Me Home*, and he joined the staff of the *Washington Post*, reporting on national affairs. He married Ann Elizabeth Weller, an editorial assistant; they divorced eighteen years later. After a year at the *Post*, he returned to his studies at Harvard but left before completing a degree in order to become a writer. In the meantime he had published his first novel.

After finishing his fourth novel, *In the Lake of the Woods*, in 1994, O'Brien stopped writing, complaining that he was "burned out." With his girlfriend and a *New York Times* photographer, he returned to Vietnam. It was an emotional visit, during which he searched for the Quang Ngai firebase of his infantry company, spoke with Vietnamese veterans, and interviewed survivors of the My Lai massacre. In a famous *New York Times Magazine* article, "The Vietnam in Me" (1994), he told how the experience brought him close to suicide but finally helped him purge some of his anxious obsession with the war. Living in an apartment near Harvard, he resumed writing, in 1998 publishing *Tomcat in Love*. Although the Vietnam War influences the plot, it does so far less than in his previous fiction.

Analysis · O'Brien draws material for his novels from his own experience. He uses imagination and fiction to find meaning in these experiences, and because he was part of defining events of the post-World War II generation, the passions and ideas in his novels appeal to American readers with broad differences in political allegiance and social background. Having fought in Vietnam, O'Brien can create fictional soldiers so realistic in attitude, speech, and behavior that readers who are veterans of the war readily identify with them. An activist in the antiwar movement of the 1960's, O'Brien likewise draws faithful imitations of the political rebels of the times. A former graduate student in political science and a campaign worker, O'Brien offers fictional politicians convincingly lifelike enough to appeal to the American passion for political scandal. Moreover, coming from a small town in the Midwest, O'Brien (and some of his characters) appears to fulfill a particularly American literary convention: the small-town kid who does well for himself in the outside world. His characters include a university professor, a wealthy geologist, and a lieutenant governor.

Some critics complain that the distinction between historical or personal facts and fiction is blurred in O'Brien's work. Indeed, the "Tim O'Brien" who narrates his two volumes of memoirs is a fictionalized construct, as the author admitted. Similarly, he incorporates historical records, apparently quoted verbatim, in the novel *In the Lake of the Woods*. This mixing of fact and fiction, as well as of memory and fantasizing, underlies O'Brien's thematic interests, all of which concern his characters' emotional struggle during events, more than the verisimilitude or logic of the events themselves. The novels are intimately personal, psychological, and exploratory. Among the major themes are the relation between storytelling and truth, father-son relationships, true courage, the psychological effect of war, loneliness, magic, and obsession.

To develop such themes, O'Brien uses narrative techniques that give readers access to the minds of characters, in order to portray their reactions to events in the plot. *Northern Lights, Going After Cacciato,* and *In the Lake of the Woods* are told from the third-person point of view either of an unnamed narrator or of a narrator whom readers are encouraged to identify with the author. This narrator recounts the thoughts and emotions of characters so that readers may empathize with their confusion and obsessions. *The Nuclear Age* and *Tomcat in Love* both employ the first-person point of view of the main character. Some episodes are told in the present tense and some in the past tense, as the characters reminisce. These techniques enable O'Brien to place the reader even more intimately in the minds of characters and display the tricky, often self-deluding action of memory. Moreover, rapid changes from past to present, changes from one story line to another within a novel's plot, intricate wordplay, and dreamlike sequences immerse readers in the mental states of the principal characters.

O'Brien told interviewers that he was obsessed with American writer Ernest Hemingway as a youth. Hemingway's influence is apparent. O'Brien writes in short, crisp sentences that often derive their power from vivid verbs. He relies on extensive dialogue and uses description more to reflect the impressions of his main characters than to construct a visually detailed setting. Unlike Hemingway, O'Brien frequently uses fragmentary sentences and questions to imitate the thought processes of characters, especially when they are under stress. Cumulatively, his style establishes an energetic narrative pace.

Going After Cacciato · *Going After Cacciato,* O'Brien's second published novel, was his first critical and popular success. A best-seller, it quickly earned notoriety as one of the first serious literary treatments of the Vietnam War, winning the National Book Award in 1979, and it remained a classic statement of the war's bewildering effects on the young Americans drafted to fight there. Paul Berlin, the point-of-view character, is a member of an infantry platoon. With his platoon he chases one of their number who has deserted, Cacciato ("the hunted" in Italian). Cacciato has vowed to escape the war and walk all the way to Paris, a crazy idea that nevertheless earns him admiration among the other soldiers. They catch Cacciato near the Laotian border, and the literal plot is over. While on guard duty, however, Berlin fantasizes. He imagines that Cacciato constantly manages to evade them, and the platoon must pursue him to Paris. He dreams up grotesque adventures in countries along the route, some hilarious escapades, some adolescent sexual fantasies, and some chilling encounters. His fantasies interrupt and blend into the literal story of the chase, giving the narrative a nightmarish quality. Berlin and his fellow soldiers are innocents trapped in a corrupt, bizarre world, but the only character who seems truly courageous in the story is Cacciato. Even though his desertion is a nonsensical gesture, it frees him from the compromises to which the others cling: acceding to the draft, fighting a war that few believe in, conforming so as to not endure shame and disapproval.

In the Lake of the Woods · *In the Lake of the Woods* is O'Brien's most disturbing novel. It is an attempt, he contends, to understand evil. The story opens at the Lake of the Woods in northern Minnesota. John and Kathy Wade are on vacation, trying to knit together an unraveling marriage and lives in disarray. Lieutenant governor of the state, Wade has just lost the primary election for the U.S. Senate because news stories have revealed that he took part in the My Lai massacre in Vietnam. As a soldier, Wade was known as Wizard, a nickname he earned for his magic tricks, but the importance of deception and illusion is deep in his psyche, and he manages to erase most records of his involvement in the massacre, escape court-martial, and keep the secret even from his wife. As the story of his war experience, political career, and family life unfolds, the distinction between truth and the illusions he creates blur in his mind— and in the reader's. However, interrupting the narrative are sections called "Evidence," which contain transcripts of actual court-martial testimony and quotations from history books. These brief sections give the story historical perspective and keep it from turning completely into Wade's illusion.

The war haunts Wade; his failure to maintain protective illusions drives him toward madness. When his wife disappears from their cabin, Wade cooperates with the authorities in searching for her, but it becomes gradually apparent that Wade himself has murdered her. What is not clear, however, is whether he understands what he has done, so lost is he in self-delusions about his past. The end of the book is ambiguous. As the authorities increasingly suspect him of murder, Wade takes a speed boat out onto the lake, and his purpose seems to be to find his wife, escape the law, and commit suicide at the same time. Since this muddled behavior resulted from a lonely childhood and the My Lai massacre, Vietnam is cast as a pervasive, mysterious, malign burden on Wade and his generation.

Tomcat in Love · *Tomcat in Love* is a comic novel in texture but a serious work in intent; it reexamines the themes of love and disaster, storytelling and truth, and obsession. Thomas H. Chippering is a tenured professor of linguistics whose wife has divorced him. Told in flashbacks, the novel is a record of their relationship, beginning in childhood and continuing with marriage, her departure, and his desperate crusade to win her back and to punish her family for causing the divorce. Chippering is pompous, vindictive, pedantic, obsessed with words, and bent on trying to seduce every woman he encounters. He is blind to to his own faults and to the feelings of those around him, constantly interpreting himself in a suave, heroic light. He has even fabricated a record as a hero in Vietnam to impress others. (Although the war does not dominate the story as it does in O'Brien's previous novel, it figures in the plot.) Much of the situational humor comes from Chippering's obvious self-delusions and the ridiculous mistakes he makes about others. His ex-wife spurns him, he loses his faculty position because of student complaints of sexual harassment, he becomes engaged to a woman whose first name he cannot bring himself to use, his ex-brother-in-law publicly humiliates him, and he eventually discovers that his ex-wife, contrary to what he always believed, is even crazier than he is. Chippering has a few redeeming features that rescue the story from simple farce. His obsession is with the human heart, and he pursues the ambiguities of love with unflagging persistence, much as Miguel de Cervantes' Don Quixote pursued chivalry. Finally, he transcends his obsession and grows spiritually, learning to treat others, women especially, as human beings rather than as objects to manipulate or adore.

Roger Smith

Other major works

SHORT FICTION: *The Things They Carried*, 1990.

NONFICTION: *If I Die in a Combat Zone, Box Me Up and Ship Me Home*, 1973, rev. 1989; "The Vietnam in Me" (*The New York Times Magazine*, October 2, 1994).

Bibliography

Beidler, Philip D. *American Literature and the Experience of Vietnam.* Athens: University of Georgia Press, 1982. Beidler devotes chapters to *If I Die in a Combat Zone, Box Me Up and Ship Me Home* and *Going After Cacciato.* He treats both as O'Brien's attempt to solidify some meaning from the nightmare of combat in a war with an unclear purpose.

Herzog, Tobey C. *Tim O'Brien.* New York: Twayne, 1997. Herzog explains the autobiographical elements in O'Brien's novels and the role of imagination in understanding their meaning. Chapters concern O'Brien's background, writing style, portrayal of soldiering, treatment of love, and the anti-Vietnam War movement. Herzon emphasizes that mystery and ambiguity are fundamental characteristics of O'Brien's fiction. A chronology and bibliography accompany the discussions.

Kaplan, Steven. *Understanding Tim O'Brien.* Columbia: University of South Carolina Press, 1994. In the introductory chapter, Kaplan stresses the importance of storytelling, memory, and imagination in O'Brien's life and fiction. Subsequent chapters explicate O'Brien's first five books, particularly their theme of courage. Generous bibliography. A concise, lucid introduction to O'Brien's work.

Myers, Thomas Robert. *Walking Point: American Narratives of Vietnam.* New York: Oxford University Press, 1988. Myers surveys the American literary reaction to Vietnam, discussing *If I Die in a Combat Zone, Box Me Up and Ship Me Home* in the context of personal narratives about the war. As well as explaining the theme of courage, the book provides critical background for readers interested in comparing O'Brien's contribution with those of his contemporaries.

FLANNERY O'CONNOR

Born: Savannah, Georgia; March 25, 1925
Died: Milledgeville, Georgia; August 3, 1964

Principal long fiction · *Wise Blood*, 1952; *The Violent Bear It Away*, 1960.

Other literary forms · Flannery O'Connor, most renowned as a writer of short fiction, published the short-story collection *A Good Man Is Hard to Find* in 1955; her canon also includes two posthumous collections, *Everything That Rises Must Converge* (1965) and *The Complete Stories* (1971). Three posthumous nonfiction works provide insight into her craft and thought: *Mystery and Manners* (1969), a collection of her occasional lectures and essays on literary art; *The Habit of Being: Letters* (1979), which consists of letters compiled by her literary executor, Sally Fitzgerald; and *The Presence of Grace* (1983), a collection of her book reviews.

Achievements · O'Connor's art was best suited to the medium of the short story, where her sharp, shocking, and grotesque characterizations could have full impact on the reader. Nevertheless, her depiction of the Christ-haunted Hazel Motes in *Wise Blood* ranks as the most memorable and piercing postmodern delineation of Western society's anxiety over God's absence. O'Connor's ability to create supernatural tension, to provoke the potentially hostile reader into considering the possibility of divine invasion of the human sphere, is unparalleled by any postwar writer. Seeing "by the light of Christian orthodoxy," O'Connor refused to chisel away or compromise her convictions to make them more congenial to her readers. She knew that it is difficult to place the Christian faith in front of the contemporary reader with any credibility, but her resolve was firm. She understood, in the words of the late John Gardner (*On Moral Fiction*, 1978), that "art which tries to tell the truth unretouched is difficult and often offensive," since it "violates our canons of politeness and humane compromise." O'Connor succeeded not in making Christianity more palatable but in making its claims unavoidable.

O'Connor was committed not only to telling the "truth unretouched" but also to telling a good story. This meant rejecting predetermined morals—homilies tacked onto stories and processed uncritically by her readers: "When you can state the theme of a story, when you can separate it from the story itself, then you can be sure the story is not a very good one." Instead of literary proselytizing, she offered a literature of evangelism, of incarnation, a fusing of literary form with authorial vision. Her evangelistic mode was not proselytizing, but *proclaiming*, the ancient and more honorable practice of declaring news, of heralding its goodness to a usually indifferent, sometimes hostile audience. O'Connor had a keen perception of her audience's mindset and cultural milieu; her proclamation was calculated to subvert the habitualization of faith and to make such notions as redemption, resurrection, and eternal life seem new and strange to a Western society that had reduced them to commonplaces empty of significance. Readers and critics continue to respond to O'Connor's clear spiritual vision and piercing narrative style, a style uncluttered by a false pluralism or sectarian debate. O'Connor, the devout Catholic, neither preached nor compelled; she simply proclaimed.

Biography · Mary Flannery O'Connor was born in Savannah, Georgia, in 1925 and moved with her mother to Milledgeville, Georgia, in 1938. She took her B.A. degree from Women's College of Georgia in 1945 and received an M.F.A. degree from the State University of Iowa in 1947. She published her first short story, "The Geranium" (*Accent,* 1946), during her years in Iowa. In 1947, she won the Rinehart-Iowa fiction award for a first novel with a portion of *Wise Blood.*

Joe McTyre

On the strength of this award and her promise as a writer, O'Connor was offered a fellowship by the Yaddo Foundation. She accepted and spent several months at Saratoga Springs, New York, but eventually returned to Milledgeville. A few months later, O'Connor moved in with the Robert Fitzgerald family in Connecticut to complete *Wise Blood.* A serious illness, lupus erythematosus, redirected her life in 1951 back to Milledgeville; there she would do the rest of her writing, and there she would die in 1964. From Milledgeville, she carried on a lively correspondence with friends, readers, critics, and her editors at Farrar and Giroux. When health permitted, she made trips to colleges and universities, many of them Catholic schools, to discuss her work and literary art.

O'Connor won a Kenyon Review fellowship in fiction in 1953, a National Institute of Arts and Letters grant in 1957, and an O. Henry first prize in short fiction in 1957. She also was granted honorary degrees from St. Mary's College (1962) and Smith College (1963). She spent the last months of her life completing the stories eventually published in her posthumous collection *Everything That Rises Must Converge. The Complete Stories* won the National Book Award for Fiction in 1971.

Analysis · Few postmodern writers have spoken as articulately and as compellingly about their craft and the relationship of their fiction to its perceived audience as did Flannery O'Connor. In her occasional prose, in her letters, and in her book reviews, O'Connor evinced an uncommonly perceptive grasp of her readers and the society in which they lived. Addressing the children of a demythologized and desacralized century, she confronted boldly the rancor and apathy with which modern culture meets the religious and the supernatural. To shake and sharpen the sensibilities of a culture made lethargic by the heritage of American civil religion, she turned to shock, to the literally awful and the grotesque, to proclaim her gospel: "To the hard of hearing you shout, and for the almost-blind you draw large and startling figures."

The underlying premise which informs all of O'Connor's fiction, and especially her two novels, *Wise Blood* and *The Violent Bear It Away*, is that men and women, as they are, are not *whole*. This "wholeness," lost in Eden, is now embodied and supplied to humans freely in the person of the incarnate Son of God. In order to make this now familiar theme "seeable" and creditable to her readers, O'Connor was led to herald a Christ who bore little resemblance to the "gentle Jesus, meek and mild" of childhood hymnody. Her Christ is a tiger who disturbs and terrorizes. One thinks especially of Hazel Motes, evangelist of the "Church of Christ without Christ" in *Wise Blood*, who fights ferociously to avoid that Jesus "in the back of his mind, a wild, ragged figure motioning to him to turn around and come off into the dark where he was not sure of his footing, where he might be walking on water and not know it and suddenly know it and drown."

Motes is a child of the fundamentalist South, but in O'Connor's economy, he is also Everyman; those who refuse Christ's offer to help them, force Him to haunt them. O'Connor used sudden death, disease, or trauma to depict the devastating encounter with Christ which must occur before one can be truly alive in this world. Worse things than mere death can befall a person made in God's image; her characters more often than not must be brought to the brink of crisis or death to see themselves as they are: in dire need of repentance and grace. In O'Connor's view, humankind did not accidentally stumble into rebellion against God; each man or woman deliberately chooses to do so. Consequently, she records with merciless precision the rationalizations of her protagonists, stripping them bare of their pretensions of goodness and innocence. She endeavored to confront her readers with the full scandal of Christianity. Those O'Connor characters who attempt to redeem themselves with arrant scientism or sheer intellectualism meet a savage Savior—manifested in a bull, a haunting prophecy, or a terrifying vision—who will not release them until they confess Him or utterly denounce Him.

For O'Connor, there was no middle ground, no neutral corner; all who are not with Him are against Him. Her narrative voice had little room for authorial compassion or tenderness. Relentlessly exposing human pride, avarice, and weakness, she agreed with writer C. S. Lewis that all things that are not eternal are eternally out of date. Western culture was already too sentimental, too complacent about Christ and Christianity; her mission was to pound on the table, to cast the moneychangers—sacred or secular—out of the literary temple.

One must ask how O'Connor avoided mere tractarianism, as her continuing popularity among critics and ubiquity in college literature anthologies attest she did. Part of the answer is that she frankly confronted the tenuous relationships which exist among audience, medium, story, and craft. It was her genius to lead her readers through and from the seemingly mundane and ordinary to a vision of reality as sacramental, as always pointing to a divine presence in human activity. "When I write a novel in which the central action is baptism, I am aware that for a majority of my readers, baptism is a meaningless rite . . . so I have to see that this baptism carries enough awe and mystery to jar the reader into some kind of emotional recognition of its significance." Her fiction strips away the jaded images of the faith, forcing a dynamic confrontation with the gospel as it is played out in the lives of professed believers and as it is rejected by the worldly wise. As the reader follows Hazel Motes or Francis Marion Tarwater on his journey to belief, he is confronted with grace–a grace that enlarges his perception of the world, enabling him to see both the natural and the supernatural anew, to both discover and retrieve deeper images of the *real*. As O'Connor states it, this journey frequently entails "an action in which the devil has been the unwilling instrument of grace. This is not a piece of knowledge that I consciously put into my stories; it is a discovery that I get out of them." It is this "awful rowing toward God" that is chronicled in O'Connor's two novels, *Wise Blood* and *The Violent Bear It Away*.

Wise Blood · Hazel Motes, the protagonist of *Wise Blood*, is, O'Connor says, a "Christian *malgrè lui*," a believer in spite of himself, a harried wayfarer who has been displaced from Eastrod, Tennessee, and from the religious life of the South. That religious life is distinctively Protestant, the religion of a South of beleaguered prophets and street-corner preachers, a South haunted by Jesus and by a theological definition of man's identity and destiny. Motes is determined to escape salvation and anything that smacks of supernatural origin. Like Francis Marion Tarwater in *The Violent Bear It Away*, Motes's story is a reverse *Bildungsroman*, a novel of an antiquest in which the protagonist tries to *avoid*, rather than *seek*, his destiny.

O'Connor maintained that *Wise Blood* is a "comic novel," and nonetheless so because it deals with "matters of life and death." Though many readers try to locate the integrity of Motes in his vigorous struggle to escape that "ragged figure moving from tree to tree in the back of his mind," O'Connor avers: "His integrity lies in his not being able to [escape] it." His attempted flight from Jesus begins on the train to Taulkinham. Discharged from military service, Motes parries with a Mrs. Hitchcock, challenging her claim to redemption. "If you've been redeemed," Motes snaps, "I wouldn't want to be." Later, he exclaims to no one in particular, "Do you think I believe in Jesus? . . . Well, I wouldn't even if He existed. Even if He was on this train." Motes has determined that the way to avoid Jesus is to avoid sin; one who is not a sinner needs no redemption–he is already "clean"–if he is free from transgression. This "freedom," however, does not mean that Motes can avoid becoming a preacher. When he first reaches the city and decides to look up Miss Leora Watts–who owns the "Friendliest Bed in Town"–both she and the cabdriver who brings him there accuse him of being a preacher; he simply looks the part.

Very soon, Motes encounters some potential disciples: Enoch Emery, who wants to help him find a "new jesus," and Sabbath Lily Hawks, the lustful daughter of a street preacher who feigns blindness. Following Sabbath and her father in order to ridicule their shallow evangelism, Motes declares that he will start a new church, a church *without* Christ. "I don't need Jesus," he tells the crowd gathering about him, "I got Leora Watts." Motes's obsession with the Hawks duo leads him to drive around the city in his beat-up Essex. His desperate flight from belief compels him to hound Asa Hawks, confronting him with the strange fact of his blindness–if Jesus is real, then why does He not heal His servants? Motes is tortured by his lack of a theodicy, a defense of God's absence; his only solace is to throw himself into his own "ministry": street-side preaching of the "Church of Christ without Christ" from the hood of his Essex.

His nightly forays into sermonizing yield only one "convert," a would-be Aaron to Motes's Moses, Onnie Jay Holy–a slick packager of religion and faith who knows a money-making scam when he sees it. Crediting Motes-the-prophet with changing his life, Holy drowns out the frustrated antipreacher, who learns to speak the truth in spite of himself: "Listen!" Motes screams. "It don't cost you any money to know the truth!" It is at this point that O'Connor's protagonist has begun his inexorable trek toward recognizing his true state and the call of God. When Enoch Emery answers Motes's call for a "new jesus" by stealing a mummified pygmy from a local museum and delivering it to the now domesticated Sabbath Lily Hawks, the reader is introduced to what Caroline Gordon called "the unholy family." Slinking into Motes's room, Sabbath introduces the mummy as their child. Sensing the blasphemy of the moment, Motes seizes the mummy and crushes it against the wall. The prophet must now leave this desecrated place and search for a new city in which he can begin his ministry afresh. Before he can leave, however, he must confront a false prophet–hired by Hoover Shoats, née Onnie Jay Holy–who has supplanted him on the streets of Taulkinham. Following him out onto a lonely road, Motes first knocks his car into the ditch and then runs over his counterpart, killing him and thus carrying out the Old Testament vengeance against false prophets.

From here, Motes inevitably heads for his own Calvary, his own "death unto life": The words of Jesus in Matthew 5:29, "And if thy right eye offend thee, pluck it out," are taken literally. Motes blinds himself so that he can see with a spiritual vision which bogus believers such as Asa Hawks and Hoover Shoats can never attain. He is fully focused now; there is no intent to escape or flee. His landlady, Mrs. Flood, represents the kind of "Christian" O'Connor loved to contrast with her dramatic, utterly committed antisaints such as Hazel Motes, the Misfit in "A Good Man Is Hard to Find," and Manley Pointer in "Good Country People." She cannot fathom Motes's sudden devotion–which extended to the bearing of the marks of Christ on his body: "I'm as good, Mr. Motes, not believing in Jesus as many a one that does," she boastfully proclaims. When she sees the barbed wire wrapped around his chest, she exclaims, "There's no reason for it. People have quit doing it." His reply, anthem and testimony for all latter-day believers, seals his fate: "They ain't quit doing it as long as I'm doing it." Motes's death is as anticlimactic as Christ's; the policemen who discover him in the drainage ditch, like the soldiers at the foot of the cross who bargain for Christ's robe, mouth inanities and treat Motes as a troublesome derelict, quite worthy of being put out of his misery.

The story of Hazel Motes is the tale of one of God's creatures and his struggle with the fundamental choice to serve God or deny Him. O'Connor's avowed purpose was to "deepen the mystery of free will," which is not the war between one will and another but of "many wills conflicting in one man." In *Wise Blood*, whose title comes from Enoch Emery's claim to "know things" because of his ancestral blood, O'Connor has created a parable of twentieth century man's inner debate over God's existence and presence in the modern world. It is ironic, although not too surprising, that O'Connor's Christian readers sometimes responded less enthusiastically to her achievement than did her nonreligious readers. Such a response was simply a corroboration of O'Connor's perceptions regarding the state of belief in postwar America.

The Violent Bear It Away · In her second novel, *The Violent Bear It Away*, written some ten years after she had originally begun *Wise Blood*, O'Connor once again returned to the theme of the antiquest, this time with a protagonist who tries to escape the daunting prophecy of his great-uncle. The title comes from an ambiguous passage found in Matthew 11:12: "From the days of John the Baptist until now, the kingdom of heaven suffereth violence and the violent bear it away." It is the dual message of this scripture which, in part, gives the novel its underlying power as still another O'Connor portrayal of the conflict of wills within man, a conflict of reason tempered with godly knowledge and an uncritical, gullible trust in the scientific method. The passage suggests, first, that with the coming of the promised Messiah, humankind can receive the kingdom of God; second, it suggests that there remain calloused and unprincipled unbelievers who will seek to bar the faithful from entering that hallowed ground. These two opposing forces are focused in the protagonist and antagonist of the novel: Francis Marion Tarwater and Rayber the schoolteacher.

Mason Tarwater had reared his nephew, Francis, to be "more than a Christian, a prophet." His prophetic task consisted of two matters: First, he was to make sure that the elder Tarwater had a proper burial, his gravesite marked by a cross; second, he was to baptize Bishop, the "dimwitted child" of Rayber. Mason had earlier tried to rear Rayber as a prophet, too, but he encountered a resistance which eventually turned into a vigorously antireligious posture. Mason Tarwater had finally broken off all relations with Rayber after the latter wrote a psychoanalysis of Tarwater for a "schoolteacher's magazine" which mocked his beliefs. Francis Tarwater, also, does not come easily to his prophetic office. At his great-uncle's death, he abandons the old man and burns down his house, balking at his obsession with Jesus; the choice is not between "Jesus and the devil," he resolves—"it's Jesus or me." Francis, like Hazel Motes, is nevertheless haunted by the presence of Jesus: "Jesus? He felt a terrible disappointment in that conclusion, a dread that it was true." He can no more escape his destiny than Motes could; it is "hidden in the blood."

Rayber is a familiar O'Connor character type, the rationalist who attempts to explain away religion as illusion or delusion. He will have no part of the Tarwaters' prophetic ministry. Just as the sense of sight was a potent symbol in *Wise Blood*, O'Connor here uses the sense of hearing, Rayber's need for a hearing aid, to underscore his spiritual ignorance: "Do you think in the box," Francis Tarwater ridiculed, "or do you think in your head?" The religious people of Rayber's acquaintance—the Tarwaters, the Carmody family—have all been "exploited" people, bilked by the foolish rhetoric of insane cadgers and shysters. Yet Rayber's will is not powerful enough to withstand the force of a prophet of God. True to his call, Francis must drown Bishop in baptism, the enduring Christian symbol of new life from death.

O'Connor organized the events of this novel into three distinct parts. Part 1 reveals the eccentric life of the prophet; as Elijah the Old Testament prophet gave his mantle to the younger Elisha, so Mason Tarwater passes his own "burden" to his charge. Part 2 depicts Francis Tarwater's struggle to free himself, like a latter-day Jonah, from the burden laid upon him; here the city is emblematic of all the distractions and temptations that might deter him from his task. Part 3 relates the purification and cleansing of the prophet who encounters his burning bush and receives his commission to "warn the children of God of the terrible speed of mercy" in the "dark city" beyond him.

The Violent Bear It Away develops more fully themes O'Connor explored in such short stories as "The Enduring Chill," "The Artificial Nigger," "Good Country People," and "The Lame Shall Enter First." Her consistent focus is placed upon the human will tortured by indecision, clouded by technology, and rendered impotent by its flight from knowledge of God. The only remedy offered is the laying down of weapons and the complete surrender of the soul. Francis Tarwater and Hazel Motes both discover that their only rest from this ordeal is acquiesence to the will of God.

Throughout her fiction, O'Connor defamiliarized the all-too-familiar concepts of conversion and discipleship and articulated the shallow view of Christ lurking behind modern faith. She wanted her readers to escape the jaundiced vision of their own time. In *Mystery and Manners*, she paralleled her task with that of St. Cyril of Jerusalem, who, in instructing catechumens, warned them of passing by the dragon on their way to the Father of Souls:

> No matter what form the dragon may take, it is of this mysterious passage past him, or into his jaws, that stories of any depth will always be concerned to tell, and this being the case, it requires considerable courage at any time, in any country, not to turn away from the storyteller.

O'Connor refused to turn away from the dragon or the storyteller, and she asked of her readers the same courage.

Bruce L. Edwards, Jr.

Other major works

SHORT FICTION: *A Good Man Is Hard to Find*, 1955; *Everything That Rises Must Converge*, 1965; *The Complete Stories*, 1971.

NONFICTION: *Mystery and Manners*, 1969; *The Habit of Being: Letters*, 1979; *The Presence of Grace*, 1983; *The Correspondence of Flannery O'Connor and Brainard Cheneys*, 1986.

MISCELLANEOUS: *Collected Works*, 1988.

Bibliography

Asals, Frederick. *Flannery O'Connor: The Imagination of Extremity*. Athens: University of Georgia Press, 1982. Asals' stated intention in this volume is to point out thematic patterns which he believes are consistent throughout all of O'Connor's fiction. As a result, this study is comprehensive, dealing with lesser-known works as fully as with those usually treated. Includes an introduction containing a useful analysis of O'Connor criticism, a full bibliography, and an index.

Desmond, John F. *Risen Sons: Flannery O'Connor's Vision of History*. Athens: University of Georgia Press, 1987. Traces O'Connor's artistic development in the context of her spiritual development. Desmond's assumption is that O'Connor's Christianity, and particularly her growing understanding of the principle of redemption, dominates her fiction. A complete bibliography and an index are provided.

Enjolras, Laurence. *Flannery O'Connor's Characters*. Lanham, MD: University Press of America, 1998. Chapters on O'Connor's descriptions of the body, of wicked children, of "conceited, self-righteous Christians," of "intellectuals and would-be artists." Includes notes and bibliography.

Orvell, Miles. *Flannery O'Connor: An Introduction*. Jackson: University Press of Mississippi, 1991. Chapters on the novels as well as explorations of O'Connor's treatment of the South, of belief, of art, of the American romance tradition, of prophets and failed prophets, and of comedy. Appendices include a chronological list of the fiction, book reviews by Flannery O'Connor, notes, and bibliography.

Paulson, Suzanne Morrow. *Flannery O'Connor: A Study of the Short Fiction*. Boston: Twayne, 1988. In addition to an excellent critical analysis of O'Connor's short stories, Paulson's volume contains relevant comments by O'Connor, her friends and acquaintances, and her editors. Concludes with a collection of excerpts from various critics, a bibliography, and an index.

Rath, Sura P., and Mary Neff Shaw, eds. *Flannery O'Connor: New Perspectives.* Athens: University of Georgia Press, 1996. Essays on the development and reception of O'Connor's career, her treatment of gender, race, and religion. Includes a bibliography.

Stephens, Martha. *The Question of Flannery O'Connor.* Baton Rouge: Louisiana State University Press, 1973. Stephens explores what she sees as an ambiguity in tone which is evident throughout O'Connor's fiction: on the one hand, the assertion of faith in Christianity, and on the other hand, a pervading pessimism, which suggests the improbability of redemption. Includes a useful annotated bibliography, a full list of sources, and an index.

JOHN O'HARA

Born: Pottsville, Pennsylvania; January 31, 1905
Died: Princeton, New Jersey; April 11, 1970

Principal long fiction · *Appointment in Samarra,* 1934; *Butterfield 8,* 1935; *A Rage to Live,* 1949; *The Farmer's Hotel,* 1951; *Ten North Frederick,* 1955; *A Family Party,* 1956; *From the Terrace,* 1958; *Ourselves to Know,* 1960; *Sermons and Soda Water,* 1960; *The Big Laugh,* 1962; *Elizabeth Appleton,* 1963; *The Lockwood Concern,* 1965; *The Instrument,* 1967; *Lovey Childs: A Philadelphian's Story,* 1969; *The Ewings,* 1972.

Other literary forms · John O'Hara was a prolific writer of short stories, and eleven volumes of stories were published during his lifetime. After O'Hara's death, Random House, his publisher since 1947, brought out two additional collections: *The Time Element and Other Stories* (1972) and *Good Samaritan and Other Stories* (1974). Scattered throughout the short-story collections are most of O'Hara's works in the novella form; the only novellas to be separately published are the three in *Sermons and Soda Water.* The play version of the story "Pal Joey" was published in 1952, and in 1961 it was reissued with four others in *Five Plays.* O'Hara's last complete play, *Far from Heaven* (1962), was first published posthumously in 1979, along with an unproduced original screenplay, *The Man Who Could Not Lose* (1959), under the title *Two by O'Hara.* Like many other writers of his period, O'Hara wrote and collaborated on film scripts from the 1930's through the 1950's, and several of his novels were made into films during his lifetime. O'Hara began his writing career as a journalist, and he was several times a newspaper columnist. Two collections of his columns were published: *Sweet and Sour* (1954)—columns written for the Trenton *Sunday Times-Advertiser*—and *My Turn* (1966), a series of syndicated columns written for *Newsday.* A collection of O'Hara's speeches, essays, and interviews, entitled *An Artist Is His Own Fault,* was edited by Matthew J. Bruccoli in 1977.

Achievements · Often dismissed as a popular novelist with tendencies toward sensationalism, or as a "social historian," O'Hara nevertheless secured a faithful following among many literary critics for his skill at storytelling and his evocation of times, places, and manners in American society in the first half of the twentieth century. O'Hara himself was equivocal about the label "social historian." In a speech in 1961, he said, "I deny that I am a social historian"; yet he went on to say that "before deciding to write a novel, I consider what opportunities a story offers for my comments on my times." Matthew J. Bruccoli is probably most accurate in calling O'Hara a "novelist of manners," in the sense that he was primarily concerned with the accurate depiction of a social matrix and its effect on human behavior and potential. Like William Faulkner and other twentieth century American novelists, O'Hara turned the realities of his hometown experience into a fictional world; unlike Faulkner, he probed this milieu with a dedication to social realism rather than elevating it to mythic status. In addition to his native eastern Pennsylvania, O'Hara used New York and Hollywood as frequent settings for his fiction. Although he lived and worked in both places, he is most clearly identified with the "Region" of Pennsylvania, on which he could bring to bear an insider's perceptions.

The fact that O'Hara was a realistic storyteller rather than an "experimental" novelist was detrimental to his critical reputation during his lifetime. Ironically, the explicit sexuality in much of his work (though restrained by today's standards), which was partially responsible for creating wide popular interest in his novels and which caused *Ten North Frederick* to be suppressed in several cities, overshadowed the depth of his concern with societal mores and pressures. Although he emphasized the role of fate and chance, O'Hara is usually considered a realist rather than a naturalist, largely because he allowed the possibility of moral choice. His long, detailed novels characteristically show people of a privileged socioeconomic level struggling with the realities of social class, personal worth, and complex human relationships.

O'Hara's treatment of his women characters has been overlooked by most critics, yet it may help to account for his enormous contemporary popularity. Long before it was fashionable or even allowable to do so, O'Hara realistically portrayed women as sexual human beings and even dealt openly with lesbianism in some of his novels and stories. Though several of his major female characters (such as Edith Chapin in *Ten North Frederick* and the title character of *Elizabeth Appleton*) are stereotypically manipulative, they are believable, complex people whose motivations are clearly the result of cultural pressures. It would be inaccurate to call O'Hara a feminist novelist, but he acknowledged women's power and their problems in ways that set him apart from most novelists of his period.

Whatever the eventual critical evaluation of O'Hara as a twentieth century American novelist, it is certain that his work will be used as a valuable resource for information about customs, manners, and attitudes in America from the 1920's through the 1950's, much as one consults the work of Theodore Dreiser, Sinclair Lewis, or John Updike. The ear for dialogue, the eye for detail, and the perception of human nature that made him a popular novelist will also ensure his continued importance.

Biography · John Henry O'Hara was born on January 31, 1905, in Pottsville, Pennsylvania. The town of Pottsville became the "Gibbsville" of his fiction, and the surrounding eastern Pennsylvania anthracite coal-mining area, known to residents as the "Region," was the locale of his major novels and stories. The author's father, Patrick O'Hara, was a doctor whose father had settled in the area during the Civil War, and his mother, Katharine Delaney O'Hara, was the daughter of a prosperous businessman in nearby Lykens, which became O'Hara's fictional "Lyons." Dr. Patrick O'Hara was a respected surgeon, necessarily specializing in injuries resulting from mining accidents, and he was seriously disappointed at his firstborn son's refusal to study medicine. Rather than inspiring a dedication to the medical profession, O'Hara's travels with his father to the scenes of medical emergencies provided him with regional lore which found its way into his writing.

Living on Pottsville's "best" street, Mahantongo ("Lantenengo" in the fictional Gibbsville), was a sign of the O'Hara family's relative affluence and provided O'Hara with an awareness of the rigid economic and ethnic stratification of the town. Until his father's early death in 1925, O'Hara led a fairly privileged existence, and his dream of attending Yale was thwarted less by lack of funds than by O'Hara's dismissals from three preparatory schools for low grades and disregard of discipline.

The alternative to college was a job as a reporter on the Pottsville *Journal* in 1924, which effectively launched O'Hara's career as a writer.

In 1928, O'Hara left Pottsville for New York, where he worked briefly for the *Herald-Tribune* and *Time* and began to contribute stories to *The New Yorker*, which eventually published more than two hundred of his short stories; accordingly, some have attributed to O'Hara the creation of that subgenre, the "*New Yorker* story." During these early years in New York, O'Hara established friendships with Franklin P. Adams (F. P. A.)–to whose New York *World* column "The Conning Tower" he sometimes contributed–Robert Benchley, Dorothy Parker, and F. Scott Fitzgerald. In 1931, he married Helen Ritchie Petit ("Pet"), but his heavy drinking and frequent unemployment led to a divorce in 1933.

Appointment in Samarra, the first of O'Hara's fifteen novels, was published in 1934, and his first collection of short stories, *The Doctor's Son and Other Stories,* appeared the following year. Although he was not financially secure for some time, O'Hara's reputation as a fiction writer grew steadily, and for the next twenty years, he lived alternately on the East Coast and in Hollywood, where he wrote film scripts. Although he intermittently aspired to be a playwright, O'Hara's only successful play was *Pal Joey,* based on a series of stories in *The New Yorker,* which ran on Broadway between 1940 and 1941. It was made into a film, starring Frank Sinatra and Rita Hayworth, in 1957. In 1956, O'Hara was given the National Book Award for *Ten North Frederick,* and in 1957 he was inducted into the National Institute of Arts and Letters, from which he resigned in 1961 because he had not been nominated for its Gold Medal for fiction.

In 1937, O'Hara was married for the second time, to Belle Mulford Wylie, the mother of his only child, Wylie Delaney O'Hara, born in 1945. The O'Haras moved to Princeton, New Jersey, in 1949, and in 1953, a serious ulcer condition prompted O'Hara to quit drinking permanently. Following Belle's death in 1954, O'Hara married Katharine Barnes Bryan ("Sister") in 1955, and the family moved two years later to Linebrook, a home in Princeton that O'Hara and Sister had designed. O'Hara died at Linebrook April 11, 1970, while working on a sequel to *The Ewings,* his last published novel.

Analysis · In the spring of 1960, John O'Hara wrote as part of his preface to *Sermons and Soda Water:* "The Twenties, the Thirties, and the Forties are already history, but I cannot be content to leave their story in the hands of the historians and the editors of picture books. I want to record the way people talked and thought and felt." Despite his frequent rejection of the seemingly derogatory critical label of "social historian," which seemed to separate him in the minds of critics from more "serious" novelists, O'Hara was committed throughout his career to providing accurate records of the decades and places in which he lived. The novels and novellas that resulted from this commitment are uneven in quality as examples of the art of fiction, but they provide an unmatched portrait of segments of American society in the first half of the century. The central characters of much of his fiction are wealthy, prominent people, whether they are the leading citizens of Gibbsville, Pennsylvania, or Hollywood film stars, yet O'Hara frequently illuminates their circumstances by juxtaposing them with members of other socioeconomic groups: servants, tradesmen, laborers. The result is a panoramic social canvas, consonant with O'Hara's conception of the traditional novel form. Occasionally, as in *From the Terrace,* the realist's attempt at panoramic vision overwhelms artistic control; as Sheldon Grebstein remarks in *John O'Hara* (1966), "the *tranche de vie* . . . has been cut too thick to be digestible." At his best, however, O'Hara's work reflects the rich diversity of American society, as in his counterpointing of the savvy political boss Mike Slattery and the wealthy, naïve, would-be politician Joe Chapin in *Ten North Frederick.*

As the example of politics suggests, one of O'Hara's major themes is power–not only the power of money, though that is a central metaphor, but also the power inherent in talent, morality, and sexuality. O'Hara shared with F. Scott Fitzgerald a fascination with wealth and social prestige, but his treatment of their influence is far more analytical. His novels typically trace the establishment of a family dynasty, as in *The Lockwood Concern*, or the progress of an individual's aspirations for himself or herself, as in *Ten North Frederick*, and *Elizabeth Appleton*–always within the constraints of a social web rendered palpable by realistic settings and dialogue. O'Hara is concerned particularly with showing the limits of human power, not in the face of an overwhelming fate, but as the result of miscalculation, error, or simple human frailty. When Julian English throws a drink in the face of Harry Reilly in *Appointment in Samarra*, or when George Lockwood, in *The Lockwood Concern*, builds a wall around his mansion, neither can foresee the fatal consequences, but both have made choices that dictate inevitable results.

As money is a metaphor for power in O'Hara's fiction, sexuality is an ambivalent metaphor for love. Though he was accused of sensationalism and bad taste in his relatively explicit depiction of sexual relationships, O'Hara was primarily interested in showing the potential for manipulation in the human sexual relationship. Women as well as men are portrayed as captive to sexual desire, and both sexes frequently mistake love for possession, or sex for love. From Grace Caldwell Tate's injudicious couplings in *A Rage to Live* to the tender relationship between Jim Malloy and Charlotte Sears in *The Girl on the Baggage Truck* (from *Sermons and Soda Water*), the possibility of true romantic love seems remote in O'Hara's fiction. His realistic approach assumes a basic human egotism and desire for power which renders such love rare.

Structure · The structures of O'Hara's novels and novellas reinforce the sense of inevitability of consequence. His novels frequently begin with an apparently small but significant event or action which spins out in mystery-story fashion to create the web that catches the characters and demonstrates their ultimate powerlessness. Yet he avoids the predictability of formulaic fiction by using multiple points of view and a wealth of complex, believable characters to play out the drama. In the novellas, the structure is frequently circular, the story beginning at a moment of culmination and then tracing the events which have brought the characters to that point. Common too, especially in the novellas, is O'Hara's use of a narrator, usually Jim Malloy, a journalist whose background and attitudes resemble those of O'Hara. Although these structural devices were not original with O'Hara, he used them skillfully to suit his fictional purposes.

Character is of supreme importance in O'Hara's fiction, and the achievement of adequate characterization determined the form he used. As he said in one of his Rider College lectures, "before I have finished two pages of manuscript my author's instinct has told me how much I want to tell about this character, and thus the length of the story is dictated." The majority of O'Hara's characters inhabit the Pennsylvania "Region" in which he spent his youth, and the fictional canon provides a vivid picture of relationships among people of various social levels over time. The reappearance of certain characters in many works reinforces the sense of a coherent world wherein the codes of morality and propriety dictate the shape of both society and individual human lives.

In its settings, characters, and incidents, O'Hara's fiction is strongly autobiographical, a circumstance which is a natural outgrowth of his desire to be a recorder of his times. Though he did not live in Pottsville, Pennsylvania, after 1930, the town and its people continued to serve as a microcosm of the American culture he dissected throughout his career. Like his autobiographical narrator Jim Malloy, O'Hara returned to Pottsville "only long enough to stand at a grave, to toast a bride, to spend a few minutes beside a sickbed," but the years he spent there left an indelible impression. From his vantage point as the doctor's son, O'Hara observed both the leading citizens and the transients, and later he explored, in his novels and novellas, the lives he imagined to exist behind the placid exterior of the American small town. Part of the autobiographical content of the fiction, however, comes from O'Hara's unfulfilled aspirations rather than from his actual experience. Although his dream of attending an Ivy League college was thwarted by his checkered prep school record and the death of his father, O'Hara's upper-class male characters typically attend prestigious universities and benefit from larger family fortunes than O'Hara's family ever enjoyed. His fiction, like that of Fitzgerald, thus conveys an ambivalent attitude toward the privileged: the wistfulness of the outsider and the realist's desire to reduce them to understandable human terms.

The span of O'Hara's career, from 1934 to 1970, coincided with a period of intense experimentation in literary forms. The fiction of James Joyce and William Faulkner, among others, tested the limits of the novel, and critical opinion during these years favored attempts to break the mold of traditional fiction, to push beyond the bounds of realistic documentation of recognizable human events. Thus, O'Hara's accurate rendition of dialogue lost place to stream of consciousness as an acclaimed technique, and the chronicling of successive generations was less favored than novels spanning a single day, controlled by a single consciousness. O'Hara's novels continue to be appreciated more for their documentary usefulness than for their creative force, yet within the limits of the traditional novel form, O'Hara was a master craftsman who captured and conveyed the human drama and social fabric of a complex period in American life.

Appointment in Samarra · In 1961, O'Hara referred to *Appointment in Samarra* as "a live novel twenty-five years after first publication." O'Hara's first novel would continue to "live," in several senses. It is obviously the work of a professional writer; O'Hara's powers of observation and skill in plot construction are already highly developed in this short novel. Also, *Appointment in Samarra* is set in the "Region" of eastern Pennsylvania, the setting of much of his long fiction throughout his career, and it has strong autobiographical elements. Finally, the novel deals starkly and dramatically with the themes of power and fate and demonstrates O'Hara's understanding of individual human destiny as a delicate balance between necessity and accident. The novel's title derives from a quotation from W. Somerset Maugham; the "appointment in Samarra" is an inescapable appointment with death, yet Julian English, O'Hara's main character, is doomed by his own actions–his tragedy is of his own making.

The story of Julian English is set against a richly detailed social and geographical background. O'Hara takes pains to provide the reader with the flavor of the early Depression years: the names of popular songs, the intricacies of the bootlegger's profession, and the subdued desperation of both rich and poor. To tie even further the novel to an era, there are topical references; Julian English mentions having recently read Ernest Hemingway's *A Farewell to Arms* (1929), and Irma Fleigler counts on President Herbert Hoover's promise that next year will be better for everyone, so that she and her husband can join the country club to which the Englishes belong. The club, and the town and region of which it is the social pinnacle, are treated with the same careful detail. O'Hara devotes several pages to the peculiarities of the anthracite coal region and the social hierarchy of Gibbsville, making clear that no person or action is independent of the social context. Despite the anxieties of what was called in 1930 a "slump," Gibbsville and its inhabitants are filled with self-importance, and none more so than Julian English, the doctor's son.

English and O'Hara share several biographical similarities. Julian, like O'Hara, has refused to adopt his doctor-father's profession, and his refusal has caused a serious rift in the father-son relationship. Julian English admires Franklin P. Adams (F. P. A.), to whom O'Hara dedicated *Appointment in Samarra*, and when a priest asks him whether he is a "frustrated literary man," Julian answers, "I'm not anything. I guess I should have been a doctor." The most important similarity between English and his creator is the sense of insecurity betrayed by this remark, an insecurity which leads both men to heavy drinking and defensive belligerence. The significant difference is that Julian English does not survive his own nature.

To dramatize his perception that the individual is inextricably bound up in his social context, O'Hara deftly shifts the point of view in the novel from interior to exterior views of Julian English, emphasizing the extent to which one person becomes the object of others' scrutiny. The novel covers the last three days of Julian's life, from the moment he throws a drink in Harry Reilly's face at the country-club Christmas party until he commits suicide by carbon monoxide poisoning, yet the narrative begins and ends with the observations of Luther and Irma Fleigler, a middle-class couple whose solid respectability and loving relationship contrasts sharply with the weakness and manipulation of the far wealthier Julian and Caroline English. Julian's action is, in itself, insignificant–a social error from which all parties could have recovered in time–but it becomes symbolic of Julian's misperception of his own strength and power. With the inevitability of Greek tragedy, social ostracism follows Julian's throwing of the drink; he becomes an outsider to his own group, and he fails in all his efforts to pick up the pieces of his life.

O'Hara presents, one by one, the sources of comfort to which twentieth century men turn in times of personal trouble and shows them all to be ineffective. Family, sex, work, drink, religion, even a simple apology–none provides solace to Julian, who is the isolated twentieth century man, left with nothing in which to believe. If Julian does not understand the motivation for his action, neither does anyone else around him, and neither his father, Dr. English, nor his wife can respond adequately to his anguish. Work fails as an escape because, as the president of a Cadillac dealership, Julian is dependent upon precisely the good will of potential customers, which his action has temporarily denied him, and drink leads to either self-pity or further belligerence. Monsignor Creedon, to whom Julian, a Protestant, feels obscurely drawn, confesses that he has sometimes wished he had chosen a different life's work; lacking a true vocation, he cannot provide a spiritual solution to Julian's guilt and loneliness.

Although the major conflict in the novel is that between Julian's personal responsibility for his own actions and fate and the effect of his social surroundings on that fate, O'Hara introduces a third element: heredity. Conscious of his own family heritage, and especially of his forebears' struggle through generations for greater status and respectability in the "Region," O'Hara places great importance on a sense of heritage. His characters are typically aware of where they come from, who their ancestors are, and to what this background entitles them on the social scale. Julian English's grandfather had committed suicide after embezzling money from a bank, and after Julian's suicide, Dr. English consoles himself regarding his own reputation by assuming that people "would see how the suicide strain has skipped one generation to come out in the next."

Dr. English reappears in several of O'Hara's later works, as do several other characters introduced. Jim Malloy, mentioned previously, becomes the narrator of the novellas in *Sermons and Soda Water*, and the relationship between Whit Hofman, here a minor character, and Pat Collins is the basis of the novella *Pat Collins*. In short, *Appointment in Samarra* established O'Hara's major locale, characters, and themes, and much of his fictional canon enlarged upon what was set forth in this novel.

The critical reception of O'Hara's first novel was generally favorable, though some reviewers were disturbed by its relatively explicit sexuality. This reaction was intensified by his next two major novels, *Butterfield 8* and *A Rage to Live*, both of which sold well in part because of the furor, and his collections of short stories were consistently well received. *Appointment in Samarra* had launched its author on a successful career.

Ten North Frederick · Although many of the short stories O'Hara published in the five collections between 1935 and 1947 were set in the "Region," *Ten North Frederick* was the first novel after *Appointment in Samarra* to deal with that locale. *Ten North Frederick* marked the beginning of the major phase of O'Hara's work as well as a new stage in his life. Two years before its publication, he had suffered the bleeding ulcer which convinced him to give up alcohol permanently, and a few months before, he had married Katharine Barnes Bryan, whom he referred to as "Sister." For the next fifteen years until his death, O'Hara would live a more settled, productive life than ever before. The timing of the novel's publication also began a tradition that continued for the rest of his career. Because O'Hara, always sensitive to reviews, wanted the task of reviewing *Ten North Frederick* to fall to a particular writer for *The New York Times*, the novel was issued on a Thursday in late November. The day was Thanksgiving, and the publication of an O'Hara novel or collection became an annual Thanksgiving event.

Butterfield 8 had been a *roman à clef,* based on the sensational and tragic story of Starr Faithfull, but despite certain resemblances between the lives of Joe Chapin and Franklin Delano Roosevelt, *Ten North Frederick* is not. Rather, as Matthew Bruccoli suggests, the novel is a "what-if study: what if Roosevelt had been a Gibbsville Republican?" O'Hara undoubtedly had Roosevelt in mind as he created Joe Chapin, and he used some elements of Roosevelt's life–the strong mother with ambitions for her son and a physical crippling in midlife–but his intention was not, as it was in *Butterfield 8*, to write a fictional account of a well-known person. Indeed, whereas Roosevelt's story is one of triumph over personal adversity, *Ten North Frederick* chronicles the failure of Joe Chapin's ambitions.

Those ambitions are far from modest. Joe Chapin wants nothing less than to leave each of his children a million dollars upon his death and to become president of the United States. That he achieves neither goal is in part the result of circumstances (the Depression reduces his financial assets) and in part of errors in judgment, such as his attempting to circumvent the local political system managed by Mike Slattery. Despite the magnitude of his hopes, Chapin is neither grasping nor overwhelmingly egotistical. Although he makes some ill-considered decisions about the lives of others–notably his daughter's abortion and the dissolution of her marriage to an Italian musician–he is not a power-hungry schemer. Instead, he is unaware that his own power has limits. Reared to believe in the privileges of wealth and status and trained in the proprieties of social forms, Chapin is merely inflexible. Rules and forms have taken precedence over human responsiveness, and his one extramarital affair, late in his life, seems to be the only spontaneous action of which he is capable.

Joe Chapin's life thus has an opaque surface which prevents even his closest Gibbsville associates from knowing him well. At Chapin's funeral, one of his cousins remarks, "I could never figure Joe out," to which Mike Slattery replies, "We knew exactly what Joe wanted us to know. And believe me, that wasn't much." Coming at the beginning of the novel, this exchange might have foreshadowed the revelation of a secret life that Chapin had hidden carefully from his friends, but O'Hara's intention instead is to show that the reality of Chapin's life is one with its facade. Behind the mask of respectability is a life that is just as sterile as the mask would suggest. With the exception of minor scandals, such as his daughter's elopement and pregnancy, Chapin's experience has been one of single-minded devotion to the accumulation of wealth and status.

Beginning *Ten North Frederick* with the funeral of his main character, O'Hara employed a structural device that attested to his development as a novelist. Both *Appointment in Samarra* and *Ten North Frederick* begin with a moment of crisis or transition, but whereas in *Appointment in Samarra* the rest of the novel traces the inevitable results of that moment, *Ten North Frederick* begins with the conclusion–the death of Joe Chapin–and then proceeds to explore the life that has ended. The fact that the major threads of that life are introduced in the conversations at Chapin's funeral and are later developed in all their complexity has caused Sheldon Grebstein to call this a "tapestry novel." Having revealed the significant facts about Joe Chapin's life early in the novel, O'Hara must compel the reader to continue by means other than suspense.

The major strength of *Ten North Frederick*, as of most of O'Hara's fiction, is its characterization. The novel deals with three generations of the Chapin family, begin-ning with Joe Chapin's parents, though instead of a straight chronological narrative O'Hara uses a flashback technique, weaving past and present together to emphasize the effect of family–especially women–on the formation of character and ambition. Both Joe's mother, Charlotte, and his wife, Edith, have plans for his life; both are women for whom love means power and ownership, and for whom sex is a form of manipulation. Edith Chapin articulates this persistent theme of O'Hara's novels as she thinks, on her wedding night, "It was not Love; Love might easily have very little to do with it; but it was as strong a desire as Love or Hate and it was going to be her life, the owning of this man." As clearly as anywhere in his fiction, O'Hara here portrays women who, because they are denied most masculine forms of power, participate vicariously by requiring their men to succeed in their stead.

Yet Joe Chapin is a failure. If there is a "secret" in his life, it is the depth of his desire for high political office. On the surface a personable, respected pillar of Gibbsville, highly regarded by most of its leading citizens, Chapin nurses the ambition for which his mother has groomed him, but he is not willing to play the political games required to gain the backing of Mike Slattery's organization, nor can money buy him the office he seeks. After he is forced to withdraw from the political arena, only his brief affair with his daughter's friend Kate Drummond gives his life meaning, and when that ends he slowly begins to commit suicide by drinking heavily.

Many of O'Hara's own feelings about accomplishment and aging informed his creation of Joe Chapin. O'Hara was fifty when the novel was completed. Like Chapin, he had gained the respect of many of his contemporaries, but certain measures of "success" had eluded him: in particular, recognition as a first-rate novelist. Both

O'Hara and his character had suffered frightening indications of poor health; Chapin ignored the warning that alcohol was killing him, but O'Hara did not. Time had become precious to him, and he reflects on this in the final paragraph of *Ten North Frederick*: "There is always enough to do while the heart keeps pumping. There is never, never enough time to do it all." O'Hara was rewarded for his persistence when *Ten North Frederick* received the National Book Award for 1955. The award citation read in part: "Tough-minded as usual, Mr. O'Hara has written a novel of emotional depth and moral conviction."

Sermons and Soda Water · The swift passing of time to which O'Hara referred in *Ten North Frederick* was one of the reasons he turned to the novella form in the three pieces that comprise *Sermons and Soda Water*. The novella took, he said, "a minimum of research," as compared to the "big novel" he was working on simultaneously (probably *The Lockwood Concern*). He wrote these novellas to "get it all down on paper while I can"; "at fifty-five I have no right to waste time." The novella, in other words, could be written quickly, from memory, rather than requiring years of research and writing. This distinction between the novel and the novella suggests that the material for the latter was more likely to be autobiographical, and his use of Jim Malloy as narrator in these three novellas adds to the impression that these are personal narratives.

Although O'Hara never fully defined the terms "novella" and "novelette" as he used them, he suggested in 1968 that the important consideration was character. The form, he said, "tells all that you need to know about certain people in certain circumstances so that those people become figures in the reader's personal library." He had first experimented with a form midway in length between the short story and the novel in the title story of *The Doctor's Son and Other Stories*, his first collection of short stories, but during the last decade of his career, beginning with *Sermons and Soda Water*, he developed the novella form as a means of disentangling one thread from the usual complex tapestry of his novels. The novella as O'Hara conceived of it has an episodic structure. It follows one conflict, relationship, or problem through a lengthy time span, isolating for dramatic attention only the crucial periods, and briefly summarizing intervening months or years. There are no subplots, and minor characters are functional rather than centers of interest in their own right.

The use of a first-person narrator with a limited consciousness, rather than the omniscient point of view O'Hara employed in most of his novels, helps to ensure the sharp focus required for the novella. Jim Malloy, the narrator of *Sermons and Soda Water*, tells the reader about the people he has known in his hometown of Gibbsville or those he meets as a journalist in New York. He is a thin mask for O'Hara in the early days of the author's career: the young man from the coal region who begins his career in New York, encounters the wealthy and famous, and keeps up with a few of the people back home. Yet, Malloy has the mature vision of O'Hara at fifty-five, and his perspective on the characters' lives is that of a concerned friend rather than an impressionable young man. Malloy, like O'Hara, is a shrewd observer of human nature, one who finds patterns in life. In *We're Friends Again*, the third novella in *Sermons and Soda Water*, he comments on this ability: "The way things tie up, one with another, is likely to go unnoticed until a lawyer or a writer calls our attention to it." Malloy's function in these novellas is to demonstrate how "things tie up" while remaining more or less removed from the central stories.

In this ultimate detachment from the lives of the characters he describes, Malloy underscores the central theme of *Sermons and Soda Water*: human loneliness and

isolation. At the end of *We're Friends Again,* Malloy calls loneliness "the final condition
of us all," and O'Hara shows that it affects people at all levels of society, from
Charlotte Sears, the film star in *The Girl on the Baggage Truck,* to Pete and Bobbie
McCrea of Gibbsville in *Imagine Kissing Pete.* The solution to loneliness is love, but, as
O'Hara so often suggests, love is elusive, and one often settles for approximations:
attraction, sex, power. As Charlotte Sears says about her relationship with the wealthy,
reclusive Thomas Hunterden, "There ought to be another word for love, for people
like Hunterden and me." It is left to Malloy, as the controlling consciousness, to find
meaning in the lives he relates, and that meaning resides ultimately in his capacity as
a writer to discern patterns of inevitability in human life.

The Lockwood Concern · Of the novels written during O'Hara's last decade, *The
Lockwood Concern* is particularly interesting as a culmination of many aspects of his
career. During this period he used a variety of settings for his fiction—Hollywood in
The Big Laugh, Philadelphia in *Lovey Childs*—but in *The Lockwood Concern* he returned
to the "Region," to the characters and situations that he handled with ease and
familiarity. Throughout the early 1960's, O'Hara referred to a "big" novel on which
he was working, and at one point he projected that it would be a two-volume work.
The Lockwood Concern is in fact a one-volume work of average length, but its scope
justifies O'Hara's adjective: It is a multigenerational novel, a "century-spanning saga,"
as the jacket blurb proclaimed.

The theme of *The Lockwood Concern* is consistent with much of O'Hara's other work,
and reaches back to *Appointment in Samarra*: the ultimate powerlessness of the individual against the force of circumstance, particularly the folly of attempting to control
the destinies of others. The attempts of Abraham and George Lockwood, the second
and third generations of the Lockwood family of Swedish Haven (actually Schuylkill
Haven, near Pottsville), to establish a family dynasty break down in the fourth
generation when George Lockwood's son and daughter reject the town and the family
and adopt ways of life antithetical to dynastic responsibilities. The "concern" of the
title is a Quaker concept, denoting an overwhelming sense of mission. Abraham
Lockwood, in the late nineteenth century, has secularized this religious concept and
translated it into a vision of generations of Lockwoods enjoying increasing wealth and
prestige, including entrance to the clubs and other bastions of gentility denied him by
the uncouth background and behavior of his own father, Moses Lockwood.

The central figure of *The Lockwood Concern* is George Lockwood, who has adopted
Abraham's dream and brought it to the point of realization. George Lockwood's
children will be the first generation to enjoy full acceptance by elite society, and as
an emblem of this progress he has built a family mansion near Swedish Haven. The
high, spiked wall around the house testifies to George's sense of exclusivity; it is also
the cause of the death of a neighboring farm boy, who becomes impaled while
attempting to climb the fence before the house is completed. This tragedy, which
George Lockwood hastens to keep quiet, opens the novel, a signal of the crumbling
of the erstwhile dynasty. From this point, George struggles to maintain the "concern"
against increasing evidence of its demise until he finally falls to his death down a secret
staircase he has had built in the still-uninhabited mansion.

O'Hara here used the circular structure which he had perfected in both long and
short fiction throughout his career. The novel begins and ends in the mid-1920's, but
ranges back to the mid-nineteenth century as O'Hara details the history of the
"Lockwood concern." It opens with the death of the unnamed farm boy and closes

with the death of George Lockwood and, by implication, of the "concern." Simultaneously, the novel has the linear thrust of the historical novel. From the canny, vigorous survival of Moses Lockwood to the effete California existence of George's son Bing, the generations move through historical and cultural change, reflecting shifting values in American society. The novel argues that such change is inevitable, and that George Lockwood's attempt at consolidation and stasis is doomed from the start. Social flux is mirrored even in the names of the male Lockwoods over time, from the tradition and authority of "Moses" and "Abraham" to the frivolity of "Bing." Even with such change, however, basic human nature does not alter; George and Bing Lockwood are, in different ways, as conniving and self-interested as their ancestors, though protected by wealth and attorneys against open public disapproval.

The Lockwood Concern is a summation of much that O'Hara had tried and accomplished during thirty years of writing. Though not his best novel, it is one of his most ambitious in subject matter and scope. It provides a history of the "Region" from the time of O'Hara's ancestors until the time when he left it for New York, and it shows the growth of the region from a backwoods settlement to a thriving coal-mining and farming area that sent its sons to Princeton and Harvard. Thematically, the novel shows that O'Hara had come to some conclusions about the interplay of destiny and choice. He had shown in *Appointment in Samarra* that an individual's power over his own life was limited by the influence of society and the intervention of chance. In *Ten North Frederick*, he added great wealth and ambition to the equation and demonstrated their ineffectuality. By the time he wrote *The Lockwood Concern*, O'Hara saw the limits to human power as determined not only by conflicting wills and accidents of fate, but also by the very sweep of time and change. Human aspiration pales before the only human certainty—death—which is described as a "secret" known only to those who have experienced it.

By entitling his biography of the author *The O'Hara Concern* (1975), Matthew J. Bruccoli suggests that O'Hara felt a sense of mission similar to that of the Lockwoods. If so, O'Hara's "concern" was not related to a family dynasty but instead to establishing himself among the first rank of American novelists. His lifelong war with literary critics and reviewers over the value of his contribution is evidence that he was never secure in his own reputation. Although he rejected the terms "social realist" and "social historian," these are appropriate characterizations of his best work. O'Hara's sense of history, his precise rendering of detail and dialogue, and his command of narrative technique make him one of the most significant chroniclers of American life in the first half of the twentieth century. The fact that he was a popular novelist during his career, in part because of the more sensational aspects of his work, has detracted from his critical reputation, but his position as an important novelist of manners seems secure.

Nancy Walker

Other major works

SHORT FICTION: *The Doctor's Son and Other Stories,* 1935; *Hope of Heaven,* 1938; *Files on Parade,* 1939; *Pal Joey,* 1940; *Pipe Night,* 1945; *Hellbox,* 1947; *Assembly,* 1961; *The Cape Code Lighter,* 1962; *The Hat on the Bed,* 1963; *The Horse Knows the Way,* 1964; *Waiting for Winter,* 1966; *And Other Stories,* 1968; *The O'Hara Generation,* 1969; *The Time Element and Other Stories,* 1972; *Good Samaritan and Other Stories,* 1974.

PLAYS: *Five Plays*, pb. 1961; *Two by O'Hara*, pb. 1979 (includes *Far from Heaven*, 1962, and the screenplay *The Man Who Could Not Lose*, 1959).

NONFICTION: *Sweet and Sour*, 1954; *My Turn*, 1966; *A Cub Tells His Story*, 1974; *An Artist Is His Own Fault*, 1977.

Bibliography

Bruccoli, Matthew. *John O'Hara: A Descriptive Bibliography*. Pittsburgh: University of Pittsburgh Press, 1978. A thorough, scholarly bibliography on all aspects of O'Hara's work. A must for the serious student.

_____. *The O'Hara Concern: A Biography of John O'Hara*. New York: Random House, 1975. The expertise of Bruccoli is evident here in this comprehensive biography of O'Hara. Contains valuable background, critical references to his works, and a useful bibliography.

Eppard, Philip B., ed. *Critical Essays on John O'Hara*. New York: G. K. Hall, 1994. Divided into sections on reviews and essays. All of O'Hara's major fiction is discussed, as well as his relationship to naturalism, his view of society, his short stories, and his view of politics, the family, and small towns. Includes a comprehensive introductory chapter on O'Hara's career and the reception of his novels, but no bibliography.

Grebstein, Sheldon Norman. *John O'Hara*. New York: Twayne, 1966. This critical study both interprets and assesses O'Hara's work. Grebstein is mostly sympathetic toward O'Hara, but has some reservations about his writings. Also assesses other criticism on O'Hara.

MacShane, Frank. *The Life of John O'Hara*. New York: E. P. Dutton, 1980. Looks at O'Hara's life through his work. A thorough study well worth reading for its valuable insights.

Shannon, William V. *The American Irish*. New York: Macmillan, 1963. Deals with O'Hara's work from the point of view of his Irish ancestry and his desire to escape from it.

WALKER PERCY

Born: Birmingham, Alabama; May 28, 1916
Died: Covington, Louisiana; May 10, 1990

Principal long fiction · *The Moviegoer*, 1961; *The Last Gentleman*, 1966; *Love in the Ruins: The Adventures of a Bad Catholic at a Time Near the End of the World*, 1971; *Lancelot*, 1977; *The Second Coming*, 1980; *The Thanatos Syndrome*, 1987.

Other literary forms · As a writer of imaginative literature, Walker Percy devoted himself exclusively to the novel. However, he also wrote more than fifty reviews and essays on many of the same topics that inform his novels: existential philosophy, language theory, modern scientific method, contemporary American culture, the South, and literature. With one or two exceptions, the most important of these essays are collected in *The Message in the Bottle* (1975), which has as its peculiarly Percyean subtitle *How Queer Man Is, How Queer Language Is, and What One Has to Do with the Other*. An indispensable book, *The Message in the Bottle* not only clarifies the author's major concerns as well as his commitment to that most basic philosophical question, "What is man?," but also details the formidable intellectual foundation upon which his fiction so unpretentiously rests. That unpretentiousness is especially evident in *Lost in the Cosmos* (1983), ironically subtitled *The Last Self-Help Book*, in which Percy employs satire and semiotics in an effort to clarify the human being's social and more especially spiritual predicament as a uniquely "lost" creature needing the good news of the gospels but all too often willing to settle for the insights of scientist Carl Sagan and talk-show host Phil Donahue.

Achievements · Percy is perhaps most easily described as a Catholic-existentialist-American-southern novelist, a baggy phrase that at least has the virtue of identifying the various currents which are blended together in his distinctive works. In Percy's fiction, Mark Twain's Huck Finn from the novel *Adventures of Huckleberry Finn* (1884) and Jean-Paul Sartre's Antoine Roquentin from the play *Nausea* (1938) meet in a single character adrift in a world where, despite the formless sprawl of mass society, the possibility of grace still exists. Percy's fiction is readily identifiable by its distinctive narrative voice. That voice—laconic yet disarmingly honest and filled with wonder—gained for Percy both critical respect and a dedicated readership. Percy received the National Book Award for *The Moviegoer*, the *Los Angeles Times* Book Award for *The Second Coming*, and the St. Louis Literary Award for *Lost in the Cosmos*. Among his other literary honors were memberships in the National Institute of Arts and Letters and the American Academy of Arts and Sciences.

Biography · Walker Percy was born in Birmingham, Alabama, on May 28, 1916. When his father, lawyer Leroy Percy, committed suicide in 1929, the widow and her three sons moved to Greenville, Mississippi, where they lived with Leroy's bachelor cousin, William Alexander Percy, who adopted the boys in 1931, following their mother's death in an automobile accident. The Greenville home served as something of a local cultural center; the uncle, the author of several works, including an

©1987 Nancy Crampton

autobiographical memoir of the South entitled *Lanterns on the Levee* (1941), entertained such houseguests as William Faulkner, Carl Sandburg, Langston Hughes, David Cohn, and Harry Stack Sullivan. In the early 1930's, Percy attended Greenville High School, where he wrote a gossip column and became the close friend of Shelby Foote, who was by then already committed to a literary career. At the University of North Carolina, which was noted for its school of behaviorism, Percy majored in chemistry and received a B.S. degree in 1937. He then enrolled in Columbia's College of Physicians and Surgeons (M.D., 1941), where, in addition to his studies, Percy underwent psychoanalysis and became a frequent filmgoer. The turning point in his life came in early 1942 when, as a resident at Bellevue Hospital in New York, Percy contracted tuberculosis. During his two-year convalescence at Saranac Lake, he began reading extensively in philosophy and literature (Sartre, Albert Camus, Søren Kierkegaard, Gabriel Marcel, Fyodor Dostoevski, Nikolai Gogol, Leo Tolstoy, Franz Kafka). What he discovered was that as a medical doctor he knew much about people but had no idea what a human really is.

Following a relapse and further convalescence in 1944, Percy seemed sure of only two things: He was a doctor who did not wish to practice medicine; he was literally as well as existentially homeless (his uncle having died in 1942). In 1945, he traveled with Shelby Foote to New Mexico and then stayed on alone for a time. On November 7, 1946, he married Mary Bernice Townsend, and less than a year later they both converted to Catholicism. (The decision to convert was, Percy said, in large measure the result of their reading of Kierkegaard's essay, "The Difference Between a Genius and an Apostle.") Soon after, the Percys moved from Sewanee, Tennessee, to New Orleans, Louisiana, where Percy continued his contemplative life, financially secure—thanks to his uncle's estate—and intellectually rich—his landlord, Julius Friend, a professor of philosophy, introduced him to the writings of Charles Saunders Peirce, whose triadic theory of language formed the basis of Percy's own linguistic speculations. (Percy's interest in language had another and more personal source: The younger of his two daughters was born deaf.) In 1950, the Percys moved to Covington, Louisiana, "a pleasant non-place," Percy said, where it is possible to live as a stranger in one's own land; it is neither the "anyplace" that characterizes mass society nor the "someplace" of the New Orleans or a Richmond, where the past haunts the present.

In the 1950's, Percy began publishing essays in such journals as *Thought, Common-*

weal, and *Philosophy and Phenomenological Research.* After discarding two early novels, he began writing *The Moviegoer* in 1959, revising it four times before its publication two years later. Until his death on May 10, 1990, Percy lived quietly in Covington, Louisiana, a serious and meditative novelist who was also a Catholic, an existentialist, and a southerner, pondering the world in thought, fiction, and an occasional essay.

Analysis · Walker Percy acknowledged that Søren Kierkegaard's writings provided him with "a theoretical frame of reference," and one of the most important ideas which he adapted from this frame is Kierkegaard's rejection of Hegelian rationalism in favor of a subjective and intensely passionate commitment on the part of the individual. In Percy's view, modern science in general and the social sciences in particular have mistakenly and indiscriminately adopted the behaviorist, or biological, method and have consequently defined the human being reductively and abstractly. Existentialism, including the existential novel, on the other hand, presents an alternative to behaviorism: a "concrete" phenomenological approach whose aim is the recovery of humankind's uniqueness. Percy admits that the behaviorist method is valid to a point; ultimately, however, it must fail, because, in classifying the human as a biological organism acting in accordance with rules applicable to all biological organisms, it fails to deal with what is distinctly human, the nonbiological goals. Concerned solely with sameness, the scientific method cannot account for Fyodor Dostoevski's underground man except as a deviation from the norm. Existentialism, Percy believes, does account for this being, as does Christianity, which acknowledges the Fall of Man and his distance from God, and defines existence as "the journey of a wayfarer along life's way." Denying the Fall, modern science makes the Gnostic mistake; it attempts to build Eden, the secular city, where human guilt and anxiety are conditioned away, where all biological needs are met, and where existence is certified by experts.

Philosophy · Percy rejects this "brave new world" and calls instead for a "radical anthropology" that can account for the ontological as well as the biological aspects of human existence. Guilt and anxiety, he points out, are not symptoms of maladjustment to be gotten rid of so that the individual (as human organism) can live the life of the satisfied consumer; rather, these signs of estrangement serve to summon a person not to self-fulfillment but to authentic existence. Humanity is on earth not to have needs met, Percy says, not to surrender sovereignty to the theories of experts (a view raised again by Christopher Lasch in his controversial book, *The Culture of Narcissism,* 1979), but to be saved, and that necessitates consciousness of the human situation.

It is important to realize that Percy's sovereign wayfarer, or castaway, is not entirely identifiable with Kierkegaard's knight of faith. In place of Kierkegaard's extreme subjectivity, Percy posits the intersubjectivity of Gabriel Marcel, a Christian existentialist whose *we are* stands in stark contrast with both Kierkegaard's *I choose* and René Descartes's *I think.* We know we exist, Marcel says, by participating in the world. He does not think of being as experience, however, but as a presence within experience which is to be understood as simultaneously transcendent *and* immanent. To separate the two components of being is to pervert them and to transmogrify the individual as sovereign wayfarer into either angel—the abstract knower, the objective consciousness—or beast—a culture organism satisfying its needs. (The terms are Percy's, borrowed from Blaise Pascal.)

Marcel's quest for being, which is the quest for salvation as well, manifests itself in

Percy's theory of language as intersubjective communication, where *we name* implies the same religious affirmation as Marcel's *we are* and Martin Buber's *I-Thou*. Percy originally turned to language theory in order to answer the question "What is man?" because the answer provided by the behaviorist method was reductive and because the old theological view, along with the words in which it was couched, has been rendered ineffective by the general acceptance of the scientific method, which predisposed modern humanity to view itself as the behaviorists had defined it. Percy then set himself the task of finding "the delta factor": that which makes the human what it is and not something else. According to the old theological view, humanity's singularity is its "soul," a meaningless word in a scientific age that demands empirical proof. For soul, Percy substitutes language, which he defines not as a sign system (the behaviorist position) but as the uniquely human process of symbolization. At the heart of language (and therefore at the heart of humankind as well) is something mysterious (compare Marcel's "mystery of being"). The mystery is explained by what Percy calls the "coupling process," the intersubjective human context by which people name, or symbolize, the world and in this way come both to know it and to share it. Language is, therefore, an attempt to bridge the gap between self and other, or, considered in the religious context of the Fall of Man, between self and God. What complicates the situation is the fact that in the late twentieth century, Percy believed, language became as meaningless, as clichéd, as the old theology. Before there can be intersubjective communication, humankind must again learn how to speak.

To learn to name and therefore to know and share that knowledge with another is the basic plot of a Percy novel. As Robert Coles has pointed out, Percy's novels trace the protagonist's movement from lofty observation to active participation in the openness of life—its possibilities and the necessity of making choices. Each of his major characters feels estranged "from being, from his own being, from the being of other creatures in the world, from the transcendent being. He has lost something, but what he does not know; he only knows that he is sick to death with the loss of it." Since this quest for being is a quest for God, it involves the hero's progress through Kierkegaard's three stages: the aesthetic (the pursuit of pleasure; the self becomes an uncommitted ironic spectator detached from himself and from others); the ethical (living within a general human code, such as marriage); the religious (requiring an entirely personal and—Kierkegaard would say—absurd leap of faith). The hero's search for being begins only when he or she becomes conscious of his or her despair and tries either to understand it or to alleviate it in one of two ways: rotation or repetition. Rotation—the quest for new experiences to offset "everydayness"—makes up the comic substance of Percy's novels. Repetition—the return to the past—may be rendered comically, but more often it serves a darker purpose, for Percy's heroes are, like William Faulkner's, haunted by the past; as a result, they do not live fully in the present. Only when they confront the past directly and become conscious of it can they break its spell and become sovereign wayfarers.

Frequently, Percy equates the past with the southern stoicism his uncle espoused, which, in Percy's judgment, leads only to pessimism, obsession with death, and "the wintry kingdom of self"; in short, it is the very antithesis of Percy's Christian existentialism. Rotation and repetition provide only temporary relief from the malaise that prevails within the aesthetic stage. The only escape from "aesthetic damnation" is through ordeal, especially the death of a loved one. Ordeal brings heroes face to face with mortality and enables them to see their world and themselves as if for the first time. The search they then begin is in effect a rejection of the absurdist position of aesthetic existentialists such as Albert Camus and Jean-Paul Sartre. The world is not absurd; it is a world to be named, known, and shared by the authentic self and the other in a mode of existence that is not so much religious *or* ethical as a synthesis of the two.

There are analogues for Percy's religious-phenomenological conception of the human search for being in his method of composition and in his prose style. The author's search for narrative form parallels the hero's search for being. Beginning with a situation rather than a plot or set of characters, Percy wrote with no fixed purpose or end in mind. As he explained, the writing, while not "haphazard," involved "many false starts, many blind detours, many blind passages, many goings ahead and backing up. . . ." Stylistically, his elegantly and precisely written novels suggest wonder, humor, and forbearance rather than the ponderous solemnity of other existential novelists such as Sartre. Moreover, his prose is richly and sensuously detailed; like two other converts to Catholicism, Marcel and even more particularly Gerard Manley Hopkins, he took pleasure in a natural and human world that is, although marred by evil, essentially sacramental.

The Moviegoer · John Bickerson Bolling–"Binx"–is the narrator and main character of *The Moviegoer* and the first of Percy's spiritually "sick" protagonists. At age twenty-nine, he is a successful broker in a modern world where the church has been replaced by the brokerage house. Although financially secure, Binx feels uneasy; although adept at planning his client's futures, he has trouble living his own life from day to day, fearful that he may at any moment succumb to that worst of all plagues, the malaise of "everydayness." To counter its effects, Binx becomes a moviegoer, partly because films project a "heightened . . . resplendent reality," albeit temporarily, and partly because films provide Binx with accepted role-models; thus his impersonations of such canonized figures as Gregory Peck, Clark Gable, Dana Andrews, and Rory Calhoun (who also serves as his confidant). The impersonation can never fully satisfy the moviegoer, however, who must eventually face the fact that the reality of his own life can never attain the heightened illusion of the star's gestural perfection. Moviego-ing serves Binx in two additional ways: It enables him to view his world through the perspective of the films he has seen and, more important, to observe the world as if it were itself a film and he the passive audience.

Binx's detachment is both a virtue and a vice. As the detached spectator, he observes those around him closely and accurately, thus exposing the roles they have unknowingly adopted. Appropriately, the novel's temporal setting is the week before Mardi Gras, the period of rehearsals for New Orleans' city-wide impersonation. Instead of recognizing their situation as castaways, these others feel serenely at home in the world, whereas in fact they are, as Binx understands, "dead." Neither virtuous nor sinful, they are merely "nice"; they speak, but in clichés; they ask questions, but neither expect nor desire answers. Binx, who fears becoming invisible–losing his identity–is right to keep his distance from these shadowy others. At the same time, however, he longs to be like them, to have his identity certified for him by such spurious means as films, identity cards, *Consumer Reports*, newspaper advice columns, and radio shows such as "This I Believe," which broadcasts the meaningless affirma-tions of abstracted religionists to a half-believing, half-skeptical Binx.

If it is his ironic detachment that saves Binx from the unreflective life of mass humanity, then it is his "search" that most clearly characterizes his longing for authenticity and being. "To become aware of the possibility of the search is to be onto something," Binx says. "Not to be onto something is to be in despair." Binx distinguishes two kinds of search. The "vertical" leads to abstraction: theories that explain the world but fail to explain what humanity is. (One alternative to such abstraction is the romanticism that killed Binx's father and that the son wisely rejects.) The other is the "horizontal" or phenomenological search that Percy himself counsels in *The Message in the Bottle*. While Binx is indeed "onto something," his search is different from Percy's; it constitutes a "debased" form of the religious search because, as Percy explained, Binx, like Sartre, "has already ruled God out." His search takes a purely aesthetic form. To ease "the pain of loss," he pursues money and women, but the pursuit leads only to boredom and depression because the novelty of his possessions quickly wears off and everydayness inevitably returns to remind him of his inauthenticity and his position as a castaway. Fortunately, Binx's yearning has a deeper current. As a college student, he found himself "lost in the mystery of being alive at such a time and place"; upon his return from the Korean War, he began his eight-year "exile" in the New Orleans suburb of Gentilly, which, like Covington, is a "nonplace"; and as a broker he has taken to reading *Arabia Deserta*, by the self-styled "God's pilgrim," Charles Montagu Doughty, concealed inside a Standard & Poor binder.

Binx's search begins with the fact of his own "invincible apathy" and eventually leads, after many wrong turns, to authenticity and intersubjective relationships with his fourteen-year-old half-brother, Lonnie Smith, and his twenty-five-year-old cousin Kate Cutrer. There exists a "complicity" between Binx and the dying Lonnie, who faces life with true serenity because he understands it religiously. Like the other dying children in Percy's novels, Lonnie represents the paradox of unmerited suffering in a world ruled by a supposedly benevolent God, a paradox Percy resolves by depicting their spiritual victory in a "world full of God's grace where sorrow and death do not have the final word." Binx attends to the "good news" that Lonnie embodies because, in part, Lonnie's monotonous way of talking makes his words fresh and therefore meaningful, "like a code tapped through a wall."

Kate, unlike Lonnie, lives in pure anxiety, swinging wildly between various extremes, especially the longing to be free and the desire "to be an anyone who is anywhere." Although she lacks Binx's degree of awareness as well as his ironic detachment and is more prone to impersonation than he, Kate, like Binx, is aware of her disease, which others can only understand in psychological terms. (Thus, the novel's epigraph, taken from Kierkegaard: "the specific character of despair is precisely this: it is unaware of being despair.") Binx and Kate neatly complement each other: His childlike "simplemindedness" allows her to feel secure enough to speak honestly, while she correctly points out that in his search Binx may be overlooking something "obvious." Her request that Binx be her God—by which she means he is to tell her what to do—is not at all absurd given Marcel's brand of Christian existentialism. Significantly, her other suitors play the part of intersubjective God rather badly: One wants to send her to a high-priced psychoanalyst; the other promises an interminable vista of "niceness" and everydayness.

Binx's leap from nominal Catholic existing in despair to sovereign wayfarer and authentic being occurs very late in the novel and is effected by what, in a parallel context, Percy calls "some dim dazzling trick of grace." In fact, only a few pages from the end Binx laments that, having but one gift, "a good nose for merde," the only course for him to follow is "to fall prey to desire." There is even some justice to his Aunt Emily's judgment of him: In crucial situations, Binx invariably chooses to "default," to "exit." Yet, in the final pages, it is clear that Binx will do so no longer.

Neither, however, will he play the part his aunt has chosen for him—southern stoic. He will go to medical school, not because she wants him to but because now he knows what to do: to observe *and* to serve others. Binx's leap is reflected in the very texture of Percy's prose. Until the epilogue, which takes place one year later, Binx has narrated his tale chiefly in what may be termed his detached, matter-of-fact, movie-goer style, against which the very few lyrical passages, used to underscore Binx's wonder and the gracefulness of his world, stand in vivid contrast. In the epilogue, Binx drops the moviegoer style (and the references to films) entirely; instead, he speaks easily, authentically, authoritatively. The man who earlier had been cousin, half-brother, and ironic impersonator, now is husband, brother, and sovereign way-farer.

The Last Gentleman · The protagonist of Percy's second novel, *The Last Gentleman*, "Williston Bibb Barrett or Billy Barrett," is a modern-day version of Dostoevski's Prince Myshkin in *The Idiot* (1868). Although far less ironic than Binx Bolling, Barrett is far more disturbed, as his periodic fugue states and bouts of amnesia and déjà vu attest. Existing in a state of pure possibility, he is incapable of making any one decisive act or choice. He has tried and failed both to live the therapeutic life and to "engineer" his own destiny. Knowing something is missing in his life, Barrett seeks to recover reality and find his being in the "gap" between self and other. Specifically, these others are the members of the Vaught family, and his search is a spiritual odyssey, modeled on Mark Twain's *Adventures of Huckleberry Finn* (1884), that takes him from New York to his native Ithaca, then on to Mississippi, and finally to Santa Fe, New Mexico, and the Sangre de Cristo mountains (Holy Faith and the Blood of Christ).

The search begins when Barrett accidentally discovers Kitty Vaught and her sister-in-law, Rita, in Central Park. Rita, a secular humanist and advocate of self-fulfillment, quickly realizes she will not be able either to control or to convert Barrett and tries unsuccessfully to get rid of him. Barrett, however, has already fallen in love with Kitty, a rather pale version of Kate Cutrer—less anxiety-ridden, more successful in her impersonations. Barrett's love affair is both furthered and complicated by Kitty's younger brother, Jamie, whose traveling companion he becomes. The fact that Jamie is dying establishes definite limits to the pure possibility of his and Barrett's lives and causes Barrett to consider his search more profoundly when he meets another sister, Val, and brother, Sutter, the two "absentee experts" (as Barrett calls them) who force him to make his existential choice. Val, a convert to Catholicism and a nun, has dedicated herself to teaching mute children to speak and to believe the Catholic religion. (All people are like her children, she claims; they are waiting to be told what to do.) Whereas she is hopeful and apostolic, Sutter, a diagnostician and pathologist, is suicidal and ironically quixotic. He rejects her belief in the human as wayfarer, claiming "We are doomed to the transcendence of abstraction and I choose the only reentry into the world which remains to us": "lewdness," cynicism, and detachment.

Sutter's mistake, as Barrett well understands, is the positing of extreme alternatives such as God or no God, transcendence or immanence. Moreover, Sutter's concern for Jamie betrays his basically religious nature, and it is this, more than his medical expertise, that has led Barrett to look to him for answers. At Jamie's baptism, it is Sutter who comprehends what is happening. Barrett, although he acts as interpreter between Jamie and the priest, misses the religious significance. He does understand that something has happened, however, and to discover what that something is he tracks down Sutter, who has decided to commit suicide. Barrett's search for an answer is, as Percy noted, a search for a father, ultimately for the Father, God; his own father, Barrett finally realizes, had looked for his answer in all the wrong places–solitude, "old sad poetry," and the music of Johannes Brahms. The son's "wait" did not keep the father from killing himself, but it does save Sutter, who appears in the final tableau less as an oracle than as Barrett's self-chosen–and therefore sovereign–responsibility.

Love in the Ruins · Subtitled *The Adventures of a Bad Catholic at a Time Near the End of the World, Love in the Ruins* is a broad satire on the state of the modern world–in particular, its behaviorist assumptions and political absurdities. The novel may be flawed, as some reviewers have contended, by the author's insistent and at times rather heavy-handed social criticism; there is, however, a comic vitality in this novel that seems to offset such reservations about it as literary art. This comic vitality, quite unlike the irony and understatement that characterize Percy's earlier novels, is appropriate to a work that has the topics of community and reconciliation as two of its major concerns. As Percy explained in an essay entitled "Notes for a Novel about the End of the World," the apocalyptic novelist serves two purposes: As prophet, or canary in the coal mine, he cries out in order to avert disaster, and as coupling agent, he connects humanity with reality. It is by means of the coupling process that disaster is averted, as Percy quietly suggests in the novel's closing image of a couple "twined about each other as the ivy twineth," in which what has been a sign of ruin (the ivy) is transformed into a symbol of intersubjective love.

The story, which is spoken into a pocket tape recorder by the hero, Tom More, as he keeps watch for snipers, follows a five-part structure (July Fourth, First, Second, Third, Fourth) that progressively becomes more chaotic until, in the epilogue ("Five Years Later"), peace and order are restored. The time of the novel is a not too distant future that bears a clear, if comically exaggerated, resemblance to the American 1960's: The fifteen-year war in Ecuador continues, racial tensions and Bantu uprisings are increasing, and the Catholic Church has split into three factions. In short, "the center did not hold." The physical setting is just as perverse as the social-political: Paradise Estates, home of the well-to-do and the spiritually impoverished; Fedville, a sprawling compound which includes a Masters and Johnson Love Clinic, where ex-priest Kev Kevin reads *Commonweal* and presides over the vaginal console; Honey Island Swamp, a counterculture retreat; and the golf course, where a banner proclaims "Jesus Christ, the Greatest Pro of Them All."

Percy's hero is as troubled as his society but in a different way. Forty-five years old and a collateral descendent of Sir/Saint Thomas, he is at once a doctor and a mental patient, a diagnostician but also a metaphysician in a world of behaviorists ready and willing to condition away any remaining feelings of guilt he may have. Loving, in descending order of importance, women, music, science, God, and, "hardly at all," his fellow human, he is the type of what Kierkegaard termed aesthetic damnation. He has lost that thread in the world-labyrinth which, until the death of his daughter Samantha, made the world seem sensible and holy. His faith gone, More has his own messianic ambition, a plan to "save" America with More's Qualitative Quantitative Onotological Lapsometer. His invention–"the stethoscope of the spirit . . . the first caliper of the soul"–is designed to measure the "gap" between the outer, social self and true, inner being; he hopes to modify the lapsometer so that it can cure as well as diagnose humanity's "fall" from being, to put together what Descartes tore apart. Like Percy and, to a degree, like Sutter Vaught, More is troubled by modern human-ity's indifference to being and its willingness to define itself in half-measures: the angel that, falling prey to abstraction, is unable to "reenter the lovely ordinary world," or the beast that adapts to its environment and so becomes the organism behaviorists say the human is.

Art Immelmann—Mephistopheles to More's Faust—tempts him with spurious "good news": a multimillion dollar development grant and the Nobel Prize. The price is, of course, More's soul—his being, his sense of personal responsibility. More resists the devil and so escapes aesthetic damnation; by not committing the unpardonable sin (refusing God's grace), he puts an end to the "feasting on death" that has preoccupied him since the onset of his daughter's illness and begins to live in the "lovely ordinary world" once again. Instead of an apocalypse, the novel ends with a new beginning, a Christmas morning. Reborn, Tom More no longer loves abstractly or bestially; he has married his former nurse, Ellen Oglethorpe, a Georgia Presbyterian, whose belief takes the form of charity. Equally important, More now knows what it is he wants: not prizes or women, but "just to figure out what I've hit on. Some day a man will walk into my office as ghost or beast or ghost-beast and walk out as a man, which is to say sovereign wayfarer, lordly exile, worker and waiter and watcher."

Lancelot · Percy's fourth novel, *Lancelot,* is by far his most troubling. Structurally, it follows the odd dialogue form of Camus's *The Fall* (1956); until the last two pages, only the voice of the protagonist is heard, addressing a "you" whose responses are not given. More disturbing is the fact that, as Joyce Carol Oates pointed out, the views of the main character, a self-righteous and unrepentant murderer, are strikingly similar to those of the author. Readers must recognize, as Percy surely does, the nature of the protagonist's grotesque mistake—the sources from which it derives and the ends to which it leads.

Lancelot Andrewes Lamar speaks his Poe-like tale from the Center for Aberrant Behavior in New Orleans, where he has been confined for one year. Although in the course of his apologia/confession Lance identifies his wife Margot's infidelity as the immediate cause of his murdering her and the members of the film company with whom she was involved, the actual causes go much further back and have less to do with Margot than with his own wasted life and his position as the last in a fallen line of southern aristocrats. As a Lamar, Lance has inherited not only the family homestead, Belle Isle, but also a way of judging humankind in absolute terms. His first wife, Lucy, was (or so Lance remembers her) an angel, whereas Margot, who for a time he turned into a goddess, became beast or devil. Dividing his life into two parts—before he discovered his wife's adultery and after—he proclaims that the past is "absolutely dead" and the future will be "absolutely new." This penchant for absolutes suggests Lance's inability or unwillingness to confront the ambiguity and mystery of human existence and is related to the way the Lamars view human life in terms of individual, historically significant events. Thus, Lance's life is reduced to his 110-yard touchdown run against Alabama and his destruction of Belle Isle and everyone in it. Lance does understand that performing such feats are actually less difficult than living an ordinary life, but when he turns Margot's infidelity into a quest for the "unholy grail," he in effect sidesteps the ordinary life which is far "more complicated and ambiguous" than either the historical events venerated by the Lamars or the clichéd films of Margot and her friends.

Like their film, Lance's quest is superficial and derivative (it is cast in the mold of the Raymond Chandler detective novels he has been reading). Moreover, it leads Lance, as Cleanth Brooks has demonstrated, to commit a modern version of the Gnostic heresy. Claiming that the original sin was something God did to man and judging Christianity as much a failure as southern stoicism, Lance determines to destroy the present age, which he cannot tolerate, and start over in a new Eden with his new Eve, Anna, a fellow patient who, he believes, as the victim of a brutal gang rape, has been restored to innocence. Lance is wrong about Anna, however; she never lost her innocence. He is also wrong about Christianity, if one distinguishes as Kierkegaard did, between Christianity (as embodied in Percival, Lance's listener to whom the novel is spoken) and Christendom, which Lance is right to reject as a viable alternative to his intolerable age.

Lance's confession as well as his predicament bring his friend Percival's spiritual ambivalence into sharp focus; Percival, the "Prince Hal" of their early manhood who has since been ordained Father John, is torn between two roles—priest and psychiatrist—and two approaches to human existence—the religious and the behavioral. It is Percival's fellow psychiatrists who certify Lance as sane, even though both Lance and Percival know there is still something wrong, something missing. As a psychiatrist, Percival cannot help Lance, whose problem is ontological and spiritual rather than psychological and whose self-righteous ranting masks his deeper uncertainty and longing. When, at the very end of the novel, Lance asks, "Is there anything I can do for you before I leave?," Percival's *"Yes"* identifies him as the apostolic Father John, the bearer of the good news for which Lance has been waiting. Against such grand gestures as blowing up Belle Isle, Percy offers the power of a small, ordinary word freshly heard.

The Second Coming · *The Second Coming* was, as Percy noted, his "first unalienated novel." Instead of the ambiguity that characterizes the endings of his earlier novels, here the author celebrates the unequivocal victory of love over death. While such a conclusion did not please all reviewers, many of whom found it unconvincing or even sentimental, it is consistent with Percy's religious vision and his flexible aesthetic with its various tones and broad range of narrative structures: the novelist's version of God's plenty.

The novel picks up the life of Will Barrett some twenty years after *The Last Gentleman.* At age forty-three, Will is a retired lawyer, a wealthy widower living in Linwood, North Carolina, and recent recipient of the Rotary's man-of-the-year award; yet, he is still a sick man, subject to dizzy spells and tricks of memory. What troubles Will is not the loss of his wife Marion but the sudden realization that he has wasted his life and been "only technically alive." At the brink of the abyss, he sees himself as a total stranger; only two percent of himself, he sets out to find the missing ninety-eight percent. His search takes him in a number of directions. One is back to his father, or more specifically to the only "event" in his life. This is a hunting accident that he comes to realize was no accident at all but instead the father's attempt to kill his son and then himself and so free them both from lives not worth living.

Like his father, Will rejects the "death in life" that characterizes modern believers as well as unbelievers; Will also rejects his father's solution, suicide, because it proves nothing. Instead, he devises the "ultimate scientific experiment" which will, he believes, provide conclusive proof of either God's existence or His nonexistence/non-involvement. As the narrator points out, Will is mad; moreover, his plan (to starve himself and so force God either to save or abandon him) is badly flawed in two important ways. The language Will uses to define his experiment (actually more a "covenant") betrays his egotism as well as his legalistic frame of reference; to his "huge" bequest (his life), he attaches a "huge" condition (God's appearing to him). Not until much later in the novel does he learn "the economy of giving and getting" and the superiority of ordinary existence to his own ultimate experiments or his father's extraordinary "events." In addition, Will is looking for God in the wrong place. While waiting in the cave for "a clear yes [or] no," he misses the unambiguous beauty of Indian summer; and while he assails God's "unavailability," his own "fade outs," such as the cave experiment, preclude the very intersubjective relationships through which God manifests Himself to humankind. The sign he does receive, a toothache, is "a muddy maybe" that cuts short the experiment and sends Will howling in pain out of the wilderness of self and into a world that, while not physically new, can be seen in an original way.

The person who changes Will's angle of vision is Allison Huger (Kitty Vaught's daughter), who has just escaped her own cave, a mental hospital, and begun a new life in an abandoned greenhouse. She resembles Will in that she feels uncomfortable around other people, as well she should, for the Allison they see is the mentally disturbed organism for whom they can imagine nothing better than "the best-structured environment money can buy." Although she wants to live an entirely self-reliant life, each afternoon about four o'clock she experiences a sense of loss or emptiness. What she feels is identical to one of the symptoms of Will's disease (Hausmann's syndrome), which the doctors call "inappropriate longing." There is a pill to control Will's disease, but there is only one way to satisfy the longing, and that is by loving Allison, by finding his being in her just as she finds hers in him. As Allison explains in her characteristically melodic way, "Our lapses are not due to synapses." Percy's love story is not, therefore, simply romantic; rather, it is religious in the Christian existential sense. Their love is, to quote Allison again, "be-all" but not "end-all." When, in the novel's concluding scene, Will Barrett confronts Father Weatherbee, an old priest,

> his heart leapt with joy. What is it I want from her and him, he wondered, not only want but must have? Is she a gift and therefore a sign of the giver? Could it be that the Lord is here, masquerading behind this simple holy face? Am I crazy to want both, her and Him? No, not want, must have. And will have.

Here, as in the four earlier novels, one finds what Sartre called humanity's "useless passion," but for Percy this passionate longing is not useless at all because the world is not absurd. Percy's search is not one of Sartre's purely arbitrary "projects"; rather it is a thoroughly modern and, for many readers, an entirely convincing rendition of John Bunyan's *The Pilgrim's Progress* (1678, 1684) in an age mired in the slough of behaviorism and unbelief.

The Thanatos Syndrome · *The Thanatos Syndrome*, Percy's sixth and last novel, ends a bit differently, which is to say less insistently. Narrator-protagonist Dr. Tom More's "well well well" befits the "smaller scale" of his latter-day desires, yet this fit proves ironic, given the novel's overgrand, at times messianic ambitions (of the kind More himself had in *Love in the Ruins*). Similarities between the two novels are obvious (they share a number of the same characters and the same Futurist-fantasy approach), but both the strengths and the weaknesses of *The Thanatos Syndrome* owe far more to *Lost in the Cosmos* than to *Love in the Ruins*: the satirizing of contemporary absurdities (inauthenticity in some of its craziest manifestations) and, unfortunately, the hardening of that spiritual need, which characterizes Will Barrett and Binx Bolling, into religious dogma. What was a translation of Christian belief into psychological, cultural, and semiotic terms in the earlier novels has begun to sound here like a propounding of conservative Catholic teachings, which undermines a novel that otherwise effectively mixes Sir Thomas More's 1516 *Utopia*, medieval romance, Fyodor Dostoevski, and Robin Cook.

The novel picks up the life and times of Tom More in the mid-1990's, a short while after his release from federal prison, where he has served a two-year term for illegally selling drugs. A brilliant diagnostician, More describes himself as "a psyche-iatrist, an old-fashioned physician of the soul" who believes that it is better, psychologically and spiritually speaking, to be sick (anxious, even terrified) than well, for disease is prolapsarian man's natural state. Many of the people around him are, he realizes, anything but anxious. They are, instead, content: without inhibitions, without anxiety, without anything more than rudimentary language skills, and, most important, without a sense of self. With the help of his epidemiologist cousin Lucy Lipscomb, More discovers "Blue Boy," a clandestinely funded pilot project which involves introducing heavy sodium into the local water supply in order to stem the tide of social deterioration (crime, teenage pregnancy, even acquired immunodeficiency syndrome).

Director of Blue Boy and indeed of the entire "Fedville" complex (including an "Equalitarian Center" with facilities for "pedeuthanasia" and "gereuthanasia" and a propensity for obfuscating acronyms) is the ironically "graceful" Bob Comeaux (née Robert D'Angelo Como), who calls Blue Boy "our Manhattan Project." He tries to cajole, seduce, bribe, and threaten More into complicity, all to no avail. Although he remains a lapsed Catholic throughout, the doctor nevertheless sides with the enigmatic, certainly depressed, previously alcoholic, perhaps mad Father Simon (as in Simeon Stylites and Simon Peter) Smith, who spends all of his time up in a fire tower silently triangulating the positions of forest fires, atoning for his sins, and on one notable occasion claiming that all tenderness inevitably leads to the gas chamber (or to the Equalitarian Center, which may be the same thing in a different, more socially acceptable, guise). Comeaux would make everyone happy, at the cost of his or her freedom as well as awareness of himself or herself as a distinctly human being: a creature caught in the malaise, lost in the cosmos, in need of something other than heavy sodium, self-help, or Phil Donahue. Like Saul Bellow's *The Dean's December* (1982), *The Thanatos Syndrome* expresses More's faith (in there being "more" than Comeaux allows) in the form of a doubt concerning the modern belief that the causes and cures of humanity's problems are invariably physical. To the extent that *The Thanatos Syndrome* articulates this doubt, it, like Percy's other novels, succeeds extraordinarily well. To the extent that it propounds Catholic dogma in response to a host of topical issues (abortion, "quality of life," sexual "freedom," child abuse, bio- and behavioral engineering, among others), it fails according to the very terms that Percy himself adopted at the time of his conversion, turning the triadic mystery of Søren Kierkegaard's apostle into dyadic pronouncement, sign into signal, spiritual "predicament" into position paper.

Robert A. Morace

Other major works

NONFICTION: *The Message in the Bottle*, 1975; *Lost in the Cosmos: The Last Self-Help Book*, 1983; *Conversations with Walker Percy*, 1985; *Signposts in a Strange Land*, 1991; *The Correspondence of Shelby Foote and Walker Percy*, 1997.

Bibliography

Allen, William Rodney. *Walker Percy: A Southern Wayfarer.* Jackson: University Press of Mississippi, 1986. Allen reads Percy as a distinctly American, particularly southern writer, claiming that the formative event in Percy's life was his father's suicide, not his reading of existentialist writers or conversion to Roman Catholicism. Allen's readings of individual novels emphasize the presence of weak fathers and rejection of the southern stoic heritage on the part of Percy's protagonists.

Coles, Robert. *Walker Percy: An American Search.* Boston: Little, Brown, 1978. An early but always intelligent and certainly sensitive reading of Percy's essays and novels by a leading psychiatrist whose main contention is that Percy's work speaks directly to modern humanity. In Coles's words, Percy "has balanced a contemporary Christian existentialism with the pragmatism and empiricism of an American physician."

Desmond, John F. *At the Crossroads: Ethical and Religious Themes in the Writings of Walker Percy.* Troy, N.Y.: The Whitston Publishing Company, 1997. Chapters on Percy and T. S. Eliot; on Percy's treatment of suicide; on Percy and Flannery O'Connor; on his treatment of myth, history, and religion; and his philosophical debt to pragmatism and Charles Sanders Pierce. A useful, accessible introduction to Percy's background in theology and philosophy.

Hardy, John Edward. *The Fiction of Walker Percy.* Urbana: University of Illinois Press, 1987. The originality of this book, comprising an introduction and six chapters (one for each of the novels, including *The Thanatos Syndrome*), derives from Hardy's choosing to read the novels in terms of internal formal matters rather than (as is usually the case) Percy's essays, existentialism, Catholicism, or southern background. Hardy sees Percy as a novelist, not a prophet.

Lawson, Lewis A. *Following Percy: Essays on Walker Percy's Work.* Troy, N.Y.: Whitson, 1988. Collects essays originally published between 1969 and 1984 by one of Percy's most dedicated, prolific, and knowledgeable commentators. Discussions of *The Moviegoer* and *Lancelot* predominate.

Percy, Walker. *Conversations with Walker Percy*, edited by Lewis A. Lawson, and Victor A. Kramer. Jackson: University Press of Mississippi, 1985. This indispensable volume collects all the most important interviews with Percy, including one (with the editors) previously unpublished. The volume is especially important for biographical background, influences, discussion of writing habits, and the author's comments on individual works through *Lost in the Cosmos.*

Quinlan, Kieran. *Walker Percy: The Last Catholic Novelist.* Baton Rouge: Louisiana State University Press, 1996. Chapters on Percy as novelist and philosopher, existentialist, explorer of modern science. Recommended for the advanced student who has already read Desmond. Includes notes and bibliography.

Tharpe, Jac, ed. *Walker Percy.* Boston: Twayne, 1983. Reading Percy as a Roman Catholic novelist concerned chiefly with eschatological matters, Tharpe divides his study into ten chapters: "Biography, Background, and Influences," "Theory of Art," "Christendom," "Techniques," one chapter on each of the five novels through *The Second Coming*, and conclusion. The annotated secondary bibliography is especially good.

_____. *Walker Percy: Art and Ethics.* Jackson: University Press of Mississippi, 1980. Ten essays by diverse hands, plus a bibliography. The essays focus on settings, existential sources, Martin Heidegger, Percy's theory of language, the semiotician Charles Saunders Peirce, Percy's politics, and *Lancelot* (in terms of his essays, Roman Catholicism, medieval sources, and semiotics).

KATHERINE ANNE PORTER

Born: Indian Creek, Texas; May 15, 1890
Died: Silver Spring, Maryland; September 18, 1980

Principal long fiction · *Ship of Fools*, 1962.

Other literary forms · Katherine Anne Porter is best known for her short fiction. Her stories appear in *Flowering Judas and Other Stories* (1930), *The Leaning Tower and Other Stories* (1944), and *The Old Order* (1944) and were gathered in *The Collected Stories of Katherine Anne Porter* (1965). Criticism, essays, and poems were collected in *The Days Before* (1952) and *The Collected Essays and Occasional Writings* (1970).

Achievements · Porter's solid and lasting reputation as a writer is based on a very small output of published work: one novel, a handful of novellas, and less than two dozen stories. This slender output, however, represents only a small portion of the fiction she wrote during her lifetime. Exacting and self-critical, she discarded many more stories than she published. By the time her first story appeared in print, she had already developed her fictional techniques to near perfection, and the maturity and craft of her style in *Flowering Judas and Other Stories*, her first published collection, never was surpassed by her later fiction.

Porter early established her reputation with literary critics and only later became widely known and read. In 1931, one year after the publication of her first volume, she was granted a Guggenheim Fellowship, an award she received again in 1938. The Society of Libraries of New York University awarded her its first annual gold medal for literature in 1940 upon the publication of *Pale Horse, Pale Rider*. A Modern Library edition of *Flowering Judas and Other Stories* appeared that same year. In 1943, she was elected a member of the National Institute of Arts and Letters, and in 1949, she accepted her first appointment as writer-in-residence and guest lecturer at Stanford University. In later years, she was to hold similar positions in many other colleges and universities, including the University of Chicago, the University of Michigan, Washington and Lee University, the University of Liège, and the University of Virginia.

By the time she published *Ship of Fools* in 1962, Porter had received three more honors: a Ford Foundation grant in 1959, and in 1962, the O. Henry Memorial Award for her story "Holiday" and the Emerson-Thoreau Bronze medal of the American Academy of Arts and Sciences. *Ship of Fools* became a Book-of-the-Month Club selection and an immediate best-seller. In the face of its overwhelming popular success, some critics charged that Porter had forsaken her artistic standards in favor of writing a book that would appeal to a large audience. *Ship of Fools* also was criticized for its pessimism and for its failure to conform neatly to the structure of a novel, a supposed flaw especially irksome to those who had admired the formal perfection of Porter's earlier works. Porter herself was surprised by the book's popularity. She had abandoned the form of her earlier work—with its tight plots centered on the fate of a single character—but she had moved deliberately on to something else. She was still writing "honest," she claimed, a quality that characterized all her fiction. First and last, she was still an artist, a label she applied to herself unhesitatingly.

Although Porter published no new fiction after *Ship of Fools*, her critical and public acclaim grew. It reached its peak when she received both the Pulitzer Prize and the National Book Award for Fiction in 1966.

Biography · Katherine Anne Porter was born Collie Russell Porter in Indian Creek, Texas, on May 15, 1890. She was the third of five children born to Harrison and Mary Alice Jones Porter. When her mother died in 1892, she and her brothers and sisters moved to Kyle, Texas, where they were cared for by their paternal grandmother, Catherine Anne Porter. When Mrs. Porter senior died in 1901, Harrison Porter sold the farm in Kyle and moved with his family to San Antonio.

Washington Star Collection, D.C. Public Library

Facts about Porter's early life and education have been difficult to substantiate, partly because Porter's own accounts were evasive or inconsistent. Although her family apparently was Methodist, Porter attended convent schools, possibly for a time in New Orleans, which may be why later researchers have reported that she was a Catholic from birth. Porter denied this allegation when it appeared in a biographical sketch published by the University of Minnesota series on American writers. Precocious as a child and rebellious as a teenager, she ran away from school at age sixteen to marry. The name of her first husband is not known, although the marriage lasted three years.

After the divorce, Porter moved to Chicago, already cherishing the ambition of becoming a professional writer. She worked as a reporter on a Chicago newspaper for a time and signed on as an extra with a motion-picture company for a few months. Passing up the opportunity to travel to Hollywood with the film company, she returned to Texas, where she reported that she made a living as a traveling entertainer, singing Scottish ballads, dressed in a costume she made herself. Thereafter, she wrote drama criticism and society gossip for a Fort Worth weekly, *The Critic*. One year later, she moved to Denver, Colorado, and became a reporter for the *Rocky Mountain News*. In Denver, during the influenza epidemic of 1918, she became severely ill and almost died. This experience, which she fictionalized in *Pale Horse, Pale Rider*, affected her profoundly. "I really had participated in death," she said years later in an interview with Barbara Thompson of the *Paris Review*. She had had "what the Christians call the 'beatific vision'"; she was no longer "like other people."

In 1919 she moved to New York City, where for a brief time she worked as a hack and ghostwriter. The following year she went to study in Mexico. Again she stayed only a short time, but for the next ten years Mexico was to be the center of her intellectual and imaginative life. Returning to Fort Worth, she began to write the stories based on her experiences there. During the next decade she traveled extensively, reviewed books for leading national magazines and newspapers, and worked and reworked the stories that were published in 1930 in *Flowering Judas and Other Stories.*

Supported by a Guggenheim Fellowship granted that year, she returned to Mexico. In 1931, she sailed aboard a German ship from Veracruz to Bremerhaven. This voyage gave her the setting for *Ship of Fools,* which was not to be published for another thirty years. She lived until the mid-1930's in Paris, marrying and later divorcing Eugene Pressly, a member of the American Foreign Service, and working on her fiction. After her divorce from Pressly, she married Albert Erskine, Jr., of the Louisiana State University faculty. Until her divorce from Erskine in 1942, she lived in Baton Rouge. During this time, she continued to work on her short fiction, but not until the late 1950's did she begin sustained effort on her only full-length novel, *Ship of Fools.* Although by that time many of her acquaintances believed she never would finish it, fragments of the novel appeared in magazines, and, in 1962, *Ship of Fools* was published. Porter wrote no more new fiction after that, although *The Collected Essays and Occasional Writings* appeared in 1970. On September 18, 1980, at age of ninety, Katherine Anne Porter died in Silver Spring, Maryland.

Analysis · Katherine Anne Porter once suggested that when she sat down to write about her life as accurately as possible, it turned into fiction; indeed, she knew no other way to write fiction. Whether this anecdote is true, it is certain that capturing the past with great detail was an important ingredient in her writing. In a number of the short stories, and in two of the best short novels, Miranda, the central character, is very close to being Porter herself. These stories follow Miranda's life from infanthood in her grandmother's house in South Texas, to her scrape with death from influenza in Colorado at the age of twenty-four–her first major step toward maturity.

Concerning the time of her illness, Porter has said that it was as though a line were drawn through her life, separating everything that came before from everything that came after. She had been given up and then had survived, and in some ways all her time after that was borrowed. Perhaps that is why her overtly autobiographical stories deal with the time before that line, the time when she was "alive" and therefore had a life to record. The stories that take place after that incident present her, if at all, as an observer, as someone slightly distant and alienated from life. (It is a question of degree: Miranda is also, of course, an acute observer in the stories in which she takes part. Her name, in fact, means "observer" in Spanish.) Porter was in real life a passenger on the ship about which her novel *Ship of Fools* was written, but she speaks of herself as purely an observer, who scarcely spoke a word on the entire voyage. She does not appear directly as a character in the novel.

Old Mortality · The girl, Miranda, in the short novel *Old Mortality,* runs away from school to get married, in part to escape from her family, so suffocatingly steeped in its own past. At the conclusion of the novella, she is determined to free herself once and for all from that past, so that she can begin to consider her own future; but she determines this, the reader is told in the ironic concluding lines, "in her hopefulness, her ignorance." The irony is that Miranda/Porter herself became so obsessed with that past that much of her best work is devoted to it. The explanation for Porter's obsession with the past can perhaps be guessed from the conclusion of "Pale Horse,

Pale Rider." Everything of importance to Miranda has died; only her ravaged body, her spark of a soul somehow survives. She finds that she has no future, only the slow progression to death once again. The past, then, is all she has, yet the past is finally intangible, as the girl in *Old Mortality* discovers as she sifts through all the evidence. At last no truth can be discovered, no objectivity, only the combined and contradictory subjectives: The only truth, once again, is the truth of fiction.

Porter said that in her fiction she is not interested in actions so much as she is interested in the various and subtle results of actions. Certainly, of all her works, *Old Mortality* deals directly with the ramifications of past actions. This short novel spans ten years in the life of the protagonist, Miranda, from the age of eight to the age of eighteen. In that time, the reader learns little of Miranda's life, except that she is bad tempered and that, unlike many of the young women in her widely extended family, she is not going to be a "beauty." She is, rather, the recording center of the novel: The events are brought to her and have their effect on the person she is becoming.

The crucial actions have occurred in the preceding generation. Miranda's family is obsessed by a past event. Miranda's aunt Amy was a great beauty, the measure, in fact, against which all the current crop of beauties are found wanting. She was glamorous, racy, even though tubercular, and for a long time spurned Gabriel's devoted courtship. Gabriel was himself wild, ran a string of racehorses, and was heir to the fortune. Only when he was disinherited and Amy found herself in the terminal stage of her illness did she consent to marry him. The couple went to New Orleans on their honeymoon, and almost immediately Amy died. Miranda tries to sift out the truth of the story. She looks at the photograph of Amy and does not find her so impossibly beautiful and indeed thinks she looks silly in her out-of-fashion dress. Later, she is introduced to Gabriel, and instead of the dashing young man who had once challenged a rival to a duel over Amy, she finds him fat and drunken, down on his luck; the woman whom he married after Amy is bitter and depressed from living with a ne'er-do-well who has spent their whole married life talking about Amy. Later still, Miranda meets Eva, a homely spinster cousin from Gabriel's generation, and Eva says the real truth is that Amy was a lewd woman, who married only because someone else got her pregnant, and took her own life with an overdose of drugs.

After a moment of shock, Miranda realizes that Eva's version, in its negative way, is just as romantic as the others. Miranda does not want to know where the truth lies. By this time, she has left school and has run off to get married. Her father is cool with her, thinking she has deserted the family; indeed she has, and deliberately. She refuses to be trapped in the past, represented by this unknowable woman whose brief life still haunts the family. She wants instead to discover who she–Miranda–is; she wants her own life to exist in the present and future. This is what she determines–in the novel's ironic final line–"in her hopefulness, her ignorance."

In her ignorance, Miranda-Porter learns that her past is what she is, the result of those past actions. She has been touched by Amy even more than the others, for she has become Amy, the Amy who refused to live by the others' rules, and at last ran off, married, and never returned–just as Miranda has done. In so doing, Amy and Miranda become separated from the rest of the family, freezing its members in their moment of history just as Porter herself became separated from her family so that she could re-create them forever in her stories.

Noon Wine · *Noon Wine* is set in the rural turn-of-the-century southern Texas of Porter's childhood but does not deal with her family. The characters in this short novel are poor and uneducated farmers, but this does not stop the story from being an intricate and subtle moral allegory. The lingering effect of past actions is not the central theme, as it was in *Old Mortality*, but a sense of the cumulative force of a man's actions gives the story a tragic inevitability. Mr. Thompson is a proud man, and as a result he marries above himself. Instead of a strong woman to help him in the strenuous operation of his farm, he marries a delicate and genteel woman who quickly becomes a near invalid. Further, she insists that they have a dairy, a bit higher class than an ordinary row-crop farm. In the end, Thompson is left with a wife who cannot help him and a kind of farmwork that he does not feel is masculine, and which he therefore shirks. The farm is deteriorating, and the couple are about to go under entirely, when a strange taciturn Swede from North Dakota arrives, asking for work. Instantly there is a revolution. The Swede fixes, paints, repairs everything, and shortly the failing farm becomes productive. As the years go by, the couple are able to buy such luxuries as an icebox, and Mr. Thompson is able to sit on the porch while the work is being done. One day Hatch arrives, a thoroughly evil man. He is a bounty hunter; the Swede, it is revealed, is an escaped homicidal maniac who in a berserk fury stabbed his own brother to death. Thompson refuses to give up the Swede. There is a scuffle; the Swede suddenly appears and steps between them; Thompson believing he sees Hatch stabbing the Swede in the stomach, smashes Hatch's skull with an ax.

The confrontation is remarkably complex. Hatch, as he is presented in the story, seems a pure manifestation of evil, and so perhaps he should be killed, but ironically he has in fact done nothing. The Swede is a primal murderer, a brother-killer like Cain, and is a threat to murder again. Thompson believes Hatch has stabbed the Swede and acts to defend him, but after he has killed Hatch, the Swede does not have a mark on him, not even, perhaps, the mark of Cain, which has been transferred to Thompson.

Thompson is easily acquitted of the crime in court, but his fundamentalist neighbors in the close-knit community look on him as a murderer. Most important, he must examine his own motives. Was he defending the Swede, or was he defending the success of his farm, which, he must have guiltily realized, was not the result of his work, but of the work of another, a sinner, a primal murderer? With his mark of Cain, Thompson goes the rounds of his neighbors, trying to tell his side of the story, believing it less each time himself, until he kills himself, the final consequence of his original pride.

Pale Horse, Pale Rider · Porter has called sleep "that little truce of God between living and dying." If dreams, therefore, take place in a landscape somewhere between life and death, it is appropriate that *Pale Horse, Pale Rider* begins with one of Miranda's many dreams to be recorded. Although the story is set during World War I in a small town in Colorado where Miranda is working for a newspaper, symbolically the story takes place in the dreamlike zone between life and death. In that initial dream, Death rides alongside Miranda, but she tells him to ride on ahead; she is not quite ready to go with him. She wakes up only to be reminded of the war, which is poisoning the lives of many people, who are full of despair because of their inability to control their destinies. The streets are filled with funerals, as the influenza epidemic kills people like a medieval plague. Miranda's work on the paper is hateful, and her only release is when, after work, she meets Adam. Adam, as his name suggests, is the man who should be her companion, her mate in life. He is a soldier, however, on his way to war and committed wholly to death, and so Miranda struggles to withhold her love from him.

The war and the plague, as presented in the novel, are symbols of the struggle of life and its vulnerability. Miranda and Adam differ from others in being existentially aware; all that exists for them is the present tense of their lives. They dance together in a cheap café, knowing that it is all they will ever have. Because they have so little—a brief moment of troubled life, and then death—the integrity of their actions becomes their only value. Miranda tells Adam that he is stupid to fight in a war in which old men send young men to die. He agrees, saying, however, that if he does not go, he can no longer face himself. Miranda has her own costly sense of integrity: As a reporter for the paper, she witnesses a pathetic scandal, and when the victims beg her not to write the story, she does not. The rival papers do, however, and her editor is furious; her colleagues think she is senseless. She is demoted to writing entertainment reviews. Even there, when she writes an unfavorable review of a vaudeville act, she is confronted by the old, broken, has-been actor, and her subsequent compassion struggles against her dedication to her job. Her colleagues counsel her to fake the reviews and make everyone happy, but writing honest reviews is an important value to her.

Miranda gets the flu, and in a long delirious dream comes to the point of death and has a beatific vision. The doctor and nurse fighting to preserve her, working with their own existential integrity, bring her back, but it is so painful being taken away from her vision and back to life, that when life-giving drugs are injected into her, she feels them like "a current of agony."

Miranda had fought, with her tiny spark of consciousness, to survive, to survive for Adam. Then she learns that Adam, perhaps having caught flu from her, has himself died. Her dream of heaven had been so brilliant that the real world seems to her a monochrome, a bleak field in which, with Adam gone, she has nothing. The reader, however, can see beyond this point. Earlier, Miranda and Adam had sung an old spiritual together, of a pale horse with a pale rider, who takes a girl's lover away, leaving her behind to mourn. Miranda is the singer who is left behind to mourn and to record the story for the rest of the world.

Ship of Fools · Porter has described her fiction as an investigation of the "terrible failure of the life of man in the Western World." Her one full-length novel, *Ship of Fools*, is a bleak cross section of modern civilization. It follows the lives of literally dozens of characters, from all levels of the particular society it is observing. More than forty characters of various nationalities are presented in some detail: American, Spanish, Mexican, Cuban, German, Swiss, Swedish. The time is 1931, and chaos is spreading. Soon Adolf Hitler will be in power, the extermination camps will be in operation, and another world war will be under way. The title *Ship of Fools* is a translation of Sebastian Brant's medieval moral allegory, *Das Narrenschiff* (1494). The ship is the world; the time of the journey is the lifetime of the characters. They, of course, do not see it that way. They think of it as a temporary voyage. The lies they tell, the treacheries they enact, the hopeless relationships they form, are only temporary, have nothing to do with the course of their real lives, with the objectives they mean to obtain, the moral codes by which they mean to live.

The ship, the *Vera* (truth), leaves Veracruz, Mexico, for the nearly monthlong journey to Bremerhaven. It is a German ship, and the German passengers sit at the captain's table. From the pompous and second-rate captain on down, they are comic grotesques, guzzling their food swinishly and looking suspiciously at everyone who does not eat pork, or who has a slightly large nose, as potentially Jewish. The only seemingly human Germans are Wilhelm Freytag, concealing as long as he can the fact that he has a Jewish wife, and Dr. Schumann, the ship's doctor, the novel's most sympathetic character, urbane, gentle, wise–who, to his own horror, commits perhaps the basest act of anyone on board. The American characters are only slightly less grotesque. William Denny the Texan is pure caricature: To him everyone but a white Texan is a "nigger," "spick," "wop," or "damyankee." He devotes all his time to pursuing sexual pleasure but is fearful that he will be cheated into paying too much for it. The comic result is that he pays out everything and gets nothing in return but a severe drubbing. Mrs. Treadwell, a forty-five-year-old divorcee, is utterly selfish, yet she wonders why she gets nothing from life. David Scott and Jenny Brown, living together, fighting constantly, are, with Dr. Schumann and Wilhelm Freytag, the novel's main characters. David Scott is tied up within himself and will give up nothing to another. Jenny Brown sporadically gives up everything to mere acquaintances yet seems to have nothing of her own within.

One character after another debates humanity's nature: Are all humans basically good; are all humans naturally depraved; are the pure races good and the mongrel races evil? The characters seem intent on acting out all these possibilities. The most disciplined of them regularly lapse into helpless sentimentality. Freytag thinks that each woman he meets is the beautiful love of his life. One of these women is a Jew, whom he married during a period of extreme romanticism, and now he is déclassé among his German compatriots and cannot admit to himself how regretful he is. David and Jenny, needing everything from each other, have only gone as far as learning each other's weaknesses, of which they take full advantage to lacerate each other. They continue to cling together, always saying they will separate at some later time. Most painful is the folly of the sympathetic Dr. Schumann. He convinces himself that he is in love with a neurotic Spanish countess (he has a wife at home), and under pretense of caring for her as her doctor, he turns her into a hopeless and helpless drug addict in order to keep his power over her.

The most purely evil characters on the ship are the shoddy Spanish dance troupe. Through herculean efforts they almost take control of the ship and certainly take control of the lives of the characters, bringing out their deepest and worst traits, but at the end they sit listless and exhausted, as though the effort were immensely greater than any return they have had from it. This troupe of carnival performers cheats, steals, blackmails, and even kills right before the others, who remark on it, but do nothing to stop them, each character feeling it is not his place to do anything. At length, the troupe is sitting confidently at the captain's table, having rearranged everyone's position on the ship. In a kind of Walpurgis Night, they bring the many characters to some sort of climax in an eruption of drunken violence. It is Porter's vision of how World War II began: low thugs and gangsters taking power with the casual, half-intentional connivance of the world.

In the midst of this bleak and pessimistic picture of the Western world, there is one possibility of redemption. The rare positive moments in the novel are when the characters suddenly, often to their own surprise, come together in the act of sex–Porter emphasizing the sensuality of the contact rather than any spiritual qualities. Perhaps Porter is saying that in their fallen state human beings must start at the bottom, with earthly sensuality, in order to slowly acquire a knowledge of spiritual beauty.

Norman Lavers

Other major works

SHORT FICTION: *Flowering Judas and Other Stories*, 1930; *Hacienda*, 1934; *Noon Wine*, 1937; *Pale Horse, Pale Rider: Three Short Novels*, 1939; *The Leaning Tower and Other Stories*, 1944; *The Old Order*, 1944; *The Collected Stories of Katherine Anne Porter*, 1965.

NONFICTION: *My Chinese Marriage*, 1921; *Outline of Mexican Popular Arts and Crafts*, 1922; *What Price Marriage*, 1927; *The Days Before*, 1952; *A Defence of Circe*, 1954; *A Christmas Story*, 1967; *The Collected Essays and Occasional Writings*, 1970; *The Selected Letters of Katherine Anne Porter*, 1970; *The Never-Ending Wrong*, 1977; *Letters of Katherine Anne Porter*, 1990.

Bibliography

Brinkmeyer, Robert H. *Katherine Anne Porter's Artistic Development: Primitivism, Traditionalism, and Totalitarianism.* Baton Rouge: Louisiana State University Press, 1993. Chapters on art and memory, Porter's early years in Mexico, her vision and sense of self, her Southern heritage, and *Ship of Fools*. Includes a detailed bibliography.

Givner, Joan. *Katherine Anne Porter: A Life.* New York: Simon & Schuster, 1982. A thorough biography that was begun with Porter's blessing before she died. Contains an overabundance of information: for example, it is difficult to locate the dates of publications of her books. Nevertheless, a complete and intriguing picture of a complex life.

Hardy, John Edward. *Katherine Anne Porter.* New York: Frederick Ungar, 1973. An introduction to Porter's life and fiction that is well organized and gracefully written. Includes a bibliography and would be useful to any student.

Hendrick, George, and Willene Hendrick. *Katherine Anne Porter.* Rev. ed. Boston: Twayne, 1988. This efficient book covers Porter's life and offers criticism of most of her work. Examines her short fiction and her only novel, *Ship of Fools*. Includes an annotated bibliography.

Stout, Janis. *Katherine Anne Porter: A Sense of the Times.* Charlottesville: University Press of Virginia, 1995. Chapters on Porter's background in Texas, her view of politics and art in the 1920's, her writing and life between the two world wars, and her relationship with the Southern agrarians. Also addresses the issue of gender, the problem of genre in *Ship of Fools*, and the quality of Porter's "free, intransigent, dissenting mind." Includes notes and bibliography.

Unrue, Darlene Harbour. *Truth and Vision in Katherine Anne Porter's Fiction.* Athens: University of Georgia Press, 1985. Porter believed that people want to understand the truth of their existence, Unrue maintains, but they get distracted by the things of this world, such as romanticized love and ideology. Provides criticism of Porter's fiction based on this thesis.

Walsh, Thomas F. *Katherine Anne Porter and Mexico.* Austin: University of Texas Press, 1992. Chapters on Porter and Mexican politics, her different periods of residence in Mexico, and *Ship of Fools*. Includes notes and bibliography.

CHAIM POTOK

Born: New York, New York; February 17, 1929

Principal long fiction · *The Chosen*, 1967; *The Promise*, 1969; *My Name Is Asher Lev*, 1972; *In the Beginning*, 1975; *The Book of Lights*, 1981; *Davita's Harp*, 1985; *The Gift of Asher Lev*, 1990; *I Am the Clay*, 1992.

Other literary forms · *Wanderings: Chaim Potok's History of the Jews* (1978) is a personal reconstruction of four thousand years of Jewish history. Potok also wrote essays and book reviews for Jewish and popular periodicals and newspapers. In January, 1988, his stage adaptation of *The Chosen* opened as a short-lived Broadway musical, with music by Philip Springer and lyrics by Mitchell Bernard. Potok wrote two picture books for young children, both illustrated by Tony Auth, *The Tree of Here* (1993) and *The Sky of Now* (1995). He also published essays and stories in various magazines and a collection of short stories about troubled young people, *Zebra and Other Stories* (1998). In addition, he wrote a few full-length works of nonfiction, including *The Gates of November: Chronicles of the Slepak Family* (1996), the epic story of the families of Solomon Slepak, a Bolshevik and one of the founders of the Soviet Union, who managed to survive all Stalin's purges without being imprisoned, and his son, Volodya Slepak, a refusenik, one of the Russian Jews who applied for and was for years refused permission by the Soviet government to emigrate to Israel.

Achievements · Critical acceptance and public acclaim have greeted Potok's novelistic explorations of the conflict between Orthodox Judaism and secular American culture. Potok received the Edward Lewis Wallant Award and a National Book Award nomination for *The Chosen*, his first novel. He received the Athenaeum Award for its sequel, *The Promise*. He also received the National Jewish Book Award for Fiction for *The Gift of Asher Lev* and the National Foundation for Jewish Culture Achievement Award for Literature. His sympathetic (critics would say sentimental) portrayal of Jewish fundamentalism and those who choose to leave it highlights the poignancy of an individual's break with tradition. Indeed, Potok's novels test the ability of traditional communities to contribute to the modern world without themselves being assimilated. His evocation of Jewish life in New York in the latter two-thirds of the twentieth century has universal appeal and disturbing implications.

Biography · Born of Orthodox Jewish parents in the Bronx in 1929, Chaim Potok was reared in a fundamentalist culture. Potok's father, Benjamin Potok, was a Polish émigré and no stranger to the pogroms of Eastern Europe. The young Potok was taught that the profound suffering of the Jews would one day transform the world. Yet, as Potok suggests in *Wanderings*, his service as a Jewish chaplain with the United States Army in Korea (1956-1957) confronted him with a world of good and evil that had never heard of Judaism. His attempt to come to terms with this larger world led Potok to a critical   investigation of his own Jewish heritage and the limitations of the fundamentalist perspective. Though he was ordained a Conservative rabbi in 1954, attracted by doctrines more liberal than those of strict Jewish Orthodoxy, Potok

continued his struggle to reconcile fundamental Judaism
with the findings of science
(as historiography and textual criticism shed new light
on ancient traditions). *The
Chosen* inaugurated his public search for a voice with
which to speak to his heritage
as well as to the larger world.

In the early 1960's, Potok
taught at the Jewish Theological Seminary in New
York, edited *Conservative Judaism*, and in 1965 became
editor-in-chief with the Jewish
Publication Society of Philadelphia. In 1975 he became
special projects editor. He was
married to Adena Mosevitzky
in 1958, and they took up residence in Merion, Pennsyl-
vania. The Potoks had three
children: Rena, Naama, and

©Jerry Bauer

Akiva. Potok served as a visiting professor at the University of Pennsylvania, Bryn
Mawr College, and The Johns Hopkins University.

Analysis · In his novels, Chaim Potok returns again and again to the story of a young
protagonist coming of age in a culture (usually Jewish) at once mysterious, beautiful,
sad, and somehow inadequate. Usually told in the first person, Potok's stories surround
the reader with forebodings of the larger, evil world (news of pogroms in Europe, the
Holocaust, the first atom bomb) into which his characters are plunged. Potok creates
a microcosm of feeling and reaction to events that shake the world. His sentences are
simple and reportorial, at times almost a parody of the staccato style of Ernest
Hemingway. The stories develop chronologically, though they are frequently invaded
by dreams, visions, or voices from the "Other Side."

In each of his stories, Potok sets for himself a question to be answered and reworks
his own experiences until he is satisfied with at least a provisional resolution. Controlling metaphors help shape the questions. In *The Chosen*, the baseball game symbolizes
the competition between two Jewish cultures, the very strict Hasidic and the more
openly assimilationist. What happens to those caught in between those two traditions?
The vision of pups being born in *The Book of Lights* represents the entrance of fertile
Cabala mysticism into a world of strict Jewish law. How can Jewish mysticism enrich
Orthodoxy? Asher Lev's dreams of his mythical ancestor foreshadow the young
artist's confrontation with his own culture. What happens when art brings great hurt?
The sound of a little door harp symbolizes the transforming power of the imagination
for Ilana Davita Chandal of *Davita's Harp*. What is the place of the imagination in
Jewish Orthodoxy? What is the place of women? (Davita is Potok's first female
protagonist.)

The Chosen · *The Chosen* recounts the story of Danny Saunders, brilliant son of a Hasidic rabbi, chosen by tradition to one day succeed his father as leader of the fundamentalist community in Brooklyn, New York. Yet Danny is less interested in studying the Talmud (Jewish law) than in probing the works of Sigmund Freud and other secular psychologists. The story closes with the inevitable confrontation between Danny and his father, which is mediated by Danny's friend Reuvan Malter. In the climactic scene in Reb Saunders's office, the old rabbi turns to his son and addresses him as a father for the first time. (For years, Danny had been reared in silence, except for times of Talmud study.) With fatherly tears, Reb Saunders explains that the years of silence created a soul of compassion within his brilliant son. Though he may well leave the Hasidic community for secular studies, Danny will always carry with him the legacy of Jewish suffering. That legacy will provide the moral force to change the world.

Reuvan, son of a Talmud scholar of the new school of textual criticism, chooses to become a rabbi. The choices, for Reuvan and for Danny, do not, however, come easily. Reuvan faces ostracism by the Hasidic community for suggesting that some Talmudic texts were of inferior quality and subject to misinterpretation. Danny must seemingly turn against his father if he is to pursue secular studies and abandon his leadership obligations.

The novel is structured almost as a diary, with pages of detailed descriptions of schoolwork in the Jewish high school, visits to the local synagogue, and the ebb and flow of Reuvan's life. Though at times tedious, the very innocence of the language contributes to a certain dramatic intensity. The conflict in the novel is mirrored in the frequent news reports of World War II and in the ensuing controversy over the creation of a Jewish state, Israel, in 1949. The Hasidic community is content to wait for the Messiah to create such a state; Reuvan's father calls for an immediate political settlement. Political questions are present in each of Potok's novels and are of central interest in *Davita's Harp*.

The Promise · Silence is again present in Potok's second novel, *The Promise*, which continues the story of Danny Saunders and Reuvan Malter as they enter their professional lives. The novel begins with shouts of rage from young Michael Gordon, the son of Professor Abraham Gordon, a controversial Jewish philosopher. Michael has been cheated at a carnival booth by an old Jewish man, and both Reuvan and his date, Rachel Gordon, Michael's cousin, stare in horror as Michael angrily denounces Orthodoxy. Michael's father had questioned the supernatural accounts in the Hebrew Bible and, as a result, was excommunicated from the Orthodox community; now Michael is releasing his hate on those who persecuted Professor Gordon. Subsequently, Michael is taken to Danny Saunders, now a psychologist at a residential treatment center. When the boy refuses to speak, Danny isolates him. The agonizing silence breaks Michael's will and he reveals the hate he feels for his father and his writings, writings that have brought condemnation to them both. Eventually, Michael is finally able to accept his own feelings and reconcile with his parents, and Danny and Rachel are married, the powerful coupling of the brilliant Hasid with the cosmopolitan daughter of a secularist philosopher.

The Promise continues the exploration of Reuvan's choice to receive his rabbinate from an Orthodox seminary and his refusal to become a secular Jew, as Professor Gordon has done. Yet Reuvan is uneasy with the traditional method of Talmud study advanced by Rav Kalman, one of his teachers. If the Talmud is the sacred oral tradition of the Jews in written form, contradictory commentaries from rabbis down through the centuries must always be reconciled by newer interpretations, so as not to call God's Word into question. For Reuvan, there is another possibility; a corrupt text could be the source of confusion. Any correction, however, would mean violence to sacred scripture. Reuvan will become a rabbi so that he might debate Rav Kalman and the others from within a common tradition.

Reuvan's father, David Malter, is the voice of quiet wisdom throughout both books. Though a proponent of the new Talmud studies, he is sympathetic toward those whose tightly knit culture is being threatened. As he tells Reuvan in *The Promise*, "We cannot ignore the truth. At the same time, we cannot quite sing and dance as they do. . . . That is the dilemma of our time, Reuvan. I do not know what the answer is." Earlier, Reuvan's father had challenged his son to make his own meaning in the world. Those who had committed themselves to the Hasidic traditions had kept the faith alive through incomprehensible persecution. Now Reuvan must also choose with the greatest seriousness and fervency, for he, too, must make a mark on the world and endure hardship of his own.

My Name Is Asher Lev · Potok picks up this theme in his third novel, *My Name Is Asher Lev*. Covering the period of the late 1940's through the late 1960's, the book is an apologia for the artist. The Orthodox Jewish surroundings are familiar, but this time the controversy is not over textual criticism but rather representational art. Painting is not strictly forbidden to the Orthodox Jew, but it is regarded as useless, as foolishness, as a waste of time better devoted to the study of the Torah, the five books of Moses. Moreover, certain pictures could come close to violating the commandment forbidding graven images. Asher Lev is a born painter, however, and throughout the novel, as he develops his talent, he is increasingly isolated from his family and culture. Asher is born in Crown Heights in Brooklyn in 1943. His father travels extensively for the local Rebbe in an effort to establish Ladover Hasid communities throughout Europe and to aid families emigrating to the United States. Asher's mother must stay with her son in New York because Asher refuses to leave his familiar streets to join his father in Europe.

There are long nights of loneliness, waiting for Asher's father to return from some mission or other. Asher's mother suffers a breakdown when her brother, also on a mission for the Rebbe, is killed. She begins to find herself again by plunging into her Russian studies, picking up the work her brother left unfinished. Metaphors of things unfinished and things completed permeate the novel. Asher's father is continually on the move because of the great unfinished work of the Ladover. Asher himself finds that he must bring some kind of completeness to the world by painting not only what he sees with his eyes but also what his inner vision reveals to him. Those visions are not always beautiful; his paintings can be like knives, plunging the reality of evil into the soul of the onlooker. The wise Rebbe, sensing Asher's vast talent, entrusts him to Jacob Kahn, himself an artistic genius and a nonobservant Jew. Kahn forces Asher to absorb the work of Pablo Picasso, especially *Guernica* (1937), a painting inspired by the German bombing of the Basque capital during the Spanish Civil War. In time, Asher begins to surpass his teacher.

Asher becomes virtually a stranger to his father. At the end of the novel, Asher's parents stare with mixed rage and amazement at the two crucifixions he has painted. Both are of his mother, looking in abstract fashion at Asher the stranger on one side and at the always-traveling husband on the other. The image of the cross for Asher has become the supreme symbol of suffering, devoid of any Christian preoccupation. The image is too much, however, for his parents, Orthodox Jews. As the Rebbe tells him, "You have crossed a boundary. I cannot help you. You are alone now. I give you my blessings."

There is a marked contrast between Asher's sensitive paintings (an effort to say what must be said about the evil in the world) and his selfish behavior toward his parents. He is one of the least sympathetic of Potok's protagonists because he struggles less with his own anguish than with his need to express his artistic gift at whatever cost. Jacob Kahn's advice, "Be a great painter, Asher Lev. . . . That will be the only justification for all the pain your art will cause," seems too facile. Asher is determined to remain an observant Jew, but he will do so on his own terms. The commandment about honoring one's parents must be radically reinterpreted. The book suffers from the technical difficulty that Asher Lev must be identified as a genius early in the story in order for Potok to create the kind of tension he needs to interest a reader. A mediocre artist who causes pain is merely self-indulgent.

Yet the book reveals something of Potok's larger purpose. Art must be true to itself even if that means surprise or hurt. The artist, painter, or writer must speak from the heart; anything else is mere propaganda. Potok is seeking to provide a rationale for his novelistic critiques of fundamentalist communities.

Potok introduces something else into Asher's story: Asher often dreams of his "mythic ancestor," a Jew who served a nobleman only to have the nobleman unleash evil upon the world. Just as Asher envisioned that ancient Jew traveling the world, seeking to redress the wrong he had a part in, so must the artist reshape evil into art and so bring a kind of balance to the world. Asher's visions are forerunners of Potok's use of mysticism or imaginative visions themselves as ways of coming to terms with a world gone crazy.

In the Beginning · *In the Beginning* is the story of young David Lurie and his childhood in an Orthodox family in the Bronx in the 1920's. The novel is patterned after the Book of Genesis: David falls from his mother's arms, develops a keen interest in the accounts of the Flood, and learns through the study of the Torah the power of words to shape a world. Potok's fourth novel was his most complex to date, departing from the forthright exposition found in *The Chosen* in favor of a more subtle panoply of impressions of growing up. Like all Potok's protagonists, David is precocious, constantly questioning the world around him, trying to have it make sense. He is sickly, bullied by other boys, and plagued with recurring nightmares. David functions in the novel as an idealized figure to focus the reader's attention on how Orthodoxy confronts anti-Semitism and growing secularization. David imagines the Golem of Prague crushing those who would harm the Jews like some powerful living robot; as David grows, though, he learns that words can be more powerful than the Golem. Eventually, helped by those who practice textual critique of the Torah, David heads for graduate study at the University of Chicago. Yet, as in Potok's other works, there must also be some kind of reconciliation of the demands of Jewish Orthodoxy with those of secular learning. It is achieved through a vision David has years later as he tours the site of the Bergen-Belsen death camp. David's vision of his dead father, and of his father's brother, David's namesake, is a moving conclusion to the book. David's father despairs that he has lost his son to the evil world, to the very world that took the lives of millions of Jews. He is reassured by David's uncle, however, that the son must journey into that world in order to bring something back to enrich Orthodoxy, which has become moribund. The son must venture out but must never forget his own roots. No anger of humanity can strike evil from the world. Only the patient use of words, with faith in their power to transform creation, can accomplish the task. That will be a new beginning for the world, and for Orthodoxy.

Potok's earlier novels tell the story of those in conflict with their Orthodox heritage. For the first time, *In the Beginning* pictures a reconciliation as a vision or story within the context of the novel. It is a kind of blessing from the beyond; here is the artist at work, crafting the resolution to the story.

The Book of Lights · *The Book of Lights*, narrated in the third person, uses the technique of mystical reconciliation for a more universal purpose. If the Master of the Universe truly exists, how is a believer to accept the death light of the twentieth century, the atomic bomb? Potok's answer is that through the imaginative use of Jewish mysticism, the spark of God can be found in an evil world.

The story departs from Potok's previous novels, which traced the childhood of the protagonist. Only a few pages are devoted to Gershon Loran's early life before his seminary days and subsequent chaplaincy in Korea. Those first pages, however, are significant. Gershon witnesses the birth of some pups on a rooftop in the midst of his rundown neighborhood; he is awed by the presence of life even amid wreckage.

In seminary, Gershon is introduced to the study of the Cabala and its *Zohar*, a Jewish mystical work from the thirteenth century. The *Zohar* is the book of lights of the novel's title, describing the creation of the world through the emanations of God. There are places where God has withdrawn His light; that has enabled humankind to come on the scene but it has also ushered in great evil. Now the mystic is called to ascend through those emanations to find God.

Such mystical tradition is complex and even contradictory. For Gershon, however, it is the pounding heart of a living faith. Gershon's quiet moments of reverie serve him well during his chaplaincy. Though Potok paints a detailed picture of Gershon's activities in Korea, the crucial story is elsewhere. Gershon's seminary friend, Arthur Leiden, travels with him to Kyoto and Hiroshima. At the Hiroshima monument, Arthur reads from the Psalms and pleads to God in vain for some kind of atonement. Arthur's father had worked with other scientists in developing the atom bomb, and Arthur is haunted by the memory. Later, Arthur is killed in a plane crash; Gershon, visiting Arthur's parents, hears a portion of one of Arthur's letters: "All the world, it seems, is a grayish sea of ambiguity, and we must learn to navigate in it or be drowned." That is Potok's message in the novel; "Loran" is itself a navigational acronym. If Judaism were merely the law, the faith would break on the shoals of the gritty world. Its mystical tradition infuses the faith with the ambiguity of real life. It does not explain but rather affirms the nature of God's creation. The *Zohar* is an imaginative understanding of the nature of God; in it, God enfolds both good and evil. It is a light by which to view a decaying civilization, a light that will survive the death light. In his final mystical vision of his old cabala teacher, Gershon learns that the mystical light will help mend the world so that it can be broken again in yet new acts of creation.

Davita's Harp · It is the "mending power" of imagination that is at the heart of *Davita's Harp*. The harp referred to is a small instrument that fits on a door, with little balls that strike piano wires when the door is opened or closed. Here Potok returns to the first-person narrative, tracing the childhood of Ilana Davita Chandal, his first female lead character. She is the daughter of a nonbelieving Jewish mother and a nonbelieving Christian father. Spanning the years from the mid-1930's to 1942, the novel speaks with a new voice yet recapitulates some familiar themes. Davita grows up in the New York area; she remembers frequent moves, strange people coming and going, and the constant singing of the door harp. Her parents are involved in the Communist Party, attempting to fight Fascism in Spain and in the United States. Davita is precocious and inquisitive and her mother intelligent and cool, forever supplying Davita with the meaning of new words: proletariat, strike, idea, magic, war. Davita is spurred in her imaginative development by Aunt Sarah, a devout Episcopalian nurse, who tells her Bible stories, and by Jakob Daw, an Austrian writer, now suffering from having been gassed in World War I, who had loved Davita's mother when they were both in Vienna. Daw is sheltered for a time by Davita's parents and spins odd stories for her. There is the story of the little bird, flying to find the source of a beautiful music that soothes the world of the horrors of war. Only if the bird could stop the deceitful music would the world wake to its pain.

Davita's father, Michael Chandal, a journalist with *New Masses*, is killed during the bombing of Guernica during the Spanish Civil War. Soon after, both Jakob Daw and Davita's mother, Channah, become disillusioned with the Stalinists because the Communists, too, have committed atrocities. Davita has taken to attending a Jewish high school and becomes an outstanding student. Jakob Daw returns to Europe, where he dies, though his stories live in Davita's heart. Not long afterward, Ezra Dinn, an Orthodox Jew who had loved Davita's mother years before, marries Channah. Slowly, Davita's mother regains her sense of place.

Davita's time of innocence is over. Before Jakob Daw left for Europe, he finished his strange story of the bird. The bird, he said, gave up searching for the music of the world and became very small to fit inside the door harp. There, said Daw, the music was not deceitful but full of innocence. Now, however, Davita encounters something sinister in her adopted tradition. She is the most brilliant student at her yeshiva but she is passed over for the Akiva Award because, she is told, she is a woman. It is 1942. Another student is selected for the award but learns the truth and refuses it. He is Reuvan Malter, first introduced in *The Chosen*.

Ilana Davita had wanted the prize because it would have given her the opportunity to tell her Jewish community a few words of farewell. "I had made this community my home, and now I felt betrayed by it. . . . I felt suddenly alone. And for the first time I began to understand how a single event could change a person's life." Later, in a vision, Jakob Daw and Davita's father appear, as well as Aunt Sarah. They want to hear her words, and so Davita speaks. She does not understand a world that kills its very best. She had wanted to speak public words of good-bye to her father and Jakob Daw the storyteller. The harp appears in her vision as well, singing in memorial to all the Davitas who would never have an opportunity to "speak their few words to this century."

In the end, Davita will go on to public school, angry with "sacred discontent." In an interview, Potok explained that Davita's experience was based on that of his wife, who was passed over as valedictory speaker because of her sex. *Davita's Harp* is a new exploration for Potok, that of Orthodoxy and feminism. Yet the novel also draws from Gershon Loran, David Lurie, and Asher Lev in recognizing the power of the artist's imagination to transform pain and ambiguity into some kind of meaning. A writer is a kind of harp, playing new music that mends the world.

The Gift of Asher Lev · *The Gift of Asher Lev* is framed by death. It begins with the funeral of Yitzchok Lev, Asher's uncle, and the ending of Asher's exile in France to attend the services in Brooklyn. Asher Lev is forty-five; he is joined by his wife Devorah, their daughter Rocheleh, eleven, and five-year-old son Avrumel. Though his family adapts well to the life of the Brooklyn Hasidim, Asher is haunted by the memory of a strange telephone call he received eighteen years earlier, the last time he had visited his parents in New York. It was a voice from the "Other Side," threatening death.

Asher is unable to paint (though he is given to sketching) and he seems to wander aimlessly through the local shops and galleries, as if waiting for a renewal of his gift. In the last year, critics had detected Asher's repetition of old themes, and he feels in danger of losing his gift should he become acclimated to his parents' community. Morose and determined to flee to France again, Asher is asked by the Rebbe to stay, at least for a while. Eventually it becomes clear to Asher that he and the aging Rebbe are woven inextricably together, as darkness and light. The Rebbe has no heir, and it is apparent that the leadership of the Ladover must pass soon to Asher's father; but there can be stability in the community only if there is assurance of the line of succession. If not Asher, then the next heir must be Avrumel, Asher's only son.

By the end of the novel, which takes Asher's story to the late 1980's, the artist has exiled himself again to France, but not without sacrifice. He has left his wife and children in New York, promising to return to them several months hence; yet in his isolation he has begun to paint again. "What kind of God creates such situations?" Asher asks himself as he walks with Devorah. "He gives me a gift and a son, and forces me to choose between them." Later, in France, Asher is visited by the image of the far-away Rebbe: "Slowly you begin to unravel the riddle," the vision says. "Your answer may save us and return you to your work. . . . It is sometimes possible for a man to acquire all of the world to come by means of a single act in this world. . . . You will redeem all that you have done and all that you are yet to do." Paradoxically, the sacrifice of Avrumel for the good of the community is a kind of death that redeems that artist himself; a gift on behalf of the world to come in exchange for the gift of the world as it is, in all its ambiguity and horror, and the ability to capture it on canvas.

I Am the Clay · Like *The Book of Lights, I Am the Clay* is a third-person narrative that grew in part from Potok's experiences in Korea. As they flee the North Korean and Chinese armies, a nameless old man and a woman named Gyu find a boy, Kim Sin, who is terribly wounded. The man wants to leave the boy, but the woman insists on taking him with them and heals him of his wounds. Eventually, they return to the village of the old couple to discover that it has not been destroyed. The boy then travels to his village, discovers that it is razed, and returns to the village of the man and woman. Nearby is an American military installation where the boy gets a job, eventually working for a Jewish chaplain. After the boy reluctantly gets involved with a thief, the chaplain helps him escape by finding him a job in Seoul. By this time, the woman is dead, and the man has learned to love the boy.

The book treats the conflicts between the old, rural way of life and the new, technological way of life as well as between the old religious ideas and the reality of war. When the old man and woman return to their village, they think things will be the same because it has been spared, but they are wrong.

Like the biblical Job, to whom the novel's title alludes, the man, woman, and boy do not understand why they suffer. The woman has learned the words "I am the clay" from a missionary, from whom she has also learned to make the sign of the cross. Blending the sign of the cross into her own ideas about magic, she illustrates Potok's idea of the unity of all people. Although the novel has little to do with Jews, *I Am the Clay* treats one of Potok's central problems: testing one's beliefs in the face of an ambiguous, often harsh, and rapidly changing reality.

Dan Barnett, updated by Richard Tuerk

Other major works

SHORT FICTION: *Zebra and Other Stories*, 1998.

NONFICTION: *Wanderings: Chaim Potok's History of the Jews*, 1978; *Tobiasse: Artist in Exile*, 1986; *The Gates of November: Chronicles of the Slepak Family*, 1996.

CHILDREN'S LITERATURE: *The Tree of Here*, 1993; *The Sky of Now*, 1995.

Bibliography

Abramson, Edward A. *Chaim Potok*. Boston: Twayne, 1986. The first book-length study of Potok, this volume is the fullest available introduction to his life and works. After a biographical sketch, Abramson discusses each of Potok's novels through *Davita's Harp* and also devotes a chapter to *Wanderings*. Supplemented by a chronology, notes, a good selected bibliography (including a list of secondary sources with brief annotations), and an index.

Potok, Chaim. "An Interview with Chaim Potok." Interview by Elaine M. Kauvar. *Contemporary Literature* 27 (Fall, 1986): 290-317. In this lengthy and wide-ranging interview, Potok discusses his work through *Davita's Harp*. He is revealed as a novelist who, more than most, writes with a clearly formed plan in mind. Of particular interest is his intention to take up the stories of the protagonists of his first six novels and interweave them in subsequent works.

_____. "Judaism Under the Secular Umbrella." Interview by Cheryl Forbes. *Christianity Today* 22 (September 8, 1978): 14-21. In this excellent interview, Potok defines his concept of "core to core culture confrontation" and explains how each of his novels through *In the Beginning* deals with such a confrontation. In *The Chosen*, for example, the confrontation is between Orthodox Judaism and Freudian psychoanalysis (which Potok identifies with "the core of Western secular humanism"); in *My Name Is Asher Lev*, there is a conflict between Judaism and art's claim to autonomy.

Shaked, Gershon. "Shadows of Identity: A Comparative Study of German Jewish and American Jewish Literature." In *What Is Jewish Literature?*, edited by Hana Wirth-Nesher. Philadelphia: Jewish Publication Society, 1994. Briefly places *The Chosen* in the context of literature in which Jewish authors and their characters have a dual identity: Jewish as well as that of the country in which they live.

Studies in American Jewish Literature 4 (1985). This special issue devoted to Potok includes several valuable critical essays, an interview with Potok conducted in 1981 by S. Lillian Kremer, and an autobiographical essay by Potok, "The First Eighteen Years." An indispensable source.

REYNOLDS PRICE

Born: Macon, North Carolina; February 1, 1933

Principal long fiction · *A Long and Happy Life*, 1962; *A Generous Man*, 1966; *Love and Work*, 1968; *The Surface of Earth*, 1975; *The Source of Light*, 1981; *Mustian: Two Novels and a Story, Complete and Unabridged*, 1983; *Kate Vaiden*, 1986; *Good Hearts*, 1988; *The Tongues of Angels*, 1990; *The Foreseeable Future: Three Long Stories*, 1991; *Blue Calhoun*, 1992; *The Honest Account of a Memorable Life: An Apocryphal Gospel*, 1994; *The Promise of Rest*, 1995.

Other literary forms · Although he is best known as a novelist, Price's short fiction is sensitively written and helps to give readers a balanced picture of his writing. His poetry, his retelling of biblical stories, and his dramas, while they are not consistently of the quality of his best novels, are all clearly the work of an author with a strong sense of what he is doing. His collections of essays include some extremely interesting insights into what Price is trying to accomplish philosophically and stylistically in his long fiction. *Late Warning: Four Poems* (1968), *Lessons Learned: Seven Poems* (1977), *Vital Provisions* (1982), and *The Laws of Ice* (1986) are collections of Reynolds Price's poetry. *The Names and Faces of Heroes* (1963) is an early collection of his short stories; it was followed by *Permanent Errors* (1970). *Things Themselves: Essays and Scenes* (1972) and *A Common Room: Essays 1954-1987* (1987) contain his most salient essays on writing. Among Price's retellings of biblical stories are *Presence and Absence: Versions from the Bible* (1973), *Oracles: Six Versions from the Bible* (1977), and *A Palpable God: Thirty Stories Translated from the Bible with an Essay on the Origins and Life of Narrative* (1978). His dramas include *Early Dark* (1977), *Private Contentment* (1984), and the teleplay *House Snake* (1986). Price's autobiography is *Clear Pictures: First Loves, First Guides* (1989).

Achievements · Early in his career Price won the literature award from the National Institute of Arts and Letters, and he has received the Sir Walter Raleigh Award five times. In 1986 *Kate Vaiden* won the National Book Critics Circle Award, and in 1994 Price's *The Collected Stories* (1993) was a finalist for the Pulitzer Prize in fiction. In 1988, in recognition of his achievements, Price was elected to the American Academy of Arts and Letters.

Biography · Born on February 1, 1933, in the rural North Carolina town of Macon, the son of William Solomon and Elizabeth Rodwell Price, Edward Reynolds Price was a child of the Depression. Although because of the closeness of his family structure his welfare was not seriously threatened by it, the boy was aware of the social dislocations around him and had what his biographer, Constance Rooke, calls Dickensian terrors of abandonment and destitution. His parents, hard pressed economically, lost their house when the father could not raise a fifty-dollar mortgage payment.

Upon graduation from Needham-Broughten High School in Raleigh, Price became an English major at Duke University in 1951, where he came under the influence of William Blackburn, who taught creative writing. Through Blackburn, he met Eudora

Welty, who respected his work and ten years later was instrumental in helping to get Price's first book, *A Long and Happy Life*, published.

Upon receiving the bachelor's degree from Duke, Price attended Merton College, University of Oxford, as a Rhodes Scholar; there he received the bachelor of letters degree in 1958. He returned to Duke University in that year as an assistant professor of English and, except for brief intervals, continued to teach there. Beginning in 1977, he served as James B. Duke Professor of English at that institution, where he regularly taught courses in creative writing and on the poetry of John Milton.

Price, who never married, burst on the literary scene auspiciously when *Harper's* magazine devoted the whole of its April, 1962, issue to printing *A Long and Happy Life*, which was being released in hardcover at about the same time. The critical reception of this first novel was enthusiastic and brought Price the prestigious Faulkner Foundation Award for a first novel.

In 1963, he visited England, and in the same year a collection of his short stories, *The Names and Faces of Heroes*, was released. This collection included "Michael Egerton," the short story that had first impressed Eudora Welty when she gave a reading at Duke in the early 1950's. The title story, told from the perspective of a young boy, is an especially sensitive study in point of view.

Price's second novel, *A Generous Man*, appeared in 1966 and focused on the Mustain family, as had his first book. The second book is a warm, rollicking story based on a hunt for a python named Death that has escaped from a snake show after being bitten by a dog diagnosed as rabid. The concept is openly allegorical, and Price drives home the allegory well while also presenting an extremely amusing story, with the hydrophobic python constituting the most outrageous phallic symbol in American literature. In 1977, Price produced a play, *Early Dark*, based on the Mustian cycle, and, in

1983, *Mustian: Two Novels and a Story, Complete and Unabridged* was issued, consisting of the first two novels and "The Chain of Love," a short story.

Love and Work and the loosely woven collection *Permanent Errors* both explore matters of heredity and its effect upon people. Neither received overwhelming praise, although they had support among some critics. Price, however, was busy with a much larger project, an ambitious saga of the Kendal-Mayfield family through four generations. The first novel of this story, *The Surface of Earth*, was received with skepticism by some critics when it appeared in 1975, but few could deny the creative zeal it reflected. The second volume of the Kendal-Mayfield story was published in 1981 under the title *The Source of Light*, and it, too, received mixed reviews.

A turning point in Price's life came in 1984, when he was in the middle of writing *Kate Vaiden*. He was stricken with spinal cancer, and the surgery that saved his life also left him a paraplegic. Pain drove Price to seek the help of a psychiatrist, who used hypnosis to control Price's pain. Little did he suspect that through hypnosis he would be put in touch with a distant past that he had not realized existed. Suddenly details of his earliest childhood and of his family surfaced. When *Kate Vaiden* was published in 1986, it was, because of these unexpected insights, a quite different novel from the one Price had originally projected. Price's hypnosis unlocked the memories from which his autobiography, *Clear Pictures: First Loves, First Guides*, published in 1989, evolved. *The Tongues of Angels*, a novel published in 1990, is also a product of Price's hypnotic communication with his past.

A further literary product of Price's painful illness is his personal narrative *A Whole New Life* (1994). The book not only offers a detailed account of his "mid-life collision with cancer and paralysis" but also celebrates his emergence from that trial into a new and, he affirms, better life. Price's own confrontation with mortality no doubt adds resonance to all his subsequent writings, such as the poignant description of Wade's suffering and death in *The Promise of Rest*. Furthermore, as an affirmation of God's strange grace, *A Whole New Life* displays kinship with Price's numerous retellings of stories from the Bible.

While focusing on long fiction, Price continued to produce notable works in other genres. The plays in his trilogy *New Music* premiered in 1989 and have subsequently been produced throughout the country. Price also wrote a television play, *Private Contentment* (1983), for the American Playhouse series aired by the Public Broadcasting Service (PBS). Along with his lyric poems, Price wrote the texts of songs ("Copperline" and "New Hymn") for his fellow North Carolinian, James Taylor.

Analysis · Any reading of all Reynolds Price's novels quickly demonstrates that Price's work, throughout his career, grapples with puzzling questions. Preeminent among these questions is the effect that families have on communities and on the broader societies outside the isolated communities that provide Price with his microcosms.

Focusing on a single region of North Carolina just south of the Virginia border, Price moved beyond the limitations one sometimes finds in regional writers and in his work deals with universal themes, particularly with those that concern original sin and free choice; biological determinism, particularly as it is reflected in heredity; and the meanings of and relationships between life and death. In Price's novels, children inherit the burden of sin passed on by their parents, and, try as they will, they cannot escape this burden. They have free will, they can make choices, but the choices they make are almost identical to the choices their progenitors have made before them, so they grow up to be like those who have spawned them, no matter how much they struggle to avoid such a resemblance.

Kate Vaiden · Price harbored from his earliest memories questions about his mother and about his parents' relationship to each other. He seldom forgot that his mother almost died in bearing him and that she was left mutilated by his difficult birth. His later relationships with her were always colored by that recollection and by the feeling of guilt it caused him. The guilt of the child is reflected most clearly in *Kate Vaiden*, where Kate blames herself for an act that was as much out of her control as was Elizabeth's difficult confinement out of Reynolds's control.

Despite Kate's innocence of any blame, she continues to blame herself after her father murders her mother and then turns the gun on himself, and her entire adult life—indeed, her life from age eleven onward—is so profoundly impacted by that single event, which brought an end to her childhood innocence, that it takes her forty-five years to begin to come to grips with her problems in any effective way. *Kate Vaiden* does not end on any realistic note of hope or promise; rather, it ends with a large question mark. Through writing the novel, however, Price presumably enhanced his understanding of his mother, who, like Kate, was orphaned at an early age.

Love and Work · Price was working toward the solution of problems like those that *Kate Vaiden* poses in his earlier *Love and Work*, in which Thomas Eborn, like Price himself a novelist and a professor, is forced to examine his relationship to his mother and his parents' relationship to each other and to society when his mother dies unexpectedly. Tom has been a dutiful son; he has helped provide for his mother financially. Yet he is also a compulsive writer who husbands his time and guards it jealously, organizing his life in such a way that he will always be able to write.

Because of this dedication, he misses his mother's last telephone call; he is busy writing and will not talk with her. Shortly thereafter, she is dead. Price creates in this novel a story that uses place most effectively. Tom Eborn teaches in a southern town not unlike Durham, North Carolina, where Price spent his professional career. Tom has arranged his life to eliminate from it any unnecessary distractions, and in doing this he has excluded from it as well much human contact. Tom's turf—completely his own—is his study, his inviolable space where he can be alone, where he can create. No one dare intrude upon it. His mother's unanticipated death, however, makes Tom realize the wrongness of isolating himself as fully as he has from humankind.

It is clear that one can find much of Reynolds Price in Tom Eborn. To make a simple equation between the two, however, would be fatuous and misleading. *Love and Work* is a novel, and although Price once said that a writer's experience and background have as much to do with writing fiction as has imagination, he also warned that writers slip in and out of autobiography, so that their novels cannot be read as accurate autobiographical statements.

One can profitably read *Love and Work* against Price's consciously constructed autobiography, *Clear Pictures: First Loves, First Guides*, and can find the correspondence between his life and Tom Eborn's. Such a comparison will show Price's departures from autobiographical revelation in this novel. The same caveat must be made for *Kate Vaiden*, which strongly reflects Price's background but which is far from an authentic autobiographical representation.

A Long and Happy Life · Price's consuming interest in the family as the fundamental unit of society is found in his first novel, *A Long and Happy Life*, and pervades his future writing. *A Long and Happy Life* and *A Generous Man*, along with several of Price's short stories and his novel, *Good Hearts*, have to do with the Mustian family, who live in Macon, North Carolina, the town on the Virginia border in which Price was born and reared. *A Long and Happy Life* revolves around the romance between twenty-year-old Rosacoke Mustian and her boyfriend of six years, Wesley Beavers, two years her senior.

Wesley motorcycles to his native Macon to visit Rosacoke whenever he can take a weekend away from the naval base in Norfolk, 130 miles to the northeast. Wesley is sexually experienced but Rosacoke is a virgin when the story opens in July. On a scorching day, Rosacoke rides on the back of Wesley's motorcycle to the black church from which her friend Mildred Sutton is to be buried. Mildred has died while giving birth to her child Sledge.

Wesley roars up to the church, deposits Rosacoke, and stays outside polishing his bike. The church moans in ecstasies of religious transport. One woman cries, "Sweet Jesus," and Wesley, hearing her cry, is transported to a sweaty bed in Norfolk, where one of his many women uttered an identical cry at a crucial point in their lovemaking.

Reminded of this, Wesley zooms off in a cloud of red dust so dry and thick that reading about it almost makes one want to wash it off. Wesley has to get ready for the afternoon, for the church picnic that he and Rosacoke will attend. Price's descriptions in this portion of the book are masterful and memorably comic, although the import of what is being communicated is deadly serious and universally significant.

At the church picnic, Wesley tries to seduce Rosacoke, but she resists him, as she always has in the past. The picnic itself is a jolly affair. As the picnickers are about to sit down to their meals, Uncle Simon discovers that his false teeth are missing. Those who have not already begun to consume their barbecued pork and Brunswick stew help Simon look for his teeth. Someone asks him when he last remembers having them.

Simon, after due deliberation, proclaims that he took them out while he was stirring the large kettle of Brunswick stew. With this revelation, all eating comes to an abrupt halt. Simon eventually finds his teeth–they were in his back pocket all along. Still, the eating never quite gets back to normal, because of the general uncertainty about where the lost denture was. Vignettes like this help Price to convey a deeply philosophical message to readers without immersing them in specialized terminology or in abstruse and abstract thinking.

A Generous Man · In *A Generous Man*, published four years after *A Long and Happy Life*, Price goes back several years in time and writes about the Mustian family before Wesley Beavers was known to them. Rosacoke is only eleven years old during the action of the later novel. The basic concept of the book is so outrageous that it would have seemed completely ridiculous if not handled delicately and well.

This novel essentially takes up a young boy's coming-of-age. Milo, Rosacoke's fifteen-year-old brother, has just lost his virginity to Lois Provo, the girl who runs the snake show at the Warren County Fair. Years ago, Lois's mother was impregnated by a bounder, who proves to be Milo's cousin. Once the truth was known, he abandoned the woman, leaving her only her memories and his eighteen-foot python, Death, which still thrives.

Milo, the morning after his maiden voyage with Lois, wakens to find that his dog, Phillip, is ill. The family gathers for a trip to the alcoholic veterinarian, who promptly diagnoses the dog's illness as rabies. For reasons unrevealed, he neither confines the dog nor destroys it. Instead, he provides a muzzle, and the Mustians leave with their muzzled mutt to go to the fair.

Rato, the retarded son, takes the dog's muzzle off. Despite his retardation, Rato has known all along that the dog does not have rabies but is merely suffering from worms, a bit of information he keeps to himself, not wanting to put his knowledge of dogs and their maladies up against the vet's.

As it turns out, Phillip has a prejudice against snakes, and when he encounters Death, he attacks it. By the time the dust has settled, the dog, the snake, and the retarded Rato have disappeared into the woods. Sheriff Rooster Pomeroy, citing the dangers of having a hydrophobic snake abroad among the loblolly and kudzu, collects a posse, a group of men keen for excitement and camaraderie, to hunt down the missing boy, the dog, and, most urgently, the snake. Spirits are high, and liquor flows freely.

In the course of the hunt, Milo, unaccustomed to alcohol, gets drunk enough to wander out of the woods, straight to Pomeroy's house, where Mrs. Pomeroy has been left alone. Because the sheriff is impotent, Mrs. Pomeroy finds her sexual satisfaction wherever she can, and Milo looks very good to her. They end up in her bed, where, during their pillow talk, Milo learns that Mrs. Pomeroy's first sexual encounter was with his cousin, the same bounder who sired Lois and gave Death to her mother.

Despite his prurient intentions, Milo cannot complete his act because the doorbell rings, prompting him to bolt through the open window, carrying his clothing with him. He rejoins the unlikely search, and it is he who finds Death. The snake wraps itself around Milo, almost choking the life out of him, but ironically Sheriff Pomeroy comes to the rescue and defeats Death with a well-placed gunshot.

Soon Milo wants to resume his lovemaking with Lois, but she is unwilling, because their first encounter left her quite unsatisfied. She classifies Milo among those men who are takers rather than givers in love encounters, and she lets him know it. He promises to reform; in his second encounter with her, his performance is indeed altered. Thus the book's title: Milo has become a man, but, having learned that he must give as well as take, he must mature further to become a generous man.

The Kendal-Mayfield saga · Price's difficulties with the critics when he produced the first volume of the Kendal-Mayfield saga, *The Surface of Earth*, stemmed largely from an inability of many northeastern critics to respond with understanding to a convoluted familial saga that had heavy biblical overtones, that had to do fundamentally with original sin, guilt, conflicted race relations, incestuous feelings, incredibly frequent suicides, and much that is a more common part of rural southern experience than of urban northern experience. Southern families like the two Price writes about in the Kendal-Mayfield novels are smothering families. Their members sometimes try to escape, but the magnetic pull back into the decaying bosom of the family is too strong for them to resist. In that respect, this saga is not unlike William Faulkner's *The Sound and the Fury* (1929), in which the Compsons can never escape their heredity and all that it has predestined for them.

It is significant that the family members in the Kendal-Mayfield saga (including those in *The Source of Light* and *The Promise of Rest*, sequels to *The Surface of Earth*) resemble one another so closely. Not only do they sound alike but, more tellingly, they also think alike and act alike from generation to generation. Readers become particularly aware of this because of the compression of the novels: a large time span is telescoped into a few hundred pages.

On a literal level, the events of the saga might seem unlikely; taken symbolically, they assume a broader and deeper meaning and a greater artistic plausibility. Perhaps reflection on the outrageous unreality of parts of *A Generous Man* can help readers to understand some of the quintessential symbolic elements of the Kendal-Mayfield saga. Such comparable sagas as the five novels that make up John Galsworthy's *The Forsyte Saga* (1922) or the three novels of Sigrid Undset's *Kristin Lavransdatter* (1920-1922) suffer from a similar sense of unreality if they are read without conscious consideration of their symbolic contexts.

A considerable amount of the symbolic content of Price's Kendal-Mayfield novels can be found in the dream sequences that are integral to the books. There are more than twenty of them in the first novel, and these sequences serve many purposes beyond suggesting the subconscious state of the characters who have the dreams.

The Surface of Earth · The beginning of the Kendal family history as Price reveals it in *The Surface of Earth* is Bedford Kendal's rendition to his children of their grandparents' tragedy. Their grandmother died while giving birth to their mother. Their grandfather, considering himself responsible for his wife's death, killed himself, leaving his newborn daughter (like Price's own mother) an orphan. Bedford, having married this orphan when she grew to adulthood, soon realized that she was consumed by guilt and that she had a strong aversion to sex, all tied up with the guilt she suffered at the thought of having, through her birth, killed her own mother and driven her father to suicide.

Bedford's children, hearing this story, build up their own guilt feelings and their own aversions to sex. His daughter Eva, the strongest student of thirty-two-year-old Latin teacher Forrest Mayfield, elopes with him. Forrest is looking for family ties and thinks that he has found them among the Kendals, who, on the surface, seem to be an enviable family. Yet his marrying Eva disrupts the family's delicate balance, so all that Forrest hopes for in the marriage is not available to him.

The title of book 1 in the novel, "Absolute Pleasures," seems to be both an irony and a warning. Eva has her absolute pleasure, her unremitting sexual release on her wedding night, but then guilt possesses her. She dreams an Electra dream of her father stretched out over her body, and she is never able to enjoy sex again. She passes on her sexual aversion to her children, suggesting to her son Rob that he masturbate rather than become ensnared in love relationships with women.

Forrest, meanwhile, has his own hereditary baggage to carry. Forrest and Eva, whose names, as Rooke notes, suggest something primal and essentially sexual, ironically are trapped by their pasts. Price emphasizes another theme on which he has dwelt before: marriage disrupts the family balance, but guilt over that disruption–at least among the Kendals and the Mayfields–in turn disrupts the marriage. The family and heredity are exacting taskmasters, and they are inescapable.

Eva, like many of Price's women, barely survives the birth of her son Rob, and in this difficult birth, which also severely threatens the life of the infant, one sees an entire cycle recurring. The mother, with her cargo of guilt about sex and about her mother's death in childbirth, has a difficult delivery that will increase her aversion to sex and that will impose upon her newborn child the same guilt with which she has lived. So has it always been with the Kendals; so presumably will it always be.

Eva and Forrest both settle for lives of frequent masturbation, and their masturbation fantasies are tied to their respective father and mother. Forrest, having abjured further sexual encounters with Eva, meditates on a poem by Gaius Valerius Catullus that has to do with ritual castration. He ultimately leaves Eva and makes a ritualized journey back to Bracey, his hometown, to live with his sister Hatt, a widow.

Book 2 of *The Surface of Earth*, the real heart of the novel, is the story of Eva and Forrest's son, Rob Mayfield, named for his paternal grandfather. Rob, now seventeen, is leaving the family nest, but the family surges within him. He has no more hope of leaving it than did any of the Kendals before him. There is no escape from either the biological heredity or the strong pull of memory and custom that families impose.

Rob, obsessed with Oedipal feelings since the onset of puberty, hopes that contact with other women will help him to overcome the shameful feelings that disturb his equilibrium. He tries to seduce his date for the senior prom, but she denies him, whereupon he sheds her. Like Milo in *A Generous Man*, his sexual thoughts are only of his own gratification, and his masturbation gives him an independence when he is rebuffed.

Rob contemplates suicide several times in his period of flight from the nest. He comes closest to it when he sees a clutch of boys shooting at a turtle, trying to kill it. The turtle comes to represent for Rob all the isolation and insensitivity that have plagued his recent life, that have brought him closer to suicide than ever in the past.

Rob seeks to overcome his problems by marrying Rachel, whose father manages a hotel, Panacea Springs, in Goshen. Not in love with Rachel, Rob wavers in his commitment to marry her, and he goes—as his father before him had gone to the first Rob—to his father for counsel. Forrest is now living in a heterodox arrangement with Polly, a woman with whom he makes love only ten times a year, fearing that more frequent contact would jeopardize what they have struggled to achieve. Having seen his father's relationship, Rob can now return to Rachel and marry her.

The dinner on the night before the wedding brings together all the elements of the family that Price needs to show to make his story work. In this evening of premarital celebration, the family history and all that it implies is made clear. That being done, the only task remaining to Price artistically is to kill Rachel off in childbirth, which he promptly does. Rachel dies giving birth to Hutch, whose story becomes the next portion of the saga.

The Source of Light · The Source of Light is a more optimistic book than its predecessor. It focuses on Hutch and on the aging and death of his father. In *The Source of Light*, both Hutch and Rob seem to have reached an accord in their lives, to have matured into acceptance of what seems for them inevitable. The pull of the family and the inevitability of their heredity are both still operative, but they are less oppressive than they were in the earlier book.

The Tongues of Angels · Set primarily at a summer camp for boys in western North Carolina, *The Tongues of Angels* is the story of a young man's rite of passage and a commentary on his continuing source of inspiration as a mature artist. Bridge Boatner is now a successful painter, but when his sons ask about the inscription on the back of his first significant landscape, he recounts the circumstances under which he produced it. At the age of twenty-one, Bridge recoiled from the recent death of his father by becoming a counselor at Camp Juniper. There he formed a brief but intense friendship with a troubled but immensely gifted camper, Raphael (Rafe) Noren, for whom the painting was intended as a gift.

Rafe's angelic name suggests the mysterious nature of his great talents (especially in Native American dancing), but he also exhibits a profound need for love. Having seen his own mother murdered, Rafe is drawn toward Bridge even though he confides little. Bridge enlists Rafe as a model for sketches of angels, and in so doing he perhaps inadvertently contributes to the camper's death. In recalling that traumatic event, however, Bridge observes that even now he creates as an artist not merely because of his past errors but by actually using those errors as instruments.

The Promise of Rest · With *The Promise of Rest* Price returns to the Mayfield family saga and completes the trilogy collectively titled A Great Circle. This final novel in the series boldly confronts the twin furies of sexuality and race that have tormented the Mayfields for nine decades.

After more than thirty years of marriage, Ann has left Hutch. Although Hutch has been faithful to her, she feels isolated because of his close friendship with Strawson Stewart, who was once Hutch's student and lover and is still the tenant on the Mayfield homeplace.

Hutch remains a successful poet and teacher at Duke University, but he is devastated by news that his only son, Wade, is suffering from acquired immunodeficiency syndrome (AIDS) in New York City. Wade was estranged from his family, not because of his homosexuality but because his black lover, Wyatt, condemned Hutch and Ann as racists. After Wyatt commits suicide, Hutch brings Wade home to die. At first Hutch tries to exclude Ann from the deathbed watch, but their mutual pain eventually pulls them back together. After Wade's death they learn that he loved not only Wyatt but also Wyatt's sister, Ivory, and with her he fathered a child.

This child, Raven, bears the given name of both Hutch and Wade, and he is proof that the Mayfield clan will not soon become extinct. Raven's link with his grandparents remains tenuous, but in the final scene of the novel he goes with Hutch to visit an aging black cousin and to spread Wade's ashes on the Mayfield farm. Thus, the book affirms racial unity and solace after the pain of death. With a long heritage of sexual confusion and miscegenation, the Mayfields may not readily achieve peaceful rest, but its promise is surely genuine.

Throughout his writing, Price is concerned with showing that people cannot outrun their past. Price's characters are dots on a long, seemingly infinite continuum, and the continuum assumes a life of its own. It is like a steadily flowing river that moves unrelentingly toward the sea. Anything in it that tries to swim upstream is destined to be defeated. Even the strongest of swimmers, the ones who make a little progress against the inevitable flow, will be caught ultimately by the flow and swept along with it.

Underlying this theme of the strength of the family and the inability of people to resist their heredities is a pervasive theme of guilt, all of it tied up with pleasure, as manifested by sex, versus death or mutilation, as represented by the childbirth catastrophes of many of Price's characters.

Price's intimate and sensitive knowledge of southern rural life enables him to write some of the most accurate and memorable descriptions in print of the locale in which most of his stories are set. He has grasped the speech rhythms, vocabulary, and syntax of northern North Carolina with an authenticity that remains consistent throughout his novels and stories, as do the unshakably consistent points of view of his characters.

R. Baird Shuman, updated by Albert Wilhelm

Other major works

SHORT FICTION: *The Names and Faces of Heroes*, 1963; *Permanent Errors*, 1970; *The Collected Stories*, 1993.

PLAYS: *Early Dark*, pb. 1977; *Private Contentment*, pb. 1984; *New Music: A Trilogy*, pr. 1989; *Full Moon and Other Plays*, pb. 1993.

TELEPLAYS: *Private Contentment*, pr. 1983; *House Snake*, 1986.

POETRY: *Late Warning: Four Poems*, 1968; *Lessons Learned: Seven Poems*, 1977; *Nine Mysteries (Four Joyful, Four Sorrowful, One Glorious)*, 1979; *Vital Provisions*, 1982; *The Laws of Ice*, 1986; *The Use of Fire*, 1990.

NONFICTION: *Things Themselves: Essays and Scenes*, 1972; *A Common Room: Essays 1954-1987*, 1987; *Clear Pictures: First Loves, First Guides*, 1989; *A Whole New Life*, 1994; *Three Gospels*, 1996.

TRANSLATIONS: *Presence and Absence: Versions from the Bible*, 1973; *Oracles: Six Versions from the Bible*, 1977; *A Palpable God: Thirty Stories Translated from the Bible with an Essay on the Origins and Life of Narrative*, 1978.

Bibliography

Kreyling, Michael. "Reynolds Price." In *The History of Southern Literature*, edited by Louis D. Rubin et al. Baton Rouge: Louisiana State University Press, 1985. Although this article is brief, it is easily accessible and does much to update the earlier sources about Price. It appeared too early to deal with his post-hypnotic years and with such books as *Kate Vaiden* and *Good Hearts*, but it is a fresh point of view clearly expressed.

Price, Reynolds. "A Conversation with Reynolds Price." Interview by Wallace Kaufman. *Shenandoah* 17 (Summer, 1966): 3-25. The most important early interview with Price, and one of the most extensive. It is reproduced in its entirety under the title "Notice, I'm Still Smiling," in *Kite Flying and Other Irrational Acts*, edited by John Carr (Baton Rouge: Louisiana State University Press, 1972). Kaufman has excellent insights into Price's southernness but realizes that his writing goes far beyond regionalism.

_____. "Reynolds Price on Writing." Interview by Ashby Bland Crowder. *Southern Review* 22 (Spring, 1986): 329-341. Anyone interested in Price as a stylist must read this interview, for it is the best brief treatment in print of how Price approaches his writing, both physically and philosophically. Crowder is an excellent interviewer. The piece is easily accessible to the reader not overly familiar with Price's work.

Rooke, Constance. *Reynolds Price*. Boston: Twayne, 1983. An early full-length treatment of Price. Despite its excellent coverage and intelligent analysis, it is badly dated because some of Price's most interesting work came after his hypnosis in 1984. One hopes that Rooke will bring out a revised edition or that some other scholar will do a solid analytical study of this author whose versatility continues to amaze and whose command of his major medium has not waned.

Sadler, Lynn Veach. "Reynolds Price and Religion: The 'Almost Blindingly Lucid' Palpable World." *Southern Quarterly* 26 (Winter, 1988): 1-11. Religion, both traditional and nontraditional, plays a fundamental part in Price's novels, and this article intelligently assesses some of his central religious beliefs, partly as shown through his translated biblical stories but also as they are revealed in some of his other work.

Schiff, James, ed. *Critical Essays on Reynolds Price*. New York: G. K. Hall, 1998. After a section of personal tributes and reminiscences, this volume provides twenty-three reviews and twelve critical essays (three of which are not available elsewhere). One essay deals with the play trilogy *New Music*, but most focus on Price's fiction, especially *A Long and Happy Life.*

_____. *Understanding Reynolds Price.* Columbia: University of South Carolina Press, 1996. While devoting brief attention to Price's essays, memoirs, plays, poems, and short stories, Schiff focuses mainly on the long fiction. Intended as an introductory work, this volume provides concise but perceptive commentary on the major novels.

THOMAS PYNCHON

Born: Glen Cove, New York; May 8, 1937

Principal long fiction · *V.*, 1963; *The Crying of Lot 49*, 1966; *Gravity's Rainbow*, 1973; *Vineland*, 1989; *Mason and Dixon*, 1997.

Other literary forms · Before his novels began to come out, Thomas Pynchon published a handful of short stories: "The Small Rain" (1959), "Mortality and Mercy in Vienna" (1959), "Low-Lands" (1960), "Entropy" (1960), and "Under the Rose" (1961–an early version of chapter 3 of *V.*). With the exception of "Mortality and Mercy," these stories appear in the 1984 collection *Slow Learner*, which also includes "The Secret Integration," originally published in 1964. Two magazine publications, "The World (This One), the Flesh (Mrs. Oedipa Maas), and the Testament of Pierce Inverarity" (1965) and "The Shrink Flips" (1966), are excerpts from *The Crying of Lot 49*. Pynchon also published some pieces in *The New York Times Book Review*, including a 1984 meditation on distrust of technology ("Is It O.K. to Be a Luddite?"), a 1988 review of Gabriel García Márquez's *Love in the Time of Cholera*, and a 1993 sketch, "Nearer, My Couch, to Thee," on the sin of sloth (included in the collection *Deadly Sins*, by various hands). He penned introductions to a reissue of Richard Fariña's 1966 novel *Been Down So Long It Looks Like Up to Me* (1983), to a posthumous collection of writings by Donald Barthelme, *The Teachings of Don B.* (1992), and to a reissue of Jim Dodge's 1990 novel *Stone Junction* (1998). Pynchon also wrote liner notes for the albums *Spiked! The Music of Spike Jones* (1994) and *Nobody's Cool*, by the rock group Lotion (1995).

Achievements · Among those contemporary novelists who enjoy both a popular and an academic following, Thomas Pynchon stands out as a virtual cult figure. His novels and stories stand up to the most rigorous critical analysis; they prove, like all great works of art, to be the product of a gifted sensibility and careful craftsmanship. At the same time, Dr. Samuel Johnson's "common reader" cheerfully wades through much abstruse matter because this author never fails to entertain—with bizarre plots, incandescent language, anarchic humor, and memorable characters.

Pynchon has an enormous, diverse, and fanatically loyal following. There are more than thirty books on his work, not to mention scholarly journals. Some of the fascination he holds for readers is derived from his reclusive habits. He refused to be interviewed, photographed, or otherwise made into a darling of the media. It finally became known that he made his home in New York City thirty years after the publication of his first novel.

Pynchon was honored with a number of literary awards. He received the William Faulkner Foundation Award for *V.*, the 1967 Rosenthal Foundation Award of the National Institute of Arts and Letters for *The Crying of Lot 49*, and the National Book Award for *Gravity's Rainbow* in 1974. Though the judging committee unanimously voted to award the Pulitzer Prize in fiction to Pynchon for *Gravity's Rainbow*, the committee was overruled by an advisory board which found the novel immoral and "turgid." The Howells Medal, awarded once every five years, was offered to Pynchon in 1975, but he declined it.

Pynchon occupies a place in the front rank of twentieth century American fiction writers, and more than one distinguished critic has declared him America's finest novelist.

Biography · Because of Thomas Pynchon's passion for privacy, little is known about his life. His father was an industrial surveyor, and the family lived in Glen Cove, East Norwich, and Oyster Bay—all on Long Island in New York. His father, a Republican, eventually served as town supervisor of Oyster Bay. Pynchon was sixteen when he graduated from Oyster Bay High School in 1953. He was class salutatorian and winner of an award for the senior attaining the highest average in English. With a scholarship at Cornell University, he first majored in engineering physics but, though he was doing well academically, abandoned that curriculum after the first year. A year later, he decided to do a hitch in the Navy before completing his baccalaureate degree. He attended boot camp at Bainbridge, Maryland, and did advanced training as an electrician at Norfolk, Virginia. The two years in the Navy, partly spent in the Mediterranean, provided Pynchon with a number of comic situations and characters, which he has exploited in "Low-Lands," *V.*, *Gravity's Rainbow*, and *Mason and Dixon*. Pynchon finished at Cornell as an English major and was graduated in 1959. While at Cornell, Pynchon took a class taught by Vladimir Nabokov; Nabokov's wife, Vera, who did her husband's grading, remembered Pynchon for his distinctive handwriting.

Pynchon lived briefly in Greenwich Village and in uptown Manhattan before taking a job with the Boeing Company and moving to Seattle. With Boeing for two and a half years (until September, 1962), he worked in the Minuteman Logistics Support Program and wrote for such intramural publications as "The Minuteman Field Service News" and *Aerospace Safety*. After leaving Boeing, he lived in California and Mexico and completed *V.*, which was published in 1963 and hailed as a major first novel.

Over the years Pynchon was rumored to be living in various places, including California, Mexico, and Oregon. In the late 1970's, he made a trip to England that mysteriously was noted in the national newsmagazines. For a long time the author eluded his pursuers, but in the 1980's he supplied a few tantalizing autobiographical facts in the introductory essays he wrote for his *Slow Learner* collection and for the 1983 Penguin reprint of *Been Down So Long It Looks Like Up to Me*, the 1966 novel by his Cornell classmate Richard Fariña.

In 1996, Nancy Jo Sales, writing for the magazine *New York*, traced Pynchon to the Manhattan apartment he shared with his wife, Melanie Jackson (also his agent), and their son. The following year a photograph taken by James Bone appeared in the London *Times Magazine*, and a camera crew from CNN taped Pynchon walking down a street. In these instances, Pynchon fought unsuccessfully to suppress publication or broadcast of his likeness.

Analysis · The quest would seem to be the one indispensable element in the fiction of Thomas Pynchon, for each of his novels proves to be a modern-dress version of the search for some grail to revive the wasteland. Pynchon's characters seek knowledge that will make sense of their unanchored lives and their fragmented times; Pynchon hints that questing has a value irrespective of the authenticity of that for which one quests. The quest lends purpose to life, enabling one to function, to see life as worthwhile. At the same time, however, Pynchon invites his more privileged reader to recognize that the ordering principle thus projected is factitious. What is real is the gathering dissolution, the passing of human beings and whole civilizations. All attempts to discover or create order and system are doomed.

Even so, as Pynchon's career developed, one notes what may be a tendency to define some grail of his own, an inclination to search for a way out of the cul-de-sac of a metaphysics perhaps unduly in thrall to the principle of entropy (broadly defined as the gradual deterioriation of the universe caused by irreversible thermodynamic equalization). Pynchon's critics disagree sharply on this point. Some maintain that the intimation of counter-entropic orders in *The Crying of Lot 49* and *Gravity's Rainbow* is merely a hook by which to catch the unwary reader, a means of seducing him or her into system-making as delusive as that of any of Pynchon's characters. Other critics, unwilling to believe that Pynchon's frequently noted affinity with modern science has been frozen at a point attained some time in the 1950's, suspect that Pynchon means to hint at transcendental alternatives implicit in the vast mysteries of contemporary astronomy and particle physics.

Regardless of whether Pynchon is on a grail quest of his own (with all the propensity for mysticism that seems indispensable to such a quester), he continues to create intricate labyrinths in which readers experience the paranoia that also figures as a prominent theme in his work. Paranoia is the conviction that mighty conspiracies exist, that all things are connected "in spheres joyful or threatening about the central pulse of [one]self." Pynchon's protagonists come to believe in this infinite reticulation of conspiracy because it is preferable to the possibility that "nothing is connected to anything." Pynchon's readers, by the same token, encounter fictive structures that formally imitate the paranoid premise: All is connected in great, seamless webs of interdependent detail.

The dialectic between order and disorder is the dialectic between art and life, and it is with reference to this neglected commonplace that one should analyze Pynchon's artifice. In art, traditionally, humanity lays claim—sometimes piously, sometimes impiously—to the divine prerogative of creation, the establishment of order where all before was without form and void. Pynchon gives evidence, since the almost nihilistic *V.*, of a fascination with the religious belief that there are "orders behind the visible," orders analogous to those found beneath the surface in works of art ostensibly reflecting life in all its chaotic aspects. *Gravity's Rainbow*, for example, strikes one at first as a complete mishmash, a welter of all-too-lifelike confusion, but one subsequently discovers it to be as finely crafted as James Joyce's *Ulysses* (1922) or *Finnegans Wake* (1939). Perhaps Pynchon can best be imagined like William Blake, William Butler Yeats, and D. H. Lawrence, as countering the smugness and complacency of a scientific age with a calculated antirationalism.

These remarks adumbrate the last major topic in Pynchon's work—science and art. Pynchon knows and makes artistic use of science. He has, if nothing else, dispatched legions of humanists in search of information about modern physics, chemistry, engineering, and cartography—disciplines to which they had previously been indifferent. As suggested above, however, science serves vision, not the other way around. Pynchon's work does more than that of any other writer—scientific or literary—to reverse the widening "dissociation of sensibility" that poet T. S. Eliot noted as part of the intellectual landscape since the seventeenth century. In Pynchon, and in his readers to a remarkable extent, C. P. Snow's "two cultures" become one again.

V. · In his first novel, *V.*, Pynchon brilliantly interweaves two narratives, one in the present (mid-1950's), the other in the period 1880 to 1943. The historical narrative, presented obliquely, concerns an extraordinary woman who appears originally as Victoria Wren and subsequently under *noms de guerre* in which the letter *V* of the alphabet figures prominently: Veronica Manganese, Vera Meroving. This is V., who turns up whenever there is bloodshed in the course of the twentieth century. In 1898, for example, she appears at the periphery of the Fashoda crisis in Egypt, and the following year she gravitates to Florence, where the spies of several nations are jockeying for position, engaging in what Pynchon calls "premilitary" activity. In 1913, she is in Paris, involved in a bloody theater riot which, like the crises in Egypt and Florence earlier, proves an earnest of World War I–a kind of fulfillment for V. in her early phase. When World War I ends with Western civilization intact, though permanently altered, V. begins to be involved with those elements that will figure in the more satisfying carnage of the century's real climacteric, World War II. In 1922, she is in German southwest Africa, where the massacre of the native Hereros reenacts the even greater massacre of two decades earlier and anticipates the really accomplished genocide in Europe between 1933 and 1945. On and off after 1918, she is on Malta, consorting with a group sympathetic to Mussolini and his Fascists. V. dies in an air raid on Malta in 1943–just as the tide turns against the Fascist cause with which she has become increasingly identified.

V.'s affinity with Fascism complements a decadent religiosity, and she comes to personify the drift to extinction of Western culture and of life itself. She gradually loses parts of her body and becomes more and more the sum of inanimate parts: false eye, false hair, false foot, false navel. She is a brilliant metaphor for entropy and the decline of civilization, and her baleful influence is projected in the novel's present in the decadence of the contemporary characters, most of whom are part of a group called the Whole Sick Crew. The Crew is exemplified by its newest member, the winsome schlemiel Benny Profane. Profane is incapable of love and emotional involvement; he is also perennially at war with inanimate objects. His dread of the inanimate suggests that he intuits the cultural situation as the century wanes. Though he is no thinker, he realizes that he and his fellows are Eliot's hollow men, on the way to their whimpering end. His inability to love is presented in comic terms–though fat, he is doted on by various desirable women, including the Maltese Paola Maijstral and the beautiful Rachel Owlglass. The failure is that of his entire circle, for though there is much sex among the Whole Sick Crew, there is no commitment, no love, no hope. The one baby generated by all the sexual freedom is aborted.

The Whole Sick Crew is what Western civilization has become as a result of entropic processes that are utterly random and mindless. The meaninglessness of entropy is something difficult for the human mind to accept, however, and in Herbert Stencil, a marginal member of the Crew, Pynchon presents what becomes his standard character, a person who must discover conspiracy to deal with the fragmentation of life and culture. It is Stencil who does the mythmaking, the elevating of Victoria Wren from mere perverted adventuress to something awesome and as multifaceted as Robert Graves's White Goddess. Nor is Stencil alone, for the undeniable desire for connectedness is quintessentially human. It is also shared by the sophisticated reader, who flings himself or herself into the literary puzzle and becomes himself a Stencil, a quester for meaning in the convoluted plot of *V.* and in the identity of the mysterious personage who gives the novel its name. Pynchon's genius manifests itself in his ability to keep his readers suspended between his two mutually exclusive alternatives: that the clues to V.'s identity are the key to meaning and that V. is nothing more than a paranoid fantasy, the product of a mind that cannot deal with very much reality.

The fascination with which readers have responded to *V.* indicates that Pynchon is himself a brilliant mythmaker. Even after one has "solved" the mystery of V. and arrived at an enlightenment that Stencil explicitly rejects as a threat to his emotional and mental stability, one still finds the myth trenchant, moving, even terrifying. The decline of the West is a theme that one has encountered before, but never has one encountered it so cogently as in this woman who loves death and the inanimate. The real conspiracy, then, is an artistic one; the connectedness is that of the novel, the cabal between author and reader.

The Crying of Lot 49 · Pynchon's second novel, *The Crying of Lot 49*, seems slight between *V.* and *Gravity's Rainbow*, and Pynchon himself seems to consider it something of a potboiler. Some readers, however, believe it to be his most perfect work of art. It is the story of Oedipa Maas, who is named "executor, or she supposed executrix" of the estate of an ex-lover, the millionaire Pierce Inverarity. In carrying out her duties, she stumbles upon evidence of a conspiracy to circumvent the United States Postal Service. She discovers Tristero, a *sub rosa* postal system at war for centuries with all officially sanctioned postal services, first in the old world, then in the new. Tristero subsumes an extraordinary number of revolutionary or simply alienated groups. In its new-world phase, it seems to bring together all those within the American system who are disfranchised, disaffected, or disinherited–all those defrauded of the American Dream.

Oedipa, like Herbert Stencil, finds that the harder she looks, the more connections to Tristero she discovers, until the connections start revealing themselves in such number and variety that she begins to doubt her sanity. Oedipa's mental condition, in fact, becomes the book's central conundrum. She first confronts the question in a flashback early in the story. She recalls visiting a Mexico City art gallery with Pierce Inverarity and seeing a disturbing painting by Remedios Varo. In the painting, a group of girls are imprisoned at the top of a circular tower and made to embroider *el Manto Terrestre*–the earth mantle. The tapestry they create, extruded through the tower's windows, contains "all the other buildings and creatures, all the waves, ships and forests of the earth," for "the tapestry was the world." Oedipa recognizes in the painting a representation of the fact that she–like any other human being–is imprisoned mentally and perceptually in the tower of her own consciousness. External reality, in other words, may be nothing more than what one weaves or embroiders in one's cranial tower. Oedipa weeps at human isolation. Later, tracking down the clues to Tristero (which seem coextensive with Inverarity's estate and enterprises), she cannot free herself from the suspicion that the proliferating connections she is discovering all have their throbbing ganglion in her own mind. She realizes that she is becoming a classic paranoid.

Though Pynchon does not resolve the question of Oedipa's sanity, he hints that becoming sensitized to the problems of twentieth century American culture (and to the horrors of the spiritual void contingent on certain twentieth century habits of mind) involves a necessary sacrifice of sanity or at least serenity. At the end, Oedipa is faced with a harrowing choice: Either she is insane, or Tristero–with its stupendous reticulation–really exists. When Oedipa attempts to rephrase the dilemma, she finds that the paranoia is somehow inescapable:

> There was either some Tristero beyond the appearance of the legacy America, or there was just America and if there was just America then it seemed the only way she could continue, and manage to be at all relevant to it, was as an alien, unfurrowed, assumed full circle into some paranoia.

Pynchon implies that Tristero, whatever its status as literal reality, is in effect a necessary fiction, a metaphor for the idea of an alternative to a closed system.

Oedipa's experiences are almost certainly an imaginative version of Pynchon's own. At the time of the novel, 1964, Oedipa is twenty-eight years old–the same age as Pynchon was in that year. Like Pynchon, she has attended Cornell and then gravitated to the West Coast. Like Pynchon, too, she comes to view herself as an "alien," unable to fit into the furrow of American success, prosperity, and complacency. Thus, one can read the novel as Pynchon's account of why he has gone underground. He has made common cause with America's disadvantaged; in all of his fiction, not to mention his article "A Journey into the Mind of Watts," one notes an obvious sympathy with minorities and something like loathing for the mechanisms of corporate greed responsible for the spoilage of the American landscape, both literal and psychic. *The Crying of Lot 49*, then, is a fictional hybrid of the spiritual autobiography–in the same tradition as St. Augustine's *Confessions* (397-401) and William Wordsworth's *The Prelude* (1850).

These speculations–the need for an alternative to a closed system, the hints of spiritual autobiography–are supported by Edward Mendelson's brilliant essay "The Sacred, the Profane, and *The Crying of Lot 49*" (the single most satisfying reading of the novel, this essay has been reprinted in Mendelson's *Pynchon: A Collection of Critical Essays*, 1978). Mendelson points out the novel's high density of language with religious connotations; he argues that what Oedipa really searches for–and behind her twentieth century humankind–is a new species of revelation, a way out of the agnostic, positivistic cul-de-sac of contemporary rationalism. He also provides an explanation of the novel's odd title. "Lot 49" is a group of stamps–Tristero forgeries–to be sold as part of the settlement of Pierce Inverarity's estate. The novel ends as lot 49 is about to be "cried" or auctioned. Oedipa, present at the auction, expects to confront some representative of the mysterious Tristero, who will attempt to acquire the evidence of the secret organization's existence. Mendelson suggests that the number "49" refers obliquely to the forty-nine-day period between Easter and the descent of the Holy Spirit at Pentecost; the revelation that awaits Oedipa at the crying of lot 49 is symbolically the revelation awaited by the modern world, whose existence so tragically lacks a numinous dimension. Thus, Pynchon ends his novel on a note of expectation, a yearning for some restoration of mystery, some answer to what the narrator calls "the exitlessness, the absence of surprise to life" in the modern age.

Gravity's Rainbow · All of Pynchon's books are filled with bizarre characters and incidents, but *Gravity's Rainbow* is especially dense and demanding. The hero is Tyrone Slothrop, an American army lieutenant attached to an allied intelligence unit in World War II. Slothrop's superiors become aware that the map of his sexual conquests (or his sexual fantasies; this is kept ambiguous) coincides with the distribution of German V-2 rockets falling on London. Significantly, the erection *precedes* the arrival of the rocket. This fact, which calls into question the usual mechanism of cause and effect (it complements the fact that the rocket, traveling faster than the speed of sound, is heard falling *after* it has exploded) is of central importance to the novel, for Pynchon means to pit two scientific models against each other. The older model, still seldom questioned, posits a mechanistic universe that operates according to the laws of cause and effect.

The character associated with this worldview is the sinister Dr. Pointsman, a diehard Pavlovian threatened by the new model, which posits a universe in which physical phenomena can be plotted and predicted only in terms of uncertainty and probability (Pynchon is on sound theoretical ground here; he is presenting the physics of Werner Heisenberg and Max Planck). The character who embraces the more up-to-date worldview is the sympathetic Roger Mexico, a statistician. Between these two, poor Slothrop–a kind of Everyman–tries to stay alive and if possible free. Pointsman and his minions concoct an experiment with Slothrop; they will provide him with the best information they have on the German rocket and then observe him closely for further revelations. Slothrop, aware that he is being used, goes AWOL to embark on a private quest to discover the truth of his personal destiny–and perhaps the destiny of his age as well.

Pynchon picks his historical moment carefully, for World War II was the moment when the technological world came of age. Technology offers humanity complete control of its environment and its destiny; techology offers something very like transcendence–or it offers annihilation. Pynchon's novel is a meditation on the choice, which is seen nowhere more clearly than in the new rocket technology. Will humanity use the rocket transcendentally, to go to the stars, or will people use it to destroy themselves? The answer has been taking shape since the German rocket scientists were sent east and west after World War II, and Pynchon concludes his great narrative with the split second before the ultimate cataclysm: The apocalyptic rocket plunges toward the "theatre" in which the film *Gravity's Rainbow* has unreeled before the reader. Critical opinion is split on the degree of bleakness in this ending. Figuratively, says Pynchon, the world is separated from its end only by "the last delta-t," the last infinitesimal unit of time and space between the rocket and its target. The delta-t, however, is a relative unit of measure. Modern human folly has indeed set in motion the process of his own destruction, but the process might still be arrested by a reordering of priorities, human and technological.

As for Slothrop, he simply fades away. Pynchon says he becomes "scattered," and the world reveals a characteristic aspect of Pynchon's genius. Just as Joyce forced religious and liturgical language to serve his aesthetic ends, Pynchon forces technological language to serve humanistic and spiritual ends. "Scattering," a trope from particle physics, refers to the dispersal of a beam of radiation, but it also evokes *sparagmos*, the ritual dismemberment and dispersal of the divine scapegoat. Slothrop has been associated all along with Orpheus, whose dismemberment became the basis of one of the many fertility cults in the Mediterranean and Near East. In a sense, Slothrop dies for the sins of the modern world, and his scattering coincides with the founding of the Counterforce, a group of enlightened, anarchic men and women devoted to reversing the technology of violence and death. The Counterforce, which has affinities with various countercultural movements waxing at the moment of this novel's composition, is not particularly powerful or effective, but it offers hope for a planet hurtling toward destruction.

After *Gravity's Rainbow*, Pynchon published no new fiction for seventeen years. During this period, the counterculture retreated as the forces of reaction, complacency, and materialism took over, and perhaps it was this frightening and disheartening development that was behind Pynchon's long silence. He may have abandoned a book or books that came to seem unattuned to the post-1960's *Zeitgeist*. Yet when the novelistic silence was at last broken, it was with a meditation on the historical polarization of the 1960's and the 1980's.

Vineland · In his long-awaited fourth novel, *Vineland*, Pynchon returns to the California setting of *The Crying of Lot 49*. As in *V.*, Pynchon sets up a dual historical focus. He imagines characters in the present–the portentous year 1984–trying to come to terms with the period, twenty years earlier, when they and the whole country underwent a searing passage. Broadly, then, Pynchon here reflects on the direction the country's history has taken–from anarchic but healthy self-indulgence to neo-Puritan repression. These poles are visible in the People's Republic of Rock and Roll, with its ethic of freedom, pleasure, dope, music, and self-expression, and in the Nixonian and Reaganite reaction that put an end to the polymorphous perversity of the 1960's and ushered in the return to materialism and political conservatism.

The novel is structured–somewhat more loosely than is usual with Pynchon–around the quest of a girl named Prairie for the mother, Frenesi Gates, who abandoned her shortly after her birth. Prairie's father, Zoyd Wheeler, still loves Frenesi, as does the man with whom she was involved before him–the sinister Brock Vond, a federal agent who had used her to infiltrate and subvert PR[3] and other radical causes. Zoyd accepts his misery, but Vond will stop at nothing to get Frenesi back in his clutches–not even at kidnapping Prairie, who could be made into an instrument of renewed control. Also involved in the action are female Ninja Darryl Louise–DL–Chastain, an old friend of Frenesi, and DL's companion, the "karmic adjuster" Takeshi Fumimota, a kind of Zen private eye.

The centrality of Prairie, Frenesi, and DL, not to mention the narrational attention to Frenesi's mother and grandmother (Sasha Gates and Eula Traverse), make this essay Pynchon's first in feminist fiction. (Though a woman, V., was central to his first novel, it was really a parody of the kind of matriarchal vision associated with Robert Graves and the White Goddess.) It is in terms of this feminism that he is able in *Vineland* to move beyond the apocalyptic obsession that characterizes all three of his previous novels, as well as the stories "Mortality and Mercy in Vienna" and "Entropy." *Vineland* ends with a vision of familial harmony that is nothing less than mythic–an augury of what an America-wide family might be. Here the reader sees Prairie reunited with her mother and half-brother, as Zoyd and others are also integrated. Vond alone is excluded (his surname is an apocope of the Dutch word *vondeling*, a foundling–as if to hint at his inability to be integrated into family wholeness). The reunion of the Traverse-Becker clans, which seem to center in their women, is Pynchon's Vonnegut-like imagining of the millennium, the era of peace and harmony that ironically succeeds the apocalyptic disruptions everywhere expected in the novel.

Herein, too, is the meaning of Pynchon's setting, the imaginary community of Vineland that provides the novel with its title. Vineland is the name given to the American continent by the Vikings, its first European visitors, at the end of the first millennium. Pynchon's novel reminds American readers that their land has been known to history for one thousand years.

Mason and Dixon · A more proximate past figures in *Mason and Dixon*. In this most massive of his novels, Pynchon ranges over the eighteenth century, with particular attention to the careers of Charles Mason and Jeremiah Dixon, who are sent by the Royal Society to the far corners of the earth to observe the 1761 and 1769 transits of Venus. Between these two assignments Mason and Dixon accept a commission to establish the much-contested boundary between Pennsylvania and Maryland. The central part of Pynchon's mammoth novel concerns this project, which occupies his protagonists from 1763 to 1767.

The dates are important: Mason and Dixon do their work on the very eve of the American Revolution. Pynchon looks at the America they traverse for the switching points of the great railroad called history. He sees colonial America as a place where Western civilization paused one last time before following its Faustian course toward more rationalism, greater dependence on technology, and the throwing out of spiritual babies with the bathwater of magic and superstition. The religious freedom it offered notwithstanding, America has always, Pynchon suggests, been a place of struggle between the spiritual and material energies of the West. By the latter part of the eighteenth century, with the Revolution in the offing, the secularizing tendencies of the Enlightenment (notably Deism) made America the conservator, merely, of a few "poor fragments of a Magic irreparably broken." No longer the setting of "a third Testament," the New World remained only sporadically the "object of hope that Miracles might yet occur, that God might yet return to Human affairs, that all the wistful Fictions necessary to the childhood of a species might yet come true. . . ." Though aware that popular religion would always figure prominently in the moral economy of the emergent American nation, Pynchon suggests that some more genuine and legitimate spirituality was elbowed aside by the less-than-idealistic interests that fostered revolution (and he offers largely unflattering sketches of figures such as Presidents Ben Franklin and George Washington). In the end, America became merely "one more hope in the realm of the Subjunctive, one more grasp at the last radiant whispers of the last bights of Robe-hem, billowing Æther-driven at the back of an ever-departing Deity." Pynchon seems, in *Mason and Dixon*, to reconceptualize the hallowed myth of a quest for religious freedom.

Indeed, he rewrites more than one archetypal American narrative. Thus he intimates, as in *The Crying of Lot 49*, some betrayal of the original American Dream; thus his protagonists, who twin the American Adam, must like so many of their literary predecessors decide whether to reenact the Fall. Pynchon also revisits the captivity narrative, with emphasis not on the godless savagery of the captors but on the nefarious scheming of the Europeans they serve. When American Indians kidnap Eliza Fields of Conestoga, they do so on behalf of evil Jesuits who seek to staff a bizarre convent-brothel called Las Viudas de Cristo: the Widows of Christ. Even more bizarre, perhaps, is Fields's escape with Captain Zhang, a Chinese Feng Shui master who objects to the severely rationalistic mensuration (and cartography) of the arch-Jesuit Padre Zarpazo.

Presently joining the crew of lumberjacks, roustabouts, and hangers-on accompanying Mason and Dixon, Zhang provides an important non-Western perspective on their project. "Boundaries," he declares, should "follow Nature,–coast-lines, ridge-tops, river-banks,–so honoring the Dragon or *shan* within, from which the Land-Scape ever takes its form. To mark a right Line upon the Earth is to inflict upon the Dragon's very flesh a sword-slash, a long, perfect scar. . . ." Zhang characterizes the Visto (the unnaturally straight ten-yard-wide swath the surveyors cut through the wilderness) as a conductor of *Sha*, the "Bad Energy" that will bring in its train "Bad History." As Zhang subsequently observes, "Nothing will produce Bad History more directly or brutally, than drawing a Line, in particular a Right Line, the very Shape of Contempt, through the midst of a People,–to create thus a Distinction betwixt 'em,–'tis the first stroke.–All else will follow as if predestin'd, unto War and Devastation." The American Civil War, half a century later, would validate Zhang's remark as prophecy.

Sir Francis Bacon, describing the Idols of the Theater, long ago recognized how received ways of knowing within a given historical period make certain kinds of thinking difficult, if not impossible. Mason, for example, aspires to membership in the Royal Society even as he desperately tries to believe that death–especially the death of his beloved wife Rebekah–is not final. Yet the scientific calling that he shares with Dixon affords little latitude for such hope. Pynchon ingeniously imagines his protagonists as imperfectly amphibious men of their age. Each struggles to reconcile a propensity for supernatural or magical thinking with professional obligations to the new, rationalist order. Whether in South Africa, on the island of St. Helena, in America, or at the North Cape, Dixon and Mason sense that they are the inconsequential pawns of forces indifferent or hostile to them. Servants of the powerful and remote Royal Society, the surveyors suffer from a paranoia somewhat different from the usual Pynchon article–or perhaps they simply show us, belatedly, the positive side of a putative psychopathology. Pynchon hints, that is, at something admirable, even redemptive, in the paranoia of his eighteenth century Rosencrantz and Guildenstern. Mason and Dixon resist the coercive intellectual forces of their age.

As brilliantly realized as that age is in these pages, Pynchon delights in anachronistic violation of his historical frame. At a number of points the reader realizes that some piece of elaborately rendered eighteenth century foolery actually mirrors a twentieth century counterpart, for Pynchon frequently circumvents historical constraint to offer droll glimpses of what America and American culture will become. Hilarious, lightly veiled allusions to Popeye, Daffy Duck, the Jolly Green Giant, and *Star Trek* abound, not to mention numerous clever periphrases of a later vernacular. There are no cheap shots here, only the occasional "inexpensive salvo." Characters do not get their backs up–they suffer "Thoracick Indignation." Those hoping to keep costs down are reminded that *"prandium gratis non est"* ("there's no such thing as a free lunch"). The reader smiles, too, at "teton dernier," "aviating swine," "coprophagously agrin," and (of Fenderbelly Bodine exposing his buttocks to a foe) "pygephanous."

Pynchon fills his pages with the imaginative conceits his readers have come to expect. There is, for example, a wonderful talking canine, the Learned English Dog. There is also a character who, at the full moon, turns into a were-beaver. An eighteenth century Valley Girl's every sentence features "as," rather than the "like" that would characterize the speech of her twentieth century sister. A chef with the punning name of Armand Allegre fends off the amorous attentions of a mechanical duck–part Daffy, part Frankenstein's Monster–invented by Jacques de Vaucanson. Such joking has its serious side: de Vaucanson's punch-card technology would be refined in the Jacquard loom and other automated weaving machines that played an important role in the Industrial Revolution, centerpiece of the Enlightenment. Subsequently, punch cards would play their role in the Age of Information.

In *Mason and Dixon*, then, Pynchon characterizes the eighteenth century as the moment in Western history when rationalism became a cultural juggernaut, crushing spiritual alternatives to Enlightenment thinking. As in *V.*, *Gravity's Rainbow*, and the 1984 essay "Is It O.K. to Be a Luddite?," the author focuses on the reification of Faustian appetite in scientific and technological advance, here symbolized in the profoundly unnatural Line that, arrowing its way into the mythic American West, consecrates the new world to reason–and to its abuses.

David Cowart

Other major works

SHORT FICTION: *Slow Learner: Early Stories*, 1984.
NONFICTION: *Deadly Sins*, 1993.

Bibliography

Berressem, Hanjo. *Pynchon's Poetics: Interfacing Theory and Text.* Urbana: University of Illinois Press, 1993. The most theoretically sophisticated treatment of Pynchon.

Chambers, Judith. *Thomas Pynchon.* New York: Twayne, 1992. A solid overview of Pynchon and his work, well suited to the student approaching Pynchon for the first time.

Cowart, David. *Thomas Pynchon: The Art of Allusion.* Carbondale: Southern Illinois University Press, 1980. This book contains some early biographical scourings, as well as an examination of Pynchon's use of art, cinema, music, and literature—especially as they define the pull in Pynchon between an "entropic" and a transcendental vision. Useful to beginning and advanced readers of Pynchon.

Grant, J. Kerry. *A Companion to "The Crying of Lot 49".* Athens: University of Georgia Press, 1994. Glosses allusions and major themes. Bibliographical references and index.

Green, Geoffrey, Donald J. Greiner, and Larry McCaffery, eds. *The Vineland Papers: Critical Takes on Pynchon's Novel.* Normal, Ill.: Dalkey Archive Press, 1994. First-rate essays and a *Vineland* bibliography by thirteen scholars, including N. Katherine Hayles, David Porush, Molly Hite, and Stacey Olster.

Hume, Kathryn. *Pynchon's Mythography: An Approach to Gravity's Rainbow.* Carbondale: Southern Illinois University Press, 1987. A highly readable and important challenge to the critical argument that Pynchon, as post-modernist, relentlessly deconstructs myth.

Levine, George, and David Leverenz, eds. *Mindful Pleasures: Essays on Thomas Pynchon.* Boston: Little, Brown, 1976. Twelve important essays, by such critics as Richard Poirier, Tony Tanner, Edward Mendelson, and the editors themselves. Mathew Winston's biographical essay is especially useful for genealogical information.

McHoul, Alec, and David Wills. *Writing Pynchon: Strategies in Fictional Analysis.* Urbana: University of Illinois Press, 1990. An intriguing if not altogether successful reversal of the usual critical approach: The authors use Pynchon's writings as the theory by which to read Derrida.

Mendelson, Edward. *Pynchon: A Collection of Critical Essays.* Englewood Cliffs, N.J.: Prentice-Hall, 1978. Part of the reliable Twentieth-Century Views series, this collection contains fourteen essays and reviews, by such important critics as Tony Tanner, Frank Kermode, Richard Poirier, Paul Fussell, and Mendelson himself.

Newman, Robert D. *Understanding Thomas Pynchon.* Columbia: University of South Carolina Press, 1986. From a series aimed at readers seeking basic introductions, this book is a good starting place for the beginner.

Schaub, Thomas. *Pynchon: The Voice of Ambiguity.* Urbana: University of Illinois Press, 1981. A reliable account of how entropy and uncertainty figure in Pynchon. Includes discussion of Marshall McLuhan's influence on *Lot 49* and the ironies attendant on Ivan Pavlov's role in *Gravity's Rainbow.* Places Pynchon in American literary tradition.

Slade, Joseph. *Thomas Pynchon.* New York: P. Lang, 1990. The first book on Pynchon (originally appeared in 1974) and still one of the best, despite nearly thirty volumes of competition. A balanced and readable discussion, but especially strong on Pynchon's uses of science. Lack of an index reduces usefulness to the browser.

Tanner, Tony. *Thomas Pynchon.* London: Methuen, 1982. Tanner is one of Pynchon's most incisive—and earliest—critics. A short and readable introduction.

Weisenburger, Steven. *A "Gravity's Rainbow" Companion: Sources and Contexts for Pynchon's Novel.* Athens: University of Georgia Press, 1988. A superb and indispensable *vade mecum.*

AYN RAND

Born: St. Petersburg, Russia; February 2, 1905
Died: New York, New York; March 6, 1982

Principal long fiction · *We the Living*, 1936; *Anthem*, 1938, rev. ed. 1946; *The Fountainhead*, 1943; *Atlas Shrugged*, 1957; *The Early Ayn Rand: A Selection from Her Unpublished Fiction*, 1984 (Leonard Peikoff, editor).

Other literary forms · In addition to her three novels and one novelette, Ayn Rand published a play and several philosophical disquisitions. An early critique, *Hollywood: American Movie City*, was published in the Soviet Union in 1926 without Rand's permission.

Achievements · Rand won the Volpe Cup at the Venice Film Festival in 1942 for the Italian motion-picture dramatization of *We the Living*, a novel about the failures of the Soviet system. The sole honorary degree, of doctor of humane letters, awarded to Rand by Lewis and Clark College in Portland, Oregon, in 1963 does not reflect the significance of her influence on America's philosophic and political-economic thought.

Biography · Alisa (Alice) Zinovievna Rosenbaum was born the eldest of three children into a Russian Jewish middle-class family in czarist Russia. When her father's pharmacy was nationalized following the Bolshevik Revolution of 1917, Alisa, who had been writing stories since she was nine, found a calling: She turned against collectivism, and she elevated individualism—personal, economic, political, and moral—into a philosophy that eventually attracted a large, occasionally distinguished, following. Early in her career she declared herself to be an atheist.

At the University of Petrograd (now St. Petersburg), Alisa studied philosophy, English, and history, graduating with highest honors in history in 1924. By then the works of French writers Victor Hugo and Edmond Rostand, and of Polish writer Henryk Sienkiewicz, had inspired her passion for the heroic and the ideal. Fyodor Dostoevski and Friedrich Nietzsche also left their mark.

Unhappy because the Soviet system was not moving in the direction of her republican ideals and because she had a dead-end job, Alisa accepted an invitation from relatives and went to Chicago in 1926. In the United States she restyled herself Ayn (the pronunciation rhymes with "mine") Rand and within a few months moved to Hollywood, California.

Working as a film extra, a file clerk, and a waitress and doing other odd jobs from 1926 to 1934, Rand perfected her language skills and became a screenwriter at various motion-picture studios. In 1937, she worked as an unpaid typist for Eli Jacques Kahn, a well-known New York architect, in preparation for her first major novel, *The Fountainhead*. Given her early experience in totalitarian Russia, Rand soon became known as the most driven of American anticommunists. She had acquired U.S. citizenship in 1931. In 1947, she appeared as a "friendly witness" before the House Committee on Un-American Activities (HUAC) during the period of the communist witch-hunts—an event she later admitted regretting. Along the way, in 1929, Rand married Charles Francis (Frank) O'Connor, a minor actor and amateur painter. He died in 1979.

After her major literary successes, Rand devoted herself exclusively to philosophizing, writing, and lecturing. She spoke on numerous Ivy League university campuses. She became a regular at the Ford Hall Forum and a columnist for the *Los Angeles Times*. She was coeditor or contributor to several philosophical publications. Rand was active in the Nathaniel Branden Institute, created to spread her philosophy of "objectivism," until her personal and professional break with Nathaniel and Barbara Branden in 1968. This triangular relationship had played an important part in Rand's life, for the Brandens formed the nucleus of a close group of followers, ironically known as "the collective."

In her seventies Rand, a chain smoker whose loaded cigarette holder had become a symbol of her persona, was diagnosed with lung cancer. She died in March, 1982, in the New York City apartment in which she had lived since 1951. Her wake was attended by hundreds, including Alan Greenspan, an early Rand devotee and later chairman of the Federal Reserve Board Bank. Philosopher Leonard Peikoff, Rand's intellectual and legal heir, was also present.

Rand's publications have sold well over twenty million copies in English and in translation even as literary critics generally dismissed her ideas as reactionary propaganda or pop philosophy. Rand was a paradox. She was a writer of romantic fiction whose ideas were often taken seriously, but she was also a controversial individualist and a contrarian who defied the moral, political, social, and aesthetic norms of her times.

Analysis · In her two major works of fiction, Rand explicated her philosophy of objectivism in dramatic form. Thus, in *The Fountainhead* and especially in *Atlas Shrugged*, Rand argues that reality exists independent of human thought (objectively), that reason is the only viable method for understanding reality, that individuals should seek personal happiness and exist for their own sake and no other, and that individuals should not sacrifice themselves or be sacrificed by others. Furthermore, unrestricted laissez-faire capitalism is the political-economic system in which these principles can best flourish. Underlying this essence is the philosophy of unadulterated individualism, personal responsibility, the power of unsullied reason, and the importance of Rand's special kind of morality.

In her long fiction the philosopher-novelist spells out her concept of the exceptional individual as a heroic being and an "ideal man," with his happiness as the highest moral purpose in life, with productive achievement the noblest activity, and reason the only absolute. Rand advocates minimal government intrusion and no initiation of physical force in human interactions. She represents such a system as enshrining the highest degree of morality and justice.

Because Rand also focuses on the denial of self-sacrifice and altruism, a staple of conventional morality and welfarism, she opposes both Christianity and communism. She finds it irrational to place the good of others ahead of one's own rational self-interest. Likewise, she denies mysticism but rather promotes the Aristotelian view that the world which individuals perceive is reality and there is no other. Both her major novels can be considered elitist and antidemocratic in that they extol the virtues of a few innovative, far-thinking individuals over the mediocre majority, which is either ignorant and uncaring or, even worse, actively striving to destroy the brilliant individuals of great ability. Besides disparaging mediocrity, Rand also decried the power of connections, conformity with what has been done before, a trend she found far too evident in the American welfare state, and the intellectual bankruptcy she deemed it to have fostered.

Rand considered herself a practitioner of Romanticism who was concerned with representing individuals "in whom certain human attributes are focused more sharply and consistently than in average human beings." Accordingly, in both these novels the characters of the heroes, sharply drawn, are idealized creations–not depictions of real individuals–who are in control of their own destinies despite major odds.

The Fountainhead · *The Fountainhead* is the story of Howard Roark, Rand's ideal man, an architect who has a vision of how buildings should really be designed. He is innovative and efficient; he also has a strong aesthetic sense and has integrity–in short, he is a man of principle and artistic individuality. Roark is contrasted with Peter Keating, a former classmate and fellow architect but a "second-hander," constantly replicating conventional styles since he has no originality of his own. He achieves a seeming success by manipulating others. Unlike Roark, whom he envies, Keating does not know who he really is.

Another of Roark's adversaries is Ellsworth Toohey. He writes a column for the *Banner*, arguing that architecture should reflect the art of the people. Gail Wynand is the *Banner*'s owner and newspaper magnate; he appreciates Roark's creativity but buckles under societal pressures, disregards his vision, and thereby engineers his own downfall as a worthy human being.

The love interest is embodied in Dominique Francon, the daughter of Guy Francon, the principal owner of the architectural firm that employs Peter Keating. She is a typical Rand heroine, a self-reliant idealist alienated by the shallow conventions of her day in interwar America and convinced that a life of principle is impossible in a world ruled by mediocrity. Her affair with Roark is motivated, not by physical or emotional passion, but by the recognition that he is a man of great worth. Along the way, in between and sometimes during other affairs, she marries Keating and then Wynand before finally becoming Mrs. Howard Roark. Dominique seems inconsistent in her ideals, attitudes, and critiques of architectural designs, but the inconsistencies are all part of her effort to spare Roark from ultimate destruction.

Roark, long professionally unsuccessful because he is unwilling to compromise the integrity of his creations, preferring not to work at all or to do menial tasks, eventually overcomes not only financial difficulties but also numerous intrigues by the likes of Keating. For instance, through the mean-spirited Toohey, Roark is assigned to build an interdenominational temple for a patron, Hopton Stoddard, a traditionalist who is abroad at the time. Toohey knows that Stoddard will hate Roark's radically innovative design. Roark makes the building's centerpiece Dominique's nude figure. Toohey incites public condemnation and persuades the patron to sue Roark for breach of contract. Stoddard wins the case, as Roark fails to defend himself in court.

Paradoxically, a friendship develops between Roark and Wynand, attracted to each other for different reasons. Wynand helps Roark in his defense at a second trial, which follows Roark's dynamiting a low-income housing project that Keating had commissioned. The latter had agreed not to alter Roark's design in any way in exchange for Roark's allowing Keating to claim credit for the former's innovative and cost-effective blueprint. When Keating fails to keep his promise and adulterates the design, Roark, with Dominique Francon's assistance, destroys the structure. The trial gives Roark the opportunity to spell out his—that is, Rand's—defense of ethical egoism and opposition to a world perishing from an "orgy of self-sacrifice" and conventional morality. After Roark's exoneration, Wynand commissions him to build the tallest skyscraper in New York City despite Wynand's losing Dominique to Roark.

Ultimately, *The Fountainhead* is a novel of ideas, of heroic characters who are the fountainhead of human progress and of their opposites, who live second-hand, second-rate lives and constantly seek social approval for their beliefs. The philosophy in the novel alternates with the action, and neither can be understood without the other.

Atlas Shrugged · Rand's philosophy extolling the myth of absolute, rugged individualism and its relationship to society is most fully explicated in what proved to be her last work of fiction, several years in the making: the twelve-hundred-page *Atlas Shrugged*. In this novel, Rand tries to answer the question raised by one of her earlier heroes: "What would happen to the world without those who do, think, work, produce?" In this apocalyptic parable, it is John Galt of Twentieth Century Motors, a physicist, engineer, inventor, and philosopher, who is Rand's ideal man and leads the other "men of the mind" on a strike against the exploitation of the genuine creators of wealth by all the leeches and parasites—the nonproducers—whom they had been sustaining.

Rand's philosophy is played out through the stories of the four heroes, the authentic moneymakers. They are the Argentine Francisco d'Anconia, heir to the world's leading copper enterprise; the Scandinavian Ragnar Danneskjold, a onetime philosopher who turns pirate in order to steal wealth back from the looters and return it to the producers of legitimate values; Henry (Hank) Rearden, an American steel magnate and inventor of a metal better than steel; and finally, the other American, John Galt, who, with the others, stops the ideological motor of the world in a strike before rebuilding society. The heroine, rail heiress Dagny Taggart, spends much of the novel wondering where the individuals of ability have gone.

Confronting them is an array of villains, manipulative appropriators, enemies of individualism and free enterprise, scabs, and moochers profiting from the achievements of the producers and united by their greed for unearned gains. Especially, there is Dr. Robert Stadler, the counterpart of Gail Wynand in *The Fountainhead*. Stadler, once the greatest physicist of his time, fully cognizant of the value of the human mind, fails to stand up for his principles. The progressive decay of James Taggart, Dagny's brother and the titular president of Taggart Transcontinental Railroad, parallels that of the society in which he lives.

In the novel, set some time in the vaguely defined future, America is following Europe down the long, hopeless path of socialism, government regulation, and a predatory state into a new Dark Age. The heroes join forces with other intelligent, freedom-loving leaders of commerce, industry, science, and philosophy to reverse the slide. They do this as Atlas may have done had he grown tired of holding the world on his shoulders without reward.

Eventually, the heroes repair to a secret Colorado mountain citadel, where they wait for their time to rebuild the decaying collectivist society whose end their "strike of the mind" against productive work is hastening. Galt, arrested and tortured by the looters but finally freed by the other heroes, delivers a thirty-five-thousand-word oration via a commandeered radio, epitomizing Rand's objectivism and views of the ideal man. Galt's (Rand's) philosophy then becomes that of the new society: "I swear by my life and my love of it that I will never live for the sake of another man, nor ask another man to live for mine." By the end of the novel, socialism has produced a bankrupt world pleading for the return of the men of the mind, who, after a confrontation with the parasites, start to rebuild society. *Atlas Shrugged* is Rand's most thorough exploration of the social ramifications of politics, economics, psychology, metaphysics, epistemology, aesthetics, religion, and ethics.

Peter B. Heller

Other major works

PLAYS: *Night of January 16th* (also titled *Woman on Trial* and *Penthouse Legend*), pr. 1934; *The Unconquered* (adapted from *We the Living*), 1940.

NONFICTION: *For the New Intellectual: The Philosophy of Ayn Rand*, 1961; *The Virtue of Selfishness: A New Concept of Egoism*, 1964; *Capitalism: The Unknown Ideal*, 1966; *Introduction to Objectivist Epistemology*, 1967, 2d enlarged ed., 1990 (Harry Binswanger and Leonard Peikoff, editors); *The Romantic Manifesto: A Philosophy of Literature*, 1969, rev. ed. 1971, 2d rev. ed. 1975; *The New Left: The Anti-Industrial Revolution*, 1971; *Philosophy: Who Needs It?*, 1982; *The Ayn Rand Lexicon: Objectivism from A to Z*, 1984 (Leonard Peikoff, editor); *The Voice of Reason: Essays in Objectivist Thought*, 1988 (Leonard Peikoff, editor); *The Ayn Rand Column*, 1991; *Letters of Ayn Rand*, 1995 (Michael S. Berliner, editor); *Journals of Ayn Rand*, 1997 (David Harriman, editor).

MISCELLANEOUS: *The Objectivist Newsletter*, 1962-1965; *The Objectivist*, 1966-1971; *The Ayn Rand Letter*, 1971-1976.

Bibliography

Baker, James T. *Ayn Rand.* Boston: Twayne, 1987. An academic's brief but objective and highly readable treatment of the novelist's life and work, with a chronology, references, and bibliography.

Branden, Barbara. *The Passion of Ayn Rand.* Garden City, N.Y.: Doubleday, 1986. A provocative assessment, by one of her former inner circle, of Rand's life as an author, philosopher, and especially a woman with strong loves and hates. Includes photographs.

Branden, Nathaniel. *Judgment Day: My Years with Ayn Rand.* Boston: Houghton Mifflin, 1989. A personal account by Rand's disciple, organizer, spokesman, lover, and, ultimately, enemy. Includes photographs.

Gladstein, Mimi Reisel. *The Ayn Rand Companion.* Westport, Conn.: Greenwood Press, 1984. A compendium of the plots and major characters of Rand's fiction.

Rand, Ayn. *Journals of Ayn Rand.* Edited by David Harriman. New York: Penguin-Dutton, 1997. The author-philosopher's thoughts and feelings about her life and work, including a cavalcade of events and people. Foreword by her designated intellectual heir, Leonard Peikoff.

Sciabarra, Chris M. *Ayn Rand: The Russian Radical.* University Park: Pennsylvania State University Press, 1995. The evolution of the author as a philosopher, of her dialectics, and of her objectivism, beginning with her early years. Includes a bibliography and photographs.

ISHMAEL REED

Born: Chattanooga, Tennessee; February 22, 1938

Principal long fiction · *The Free-Lance Pallbearers*, 1967; *Yellow Back Radio Broke-Down*, 1969; *Mumbo Jumbo*, 1972; *The Last Days of Louisiana Red*, 1974; *Flight to Canada*, 1976; *The Terrible Twos*, 1982; *Reckless Eyeballing*, 1986; *The Terrible Threes*, 1989; *Japanese by Spring*, 1993.

Other literary forms · Ishmael Reed may be best known as a satirical novelist, but he also gained a reputation as a respected poet, essayist, and editor. His poetry collections, which include *Catechism of D Neoamerican Hoodoo Church* (1970), *Conjure: Selected Poems 1963-1970* (1972), *Chattanooga* (1973), *A Secretary to the Spirits* (1977), and *New and Collected Poems* (1988), established him as a major African American poet, and his poetry has been included in several important anthologies. In well-received collections of essays, including *Shrovetide in Old New Orleans* (1978), *God Made Alaska for the Indians* (1982), and *Writin' Is Fightin'* (1988), Reed forcefully presented his aesthetic and political theories. He also proved to be an important editor and publisher. *Nineteen Necromancers from Now* (1970) was a breakthrough anthology for several unknown black writers. *Yardbird Lives!* (1978), which Reed edited with novelist Al Young, includes essays, fiction, and graphics from the pages of the *Yardbird Reader*, an innovative periodical that published the work of minority writers and artists. Reed's most ambitious editing project resulted in *Calafia: The California Poetry* (1979), an effort to gather together the forgotten minority poetry of California's past.

Achievements · Reed earned a place in the first rank of contemporary African American authors, but such recognition did not come immediately. Most established reviewers ignored Reed's first novel, *The Free-Lance Pallbearers*, and many of the reviews that were written dismissed the novel as offensive, childish, or self-absorbed. Although *Yellow Back Radio Broke-Down* was even less traditional than its predecessor, it received much more critical attention and became the center of considerable critical debate. Some reviewers attacked the novel as overly clever, bitter, or obscure, but many praised its imaginative satire and technical innovation. Moreover, the controversy over *Yellow Back Radio Broke-Down* stirred new interest in *The Free-Lance Pallbearers*. Reed's increasing acceptance as a major African American author was demonstrated when his third novel, *Mumbo Jumbo*, was reviewed on the front page of *The New York Review of Books*. Both *Mumbo Jumbo* and *Conjure*, a poetry collection published in the same year, were nominated for the National Book Award.

Subsequent novels maintained Reed's position in American letters. In 1975, Reed's *The Last Days of Louisiana Red* received the Rosenthal Foundation Award, and some reviewers viewed *Flight to Canada* as Reed's best novel. Yet his work proved consistently controversial. His novels have, for example, been called sexist, a critical accusation that is fueled by comparison of Reed's novels with the contemporary powerful fiction written by African American women such as Alice Walker and Toni Morrison. The charge of sexism is further encouraged by Reed's satirical attack on feminists in *Reckless Eyeballing*. Reed has also been called a reactionary by some critics because of his uncomplimentary portrayals of black revolutionaries. His fiction has been translated into three languages, and his poetry is included in *Poetry of the Negro, New Black Poetry, The Norton Anthology of Poetry*, and other anthologies. In 1998, Ishmael Reed was awarded the MacArthur "genius" fellowship. This is fitting recognition for a writer who consciously attempted to redefine American and African American literature.

James Lerager

Biography · The jacket notes to *Chattanooga* glibly recount Ishmael Scott Reed's life: "born in Chattanooga, Tennessee, grew up in Buffalo, New York, learned to write in New York City and wised up in Berkeley, California." Each residence played a crucial role in Reed's development.

Reed was born the son of Henry Lenoir and Thelma Coleman, but before he was two years old, his mother remarried, this time to autoworker Bennie Reed. When he was four years old, his mother moved the family to Buffalo, New York, where she found factory work. Reed was graduated from Buffalo's East High School in 1956 and began to attend Millard Fillmore College, the night division of the University of Buffalo, supporting himself by working in the Buffalo public library. A satirical short story, "Something Pure," which portrayed Christ's return as an advertising man, brought Reed the praise of an English professor and encouraged him to enroll in day classes. Reed attended the University of Buffalo until 1960, when he withdrew because of money problems and the social pressures that his financial situation created. He married Priscilla Rose Thompson and moved into the notorious Talbert Mall Projects. The two years he spent there provided him with a painful but valuable experience of urban poverty and dependency. His daughter, Timothy Bret Reed, was also born there. During his last years in Buffalo, Reed wrote for the *Empire Star Weekly*, moderated a controversial radio program for station WVFO, and acted in several local stage productions.

From 1962 to 1967, Reed lived in New York City. As well as being involved with the Civil Rights movement and the Black Power movement, Reed served as editor of *Advance*, a weekly published in Newark, New Jersey. His work on the *Advance* was admired by Walter Bowart, and together they founded the *East Village Other*, one of the first and most successful "underground" newspapers. An early indication of Reed's commitment to encouraging the work of minority artists was his organization in 1965 of the American Festival of Negro Art.

In 1967, Reed moved to Berkeley, California, and began teaching at the University of California at Berkeley. In 1970, Reed and his first wife divorced (after years of separation), and he married Carla Blank. In 1971, with Al Young, Reed founded the Yardbird Publishing Company, which from 1971 to 1976 produced the *Yardbird Reader*, an innovative journal of ethnic writing and graphics. The Reed, Cannon, and Johnson Communications Company, which later became Ishmael Reed Books, was founded in 1973 and has published the work of William Demby, Bill Gunn, Mei Mei Bressenburge, and other ethnic writers. In 1976, Reed and Victor Cruz began the Before Columbus Foundation. In 1977, Ishmael Reed's daughter Tennessee was born, and he was denied tenure in the English department at the University of California at Berkeley. He continued to serve as a lecturer at Berkeley, however, and also taught at Yale, Harvard, Columbia, Dartmouth, and a number of other colleges and universities. In 1995, he was awarded an honorary doctorate in letters from the State University of New York at Buffalo.

Reed made important contributions as a poet, novelist, essayist, playwright, and as an editor and publisher. He stated that he considers himself a global writer, and his success at writing poetry in the African language of Yoruba and his study of Japanese language and culture for his novel *Japanese by Spring* supports this assertion. He also extended his literary range to include plays, such as *The Preacher and the Rapper* (pub. 1997), and jazz albums, such as *Conjure I* (1983) and *Conjure II* (1989), and he even completed a libretto and served as the executive producer for a cable television soap opera called *Personal Problems* (1981).

In the early 1990's, Reed was, perhaps, best known for his controversial essays on such issues as the Rodney King and O. J. Simpson trials and the U.S. Justice Clarence Thomas hearings, some of which were collected in *Airing Dirty Laundry* (1993). However, his most important contribution to American letters may well be his work as an editor and publisher for other ethnic writers. In all of his publishing ventures, Reed tries to expose readers to the work of Asian Americans, African Americans, Chicanos, and Native Americans in an effort to help build a truly representative and pluralistic national literature.

Analysis · Ishmael Reed is consciously a part of the African American literary tradition that extends back to the first-person slave narratives, and the central purpose of his novels is to define a means of expressing the complexity of the African American experience in a manner distinct from the dominant literary tradition. Until the middle of the twentieth century, African American fiction, although enriched by the lyricism of Jean Toomer and Zora Neale Hurston, concentrated on realistic portrayals of black life and employed familiar narrative structures. This tendency toward social realism peaked with Richard Wright's *Native Son* (1940) and *Black Boy* (1945), but it was continued into the late twentieth century by authors such as James Baldwin. Reed belongs to a divergent tradition, inspired by Ralph Ellison's *Invisible Man* (1952), a countertradition that includes the work of Leon Forrest, Ernest Gaines, James Alan McPherson, Toni Morrison, and Alice Walker.

Believing that the means of expression is as important as the matter, Reed argues that the special qualities of the African American experience cannot be adequately communicated through traditional literary forms. Like Amiri Baraka, Reed believes that African American authors must "be estranged from the dominant culture," but Reed also wants to avoid being stifled by a similarly restrictive countertradition. In *Shrovetide in Old New Orleans,* Reed says that his art and criticism try to combat "the consciousness barrier erected by an alliance of Eastern-backed black pseudo-nationalists and white mundanists." Thus, Reed works against the stylistic limitations of the African American literary tradition as much as he works with them. Henry Louis Gates, Jr., compared Reed's fictional modifications of African American literary traditions to the African American folk custom of "signifying," maintaining that Reed's novels present an ongoing process of "rhetorical self-definition."

Although Reed's novels are primarily efforts to define an appropriate African American aesthetic, his fiction vividly portrays the particular social condition of black Americans. In his foreword to Elizabeth and Thomas Settle's *Ishmael Reed: A Primary and Secondary Bibliography* (1982), Reed expresses his bitterness over persistent racism and argues that the personal experience of racism that informs his art makes his work inaccessible and threatening to many readers: "I am a member of a class which has been cast to the bottom of the American caste system, and from those depths I write a vision which is still strange, often frightening, 'peculiar' and 'odd' to some, 'ill-considered' and unwelcome to many." Indeed, Ishmael seems to be an ironically appropriate name for this author of violent and darkly humorous attacks on American institutions and attitudes, for the sharpness and breadth of his satire sometimes make him appear to be a man whose hand is turned against all others. His novels portray corrupt power brokers and their black and white sycophants operating in a dehumanized and materialistic society characterized by its prefabricated and ethnocentric culture. Yet Reed's novels are not hopeless explications of injustice, for against the forces of repression and conformity he sets gifted individuals who escape the limitations of their sterile culture by courageously penetrating the illusions that bind them. Moreover, in contrast to many white authors who are engaged in parallel metafictive experiments, Reed voices a confident belief that "print and words are not dead at all."

Reed's narrative technique combines the improvisational qualities of jazz with a documentary impulse to accumulate references and allusions. In his composite narratives, historical and fictional characters coexist in a fluid, anachronistic time. In an effort to translate the vitality and spontaneity of the oral, folk tradition into a literature that can form the basis for an alternative culture, Reed mixes colloquialisms and erudition in novels which are syncretized from a series of subtexts. The literary equivalent of scat singing, his stories-within-stories parody literary formulas and challenge the traditional limits of fiction.

Reed claims that his novels constitute "an art form with its own laws," but he does not mean to imply that his work is private, for these "laws" are founded on a careful but imaginative reinterpretation of the historical and mythological past. The lengthy bibliography appended to *Mumbo Jumbo* satirizes the documentary impulse of social realist authors, but it also underscores Reed's belief that his mature work demands scholarly research in order to be decoded. This artistic process of reinterpretation often requires the services of an interlocutor, a character who explicitly explains the events of the narrative in terms of the mythological past. Reed's novels describe a vision of an Osirian/Dionysian consciousness, a sensuous humanism that he presents as an appropriate cultural alternative for nonwhite Americans. His imaginative reconstructions of the American West, the Harlem Renaissance, the American Civil War, and contemporary American politics, interwoven with ancient myths, non-European folk customs, and the formulas of popular culture, are liberating heresies meant to free readers from the intellectual domination of the Judeo-Christian tradition.

The Free-Lance Pallbearers · Reed's first novel, *The Free-Lance Pallbearers*, takes place in a futuristic America called HARRY SAM: "A big not-to-be-believed out-of-sight, sometimes referred to as O-BOP-SHE-BANG or KLANG-A-LANG-A-DING-DONG." This crumbling and corrupt world is tyrannized by Sam himself, a vulgar fat man who lives in Sam's Motel on Sam's Island in the middle of the lethally polluted Black Bay that borders HARRY SAM. Sam, doomed by some terrifying gastrointestinal disorder, spends all of his time on the toilet, his filth pouring into the bay from several large statues of Rutherford B. Hayes.

The bulk of the novel, although framed and periodically informed by a jiving narrative voice, is narrated by Bukka Doopeyduk in a restrained, proper English that identifies his passive faith in the establishment. Doopeyduk is a dedicated adherent to the Nazarene Code, an orderly in a psychiatric hospital, a student at Harry Sam College, and a hapless victim. His comically futile efforts to play by the rules are defeated by the cynics, who manipulate the unjust system to their own advantage. In the end, Doopeyduk is disillusioned: He leads a successful attack on Sam's Island, uncovers the conspiracy that protects Sam's cannibalism, briefly dreams of becoming the black Sam, and is finally crucified.

The Free-Lance Pallbearers is a parody of the African American tradition of first-person, confessional narratives, a book the narrator describes as "growing up in soulsville first of three installments—or what it means to be a backstage darky." Reed's novel challenges the viability of this African American version of the *Bildungsroman*, in which a young protagonist undergoes a painful initiation into the darkness of the white world, a formula exemplified by Wright's *Black Boy* and James Baldwin's *Go Tell It on the Mountain* (1953). In fact, the novel suggests that African American authors' use of this European form is as disabling as Doopeyduk's adherence to the dictates of the Nazarene Code.

The novel is an unrestrained attack on American politics. HARRY SAM, alternately referred to as "Nowhere" or "Now Here," is a dualistic vision of an America that celebrates vacuous contemporaneity. The novel, an inversion of the Horatio Alger myth in the manner of Nathanael West, mercilessly displays American racism, but its focus is the corruptive potential of power. Sam is a grotesque version of Lyndon B. Johnson, famous for his bathroom interviews, and Sam's cannibalistic taste for children is an attack on Johnson's Vietnam policy. With *The Free-Lance Pallbearers*, Reed destroys the presumptions of his society, but it is not until his later novels that he attempts to construct an alternative.

Yellow Back Radio Broke-Down · *Yellow Back Radio Broke-Down* is set in a fantastic version of the Wild West of popular literature. Reed's protagonist, the Loop Garoo Kid, is a proponent of artistic freedom and an accomplished Voodoo *houngan* who is in marked contrast to the continually victimized Doopeyduk. Armed with supernatural "connaissance" and aided by a white python and the hip, helicopter-flying Chief Showcase, the Kid battles the forces of realistic mimesis and political corruption. His villainous opponent is Drag Gibson, a degenerate cattle baron given to murdering his wives, who is called upon by the citizens of Yellow Back Radio to crush their rebellious children's effort "to create [their] own fictions."

Although *Yellow Back Radio Broke-Down* satirizes Americans' eagerness to suspend civil rights in response to student protests against the Vietnam War, its focus is literature, specifically the dialogue between realism and modernism. The Loop Garoo Kid matches Reed's description of the African American artist in *Nineteen Necromancers from Now*: "a conjurer who works JuJu upon his oppressors; a witch doctor who frees his fellow victims from the psychic attack launched by demons." Through the Loop Garoo Kid, Reed takes a stand for imagination, intelligence, and fantasy against rhetoric, violence, and sentimentality. This theme is made explicit in a debate with Bo Shmo, a "neo-social realist" who maintains that "all art must be for the end of liberating the masses," for the Kid says that a novel "can be anything it wants to be, a vaudeville show, the six o'clock news, the mumblings of wild men saddled by demons."

Reed exhibits his antirealist theory of fiction in *Yellow Back Radio Broke-Down* through his free use of time, characters, and language. The novel ranges from the eighteenth century to the present, combining historical events and cowboy myths with modern technology and cultural detritus. His primary characters are comically exaggerated racial types: Drag Gibson represents the white's depraved materialism, Chief Showcase represents the American Indian's spirituality, and the Loop Garoo Kid represents the African American's artistic soul. Reed explains the novel's title by suggesting that his book is the "dismantling of a genre done in an oral way like radio." "Yellow back" refers to the popular dime novels; "radio" refers to the novel's oral, discontinuous form; and a "broke-down" is a dismantling. Thus, Reed's first two novels assault America in an attempt to "dismantle" its cultural structure.

Mumbo Jumbo · In *Mumbo Jumbo*, Reed expands on the neo-hoodooism of the Loop Garoo Kid in order to create and define an African American aesthetic based on Voodoo, Egyptian mythology, and improvisational musical forms, an aesthetic to challenge the Judeo-Christian tradition, rationalism, and technology. Set in Harlem during the 1920's, *Mumbo Jumbo* is a tragicomical analysis of the Harlem Renaissance's failure to sustain its artistic promise. Reed's protagonist is PaPa LaBas, an aging hoodoo detective and cultural diagnostician, and LaBas's name, meaning "over there" in French, reveals that his purpose is to reconnect African Americans with their cultural heritage by reunifying the Text of Jes Grew, literally the Egyptian Book of Thoth. Reed takes the phrase Jes Grew from Harriet Beecher Stowe's Topsy and James Weldon Johnson's description of African American music's unascribed development, but in the novel, Jes Grew is a contagion, connected with the improvisational spirit of ragtime and jazz, that begins to spread across America in the 1920's. Jes Grew is an irrational force that threatens to overwhelm the dominant, repressive traditions of established culture. LaBas's efforts to unify and direct this unpredictable force are opposed by the Wallflower Order of the Knights Templar, an organization dedicated to neutralizing the power of Jes Grew in order to protect their privileged status. LaBas fails to reunify the text, a parallel to the dissipation of the Harlem Renaissance's artistic potential, but the failure is seen as temporary; the novel's indeterminate conclusion looks forward hopefully to a time when these artistic energies can be reignited.

The novel's title is double-edged. "Mumbo jumbo" is a racist, colonialist phrase used to describe the misunderstood customs and language of dark-skinned people, an approximation of some critics' description of Reed's unorthodox fictional method. Yet "mumbo jumbo" also refers to the power of imagination, the cultural alternative that can free African Americans. A text of and about texts, *Mumbo Jumbo* combines the formulas of detective fiction with the documentary paraphernalia of scholarship: footnotes, illustrations, and a bibliography. Thus, in the disclosure scene required of any good detective story, LaBas, acting the part of interlocutor, provides a lengthy and erudite explication of the development of Jes Grew that begins with a reinterpretation of the myth of Osiris. The parodic scholarship of *Mumbo Jumbo* undercuts the assumed primacy of the European tradition and implicitly argues that African American artists should attempt to discover their distinct cultural heritage.

The Last Days of Louisiana Red · In *The Last Days of Louisiana Red*, LaBas returns as Reed's protagonist, but the novel abandons the parodic scholarship and high stylization of *Mumbo Jumbo*. Although LaBas again functions as a connection with a non-European tradition of history and myth, *The Last Days of Louisiana Red* is more traditionally structured than its predecessor. In the novel, LaBas solves the murder of Ed Yellings, the founder of the Solid Gumbo Works. Yellings's business is dedicated to combating the effects of Louisiana Red, literally a popular hot sauce but figuratively an evil state of mind that divides African Americans. Yelling's gumbo, like Reed's fiction, is a mixture of disparate elements, and it has a powerful curative effect. In fact, LaBas discovers that Yellings is murdered when he gets close to developing a gumbo that will cure heroin addiction.

In *The Last Days of Louisiana Red*, Reed is examining the self-destructive forces that divide the African American community so that its members fight one another "while above their heads . . . billionaires flew in custom-made jet planes." Reed shows how individuals' avarice leads them to conspire with the establishment, and he suggests that some of the most vocal and militant leaders are motivated by their egotistical need for power rather than by true concern for oppressed people. Set in Berkeley, California, *The Last Days of Louisiana Red* attacks the credibility of the black revolutionary movements that sprang up in the late 1960's and early 1970's.

Flight to Canada · *Flight to Canada*, Reed's fifth novel, is set in an imaginatively redrawn Civil War South, and it describes the relationship between Arthur Swille, a tremendously wealthy Virginia planter who practices necrophilia, and an assortment of sociologically stereotyped slaves. The novel is presented as the slave narrative of Uncle Robin, the most loyal of Swille's possessions. Uncle Robin repeatedly tells Swille that the plantation is his idea of heaven, and he assures his master that he does not believe that Canada exists. Raven Quickskill, "the first one of Swille's slaves to read, the first to write, and the first to run away," is the author of Uncle Robin's story.

Like much of Reed's work, *Flight to Canada* is about the liberating power of art, but in *Flight to Canada*, Reed concentrates on the question of authorial control. All the characters struggle to maintain control of their stories. After escaping from the plantation, Quickskill writes a poem, "Flight to Canada," and his comical verse denunciation of Swille completes his liberation. In complaining of Quickskill's betrayal to Abraham Lincoln, Swille laments that his former bookkeeper uses literacy "like that old Voodoo." In a final assertion of authorial control and the power of the pen, Uncle Robin refuses to sell his story to Harriet Beecher Stowe, gives the rights to Quickskill, rewrites Swille's will, and inherits the plantation.

The Terrible Twos · In *The Terrible Twos*, Reed uses a contemporary setting to attack Ronald Reagan's administration and the exploitative nature of the American economic system. In the novel, President Dean Clift, a former model, is a mindless figurehead manipulated by an oil cartel that has supplanted the real Santa Claus. Nance Saturday, another of Reed's African American detectives, sets out to discover Saint Nicholas's place of exile. The novel's title suggests that, in its second century, the United States is acting as selfishly and irrationally as the proverbial two-year-old. The central theme is the manner in which a few avaricious people seek vast wealth at the expense of the majority of Americans.

Reckless Eyeballing · *Reckless Eyeballing* takes place in the 1980's, and Reed employs a string of comically distorted characters to present the idea that the American literary environment is dominated by New York women and Jews. Although *Reckless Eyeballing* has been called sexist and anti-Semitic by some, Reed's target is a cultural establishment that creates and strengthens racial stereotypes, in particular the view of African American men as savage rapists. To make his point, however, he lampoons feminists, using the character Tremonisha Smarts, a female African American author who has written a novel of violence against women. Reed's satire is probably intended to remind readers of Alice Walker's *The Color Purple* (1982).

Because the novel's central subject is art and the limitations that society places on an artist, it is appropriate that Reed once again employs the technique of a story-within-a-story. Ian Ball, an unsuccessful African American playwright, is the novel's protagonist. In the novel, Ball tries to succeed by shamelessly placating the feminists in power. He writes "Reckless Eyeballing," a play in which a lynched man is posthumously tried for "raping" a woman with lecherous stares, but Ball, who often seems to speak for Reed, maintains his private, chauvinistic views throughout.

The Terrible Threes · *The Terrible Threes*, a sequel to *The Terrible Twos*, continues Reed's satirical attack on the contemporary capitalist system, which, he argues, puts the greatest economic burden on the least privileged. (Reed was also planning a third book in the series, *The Terrible Fours*.) In the first book, there appears a character named Black Peter—an assistant to St. Nicholas in European legend. This Black Peter is an imposter, however, a Rastafarian who studied and appropriated the legend for himself. In *The Terrible Threes*, the true Black Peter emerges to battle the false Peter but is distracted from his mission by the need to do good deeds. Black Peter becomes wildly popular because of these deeds, but a jealous St. Nick and concerned toy companies find a way to put Santa Claus back on top. Capitalism wins again.

Japanese by Spring · *Japanese by Spring* is postmodern satire. Like much of Reed's imaginative work, the book mixes fictional characters with "fictionalized" ones. Ishmael Reed himself is a character in the book, with his own name. The protagonist of *Japanese by Spring* is Benjamin "Chappie" Puttbutt, a teacher of English and literature at Oakland's Jack London College. Chappie dabbled in activist politics in the mid-1960's, but his only concern in the 1990's is receiving tenure and the perks that accompany it. He will put up with virtually anything, including racist insults from students, to avoid hurting his chances at tenure. As in many of Reed's books, Chappie is passive in the face of power at the beginning of his story. He is a middle-class black conservative, but only because the climate at Jack London demands it. Chappie is a chameleon who always matches his behavior to the ideology of his environment. However, when he is denied tenure and is about to be replaced by a feminist poet who is more flash than substance, Chappie's hidden anger begins to surface. Chappie has also been studying Japanese with a tutor named Dr. Yamato. This proves fortuitous when the Japanese buy Jack London and Dr. Yamato becomes the college president. Chappie suddenly finds himself in a position of power and gloats over those who denied him tenure. He soon finds, however, that his new bosses are the same as the old ones. Dr. Yamato is a tyrant and is eventually arrested by a group that includes Chappie's father, a two-star Air Force general. Dr. Yamato is released, though, and a surprised Chappie learns that there is an "invisible government" that truly controls the United States. Chappie has pierced some of his illusions, but there are others that he never penetrates, such as his blindness to his own opportunism.

The novel's conclusion moves away from Chappie's point of view to that of a fictionalized Ishmael Reed. This Reed skewers political correctness but also shows that the people who complain the most about it are often its greatest purveyors. Reed also lampoons American xenophobia, particularly toward Japan, but he does so in a balanced manner that does not gloss over Japanese faults. Ultimately, though, Reed uses *Japanese by Spring* as he used other novels before, to explore art and politics and the contradictions of America and race.

Carl Brucker, updated by Charles A. Gramlich

Other major works

PLAY: *The Preacher and the Rapper*, pb. 1997.

POETRY: *Catechism of D Neoamerican Hoodoo Church*, 1970; *Conjure: Selected Poems, 1963-1970*, 1972; *Chattanooga*, 1973; *A Secretary to the Spirits*, 1977; *Cab Calloway Stands In for the Moon*, 1986; *New and Collected Poems*, 1988.

NONFICTION: *Shrovetide in Old New Orleans*, 1978; *God Made Alaska for the Indians*, 1982; *Writin' Is Fightin'*, 1988; *Airing Dirty Laundry*, 1993.

EDITED TEXTS: *Nineteen Necromancers from Now*, 1970; *Yardbird Lives!*, 1978 (with Al Young); *Calafia: The California Poetry*, 1979; *The Before Columbus Foundation Fiction Anthology: Selections from the American Book Awards, 1980-1990*, 1992 (with Kathryn Trueblood and Shawn Wong); *MultiAmerica: Essays on Cultural Wars and Cultural Peace*, 1997.

Bibliography

Dick, Bruce, and Amritjit Singh, eds. *Conversations with Ishmael Reed.* Jackson: University Press of Mississippi, 1995. A collection of twenty-six interviews with Ishmael Reed, which cover the years 1968-1995. Includes one self-interview and a chronology of Reed's life.

Fabre, Michel. "Postmodern Rhetoric in Ishmael Reed's *Yellow Back Radio Broke-Down.*" In *The Afro-American Novel Since 1960*, edited by Peter Bruck and Wolfgang

Karrer. Amsterdam: Gruener, 1982. A valuable addition to the study of Reed regarding his postmodernism.

Fox, Robert Elliot. *Conscientious Sorcerers: The Black Post-Modern Fiction of LeRoi Jones/Amiri Baraka, Ishmael Reed, and Samuel R. Delaney*. New York: Greenwood Press, 1987. Situates Reed within both the tradition of black fiction and the self-conscious style of contemporary postmodernist fiction.

Gates, Henry Louis, Jr. *The Signifying Monkey: A Theory of Afro-American Literary Criticism*. New York: Oxford University Press, 1988. The section on Reed examines his fiction, especially the novel *Mumbo Jumbo*, as an extension of the tendency of black English to play deliberately with language.

Lee, A. Robert, ed. *Black Fiction: New Studies in the Afro-American Novel Since 1945*. New York: Barnes & Noble Books, 1980. Frank McConnell's essay on Reed uses a quotation about him from Thomas Pynchon's novel, *Gravity's Rainbow*, in order to speak broadly about parody in Reed's novels.

McGee, Patrick. *Ishmael Reed and the Ends of Race*. New York: St. Martin's Press, 1997. Looks at Reed's refusal to meet expectations associated traditionally with African American writers, and examines his use of satire and his antagonism toward political correctness.

Martin, Reginald. *Ishmael Reed and the New Black Aesthetic Critics*. New York: St. Martin's Press, 1988. A comprehensive and important look at Reed's work and theories in relation to the evolution of the black aesthetics movement.

The Review of Contemporary Fiction 4 (Summer, 1984). A special issue devoted to Reed. Especially important is an essay by James Lindroth, "From Krazy Kat to Hoodoo: Aesthetic Discourse in the Fiction of Ishmael Reed," and an interview with Reed by Reginald Martin.

ANNE RICE

Born: New Orleans, Louisiana; October 4, 1941

Principal long fiction · *Interview with the Vampire*, 1976; *The Feast of All Saints*, 1979; *Cry to Heaven*, 1982; *The Claiming of Sleeping Beauty*, 1983 (as A. N. Roquelaure); *Beauty's Punishment*, 1984 (as Roquelaure); *Beauty's Release: The Continued Erotic Adventures of Sleeping Beauty*, 1985 (as Roquelaure; collective title for this volume and the previous two, *Sleeping Beauty Trilogy*); *Exit to Eden*, 1985 (as Anne Rampling); *The Vampire Lestat*, 1985; *Belinda*, 1986 (as Rampling); *The Queen of the Damned*, 1988; *The Mummy: Or, Ramses the Damned*, 1989; *The Witching Hour*, 1990; *The Tale of the Body Thief*, 1992; *Lasher: A Novel*, 1993; *Taltos: Lives of the Mayfair Witches*, 1994; *Memnoch the Devil*, 1995 (together with *Interview with the Vampire*, *The Vampire Lestat*, *The Queen of the Damned*, and *The Tale of the Body Thief* also known by the collective title The Vampire Chronicles); *The Servant of the Bones*, 1996; *Violin*, 1997; *Pandora: New Tales of the Vampires*, 1998; *The Vampire Armand*, 1998.

Other literary forms · Anne Rice is known primarily for her novels. In addition to her historical fiction and her well-known vampire and witch novel series, Rice published erotic novels. *The Claiming of Sleeping Beauty*, *Beauty's Punishment*, and *Beauty's Release: The Continued Erotic Adventures of Sleeping Beauty* appeared under the pseudonym A. N. Roquelaure, while Rice used the pen name Anne Rampling for *Exit to Eden* and *Belinda*. Rice also penned the screenplay for the film *Interview with the Vampire* (1994), based on her novel.

Achievements · Anne Rice experimented with several different literary genres and acquitted herself well in each: gothic horror, historical fiction, erotica, romance. The conventions of gothic fiction, however, best conform to Rice's obsessions with eroticism, androgyny, myth, and the nature of evil. Clearly, for critics and fans alike, the novels that constitute The Vampire Chronicles are her greatest achievement. Gothic horror, like all popular fiction, is customarily slighted by commentators, who peg it as nothing more than a barometer of its own time, devoid of resonance. Paradoxically perhaps, Rice's success grows out of her ability to revamp the vampire, to update the hoary edifice first built by Horace Walpole in 1765 in *The Castle of Otranto*. Yet she does more than merely put her archetypal hero, the vampire Lestat, in black leather on a motorcycle; she makes him, in all his selfishness and soul searching, emblematic of the waning days of the twentieth century. If horror can be defined as the sense that the world is on the verge of primeval chaos, Rice might be considered the novelist for the millennium.

Biography · Anne Rice—then named Howard Allen Frances O'Brien—was born on October 4, 1941, in New Orleans, Louisiana, to Howard O'Brien and Katherine Allen O'Brien. Howard O'Brien's reasons for bestowing his own name on his daughter remain obscure, but bearing a masculine name clearly had a profound effect on her. When she entered first grade, the little girl christened herself Anne. The name stuck, as did a lifelong obsession with androgyny.

The exotic, decadent, intoxicating atmosphere of her hometown must also be counted among Anne Rice's early influences—as must her mother's alcoholism. As she approached puberty, Anne devoted much of her time to reading in a darkened bedroom to the increasingly incapacitated Katherine. It was there, perhaps, that Anne acquired an affinity for vampires. She would later recall how her mother first explained alcoholism as a "craving in the blood" and then asked her to say the rosary. Anne watched her mother alternate between wild exhilaration and collapse and finally waste away, her body drained by addiction and an inability to eat. When Katherine died in 1956, the nexus between blood, religion, and death must have taken root in her young daughter's psyche.

Anne's father remarried when she was sixteen, and, after Anne's sophomore year in high school, he moved the family to Richardson, Texas, where Anne met Stan Rice. Stan was a year younger than Anne, and at first he did not seem to share her romantic feelings about their relationship. It was not until after Anne graduated and moved away to San Francisco that Stan finally realized his feelings. They were married on October 14, 1961, when Anne was twenty.

The couple took up residence in the San Francisco Bay Area, where they would remain for the next twenty-seven years. Stan, a poet, completed his undergraduate education and began teaching creative writing. Anne, too, completed her B.A., majoring in political science. After receiving a master's degree in creative writing in 1972, she devoted herself full time to her writing career.

In the meanwhile, however, a momentous event had occurred in the Rices' lives. Their daughter, Michele, who was born in 1966, developed a rare form of leukemia and died two weeks before her sixth birthday. The trauma of this loss seems to have plunged Anne into depression. The old association between blood and death had returned to haunt her, but Rice fought off her demons by submersing herself in her writing. The result was her first published novel, *Interview with the Vampire*.

In 1978, the Rices had a son, Christopher, and a decade later they moved to New Orleans. With the proceeds of many best-selling books and the lucrative sale of film rights, Anne Rice purchased a mansion in the Garden District, which later became the setting of one of her novels and the scene of such memorable parties as the 1995 Memnoch Ball.

Analysis · Rice discovered her strong suit early. Written in five weeks, *Interview with the Vampire* introduced the themes of compulsion, exoticism, and eroticism that would inform all her later works. Although she explored these themes against a wide variety of backdrops, it is her revival of the gothic—and of the vampire, in particular—that both brought her critical attention and transformed her into a popular cultural icon.

The Vampire Chronicles · *Interview with the Vampire* is the first of the books Anne Rice produced in her Vampire Chronicles series. The Vampire Chronicles shift back and forth in time, from the prevampire life of Lestat in eighteenth century rural France to his escapades in twentieth century New Orleans, and then, in *Memnoch the Devil*, to the time of the creation of heaven and hell.

Interview with the Vampire introduces Lestat through the narrative of Louis, a vampire Lestat has "made." Louis relates his story to Daniel, a young reporter. Even as Louis grieves for his mortal life, Daniel craves Louis's power and immortality. Daniel has to overcome his initial horror and skepticism before accepting the truth of what Louis says, but by the end of Louis's long story, Daniel is begging to be made a vampire, too. In *The Vampire Lestat*, Lestat relates his own version of his life. Lestat's narrative, like Louis's, is published as a book. (Indeed, Lestat has written his in order to correct several of Louis's errors.) Lestat, always a show-off, revels in publicity, and he uses the book to launch his career as a rock star. Like so many of Lestat's grand schemes, however, this plan crashes, ending when Lestat barely escapes his fellow vampires' murderous attack as they seek revenge for his unpardonable publication of a book that reveals their secrets.

In *The Queen of the Damned*, Lestat becomes the consort of Akasha, the Egyptian ruler who became the mother of all vampires when a demon wounded and invaded her body, giving her immortal life. Marius, an old Roman sage and vampire, has kept Akasha intact for over two thousand years, but it is Lestat's energetic wooing that brings her out of her long stupor. She revives determined to rid the world of men, whose violence has made them unfit to survive. Only a remnant will endure for breeding purposes, she declares. Having partaken of her blood and fallen deliriously in love with her, Lestat nevertheless struggles against her insane project. He is finally saved from Akasha's wrath by Maharet and Mekare, witches who are also twin sisters and who destroy Akasha.

In *The Tale of the Body Thief*, Lestat, suffering from ennui, succumbs to the temptations of a body thief, Raglan James. The body thief offers Lestat a day of adventure in a mortal body in exchange for his own. Stupidly, Lestat accepts, even paying James twenty million dollars for the privilege of enjoying one day of mortality. James then absconds with both the money and Lestat's body, which Lestat is able to repossess only with the help of David Talbot, head of the Talamasca, a society dedicated to investigating the occult. Lestat, who is in love with David, then makes the resistant David into a vampire.

In *Memnoch the Devil*, a terrified Lestat discovers that he is being stalked by Satan, who calls himself Memnoch because he does not regard himself as a rebel angel or as God's accuser. Memnoch invites Lestat to become his lieutenant—not to gather souls for hell, but to redeem those awaiting enlightenment and salvation. Memnoch's argument is that he is offering God a grander creation, a purer vision of humankind, than God himself has conceived. In the end, Lestat repudiates Memnoch, doubting the devil's word and wondering if what he has "seen" is only what he has imagined.

The Vampire Chronicles rejuvenate the conventions of gothic romance and the horror novel. Like earlier heroes, Lestat is a nobleman of surpassing courage and physical attractiveness. Indeed, the vampire elder, Magnus, makes him into a vampire because he has seen the handsome Lestat on the stage in Paris and admired his indomitable spirit. As in William Godwin's novel, *Caleb Williams* (1794), Lestat is an insatiably curious protagonist attached to an older hero who represents both good and evil. Lestat must know the origins of vampirism, and he must follow his desires regardless of the cost to himself and others.

Lestat's eroticism also partakes of the gothic tradition. Reflecting Anne Rice's abiding interest in androgyny, he finds himself attracted to both men and women, to the goddess Akasha, and to the head of the Talamasca, David Talbot. Deeply devoted to his mother, Gabrielle, he takes her as his vampire lover. Incestuous and homoerotic elements that are veiled or only hinted at in earlier gothic fiction explode in Rice's chronicles. Rice also succeeds in making gothicism contemporary by making Lestat into a rock star, thus underscoring parallels between the cult of celebrity and the allure of the vampire.

The Mayfair Witches series · Rice conceived the first installment of the Mayfair Witches cycle, *The Witching Hour*, in 1985 after concluding *The Vampire Lestat*. She had generated some new characters which she at first envisioned as playing parts in the next Vampire Chronicle. She soon reached the conclusion, however, that these characters–a family of witches and their presiding spirit–deserved an entirely separate book, one set in New Orleans.

The protagonist of *The Witching Hour*, Michael Curry, is a successful forty-eight-year-old businessman who has his life blighted by a near-death experience. After nearly drowning in San Francisco Bay, he is rescued by a mysterious woman in a passing boat. He then discovers that simply by touching objects and people with his hands he has access to other lives and events. His insights, however, are fragmentary–as is his memory of an encounter with otherworldly beings during his drowning episode, when he promised to fulfill a mission for them.

One of Michael's doctors puts him in touch with his rescuer, who Michael believes will help him understand what he is meant to do. When he meets Dr. Rowan Mayfair, a thirty-year-old blonde beauty and a superb surgeon, Michael falls in love with her. Like Michael, Rowan is searching for answers. She has the power both to hurt and to heal people. She can stop a patient's bleeding simply by a laying on of hands; she can also cause a heart attack or stroke if she does not control her rage. Her obsession with saving people is her effort at self-redemption. Just as Michael hopes that touching Rowan and her boat will bring back his sense of mission, Rowan hopes that Michael will help reveal her past, which remains a mystery to her.

Rowan and Michael realize that their fates are linked to New Orleans, where as a boy Michael developed a fixation on a Garden District mansion that turns out to be Rowan's ancestral home. There he saw a spectral man, the Mayfairs' presiding spirit. Michael's intense memories of his childhood are connected, he is sure, with his near-death experience. When Rowan's birth mother dies, Rowan is visited by a spectral man, and she decides that she must return to the Crescent City.

Hovering around this couple is Aaron Lightner, an agent of the Talamasca. Through Aaron, Michael learns that Rowan is the descendant of a matriarchal family of witches that has fascinated the Talamasca for nearly three hundred years. A strong woman, Rowan believes she can destroy Lasher, the spectral man who has maddened the Mayfairs in an attempt to possess them. Like the others, however, Rowan loses control of Lasher, who invades the cells of the fetus growing within her and emerges as a powerful boy-man.

Rowan is rather like a female Dr. Faustus, determined to conquer the secrets of nature. She wants to heal, but the extremity of her desire cuts her off from her own humanity. Like Faust, she risks damnation. She is in thrall to her Mephistopheles, Lasher. When Michael playfully calls his lover Dr. Mayfair, the epithet suggests not only Dr. Faustus but also Dr. Frankenstein. Indeed, although Rowan finds Lasher's proposal that they create a super-race seductive, once their offspring is born, she plans to submit its cells to laboratory tests, thus reducing it to the status of a research subject.

In *Lasher*, the second installment in the series, Rowan has begun to help Lasher fulfill his desire. Together they have a girl child, Emaleth. The central revelation of the book is that the Mayfairs can, by interbreeding, produce a genetic aberration–a legendary race of nearly immortal giants known as Taltos, of which Lasher is a member. The Talamasca believe that Lasher is possessed of a unique genome, so when at the end of the book Michael Curry destroys him and Rowan does away with her demoniac girl child, it seems that Lasher's kind is no more.

However, *Taltos*, the third installment of the series, features another Taltos, Ashlar Templeton, an eccentric and reclusive billionaire toy maker. Ashlar's profession indicates that his nature is far more benign than Lasher's. Indeed, he more closely resembles Rice's vampires than his own protean kind. Unlike Lasher, he is not devoured by a need to propagate his supernatural breed; instead, he yearns—as much as Louis and, in his weaker moments, Lestat—for integration with humanity.

Lisa Paddock

Other major work

SCREENPLAY: *Interview with the Vampire*, 1994.

Bibliography

Dickinson, Joy. *Haunted City: An Unauthorized Guide to the Magical, Magnificent New Orleans of Anne Rice*. New York: Citadel Press, 1995. Chapters on the city's Creole history, the French Quarter, the Garden District, the cemeteries and tombs, the churches, swamps, and plantations, and the nineteenth century milieu of Lestat.

Hoppenstand, Gary, and Ray B. Browne, eds. *The Gothic World of Anne Rice*. Bowling Green, Ohio: Bowling Green State University Press, 1996. Essays by the most important Rice critics on all aspects of her fiction: The Vampire Chronicles, the romances, and her stories of the supernatural.

Ramslund, Katherine, ed. *The Anne Rice Reader*. New York: Ballantine, 1997. Part 1 concentrates on interviews with Rice, her personal essays, and articles about her life and career. Part 2 focuses on literary critiques, assessing Rice's contribution to the literature about vampires, her relationship to the gothic tradition, the film of *Interview with the Vampire*, and her other horror novels.

_____. *Prism of the Night: A Biography of Anne Rice*. New York: Dutton, 1991. Written with her cooperation, this is the most complete source of information about Rice.

Roberts, Bette B. *Anne Rice*. New York: Twayne, 1994. A solid introductory study with chapters on Rice's life and art, her relationship to the gothic tradition, her vampire series, her historical novels, and her erotic fiction.

PHILIP ROTH

Born: Newark, New Jersey; March 19, 1933

Principal long fiction · *Letting Go*, 1962; *When She Was Good*, 1967; *Portnoy's Complaint*, 1969; *Our Gang*, 1971; *The Breast*, 1972, revised 1980; *The Great American Novel*, 1973; *My Life as a Man*, 1974; *The Professor of Desire*, 1977; *The Ghost Writer*, 1979; *Zuckerman Unbound*, 1981; *The Anatomy Lesson*, 1983; *Zuckerman Bound*, 1985 (includes *The Ghost Writer, Zuckerman Unbound, The Anatomy Lesson*, and *Epilogue: The Prague Orgy*); *The Counterlife*, 1986; *Deception*, 1990; *Operation Shylock: A Confession*, 1993; *Sabbath's Theater*, 1995; *American Pastoral*, 1997; *I Married a Communist*, 1998.

Other literary forms · Five of Philip Roth's short stories are collected along with his novella *Goodbye, Columbus* in a volume bearing that title (1959). A number of his essays, interviews, and autobiographical pieces appear in *Reading Myself and Others* (1975). An unproduced screenplay, *The Great American Pastime*, was anthologized in 1968, and two of his works, *Goodbye, Columbus* and *Portnoy's Complaint*, have been made into films by others. In 1975, Roth began editing a series called Writers from the Other Europe for Penguin Books, to which he contributed several introductions. *The Facts: A Novelist's Autobiography* appeared in 1988. *Patrimony*, a memoir of his father's life, was published in 1991.

Achievements · Philip Roth emerged as a leading Jewish American writer when his first published book, *Goodbye, Columbus*, won the National Book Award in 1960. Many of his subsequent works involved Jewish characters and specifically Jewish American dilemmas; novels such as *Portnoy's Complaint, The Counterlife*, and *Operation Shylock*, in particular, involve characters struggling to reconcile their desires to be fully American during the age of American triumphalism with their deeply ingrained sense of separateness. More than a touch of local color, his depictions of Jewish communities form a base from which to spin—and unspin—national and personal narratives. Along with contemporary writers such as John Barth and Norman Rush, Roth created some of American literature's most memorable and most self-conscious storytellers, the angst-ridden Alexander Portnoy, the irrepressible Nathan Zuckerman, and the outwardly controlled, inwardly crumbling Swede Levov.

Roth's special concern in his work is the relationship between a writer and his subject, which is often closely drawn from his own personal life. His fictional accounts of smothering Jewish mothers, harried Jewish fathers, and illicit love affairs involving Jews in his early work made him notorious among the conservative Jewish establishment during the 1970's. Subsequent depictions of family relationships bearing a close resemblance to his own drew fire from his ex-wife Claire Bloom, among others. In his later work, Roth brilliantly presented the fascinating relationship between fiction and autobiography, using fictional surrogates, such as Nathan Zuckerman, to explore what he called "counterlives," or the proliferation of possible lives one single person might have lived.

Throughout his fiction, Roth exhibits the abilities of a master comedian. His ear is arguably the best of any contemporary writer, capturing the spoken voice in a wide variety of accents, intonations, and cadences, but his facility with dialogue sometimes leads critics to miss the serious undercurrents of his work. Roth's fiction covers a variety of satiric modes, from the social (*Portnoy's Complaint*) to the political (*Our Gang*) to the literary and academic (*The Professor of Desire*). Whatever mode he adopts, he presents the objects of his satire or comedy in vivid and compelling fashion. Once referred to as preeminently a social realist (as in *Goodbye, Columbus*), he transcended that mode successfully in such works as *The Counterlife* and *Deception*, which show him, as ever, both a consummate craftsman and a tireless experimenter with his medium.

Roth won numerous prestigious awards for his work, including the National Book Critics Circle Award for *Patrimony*, the PEN/Faulkner Award for *Operation Shylock*, the National Book Award for *Sabbath's Theater* and the Pulitzer Prize for *American Pastoral.*

Biography · Born in the Weequahic section of Newark, New Jersey, on March 19, 1933, Philip Roth learned very early what it was like to grow up Jewish in a lower-middle-class neighborhood of a large metropolitan area. His parents were Beth Finkel and Herman Roth, a salesman for the Metropolitan Life Insurance Company. After he was graduated from Weequahic High School in 1950, Roth worked for a while at the Newark Public Library and attended Newark College of Rutgers University. A year later, he transferred to Bucknell University. Although the family could ill afford the expense of a private college, Herman Roth determined that if his son wanted to go there, he

Nancy Crampton

would go. At Bucknell, Roth began writing stories and edited the school's literary magazine. He also had his first love affairs, from which he drew incidents (fictionally transformed, of course) for his subsequent novels. He received his B.A. in English, magna cum laude, in 1954, and he accepted a teaching fellowship at the University of Chicago for graduate work in English.

After receiving his M.A. in English from Chicago, Roth enlisted in the United States Army, but a back injury suffered during basic training resulted in an early discharge. He returned to Chicago to pursue doctoral studies in English but continued writing short stories, which had begun to get published as early as the fall of 1954 in small literary journals such as the *Chicago Review* and *Epoch*. Several of his stories were anthologized in Martha Foley's *Best American Short Stories* and in *The O. Henry Prize Stories*. These awards, the success of his first published volume, *Goodbye, Columbus*, a

Houghton Mifflin Literary Fellowship, and a Guggenheim Fellowship persuaded Roth to abandon graduate work in English for a career as a creative writer.

While a graduate student and instructor at the University of Chicago, Roth met and later married his first wife, Margaret Martinson Williams. The relationship was never a happy one, and after a few years they separated, Margaret steadfastly refusing to agree to a divorce. Meanwhile, they spent one year of their marriage (1960) at the Writers' Workshop at the University of Iowa, where Philip served on the faculty. After his first full-length novel, *Letting Go*, was published in 1962, he became writer-in-residence at Princeton University. He later taught English literature at the University of Pennsylvania. His experiences as an academic provided much material for novels, many of which have a university setting or are otherwise peopled by academics.

The publication of *Portnoy's Complaint* in 1969, a year after his estranged wife was killed in an automobile accident, launched Roth's greatest notoriety, especially among the conservative Jewish community in America, and assured his fame as a novelist. He became an increasingly prolific writer, spending part of the year in his Connecticut home and part in London in an apartment near his writing studio. For years he shared his life with the British stage and screen actress Claire Bloom, whom he married in April, 1990. Their difficult relationship and 1995 divorce became a subject of Bloom's memoir, *Leaving a Doll's House*, and received fictionalized treatment in Roth's 1998 novel, *I Married a Communist*.

Analysis · While his early works clearly show the influence of his literary idols—Henry James, Leo Tolstoy, Gustave Flaubert, Thomas Wolfe, and Theodore Dreiser—Philip Roth came into his own as a novelist beginning with *Portnoy's Complaint*, which reveals a unique voice in American literature. His subsequent development parallels his growing interest in other Continental writers, such as Anton Chekhov, Franz Kafka, Fyodor Dostoevski, and particularly contemporary writers such as Milan Kundera, whom Roth assisted in getting his works published in America. Roth's first novels are set squarely in his native land: in Newark, where he was born and reared; in the great Midwest, where he went to graduate school; and in New York and Philadelphia, where he lived, wrote, and taught literature at several universities. The protagonists of his later fiction travel abroad to Western and Eastern Europe and as far as Hong Kong. Roth's development as a novelist is thus the development, in part, of a growing cosmopolitanism along with a deepening interest in basic human concerns and predicaments.

Chief among those predicaments is the endless struggle between the id and the superego or, in less Freudian terms, between the drive for sensual gratification and the drive for moral uprightness. On the one hand, pulling at his protagonists (all but one of whom are men) is the powerful desire for sexual conquest; on the other is the almost equally powerful desire to lead a morally self-fulfilling and decent life. These drives, conflicting at almost every turn, nearly tear his protagonists apart. Even when, as at the end of *The Professor of Desire*, David Kepesh believes that he has at least achieved a reasonable equilibrium and found peace, a nagging unease enters the picture, upsetting his contentment and providing a presentiment of doom.

Indeed, Roth's heroes, if one can apply that term to such unlikely characters, all seem doomed in one way or another. Their pervasive sense of disaster, however, does not destroy Roth's comedy; it deepens it. The sense of the absurd, of the incongruities of human experience, also pervades Roth's novels and is the source of much rich humor. Moreover, his protagonists usually are fully self-aware; they understand their predicaments with uncommon self-perception, if (more often than not) they are utterly baffled in trying to find a solution to or resolution of their dilemmas. Again, their awareness and frustration combine to make the reader laugh, though the reader must be careful not to let the laughter obscure or nullify the compassion that is also the character's due.

Letting Go · Roth's first full-length novel, *Letting Go*, sets out all these themes and influences. The principal character, Gabe Wallach, is the educated, sophisticated son of well-off middle-aged Easterners, who after a brief stint in the army pursues graduate studies in the Midwest. His mother has recently died, leaving her son with a heavy moral burden: not to interfere in the lives of others as she, regretfully, has done. It is a legacy Gabe finds almost impossible to live up to, until the very end, after he has nearly ruined the lives of several people close to him. Before that, he succeeds, however, in remaining aloof from his widower father, who is lonely and adrift and tries to persuade Gabe to return home. This is Gabe's only success, however, as eventually his father meets and marries a widow who helps him rediscover life's pleasures.

Meanwhile, Gabe has his affairs, none of which works out happily, and his friendships, especially with Paul and Libby Herz, whom he meets during graduate school in Iowa. Paul is a hardworking, highly principled young man who married Libby while they were still undergraduates at Cornell. Their mixed marriage—Paul is Jewish, Libby Catholic—is mainly the result of Paul's misguided sense of devotion and responsibility. Although the passion has long since gone out of their relationship, owing to Libby's poor health and neurotic disposition, Paul remains loyal. Together, they struggle with financial and other problems, including opposition from both sets of parents.

Gabe's life and the Herzes' intersect at various points, invariably with well-intentioned but almost disastrous consequences. At Iowa, Gabe tries to befriend the couple, offers various forms of assistance to them, and finds an unusual attractiveness in Libby, which culminates in little more than a kiss. Their affair, such as it is, focuses partly on Henry James's novel *The Portrait of a Lady* (1880-1881), which Gabe lends to Paul; Libby reads the book, finding in it the last letter Gabe's mother had written him when she lay dying. Both the novel and the letter help to form a bond between Gabe and Libby that endures. Later, when Gabe is teaching at the University of Chicago, their relationship resumes when Gabe helps Paul get a job in his department.

Through Martha Reganhart, with whom Gabe has begun to live, Gabe finds someone who is willing to let her unborn baby be adopted by the Herzes. Paul and Libby have wanted a child and nearly had one, but poverty-stricken as they were, Paul persuaded Libby to have an abortion. The incidents surrounding that event are both comical and dreadful. Afterward, Libby's health never becomes robust enough for her to risk conceiving another child; hence, they hope to adopt one. The circumstances of trying to adopt a baby involve episodes best referred to as "deadly farce," including several in which Gabe intervenes on their behalf. At the same time, Gabe's relationship with Martha, a divorcee with two young children, deepens and then falls apart, largely the result of his inability to make a full and lasting commitment.

Gabe and Paul thus represent contrasting studies in personality. At the end, Gabe finally learns to "let go," the lesson his mother tried to teach him from her deathbed, but letting go for him means abandoning lover, friends, family, and career to become a wanderer in Europe, whence he writes Libby a final letter. Forwarded many times, an invitation to her adopted daughter's first birthday party arrives with no other message in it. This Gabe takes as "an invitation to be forgiven" for his nearly catastrophic interference in their lives. Gabe, however, feels unable to accept forgiveness—not yet, anyway. He is not "off the hook," he says, and does not want to be let off it, not until he can make some sense of the "larger hook" he feels he is still on.

The larger hook on which Roth's later protagonists wriggle is precisely the dilemma between commitment and freedom that they all experience. Thus, Alexander Portnoy finds himself torn between his desire to maintain his position as New York's Assistant Commissioner for Human Opportunity, a job of considerable responsibility as well as prestige, and his desire to enjoy the full sexual freedoms heralded by the 1960's. For a while he seems to manage both, until his affair with Mary Jane Reed develops into something else—Mary Jane's wish to get married. Her sexual adroitness—she is called "the Monkey"—has kept them together for more than a year, but this demand for full commitment proves too much for Alex, who abandons her in Athens during a trip to Europe in which they have experienced the ultimate of their sexual adventures. Alex flees to Israel, the land of his forefathers, only to find that when he tries to make love there he is impotent. The experience drives him to seek help from Dr. Otto Spielvogel, a New York psychiatrist.

The novel, in fact, is told as a series of confessions, or therapy sessions, and derives its title from the name Dr. Spielvogel gives to his patient's illness. "Portnoy's Complaint" is "a disorder in which strongly felt ethical and altruistic impulses are perpetually warring with extreme sexual longings, often of a perverse nature." The symptoms of the illness, Spielvogel believes, can be traced to the mother-child relationship, and indeed Portnoy's boyhood has been fraught with problems, often hilarious ones as he recounts them, occasioned by his stereotypical Jewish mother. Sophie Portnoy is a domineering, overprotective mother who frequently drives her young son to distraction, as he tries in vain to understand her demands upon him and her suffocating affection. Jack Portnoy, his father, long-suffering (mostly from constipation) and hardworking, seems unable to mitigate the family relationship, exacerbating Alex's quandary. No wonder he grows up as he does, afflicted with the dilemma, or the condition, Dr. Spielvogel describes. By the end of the novel, after the long unfolding of his tales of woe, all Alex hears from his therapist is, "Now vee may perhaps to begin. Yes?"

In a sense, that *is* just the beginning. Roth tried hard to progress further in his next "family" novel, *My Life as a Man*, which took him years to write. Meanwhile, he wrote the pre-Watergate Nixon satire *Our Gang* and the satirical burlesque of American culture *The Great American Novel*, which takes the great American pastime, baseball, as its focus and its vehicle. Yet it was the fictionalized account of his marriage—or rather, the affair which turned into marriage through a masterful trick—that really preoccupied Roth in the years following *Portnoy's Complaint*. Roth invents not one fictional surrogate but two: Peter Tarnopol, a writer, and Tarnopol's own fictional surrogate, Nathan Zuckerman. The two "useful fictions" that precede "My True Story," or the novel proper, are Roth's early experiments with "counterlives" developed at greater length and complexity in his finest novel, *The Counterlife*. They provide alternative, "possible" accounts of Peter Tarnopol's early life—and, through Tarnopol's, Roth's.

Peter's problem is trying to discover how he ever got involved with Maureen, his wife of ten years, from whom he is finally separated but who refuses to grant him a divorce. Related to this problem is the current one he experiences with his beautiful and dutiful lover, Susan Seabury McCall, a young widow who provides Peter with apparently everything he wants; however, she is essentially too submissive, too dull. One part of Tarnopol misses the excitement–no, the frenzy–that Maureen brought into his life, while another part hates it. Though it does not follow a strict chronological sequence, the novel becomes an account of his experience first with Maureen, then with Susan, whom he finally also leaves and determines to give up, despite her attempted suicide. Writing the novel in guarded solitude at an artist's colony called Quahsay, Tarnopol retrospectively tries to understand his plight.

The Breast · *The Breast* is another novel written during this period when Roth was trying to compose *My Life as a Man*. This book is the sequel to *The Professor of Desire*, written a few years later. Like Portnoy, Zuckerman, and Tarnopol, Kepesh is a nice Jewish young man brought up by caring parents in a sheltered Jewish environment, who early in life experiences the pleasures of emancipation and of the flesh, first as a Fulbright scholar living in London, then as a graduate student at Stanford University. Like Tarnopol, he becomes the victim of a femme fatale, a woman who, like Maureen, has "lived." Helen Baird is a striking beauty, but more than her beauty, her experience living abroad as the lover of a Hong Kong millionaire attracts Kepesh. They become lovers and later, disastrously, husband and wife. Gradually, Kepesh sinks into the condition of becoming Helen's servant, if not slave, until she flees once more to Hong Kong, hoping to reunite with her erstwhile lover. He will not have her, and David must rescue her, but in the process he becomes aware that their life together is over, and they get divorced.

David now moves back to New York, where he gets a job teaching comparative literature, meets Claire, a young schoolteacher, and falls in love with her. During this period he undergoes psychotherapy to "demythologize" his marriage to Helen; Dr. Klinger becomes Claire's advocate against David's brooding over Helen. During this period also, David's mother dies, and like Gabe Wallach in *Letting Go*, Kepesh has a widowed father on his hands. Yet the elder Mr. Kepesh is by no means as demanding as Dr. Wallach; on the contrary, he is delighted with his son's liaison with Claire (as he was not with the marriage to Helen) and hopes that they will marry. The novel ends as the young couple along with the elder Mr. Kepesh and a friend of his, a concentration camp survivor, spend a weekend in a bungalow in the Catskills, not far from where David grew up, and where he now ponders his future. He seems to have everything he wants or needs, but somehow he feels dissatisfied, anxious, afraid that ennui will set in and destroy everything or that some other disaster will overtake them.

It does, but the disaster is hardly anything that David Allen Kepesh anticipates. About a year later, as his lovemaking with Claire has almost ceased, he turns into a six-foot, 155-pound breast. In *The Breast*, Roth partly follows Franz Kafka's "The Metamorphosis" (1915), an obvious, but not exact, source for this novella. Unlike Kafka, Roth tells the story from Kepesh's point of view, using the first-person narrator to convey something of the real anguish Kepesh feels and his amazement at his condition. If he was beset by a dilemma at the end of *The Professor of Desire*, his bafflement there is nothing to what he experiences now. Despite the aid and comfort that everyone–Claire, his father, Dr. Klinger–tries to give him, he remains at the end as bitterly confused and disturbed as ever, thoroughly unreconciled to his lot except as he vainly tries to persuade everyone that what has happened has not happened, that it is all a bad dream from which eventually he will awake, or that he has simply gone mad.

The Ghost Writer · Roth's next novels form a trilogy to which he appends an epilogue, all under the title of *Zuckerman Bound.* Again, Roth borrows from autobiography to write his fiction, his own "counterlife." In *The Ghost Writer*, the first of the series which make up this portrait novel, Nathan Zuckerman is at the beginning of a promising career as a writer. He has published a few short stories and is now staying at an artist's colony (Quahsay again), trying to write more. Since he is not far from the home of E. I. Lonoff, a writer he much admires, he visits and is welcomed by the older writer and his wife. Zuckerman is surprised by them in many ways: first by Lonoff's austere life as a writer, spent endlessly turning his sentences around, and then by Hope Lonoff's conviction that her husband would be better off without her. By birth and upbringing far different from him–she is a New England Yankee as opposed to his immigrant origins–she is temperamentally unsuited to the kind of life they have led for many years. She is convinced, moreover, that Lonoff would be better off living with a younger woman, like Amy Bellette, a former student from the nearby women's college where Lonoff teaches, who obviously adores him. Lonoff refuses, however, to entertain any such thoughts of abandoning Hope or realizing his fantasy of living abroad in a villa in Italy with a younger woman.

Nathan is persuaded to stay the night, especially after meeting Amy Bellette, who is also staying there on a brief visit. Nathan has his own fantasy that evening, that Amy is really Anne Frank, author of the famous diary, who has miraculously survived death camps. They fall in love, get married, and thus show his parents and other relatives that, despite what they may think from some of his stories, he is a good Jewish man, the worthy husband of the famous Jewish heroine. As a tribute to Roth's skill as a writer, the account of Amy's survival is quite credible; moreover, it shows Roth's understanding of compassion for the suffering in the death camps. At the same time, it supports Nathan Zuckerman's qualifications as a writer, justifying Lonoff's praise and encouragement of the young man.

Zuckerman Unbound · Lonoff's belief in Nathan is borne out in *Zuckerman Unbound,* the second novel in the trilogy. By now Zuckerman is the author of several novels, including the notorious *Carnovsky.* This novel is to Zuckerman what *Portnoy's Complaint* was to Philip Roth, and *Zuckerman Bound* recounts experiences similar to those Roth most have had, such as the notoriety that involved mistaking his fictional characters for his real mother and father. Zuckerman is accosted in the streets, on the telephone, and apparently everywhere he goes by people who think they know him because they mistake his confessional novel for actual autobiography. Yet fiction and autobiography are at best distant relatives; for example, unlike Zuckerman's father, who is extremely upset by his son's novel and turns on him at his death, Roth's parents remained proud of their son's accomplishments and never took offense at what he wrote, notwithstanding the uproar in the Jewish community.

Zuckerman is beset by would-be hangers-on, such as Alvin Pepler, the Jewish marine, once a quiz-show winner but deprived of full fame by a scam reminiscent of the Charles Van Doren scandal. Zuckerman's brief affair (actually, no more than a one-night stand) with the Irish actress Caesara O'Shea is a comic treatment of the adventures attributed to Roth by columnists such as Leonard Lyons, who insisted he was romantically involved with Barbra Streisand, though actually Roth at that time had not so much as met her. Finally, Zuckerman's trip to Miami with his brother, Henry, which ends with their estrangement on the way home after their father dies of a stroke, is totally different from actual events in Roth's life. All these incidents are, after all, "counterlives," imaginative renderings of what might have or could have happened, not what did.

The Anatomy Lesson · Similarly, in *The Anatomy Lesson*, the third novel in the series, Roth borrows from incidents in his own life but fictionalizes them so that no one-to-one equivalence can be made. Now, some years later, Zuckerman is afflicted with a strange ailment that causes him intense pain, from which he gets temporary relief only from vodka or Percodan. He can no longer write, but four different women tend to his other needs, including his sexual ones. Among them are a young Finch College student, who also works as his secretary; his financial adviser's wife; an artist in Vermont who occasionally descends from her mountaintop to visit; and a Polish émigrée, whom Zuckerman meets at a trichological clinic (in addition to everything else, Zuckerman is losing his hair).

In despair of his life and his calling, Zuckerman decides to give up writing and become a doctor. He flies to Chicago, where he hopes his old friend and classmate, Bobby Freytag, will help him get admitted to medical school. En route on the plane and later from the airport, Zuckerman impersonates Milton Appel, a literary critic modeled on Irving Howe, who early praised Roth's work and then turned against it. In this impersonation, however, Zuckerman pretends that Appel is a pornography king, editor and publisher of *Lickety Split* and an impresario of houses of pleasure. The impersonation is triggered by Appel's appeal, delivered through an intermediary, to Zuckerman to write an op ed article on behalf of Israel.

Zuckerman as the porn king Appel provides plenty of material for those who like to see Roth as antifeminist but who thereby miss the point of his fiction. It is a tour de force, a persona adopting a persona–miles away from the real Roth. At his office in the hospital, Bobby Freytag reminisces with Zuckerman for a bit and then tries to talk him out of his scheme. Only the next day when, under the influence of too much Percodan and vodka, Zuckerman falls and fractures his jaw, does the healing begin, in soul as well as body. Zuckerman learns what real pain and loss are, as he walks the corridors of the hospital watched over by his friend, who also weans him from his drug addiction. At the end, Zuckerman is a chastened and more altruistic individual, though still deluded into thinking he could change into a radically different person.

The Prague Orgy · The epilogue, *The Prague Orgy*, shows Zuckerman not as a doctor but as a famous novelist undertaking an altruistic mission on behalf of an émigré Czech writer whose father had written some excellent, unpublished stories in Yiddish. Unfortunately, the Czech's estranged wife holds the stories but will not release them. Zuckerman manages to fetch them without having to sleep with her, despite her pleas, but the stories are immediately confiscated by the police, who then escort him out of the country (this is pre-1989 Czechoslovakia). Zuckerman thus learns to accept his limitations and to become reconciled to them. He accepts that he will not become "transformed into a cultural eminence elevated by the literary deeds he performs."

The Counterlife · In *The Counterlife*, Nathan and his brother are briefly reunited, mainly so that Roth can explore alternative versions of a fate that first befalls one and then the other. The plot thus doubles back on itself more than once and is too complex for summary treatment. Despite its complexity, the novel is not difficult to follow and is full of surprises that intellectually stimulate as they also amuse the reader. Particularly interesting are the episodes in Israel, where Henry has fled to start a new life, bringing Nathan after him to discover what is going on. Much is going on, including a considerable amount of discussion from characters on the political Left and Right, with Nathan clearly in the middle. The latter part of the novel finds Nathan in London, married to a English divorcee with a child and trying to come to grips with British anti-Semitism, including some in his wife's family. Throughout the novel, Roth implicitly and sometimes explicitly raises questions about the nature of fiction and the characters that inhabit it.

He does so, too, in *Deception*, though in that novel, written almost entirely in dialogue, the experiment takes on a different form. Here, Roth drops his surrogate, Nathan Zuckerman; his main character, present in all the dialogue, is called Philip, who also happens to be a novelist who has written about a character named Zuckerman. Thus Roth seems here to speak in his own voice, though of course he does not, quite: He merely makes the partition separating him from his characters that much thinner, almost to the point of transparency, as when he takes on the critics who claim that when he writes fiction, he does autobiography, and vice versa. The novel is filled with discussions between "Philip" and his lover, who proves to be the woman Nathan married in *The Counterlife*; thus, much of the talk is naturally about fiction.

Sabbath's Theater · Roth turned away briefly from his various author personas to write the wickedly funny *Sabbath's Theater*, a novel about an aging pornographic puppeteer obsessed with death and socially proscribed forms of sex. Mickey Sabbath's perverse confessions and the absurd situations Sabbath creates for himself may remind some of Roth's early novel *Portnoy's Complaint*. Yet whereas Alexander Portnoy was tortured by his conflicting desires to be a model American and to satisfy his sexual longings, there is no such conflict in Sabbath. He revels in his capacity to break bourgeois mores, becoming a *cause célèbre* for First-Amendment defenders in the 1950's, when running his randy street theater resulted in his arrest. Since that time, he has lived in a small New England town teaching college drama, until he is forced to resign for sexually harassing female students. Now he is locked in an acrimonious marriage with his wife Roseanna, a recovering alcoholic, and mourning the death of his sexually adventurous mistress, Drenka. If *Portnoy's Complaint* revolved around Portnoy's confessions, *Sabbath's Theater* revolves around Sabbath's unapologetic reveling in nastiness. Through Sabbath's repellent diatribes against the Japanese, women, and self-help groups, Roth draws a figure for whom readers will find little sympathy. Because Sabbath himself seems so thoroughly jaded, many critics have decried the novel's sentimental turn toward Sabbath's past, into the death of his much admired brother in World War II and the resulting demise of his mother, to contextualize Sabbath's bitterness.

American Pastoral · Roth portrays another bitter and obsessed character in *American Pastoral*, but in this novel the stakes are higher and the perspective a degree removed. Merry Levov is the stuttering teenage daughter of a beauty queen and a successful assimilated American Jew. She grows up in a prosperous New Jersey suburb in a loving home, the center of her father Swede's ideal, his "American pastoral." Then life changes. Merry's protests against the Vietnam War turn into ever more violent, clichéd complaints against American imperialism, capitalism, bourgeois complacency, and, finally, her family's own success story. She bombs the town's post office, killing a well-loved doctor and challenging her father's understanding of his life and his country. The story is told through her father's tortured pursuit of both his daughter and the reasons for her rage. Roth deftly weaves social criticism into this compelling story for an insightful depiction of an entire generation blindsided by the great upheavals of the 1960's. Zuckerman reappears to interpret Swede Levov's story as an epic clash between the American innocent pursuing upward mobility and the return of the repressed violence inherent in that American Dream. Merry Levov, Zuckerman says, "transports him out of the longed-for American pastoral and into everything that is its antithesis and its enemy, into the fury, the violence, and the desperation of the counterpastoral—into the indigenous American berserk."

I Married a Communist · Just as ambitious as *American Pastoral,* Roth's next book, *I Married a Communist,* takes the 1950's as its historical backdrop. Nathan Zuckerman again acts partly as interpreter and partly as scribe, this time to his former high school teacher, Murray Ringold. Murray tells the story of his brother Ira, a radio actor who was blacklisted during the era of McCarthyism. Ira becomes a populist hero to many, including young Nathan, until his actress wife, exasperated by Ira's repeated betrayals with other women, exposes him by publishing a tell-all book, *I Married a Communist.* The book destroys not only Ira's heroic profile but also his career, for he becomes blacklisted. The plot once again alludes to events in Roth's own life, particularly to his divorce from Claire Bloom. Like the character Eve Frame, Bloom had a talented teenage daughter who caused friction in the marriage. Also like Eve Frame, Bloom published a memoir in which she, like Roth in several of his novels, exposed intimate details of their personal life. Ira's unthinking acceptance of the Communist Party and his subsequent devolution into an angry, bitter cynic give this political novel a decidedly conservative overtone.

Surveying the corpus of Roth's longer fiction, one may conclude that he is a novelist who rarely repeats himself, even as he reworks ideas, issues, and dilemmas or reintroduces characters and locales. This is the essence of the "counterlife" motif that was present in Roth's work from the start but became explicit only later on.

Jay L. Halio, updated by Julie Husband

Other major works
SHORT FICTION: *Goodbye, Columbus,* 1959.
NONFICTION: *Reading Myself and Others,* 1975; *The Facts: A Novelist's Autobiography,* 1988; *Patrimony,* 1991.

Bibliography
Cooper, Alan. *Philip Roth and the Jews.* Albany: State University of New York Press, 1996. Part of the SUNY series in modern Jewish literature and culture, this work examines Judaism in literature and Roth's handling of Jewish characters. Includes bibliographical references and an index.
Halio, Jay L. *Philip Roth Revisited.* New York: Twayne, 1992. This solid overview is excellent for the beginning student of Roth. Replaces the 1978 Twayne edition, with much biographical and critical data.
Jones, Judith Paterson, and Guinevera A. Nance. *Philip Roth.* New York: Frederick Ungar, 1981. This slim volume traces three themes throughout Roth's work: the "good" Jewish child's struggle to free him- or herself from parental coercion and guilt, the "conflict between high-minded moral responsibility and sensuous self-assertion," and the absurdities of contemporary American society, which elicit

satirical treatment from the novelist. Each essay contains discrete sections devoted to individual novels and is very accessible.

McDaniel, John M. *The Fiction of Philip Roth*. Haddonfield, N.J.: Haddonfield House, 1974. An early review of Roth's work, the volume's concern with the "Jewish question" and "fictional hero types" may seem dated, but it is valuable for its close reading of Roth's early stories.

Milbauer, Asher Z., and Donald G. Watson, eds. *Reading Philip Roth*. New York: St. Martin's Press, 1988. Borrowing its title from Roth's own collection of essays, this book begins with an informative interview with Roth and includes essays by writers such as Roth's friends Aharon Appelfeld and Milan Kundera. Most of the volume, however, contains fairly heavy readings of Roth's fiction by European and American critics such as Clive Sinclair, Martin Green, Sam B. Girgus, Donald Gartiganer, and Hana Wirth-Nesher. Indexed, but no bibliography.

Pinsker, Sanford. *The Comedy That "Hoits": An Essay on the Fiction of Philip Roth*. Columbia: University of Missouri Press, 1975. A witty, learned, and perceptive short book on Roth by a Jewish scholar who understands the language and structure of Roth's novels exceptionally well. No index or bibliography, but secondary references are footnoted.

_____, ed. *Critical Essays on Philip Roth*. Boston: G. K. Hall, 1982. An outstanding collection of some of the best essays and reviews on Roth. It includes excellent essays by Mark Schechner, Sarah Blacher Cohen, and Morton Levitt, as well as a personal memoir by Theodore Solotaroff and the famous attack by Irving Howe called "Philip Roth Reconsidered." Contains an index but no bibliography.

Rodgers, Bernard F., Jr. *Philip Roth*. Boston: Twayne, 1978. This solid critical study by Roth's bibliographer contains a wealth of biographical and other information, along with clear and perceptive readings of the novels. Fully annotated and indexed, it also contains a "Select Bibliography" of both primary and secondary sources.

J. D. SALINGER

Born: New York, New York; January 1, 1919

Principal long fiction · *The Catcher in the Rye*, 1951.

Other literary forms · Little, Brown and Company has published three collections of J. D. Salinger's short fiction: *Nine Stories* (1953), *Franny and Zooey* (1961), and *Raise High the Roof Beam, Carpenters, and Seymour: An Introduction* (1963). An unauthorized paperback collection of his stories in two volumes, apparently published by an unidentified source in Berkeley, California, *The Complete Uncollected Short Stories of J. D. Salinger*, was issued in 1974. It provoked Salinger's first public statement in some years, denouncing the collection, which was suppressed by the copyright holders. There has been one film adaptation of his work, produced by Samuel Goldwyn and adapted by Julius J. and Phillip G. Epstein from Salinger's "Uncle Wiggily in Connecticut," renamed *My Foolish Heart* (1950) and starring Susan Hayward and Dana Andrews. Salinger was so upset by the screen version that he banned all further adaptations of his work into any other medium.

Achievements · In the post-World War II years, Salinger was unanimously acclaimed by both literate American youth and the critical establishment. His only novel has sold steadily since its publication, and it not only still generates high sales but also generates intense discussion as to its appropriateness for classroom use. Although his productivity has been slow, his popularity in terms of both sales and critical articles and books written about him has continued unabated since the early 1950's.

The Catcher in the Rye has been one of the most widely read and influential postwar novels and has entered the culture as a statement of youth's view of the complex world. The novel has been translated into German, Italian, Japanese, Norwegian, Swedish, French, Dutch, Danish, Hebrew, Czechoslovakian, Yugoslavian, and Russian and has been highly successful. In Russia, possession of a copy of *The Catcher in the Rye* became something of a status symbol for young intellectuals. Although there have been problems in translating the particularly American idiom into foreign languages, the story touches a nerve that cuts across cultural and global lines. The novel has also been favorably compared to Mark Twain's *Adventures of Huckleberry Finn* (1884) in terms of its portrayal of the "phoniness" of society, the coming of age of a young man, and its use of colloquial language.

Salinger's reputation, paradoxically, has been aided by his refusal to give interviews or to be seen in public. Critics and magazine writers have pursued him relentlessly, trying to discover his thoughts, concerns, and approaches to literature and writing.

Biography · Jerome David Salinger was born in New York, New York, on January 1, 1919, the second child and only son of Sol and Miriam (Jillich) Salinger, although details on Salinger and his parents' life is clouded. Salinger's father was born in Cleveland, Ohio, and has been noted as being the son of a rabbi, but he drifted far enough away from orthodox Judaism to become a successful importer of hams and to marry a Gentile, the Scotch Irish Marie Jillich, who changed her name soon after to Miriam to fit in better with her husband's family. During J. D.'s early years the Salingers moved several times, to increasingly affluent neighborhoods.

Salinger attended schools on Manhattan's upper West Side, doing satisfactory work in all subjects except arithmetic. He probably spent most of his summers in New England camps like most sons of upper-middle-class New York families; he was voted the "most popular actor" in the summer of 1930 at Camp Wigwam in Harrison, Maine. When he reached high school age, he was placed in Manhattan's famed McBurney School, a private institution, where he was manager of the fencing team, a reporter on the *McBurnean,* and an actor in two plays; however, he flunked out after one year. In September of 1934, his father enrolled him at Valley Forge Military Academy in Pennsylvania.

During his two years at Valley Forge, Salinger did satisfactory, but

Washington Star Collection, D.C. Public Library

undistinguished, work. He belonged to the Glee Club, the Aviation Club, the French Club, the Non-Commissioned Officers' Club, and the Mask and Spur, a dramatic organization. He also served as literary editor of the yearbook, *Crossed Sabres,* during his senior year. He is credited with writing a three-stanza poetic tribute to the academy that has since been set to music and is sung by the cadets at their last formation before graduation. Although not yet the recluse that he would later become, Salinger began to write short stories at that time, usually working by flashlight under his blankets after "lights out." Astonishingly, he also appeared interested in a career in the motion-picture business, as either a producer or a supplier of story material. He graduated in June of 1936.

It is unclear what Salinger did after graduation, but he enrolled at least for the summer session of 1937 at Washington Square College in New York. Salinger, in one of his rare interviews, mentioned that he spent some time in Vienna, Austria, and Poland learning German and the details of the ham importing business; it is not clear if his father accompanied him or not, but his trip probably occurred before Adolf Hitler's Anschluss, possibly in the fall of 1937.

On his return, Salinger enrolled at Ursinus College, a coeducational institution sponsored by the Evangelical and Reformed Church at Collegeville, Pennsylvania, not far from Valley Forge. Although he remained only one semester, he wrote a humorous and critical column, "The Skipped Diploma," for the *Ursinus Weekly.* He returned to New York and enrolled in Whit Burnett's famous course in short-story writing at Columbia University. It has been noted that Burnett was not at first impressed with the quiet boy who made no comments in class and seemed more interested in playwriting. Yet Salinger's first story, "The Young Folks," was impressive enough to be published in the March, 1940, issue of *Story*, edited by Burnett.

After publishing in a magazine famous for discovering new talent, Salinger spent another year writing without success until, at age twenty-two, he broke into the well-paying mass circulation magazines with a "short, short story" in *Collier's* and a "satire" in *Esquire*; he even had a story accepted by *The New Yorker*, which delayed publication of "Slight Rebellion off Madison," until after the war. This story proved to be one of the forerunners to *The Catcher in the Rye*.

During 1941, he worked as an entertainer on the Swedish liner MS *Kungsholm*. Upon his return to the United States, he wrote to the military adjunct at Valley Forge, Colonel Milton G. Baker, to see if there was some way that he could get into the service, even though he had been classified as 1-B because of a slight cardiac condition. After Selective Service standards were lowered in 1942, Salinger was inducted and attended the Officers, First Sergeants, and Instructors School of the Signal Corps. He also reportedly corrected papers in a ground school for aviation cadets. He applied for Officers' Candidate School but was transferred to the Air Service Command in Dayton, Ohio, and wrote publicity releases. Finally, at the end of 1943, he was transferred to the Counter-Intelligence Corps. He also conducted a long correspondence with Eugene O'Neill's daughter Oona (later the last Mrs. Charles Chaplin).

He continued to write whenever he found the opportunity, publishing again in *Collier's, Story*, and at last in the well-paying and highly celebrated *Saturday Evening Post*. One of the *Saturday Evening Post* stories marks the first mention of the character Holden Caulfield. Salinger also sent Whit Burnett two hundred dollars from his earnings from the "slicks" to be used to encourage young writers and be applied to future writing contests for college undergraduates, such as the one won by Norman Mailer in 1941.

After training in Tiverton, Devonshire, he joined the American Fourth Division and landed on Utah Beach five hours after the initial assault wave on D-Day. He served with the Division through five European campaigns as a special agent responsible for security of the Twelfth Infantry Regiment. There is an unsupported story that Salinger had an audience with author and war correspondent Ernest Hemingway, who shot off the head of a chicken either to impress Salinger or to demonstrate the effectiveness of a German Luger. This incident has been used to explain why Salinger has written about Hemingway in a bad light in his stories and has Holden Caulfied in *The Catcher in the Rye* detest Hemingway's *A Farewell to Arms* (1929). There are also reports that during the war Salinger married a French woman, Sylvia, who was a doctor, possibly a psychiatrist. The two returned together to the United States after the war, according to biographer Ian Hamilton, but the marriage, which took place in September, 1945, lasted only eight months.

After the war, Salinger decided to make a living by selling stories to the so-called "slicks," publishing again in the *Saturday Evening Post* and *Collier's*, which issued "I'm Crazy" in its Christmas issue. "I'm Crazy" featured the long-delayed debut of Holden Caulfield, who had been mentioned as missing in action in several of Salinger's wartime stories. *Mademoiselle, Good Housekeeping*, and *Cosmopolitan* also published Salinger's work. *Cosmopolitan* featured a short novelette, "The Inverted Forest," an involved, obscure allegory of an artist, his possible muses, and his fate. During part of this period, Salinger lived with his parents but also kept a Greenwich Village apartment to entertain various young women. He also, supposedly, began to develop an interest in Zen Buddhism that is illustrated in his stories following publication of *The Catcher in the Rye*, especially the Glass family saga, but there is no suggestion that he actually converted to Buddhism.

After the disastrous film version of "Uncle Wiggily in Connecticut" and stories in *Harper's* and *World Review*, he settled down with a contract to produce stories solely for *The New Yorker* and thereafter published exclusively for that magazine. At that time, Salinger was also his most public: He lived in Tarrytown, New York, and even visited a short-story class at Sarah Lawrence College. Although he seemed to enjoy the conversation and interaction, he never repeated it. It was during that period that he decided to avoid all public appearances and concentrate his efforts on writing.

The Catcher in the Rye finally made its appearance on July 16, 1951, although years earlier Salinger submitted, had accepted, and then withdrew a much shorter version. It was not the immediate hit that time suggests, but it did gain Salinger enormous critical praise and respect. The novel was successful enough to cause Salinger to have his picture removed from the dust jacket of the third edition and all subsequent editions; annoyed by the letters, autograph seekers, and interviewers that sought him, he apparently sailed to Europe to keep his composure and avoid publicity.

In 1952 Salinger settled in Cornish, New Hampshire, a small town across the Connecticut River from Windsor, Vermont. His first house in Cornish was a small saltbox on ninety acres with no furnace, no electricity, and no running water. In 1953, Salinger met his future wife, Claire Douglas, at a cocktail party in Manchester, Vermont. The daughter of a well-known British art critic, she was then a nineteen-year-old Radcliffe student. During his first two years in Cornish, Salinger fraternized with high school students in the area, attended their basketball games, and entertained them in his home. In November of 1953 he granted Shirley Blaney an interview for the high school page of the Claremont, New Hampshire, *Daily Eagle*. He became upset when the interview was printed prominently on the editorial page of the paper instead. Thereafter he ceased entertaining area students and built a fence around his home.

In January, 1955, he returned to print in *The New Yorker* with the publication of "Franny," the first of the Glass Family series that occupied all of his forthcoming stories. He supposedly dedicated it to his new bride, whom he married in Barnard, Vermont, on February 17, 1955. On December 10 of that year, the Salingers became the parents of their first child, Margaret Ann; on February 13, 1960, his only son, Matthew, was born. Afterward, Salinger concentrated his efforts on rearing his family and documenting the Glass family. Little was heard or read from Salinger after the 1965 publication of "Hapworth 16, 1924" in *The New Yorker*. He was divorced from his wife in November, 1967.

The reclusive Salinger, dubbed "the Greta Garbo of American letters" by *People Weekly* in reference to another famous but hermitic figure, was thrust into the media limelight in the mid-1980's because of disputes over the content of a biography being published by Ian Hamilton. Thwarted in his quest for an interview with Salinger, Hamilton had nevertheless found two valuable—and hitherto untapped—research sources: collections of Salinger letters in Princeton University's Firestone Library and the library of the University of Texas. Galleys of Hamilton's book were slipped to Salinger by a book dealer in 1986, and Salinger immediately protested the use of his unpublished letters. Attempts at compromise failed, and Salinger filed suit against

Hamilton and his publisher, Random House. Eventually, a U.S. Court of Appeals ruling decreed that the letters were indeed Salinger's property and could not be quoted, or even paraphrased, without his permission. The Supreme Court declined to hear an appeal, and Salinger returned to his seclusion. Hamilton's book *In Search of J. D. Salinger*, minus the content of the letters but filled out with a detailed account of the controversy, was finally published in 1988.

Analysis · J. D. Salinger's characters are always extremely sensitive young people who are trapped between two dimensions of the world: love and "squalor." The central problem in most of his fiction is not finding a bridge between these two worlds but bringing some sort of indiscriminate love into the world of squalor: to find a haven where love can triumph and flourish. Some characters, such as the young, mixed-up Holden Caulfield, adopt indiscriminate love to aid them in their journey through the world of squalor, while others, such as Seymour Glass, achieve a sort of perfect love, or satori, and are destroyed, in Seymour's case by a bullet through his head. Each of these characters is metropolitan in outlook and situation and is introverted: Their battles are private wars of spirit, not outward conflicts with society. The characters' minds struggle to make sense of the dichotomy between love and squalor, often reaching a quiet peace and transcending their situation through a small act.

Frederick L. Gwynn and Joseph L. Blotner, in *The Fiction of J. D. Salinger* (1958), offer an analysis of Salinger that claims he is the first writer in Western fiction to present transcendental mysticism in a satiric mode, or simply to present religious ideas satirically. Although much has been made of Salinger's Zen Buddhism, the stories do not seem to be about applying Buddhist principles to modern life, nor do they present a clear and coherent statement of what these principles entail or signify. Holden Caulfied does not react as a Buddhist would, nor does he seek consolation from Buddhism. The Glass family may mention Buddhism, but because of their acquaintance with all religions and their high intelligence and hyperkinetic thirst for knowledge, Salinger suggests they they have picked and chosen aspects from various religions and created a composite of them all. If anything, Salinger's characters seem to move toward a "perfect" Christian ideology—indiscriminate love.

The normality of the characters in Salinger's stories is a primary attraction for readers. Holden Caulfield is no better or no worse than any young high school boy; he is merely a bit more articulate and honest in his appraisals, more open with his feelings. Even though the Glasses are brilliant, they are not cerebral or distanced from the reader because of their brilliance; and all the characters live in the same world and environment as the readers do. Their moments of pain and delight are the same as the readers', but Salinger's characters articulate these moments more naturally and completely.

Another element that draws readers into Salinger's world is his use of satire. The satire not only touches upon the characters' descriptions and reactions to the world but also touches on the characters themselves. Holden Caulfield's confrontation with Maurice, the brawny Edmont Hotel elevator operator/pimp, shows not only the ridiculousness of the antagonist but also Holden's stupidity for attempting to reason with him. Even if he does not realize it, Holden does many of the things that he tells readers he hates. He is critical enough, however, to realize that these things are wrong.

All of Salinger's work has also a strong focus on the family; it is held as an ideal, a refuge, and a raft of love amid a sea of squalor. Although the family does not provide the haven that Salinger suggests it might, it is through coming home that the characters flourish, not by running away. Holden Caulfield, in *The Catcher in the Rye*, never realistically considers running away, for he realizes that flight cannot help him. At the critical moment his family may not be ready to grant him the salvation that he needs, but it is his only security. If the world is a place of squalor, perhaps it is only through perfect love within the family unit that an individual can find some kind of salvation. It is important to notice that the family unit is never satirized in Salinger's fiction.

The Catcher in the Rye · The basic story of *The Catcher in the Rye* follows the adventures of sixteen-year-old Holden Caulfield, an independent, self-indulgent, idealistic, and sentimental figure of adolescent rebellion, during a forty-eight-hour period after he has been expelled from Pencey Prep, the latest of three expulsions for Holden. After confrontations with some fellow students at Pencey, Holden goes to New York City, his hometown, to rest before facing his parents. During the trip he tries to renew some old acquaintances, attempts to woo three out-of-towners, hires a prostitute named Sunny, and copes with recurring headaches. Eventually, after two meetings with his younger sister, Phoebe, he returns home. At the beginning of the novel he has told us that he is in California recovering from an illness and that he is reconciled with his family. The entire story of Holden's exploits comes to us through a first-person narration, one which contains youthful phrasing and profanity and has many digressions, but one which has a mesmerizing flow to it.

Holden Caulfield is a confused sixteen-year-old, no better and no worse than his peers, except that he is slightly introverted, a little sensitive, and willing to express his feelings openly. His story can be seen as a typical growing process. As he approaches and is ready to cross the threshold into adulthood, he begins to get nervous and worried. His body has grown, but his emotional state has not. He is gawky, clumsy, and not totally in control of his body. He seeks to find some consolation, some help during this difficult time but finds no one. The school cannot help him, his peers seem oblivious to his plight, his parents are too concerned with other problems (his mother's nerves and his father's business activities as a corporate lawyer). His girlfriend, Sally Hayes, who has a penchant for using the word "grand" and whom Holden calls the "queen of the phonies," is no help, and his favorite teacher, Mr. Antolini, merely lectures him drunkenly. The only people with whom he can communicate are the two young boys at the museum, the girl with the skates at the park, and his younger sister Phoebe: All of them are children, who cannot help him in his growing pains but remind him of a simpler time, one to which he wishes he could return. Eventually, he does cross the threshold (his fainting in the museum) and realizes that his worries were unfounded. He has survived. At the end of the book, Holden seems ready to reintegrate himself into society and accept the responsibilities of adulthood.

Through Holden's picaresque journeys through New York City, he grows spiritually. He slowly begins to recognize the "phoniness" around him and the squalor that constantly presses down on him. Although he castigates himself for doing some of the phony things, lying especially, Holden does realize that what he is doing is incorrect: This understanding sets him above his fellows; he knows what he is doing. Holden never hurts anyone in any significant way; his lies are small and harmless. Conversely, the phony world also spins lies, but they are dangerous since they harm people. For example, Holden mentions that Pencey advertises that it molds youth, but it does not. He is angry with motion pictures because they offer false ideals and hopes. Yet, his lies help a mother think better of her son. Like Huck Finn, he lies to get along, but not to hurt, and also like Huck, he tries to do good. Near the end of the novel Holden dreams of fleeing civilization and building a cabin out west, something which belies his earlier man-about-town conduct.

By the end of the book, Holden has accepted a new position—an undiscriminating love for all humanity. He even expresses that he misses all the people who did wrong to him. Although not a Christ-figure, Holden does acquire a Christlike position—perfect love of all humankind, good and evil. He is not mature enough to know what to do with this love, but he is mature enough to accept it. In this world, realizing what is squalor and what is good and loving it all is the first step in achieving identity and humanity: Compassion is what Holden learns.

Recalling all the suffering and pain that he has witnessed, Holden develops a profound sense of the human condition and accepts Christ's ultimate commandment. In the passage regarding Holden's argument with his Quaker friend Arthur Childs, Holden argues that Judas is not in hell because Jesus would have had the compassion and love not to condemn Judas to hell. Also, Jesus did not have time to analyze who would be perfect for his Disciples; thus, they were not perfect and would have condemned Judas if they had had the chance. In this discussion, Holden points out his own dilemma, not having time to analyze his decisions, and his belief in the perfect love that he embraces at the end of the book. Although not a would-be saint, Holden does become a fuller human being through his experiences.

The title symbol of the novel comes from Holden's misreading of a line from a song of Robert Burns. Holden's wish, as expressed to his sister, is to be a catcher in the rye, one standing beneath a cliff waiting to catch any child who falls over it: He seeks to spare children the pain of growing up and facing the world of squalor. He also hopes to provide some useful, sincere activity in the world. The catcher-in-the-rye job is one that Holden realizes is impractical in the world as it is. Only by facing the world and loving it indiscriminately can anyone live fully within it and have any hope of changing it.

In the novel, Holden is also constantly preoccupied with death. He worries about the ducks in Central Park's lagoon freezing in winter, about Egyptian mummies, and about his dead brother Allie. He cries to Allie not to let him disappear. This symbolizes Holden's wish not to disappear into society as another cog in the great machine, and his desire not to lose what little of himself he feels that he has. To Holden, the change from childhood to adulthood is a kind of death, a death he fears because of his conviction that he will become other than he is. This fear proves groundless by the end of the book. His name also provides a clue: Holden—hold on. His quest is to hold on to his adolescent self and to save other children from the pain of growth. His quest fails, but his compassion and the growth of his humanity provide him with better alternatives.

Regarding sex, Holden tends to be puritanical. His trouble lies in the fact that he begins to feel sorry for the girls he dates, and he has too much compassion for them to defile their supposed virtue. This problem ties in with his compassion: He tries to see people as they are and not as types. He looks quickly and may make rash judgments, but once he talks to or acquaints himself with someone, he sees him or her as an individual. His mentioning of the boring boy he knew in school who could whistle better than anyone is the perfect example: Holden cannot help but confront people as individuals. Again, this shows his growing compassion and indiscriminate love. He sympathizes with the girl's position, which is a very mature quality for a teenager. At Pencey, for example, he wants to protect a childhood friend named Jane

Gallagher from Ward Stradlater, remembering that she always kept her kings in the back row in checker games and never used them.

The Catcher in the Rye also reflects the art of a maturing author. Although there is no indication that Holden will become a novelist, there are clues scattered throughout the novel that he has an artistic sensibility. His sensitivity, his compassion, his powers of observation, and his references to himself as an exhibitionist are several such clues.

Later, Salinger more fully develops the contrast between squalor and love in the world and reintroduces various elements of his Caulfield family saga in his grand design of charting the story of the Glass family. The compassion, the satire, the heights of perfect love, the love of the family unit, and the use of brilliant conversational language that characterized Salinger's great novel, *The Catcher in the Rye*, will continue to set his fiction apart.

Domenic Bruni, updated by James Norman O'Neill

Other major works

SHORT FICTION: *Nine Stories*, 1953; *Franny and Zooey*, 1961; *Raise High the Roof Beam, Carpenters, and Seymour: An Introduction*, 1963.

Bibliography

Belcher, William F., and James W. Lee, eds. *J. D. Salinger and the Critics.* Belmont, Calif.: Wadsworth, 1962. This collection of critical essays could function as a casebook for Salinger study. Part 1 contains thirteen essays exclusively on *The Catcher in the Rye*; the smaller part 2 covers his stories and contains general studies. Suggests topics for essays and includes a bibliography.

French, Warren. *J. D. Salinger, Revisited.* New York: Twayne, 1988. This revision offers a detailed introduction to Salinger and analyzes all of his work. Includes an annotated bibliography and a thorough chronology.

Gwynn, Frederick L., and Joseph L. Blotner. *The Fiction of J. D. Salinger.* Pittsburgh, Pa.: University of Pittsburgh Press, 1958. This tiny book provides capsule introductions to Salinger's fiction and is most useful in its discussion of his early stories. Contains a short bibliography.

Laser, Marvin, and Norman Furman, eds. *Studies in J. D. Salinger: Reviews, Essays, and Critiques of "The Catcher in the Rye" and Other Fiction.* New York: Odyssey Press, 1963. Although the collection concentrates on *The Catcher in the Rye*, it includes four explications of "For Esmé—with Love and Squalor," a section on censorship of *The Catcher in the Rye*, some negative evaluations of Salinger's work, and some suggested writing topics.

Lundquist, James. *J. D. Salinger.* New York: Frederick Ungar, 1979. Discusses Salinger's work as exhibiting four stages of development: alienation resulting from World War II, isolation ended through "Zen-inspired awakening," Zen art applied to the short story, and philosophical experimentation. Especially strong on Salinger's later work, the book also contains an exhaustive bibliography.

Maynard, Joyce. *At Home in the World: A Memoir.* New York: Picador USA, 1998. This memoir reveals many details of Salinger's private life, which he struggled to suppress. Best source for biographical information.

Pinsker, Sanford. *"The Catcher in the Rye": Innocence Under Pressure.* New York: Twayne, 1993. Argues that *The Catcher in the Rye* has affinities with several great American novels told by a retrospective first-person narrator and that it is perhaps the best portrait of a sixteen-year-old American boy ever written.

Salzman, Jack, ed. *New Essays on "The Catcher in the Rye."* Cambridge, England: Cambridge University Press, 1991. Has an introduction, a selected bibliography, and five essays on the novel. The essays deal with the book's subliminal war features, its narrator and audience, its cultural codes, its spirit of protest, and its themes of love and death.

WILLIAM SAROYAN

Born: Fresno, California; August 31, 1908
Died: Fresno, California; May 18, 1981

Principal long fiction · *The Human Comedy*, 1943; *The Adventures of Wesley Jackson*, 1946; *Rock Wagram*, 1951; *Tracy's Tiger*, 1951; *The Laughing Matter*, 1953 (reprinted as *The Secret Story*, 1954); *Mama I Love You*, 1956; *Papa You're Crazy*, 1957; *Boys and Girls Together*, 1963; *One Day in the Afternoon of the World*, 1964.

Other literary forms · Despite his many novels, William Saroyan is more famous for his work in the short story, the drama, and autobiography. Each of these areas received emphasis at different stages in his career. In the 1930's, he made a spectacular literary debut with an avalanche of brilliant, exuberant, and unorthodox short stories. Major early collections were: *The Daring Young Man on the Flying Trapeze and Other Stories* (1934), *Inhale and Exhale* (1936), *Three Times Three* (1936), and *Love, Here Is My Hat and Other Short Romances* (1938). *My Name Is Aram* (1940), a group of stories detailing the experiences of Aram Garoghlanian growing up in a small California town, marks the culmination of his short-story artistry.

Most of Saroyan's plays and his productions on Broadway were concentrated in the years between 1939 and 1942. *My Heart's in the Highlands* was produced by the Group Theatre in April, 1939. His second major production, *The Time of Your Life* (1939), was awarded both the Pulitzer Prize and the New York Drama Critics' Circle Award and is still considered Saroyan's best play. *Hello Out There* (1941), a one-act play, is also regarded as a fine drama.

In 1951, Saroyan and Ross Bagdasarian published a very popular song, "Come On-a My House." Saroyan also wrote several television plays, including an adaptation of *The Time of Your Life*. Starting with *The Bicycle Rider in Beverly Hills* (1952), Saroyan composed extensive memoirs, including *Here Comes, There Goes, You Know Who* (1961), *Not Dying* (1963), *Days of Life and Death and Escape to the Moon* (1970), *Places Where I've Done Time* (1972), *Sons Come and Go, Mothers Hang in Forever* (1976), *Chance Meetings* (1978), and *Obituaries* (1979).

Achievements · A thorough evaluation of Saroyan's achievement as a writer has yet to be made. By the age of twenty, he had already decided his role in life was to be that of a professional writer, and throughout his remaining fifty years he dedicated himself to that vocation, publishing voluminously in all literary forms, with the exception of poetry. The sheer bulk of his work and his admission that much of it was done merely to earn money have worked against him. Further, his frequent arguments with his critics and his increasingly difficult personality left him with few strong critical advocates.

Saroyan's lasting literary achievement is in the area of the short story, where he expanded the genre by linking narrative form to the essay and infusing his work with a highly individual vision of poetic intensity. Many of his stories feature a character modeled on Saroyan, a writer-persona who, though often obsessed with his own ideas and feelings, is vitally alive to the world of his immediate experience. Several of the most successful stories concern childhood experiences in an ethnic, small-town environment modeled on Saroyan's Fresno. Saroyan impressed his early readers with his rediscovery of the wondrous in the texture of ordinary American life. *The Saroyan Special: Selected Stories* (1948) is a collection of his best stories. *My Name Is Aram* delineates with some beautiful character portraits Saroyan's sense of the poetic interplay of values in the ethnic community.

Saroyan's plays oppose the vitality of personality and individual dreams to the force of social institutions and the threats of war. In their sense of improvised movement, his plays were a deliberate challenge to the strictly plotted productions of the commercial theater.

Starting in the mid-1940's, Saroyan turned his attention to longer fiction, writing over the next two decades a series of novels concerned with marriage and divorce. Apparently inspired by his own experiences, the books become increasingly skeptical about romantic love and reflect Saroyan's growing cynicism about the man-woman relationship while retaining his fondness for the charm of childhood.

Saroyan's longer fiction grows gradually out of those short stories concerned with growing up in a small town. *My Name Is Aram*, a story collection moving toward novelistic unity, leads directly to *The Human Comedy*, where Saroyan finally succeeds in making a novel out of his childhood material. While *The Adventures of Wesley Jackson* must be regarded as a failed attempt to write in the picaresque mode, *Rock Wagram* is a surprisingly mature handling of the thematic scope provided by the novel form. Whereas *The Adventures of Wesley Jackson* presents marriage as an idyllic goal for the solitary man, *Rock Wagram* focuses on the crushing effect of the title character's failed marriage. Several shorter book-length works—*Tracy's Tiger, Mama I Love You*, and *Papa You're Crazy*—seem more tied to Saroyan's earlier material in their confinement to the perspectives of childhood and youth and, for the most part, are limited in theme and story situations. Saroyan's other novels—*The Laughing Matter, Boys and Girls Together*, and *One Day in the Afternoon of the World*—are deliberate forays into social areas where relationships are often intense and events are somber in their finality. Like *Rock Wagram*, each of these books centers on a male's struggle with marriage, death, and divorce. The last novel, *One Day in the Afternoon of the World*, features a character who at last seems to have acquired the wisdom to deal with such personal crises. Though his longer fictions are professionally wrought, Saroyan's achievements in the novel form are limited.

The mood of the later novels is picked up and carried to greater extremes in Saroyan's memoirs, a series whose loose formats encourage the author to reveal, often in free associations, his deep anxiety about his relationship to his society. Saroyan's memoirs, generally his weakest works, become increasingly preoccupied with death, the significance of his literary achievements, and with his struggle to ward off a bitterness that he occasionally admits but wants to deny.

Biography · So much of William Saroyan's work—especially his fiction—is drawn from the circumstances of his life that it has a biographical dimension. He was born in 1908, in Fresno, California, the city where he died on May 18, 1981. The child of Armenian immigrants, he faced his first hardship when, at his father's death in 1911, he was placed for four years in the Fred Finch orphanage in Oakland. During these years, his mother worked in San Francisco as a maid, finally gathering the money to move back to a house in Fresno with her four children. Here Saroyan lived from age seven to seventeen, learning Armenian, acquiring an irreverence for the town's chief social institutions, the church and the school, and working as a newspaper boy and as a telegraph messenger to help support the family. At fifteen, he left school permanently to work at his Uncle Aram's vineyards. In 1926, he left Fresno, first to go to Los Angeles, then, after a brief time in the National Guard, to move to San Francisco, where he tried a number of jobs, eventually becoming at nineteen, the manager of a Postal Telegraph branch office. In 1928, determined to make his fortune as a writer, he made his first trip to New York. He returned to San Francisco the following year, somewhat discouraged by his lack of success. In the early 1930's, however, he began to write story after story, culminating with his decision in January, 1934, to write one story a day for the whole month. That year, *Story* pub-

D.C. Public Library

lished "The Daring Young Man on the Flying Trapeze," and suddenly Saroyan stories were appearing in many of the top periodicals. His first book of stories was published that year, and the following year he had enough money to make an ethnic return, a trip to Soviet Armenia.

Except for a few months in 1936 spent working on motion pictures at the Paramount lot, Saroyan spent the majority of the 1930's in San Francisco. By 1939, he had shifted his activities to drama, writing and producing plays on Broadway. After *The Time of Your Life* won both the New York Drama Critics' Circle Award for the best play of 1939 to 1940 and the Pulitzer Prize, Saroyan made headlines by rejecting the Pulitzer on the grounds that he was opposed to prizes in the arts and to patronage. More controversy followed when he wrote *The Human Comedy* as a screenplay for Metro-Goldwin-Mayer, then argued about directing the film and tried to buy his work back for twenty thousand dollars, more than he was paid for it. At that time he was also, in a letter to *The New York Times*, publicly denouncing the Broadway theater.

Even though he had pacificist sympathies, Saroyan was inducted into the United States Army in October, 1942, serving until 1945. His most traumatic experience in the 1940's, however, was his marriage to Carol Marcus, which lasted from 1943 to 1949, and which was resumed briefly from 1951 to 1953, before a final divorce. The couple had two children, Aram and Lucy.

In the 1950's, Saroyan began to write more long fiction, much of it dealing with marital difficulties. In addition, in 1951, he was the coauthor of a hit song, "Come On-a My House," and in the late 1950's, he began writing television plays. From 1952 to 1959, he lived in a Malibu beach house, an environment which encouraged him to work very steadily. During this time, he lived a less public existence and, feeling monetary pressure because of his gambling and his huge income tax debt, he increasingly developed a reputation as a difficult personality.

In 1960, after some travel about the world, he settled in a modest apartment at 74 Rue Taitbout, Paris. The following year he was briefly a writer-in-residence at Purdue University. By 1962, he arranged to buy two adjacent houses in Fresno and thereafter alternated living between Fresno and Paris. He spent most of the last fifteen years of his life working on various volumes of memoirs. Five days before his death he called the Associated Press to give this statement: "Everybody has got to die, but I have always believed an exception would be made in my case. Now what?" After much success (much money earned by writing, much money lost by gambling), much international travel, much controversy, much fame, and much obscurity, William Saroyan died of cancer in his hometown, Fresno, in 1981.

Analysis · William Saroyan's work habits were a major determinant (for better or worse) of his unique literary effects. He regarded writing as work, something that required disciplined effort, but also as an activity whose chief characteristic was the free play of the mind. As he explained his practice, Saroyan would often give himself assignments, a story or a chapter a day (or so many hours of writing), but would seldom work from a detailed organizational plan. Uncomfortable with mulling over possible styles, attitudes, narrative directions, he would often prefer to plunge into writing, fueled by coffee and cigarettes, hoping that whatever got down on paper would inspire the story to "take off on its own." Whatever relationships would be worked out would be those of deep structure, drawn from his inner being rather than from rhetoric. At times he would begin with a "theory" or abstract idea. (For example, the theory stated at the end of "War" is that hatred and ugliness exist in the heart of everyone.) The act of writing itself was to clarify and refine the idea for the writer. In "Myself upon the Earth," the writer's own situation, his dead father, and his attitudes toward the world begin to weave into the free connections that substitute for a conventional plot. Thematically, the apparently undisciplined becomes the true discipline as the dedication expressed in an attitude toward life–toward humanity–is transformed through the narration into a dedication to art.

There are obvious difficulties with this method of composition. "The Man with His Heart in the Highlands" begins in the course of its improvisation to split in two; when Saroyan puts it into the form of a full-length play, the theme of the importance of acceptance in forming the new American community is finally seen as a basic articulation in the material. Saroyan also acknowledged revision as an important stage in the writing process, but much of his work suffers from a lack of objectivity, the ability to see his own work clearly and revise it accordingly.

While the act of writing was for Saroyan both a kind of thinking and a performance, the materials of his art were usually the materials of his life. Much in the manner of Thomas Wolfe (an early influence), Saroyan's fiction was often drawn directly from his experience. A letter to Calouste Gulbenkian (in *Letters from 74 Rue Taitbout*, 1969) shows how Saroyan drew in detail on his external experience and his frame of mind for most of the content of "The Assyrian." Writing, he came to believe, was connected with "noticing" life and with the sense that life itself was theatrical. Although Saroyan acknowledged that the process of writing had to discover form in its materials and that the writer had to be transformed into a character framed by his art, the sense of witnessed scene and character in his best work lends a necessary solidity to his creative exuberance.

The favorite writer-personas in Saroyan's early fiction were poet-philosophers in the manner of Walt Whitman; American wiseguys (the young grown suddenly smarter about the ways of the world than their elders); or combinations of the two. His later long fiction featured the writer as a veteran of life, sometimes bitter but with his own philosophic resignation, a mode of stoic humility about what he might be able to accomplish. Saroyan's typical themes–the advocacy of love and a condemnation of war and violence–are less important than the way in which he plays the narrator (usually a writer) against the narrator's circumstances. In the most deep-seated manifestation of this paradigm–the ethnic boy responding to his American environment–Saroyan associates the ethnic self in the ethnic community with naturalness, lack of self-consciousness, true being, and dignity of person. The American environment, while it promises opportunity with its training and its competitive games, also has institutions which seem to specialize in modes of restriction, punishment, and prejudice.

The ethnic responds to his environment with a complex involvement and detachment. On the one hand, he is willing, even eager, to be assimilated; on the other hand, however, he is always aware of a kind of existence that has no adequately defined relationship to the American world of conventional social fact. The ethnic's psychological relationship to the world recalls Whitman's democratic paradox of people being intensely individual and at the same time like everyone else. In Saroyan's fiction, there is at times an emphasis on the individual's alienation–as when the protagonist in "The Daring Young Man on the Flying Trapeze" feels "somehow he had ventured upon the wrong earth" and the central character in "1,2,3,4,5,6,7,8" feels the room he is living in is not a part of him and wants a home, "a place in which to return to himself." Invariably, however, the ethnic family and its small-town environment expand quite naturally for Saroyan into a version of the democratic family of people.

This sense of communal home, however, is not easily preserved–as Saroyan's novels with their marital catastrophes and lonely protagonists repeatedly demonstrate. From the beginning, the fate of Saroyan's ethnic was complicated by the fact that his deepest allegiance was to a national community that no longer existed. In an early story, "Seventy Thousand Assyrians," the Assyrian states, "I was born in the old country, but I want to get over it . . . everything is washed up over there." Though Saroyan could be sympathetic to such practicality, he tried to achieve, often with a deliberate naïveté, a poetic point of view that would embrace both existence in the old community of family values (which was a basic part of his being) and existence in the practical new world (which offered the only opportunity for becoming).

From the perspective of Saroyan's writer-persona, the world outside is continually new, funny, sometimes strange, often wonderful, a place of innocent relationships and suspended judgments. A recurring situation in his work has someone who is apprehended for theft trying to explain that he is not guilty because his value system is different from that of his accusers. On the one hand, Saroyan believes in an attitude of joyful acceptance: Here he sees man "on the threshold of an order of himself which must find human reality a very simple unavoidable majesty and joy, with all its complications and failures." On the other hand, he imagines, like Whitman, a more somber mystic vision based on "the joyous sameness of life and death." In this mysterious crucible, life is fate, perhaps only glimpsed fully when "drawing to the edge of full death every person is restored to innocence–to have lived was not his fault." Saroyan's basic impulse is to preserve, recapture, and restore the innocence that the world has lost that state of being which sees experience only as a fantastic fate which serves ultimately to redeem the primal self.

My Name Is Aram · Like Sherwood Anderson's *Winesburg, Ohio* (1919) and William Faulkner's *The Unvanquished* (1938), *My Name Is Aram* is a book that falls midway between short-story collection and novel. The stories are separate and distinct, but they all concern the small-town experiences of the same boy, Aram, with his Armenian relatives. There is little sense of sequence but rather an accumulated manifestation of the potential wisdom in this world. Saroyan emphasizes the preservation of innocence, the warding off of the absolute element in the values of the adult culture. Aram and his friends turn social rituals into human games, and in the course of their experiences demonstrate that the many social failures in these stories have really two constituents, the innocent immediacy of the experience (its essential value) and the cultural "truths" and judgments applied to it. Through vital participation in their world, Aram and his friends begin to negotiate its preconceived ideas.

The Human Comedy · The setting, the characters, and the young man's perspective which predominate in *The Human Comedy* all have their sources in Saroyan short stories. The background is World War II, and the California small town has accordingly become "the home front." In the book's basic drama, the innocence in this environment–its vulnerable children, young people, and women and its emotional closeness–must come to terms with death and its finalities.

Within the context of the small-town milieu, the novel focuses primarily on the Macauley family and most often on Homer Macauley, a fourteen-year-old telegraph messenger boy. As Homer delivers telegrams announcing the deaths of soldiers, he finds himself getting caught up psychologically in the shock of the family reactions. On his first such delivery, to Rosa Sandoval, the woman responds with an eerie, calm hysteria in which she confuses Homer with her dead son and begins to think of both as little boys. Feeling at first both compassion and an urge to flee, Homer gradually arrives at an awareness of the meaning of death. With the help of his mother (whose husband has recently died), he fights through feelings of loneliness and isolation toward the idea that death and change afford perspectives for redeeming the values of innocence, love, and life itself.

The ideal of the community dominates the book. The novel implies in its moments of crisis and healing–Homer becoming briefly transformed into the son of another woman; Tobey taking the place of the dead Marcus in the Macauley family–that humankind is a single family. Though the fact of death and the awareness of death are constant threats to the individual, the book, as the allusions to Homer's *Odyssey* (c. 800 B.C.E.) imply, is about to return home, the coming back from the ugly realities of the outside world to the love and security which humankind can provide.

The book seems intent on assuring its readers that despite economic tribulations, the discontent of restless desire, the anxiety connected with competition, and the confining tendency of its institutions, the community is an active, positive force. A working out in the rhythms of experience of the differences between people–age, sex, degrees of formality–invariably shows positive contrasts. The many relationships

Homer has with older people are all thematically active ingredients for dramatizing the closeness of the community. *The Human Comedy* insists—perhaps too facilely at times—on the capacity of the American community to regulate the experience of life and the encounter with death.

The Adventures of Wesley Jackson · *The Adventures of Wesley Jackson* may be Saroyan's worst novel. It is marred by two closely related problems, an uncertain grasp of form and a confusion about its issues. Saroyan's indiscriminate use of his own military experience takes the novel hopelessly out of control. Evidently attempting to give himself ample latitude with the novel form, Saroyan chose to employ the picaresque form, referring in his comments on the novel to Mark Twain's *Adventures of Huckleberry Finn* (1884). Unfortunately, Wesley is much too introverted to be an effective picaro of any kind. He is intended to be a nonconformist, but, except for a few anti-Army establishment opinions, his personal idealism and prosaic earnestness only serve to make him seem as remote from the realities of Army life as from the realities of war. Lacking a feeling for the actual operations of the Army, the book meanders haphazardly from the bureaucratic to the personal, from one location to another, from family concerns to writing ambitions, succeeding finally in giving the impression of an Army journal rather than a picaresque novel.

At times the book develops an antiwar theme; at times the theme seems to be the pettiness of the Army bureaucracy. No one theme, however, is developed consistently. Wesley's self-absorbed narration does provide some shaping by turning the officers into bad fathers (cruel figures of authority), the women into sympathetic (though vague) images, and his fellow soldiers into boys, sometimes naughty but basically innocent. In sporadic, almost desultory, fashion the first part of the book features Wesley's search for his father, the essentially good man who has been displaced and ignored by organized society. The last part of the book becomes concerned with Wesley's search for a son (actually a search for a woman to bear him a son). Were Wesley's narration less limited, less egotistical, these thematic threads might have made firmer connections.

Rock Wagram · The split structure of *Rock Wagram*—approximately half the novel taking place in September, 1942, and half in February, 1950—emphasizes the drive of Rock Wagram (pronounced Vah-GRAM) to be married to Ann Ford and his resultant puzzled desperation when that marriage fails. The chronological gap, by omitting the marriage and Rock's military experience, accents the negative quality of this part of his life. Yet by leaving out the specific difficulties that are so much a part of his later depression, the novel makes Rock's psychology a problematic frame for understanding events instead of using the events of the past to put his psychology in an understandable perspective. At times, the failure of the marriage seems explained by Ann's frivolous, lying character. At other times, the failure seems to grow out of Rock's ethnic assumption that people must become involved in a family existence.

Rock Wagram explores the tensions between people as individuals and people as social animals. In his motion-picture career, Rock has become successful as an individual star, but his acquaintance with Ann Ford kindles his memories of certain values from his Armenian background, particularly the notion that a man is not complete until he had founded his own family, been husband to his wife, father to his children. Unhappily for him, Ann turns out to be like so many other characters whose departures from their true natures disturb him; her lies signify to him that she is refusing to be herself, hoping for something better. Earlier Rock has met a series of males rebelling against their heritage: Paul Key, the Hollywood producer who hates being a Jew; Sam Schwartz, Paul's nephew, who devotes himself to becoming the image of success; and Craig Adams, the completely assimilated Armenian. Although these men are denying both their heritage and their own individuality, they are better adapted to the world of casual social relationships than he, and the book raises doubts about the possibilities of a deeply authentic existence.

Rock chooses to see his life—and the life of man—as involving continual adjustment to a Shavian life force, a power which, once he begins to perceive it through his Armenian ethnic environment, becomes his ultimate guide to true being. To get in tune with this force, he tries to be uninhibited in his social relationships, to go with the flow of events, to pay attention to his circumstances and to the people he is with, and to be, as he puts it, "a good witness" to his own experience and to his world.

Part of Rock's effort to live in terms of true being is a half-conscious cultivation of strategies toward death. His reaction to the death of his brother Haig is rage; at the death of his friend Paul Key, he affects a Hemingwayesque stocisim; and to his mother's death, he responds by plunging deeply and intensely into his subjective nature. In spite of all attempts to come to terms with the reality of death, he seems at last depressed, left with a sense of being part not only of a dying culture, but also of a dying world. As he goes back to acting at the end of the narrative, his feeling for his art is one of obligation rather than enthusiasm for an individualized expression of himself. Yet, as the humor in his last statement indicates, he is finally not without hope in probing his lonely situation for its satisfactions.

The Laughing Matter · The laughter of *The Laughing Matter* is that of black comedy. From the time Swan Nazarenus announces to her husband that she is pregnant with another man's child, *The Laughing Matter* moves powerfully but erratically toward what seems an almost self-indulgently gruesome ending. The story line is captive to the emotional tensions and explosions of Evan Nazarenus as he attempts to sort out a future direction for himself, Swan, and their two children, Red and Eva. As he resorts successively to drink, violence, a return to family harmony, an abortion, and more violence, the problem-pregnancy tends to be obscured by his confusing attempts at solution. Since his personality is never clarified in the characterization, and since he often gives the impression of running aimlessly about the countryside, Evan becomes progressively less sympathetic in his shifting relationship to people and events.

The accompaniment to the mad rhapsody of his behavior is more carefully controlled. The children are innocent victims, becoming increasingly aware that something is wrong and even acting out some of the tensions themselves. The Walzes, a neighbor couple, have their own fights, and Evan's brother, Dade, who has, after years of domestic turbulence, lost his family entirely, conveniently defines one possible outcome.

Complicating the question of what to do is the issue of who is to blame. In one scene between Evan and Dade, the two brothers—who often speak in an old-country tongue—review their ethnic fate as heads of families, Evan wondering what they as males have done wrong. Evan debates whether he ought to be more feminine, more kindly, or strive to retain his masculine pride in the face of what may be an essential challenge to his person. His solution, the abortion, is less an act of harsh morality (as he later views it) than the result of a desire to begin again, to regain a kind of innocence by reversing events.

The ironies and the deaths pile up so rapidly at the conclusion that they achieve only a blurred effect. The fact that so much violence results from simple ignorance begins to make the characters comic rather than tragic, and this may have been the prompting behind Saroyan's title. When Evan accuses the wrong man as the adulterer (pushing the poor lonely man toward suicide), and when he shoots and kills his brother Dade under the mistaken notion that they have been responsible for Swan's death from abortion, Evan seems more the incompetent than the grief-stricken victim. His own death in an auto accident may have been meant to suggest that the whole chain of events was merely a series of accidents, but this must be weighed against the remarks of the doctor who explains to Dade that Swan committed suicide and that she had evidently had a strong death wish for several years. For all its masculine madness, this book begins and ends by pointing an accusing finger at the woman.

Boys and Girls Together · *Boys and Girls Together* is a realistic study of a husband-wife relationship that moves with an understated satire toward black humor. The husband, Dick, is a writer who finds that his current domestic relationship has made it impossible for him to work, thus heaping financial strain upon his already turbulent marriage to Daisy. In the course of their sporadic fighting, the couple discovers greater and greater depths of incompatibility. Dick comes to the conclusion that she is ignorant, trivial, and selfish; Daisy accuses him of being egotistical and immature. Were it not for the two children (Johnny, five, and Rosey, two and a half), the writer, who is a family man, would undoubtedly leave.

As this account of a few days in their lives demonstrates, what keeps the marriage together is their socializing with other couples. The slight story line follows the meeting of Dick and Daisy with two other couples for a few days of fun in San Francisco. Though only casual friends, all the couples have common characteristics: In each instance, the husband has achieved prominence in the arts; in each case, the husband is many years older than the wife; and in each instance, the difference in age seems part of the strain on the marriage. Before all six can get together, the oldest husband, Leander, dies of a heart attack, an episode witnessed by Oscar Bard (the actor) and his wife, and by Leander's wife Lucretia. Dick and Daisy arrive soon after the attack and seem generally ineffective in preventing the scene from sliding from seriousness to farce. Dick eventually begins to act as satiric observer, commenting on Oscar's egotistical discomfort and on Lucretia's performance as grieving widow. The scene has its climax in Oscar's long speech on the difficulties of their kind of marriage. While he begins by pointing out realistically that the women they have married are not for them, he finally comes to the conclusion that it is sexual attraction that gives the necessary life to all partners in such marriages and which makes them continue to put up with each other. Dick does not disagree. Soon the survivors are planning a trip to Reno as another distraction from the harsh realities around them. Earlier, Dick had resented it when his wife teased him about being a fool for sex. In the last part of the novel, his understated satiric vision outlines them all as characters in a sexual farce.

If all of William Saroyan's writing can be regarded as his attempt to understand and define his position in the world, his long fiction must be seen as his deliberate recognition of the crueler circumstances in that world—death, the failure of love, divorce, the recalcitrant details of life itself. His own marital troubles undoubtedly inspired the novels of the 1950's and 1960's with their fragmented families, and while the intently masculine perspective in these books reveals a serious but virtually unexamined reverence for love and marriage, it also demonstrates the author's own very personal irritation with wives. In nearly all of his novels, the formal problem tends to be the male protagonist's varied reactions to his situation. In *Rock Wagram* and *The Laughing Matter*, Saroyan is successful in focusing these reactions by means of intense emotional pressures, but his confusion about final blame for the marital breakdown makes a fictional closure difficult. With *Papa You're Crazy* and *Mama I Love You*, he moves to the detachment of the child's point of view but is still uncertain about the extent to which the world's facts ought to–and must–impinge on the individual family member. (To what degree, for example, does the particular existence of the parent doom or mold the life of the child?) In *Boys and Girls Together* and *One Day in the Afternoon of the World*, Saroyan gets mixed results from mining the attitudes of his male protagonists for a perspective that would be both a consistent and legitimate interpretation of their marital situations. In Saroyan's long fiction, as well as in his other writing, both his strengths and his weaknesses derive from his insistent emotional presence.

Walter Shear

Other major works

SHORT FICTION: *The Daring Young Man on the Flying Trapeze and Other Stories*, 1934; *Inhale and Exhale*, 1936; *Three Times Three*, 1936; *The Gay and Melancholy Flux: Short Stories*, 1937; *Little Children*, 1937; *Love, Here Is My Hat and Other Short Romances*, 1938; *The Trouble with Tigers*, 1938; *Three Fragments and a Story*, 1939; *Peace, It's Wonderful*, 1939; *My Name is Aram*, 1940; *Saroyan's Fables*, 1941; *The Insurance Salesman and Other Stories*, 1941; *Forty-eight Saroyan Stories*, 1942; *Some Day I'll Be a Millionaire: Thirty-four More Great Stories*, 1944; *Dear Baby*, 1944; *The Saroyan Special: Selected Stories*, 1948; *The Fiscal Hoboes*, 1949; *The Assyrian and Other Stories*, 1950; *The Whole Voyald and Other Stories*, 1956; *William Saroyan Reader*, 1958; *Love*, 1959; *After Thirty Years: The Daring Young Man on the Flying Trapeze*, 1964; *Best Stories of William Saroyan*, 1964; *The Tooth and My Father*, 1974.

PLAYS: *The Hungerers: A Short Play*, pb. 1939; *My Heart's in the Highlands*, pr., pb. 1939; *The Time of Your Life*, pr., pb. 1939 (also includes essays); *Love's Old Sweet Song*, pr., pb. 1940; *Three Plays: My Heart's in the Highlands, The Time of Your Life, Love's Old Sweet Song*, pb. 1940; *Subway Circus*, pb. 1940; *The Ping-Pong Game*, pb. 1940 (one act); *The Beautiful People*, pr. 1940; *The Great American Goof*, pr. 1940; *Across the Board on Tomorrow Morning*, pr., pb. 1941; *Three Plays: The Beautiful People, Sweeney in the Trees, Across the Board on Tomorrow Morning*, pb. 1941; *Hello Out There*, pr. 1941 (one act); *Jim Dandy*, pr., pb. 1941; *Razzle Dazzle*, pb. 1942 (collection); *Talking to You*, pr., pb. 1942; *Get Away Old Man*, pr. 1943; *Sam Ego's House*, pr. 1947; *A Decent Birth, a Happy Funeral*, pb. 1949; *Don't Go Away Mad*, pr., pb. 1949; *The Slaughter of the Innocents*, pb. 1952; *The Cave Dwellers*, pr. 1957; *Once Around the Block*, pb. 1959; *Sam the Highest Jumper of Them All: Or, The London Comedy*, pr. 1960; *Settled Out of Court*, pr. 1960; *The Dogs: Or, The Paris Comedy and Two Other Plays*, pb. 1969.

NONFICTION: *Harlem as Seen by Hirschfield*, 1941; *Hilltop Russians in San Francisco*, 1941; *Why Abstract?*, 1945 (with Henry Miller and Hilaire Hiler); *The Twin Adventures: The Adventures of William Saroyan*, 1950; *The Bicycle Rider in Beverly Hills*, 1952; *Here Comes, There Goes, You Know Who*, 1961; *A Note on Hilaire Hiler*, 1962; *Not Dying*, 1963; *Short Drive, Sweet Chariot*, 1966; *Look at Us: Let's See: Here We Are*, 1967; *I Used to Believe I Had Forever: Now I'm Not So Sure*, 1968; *Letters from 74 Rue Taitbout*, 1969; *Days of Life*

and *Death and Escape to the Moon*, 1970; *Places Where I've Done Time*, 1972; *Sons Come and Go, Mothers Hang in Forever*, 1976; *Chance Meetings*, 1978; *Obituaries*, 1979; *Births*, 1983.
CHILDREN'S LITERATURE: *Me*, 1963; *Horsey Gorsey and the Frog*, 1968.

MISCELLANEOUS: *My Name Is Saroyan*, 1983 (stories, verse, play fragments, and memoirs).

Bibliography

Balakian, Nona. *The World of William Saroyan.* Lewisburg, Ohio: Bucknell University Press, 1998. Balakian, formerly a staff writer for *The New York Times Book Review*, knew Saroyan personally in his last years, and her observations of him color her assessment of his later works. She viewed it as her mission to resurrect his reputation and restore him among the finest of twentieth century American writers. Traces his evolution from ethnic writer to master of the short story, to playwright, and finally to existentialist.

Calonne, David Stephen. *William Saroyan: My Real Work Is Being.* Chapel Hill: University of North Carolina Press, 1983. A good introduction to Saroyan's work. Calonne balances his examination of Saroyan's short stories, plays, novels, memoirs, and essays. Includes excellent notes, a bibliography, and an index.

Foster, Edward Halsey. *William Saroyan: A Study of the Short Fiction.* New York: Twayne, 1991. This volume separates into three parts. The first is devoted to Foster's assessment of Saroyan's career as a short-story writer, the second focuses on Saroyan himself—and reprints an interview with the writer as well as several of his nonfiction pieces—and the third reprints essays on Saroyan written by other critics.

Keyishian, Harry, ed. *Critical Essays on William Saroyan.* New York: G. K. Hall & Co., 1995. Like other volumes in this series, this book includes contemporaneous reviews, outstanding extant criticism, and original commissioned essays. In addition to a preface by Keyishian and a substantial introduction to Saroyan and his critics by Alice K. Barter, the volume contains valuable new comparative studies of Saroyan and Walt Whitman and of Saroyan and Gertrude Stein.

Lee, Lawrence, and Barry Gifford. *Saroyan: A Biography.* New York: Harper & Row, 1984. A vivid biography of Saroyan that concentrates on the writer. Its unusual three-part structure opens at the height of his career (1940-1950), shifts to his roots and early literary struggles (1908-1939), and concludes with his last years (1950-1981).

LESLIE MARMON SILKO

Born: Albuquerque, New Mexico; March 5, 1948

Principal long fiction · *Ceremony*, 1977; *Almanac of the Dead*, 1991; *Gardens in the Dunes*, 1999.

Other literary forms · Leslie Marmon Silko's first published book, *Laguna Woman* (1974), is a collection of poems. Her earliest published works were short stories, published in magazines, most of which were later included in *Storyteller* (1981). This book defies genre classification by including short fiction, poetry, retellings of traditional stories, and family photographs, all linked by passages of commentary and memoir. Her interest in images interacting with words led Silko to produce a film in 1980 with Dennis Carr entitled *Estoyehmuut and the Gunnadeyah* (Arrowboy and the Destroyers). In shooting the film at Laguna, New Mexico, using pueblo residents and elders instead of professional actors, Silko documented a time and place that no longer exist.

Silko's nonfiction works include *The Delicacy and Strength of Lace: Letters Between Leslie Marmon Silko and James Wright* (1986; edited by Ann Wright), and *Yellow Woman and a Beauty of the Spirit: Essays on Native American Life Today* (1996), a collection of essays. In *Sacred Water: Narratives and Pictures* (1993), she self-published her essay on water interwoven with her Polaroid photographs. The first edition was hand sewn and glued by Silko; a subsequent edition was conventionally bound.

Achievements · The publication of Silko's first novel, *Ceremony*, along with N. Scott Momaday's winning of the 1969 Pulitzer Prize for *House Made of Dawn*, marked the beginning of a surge in publishing by Native American authors–the "Native American renaissance" of the late 1960's and early 1970's. Yet just as her works defy genre classification, Silko transcends the category of Native American writer. Her earlier works draw heavily on her own experiences and the traditional stories of Laguna Pueblo; later works move beyond the pueblo while maintaining a strong connection with the Southwest and with traditional and autobiographical materials. Her first two novels, *Ceremony* and *Almanac of the Dead*, are experimental in form, testing the limits of the novel as a genre and format. Indeed, Silko once said that she loves working in the novel form because its flexibility imposes so few limitations on the writer. Her third novel, *Gardens in the Dunes*, adheres more closely to conventional novel form, but like the previous two, it is highly political, reflecting Silko's activism.

Her books, particularly *Ceremony* and *Storyteller*, are widely taught in colleges and universities; her short fiction and poetry are widely anthologized. Her works have been translated into Italian and German and are popular internationally, both in translation and in the original English.

Silko's works in fiction, nonfiction, and poetry earned her a National Endowment for the Arts (NEA) Discover Grant (1971), *The Chicago Review* Poetry Award (1974), the Pushcart Prize for Poetry (1977); a MacArthur Prize Fellowship (1981); the *Boston Globe* prize for nonfiction (1986); a New Mexico Endowment for the Humanities "Living Cultural Treasure" Award (1988); and a Lila Wallace *Reader's Digest* Fund

Writers Award (1991). Her story "Lullaby" was selected as one of twenty best short stories of 1975.

Biography · Leslie Marmon Silko was born to Leland (Lee) Howard Marmon and Mary Virginia Leslie in 1948. Her extended mixed-heritage family (Laguna, Mexican, white) had a rich history of tribal leadership and a rich tradition of storytelling. Growing up at Laguna Pueblo, Silko rode horses, hunted, and was free to explore the land of her ancestors, land that was inextricably tied to the traditional stories told by her aunts and grandmother.

In 1964 she entered the University of New Mexico. In 1966, she married Richard Chapman and gave birth to Robert William Chapman. During her sophomore year, she took a creative writing class. Despite the success of a short story written for that class, "The Man to Send Rainclouds," which was published first in *New Mexico Quarterly* and then in Kenneth Rosen's anthology of Native American writing as the title piece, Silko did not yet see herself primarily as a writer. After receiving her B.A. in 1969, she entered the University of New Mexico law school in the American Indian Law Fellowship program. During the same year, she separated from and eventually divorced Chapman.

In 1971, she left law school. Convinced that the American justice system was inherently unjust, and believing that her own role was to call attention to this injustice by telling stories, she entered graduate school in English at the University of New Mexico. She soon left to teach at Navajo Community College. During the same year, she married John Silko (whom she would also later divorce) and gave birth to her second child, Cazimir Silko.

Leaving the Southwest for the first time, Silko moved with her husband and children to Ketchikan, Alaska, in 1973. The impact of the Alaskan landscape and climate can be seen in her short story "Storyteller," written during this time, and it resurfaces in *Almanac of the Dead.* She also began writing *Ceremony* while in Alaska, re-creating her beloved southwestern landscape.

Silko returned to Laguna for a short time before moving to Tucson in 1978, where she taught at the University of Arizona. She eventually settled on a ranch outside Tucson, enjoying the physical labor of ranch life. In 1981, the year in which *Storyteller* was published, Silko was awarded the MacArthur Prize Fellowship. Sometimes called the "genius award," the MacArthur Prize provided five years of financial support, allowing her, for the first time, to devote all of her efforts to writing. While writing *Almanac of the Dead,* she became incensed about Arizona politics, leading her to paint a mural of a snake with political graffiti on the outside wall of her Stone Avenue office. Though later owners painted over the mural, it was well received by the people of the neighborhood and was important both in helping Silko (who describes herself as a "frustrated painter") to overcome writer's block and to develop further her technique of combining images with words. After the publication of *Almanac of the Dead* in 1991, Silko's desire for independence from the publishing world and her experiments with photography (in part inspired by her father, a professional photographer) led her to self-publish *Sacred Water: Narratives and Pictures.*

Analysis · Leslie Marmon Silko once stated that she tries to write a very different book every time. Indeed, her novels are as different from one another as they are from her books in other genres. Despite such diversity, however, Silko's novels share certain common traits. All draw heavily on her personal experiences, but they are not conventionally autobiographical. Although only *Ceremony* deals exclusively with Native American themes and characters, Native American themes and characters are central in the other two novels as well.

Silko was so attuned to the political situation in northern Mexico that, in *Almanac of the Dead*, published two years before the Zapatista uprising in Chiapas, her description of an uprising in northern Mexico seems prophetic. Silko's work makes use of her eclectic reading on topics as diverse as the Gnostic gospels and orchid collecting.

Silko uses very little dialogue, yet her characters are richly drawn through the use of an omniscient narrator who reveals their inner thoughts and reactions. Her descriptions are vivid and detailed. Though predominantly serious, all of Silko's novels display her wry, ironic sense of humor. An important recurring theme in all of Silko's novels is the conflict between the "destroyers," those whose disregard for the land leads them to exploit it and its people for profit, and those who are in touch with and respect the land. Although those in touch with the land are usually the indigenous people who have not separated themselves from nature, indigenous people can be destroyers, and whites can be in touch with the land.

Ceremony · Tayo, a young veteran of mixed Laguna and white ancestry, returns from World War II with what would now be called post-traumatic stress syndrome. When the Veterans Administration hospital sends him home to the pueblo uncured, his family asks the tribal healer, old Ku'oosh, to perform the traditional ceremony for reincorporating warriors into the community. The ceremony is only partially successful; Tayo is still deeply disturbed, blaming himself for his cousin and friend Rocky's death and turning to alcohol along with a group of friends who are also veterans. After a fight with his friend Emo, Tayo is sent back to the V.A. hospital, but his treatment is no more successful than it was the first time.

Betonie, a Navajo medicine man who uses unconventional methods, is more successful. He conducts a Navajo healing ceremony for Tayo that sets him on the road to recovery. When Tayo leaves, Betonie says that to complete the ceremony Tayo must recover the spotted cattle that Tayo and his Uncle Josiah had planned to raise but that had presumably wandered off in Tayo's absence after Josiah died. Tayo discovers that the cattle were stolen by white ranchers and realizes that he had believed the lie that only Indians and Mexicans stole because whites did not need to steal. With the help of Ts'eh, a mysterious woman who turns out to be the spirit of the sacred mountain, Tayo takes the cattle home.

Meanwhile, Emo has become one of the destroyers, a participant in witchery, and he convinces the rest of the group to cooperate in his plan to kill Tayo. Warned by Ts'eh, Tayo is able to resist the witchery. He returns home and tells his story to the elders in the kiva, who recognize Ts'eh as the spirit who brings rain and healing to their drought-stricken land. Tayo's separation from his community, in part caused by the war but also caused by his rejection as an illegitimate "half-breed," was symptomatic of a larger rift in the community. His healing demonstrates that things must change, that the new must be incorporated into the old, and that the "half-breed" can act as a mediator between the old traditions and the new world. Much of *Ceremony* is told in flashbacks. Traditional Laguna stories are woven throughout, set off from the text. The language is lyrical, and the message is of healing and conciliation.

Almanac of the Dead · When Silko read from this novel at the time of its publication, she announced, "This book attempts to crush linear time." It succeeds by repeatedly shifting time frames. Silko interweaves an enormous cast of characters involved in multiple subplots. They tell the story, in an indeterminate time in the not-too-distant future, of a spontaneous uprising across the Americas of dispossessed indigenous people who move throughout the novel toward an apocalyptic convergence on Tucson, Arizona.

Lecha and Zeta are twins, mixed-blood Yaquis, who have been given pieces of an old Mayan book (the almanac of the title). Unlike the Mayan Codices, this book has stayed in the hands of the people. As they work to transcribe the pieces, they discover that the Mayans foretold the coming of the white European invaders—and foretold their demise as well. Seese, a young white woman whose baby has been kidnapped, consults Lecha, who is a psychic, and stays to work for her. Sterling, an old man who is exiled for revealing tribal secrets, also comes to work at the twins' ranch.

Other characters include Allegria, a mercenary architect, and her husband, Menardo, who live near Mexico City; the Tucson branch of the Blue family, mafiosi who dominate the Tucson real estate market; the Indian twin brothers Tacho and Wacah, who embody the mysterious power of twins and lead the people north toward Tucson; and Marxist Mexican revolutionaries Angelita (La Escapia) and El Feo. Their stories intertwine as they converge on Tucson, where the Barefoot Hopi warns that the familiar way of life on earth will end unless the destroyers change their ways and respect the earth. "Eco-warriors" to the north threaten a suicide bombing of a dam. The novel ends as all are poised on the brink of revolution.

Gardens in the Dunes · In an unpublished interview, Silko described her third novel as "full of flowers and light." Set in the time immediately following the stock market crash of 1893, *Gardens in the Dunes* tells the story of Indigo and Sister Salt. The young sisters are the last of the Sand Lizards, a fictional tribe based loosely on the Colorado River tribes that were wiped out around the beginning of the twentieth century. After a Ghost Dance they are attending is raided by the police, the girls are separated from their mother as they flee. Later, their grandmother dies and Indigo is captured by the police. She is sent to boarding school in Riverside.

There she is befriended by Hattie and Edward, a wealthy couple who live near the school. Before marrying Edward, Hattie attended Harvard University until her unconventional thesis proposal on the Gnostic gospels was rejected. Edward is a professional plant collector who sells rare specimens to wealthy buyers. They take Indigo along on their European trip during the school's summer break. Indigo sees the Jesus of the European churches as another manifestation of Wovoka, the prophet of the Ghost Dance. Edward's scheme to steal citron cuttings fails; Hattie, disgusted by his greed, divorces him and vows to help Indigo find her family.

Meanwhile, Sister Salt is befriended by Big Candy, who fathers her baby, the "little black grandfather." When Big Candy's preoccupation with wealth causes him to neglect Sister Salt and the baby, she and the Chemehuevi twins leave to farm land that the twins acquired from an aunt. The sisters are reunited, returning to the old gardens. Indigo plants the seeds and bulbs she collected on her journey, mixing the impractical but beautiful flowers with the traditional food crops. As in earlier works, Silko emphasizes the need to live in harmony with the land, the dangers of capitalism, and the need to use the new along with the old.

Robin Payne Cohen

Other major works

SHORT FICTION: *Yellow Woman,* 1993.

POETRY: *Laguna Woman,* 1974.

NONFICTION: *The Delicacy and Strength of Lace: Letters Between Leslie Marmon Silko and James Wright,* 1986; *Sacred Water: Narratives and Pictures,* 1993; *Yellow Woman and a Beauty of the Spirit: Essays on Native American Life Today,* 1996.

MISCELLANEOUS: *Storyteller,* 1981 (includes prose and poetry).

Bibliography

Allen, Paula Gunn. *The Sacred Hoop: Recovering the Feminine in American Indian Traditions.* Boston: Beacon Press, 1986. In the chapter entitled "The Feminine Landscape of Leslie Marmon Silko's *Ceremony,*" Allen traces the traditional origins of the novel's female characters, illuminating their symbolism.

Coltelli, Laura. *Winged Words.* Lincoln: University of Nebraska Press, 1990. A collection of interviews with Native American authors. The interview with Silko gives insight into her experiences and influences in writing *Almanac of the Dead* in addition to reviewing her earlier work.

Owens, Louis. *Other Destinies: Understanding the American Indian Novel.* Norman: University of Oklahoma Press, 1992. 167-191. In the chapter entitled "The Very Essence of Our Lives: Leslie Silko's Webs of Identity," Owens analyzes *Ceremony* as a search for identity through memory and returning home.

Salyer, Greg. *Leslie Marmon Silko.* New York: Twayne, 1997. A useful overview of Silko's life and work prior to *Gardens in the Dunes.* Good chronology and bibliography.

Studies in American Indian Literatures (SAIL) 2, no. 10. Fall, 1998. Special issue on *Almanac of the Dead.* Includes excellent essays as well as Ellen Arnold's interview, in which Silko discusses *Gardens in the Dunes.*

UPTON SINCLAIR

Born: Baltimore, Maryland; September 20, 1878
Died: Bound Brook, New Jersey; November 25, 1968

Principal long fiction · *Springtime and Harvest*, 1901; *Prince Hagen*, 1903; *The Journal of Arthur Stirling*, 1903; *Manassas*, 1904 (as *Theirs Be the Guilt*, 1959); *The Jungle*, 1906; *A Captain of Industry*, 1906; *The Overman*, 1907; *The Metropolis*, 1908; *The Moneychangers*, 1908; *Samuel the Seeker*, 1910; *Love's Pilgrimage*, 1911; *Sylvia*, 1913; *Sylvia's Marriage*, 1914; *King Coal*, 1917; *Jimmie Higgins*, 1919; *100%*, 1920; *They Call Me Carpenter*, 1922; *Oil! A Novel*, 1927; *Boston*, 1928; *Mountain City*, 1930; *Roman Holiday*, 1931; *The Wet Parade*, 1931; *Co-op*, 1936; *The Flivver King*, 1937; *No Pasaran!*, 1937; *Little Steel*, 1938; *Our Lady*, 1938; *World's End*, 1940; *Between Two Worlds*, 1941; *Dragon's Teeth*, 1942; *Wide Is the Gate*, 1943; *Presidential Agent*, 1944; *Dragon Harvest*, 1945; *A World to Win*, 1946; *Presidential Mission*, 1947; *One Clear Call*, 1948; *O Shepherd, Speak!*, 1949; *Another Pamela: Or, Virtue Still Rewarded*, 1950; *The Return of Lanny Budd*, 1953; *What Didymus Did*, 1954; *It Happened to Didymus*, 1958; *Affectionately Eve*, 1961.

Other literary forms · Between 1901 and 1961, Upton Sinclair wrote or rewrote more than forty novels, but in addition to his longer fiction, Sinclair also wrote and published a massive amount of nonfiction, including pamphlets, analyses of diverse subjects, memoirs, twelve plays, and letters by the thousands. The bibliography of his works is testimony to his amazing fluency, but no one who is so prolific can escape being uneven, and this is indeed the case with Sinclair. His career, which spanned more than six decades, was unified in one respect, however, for both his fiction and his nonfiction were devoted to a single aim–the achievement of social justice. Everything that he wrote was written primarily as a means to attain the end he sought, bettering the conditions of life for all people. Thus, much of what Sinclair produced is not belletristic in any full sense, but propaganda to spread his ideas about politics and economics. In books such as *The Industrial Republic* (1907), he tries to explain how socialism will be arrived at by a natural process in America; the theory is based on the premise that social revolutions are bound to be benevolent. During the period following World War I to the onset of the Depression, most of Sinclair's writing was nonfiction. In a number of books, which he called his Dead Hand series, an ironic allusion to Adam Smith's "Invisible Hand" of *laissez-faire* economics, Sinclair deals with the destructive influence of capitalism on numerous American institutions: *The Profits of Religion* (1918) treats the abuses of institutional religions, showing how the established church supports the ruling classes in exchange for economic advantages; *The Brass Check: A Study in American Journalism* (1919) details the operation of class bias in American journalism; *The Goose-Step: A Study of American Education* (1923) reveals higher education's lackeylike relationship to capitalism, fostered by grants and endowments made to the universities by wealthy families and industry. In *The Goslings: A Study of the American Schools* (1924), the same kind of servile relationship with the capitalist status quo is exposed as existing in elementary and high schools, and in *Mammonart* (1925), Sinclair shows how artists and writers down through history have been duped into serving oppressive economic and political power structures. Not even

William Shakespeare, Fyodor Dostoevski, or Joseph Conrad were their own men according to Sinclair's ideological criticism. Although the Dead Hand series is flawed by an excess of socialist polemics, Sinclair did an extensive amount of research to produce each book, and though the case is overstated, there is a grain of truth in his analysis of the all-pervasive influence of the economic and political structure of America on those areas that should be most independent of such pressure–the Church, the press, the educational system, the arts.

Of more interest to the general reader are Sinclair's autobiographical works *American Outpost: A Book of Reminiscences* (1932) and *The Autobiography of Upton Sinclair* (1962), which updates his life for the thirty years intervening between the two books. In his accounts of his life, Sinclair reveals himself to be an honest but self-centered idealist. He chronicles his victories and defeats through childhood, youth, and marriage as the educational experiences of a genius; he offers in generally positive and optimistic terms his lifelong belief in progress and his hatred of social inequality and social exploitation.

Achievements · Sinclair's literary remains weighed in at eight tons when being collected for donation to Indiana University Library. Of modern American writers, he is among the most widely translated, his works having been translated into forty-seven languages in thirty-nine countries, yet his literary reputation steadily declined after the 1940's, despite the fact that *The Jungle* was still widely read in high school and college classrooms. Moreover, Sinclair himself has historical importance for the role he played in the American radical movement.

Sinclair's recurring theme as a novelist was class-conflict, the exploitation of the poor by the rich, of labor by management, of the have-nots by the haves. With few exceptions, the rich are depicted as useless, extravagant, and unprincipled, while the poor are essentially noble characters who are the victims of capitalistic society. Sinclair's literary method, which came to be called "muckraking," was intended to expose the evils of such a society. Apart from *The Jungle*, which is the best-known example of this genre, there is the Lanny Budd series–ten historical novels that trace the history of the world from 1913 to 1946. *Dragon's Teeth*, the third in the series, won the Pulitzer Prize for Fiction in 1942 by virtue of its vivid portrayal of conditions in Nazi-dominated Europe. In addition to these, the most widely read of Sinclair's novels, he produced novels on almost every topic of then-current social history, including coal strikes in Colorado in *King Coal*, exploitation by the oil industry in California in *The Wet Parade*, and the legal injustices of the Sacco-Vanzetti case in *Boston*. All of Sinclair's fiction was aimed at the middle-class liberal, whom he hoped to convert to his idealistic vision of a brotherhood of labor. Sinclair was thus a spokesman for the progressive era of American history; a chronic protester and iconoclast, he tried to stir the conscience of his nation and to cause change. In only one case, *The Jungle*, was he successful in prompting the desired changes through legislation. As a propagandist writing in the spirit of Thomas Paine and in the idiom of Karl Marx, Sinclair made a permanent impact by what he said, if not by how he wrote, and to this day, he still serves as one of the chief interpreters of American society to other nations.

Biography · Upton Beall Sinclair was born in Baltimore, Maryland, but reared in New York. Finishing high school at the age of twelve, he was too young for college and had to wait until he was fourteen before he could enter the City College of New

York. While an undergraduate, he helped support himself by writing stories and jokes for pulp magazines. In one span of a few weeks, he turned out fifty-six thousand words, an incredible feat even for a prolific prodigy such as Sinclair. In 1898, after taking his B.A. from CCNY, Sinclair enrolled as a special student in the Graduate School of Columbia University, but withdrew after a professor told him "you don't know anything about writing." In 1900, Sinclair married Meta Fuller and began work on his first novel, *Springtime and Harvest,* which was written in Canada. Shortly afterward, in 1902, he joined the Socialist party. The reception of his early fiction gave him little critical encouragement and no cash of which to speak. His first four

Library of Congress

novels brought him less than one thousand dollars, and the threat of poverty put a strain on his marriage. In 1905, Sinclair, with Jack London, formed the Intercollegiate Socialist Society, an indication of his growing political radicalism.

Sinclair's first fame came with his fifth novel, *The Jungle;* he was even invited to the White House by President Theodore Roosevelt to discuss the book. With the thirty thousand dollars that *The Jungle* earned for him, Sinclair founded a utopian community, Helicon Colony, in New Jersey. In 1907, an arsonist burned down the Colony and Sinclair's fortune with it. This was the first actual persecution that Sinclair had experienced for professing unpopular views. In private life, he faced further difficulties; his wife divorced him in 1911; he remarried in 1913 and moved West with his new wife, Mary Kimbrough, in 1915. Continuing to write at a furious pace, Sinclair became a publisher during World War I with the *Upton Sinclair Magazine.* He also issued a series of tracts on the effects of capitalism, objecting to its effects on education, art, journalism, and literature.

Not all of Sinclair's energies went into writing. He was instrumental in creating The League for Industrial Democracy and the American Civil Liberties Union. Three times he ran for the California state legislature and three times for governor, usually on the Socialist party ticket but also as a Democrat. In *I, Governor of California and How I Ended Poverty* (1933), he set forth his platform, "End Poverty in California" or "E.P.I.C.," which explained the Depression as a result of private ownership and the economic insanity of limited production. His ideas found a large degree of public acceptance in the early days of the New Deal and he came close to being elected despite the mudslinging of his opponent. Some critics believe that the chief reason for Sinclair's decline as a novelist was his involvement in electoral politics in the 1930's. His novels of that decade are about specific political situations. *The Flivver King* attacks Ford Motor Company and makes a case for labor unions. "Little Steel" is a story about the organization of steel-mill owners against unions. "Pasaram!" is another short story from the 1930's about the brave fight in the Spanish Civil War against right-wing dictators.

During World War II, Sinclair began the historical record of his times in the Lanny Budd series. The novels in this ten-book series show the metamorphosis of the hero, Lanny, from an espouser of socialist causes to an anti-Communist, a change that reflected Sinclair's own changed sympathies.

By the decade of the 1950's, Sinclair had entered semiretirement, during which he nevertheless managed to expand his autobiography and finish six books, including a clever parody of Samuel Richardson's epistolary novel *Pamela* (1740-1741), entitled *Another Pamela*, and a biography of Jesus. In these years, Sinclair finally settled his quarrel with the status quo. In his old age, he came to approve of the American establishment's foot-dragging on civil rights and supported American intervention in Vietnam. The old radical had, like so many before him, softened his position.

Analysis · Upton Sinclair was a prodigy as a writer and wrote with great fluency and consequent unevenness. For him, the essential purpose of literature was to expose social evils and promote change; his end as a writer was the improvement of the condition of humankind. Thus, his literary reputation is not really germane to what he was trying to do as a writer. His fiction has more relevance when it is regarded in a political and historical light rather than as literature per se. As the social and economic issues of his time recede into history, so does interest in those books that were simply propaganda.

Although Sinclair was regarded as a literary rebel for his iconoclastic attacks on America's economic, intellectual, and political institutions, he was not in any way an avant-garde writer in terms of style and structure. His subject was society rather than the individual human consciousness. It is necessary in any analysis of Sinclair's fiction to admit at once the defects in his writing. Most of it is journalistic in quality rather than belletristic. In fact, he deliberately wrote against the genteel tradition in American letters. Sinclair employed his rhetoric for practical results rather than to achieve poetic effects. His polemics were couched in fictional form because he believed the novel was a particularly effective medium for his idealistic radicalism.

Sinclair's first four novels were produced between 1900 and 1904. These early works were awkward but full of passionate idealism. In *Prince Hagen* and *The Overman*, which were written before Sinclair discovered socialism, there is already a conflict between the pure-minded and the corrupt oppressors, but no solutions for the problems are proposed. The ideology of socialism provided him with solutions, although Sinclair was not a traditional Socialist; to him, socialism was the purest expression of the American Dream. He did not see himself as an overthrower of American values, but as a writer who was helping his countrymen return to a vision of human brotherhood.

Manassas · Prior to *Manassas*, Sinclair's fiction had been based on personal experience. In this novel about the Civil War, a young southerner, Alan Montague, the son of a Mississippi plantation owner, becomes a supporter of abolition. The protagonist is present at many historic moments—the raid at Harper's Ferry, the bombardment of Fort Sumter—and encounters many historical figures, such as Abraham Lincoln, Jefferson Davis, Frederick Douglass, and John Brown. *Manassas* differed from Sinclair's early books in that it was more realistic and objective. As a work of art, however, *Manassas* is not remarkable. The plot is often an inert review of historical facts, the characterizations are shallow, and the story is too filled with coincidence to be plausible. Despite its flaws, *Manassas* marked a turning point in Sinclair's career. In this novel, he revealed attitudes that pointed toward his development as a writer of exposés.

The Jungle · In 1904, Sinclair was asked by the editor of *The Appeal*, a radical paper, to write a novel about wage-slavery and the oppressive conditions of industrial workers which would show that their plight was analogous to that of the black in the Old South. Responding to this offer, Sinclair spent two months in the meat-packing houses of Chicago talking to the workers; he visited the plants also as an official tourist, and in disguise as a worker. The impressions and information Sinclair gathered from this experience were extremely distressing to him. His personal reaction to the corruption he saw was outrage; it is his identification with the exploited workers and his naturalistic descriptions of the oppressive industrial conditions that make *The Jungle* so gripping.

As Sinclair explains in his memoirs, *American Outpost*, he returned to his farm in New Jersey after he had collected his data on the meat-packing industry in Chicago and started writing the novel on Christmas Day, completing it in the summer of 1905 after less than six months' work. Although it was published in serial form as it was being written, Sinclair had trouble finding a publisher for the book; it was refused by five houses before Doubleday & Company took it after their lawyers made a careful investigation to avoid any possible libel suits. When *The Jungle* was published in February, 1906, the public was horrified, not by the novel's account of the conditions of the workers as Sinclair and his socialist friends expected, but by the naturalistic descriptions of the slaughterhouses and the evidence of criminal negligence in meat inspection. *The Jungle*, like most of Sinclair's fiction, straddles genres; it is partly a novel and partly exposé journalism. Sinclair's purpose in writing the book was to protest the exploitation of the workers and to recommend socialism as a corrective ideology to capitalism; the revelations of unsanitary packing-plant procedures were only a means to those ends. Hardly a dozen pages of this long novel are explicitly concerned with the repugnant details of the slaughterhouse, yet what remains in the reader's mind long after the plot line and thematic intentions fade are the scenes of grinding up poisoned rats, children's fingers, and carcasses of steers condemned as tubercular for canning meats; and the rendering of hogs dead of cholera for a fine grade of lard. Most dramatic of all, however, was Sinclair's report that the men who served in the cooking room occasionally fell into the boiling vats and were returned to the world transubstantiated into Durham's Pure Leaf Lard. The vividness of the author's descriptions had two effects: The first was an immediate drop in meat sales across America and Europe; the second was a summons to the White House to detail the abuses in the meat industry to President Theodore Roosevelt. The outraged public brought pressure to bear on politicians, and Congress enacted the Federal Pure Food and Drug Act of 1906.

The sensational revelations of *The Jungle* have drawn attention from the book's literary qualities. *The Jungle* has been compared to the polemical late works of Leo

Tolstoy and to the naturalistic fiction of Émile Zola because of its pessimistic determinism. The setting is the grim slums of Chicago and the gory stockyards. The novel tells the story of a group of recent Lithuanian immigrants who have been lured to America from their old-world villages with promise of high wages.

Jurgis Rudkus, the novel's principal character, comes to the stockyard district, along with several of his friends and relatives, expecting to realize the American Dream, little aware that they have entered a jungle. Unable to speak English, the immigrants are exploited by almost everyone in power—the politicians, the police, the landlords, and the "Beef Trust" bosses. Jurgis has to pay his foreman part of his low salary to keep his job. He is cheated by a crooked real-estate agent, who sells him a house with a hidden clause which allows the mortgage company to foreclose on Jurgis. After losing his house, Jurgis and his family are afflicted with misery. His job is taken away after he is blacklisted; he serves a jail term for slugging his wife's lascivious boss, who has compromised her honor. In turn, his father dies of disease, his wife and infant son die in childbirth, and finally, he loses his last son in a drowning accident. Jurgis is left without anything; alone and in ill health, he is a broken man. He becomes a hobo, a petty criminal, and a strike-breaking scab—the lowest form of degradation for him.

In his extremity, Jurgis for the first time reflects upon how unjustly he has been treated by society, which he begins to regard as his enemy, but his views are inchoate. One day, by chance he hears a Socialist speak. The lecture transforms his conception of the world; socialism is like a revelation, for now there is a way by which the workers of the world can win respect. With Jurgis's conversion, the novel as a narrative ends for all practical purposes. The last chapters are devoted to socialist propaganda and socioeconomic analysis. The optimistic conclusion of the novel contrasts sharply with the pessimistic naturalism of the first chapters. Ironically, and to Sinclair's disappointment, the appeal to socialism and the protest against wage-slavery did not win the hearts and minds of his audience, but his realistic portrayal of conditions in the meatpacking industry (as he once remarked) surely turned the stomach of the nation.

The Jungle will never be placed in the first rank of American fiction because of its mixture of fictional and journalistic elements, its unresolved contradictions in theme, and its melodramatic plot and bifurcated structure. Sinclair tried to do too many things at once, and he was only partially successful. Most readers think that the true significance of Sinclair's achievement in *The Jungle* lies in the uncensored presentation of the conditions of working-class life. Only Stephen Crane in *Maggie: A Girl of the Streets* (1893) had dealt with slum subjects with such integrity, and Sinclair had no models to follow in depicting this strata of society. In his firsthand observations and deep compassion for the oppressed, he was breaking new ground for literary treatment, which Theodore Dreiser would follow to different purposes.

The Metropolis, The Moneychangers, and *Love's Pilgrimage* · Following the success of *The Jungle* was difficult for Sinclair. He spent the next eight years trying to repeat what he had done with his first and best "muckracking" book. He produced a number of novels focused on specific problems, but at the other end of the social scale. *The Metropolis* is an exposé of conspicuous consumption among upper-class New York socialites. It is a poor book by Sinclair's own admission and is remarkable only for the absence of socialistic sermons by the author. Sinclair, like F. Scott Fitzgerald, apparently believed that money sets the very wealthy quite apart from the rest of society, but, rather than seeking rapport with his wealthy characters, as Fitzgerald did,

Sinclair hoped to reform them. Another novel of this period, *The Moneychangers*, is a story of the machinations of a high financier, obviously patterned on J. P. Morgan; the story tells of the exploits of Dan Waterman, the elderly head of the Steel Trust, who creates a panic on Wall Street purely for personal revenge against a rival steel magnate. Although *The Moneychangers* is not very good fiction, it does have an interesting premise, suggesting a connection between sexual desire and the drive for financial power.

Another novel of this period that deserves mention for its subject is *Love's Pilgrimage*; neofeminist in theme, this work examines the pressures on Sinclair's own marriage because of his male insensitivity to his wife's personal, sexual, and intellectual needs. The novel is also interesting for the insight it offers into Sinclair's personality, for he candidly implies that the divorce his first wife sought was deserved because he prudishly withheld from sexual relations on the theory that it would decrease his creative energy.

King Coal · In 1914, Sinclair was remarried and living in California. The transition in his life resulted in a change in his writing. In the West, Sinclair was drawn back to the problems of the proletariat by labor strife in the Colorado coal mines. As a result of the attempt by the United Mine Workers to organize the miners, the govenor of Colorado had called up the state militia to break up strikes. In 1914, in the town of Ludlow, National Guard troops fired into a camp of strikers and their families, killing eleven women and two children. This shocking event outraged Sinclair as nothing had since he had witnessed the brutal conditions of the stockyards. Following the methods he had used to collect background material for *The Jungle*, he went to Colorado, visited the miners and their families, and talked with the mining officials and labor leaders. His direct contact with the working-class people stirred his emotions and gave him a more realistic point of departure for his next novel, *King Coal*, than any he had employed since *The Jungle*. In fact, *King Coal* was an attempt to repeat the same sort of muckraking performance that had succeeded so well in the former case. Unfortunately for Sinclair, *King Coal* did not create the response aroused by *The Jungle*, a fact largely resulting from the lag time in the publication of the novel. When *King Coal* appeared in 1917, the events in Ludlow were three years old and yesterday's news. America had just entered World War I, and the nation's mind was on "doughboys" rather than on coal miners.

The poor reception of *King Coal* was a great disappointment to Sinclair, because he knew he had produced the kind of novel he wrote best. *King Coal*, while not as powerful as *The Jungle*, has the rhetorical strength and the factual validity of the earlier book. Sinclair tells the story of a rich young man named Hal Warner, who impersonates a coal miner in order to investigate working conditions in the western coal camps. He becomes a union sympathizer and labor agitator after he becomes convinced that the mine owners are denying the miners their legal rights and are cheating them out of their wages by rigged scales. After witnessing the futility of getting justice for working men inside the legal system, the miners go on a wildcat strike. Hal convinces his coworkers to join the union, and the novel ends with the lines drawn between labor and management while Hal returns to college, vowing to continue his fight for the working people of America.

Although *King Coal* is not as powerful in its naturalistic details as *The Jungle* and lacks the pessimistic determinism of that novel, it is in the opinion of most critics Sinclair's second-best effort at muckraking. If very few Americans responded to

Sinclair's account of the dangers of cave-ins, coal dust, and explosions, this result may be because they were never exposed to such perils, whereas all were subject to health hazards as a result of unsanitary food processing. For this reason, the exposé of negligence in Chicago meat-packing plants had a much more profound and practical effect than the exposé of the inhuman conditions in the coal camps of Colorado.

Oil! A Novel **and** *Boston* · Between World War I and the start of the Depression, Sinclair wrote two remarkable novels based on topical social or political situations. *Oil! A Novel* delves into the Tea Pot Dome and other oil scandals of the Harding administration, and thus has considerable historical significance as well as being one of Sinclair's most readable books. *Boston*, on the other hand, represents Sinclair's best use of a contemporary event for fictional purposes. This novel enfolds the drama of the Sacco-Vanzetti case, but it also encompasses the whole of Boston's society, suggesting that the city itself was responsible for what happened in this tragic case. The central character is again from the upper classes, an elderly Back Bay aristocrat, Cornelia Thornwell, wife to a governor. Full of vitality and intelligence, she thinks that she has spent her life as an artificial adornment to a great family. She determines late in life to emancipate herself from mores and manners of the mansion, and moves out to board with the Brini family, who are honest Italian mill hands, and starts to earn her own living in a factory.

At this point, Vanzetti enters the story. During a strike in the mill, he plays an important role in keeping up the workers' spirits. He also prevents them from organizing, because as an anarchist, Vanzetti did not support unions. Afterward, Vanzetti and his friend Sacco are marked as "anarchist wops" by the police. They are picked up as suspects in a payroll robbery, and in the midst of the deportation mania of the postwar period, the city's reason and sense of justice are beclouded. The courts, judge, jury, and prosecutor seem determined to make the foreigners pay—if not for the crime, then for their politics. The climax of the novel comes when the cogs of justice bring the proletarian saints, Vanzetti and Sacco, to the electric chair with many doubts about their guilt still lingering.

Through a blending of fact and fiction, Sinclair is able to record a complex and tragic story of social injustice, although the story of the runaway grandmother does get lost in the final pages as the historical facts dominate the plot. As a novel, the two-volume *Boston* is too long except for readers with some special interest in the Sacco-Vanzetti case. As usual, Sinclair was writing for a mass audience, and the novel employs many stock characters and a melodramatic plot; furthermore, a statement of socialist doctrine forms a coda to the novel. Sinclair does, however, create a convincing portrait of Vanzetti. It is in Sinclair's account of the death of this man of dignity and intelligence that the novel gains its greatest power.

Lanny Budd series · The major literary effort of Sinclair's career was launched just before the outbreak of World War II: a ten-novel series offering a fictionalized history of the Western world in the first half of the twentieth century. The series is unified by its central character, Lanny Budd, and is known collectively by his name. One of the Lanny Budd novels, *Dragon's Teeth*, won for Sinclair a Pulitzer Prize in 1943. A chronicle of Germany's slide into Nazism, *Dragon's Teeth* is a scrupulous study of the fateful years between 1930 and 1934, and reflects an extensive research effort on Sinclair's part. In fact, several critics claimed that if the book were stripped of its fictional ingredient, it might well serve as a history text.

Sinclair creates an air of impending doom as he shows how quickly Europe was led to the abyss. His protagonist, Lanny Budd, is a neutral observer traveling the Continent with his millionaire wife, Irma, who is especially obtuse about economics, politics, and national traits. She is a foil to the sensitive and intelligent Lanny, who is aware of the coming crisis. Irma and her upper-class female friends refuse to believe that their smug routine of bridge and dinner parties will be disrupted. The reader in 1942 received these opinions with a great deal of dramatic irony. Meanwhile, Lanny grows increasingly concerned about the absence of morality in the political climate of Germany. Lanny has rather improbable meetings with the big-wigs of the Nazi regime. He goes hunting with Hermann Göring, has cocktails with Joseph Goebbels, and a discussion with Adolf Hitler about the Jewish question. His interest in this topic is not merely academic, since his sister is married to one of Germany's most prominent Jews. The Jews in Germany, however, are like Irma's circle; they refuse to face the realities of Nazism. The novel ends with Lanny's contriving to help his brother-in-law escape the dragon's teeth of the Nazi menace, closing the story on an exciting climax, somewhat like that of a cliffhanger film of the 1940's.

Sinclair continued the adventures of Lanny Budd, interweaving fiction with fact as he related the sequence of world events in *World's End* which covers the years 1913 to 1919; *Between Two Worlds* deals with the events between the Versailles Treaty and the stock market crash of 1929; the author then covers the Nazi "Blood Purge" of 1934 to the Spanish Civil War in *Wide Is the Gate*; the annexation of Austria, the invasion of Czechoslovakia, and the Munich pact in *Presidential Agent*; the fall of France in *Dragon Harvest*; and America's entry into the war in *A World to Win*. The years of Allied setbacks, 1941-1943, are covered in *Presidential Mission; One Clear Call* and *O Shepherd, Speak!* deal with the Normandy Invasion and the defeat of the German military machine; and in the sequel to the series, *The Return of Lanny Budd*, Sinclair brings events up to 1949 and the onset of the Cold War between the United States and the Soviet Union.

As a whole, this group of novels is interesting, in part simply because the series surveys a dramatic period of history in considerable detail. Throughout the series, Sinclair's careful research is evident, but the popularity of these novels was also a result of their appeal to patriotism. America's role as the savior of civilization is increasingly emphasized in the later novels in the series. During this period, Sinclair's confidence that progress was represented by socialism and Communism was shaken by the example of the Soviet Union. Like so many early twentieth century political radicals, he became an anti-Communist in the 1950's.

Sinclair was a propagandist first and a novelist second, if propaganda is defined as an "effort directed systematically toward the gaining of support for an opinion or course of action." He wrote millions of words trying to change, improve, or expose oppressive conditions. Because Sinclair so obviously used literature for ulterior purposes and because he was so prolific, serious critics have unduly neglected him; on the other hand, he has been overrated by those foreign critics who delight in finding indictments of America by an American writer. As time puts Sinclair's contribution to American literature into perspective, it seems certain that he will never be regarded as a great novelist, but he will fairly be judged an honest, courageous, and original writer.

Hallman B. Bryant

Other major works

PLAYS: *Plays of Protest*, pb. 1912; *Hell: A Verse Drama and Photo-Play*, pb. 1923; *The Millennium*, pb. 1924; *The Pot Boiler*, pb. 1924; *Singing Jailbirds*, pb. 1924; *Bill Porter*, pb. 1925; *Wally for Queen!*, pb. 1936; *Marie Antoinette*, pb. 1939; *A Giant's Strength*, pr., pb. 1948.

NONFICTION: *Our Bourgeois Literature*, 1904; *The Industrial Republic*, 1907; *The Fasting Cure*, 1911; *The Profits of Religion*, 1918; *The Brass Check: A Study in American Journalism*, 1919; *The Book of Life, Mind, and Body*, 1921; *The Goose-Step: A Study of American Education*, 1923; *The Goslings: A Study of the American Schools*, 1924; *Mammonart*, 1925; *Letters to Judd*, 1925; *Money Writes!*, 1927; *Mental Radio*, 1930; *American Outpost: A Book of Reminiscences*, 1932; *I, Governor of California and How I Ended Poverty*, 1933; *The Way Out—What Lies Ahead for America?*, 1933; *The EPIC Plan for California*, 1934; *What God Means to Me*, 1936; *Terror in Russia: Two Views*, 1938; *Expect No Peace!*, 1939; *A Personal Jesus*, 1952; *The Cup of Fury*, 1956; *My Lifetime in Letters*, 1960; *The Autobiography of Upton Sinclair*, 1962.

CHILDREN'S LITERATURE: *The Gnomobile: A Gnice Gnew Gnarrative with Gnonsense, but Gnothing Gnaughty*, 1936.

Bibliography

Colburn, David R., and George E. Pozzetta, eds. *Reform and Reformers in the Progressive Era*. Westport, Conn.: Greenwood Press, 1983. An essay by Judson Grenier examines Sinclair's position as a muckraker and his role in inspiring Progressive reforms. Unlike other journalistic writers, Sinclair was personally and ideologically committed.

Dell, Floyd. *Upton Sinclair: A Study in Social Protest*. New York: AMS Press, 1970. Dell's treatment of Sinclair's career analyzes the apparent discrepancy between his literary position in the United States and throughout the rest of the world. Personal incidents and psychological insights are intertwined with evaluations and interpretations of specific works. Contains a bibliography of out-of-print books and an index.

Harris, Leon. *Upton Sinclair: American Rebel*. New York: Thomas Y. Crowell, 1975. This biography traces Sinclair's rise from obscurity to fame, with his subsequent decline in popularity. The text provides interesting information regarding source materials for some of his novels. A section of photographs, extensive notes, a list of Sinclair's books, and an index complete the book.

Mookerjee, R. N. *Art for Social Justice: The Major Novels of Upton Sinclair*. Metuchen, N.J.: Scarecrow, 1988. Mookerjee, a critic of writers of the 1930's, provides a reevaluation of *The Jungle, King Coal, Oil! A Novel, Boston*, and the Lanny Budd series. This slender volume is a valid reminder of the pioneer role of Sinclair in the "documentary novel." Contains a good selected bibliography.

Scott, Ivan. *Upton Sinclair: The Forgotten Socialist*. Lewiston: Edwin Mellen Press, 1997. See especially chapters 1 and 2, "The Formation of Genius" and "*The Jungle*." In his introduction, Scott makes a good case for Sinclair's importance. A sound scholarly biography drawing extensively on the Sinclair collection at Lilly Library, the University of Indiana.

Yoder, Jon A. *Upton Sinclair*. New York: Frederick Ungar, 1975. Like some other critics, Yoder attributes Sinclair's "meager reputation" in part to his socialistic views. Five chapters in this slim volume examine various facets of the novelist's life and career. A chronology, notes, a bibliography, and an index supplement the text.

WALLACE STEGNER

Born: Lake Mills, Iowa; February 18, 1909
Died: Santa Fe, New Mexico; April 13, 1993

Principal long fiction · *Remembering Laughter*, 1937; *The Potter's House*, 1938; *On a Darkling Plain*, 1940; *Fire and Ice*, 1941; *The Big Rock Candy Mountain*, 1943; *Second Growth*, 1947; *The Preacher and the Slave*, 1950; *A Shooting Star*, 1961; *All the Little Live Things*, 1967; *Angle of Repose*, 1971; *The Spectator Bird*, 1976; *Recapitulation*, 1979; *Joe Hill*, 1980; *Crossing to Safety*, 1987.

Other literary forms · Wallace Stegner also published two collections of short fiction, *The Women on the Wall* (1950) and *The City of the Living and Other Stories* (1956); two biographies, *Beyond the Hundredth Meridian: John Wesley Powell and the Second Opening of the West* (1954) and *The Uneasy Chair: A Biography of Bernard De Voto* (1974); a collection of critical essays, *The Writer in America* (1951); a historical monograph, *The Gathering of Zion: The Story of the Mormon Trail* (1964); and two volumes of personal essays on the Western experience. *Wolf Willow: A History, a Story, and a Memory of the Last Plains Frontier* (1962) and *The Sound of Mountain Water* (1969). Stegner also published a number of edited works, both nonfiction and fiction.

Achievements · Stegner would have three distinct audiences after the start of his career: the popular magazine audience; readers interested in modern American literature; and a regional audience interested in the culture and history of the American West. From the 1930's, he published seventy-two short stories, with fifty of them appearing in such magazines as *Harper's, Mademoiselle, Collier's, Cosmopolitan, Esquire, Redbook, The Atlantic Monthly, The Inter-Mountain Review,* and the *Virginia Quarterly*. Bernard De Voto, Van Wyck Brooks, and Sinclair Lewis recognized his talent early, and De Voto was instrumental in encouraging Stegner to continue writing. Stegner enjoyed a solid critical reputation as a regional American writer concerned largely with the problems and themes of the western American experience.

He also won numerous honors throughout his career. He was elected to the American Academy of Arts and Sciences and the National Academy of Arts and Letters, and he was awarded fellowships by Phi Beta Kappa, the Huntington Library, The Center for Advanced Studies in the Behavioral Sciences, and by the Guggenheim, Rockefeller, and Wintergreen Foundations. In 1937, he won the Little, Brown Novelette Prize for *Remembering Laughter*. He also won the O. Henry Memorial Award for short stories in 1942, 1948, and 1950, and in 1971 he won the Pulitzer Prize for Fiction for his *Angle of Repose*. Other awards for his work include the Houghton Mifflin Life-in-America Award in 1945 and the Commonwealth Club Gold Medal in 1968. In 1981, he became the first recipient of the Robert Kirsch Award for Life Achievement in the *Los Angeles Times* Book Awards.

As a master of narrative technique and a respected literary craftsman, Stegner had the opportunity to influence many young writers associated with the Stanford University Creative Writing Program, where he taught from 1945 to 1971, including Eugene Burdick, one of the authors of *The Ugly American* (1958), Ken Kesey, and Thomas

McGuane. His own theory of literature is rather traditional and appears in his only extended piece of criticism, *The Writer in America.* The creative process, he believed, is basically the imposition of form upon personal experience. The committed writer must discipline himself to the difficult work of creation, choosing significant images from the insignificant and selecting significant actions for his characters. The writer must change the disorderliness of memory into symmetry without violating his readers' sense of what is true to life.

Biography · Wallace Earle Stegner was born on February 18, 1909, in Lake Mills, Iowa, the second son of George and Hilda Paulson Stegner. He was descended from Norwegian farmers on his mother's side and unknown ancestors on his father's side. His father was a drifter and a resourceful gambler–a searcher for the main chance, the big bonanza. In Stegner's early years, the family moved often, following his father's dream of striking it rich, from Grand Forks, North Dakota, to Bellingham, Washington, to Redmond, Oregon, to East End Saskatchewan, where they lived from 1914 to 1921. East End left him with memories of people and landscapes that played an important role in *The Big Rock Candy Mountain.* The family moved in 1921 to Salt Lake City, Utah, where Stegner attended high school and began college. Here, Stegner went through the pains of adolescence and, although not himself a Mormon, he developed a strong attachment to the land and a sympathy for Mormon culture and values, which are reflected in his later books such as *Mormon Country* (1942), *The Gathering of Zion,* and *Recapitulation.*

From 1925 to 1930, Stegner attended the University of Utah, where he balanced his interest in girls and his studies with a job selling rugs and linoleum in the family business of a close friend. By a fortunate chance, he studied freshman English with Vardis Fisher, then a budding novelist, and Fisher helped stimulate Stegner's growing interest in creative writing. In 1930, he entered the graduate program at the University of Iowa, completing his M.A. in 1932 and completing his Ph.D. in 1935 with a dissertation on the Utah naturalist Clarence Dutton, entitled "Clarence Edward Dutton: Geologist and Man of Letters," later revised and published as *Clarence Edward Dutton: An Appraisal* by the University of Utah in 1936. This work fed his interest in the history of the American West and the life of the explorer John Wesley Powell, the subject of his *Beyond the Hundredth Meridian.* Teaching English and creative writing occupied him for several years, beginning with a one-year stint at tiny Augustana College in Illinois in 1934. Next, he went to the University of Utah until 1937, moving from there to teach freshman English at the University of Wisconsin for two years. He also taught at the Bread Loaf School of English in Vermont for several summers and enjoyed the friendship of Robert Frost, Bernard De Voto, and Theodore Morrison. In 1940, he accepted a part-time position at Harvard University in the English writing program. There, during the Depression, he was involved in literary debates between the literary left, led by F. O. Matthiessen, and the conservative De Voto.

In 1945, Stegner accepted a professorship in creative writing at Stanford University, where he remained for twenty-six years until his retirement in 1971. The Stanford years were his most productive; he produced a total of thirteen books in this period. In 1950, he made an around-the-world lecture tour, researched his family's past in Saskatchewan and Norway, and spent much of the year as writer-in-residence at the American Academy in Rome. He was also an active environmentalist long before ecology became fashionable. During the Kennedy administration, he served as Assistant to the Secretary of the Interior (1961) and as a member of the National Parks Advisory Board (1962).

Analysis · Wallace Stegner was a regional writer in the best sense. His settings, his characters, and his plots derive from the Western experience, but his primary concern is with the meaning of that experience. Geographically, Stegner's region runs from Minnesota and Grand Forks, North Dakota, through Utah and northern Colorado. It is the country where Stegner lived and experienced his youth. Scenes from this region appear frequently in his novels. East End, Saskatchewan, the place of his early boyhood, appears as Whitemud, Saskatchewan, in *The Big Rock Candy Mountain*, along with Grand Forks and Lake Mills, Iowa, his birthplace. Salt Lake City figures prominently in *Recapitulation* and *The Preacher and the Slave*, the story of Joe Hill, a union martyr. *Wolf Willow*, furthermore, is historical fiction, a kind of history of East End, Saskatchewan, where he spent his early boyhood, and *On a Darkling Plain* is the story of a much decorated and seriously wounded veteran of World War I who withdraws from society in an isolated shack on the plains outside of East End.

In a much larger sense, Stegner is concerned with the spiritual West–the West as an idea or a consciousness–and with the significance of the Western values and traditions. He is also concerned with the basic American cultural conflict between East and West and with the importance of frontier values in American history. Bo Mason, modeled after Stegner's father, the abusive head of the Mason family in *The Big Rock Candy Mountain*, is an atavism, a character who may have been at home in the early frontier, who searches for the elusive pot of gold–the main chance of the Western myth. Never content with domestic life or with stability, Bo Mason, like George Stegner, moves his family from town to town always looking for an easy fortune. As a man of mixed qualities–fierce pride, resourcefulness, self-reliance, and a short, violent temper–he is ill at ease in the postfrontier West, always chafing at the stability of community and family ties. He continually pursues the old Western myth of isolated individualism that preceded twentieth century domestication of the region. He might have made a good mountain man. Stegner stresses his impact on his family and community and shows the reader the basic tragedy of this frontier type trapped in a patterned world without easy bonanzas.

In *Angle of Repose*, Stegner explores the conflict between the values of self-reliance, impermanence, and Western optimism and the Eastern sense of culture, stability, and tradition. In a way, this is the basic conflict between Ralph Waldo Emerson's party of hope (the West) and the party of the past (the East). He also explores the idea of community as a concept alien to the Western myth. Indeed, community as the close-knit cooperation between individuals is shown in Stegner's work as the thing that ended the frontier. In *The Big Rock Candy Mountain* and in *Recapitulation*, there is a longing for community and a pervasive feeling that the Mason family is always outside the culture in which it exists, particularly in Utah, where Mormon culture is portrayed as innocent, solid, stable, and as a result attractive. Mormon life is characterized by the absence of frontier individualism and by a belief in permanence and group experience, an anomaly in the Western experience.

The Big Rock Candy Mountain · A third major concern throughout Stegner's work is his own identity and the meaning of Western identity. Bruce Mason in *The Big Rock Candy Mountain* is much concerned with his relationship as an adolescent to the Utah culture and its sense of community.

The Big Rock Candy Mountain, Stegner's fifth novel, is an obviously autobiographical account of his childhood and adolescence. A family saga, the novel follows the history of the rootless Mason family as it follows the dreams of Bo Mason, a thinly disguised version of Stegner's father, as he leads them to Grand Forks, North Dakota, to the lumber camps of Washington, then back to Iowa and up to Whitemud, Saskatchewan, and finally to Salt Lake City and Reno. Family identity problems are played out against the backdrop of an increasingly civilized and domesticated West against which the self-reliant and short-tempered character of Bo Mason stands out in stark relief. His qualities, which might have had virtues in the early settlement of the West, create family tensions and trauma that cause Bruce Mason (Stegner) to develop a hatred for his father only partially tempered by a grudging respect. Bo Mason relentlessly pursues the American Dream and the Western myth of easy success rooted in the early frontier: He endlessly pursues the Big Rock Candy Mountain.

Throughout this odyssey, the family longs for stability and community, for a place to develop roots. Even in Salt Lake City, where Bruce spends his adolescence, Bo keeps the family changing houses to hide his bootlegging business during the Prohibition period. His activities in the midst of puritanical Mormon culture only highlight the contrast between the Masons and the dominant community. Even in his later years, Bo pursues his dream in Reno by operating a gambling house.

Stegner vividly illustrates how this rootless wandering affects family members. Else, Bo's wife, representing the feminine, domesticating impulse, is a saintly character—long-suffering, gentle, and protective of her two sons. She longs for a home with permanence but never finds it. Her initial good nature and mild optimism eventually give way to pessimism as resettlements continue. Three of the family members die: Else is destroyed by cancer; Chet, the other son, who is defeated by both marriage and career, dies young of pneumonia; and Bo, with all his dreams shattered and involved with a cheap whore after Else's death, shoots himself. Only Bruce is left to make sense of his family's experiences, and he attempts to understand his place in the family saga as he strives to generalize his family's history. In the final philosophical and meditative chapters, Stegner tries to link Bruce (and therefore himself) to history, to some sense of continuity and tradition. His family history, with its crudeness and tensions, is made to represent the history of the frontier West with its similar tensions and rough edges. Bruce, who long sought solace and identity in books, excels in school and finally follows the civilized but ironic path of going to law school at the University of Minnesota. He has, finally, reached a higher level of culture than his family ever attained. *The Big Rock Candy Mountain* has achieved a reputation as a classic of American regionalism, while it also deals with broader national themes and myths.

Angle of Repose · *Angle of Repose*, published in 1971 and awarded the Pulitzer Prize for Fiction, is regarded by many critics as Stegner's most finely crafted novel. The metaphoric title is a mining and geological term designating the slope at which rocks cease to fall, the angle of rest. Stegner uses it to apply to the last thirty years of the marriage of Susan Burling and Oliver Ward, two opposite personalities, after their often chaotic early married years. This ambitious work, covering four generations, is a fictionalized biography of the turn-of-the-century writer and illustrator Mary Hallock Foote (1847-1930) and her marriage to Arthur De Wint Foote, an idealistic pioneer and self-educated mining engineer.

Lyman Ward, the narrator, was reared by his grandparents Susan Burling Ward and Oliver Ward, fictionalized versions of the Footes, and is a retired history professor from Berkeley who was crippled in middle age by a progressively arthritic condition. He has been transformed by the disease into a grotesque creature who loses first his leg and then his wife Ellen, who runs off with the surgeon who amputated Lyman's leg. Bitter and disillusioned by his wife's behavior and his son Rodman's radical idealism and contempt for the past, he retires to Grass Valley, California, to write his grandparents' biography. Here, he is assisted by Shelly Hawkes, a Berkeley dropout who shares Rodman's attitude toward history.

As he reads through his grandparents' correspondence, he simultaneously recounts the development of their marriage and discovers the dynamics of their personalities. Susan Ward, cultured, educated in the East, and artistically talented, marries Oliver Ward, an idealistic mining engineer, her second choice for a husband. Without having resolved her disappointment at his lack of culture and appreciation for the arts, she marries him and begins two decades of following him through the West as he looks for professional and financial success in the unstable mining industry. The years in New Almeden, California, Leadville, Colorado, Michoacán, Mexico, and southern Idaho increasingly wear Susan down, despite brief interludes of stability and the frequent company of other Eastern scientists and engineers during her Western exile.

In Boise Canyon, Idaho, as Oliver's grand irrigation project falls apart, Susan falls into infidelity with Frank Sargent, Oliver's colorful assistant, and steals away to the countryside under the pretext of taking five-year-old Agnes Ward for a walk. Soon, Agnes's body is found floating in a nearby canal, and the day after her funeral, Frank Sargent commits suicide. Suspecting the worst, Oliver leaves his wife for two years until persuaded to return. For the remaining fifty years of their marriage, Oliver treats her with a kind silence and lack of physical affection, never truly forgiving her infidelity. Lyman learns that his grandparents' angle of repose was not the real thing, not a time of harmony, but a cold truce full of human weakness. His naïve image of his grandparents based on childhood memories is undercut as he comes to understand them in a more sophisticated way. He learns to respect their strength and complexity.

Lyman's discoveries are all the more poignant because of the similarities between his grandparents' experience and his own relationship with an unfaithful wife who has broken trust, and who, it is implied, will seek a reconciliation. As in *The Big Rock Candy Mountain*, the two main characters symbolize two conflicting impulses in the settlement of the West—Oliver, the dreamer and idealist, pursuing his vision of success in a world with few amenities, and Susan, the finely cultured Easterner, yearning for stability and society. Lyman discovers links between his family's past and present and encounters universals of history such as suffering and infidelity which are more poignant to him because he discovers them in his own family history. Finally, the novel suggests that frontier values and the civilizing impulses need their own angle of repose. In essence, American experience had not yet reached its angle of rest; frontier and domestic values lie instead in a kind of uneasy truce.

Recapitulation · A continuation of the family saga played out in *The Big Rock Candy Mountain, Recapitulation*, published in 1979, is the moving drama of Bruce Mason's return to Salt Lake City to face his past. Toward the end of a successful career as a diplomat in the United States Foreign Service, Mason returns to the scene of his turbulent adolescence and the death of his family to attend his maiden aunt's funeral. Upon his arrival at the funeral home, the attendant presents him with a message to call Joe Mulder, his best friend in high school and in college at the University of Utah.

Bruce was virtually a member of Joe's family for three years during the time when his father's bootlegging business threatened to jeopardize his social life.

Bruce remembers the 1920's and his adolescence before the stock market crash. Trying to find himself, he slowly remembers the time when he was an outsider in Mormon country, a time when he found many of the values that sustained him after the death of his family. Well-liked in high school by his teachers, Bruce was also picked on by the bigger boys and the less able students and acutely embarrassed by the family's house, which doubled as a speakeasy. His first major romance with Nola, a Mormon country girl who was half American Indian, led to his first sexual encounter. Bruce was infatuated with her but knew her intellectual limits—that ideas put her to sleep and art bored her. Throughout the narrative, he recounts the disintegration of his family during his adolescence.

Stegner stresses Bruce's close relationship with Joe Mulder, but Bruce is emotionally incapable of meeting Joe because he hates being treated as "The Ambassador," a visiting dignitary—a title that would only exaggerate the changes and losses of the past forty-five years. In a sense, he finds that he cannot go home again. He would have nothing in common with Joe except memories of adolescent love affairs and youthful myths. Their past could never be altered or renewed.

A second major theme in *Recapitulation* is the need to belong to some larger community. The Mormon sense of community, whatever its intellectual failings, is viewed nostalgically. Bruce envies the close-knit families of his friends. Nola's family, for example, seems like a tribe, a culture unto itself full of unspoken values and understandings. His decision to attend law school in Minnesota irrevocably removes him from Nola, Utah, his adolescence, and ultimately from his chance to belong. When he returns to Utah, he is in the later stages of a successful but lonely adult life. His first job out of law school was in Saudi Arabia—a place without available women. He finally becomes a Middle Eastern specialist and a permanent bachelor.

Stegner ends the novel with Bruce, lonely, nostalgic, and emotionally incomplete, unable to make contact with Joe Mulder and with his past in a satisfying way. Even though the act of thinking through his past has served him therapeutically, he will continue as a diplomat, making formal contacts with people, living in the surface world of protocol, unable to connect emotionally with people. As the last of his family, he is a solitary figure, a man of deep feelings which he is unable to express. He is, finally, a man who has partially tamed the frontier restlessness and anger of his father and risen above his family's self-destructive tendencies. Still, Bruce carries on the family's feeling of rootlessness, in a more formal, acceptable way. In the Foreign Service, he never develops roots and is shifted from one diplomatic post to another. In a more formal sense than his father, Bruce is still a drifter. Stegner ends the novel fittingly with Bruce Mason being called back to the diplomatic service as United States Representative to an important OPEC meeting in Caracas, Venezuela, reluctantly pulled away from his efforts to understand his past.

Crossing to Safety · *Crossing to Safety* introduces a new set of characters but also is about coming to terms with the past. Larry and Sally Morgan are a young couple who have moved to Madison, Wisconsin, because Larry has been given a teaching post for a year at the university there. Almost magically, they meet a personable young couple like themselves, Sid and Charity Lang, who also turn out to be very generous. In these Depression days, security is the most sought-after item, and all the young academics vie furiously for tenure. Yet, the Langs (though engaged as furiously in the contest as any) bestow on the Morgans a friendship rare in this backbiting atmosphere—wholehearted, sincere, and giving. Envy and jealousy are not part of their emotional makeup, though they do have their problems. Charity comes from an academic household (her father is a professor), and she wants the same for her family, including a professorship for her husband, who, however, really wants only to write poetry.

Stegner's portrayal of this lifelong friendship is neither idealistic nor blind. He reveals the human sides to his characters, keeping this paragon of *amicitia* from being falsely perfect. The ups and downs of their lives are relayed through flashback: Larry and Sally have come to visit the Langs because Charity is dying from cancer. Larry and Sally's life has not been without tragedy either. The summer after bearing their first child, Sally contracts polio and is crippled by it.

Ultimately, Larry becomes a successful writer, while Sid never becomes successful either as an academic or as a poet. Belying her name—for she is a strong personality at best, harsh and unyielding at worst—Charity never really forgives Sid for his failure. Yet, Stegner concentrates on the love these people have for one another through thick and thin, creating a compelling story without resorting to tricks of subterfuge or violence to sustain the reader's interest. Stegner's great strength lies in knowing people; he knows their quirks and foibles so well that they come alive on the page without being demeaned or caricatured. In addition, his feeling for mood and setting are twin talents that infuse his writing with life, placing Stegner firmly on the short list of great American novelists.

Richard H. Dillman

Other major works

SHORT FICTION: *The Women on the Wall,* 1950; *The City of the Living and Other Stories,* 1956; *Collected Stories of Wallace Stegner,* 1990.

NONFICTION: *Mormon Country,* 1942; *One Nation,* 1945 (with the editors of *Look*); *Look at America: The Central Northwest,* 1947; *The Writer in America,* 1951; *Beyond the Hundredth Meridian: John Wesley Powell and the Second Opening of the West,* 1954; *Wolf Willow: A History, a Story, and a Memory of the Last Plains Frontier,* 1962; *The Gathering of Zion: The Story of the Mormon Trail,* 1964; *The Sound of Mountain Water,* 1969; *The Uneasy Chair: A Biography of Bernard De Voto,* 1974; *Ansel Adams: Images 1923-1974,* 1974; *One Way to Spell Man,* 1982; *The American West as Living Space,* 1987; *On the Teaching of Creative Writing: Responses to a Series of Questions,* 1988 (Edward Connery Lathem, editor); *Where the Bluebird Sings to the Lemonade Springs: Living and Writing in the West,* 1992.

EDITED TEXTS: *An Exposition Workshop,* 1939; *Readings for Citizens at War,* 1941; *Stanford Short Stories, 1946,* 1947 (with Richard Scowcroft); *The Writer's Art: A Collection of Short Stories,* 1950 (with Scowcroft and Boris Ilyin); *This Is Dinosaur: The Echo Park and Its Magic Rivers,* 1955; *The Exploration of the Colorado River of the West,* 1957; *Great American Short Stories,* 1957 (with Mary Stegner); *Selected American Prose: The Realistic Movement,* 1958; *Report on the Lands of the Arid Region of the United States,* 1962; *Modern Composition,* 1964 (4 volumes); *The American Novel: From Cooper to Faulkner,* 1965; *Twenty Years of Stanford Short Stories,* 1966; *The Letters of Bernard De Voto,* 1975.

Bibliography
Arthur, Anthony, ed. *Critical Essays on Wallace Stegner.* Boston: G. K. Hall, 1982. Two sections divided into reviews and articles and essays. Includes treatments of several

Stegner novels, especially *Big Rock Candy Mountain* and *Angle of Repose,* and of his use of Western history. Includes an interview with Stegner and an introductory essay. No bibliography.

Burrows, Russell. "Wallace Stegner's Version of Pastoral." *Western American Literature* 25 (May, 1990): 15-25. In this article, Burrows discusses the importance of the topic of ecology in Stegner's fiction. The article includes some discussion of *Crossing to Safety,* but a more in-depth review (by Jackson J. Benson) of that book follows Burrows's article. Includes reference notes and a bibliography.

Lipson, Eden Ross. "Back to Work After Bora-Bora." *The New York Times Book Review* 92 (September 20, 1987): 14. This interview with Stegner includes his reflections on writing *Crossing to Safety* as well as a discussion of that novel.

Mosher, Howard Frank. "The Mastery of Wallace Stegner." *The Washington Post,* October 4, 1987. This review of *Crossing to Safety* includes some biographical information on Stegner as well as an in-depth discussion of the novel.

Robinson, Forrest Glen, and Margaret G. Robinson. *Wallace Stegner.* Boston: Twayne, 1977. Part of Twayne's United States Authors series, this volume provides a brief chronology of personal and professional events in Stegner's life and some general biographical information. After a discussion of his work, there are primary and secondary bibliographies and an index.

GERTRUDE STEIN

Born: Allegheny, Pennsylvania; February 3, 1874
Died: Neuilly-sur-Seine, France; July 27, 1946

Principal long fiction · *Three Lives*, 1909; *The Making of Americans*, 1925; *Lucy Church Amiably*, 1930; *A Long Gay Book*, 1932; *Ida, a Novel*, 1941; *Brewsie and Willie*, 1946; *Blood on the Dining-Room Floor*, 1948; *Things as They Are*, 1950 (later as *Quod Erat Demonstrandum*); *Mrs. Reynolds and Five Earlier Novelettes, 1931-1942*, 1952; *A Novel of Thank You*, 1958.

Other literary forms · Any attempt to separate Gertrude Stein's novels from her other kinds of writing must be highly arbitrary. Stein thought the novel to be a failed literary form in the twentieth century, claiming that no real novels had been written after Marcel Proust and even including her own novelistic efforts in this assessment. For this and other reasons, it might be claimed that few, if any, of Stein's works are novels in any traditional sense. In fact, very few of Stein's more than six hundred titles in more than forty books can be adequately classified into any traditional literary forms. Her philosophy of composition was so idiosyncratic, her prose style so seemingly nonrational, that her writing bears little resemblance to whatever genre it purports to represent. Depending on one's definition of the novel, Stein wrote anywhere between six and twelve novels, ranging in length from less than one hundred to 925 pages. The problem is that none of Stein's "novels" has a plot in any conventional sense, that few have conventionally developed and sustained characters, and that several seem almost exclusively autobiographical, more diaries and daybooks than anything else. It is not any easier to categorize her other pieces of writing, most of which are radically *sui generis*. If references to literary forms are made very loosely, Stein's work can be divided into novels, autobiographies, portraits, poems, lectures, operas, plays, and explanations. Other than her novels, her best-known works are *The Autobiography of Alice B. Toklas* (1933); *Tender Buttons* (1914); *Four Saints in Three Acts* (1934); *Lectures in America* (1935); *Everybody's Autobiography* (1937); and *Portraits and Prayers*, 1934.

Achievements · Whether towering or crouching, Stein is ubiquitous in contemporary literature. A child of the nineteenth century who staunchly adhered to many of its values halfway through the twentieth, she nevertheless dedicated her creative life to the destruction of nineteenth century concepts of artistic order and purpose. In her own words, she set out to do nothing less than to kill a century, to lay the old ways of literary convention to rest. She later boasted that "the most serious thinking about the nature of literature in the twentieth century has been done by a woman," and her claim has great merit. During the course of her career, Stein finally managed to convince almost everyone that there was indeed some point, if not profundity, in her aggressively enigmatic style. The ridicule and parody that frustrated so much of her early work had turned to grudging tolerance or outright lionizing by 1934, when Stein made her triumphant American lecture tour; for the last fifteen or so years of her life, she was published even if her editor had not the vaguest idea of what she was doing (as Bennett Cerf later admitted he had not). On the most concrete level, Stein's distinctive prose style is remarkably significant even when its philosophical dimensions are ignored. William Gass has observed, Stein "did more with sentences, and understood them better, than any writer ever has."

More important was Stein's influence on other leaders in the development of modernism. As a student of William James, a friend of Alfred North Whitehead and Pablo Picasso, Stein lived at the center of the philosophical and artistic revolutions of the twentieth century. She was the natural emblem for modernism, and in her person, career, and legend, many of its salient issues converged. In the light of more recent developments in the novel and in literary theory, it has also been argued that Stein was the first postmodernist, the first writer to claim openly that the instance of language is itself as important as the reality to which it refers. Among major writers, Ernest Hemingway was most obviously influenced by his association with her, but her genius was freely acknowledged by F. Scott Fitzgerald, Sherwood Anderson, and Thornton Wilder. William Saroyan explained her influence most directly when he asserted that no American writer could keep from coming under it, a sentiment reluctantly echoed by Edmund Wilson in *Axel's Castle* (1931), even before Stein's great popular success in the mid-1930's.

Biography · Gertrude Stein was born on February 3, 1874, in Allegheny, Pennsylvania, but she was seven before her family settled into permanent residence in Oakland, California, the city she was later to describe as having "no there there." Her birth itself was contingent on the deaths of two of her five brothers and sisters: her parents had decided to have only five children, and only after two children had died in infancy were Gertrude and her older brother, Leo, conceived. Identity was to become one of the central preoccupations of her writing career, and the tenuous nature of her own birth greatly influenced that concern.

Stein's early years were comfortably bourgeois and uneventful. Her father, a vice-president of the Union Street Municipal Railway System in San Francisco, was authoritarian, moody, aggressive, but vacillating, and he may have helped foster her sense of independence, but he undoubtedly left her annoyed by him in particular and by fatherhood in general. Her mother barely figured in her life at all: A pale, withdrawn, ineffectual woman, she left most of the rearing of her children to governesses. By the time Stein was seventeen, both parents had died and she had grown even closer to her immediate older brother, Leo. In 1893, she entered Harvard Annex (renamed Radcliffe College the following year), thus rejoining Leo, who was a student at Harvard. There, Stein studied with William James and Hugo Munsterberg and became involved in research in psychology. Together with the great influence exerted on her thinking by William James, this early work in psychology was to provide her with both a subject and a style that would continue in many forms throughout her career. She was awarded her A.B. by Harvard in 1898, almost a year after she had entered medical school at The Johns Hopkins University. Her interest in medicine rapidly waned, and she left Johns Hopkins in 1901, failing four courses in her final semester.

After leaving medical school, Stein spent two years moving back and forth between Europe and America. During that time, she was involved in an agonizing love affair with another young woman student at Johns Hopkins, May Bookstaver. The affair was painfully complicated, first by Stein's naïveté, then by the presence of a more sophisticated rival for May's love, Mabel Haynes. The resulting lover's triangle led

Stein, in an effort to understand May, to begin formulating the theories of personality that dominated her early writing. The frustration and eventual despair of this lesbian relationship profoundly influenced Stein's view of the psychology of personality and of love. Most directly, Stein's troubled affair with May Bookstaver provided her with many, if not most, of the concerns of three of her books, *Quod Erat Demonstrandum, The Making of Americans,* and *Three Lives,* the first two of which she began while living in New York in the winter of 1903.

After a brief stay in New York, she lived with Leo, first in Bloomsbury in London, and then, beginning in 1903, in Paris at 27 rue de Fleurus, the address she was to make so well known to the world. In Paris, Gertrude and Leo became more and more interested in painting, buying works by new artists such as Henri Matisse and Picasso. Leo's preference was for works by Matisse, while Gertrude favored the more experimental works of Picasso, marking the beginning of a distancing process that would lead to Leo's complete separation from his sister in 1913. Leo was bright, opinionated, and fancied himself by far the greater creative talent of the two, but his brilliance and energy never produced any creative or significant critical work, and he grew to resent both his sister's independent thinking and her emerging ability to write. Later in his life, he would dismiss Gertrude as "dumb," her writing as "nonsense."

In 1907, Stein met another young American woman in Paris, Alice Toklas, and Alice began to displace Leo as the most important personal influence in Gertrude's life. Alice learned to type so she could transcribe Stein's handwritten manuscripts, beginning with portions of *The Making of Americans* in 1908. In 1909, Alice moved in with Gertrude and Leo at 27 rue de Fleurus, and by 1913, Alice had replaced Leo as Gertrude's companion and as the manager of her household. Stein later referred to her relationship with Alice as a "marriage," and few, if any, personal relationships have ever influenced a literary career so profoundly. Apart from providing Stein with the persona for her best-known work, *The Autobiography of Alice B. Toklas,* Alice typed, criticized, and valiantly worked to publish all of Stein's work for the rest of her career and for the twenty years that Alice lived after Stein's death. While it is doubtful that Alice was directly responsible for any of Stein's writing, her influence on its composition and on Stein's life was tremendous.

Gertrude and Alice spent the first months of World War I in England as houseguests of Alfred North Whitehead, returning to Paris briefly in 1914, then spending more than a year in Spain. They joined the war effort in 1917 when Stein ordered a Ford motor van from America for use as a supply truck for the American Fund for French Wounded, an acquisition which began Stein's lifelong fascination with automobiles, particularly with Fords. She and Alice drove this van, named "Auntie," until the war ended, work for which she was later awarded the Medaille de la Reconnaissance Française.

Modernism had burst on the American consciousness when the Armory Show opened in New York in 1913, and this show, which had confronted Americans with the first cubist paintings, also led to the association in the public mind of Stein's writing with this shockingly new art, particularly since Stein's first periodical publications had been "Matisse" and "Picasso" in *Camera Work,* the year before. Stein's mammoth, 925-page novel, *The Making of Americans,* was published in 1925, and in 1926, she lectured at Oxford and Cambridge, attempting to explain her idiosyncratic writing style. Her "landscape" novel, *Lucy Church Amiably,* appeared in 1930, but it was in 1933, with the publication of the best-selling *The Autobiography of Alice B. Toklas,* that Stein first captured the public's interest. She became front page news the following year when her opera *Four Saints in Three Acts* was first performed and when she embarked on a nationwide lecture tour, later described in *Everybody's Autobiography* and *Lectures in America*.

Stein and Toklas spent World War II in Bilignin and then in Culoz, France. While Stein and Toklas were both Jewish, they were never persecuted by occupying forces, owing in part to the influence of Bernard Fay, an early admirer of Stein's work who directed the Bibliothèque Nationale for the Vichy regime. When, after the war, Fay was sentenced to life imprisonment for his Vichy activities, Stein was one of his few defenders. That her art collection survived Nazi occupation virtually intact can only have been through Fay's intercession. During the war, Stein finished another novel, *Mrs. Reynolds* (unpublished), and *Wars I Have Seen* (1945), an autobiographical work. Her novel *Brewsie and Willie*, a series of conversations among American soldiers, was published in 1946.

Stein died following an operation for cancer in the American Hospital in Neuilly-sur-Seine, France, on July 27, 1946. While Alice Toklas's account of Stein's last words may be apocryphal, it certainly is in keeping with the spirit of her life. As Alice later reconstructed their last conversation, Stein had asked her "What is the answer?" Then, when Alice remained silent, Stein added, "In that case, what is the question?"

Analysis · While Gertrude Stein's persistence finally earned her access to readers, it could never guarantee her readers who would or could take her strange writing seriously. As a result, more confusing and contradictory information surrounds her career than that of any other twentieth century writer of comparable reputation. Usually responding in any of four basic ways, readers and critics alike seemed to view her as (1) a literary charlatan of the P. T. Barnum ilk, interested in publicity or money rather than in art; (2) something of a naïve child-woman incapable of comprehending the world around her; (3) a fiery-eyed literary revolutionary, den mother of the avant-garde; or (4) an ageless repository of wisdom and genius. Ultimately, the reader's acceptance or rejection of these various categories will greatly determine his or her response to Stein's writing, which forces the reader to make as many cognitive choices as does that of any major writer.

Stein's many explanations of her writing further complicate its interpretation: Even her "explanations" frustrate as much as they reveal, explicitly setting her up in cognitive competition with her reader, a competition suggested by her favorite cryptogram, which works out to read: "I understand you undertake to overthrow my undertaking." Stein proposes a rhetoric not of misunderstanding, but of antiunderstanding; that is, her "explanations" usually argue precisely against the desirability of explaining.

As Stein bluntly put the matter, "understanding is a very dull occupation." "Understanding" has a special denotation for Stein, sometimes meaning as little as paying attention to or reading. "To understand a thing means to be in contact with that thing," she proclaimed. Central to her mistrust of explanations and interpretations was Stein's often anguished belief that her thoughts could never really be matched to anyone else's. She was deeply troubled by this doubt as she wrote *The Making of Americans*, referring in that work to "the complete realization that no one can believe as you do about anything" as "complete disillusionment in living." Starting from this assumption that no one can ever really understand what someone else says or writes because of the inherent ambiguity of language, Stein not only decided to force her readers to confront that ambiguity, but also claimed it as a primary virtue of her writing. She announced triumphantly that "if you have vitality enough of knowing enough of what you mean, somebody and sometimes a great many will have to realize that you know what you mean and so they will agree that you mean what you know, which is as near as anybody can come to understanding any one." Stein's focus here is on relationships or process rather than on product—on the act of trying to become one with, rather than focusing on the ultimate result of that act.

Stein's thinking about understanding manifests itself in a number of distinctive ways in her writing, as do her theories of perception and of human psychology. Moreover, during the nearly fifty years of her writing career, her style developed in many related but perceptibly different stages, such as her "cubist" or her "cinema" phases. As a result, no single analysis can do more than describe the primary concerns and features of one of her stylistic periods. There are, however, three central concerns that underlie and at least partially account for all of the stages in the development of her style. These concerns are with the value of individual words, with repetition as the basic rhythm of existence, and with the related concept of "movement" in writing. Her articulations of these central concerns all run counter to her reader's expectations about the purpose and function of language and of literature. Her writing surprised her readers in much the same way that her penchant for playing only the black keys on a piano surprised and frustrated all but the most patient of her listeners.

One of Stein's goals was to return full meaning, value, and particularity to the words she used. "I took individual words and thought about them until I got their weight and volume complete and put them next to another word," she explained of seemingly nonsense phrases such as "toasted Susie is my ice cream," or "mouse and mountain and a quiver, a quaint statue and pain in an exterior and silence more silence louder shows salmon a mischief intender." This sort of paratactic juxtaposition of seemingly unrelated words rarely occurs in Stein's novels, but represents a problem for her reader in many other ways in her writing. She frequently chose to stress or focus on a part or aspect of the object of her description that the reader normally does not consider. The "things" Stein saw and wrote of were not the "things" with which readers are familiar: Where another observer might see a coin balanced on its edge, Stein might choose either of the descriptive extremes of seeing it literally as a thin rectangle, or figuratively as the essence of money. Characteristically, her most opaque parataxis refers to essences or processes rather than to objects or static concepts.

A related quirk in Stein's style results from her intellectual or emotional attachment to particular words and phrases at certain stages of her career. As she admitted in *The Making of Americans,*

> To be using a new word in my writing is to me a very difficult thing. . . . Using a word I have not yet been using in my writing is to me a very difficult and a peculiar feeling. Sometimes I am using a new one, sometimes I feel a new meaning in an old one, sometimes I like one I am very fond of that one that has many meanings many ways of being used to make different meanings to everyone.

Stein said she had learned from Paul Cézanne that everything in a painting was related to everything else and that each part of the painting was of equal importance—a blade of grass as important to the composition of the painting as a tree. She attempted to apply these two principles to the composition of her sentences, taking special delight in using normally "overlooked" words, arguing that articles, prepositions, and conjunctions—the transitive elements in grammar—are just as important and more interesting than substantives such as nouns and verbs. Her reassessment both of the value of words and of the conventions of description resulted in what Michael J. Hoffman in *The Development of Abstractionism in the Writings of Gertrude Stein* (1965) has described as Stein's "abstractionism." It also resulted in her including in her writing totally unexpected information in perplexingly paratactic word-strings.

A second constant in Stein's style is the pronounced repetition of words, phrases, and sentences, with no change or with only incremental progressions of sounds or associations. Works such as *The Making of Americans* and *Three Lives* contain long passages in which each sentence is a light variation on some core phrase, with great repetition of words even within a single sentence. Stein termed this phenomenon "insistence" rather than repetition, citing her former teacher, William James, as her philosophical authority. James's argument in his *The Principles of Psychology* (1890) that one must think of the identical recurrence of a fact in a fresh manner remarkably resembles Stein's contention that "in expressing anything there can be no repetition because the essence of that expression is insistence, and if you insist you must each time use emphasis and if you use emphasis it is not possible while anybody is alive that they should use exactly the same emphasis." Repetition or insistence is perhaps the central aspect of what has been called Stein's "cinema style," based on her claim that in writing *The Making of Americans* she was "doing what the cinema was doing." She added that her writing in that book was "like a cinema picture made up of succession and each moment having its own emphasis that is its own difference and so there was the moving and the existence of each moment as it was in me."

Stein's discussion of "what the cinema was doing" appears in her *Lectures in America* and also suggests the third basic concern of her writing: movement. By "movement," she referred not to the movement of a message to its conclusion or the movement of a plot or narrative, but to "the essence of its going" of her prose, a timeless continuous present in the never-ending motion of consciousness. Stein also credits Cézanne with discovering this concern, "a feeling of movement inside the painting not a painting of a thing moving but the thing painted having inside it the existence of moving." She seemed to understand Cézanne's achievement in terms of William James's model of consciousness as an ever-flowing stream of thought. Accordingly, she used her writing not to record a scene or object or idea (products of thought), but to try to capture the sense of the process of perceiving such things. Stein's subject is almost always really two things at once: whatever attracted her attention—caught her eye, entered her ear, or crossed her mind—and the mobile nature of reality, particularly as it is perceived by human consciousness. In fact, Stein was usually more concerned with the nature of her own perception and with that of her reader than she was with its objects. She wanted to escape the conventions of linguistic representation, arbitrary arrangements similar to the "rules" for perspective in painting, and to present "something moving as moving is not as moving should be." As confusing as her resulting efforts sometimes are, her concern with motion makes sense as an attempt to mimic or evoke the nature of consciousness as she understood it.

From James at Harvard and possibly from Henri Bergson in Paris, Stein had learned that the best model for human consciousness was one that stressed the processual, ever-flowing nature of experience. She added to this belief her assumption that the essence of any subject could only be perceived and should only be represented through its motion, echoing Bergson's claim that "reality is mobility." Unfortunately, this belief led her writing into one of its many paradoxes: She could only attempt to represent the continuous stream of experience through the segmented, inherently sequential nature of language. Streams flow; words do not. Instead, they proceed one by one, like the cars pulled by a train engine. While James would certainly have objected to Stein's sequential cinema model as an approximation of the stream of consciousness, her motion-obsessed writing probably suggests the flow of consciousness as well as does any literary style.

Quod Erat Demonstrandum · Written in 1903, but put out of her mind until 1932, and not published until 1950, Stein's *Quod Erat Demonstrandum* (first published as *Things as They Are*) is her most conventional novel. Its sentences employ no unexpected syntax or diction, its central concerns are clear, its time scheme is linear, and its characters are conventionally drawn. If anything, Stein's style in this first novel is markedly old-fashioned, including highly formal sentences that frequently sport balanced serial constructions. "Adele vehemently and with much picturesque vividness explained her views and theories of manners, people and things, in all of which she was steadily opposed by Helen who differed fundamentally in all her convictions, aspirations and illusions." While its conventional style (crudely reminiscent of that of Henry James) is completely unlike that of any other Stein novel, *Quod Erat Demonstrandum* is a very significant work for the consideration of Stein's career. Apart from convincingly refuting the suspicion of some of her detractors that Stein was incapable of rational writing, this book establishes her preoccupation with psychological typecasting and vaguely hints at the importance of repetition in her thinking and writing.

Quod Erat Demonstrandum charts the growth, turbulence, and eventual dissolution of the relationships among three young women: Adele, the book's central consciousness, an obviously autobiographical figure; Helen Thomas, the object of Adele's love; and Mable Neathe, Adele's calculating rival for Helen's affection. These three characters closely parallel Stein, May Bookstaver, and Mabel Haynes, and the story of their relationship is the story of Stein's first, agonizing love affair. While the novel follows these three young women for three years, not much happens. Most of the book relates conversations and correspondence between Adele and Helen, showing Adele's torment first from her not yet understood desire for Helen, then from her growing realization that she is losing Helen to Mabel. Of principal interest to the reader is Stein's self-characterization in her portrayal of Adele.

Three Lives · *Three Lives* is easily Stein's best-known and most respected piece of fiction. Technically three novellas, this work is unified by its three subjects, by its central concern with the nature of consciousness, and by its attempt to blend colloquial idioms with Stein's emerging style, here based largely on her understanding of Cézanne's principles of composition, particularly that "one thing was as important as another thing." "The Good Anna," "Melanctha," and "The Gentle Lena" are the three sections of this work. Anna and Lena are poor German immigrants who patiently work as servants in Bridgepoint, Baltimore; Melanctha is a young black woman who discovers sexuality and love, then turns from a frustrating relationship with a sincere young black doctor to a dissipative affair with a gambler. Since all three women are essentially victimized by their surroundings and die at the end of their stories, this work is deterministic in the naturalist tradition, but *Three Lives* marks the transition from naturalism to modernism as Stein departs from nineteenth century literary conventions. She abandons conventional syntax to try to follow the movement of a consciousness rather than of events, and she develops a new narrative style only partially tied to linear chronology. The result is an interior narrative of consciousness in which Stein's prose style serves as the primary carrier of knowledge. Through the rhythms of her characters' speech and the rhythms of her narration, Stein gives her reader a sense of the basic rhythms of consciousness for these three women—what Stein would elsewhere refer to as their "bottom natures."

Possibly Stein's most widely celebrated piece of writing, "Melanctha" recasts the anguishing love triangle of *Quod Erat Demonstrandum* into the conflict between Melanctha and Jeff Campbell, whose inherently conflicting "bottom natures" or personality types parallel the conflict between Helen and Adele in the earlier work. "Melanctha" has been praised by Richard Wright, among others, as one of the first realistic and sympathetic renderings of black life by a white American author, but Melanctha's race is actually incidental to Stein's central concerns with finding a style to express the rhythms of personality and the frustrating cycles of love.

The Making of Americans · While it was not published until 1925, Stein's *The Making of Americans* occupied her as early as 1903 and was in fact begun before *Quod Erat Demonstrandum* and *Three Lives*. This mammoth novel began as a description of the creation of Americans from a representative immigrant family: "The old people in a new world, the new people made out of the old, that is the story that I mean to tell, for that is what really is and what I really know." Stein's projected family chronicle soon lost its original focus, becoming first a history of everyone, then a study of character types rather than of characters. Leon Katz, who has worked with this book more than has anyone else, calls it "a massive description of the psychological landscape of human being in its totality." Although the book ostensibly continues to follow events in the lives of two central families, the Herslands and the Dehnings, its real concern is almost always both larger and smaller, ranging from Stein's questions about her own life and identity to questions about the various personality types of all of humanity. As Richard Bridgman suggests, this is "an improvised work of no identifiable genre in which the creator learned by doing," one "full of momentary wonders and botched long-range schemes, lyrical outbursts and anguished confessions." Accordingly, Bridgman concludes that *The Making of Americans* is best thought of "not as a fictional narrative nor a philosophic tract, but as a drama of self-education." In a way, the book chronicles the "making" of Gertrude Stein, presenting a phenomenology of her mind as it works its way through personal problems toward the distinctive "cinema style."

Underlying a great part of the writing in this book is Stein's belief that human personality consists of variations on a few basic "bottom natures" or kinds of identity which can be perceived through a character's repeated actions. "There are then many things every one has in them that come out of them in the repeating everything living have always in them, repeating with a little changing just enough to make of each one an individual being, to make of each repeating an individual thing that gives to such a one a feeling of themselves inside them." There are two basic personality types, "dependent independent" and "independent dependent," polarities identified in part by the way the person fights: the first kind by resisting, the second by attacking. Concerns with character-typing dominate the book's first two sections, "The Dehnings and the Herslands" and "Martha Hersland," (the character most closely modeled on Stein's own life), while the third section, "Alfred and Julia Hersland," contains mostly digressions about contemporary matters in Stein's life. The fourth section, "David Hersland," becomes a meditation on the nature of aging and death ("He was dead when he was at the beginning of being in middle living."), and the final section, "History of a Family's Progress," is—even for Stein—an incredibly abstract and repetitive series of reflections on the concerns that had given rise to the novel. This final section contains no names, referring only to "some," "any," "every," or "very many."

Stein later described her efforts in this book as an attempt "to do what the cinema was doing"; that is, to give a sense of motion and life through a series of highly repetitive statements, each statement only an incremental change from the preceding one, like frames in a strip of film. One of the main effects of this technique is to freeze all action into a "continuous present." Not only do Stein's sentences exist in overlapping clusters, depending more for their meaning on their relationships to one another than on individual semantic content, but also her verbs in *The Making of Americans* are almost exclusively present participles, suspending all action in the present progressive tense. "The business of Art," Stein later explained, "is to live in the actual present, that is the complete actual present." As a result, while *The Making of Americans* does ostensibly present a history of four generations of the Hersland family, there exists in it little or no sense of the passage of time. Instead, the book presents a sense of "existence suspended in time," a self-contained world existing quite independently of the "real world," a basic modernist goal that has also become one of the hallmarks of postmodernism.

A 416-page version, abridged by Stein, was published in 1934, but has not been accepted by Stein scholars as adequately representative of the longer work. For all its difficulty, *The Making of Americans* is one of modernism's seminal works and an invaluable key to Stein's literary career.

Lucy Church Amiably · Described by its author as "a novel of Romantic beauty and nature and which Looks Like an Engraving," *Lucy Church Amiably* shares many characteristics with Stein's best-known opera, *Four Saints in Three Acts*, and with the several works she called "geographies." The book was Stein's response to the area around Belley, France, where she and Alice spent many summers. Stein's title plays on the existence of the church in a nearby village, Lucey. As Richard Bridgman has observed, Lucy Church refers throughout the book to both that church and to a woman who resembles a relaxed Gertrude Stein. As Bridgman also notes, "the book is essentially a long, lyric diary," with Stein including in it information about the geography, residents, and flora of the surrounding area. This information appears, however, in Stein's distinctive paratactic style:

> In this story there is to be not only white black tea colour and vestiges of their bankruptcy but also well wishing and outlined and melodious and with a will and much of it to be sure with their only arrangement certainly for this for the time of which when by the way what is the difference between fixed.

This novel can perhaps best be thought of as a pastoral and elegiac meditation on the nature of place.

The World Is Round* and *Ida, a Novel · In 1939, Stein's novel for children, *The World Is Round*, was published, with illustrations by Clement Hurd. The book focuses on a series of events in the lives of a nine-year-old girl, Rose, and her cousin, Willie. These events are more enigmatic than dramatic, but seem to move both children through several kinds of initiations. Identity worries both Rose and Willie ("Would she have been Rose if her name had not been Rose and would she have been Rose if she had been a twin"), as does the contrast between the uncertainties of their lives and the advertised verities of existence, emblemized by the "roundness" of the world. Comprising both the children's meditations and their songs, the book is, for Stein, relatively conventional. Although its sentences are highly repetitive and rhythmic, they present a compelling view of a child's consciousness, and Stein scholars agree on the importance and success of this little-known work.

Originally intended as "a novel about publicity," *Ida, a Novel* expands many of the concerns of *The World Is Round*, extending them from Ida's birth well into her adult life. As is true of all of Stein's novels, there is not anything resembling a plot, and many of the things that happen in Ida's life are surrealistically dreamlike. "Funny things" keep happening to the young Ida, and while the nature of these things is never explained, most of them seem to involve men. Frequently, these men have nothing at all to do with her, or they only glance at her, but Ida sees them as vaguely threatening, and insofar as her novel can be said to have a central concern, it is with certain problems of sexuality. Although Stein later described Ida as having been based on the Duchess of Windsor, this connection is only superficial, and Ida is better seen as another in the long line of Stein's autobiographical characters.

Brewsie and Willie · Stein's novel, *Brewsie and Willie*, redirected her revolutionary spirit from literary to social and economic problems. In this series of conversations among American soldiers and nurses awaiting redeployment from France to the United States after World War II, Stein pessimistically considered the future of her native land. Stein had long held that the United States was "the oldest country in the world" because it had been the first to enter the twentieth century. By 1945, she felt that America had grown "old like a man of fifty," and that its tired, middle-aged economic system had become stale and repressive. In *Brewsie and Willie*, she describes that economic system as "industrialism," portraying a stultifying cycle of depleting raw materials for overproduction and installment buying. This cycle also locked the worker into "job thinking," making of him a kind of automaton, tied to his job, locked into debt, and, worst of all, robbed of freedom of thought. Through conversations involving Brewsie (Stein's spokesman), Willie, and several other soldiers and nurses, Stein portrays an apprehensive generation of young Americans who see the potential dangers of postwar America but who fear they do not "have the guts to make a noise" about them. These conversations cover a wide range of subjects, from a comparison of French and American baby carriages to the tentative suggestion that the American system must be torn down before "pioneering" will again be possible.

Stein makes little or no effort in this book to differentiate the voices of her speakers, but she does rather amazingly blend her own voice with those of the soldiers. The result is a style that is characteristically Stein's but that also has the rhythm and the randomness of overheard conversation. Often overlooked, *Brewsie and Willie* is one of the most remarkable documents in Stein's writing career.

However idiosyncratic Stein's writing may seem, it must be remembered that a very strong case can be made for its substantial philosophical underpinnings. To her way of thinking, language could refuse few things to Stein, and the limitations of language were exactly what she refused to accept. She bent the language to the very uses that process philosophers such as James and Bergson and Whitehead feared it could not be put. Her stubborn emphasis on the individual word–particularly on transitive elements–her insistent use of repetition, and her ever-present preoccupation with the essential motion of words were all part of Stein's monumental struggle with a language she felt was not accurately used to reflect the way people perceive reality or the motion of reality itself. In a narrow but profound sense, she is the most serious realist in literary history. Stein was not a philosopher—her magpie eclecticism, associational flights, and thundering *ex cathedra* pronouncements ill-suited her for systematic explanation—but in her writing a wealth of philosophy appears.

Brooks Landon

Other major works

PLAYS: *Geography and Plays*, pb. 1922; *Operas and Plays*, pb. 1932; *Four Saints in Three Acts*, pr., pb. 1934; *In Savoy: Or, Yes Is for a Very Young Man (A Play of the Resistance in France)*, pr., pb. 1946; *The Mother of Us All*, pr. 1947; *Last Operas and Plays*, pb. 1949; *In a Garden: An Opera in One Act*, pb. 1951; *Lucretia Borgia*, pb. 1968; *Selected Operas and Plays*, pb. 1970.

POETRY: *Tender Buttons: Objects, Food, Rooms*, 1914; *Two (Hitherto Unpublished) Poems*, 1948; *Bee Time Vine and Other Pieces: 1913-1927*, 1953; *Stanzas in Meditation and Other Poems: 1929-1933*, 1956.

NONFICTION: *The Autobiography of Alice B. Toklas*, 1933; *Matisse, Picasso, and Gertrude Stein, with Two Shorter Stories*, 1933; *Portraits and Prayers*, 1934; *Lectures in America*, 1935; *Narration: Four Lectures*, 1935; *The Geographical History of America*, 1936; *Everybody's Autobiography*, 1937; *Picasso*, 1938; *What Are Masterpieces*, 1940; *Wars I Have Seen*, 1945; *Reflections on the Atomic Bomb*, 1973; *How Writing Is Written*, 1974.

CHILDREN'S LITERATURE: *The World Is Round*, 1939.

Bibliography

Bowers, Jane Palatini. *Gertrude Stein*. New York: St. Martin's Press, 1993. A succinct, feminist-oriented introduction to Stein, with separate chapters on *The Making of Americans* and *Tender Buttons* and on her plays. Includes notes and bibliography.

Bridgman, Richard. *Gertrude Stein in Pieces*. New York: Oxford University Press, 1970. Still an indispensable source, this was the first book to look critically at the whole Stein canon and to analyze its genesis. Bridgman remains immune from the many statements Stein made to explain her own work and arrives at honest and independent—if not always completely acceptable—judgments.

Doane, Janice L. *Silence and Narrative: The Early Novels of Gertrude Stein*. Westport, Conn.: Greenwood Press, 1986. Strong on the development of Stein's unique narrative voice with its focus on the speech of working-class women. Demonstrates Stein's sensitivity to nuance.

Hoffman, Michael J., ed. *Critical Essays on Gertrude Stein*. Boston: G. K. Hall, 1986. The most current collection of writing on Stein, representing varied points of view. A good starting point for beginners.

_____. *Gertrude Stein*. Boston: Twayne, 1976. A useful book with strong analyses of Stein's writing and interesting sidelights on its production and its relationship to the avante garde movements of the period. Especially strong on cubist influences.

Kellner, Bruce, ed. *A Gertrude Stein Companion*. New York: Greenwood Press, 1988. Kellner supplies a helpful introduction on how to read Stein. The volume includes a study of Stein and literary tradition, her manuscripts, her various styles, and biographical sketches of her friends and enemies. Provides an annotated bibliography of criticism.

Knapp, Bettina K. *Gertrude Stein*. New York: Ungar, 1990. A short introductory study, with useful chapters on her verbal portraits, *Tender Buttons*, her plays, and her use of fact and fiction. Includes chronology, notes, and bibliography.

Mellow, James R. *Charmed Circle: Gertrude Stein and Company*. New York: Praeger, 1974. A deeply felt and pleasing illustrated book by one of Stein's scholarly admirers. Contains interesting, detailed discussions of her writing, her family background and relationships, her association with artists and writers in Paris over fifty years, and her enduring relationship with Alice B. Toklas.

Neuman, Shirley, and Ira B. Nadel, eds. *Gertrude Stein and the Making of Literature*. Boston: Northeastern University Press, 1988. Offers some of the most current feminist readings of Stein, clarifying the innovations that originated with Stein and had a sweeping influence on later writers including Ernest Hemingway, Ford Madox Ford, and Sherwood Anderson.

Steiner, Wendy. *Exact Resemblance to Exact Resemblance*. New Haven, Conn.: Yale University Press, 1978. Perhaps the best book available for linking Stein's modernism to her interest in and study of psychology and philosophy.

JOHN STEINBECK

Born: Salinas, California; February 27, 1902
Died: New York, New York; December 20, 1968

Principal long fiction · *Cup of Gold*, 1929; *The Pastures of Heaven*, 1932; *To a God Unknown*, 1933; *Tortilla Flat*, 1935; *In Dubious Battle*, 1936; *The Red Pony*, 1937, 1945; *Of Mice and Men*, 1937; *The Grapes of Wrath*, 1939; *The Moon Is Down*, 1942; *Cannery Row*, 1945; *The Pearl*, 1945 (serial), 1947 (book); *The Wayward Bus*, 1947; *Burning Bright*, 1950; *East of Eden*, 1952; *Sweet Thursday*, 1954; *The Short Reign of Pippen IV*, 1957; *The Winter of Our Discontent*, 1961; *Acts of King Arthur and His Noble Knights*, 1976.

Other literary forms · In addition to his seventeen novels, John Steinbeck published a story collection, *The Long Valley* (1938), and a few other uncollected or separately printed stories. His modern English translations of Sir Thomas Malory's Arthurian tales were published posthumously in 1976. Three plays he adapted from his novels were published as well as performed on Broadway: *Of Mice and Men* (1937), *The Moon Is Down* (1942), and *Burning Bright* (1951). Three of the six film treatments or screenplays he wrote—*The Forgotten Village* (1941), *A Medal for Benny* (1945), and *Viva Zapata!* (1952)—have been published; the other three also were produced as films—*Lifeboat* (1944), *The Pearl* (1945), and *The Red Pony* (1949), the latter two adapted from his own novels. His nonfiction was voluminous, and much of it remains uncollected. The more important nonfiction books include: *Sea of Cortez* (1941, with Edward F. Ricketts), *Bombs Away* (1942), *A Russian Journal* (1948), *Once There Was a War* (1958), *Travels with Charley: In Search of America* (1962), *America and Americans* (1966), *Journal of a Novel* (1969), and *Steinbeck: A Life in Letters* (1975; Elaine Steinbeck and Robert Wallsten, editors).

Achievements · From the publication of his first bestseller, *Tortilla Flat*, in 1935, Steinbeck was a popular and widely respected American writer. His three earlier novels were virtually ignored, but the five books of fiction published between 1935 and 1939 made him the most important literary spokesman for the Depression decade. *In Dubious Battle, The Red Pony*, and *Of Mice and Men* established him as a serious writer, and his master work, *The Grapes of Wrath*, confirmed him as a major talent. During these years, his popular and critical success rivaled that of any of his contemporaries.

Although his immense popularity, public recognition, and the impressive sales of his works persisted throughout his career, Steinbeck's critical success waned after *The Grapes of Wrath*, reaching a nadir at his death in 1968, despite his Nobel Prize in Literature in 1962. During World War II, his development as a novelist faltered for many reasons, and Steinbeck never recovered his artistic momentum. Even *East of Eden*, the work he thought his masterpiece, proved an artistic and critical failure though a popular success. Since his death, Steinbeck remains widely read, both in America and abroad, while his critical reputation has enjoyed a modest revival. Undoubtedly the appreciation of his considerable talents will continue to develop, as few writers have better celebrated the American Dream or traced the dark lineaments of the American nightmare.

Biography · John Ernst Steinbeck was born on February 27, 1902, in Salinas, California. The time and place of his birth are important because Steinbeck matured as an artist in his early thirties during the darkest days of the Depression, and his most important fictions are set in his beloved Salinas Valley. In one sense, Steinbeck's location in time and place may have made him a particularly American artist. Born just after the closing of the frontier, Steinbeck grew up with a frustrated modern America and witnessed the most notable failure of the American Dream in the Depression. He was a writer who inherited the great tradition of the American Renaissance of the nineteenth century and who was forced to reshape it in terms of the historical and literary imperatives of twentieth century modernism. Steinbeck's family background evidenced this strongly American identity. His paternal grandfather, John Adolph Steinbeck, immigrated from Germany, settling in California after serving in the Civil War. His mother's father, Samuel Hamilton, sailed around Cape Horn from northern Ireland, finally immigrating to the Salinas Valley. John Ernst Steinbeck and Olive Hamilton were the first-generation descendants of sturdy, successful, and Americanized immigrant farm families. They met and married in 1890, settling in Salinas, where the father was prominent in local business and government, and the mother stayed home to rear their four children—three daughters and a son, the third child named for his father. The Steinbecks were refined, intelligent, and ambitious people who lived a quiet middle-class life in the small agricultural service town of Salinas.

Steinbeck seems to have enjoyed a happy childhood, and in fact he often asserted that he did. His father made enough money to indulge him in a small way, even to buy him a red pony. His mother encouraged him to read and to write, providing him with the classics of English and American literature. At school, he proved a popular and successful student and was elected president of his senior class.

After graduation from Salinas High School in 1919, Steinbeck enrolled at Stanford University. His subsequent history belies the picture of the happy, normal young man. He was soon in academic difficulties and dropped out of college several times to work on ranches in the Salinas Valley and observe "real life." His interests were varied, but he settled on novel-writing as his ambition, despite his family's insistence that he prepare for a more prosaic career. This traumatic rejection of middle-class values would prove a major force in shaping Steinbeck's fiction, both his social protest novels and his lighter entertainments such as *Cannery Row*.

Leaving Stanford without a degree in 1925, Steinbeck sojourned in New York for several months, where he worked as a laborer, a newspaper reporter, and a freelance writer. Disillusioned in all his abortive pursuits, Steinbeck returned to California, where a job as winter caretaker of a lodge at Lake Tahoe provided the time to finish his first novel, *Cup of Gold*. The novel, a romance concerned with the Caribbean pirate Henry Morgan, was published by a small press directly before the crash of 1929, and it earned the young writer little recognition and even less money. In 1930, he married Carol Henning and moved with her to Los Angeles and later to Pacific Grove, a seaside resort near Monterey, where he lived in his parents' summer house. Still supported by his family and his wife, the ambitious young writer churned out the manuscripts of several novels.

A friend, Edward F. (Ed) Ricketts, a marine biologist trained at the University of Chicago, encouraged Steinbeck to treat his material more objectively. Under Rickett's influence, Steinbeck modified his earlier commitment to satire, allegory, and Romanticism and turned to modern accounts of the Salinas Valley. Steinbeck's next two

novels, *The Pastures of Heaven* and *To a God Unknown*, are both set in the Valley, but both still were marked by excessive sentimentality and symbolism. Both were virtually ignored by the public and the critics. Steinbeck's short fiction, however, began to receive recognition; for example, his story "The Murder" was selected as an O. Henry Prize story in 1934.

Tortilla Flat, a droll tale of Monterey's Mexican quarter, established Steinbeck as a popular and critical success in 1935. (Unfortunately, his parents died just before he achieved his first real success.) The novel's sales provided money to pay his debts, to travel to Mexico, and to continue writing seriously. His next novel, *In Dubious Battle*, established him as a serious literary artist and began the period of his greatest success, both critical and popular. This harshly realistic strike novel followed directions established in stories such as "The Raid," influenced by the realistic impulse of American literature in the 1930's. Succeeding publications quickly confirmed this development in his fiction. His short novels *The Red Pony* and *Of Mice and Men* followed in 1937, his story collection *The Long Valley* in 1938, and his epic of the "Okie" migration to California, *The Grapes of Wrath*, in 1939. His own play version of *Of Mice and Men* won the Drama Critics Circle Award in 1938, and *The Grapes of Wrath* received the Pulitzer Prize in 1940. Steinbeck had become one of the most popular and respected writers in the country, a spokesman for an entire culture.

In 1941, Pearl Harbor changed the direction of American culture and of John Steinbeck's literary development. During the war years, he seemed in a holding pattern, trying to adjust to his phenomenal success while absorbing the cataclysmic events around him. Steinbeck's career stalled for many reasons. He left the California subjects and realistic style of his finest novels, and he was unable to come to terms with a world at war, though he served for a few months as a front-line correspondent. Personal developments paralleled these literary ones. Steinbeck divorced his first wife and married Gwen Conger, a young Hollywood starlet; no doubt she influenced his decision to move from California to New York. Steinbeck began to write with an eye on Broadway and Hollywood.

Steinbeck was forty-three when World War II ended in 1945; he died in 1968 at the age of sixty-six. Over those twenty-three years, Steinbeck was extremely productive, winning considerable acclaim—most notably, the Nobel Prize in Literature in 1962. Yet the most important part of his career was finished. The war had changed the direction of his artistic development, and Steinbeck seemed powerless to reverse his decline.

Again, his personal life mirrored his literary difficulties. Although Gwen Conger presented him with his only children—Tom, born in 1944, and John, born in 1946—they were divorced in 1948. Like his first divorce, this one was bitter and expensive. In the same year, his mentor Ricketts was killed in a car accident. Steinbeck traveled extensively, devoting himself to film and nonfiction projects. In 1950, he married Elaine Scott, establishing a supportive relationship which allowed him to finish his epic Salinas Valley novel *East of Eden*.

Steinbeck tried again and again to write his way back to the artistic success of his earlier years, notably in *The Wayward Bus*, but his commercial success kept getting in the way. *East of Eden*, Steinbeck's major postwar novel, attempted another California epic to match the grandeur of *The Grapes of Wrath*. Although the book was a blockbuster best-seller, it was an artistic and critical failure. Steinbeck himself seemed to recognize his own decline, and in his last years he virtually abandoned fiction for journalism.

Of his last novels, only *The Winter of Our Discontent* transcends mere entertainment, and it does not have the literary structures to match its serious themes. Despite the popularity of nonfiction such as *Travels with Charley*, despite awards such as the Nobel Prize and the United States Medal of Freedom, despite his personal friendship with President Lyndon Johnson as a supporter of Vietnam, Steinbeck was only the shell of the great writer of the 1930's. He died in New York City on December 20, 1968.

Analysis · John Steinbeck remains a writer of the 1930's, perhaps *the* American writer of the 1930's. Although his first novel, *Cup of Gold*, was published in 1929, its derivative "Lost Generation" posturing gives little indication of the master-piece he would publish at the end of the next decade, *The Grapes of Wrath*. Steinbeck developed from a Romantic, imitative, often sentimental apprentice to a realistic, objective, and accomplished novelist in only a decade. The reasons for this change can be found in the interplay between a sensitive writer and his cultural background.

A writer of great talent, sensitivity, and imagination, John Steinbeck entered into the mood of the country in the late 1930's with an extraordinary responsiveness. The Depression had elicited a reevaluation of American culture, a reassessment of the American Dream: a harsh realism of observation balanced by a warm emphasis on human dignity. Literature and the other arts joined social, economic, and political thought in contrasting traditional American ideals with the bleak reality of breadlines and shantytowns. Perhaps the major symbol of dislocation was the Dust Bowl; the American garden became a wasteland from which its dispossessed farmers fled. The arts in the 1930's focused on these harsh images and tried to find in them the human dimensions which promised a new beginning.

The proletarian novel, documentary photography, and the documentary film stemmed from similar impulses; the radical novel put more emphasis on the inhuman conditions of the dislocated, while the films made more of the promising possibilities for a new day. Painting, music, and theater all responded to a new humanistic and realistic thrust. The best balance was struck by documentary photographers and filmmakers: Dorothea Lange, Walker Evans (James Agee's associate), and Arthur Rothstein in photography; Pare Lorentz, Willard Van Dyke, and Herbert Kline in film. As a novelist, Steinbeck shared this documentary impulse, and it refined his art.

In Dubious Battle · *In Dubious Battle* tells the harsh story of a violent agricultural strike in the "Torgas Valley" from the viewpoint of two Communist agitators. Careful and objective in his handling of the material, the mature Steinbeck provided almost a factual case study of a strike. In a letter, he indicated that this was his conscious intention:

> I had an idea that I was going to write the autobiography of a Communist. Then Miss McIntosh [his agent] suggested I reduce it to fiction. There lay the trouble. I had planned to write a journalistic account of a strike. But as I thought of it as fiction the thing got bigger and bigger . . . I have used a small strike in an orchard valley as the symbol of man's eternal, bitter warfare with himself.

For the first time, Steinbeck was able to combine his ambition to write great moral literature with his desire to chronicle his time and place.

Significantly, the novel takes its title from John Milton's *Paradise Lost* (1667, 1674) in which the phrase is used to describe the struggle between God and Satan, but it takes its subject from the newspapers and newsreels of the 1930's. The underlying structure demonstrates the universal struggle of good and evil, of human greed and selfishness versus human generosity and idealism. Jim, the protagonist killed at the conclusion, is obviously a Christ figure, an individual who has sacrificed himself for the group. Here, Steinbeck needs no overblown symbolic actions to support his theme. He lets his contemporary story tell itself realistically and in documentary fashion. In a letter, he describes his method in the novel: "I wanted to be merely a recording consciousness, judging nothing, simply putting down the thing." This objective, dispassionate, almost documentary realism separates *In Dubious Battle* from his earlier fiction and announces the beginning of Steinbeck's major period.

Of Mice and Men · *Of Mice and Men* was written in 1935 and 1936 and first published as a novel in 1937 at the height of the Depression. Steinbeck constructed the book around dramatic scenes so that he could easily rewrite it for the stage, which he did with the help of George S. Kaufmann. The play opened late in 1937, with Wallace Ford as George and Broderick Crawford as Lennie. A film version, directed by Lewis Milestone, with Burgess Meredith and Lon Chaney, Jr., in the central roles, appeared in 1939. The success of the play and film spurred sales of the novel and created a wide audience for Steinbeck's next book, *The Grapes of Wrath.*

Like his classic story of the "Okie" migration from the Dust Bowl to the promised land of California, *Of Mice and Men* is a dramatic presentation of the persistence of the American Dream and the tragedy of its failure. His characters are the little people, the uncommon "common people," disoriented and dispossessed by modern life yet still yearning for a little piece of land, that little particle of the Jeffersonian ideal. Lennie is the symbol of this visceral, inarticulate land-hunger, while George becomes the poet of this romantic vision. How their dream blossoms and then dies is Steinbeck's dramatic subject; how their fate represents that of America in the 1930's and after becomes his theme. His title, an allusion to the Scottish poet Robert Burns, suggests that the best laid plans "of mice and men often gang a-gley"; so the American vision had gone astray in the Depression decade Steinbeck documented so movingly and realistically.

The Red Pony · *The Red Pony* involves the maturation of Jody Tiflin, a boy of about ten when the action opens. The time is about 1910 and the setting is the Tiflin ranch in the Salinas Valley, where Jody lives with his father, Carl, his mother, Ruth, and the hired hand, a middle-aged cowboy named Billy Buck. From time to time, they are visited by Jody's grandfather, a venerable old man who led one of the first wagon trains to California. "The Gift," the first section of the novel, concerns Jody's red pony, which he names Gabilan, after the nearby mountain range. The pony soon becomes a symbol of the boy's growing maturity and his developing knowledge of the natural world. Later, he carelessly leaves the pony out in the rain, and it takes cold and dies, despite Billy Buck's efforts to save it. Thus Jody learns of nature's cruel indifference to human wishes.

In the second part, "The Great Mountains," the Tiflin ranch is visited by a former resident, Gitano, an aged Chicano laborer reared in the now vanished hacienda. Old Gitano has come home to die. In a debate which recalls Robert Frost's poem "The Death of the Hired Man," Carl persuades Ruth that they cannot take Old Gitano in, but—as in Frost's poem—their dialogue proves pointless. Stealing a broken-down nag significantly named Easter, the old man rides off into the mountains to die in dignity. Again, Jody is faced with the complex, harsh reality of adult life.

In "The Promise," the third section, Jody learns more of nature's ambiguous promises when his father has one of the mares put to stud to give the boy another colt. The birth is complicated, however, and Billy Buck must kill the mare to save the colt, demonstrating that life and death are inextricably intertwined. The final section, "The Leader of the People," ends the sequence with another vision of death and change. Jody's grandfather comes to visit, retelling his time-worn stories of the great wagon crossing. Carl Tiflin cruelly hurts the old man by revealing that none of them except Jody is really interested in these repetitive tales. The grandfather realizes that Carl is right, but later he tells Jody that the adventurous stories were not the point, but that his message was "Westering" itself. For the grandfather, "Westering" was the source of American identity. With the close of the frontier, "Westering" has ended, and the rugged Westerners have been replaced by petty landholders such as Carl Tiflin and aging cowboys such as Billy Buck. In his grandfather's ramblings, Jody discovers a sense of mature purpose, and by the conclusion of the sequence, he too can hope to be a leader of the people.

The Red Pony traces Jody's initiation into adult life with both realism and sensitivity, a balance which Steinbeck did not always achieve. The vision of the characters caught up in the harsh world of nature is balanced by their deep human concerns and commitments. The evocation of the ranch setting in its vital beauty is matched only in the author's finest works, such as *Of Mice and Men*. Steinbeck's symbols grow naturally out of this setting, and nothing in the story-sequence seems forced into a symbolic pattern, as in his later works. In its depiction of an American variation on a universal experience, *The Red Pony* deserves comparison with the finest of modern American fiction, especially with initiation tales such as William Faulkner's *The Bear* (1942) and Ernest Hemingway's Nick Adams stories.

Responding to a variety of social and artistic influences, Steinbeck's writing had evolved toward documentary realism throughout the 1930's. In fiction, this development is especially clear in *In Dubious Battle, Of Mice and Men,* and *The Long Valley*. Even more obvious was the movement of his nonfiction toward a committed documentation of the social ills plaguing America during the Depression decade. Steinbeck's newspaper and magazine writing offered detailed accounts of social problems, particularly the plight of migrant agricultural workers in California's fertile valleys. The culmination of this development was *Their Blood Is Strong* (1938), a compilation of reports originally written for the *San Francisco News* and published with additional text by Steinbeck and photographs by Dorothea Lange originally made for the Farm Security Administration.

The Grapes of Wrath · It is significant that Steinbeck first conceived of *The Grapes of Wrath* as just such a documentary book. In March, 1938, Steinbeck went into the California valleys with a *Life* magazine photographer to make a record of the harsh conditions in the migrant camps. The reality he encountered seemed too significant for nonfiction, however, and Steinbeck began to reshape this material as a novel, an epic novel.

Although his first tentative attempts at fictionalizing the situation in the agricultural valleys were heavily satiric, as indicated by the early title *L'Affaire Lettuceberg*, Steinbeck soon realized that the Okie migration was the stuff of an American epic. Reworking his material, adding to it by research in government agency files and by more journeys into the camps and along the migrant routes, Steinbeck evolved his vision. A grand design emerged; he would follow one family from the Oklahoma Dust

Bowl to California. Perhaps this methodology was suggested by the sociological case histories of the day, perhaps by the haunted faces of individual families which stared back at him as he researched in Farm Security Administration files.

In discussing his plans for his later documentary film, *The Forgotten Village* (1941), Steinbeck remarked that most documentaries concerned large groups of people but that audiences could identify better with individuals. In *The Grapes of Wrath*, he made one family representative of general conditions. The larger groups and problems he treated in short interchapters which generalized the issues particularized in the Joad family. Perhaps the grand themes of change and movement were suggested by the documentary films of Pare Lorentz (later a personal friend), *The Plow That Broke the Plains* (1936) and *The River* (1938), with their panoramic geographical and historical visions. Drawing an archetypal theme from Sir Thomas Malory, John Bunyan, John Milton, and the Bible—the ultimate source of his pervasive religious symbolism—Steinbeck made the journey of the Joads into an allegorical pilgrimage as well as a desperate race along Route 66. During this journey, the Joad family disintegrates, but the larger human family emerges. Tom Joad makes a pilgrim's progress from a narrow, pessimistic view to a transcendental vision of American possibilities. The novel ends on a note of hope for a new American Dream.

The Grapes of Wrath was a sensational best-seller from the beginning. Published to generally favorable reviews in March, 1939, it was selling at the rate of more than twenty-five hundred copies a day two months later. Controversy helped spur sales. As a semidocumentary, its factual basis was subject to close scrutiny, and many critics challenged Steinbeck's material. Oklahomans resented the presentation of the Joads as typical of the state (many still do), while Californians disapproved of the depiction of their state's leading industry. The book was attacked, banned, burned—but everywhere it was read. Even in the migrant camps, it was considered an accurate picture of the conditions experienced there. Some 430,000 copies were sold in a year, and in 1940, the novel received the Pulitzer Prize and the Award of the American Booksellers Association (later the National Book Award). Naturally, all the excitement attracted the attention of Hollywood, in spite of the fact that the controversy over the novel seemed to preclude a film version, or at least a faithful film version. Nevertheless, Darryl F. Zanuck produced and John Ford directed a faithful adaptation starring Henry Fonda in 1940; the film, like the novel, has become a classic, and it gave Steinbeck's vision of America in the 1930's even wider currency.

Indeed, Steinbeck's best work was filmic in the best sense of that word—visual, realistic, objective. These qualities nicely balanced the allegorical and romantic strains inherent in his earlier fiction. During World War II, however, his work, much to its detriment, began to cater to the film industry. In fact, much of his postwar writing seems to have found its inspiration in Hollywood versions of his work. His own screen adaptation of an earlier story, *The Red Pony*, proves a sentimentalized reproduction of the original. Still, he was occasionally capable of recapturing his earlier vision, particularly in his works about Mexico—*The Pearl* and *Viva Zapata!*

The Pearl · Mexico always had been an important symbolic place for Steinbeck. As a native Californian, he had been aware of his state's Mexican heritage. Even as a boy, he sought out Chicano companions, fascinated by their unconcern for the pieties of WASP culture; he also befriended Mexican fieldhands at the ranches where he worked during his college summers. Later, his first literary success, *Tortilla Flat*, grew from his involvement with the *paisanos* of Monterey, people who would today be called Chicanos.

For Steinbeck, Mexico was everything modern America was not; it possessed a primitive vitality, a harsh simplicity, and a romantic beauty—all of which are found in *The Pearl*. Mexico exhibits the same qualities in the works of other modern writers such as Malcolm Lowry, Aldous Huxley, Graham Greene, Hart Crane, and Katherine Anne Porter. All of them lived and worked there for some time, contrasting the traditional culture they discovered in Mexico with the emptiness of the modern world. Steinbeck also was fascinated by a Mexico still alive with social concern. The continued extension of the Revolution into the countryside had been his subject in *The Forgotten Village*, and it would be developed further in *Viva Zapata!* For Steinbeck, Mexico represented the purity of artistic and social purposes that he had lost after World War II. This sense of the writer's personal involvement energizes *The Pearl*, making it Steinbeck's best work of fiction in the years following the success of *The Grapes of Wrath*. At the beginning of the novella, the storyteller states: "If this story is a parable, perhaps everyone takes his own meaning from it and reads his own life into it." The critics have read Steinbeck's short novel in a number of ways, but strangely enough, they have not considered it as a parable of the author's own career in the postwar period. Much like Ernest Hemingway's *The Old Man and the Sea* (1952), *The Pearl* uses the life of a simple fisherman to investigate symbolically an aging artist's difficult maturation.

Steinbeck was presented with the tale during his Sea of Cortez expedition in 1940. In his log, he recounts "an event which happened at La Paz in recent years." The story matches the basic outline of *The Pearl*, though Steinbeck made several major changes, changes significant in an autobiographical sense. In the original, the Mexican fisherman was a devil-may-care bachelor; in *The Pearl*, he becomes the sober young husband and father, Kino. Steinbeck himself had just become a father for the first time when he wrote the novella, and this change provides a clue to the autobiographical nature of the parable. The original bachelor thought the pearl a key to easy living; Kino sees it creating a better way of life for the people through an education for his baby son, Coyotito. If the child could read and write, then he could set his family and his people free from the social and economic bondage in which they toil. Kino is ignorant of the dangers of wealth, and *The Pearl* is the tale of how he matures by coming to understand them. Steinbeck, too, matured from his youthful innocence as he felt the pressures of success.

As in his best fiction of the 1930's Steinbeck fuses his universal allegory with documentary realism. Perhaps planning ahead for a screenplay, Steinbeck's prose in the novel often takes a cinematic point of view. Scenes are presented in terms of establishing shots, medium views, and close-ups. In particular, Steinbeck carefully examines the natural setting, often visually contrasting human behavior with natural phenomena. As in his best fiction, his naturalistic vision is inherent in the movement of his story; there is no extraneous philosophizing.

Steinbeck's characters in *The Pearl* are real people in a real world, but they are also universal types. Kino, the fisherman named for an early Jesuit explorer, Juana, his wife, and Coyotito, their baby, are almost an archetypal family, like the Holy Family in a medieval morality play. Kino's aspirations are the same universal drives to better himself and his family that took the Okies to the California valleys. Like the Joads, this symbolic family must struggle at once against an indifferent natural order and a corrupt social order. Unfortunately, aside from the screenplay of *Viva Zapata!*, Steinbeck would never again achieve the fusion of parable and realism which energizes *The Pearl.*

In his Nobel Prize speech of 1962, Steinbeck indicated what he tried to accomplish in his work:

> The ancient commission of the writer has not changed. He is charged with exposing our many grievous faults and failures, with dredging up to the light our dark and dangerous dreams, for the purpose of improvement.

No writer has better exposed the dark underside of the American Dream, but few writers have so successfully celebrated the great hope symbolized in that dream—the hope of human development. Steinbeck's best fictions picture a paradise lost but also posit a future paradise to be regained. In spite of his faults and failures, John Steinbeck's best literary works demonstrate a greatness of heart and mind found only rarely in modern American literature.

Joseph R. Millichap

Other major works

SHORT FICTION: *Saint Katy the Virgin*, 1936; *The Long Valley*, 1938.

PLAYS: *Of Mice and Men*, pr., pb. 1937; *The Moon Is Down*, pr. 1942; *Burning Bright*, pb. 1951.

SCREENPLAYS: *The Forgotten Village*, 1941; *Lifeboat*, 1944; *A Medal for Benny*, 1945; *The Pearl*, 1945; *The Red Pony*, 1949; *Viva Zapata!*, 1952.

NONFICTION: *Their Blood Is Strong*, 1938; *The Forgotten Village*, 1941; *Sea of Cortez*, 1941 (with Edward F. Ricketts); *Bombs Away*, 1942; *A Russian Journal*, 1948 (with Robert Capa); *Once There Was a War*, 1958; *Travels with Charley: In Search of America*, 1962; *Letters to Alicia*, 1965; *America and Americans*, 1966; *Journal of a Novel*, 1969; *Steinbeck: A Life in Letters*, 1975 (Elaine Steinbeck and Robert Wallsten, editors).

Bibliography

French, Warren. *John Steinbeck's Fiction Revisited.* New York: Twayne, 1994. Thoroughly revises French's two other books in this Twayne series. Chapters on Steinbeck's becoming a novelist, his relationship to modernism, his short fiction, his wartime fiction, and his final fiction. Includes chronology, notes, and annotated bibliography.

Hughes, R. S. *John Steinbeck: A Study of the Short Fiction.* Boston: Twayne, 1989. Divided into three sections: Steinbeck's short stories, the author's letters exploring his craft, and four critical commentaries. A good study of some of his lesser known works which includes a chronology, a lengthy bibliography, and an index.

Lisca, Peter. *The Wide World of John Steinbeck.* New York: Gordian Press, 1958. An indispensable guide to Steinbeck's work, published in 1958 and then updated with an "Afterword" examining the writer's last novel *The Winter of Our Discontent* (1961). Admired and imitated, Lisca's work set the standard for future Steinbeck studies.

McCarthy, Paul. *John Steinbeck.* New York: Frederick Ungar, 1980. A short biographical approach to Steinbeck's work that examines each novel against the forces that shaped his life. Includes a useful chronology, notes, a bibliography, and an index.

HARRIET BEECHER STOWE

Born: Litchfield, Connecticut; June 14, 1811
Died: Hartford, Connecticut; July 1, 1896

Principal long fiction · *Uncle Tom's Cabin: Or, Life Among the Lowly*, 1852; *Dred: A Tale of the Great Dismal Swamp*, 1856; *The Minister's Wooing*, 1859; *Agnes of Sorrento*, 1862; *The Pearl of Orr's Island*, 1862; *Oldtown Folks*, 1869; *Pink and White Tyranny*, 1871; *My Wife and I*, 1871; *We and Our Neighbors*, 1875; *Poganuc People*, 1878.

Other literary forms · In 1843, Harriet Beecher Stowe gathered a number of her sketches and stories into a volume called *The Mayflower: Or, Sketches of Scenes and Characters of the Descendants of the Pilgrims* (1843). For forty years thereafter, she published short fiction and miscellaneous essays in magazines. In *A Key to Uncle Tom's Cabin* (1853), she assembled a mass of sources and analogues for the characters and incidents of her most famous novel. Her 1869 *The Atlantic Monthly* article "The True Story of Lady Byron's Life," and a subsequent elaboration, *Lady Byron Vindicated* (1870), caused a sensation at the time. She also published a geography for children (1833, her earliest publication, issued under her sister Catharine's name), poems, travel books, collections of biographical sketches, and a number of other children's books.

Stowe's stories and sketches remain readable. Her best collection, *Sam Lawson's Oldtown Fireside Stories* (1872), differs from the novel *Oldtown Folks* mainly in degree of plotlessness. Selections from Stowe's frequently long and chatty letters can be found in the *Life of Harriet Beecher Stowe* (1889), written by her son Charles Edward Stowe, and in more recent biographies, but hundreds of her letters remain unpublished and scattered in various archives.

Achievements · Known primarily today for her antislavery novel *Uncle Tom's Cabin*, Stowe also interpreted the life of her native New England in a series of novels, stories, and sketches. Along with Ralph Waldo Emerson and Oliver Wendell Holmes, she contributed to the first issue of the *The Atlantic Monthly* (November, 1857) and for many years thereafter contributed frequently to that Boston-based magazine. As an alert and intelligent member of a famous family of Protestant ministers, she understood the Puritan conscience and outlook as well as anyone in her time, and as a shrewd observer of the commonplace, she deftly registered Yankee habits of mind and speech. All of her novels feature authentic New England characters; after *Uncle Tom's Cabin* and *Dred*, she turned to settings which included all six New England states. Despite a contradictory idealizing tendency, she pioneered in realism.

One of the first American writers to apply a talent for dialect and local color to the purposes of serious narrative, she exerted a strong influence on Sarah Orne Jewett, Mary Wilkins Freeman, and other regionalists of the later nineteenth century. Without a doubt, however, her greatest achievement was the novel which, beginning as an intended short serial in a Washington antislavery weekly, the *National Era*, forced the American reading public to realize for the first time that slaves were not only a national problem but also people with hopes and aspirations as legitimate as their own. Critics as diverse as Henry Wadsworth Longfellow, Heinrich Heine, William Dean Howells, and Leo Tolstoy in the nineteenth century, and Edmund Wilson and Anthony Burgess in the twentieth, have used superlatives to praise *Uncle Tom's Cabin.*

Library of Congress

Biography · When Harriet Elizabeth Beecher was born on June 14, 1811, the seventh child of Lyman and Roxana Beecher, her father's fame as a preacher had spread well beyond the Congregational Church of Litchfield, Connecticut. All seven Beecher sons who lived to maturity became ministers, one becoming more famous than his father. Harriet, after attending Litchfield Academy, a well-regarded school, was sent to the Hartford Female Seminary, which was founded by her sister Catharine—in some respects the substitute mother whom Harriet needed after Roxana died in 1816 but did not discover in the second Mrs. Beecher. In later years, Harriet would consistently idealize motherhood. When Catherine's fiancé, a brilliant young man but one who had not experienced any perceptible religious conversion, died in 1822, the eleven-year-old Harriet felt the tragedy. In 1827, the shy, melancholy girl became a teacher in her sister's school.

In 1832, Lyman Beecher accepted the presidency of Lane Seminary in Cincinnati, Ohio, and soon Catharine and Harriet had established another school there. Four years later, Harriet married a widower named Calvin Stowe, a Lane professor. In the years that followed, she bore seven children. She also became familiar with slavery, as practiced just across the Ohio River in Kentucky; with the abolitionist movement, which boasted several notable champions in Cincinnati, including the future Chief Justice of the United States Supreme Court, Salmon P. Chase; and with the Underground Railroad. As a way of supplementing her husband's small income, she also contributed to local and religious periodicals.

Not until the Stowes moved to Brunswick, Maine, in 1850, however, did she think of writing about slavery. Then, urged by her brother Henry, by then a prominent minister in Brooklyn, New York, and by other family members in the wake of Congress's enactment of the Fugitive Slave Act, and spurred by a vision she experienced at a church service, she began to construct *Uncle Tom's Cabin*. Even as a weekly serial in the *National Era*, it attracted much attention, and its publication in 1852 as a book made Stowe an instant celebrity. After that year, from her new base in Andover, Massachusetts, where her husband taught, she twice visited Europe, met Harriet Martineau, John Ruskin, the Brownings, and Lady Byron, among others, and the scope of her fame increased even further.

Stowe wrote another slavery novel, *Dred*, and then turned her literary attention to New England. The drowning of her son Henry, a Dartmouth student, in the summer of 1857, marred for her the successes of these years. In the fall of 1862, infuriated by the lack of British support for the North in the Civil War and skeptical that President Lincoln would fulfill his promise to issue a proclamation of emancipation, Stowe visited Lincoln, who is reported to have greeted her with the words, "So this is the little lady who made this big war." She left Washington satisfied that the president would keep his word.

Following Calvin Stowe's retirement from Andover, the family moved to Hartford, the winters usually being spent in northern Florida. Two of the most sensational scandals of the post-Civil War era involved Stowe, the first arising when she published an imprudent and detailed account of Lord Byron's sins as revealed to her some years earlier by the now deceased widow of the poet, the second being an adultery suit brought against her brother Henry in which Stowe characteristically defended him to the hilt. The Byron affair in particular turned many people against her, although her books continued to be commercial successes throughout the 1870's. The most severe personal abuse ever directed at a respectable nineteenth century woman bothered Stowe far less than another personal tragedy: the alcoholism and eventual disappearance of her son Fred in San Francisco, California, in 1870.

In the last twenty-three years of her life, Stowe became the central attraction of the Hartford neighborhood known as Nook Farm, also the home of Charles Dudley Warner and Mark Twain, the latter moving there in part because of its Beecher connections. Her circle of friends included Annie Fields, wife of *The Atlantic Monthly* publisher; George Eliot, with whom she corresponded; and Holmes, always a staunch supporter. In her final years, her mind wandered at times, but she was still writing lucid letters two years before her death on July 1, 1896, at the age of eighty-five.

Analysis · In 1869, after finishing her sixth novel, *Oldtown Folks*, Harriet Beecher Stowe began a correspondence with George Eliot by sending her a copy. Although an international celebrity, Stowe wanted the approval of this younger and less famous woman who had contributed notably to a movement just beginning to be critically recognized: literary realism. Like Stowe, Eliot came from a deeply religious background and had formed a union with an unromantic, bookish, but supportive man. Unlike the American novelist, Eliot had rejected religion for rationalism and Romanticism for realism. Had Calvin Stowe's first wife not died, it would have been unthinkable for Harriet Beecher to live with him as Eliot did with George Henry Lewes. In life, the former Miss Beecher cheerfully married the unexciting scholar; in *The Minister's Wooing*, she would not permit her heroine Mary Scudder to marry her scholarly suitor (as Eliot's Dorothea Brooke in *Middlemarch* (1871-1872) was permitted to marry hers, Dr. Casaubon).

Stowe's hope, in a measure fulfilled, that Eliot would like *Oldtown Folks* may be taken as signifying her desire to be recognized as a realist, even though her own realism was strongly tinged with the Romanticism Eliot had come to despise. The young Harriet Beecher had probably learned something from John Bunyan's *The Pilgrim's Progress* (1678, 1684), but most of her other reading—*The Arabian Nights*, Cotton Mather's *Magnalia Christi Americana* (1702), and the works of Sir Walter Scott and Lord Byron—had little to teach an incipient realist. Nor did American literature in the 1830's, when she began to write, furnish any likely models. As a result, the reader finds in her works a mingling of realistic and Romantic elements.

Stowe's settings, particularly the New England ones, ring true. She understood her cultural roots, and she proved able to recollect childhood impressions almost photographically. She possessed a keen ear for dialect and a sharp eye for the idiosyncrasies of people she scarcely seemed to have noticed until they turned up in her writing. She used the novel to probe urgent social issues such as slavery and women's rights. Although she liked nature and worked hard at describing it accurately, she disdained her native region's characteristic transcendental interpretations of it. She displayed the realist's aversion to mystery, mysticism, and the legendizing of history.

On the other hand, the Romantic tendencies of Stowe's fiction stand out against its realistic background. Her heroines are invariably saintly, as are certain of her black males such as Uncle Tom and, in *Dred*, Uncle Tiff. Her recalcitrant heroes often undergo rather unconvincing conversions. Occasionally, she introduces a mythic, larger-than-life character such as Dred. In common with most of the generation of American realists who followed her, she never renounced the heroic but sought to demonstrate its presence among humble and common people. Her heroes differ from those of Twain, William Dean Howells, and Henry James, however, in drawing their strength from a firm Christian commitment: Stowe's piety has been something of an impediment to her modern readers.

The looseness of plotting about which Stowe's critics have complained so much derives in large measure from her inability to develop convincing central characters in most of her novels. Four of her last five novels have plural nouns—words such as *neighbors* and *folks* and *people*—in their titles, but even *Uncle Tom's Cabin* is not about Uncle Tom in the sense that Charles Dickens's *David Copperfield* (1849-1850) or Gustave Flaubert's *Madame Bovary* (1857) is about its title character. In fact, Stowe changed the title of *Dred* for a time to *Nina Gordon*, a more central character but one who dies many chapters from the end. *My Wife and I* and *Oldtown Folks* are narrated by relatively colorless central characters.

One of Stowe's most persistent and indeed remarkable narrative traits also works against her realism on occasions. As she confides at the beginning of chapter 44 of *Dred*, "There's no study in human nature more interesting than the aspects of the same subject in the points of view of different characters." That she periodically allowed this interest to distract her from the task at hand is clear. Although she experimented with different points of view—omniscient, first-person, dramatic, and circulating (the last primarily through the use of the epistolary method)—she worked before the time when novelists such as Joseph Conrad, James Joyce, and William Faulkner developed techniques capable of sustaining this kind of interest. It should be pointed out that Stowe uses the expression "points of view" in the sense of "opinions," and she is more likely to present the conflict of opinions through conversations than through living, breathing embodiments of motivating ideas.

It is as a realist before her time that Stowe is most profitably considered. Even where her realism does not serve a socially critical purpose, as it does in *Uncle Tom's Cabin* and *My Wife and I*, she makes her readers aware of the texture, the complexity, of social life—particularly the conflicts, tensions, and joys of New England community life. Understanding how people grow from their geographic, social, religious, and intellectual roots, she is able to convey the reality of isolated Maine coastal villages and the jaunty postwar Manhattan of aspiring journalists. In her best work, she depicts evil not as the product of Mephistophelean schemers or motiveless brutes but of high-minded people incapacitated by a crucial weakness, such as the irresolute Augustine St. Clare of *Uncle Tom's Cabin*, the temporizing Judge Clayton of *Dred*, and the imperceptive Dr. Hopkins of *The Minister's Wooing*.

Uncle Tom's Cabin · *Uncle Tom's Cabin: Or, Life Among the Lowly*, remains one of the most controversial of novels. Extravagantly admired and bitterly detested in the 1850s, it still arouses extreme reactions more than a century later. An early barrage of challenges to its authenticity led Stowe to work furiously at the assembling of *A Key to Uncle Tom's Cabin* the next year. In 262 closely printed, double-columned pages, she impressively documented horrors that verified "the truth of the work." This book unfortunately encouraged the development of an essentially nonliterary mass of criticism, with the result that the novel early gained the reputation of a brilliant piece of propaganda—even President Lincoln supposedly accepting the Civil War as its legacy—but unworthy of serious consideration on artistic grounds.

It did not help the novel's cause that the inevitable later reaction against this enormously popular story coincided with the effort, spearheaded by Henry James, to establish the novel as a form of art rather than as a mere popular entertainment. A writer who strove too singlemindedly for mere verifiability did not merit consideration as an artist. In the same year that *Uncle Tom's Cabin* began appearing serially, Nathaniel Hawthorne—James's chief example of the American artist—prefaced his *The House of the Seven Gables* (1851) with a firm declaration of its imaginary basis which contrasted sharply with his attempt to provide a "historical" one for *The Scarlet Letter* one year earlier. Hawthorne's star as a writer of fiction gradually rose: Stowe's sank. Like "Old Ironsides," the vigorous youthful poem of Stowe's staunch friend of later years, *Uncle Tom's Cabin* was relegated to the status of a work that made things happen—important historically but damned by that very fact to the region of the second-rate.

In *A Key to Uncle Tom's Cabin*, Stowe herself called *Uncle Tom's Cabin* "a very inadequate representation of slavery," but her excuse is significant: "Slavery, in some of its workings, is too dreadful for the purposes of art." She was acknowledging a problem that would continue to bedevil realists for most of the rest of the century. The most prominent spokesman for realism, Howells, agreed with her, and until the 1890's, realists would generally exclude things considered "too dreadful." As late as 1891, Thomas Hardy induced mass revulsion by allowing his heroine to be raped in *Tess of the D'Urbervilles* (1891) while referring to her in his subtitle as "a pure woman."

Stowe sandwiched the story of Uncle Tom, the meek Christian capable of turning the other cheek even to the sadistic Simon Legree, between the resolute George and Eliza Harris's escape from slavery and the Harris family's fortuitous reunion at the end of the novel. If the plot is untidy and contrived, a number of the individual characters and episodes have remained among the most memorable in fiction. The famous scene in which Eliza crosses the Ohio River ice in early spring is "true" not because the feat had been accomplished (although Stowe knew it had) but because she makes the reader feel Eliza's desperation, the absolute necessity of the attempt, and the likelihood that a person who grew up in her hard school would develop the resources to succeed.

The meeting between Miss Ophelia and Topsy illustrates Stowe's talent for dramatizing the confrontation of stubborn viewpoints. Sold down the river by his first owner, Tom has rescued the angelic daughter of Augustine St. Clare and has been installed to the St. Clare household. Miss Ophelia, a Vermont cousin of St. Clare, has been brought south to take care of Eva, whose mother is languidly incompetent. St. Clare despises slavery but feels powerless to resist it; Ophelia's intransigent New England conscience will not permit her to acquiese in it. After listening to a considerable amount of her antislavery rhetoric, St. Clare gives his cousin a little black girl rescued from alcoholic parents. Ophelia is revolted by Topsy, so utterly different from the golden, cherubic Eva. Topsy, shrewd and skeptical beyond her years, embodies the insidiousness of slavery itself. Neither was premeditated but simply "grow'd" and now must somehow be dealt with as found. Ophelia must find room in her heart for the little "black spider" or lose face with her cousin. Her struggle with Topsy—and with her own physical aversion—is fierce and richly comical, and its successful outcome believable.

For the modern reader, the death scenes in the novel are more of a problem. Little Eva's protracted illness and beatific death exactly pleased the taste of Stowe's time. Today, her father's senseless and sudden death as a result of his attempt to mediate a tavern brawl seems more like real life—or would if Stowe had not permitted St. Clare to linger long enough to undergo a deathbed religious conversion. Modern reaction to Stowe's climactic scene is complicated by the hostility of writers such as James Baldwin to the character of Uncle Tom, who, in dying at the hands of Legree's henchmen, wins their souls in the process. Whether or not the conversion of Sambo and Quimbo convinces today's reader, Tom's character has been firmly established, and he dies in precisely the spirit the reader expects.

Far less satisfactory is the subsequent escape of two of Legree's slaves from his clutches. Stowe did nothing beforehand to induce belief in a brutal master who could melt into helpless impassivity at the sight of a lock of his dead mother's hair. Finding it expedient to make Legree superstitious, she established this side of his character belatedly and ineptly, and she failed to understand that her conception of the power of motherhood was not universally shared.

In short, the reader's admiration is interrupted by idealistic and sentimental material that does not support Stowe's goal of depicting life as it was. Nor is this inconsistency surprising. No American had ever written such a novel: realistic in impulse and directed at a current social problem of the greatest magnitude. She had no models and could not, like Twain after her, draw upon experiences as Missourian, journalist, western traveler, and–before he wrote his greatest books–neighbor of Stowe and reader of her work.

Like Twain and Howells after her, Stowe did not banish Romanticism from her novels, but her commitment to realism is clear. Thirty years before Twain's accomplishments with dialect in *Adventures of Huckleberry Finn* (1884), and nearly two decades before Bret Harte popularized the concept of local color, Stowe used dialects–not with perfect consistency but not for the conventional purpose of humor either. For the first time in major American fiction, dialect served the purpose of generating a credible environment for a serious narrative. In the process, she changed the perceptions of hundreds of thousands of readers forever.

Within a year, the book had made Stowe internationally known. When, after several years of minor literary activity, she returned to the subject of slavery, events were unfolding that led inexorably to war. Her brother Henry was outraging North and South alike by holding his own mock slave auction in his Brooklyn church. John Brown was launching his personal civil war in Kansas. In the chamber of the United States Senate, abolitionist Charles Sumner was nearly beaten to death by a southern colleague. Stowe herself had been busy with antislavery petitions and appeals.

Dred · From this context emerged *Dred*, a more somber novel. As it opens, Nina Gordon has returned to her North Carolina plantation from New York upon the death of her father. She has dallied with several suitors but has sense enough to prefer Edward Clayton, an idealistic young lawyer from another part of her native state. After successfully prosecuting a white man who had hired and then physically abused Nina's domestic slave Milly, Clayton's ambition to counteract such abuses legally is checked when an appeals judge–a man of undoubted probity and, ironically, Clayton's own father–reverses the earlier decision on the grounds that no slave has any rights under state law. Meanwhile, Nina's attempt at benign management of her plantation is set back by the appearance of her wastrel brother Tom, who especially enjoys tormenting her able quadroon steward Harry. Although bearing a strong resemblance to George Harris of *Uncle Tom's Cabin*, Harry is different in two important ways. First, Stowe develops the frustration of this educated and sensitive man much more thoroughly. Second, Harry is, unknown to Nina, the Gordon children's half-brother.

When Nina dies in a cholera epidemic, Tom asserts control over the plantation, and Clayton returns home with the resolve to press for changes in a legal code that permits a man to own and mistreat his own brother. Harry is driven to rebel and flee into the nearby swamp, where he falls under the influence of Dred, whom the author styles after the son of the famous black rebel Denmark Vesey, but who resembles even more closely that other noted rebel, Nat Turner.

What happens next exemplifies Stowe's familiarity with the clergy and her talent for controversy. Invited by his uncle to a Presbyterian ministers' conference, Clayton seeks there the moral support for legal reform. Even though he finds one minister passionately committed to rights for slaves, the majority of the brethren turn out to be complacent trimmers, and Clayton learns that he can expect no help in that quarter. Stowe strategically places the conference between two scenes of desperation, both of which illustrate the social system's assault on the family. In the former, Uncle

Tiff, the black guardian of two white children whose father is a shiftless squatter on the Gordon plantation, vows to preserve them from the corrupting influence of their slatternly stepmother and takes them to Dred's hidden fastness in the swamp. In the latter, another quadroon Gordon offshoot, Cora, confesses in court to the murder of her own two children to "save" them, as she puts it, from being sold away.

In the swamp, Tiff and the children are succored by Dred, who is one of Stowe's most bizarre creations: half Robin Hood, half self-appointed executioner for the Lord. Too mythic a hero for a realistic novel, Dred unfortunately develops quickly into a very tedious one too, ranting interminably in his guise of Old Testament prophet. Even he is no match, however, for the committed Christian Milly, although she can accomplish no more than the postponement of his planned revenge against the hated whites. When Tom Gordon organizes a party to ransack the swamp for Dred and Harry, the former is killed, and Harry and his wife, along with Tiff and his young charges, escape to the North. In an obviously Pyrrhic victory, Clayton, baffled by his neighbors in his attempt to educate the slaves on his own estate, takes them off to Canada, where they continue to work for him in their freedom.

Tiff is another saintly domestic slave, but he has no power to reclaim any Sambo or Quimbo from degradation. There are no spectacular personal conversions in *Dred* and no hope of any social one. Milly, who has had to endure the loss by death or sale of all her numerous children, seems to win a legal victory over a cruel master and a moral one over the vindictive fugitive Dred, but both turn out to be illusory. Not only the fugitive blacks but also Clayton the hero must leave the country. If *Uncle Tom's Cabin* stands as a warning to a divided society, *Dred* is a prophecy of disintegration.

The Minister's Wooing · Stowe's next two novels have much in common. Both *The Minister's Wooing* and *The Pearl of Orr's Island* are anchored in New England coastal communities, and both put Yankee manners and speech on display. Each novel boasts a saintly heroine who effects the conversion of a dashing young man with a strong affinity for the sea. Although the former novel paints Newport, Rhode Island, less colorfully than the latter does coastal Maine, *The Minister's Wooing* is a more carefully constructed novel which analyzes New England character more profoundly. More than any other Stowe novel, *The Minister's Wooing* focuses on its principals: Samuel Hopkins, Congregationalist minister of Newport, and Mary Scudder, daughter of Hopkins's widowed landlady. In several respects, the minister is the historical Dr. Hopkins, learned protégé of the great Jonathan Edwards, eminent theologian in his own right, and vigorous opponent of slavery in a town consecrated to the slave trade. In the 1780's, when the novel is set, however, the real Hopkins was in his sixties and possessed a wife and eight children; Stowe makes him middle-aged and a bachelor. Another celebrity of the time plays a significant role: Aaron Burr in the years before he became senator, vice-president, and killer of Alexander Hamilton in a duel. Burr is depicted as a charming, unscrupulous seducer of women—a distortion of the historical Burr, no doubt, but one based on the man's reputation.

Stowe's motive for involving these men in her story of pious young Mary Scudder is utterly serious. As friend and student of Edwards, Hopkins represents the stern, uncompromising Puritan past. As Edwards's wordly and skeptical grandson, Burr stands for the repudiation of the past. Mary's choice is not—what would be easy for her—between Hopkins and Burr but between Hopkins and her young lover James Marvyn, who resembles Burr only in his impatience with the hard and incomprehensible doctrines of his forebears. James has grown up with Mary but has gravitated to

the sea, and is not quite engaged to her when he is reported lost in a shipwreck. Mrs. Scudder thereafter nudges Mary toward a union with the unexciting minister, himself an admirer of the young lady's ardent–if for his taste too sunny–Christianity.

Stowe neatly balances the claims of Hopkins's exacting Old Testament theology and Mary's simpler faith in the loving kindness of Jesus. In comforting the lost James's mother, long appalled by the minister's remorseless logic and now driven to near-psychosis by her son's supposed death, Mary's cheerful faith receives its first test. She also befriends an aristocratic young Frenchwoman–Burr's intended victi–and learns of the world of adulterous intrigue. As in her previous novels, Stowe introduces a black servant who has looked on life long and maintained a practical Christianity that is proof against all temptation to despair. Having been freed by her master, Mr. Marvyn, under the minister's influence, Candace works freely for the Marvyns and venerates Dr. Hopkins, not failing, however, to draw Mrs. Marvyn gently from "the fathomless mystery of sin and sorrow" to the "deeper mystery of God's love." Meanwhile, Mary's faith deepens, Stowe probably raising more than a few Protestant eyebrows by likening her explicitly to the Virgin Mary, who "kept all things and pondered them in her heart."

In real life, Catharine Beecher's beloved did not survive his shipwreck, and Stowe's elder sister agonized long over the possibility of his having died unregenerate. In life, Henry Stowe did not miraculously escape drowning. James Marvyn, on the other hand, after a considerable interval in which he inexplicably fails to notify either Mary or his family of his survival, returns a week before Mary's scheduled wedding with the minister. After having promised herself to Hopkins, Mary will not of course renege, so it falls to Miss Prissy, her dressmaker and friend, to approach the formidable theologian with the fact–which he is incapable of divining–that James is Mary's true love. Miss Prissy is one of Stowe's well-conceived realistic characters; an incurable gossip and a hypocrite in her professed admiration for the minister's sermons, she is nevertheless willing to assume the unpleasant initiative on behalf of her friend. Apprised of the true situation, the minister releases Mary and promptly marries her to Marvyn.

As she had in her first *The Atlantic Monthly* short story, Stowe depicts in this novel the psychology of bereavement; what she refuses to present is not death itself but the possibility of a good-hearted lad's dying unregenerate. She demonstrates how the rigorous faith of a Hopkins can be a barrier, even a poison, to the unstable, but of the efficacy of Christianity to restore lost lambs, she can conceive no doubt. Even the heterodox Burr nearly succumbs to Mary's entreaties to reform. Stowe's less saintly believers, such as Miss Prissy, and her magnanimous skeptics, like Augustine St. Clare of *Uncle Tom's Cabin*, are more credible. As for Hopkins, willing to jeopardize his church financially and socially by his insistence that the most influential of his parishoners renounce his connections with the slave trade, his final renunciation of Mary is quite consistent with his previous rock-ribbed selflessness.

Oldtown Folks · *Oldtown Folks*, at which Stowe worked in the postwar years and published whole in 1869–for she refused to serialize it in the usual way–repeats many of the concerns of *The Minister's Wooing* and even reintroduces Jonathan Edwards's grandson, here known as Ellery Davenport. Longer, more varied, and much more rambling, this novel contains a considerable amount of Stowe's best writing. In the preface, her narrator, Horace Holyoke, vows to "interpret to the world the New England life and character of the early republic." Today, no one would choose a loose, leisurely narrative to achieve such an ambition, and perhaps no one but Stowe would have attempted it in the 1860's. It is no coincidence that *Oldtown Folks* attracted the attention of Perry Miller, the distinguished twentieth century interpreter of the New England tradition.

The Minister's Wooing had been a theological novel in which no one had very much fun. As if to redress the deficiency, Stowe widens her focus, invests this work with more of the engaging minor characters of *The Pearl of Orr's Island,* and shows her villagers enjoying themselves. Her twenty-seventh chapter, "How We Kept Thanksgiving at Oldtown," which has become an anthology piece in recent years, argues that Oldtown (based on her husband's hometown of Natick, Massachusetts) has fun precisely because the inhabitants take human life seriously enough "to believe they can do much with it." Sam Lawson–Stowe's most famous character outside *Uncle Tom's Cabin*–far from exemplifying the protestant work ethic, is the town idler, universally valued for his skill at "lubricating" with his humorous andecdotes and relaxed manner the "incessant streampower in Yankee life." By contrast, the character most devoted to work, Miss Asphyxia Smith, is easily the most hateful character in the book.

Sam also serves the tenuous plot interest by coming upon two of its three principals (narrator Horace Holyoke is the other) in an abandoned house to which they had fled from Miss Asphyxia's clutches, for, like Uncle Tiff's young charges in *Dred,* Harry and Tina Percival have been successively deserted by their scalawag father and subjected to the slow death of their mother. Tina, who is adopted by Mehitabel Rossiter, a woman of no physical beauty but much strength of character and intellect, grows into a beautiful, kindhearted, but willful woman–exactly the type favored by the unprincipled Davenport. Harry grows up as Horace's companion in the nearby Holyoke household.

Tina, not knowing that Davenport numbers among his previous victims Ellen Rossiter, Mehitabel's younger sister, marries him, and it appears that Stowe will not permit her protagonist the usual eleventh-hour rescue. Tina endures ten years with the erratic Davenport, generously adopting his daughter by Ellen Rossiter, but then, in a switch on the Aaron Burr story, Davenport is killed in a duel. Two years (but only three paragraphs) later, Tina and Horace marry and settle in Boston. At the end of the novel, the Horace Holyokes are discoverd back in Oldtown visiting its most durable inhabitant, Sam Lawson.

Any synopsis leaves untouched the merits of *Oldtown Folks*: the interplay of its varied and vital minor characters and the development of its seduction theme. Of the former, Miss Asphyxia, "a great threshing-machine of a woman"; Horace's peppery grandmother, "a valiant old soul, who fearlessly took any bull in life by the horns, and was ready to shake him into decorum"; and Lawson, half nuisance, half good neighbor, are only three of the most memorable. As seducer, Davenport takes advantage of several factors: the intransigence of Calvinism in its death throes, embodied in brilliant but outdated theorizers such as this novel's version of Hopkins, Dr. Stern; the Calvinist legacy of neurosis, skepticism, and rebellion (Miss Rossiter, Tina, and Davenport himself); and the ineffectuality of well-intentioned observers such as Horace and Harry. Thwarted by orthodoxy, which has become a cruel instrument in the hands of its conservative defenders, and averse to the rationalism that played such a large part in the creation of the new republic, the Oldtowners are easily taken in by Davenport, who has turned the passion and intellectual energy inherited from Edwards and the rest of his Puritan forebears to the service of selfish and worldly ends.

My Wife and I* and *We and Our Neighbors · In *My Wife and I* and its sequel, *We and Our Neighbors*, Stowe turns to contemporary Manhattan life, a frivolous and even more worldly existence dotted nevertheless by young men and women of impulses Stowe characterizes as Christian but which may strike today's reader as more generally humanitarian. The full spectrum of views on women's rights is on display, including a conviction, expressed by a young woman struggling for the opportunity to study medicine, that "marriage ought never to be entered on as a means of support." The main business of the two novels, however, is to educate Harry Henderson for marriage and thus to provide a base of operations for his wife, who dedicates herself to neighborliness and charitable offices. Stowe retains her observant eye and spicy descriptive powers, but her narrator cannot "interpret" the Gilded Age as Horace Holyoke in *Oldtown Folks* could interpret post-Revolutionary New England.

Poganuc People · *Pink and White Tyranny*, the story of a man who married and must endure a selfish and demanding woman, must rank, along with the earlier *Agnes of Sorrento*, among Stowe's weakest books. Finally, in *Poganuc People*, she returns to the milieu of *The Minister's Wooing, The Pearl of Orr's Island*, and her Oldtown books. Poganuc is the Litchfield of her childhood and Dolly Cushing her closet approximation to an autobiographical heroine. The principal conflict is not between the old religion and the new worldliness but between entrenched Congregationalism and upstart Episcopalianism. The novel begins and ends at Christmas when the liturgical and social differences between the two denominations stand out most sharply. Like Maggie Tulliver in Eliot's *The Mill on the Floss* (1860) Dolly is precocious, sensitive, and consequently often uncomfortable, but instead of developing the crises of her heroine's maturation, as does Eliot, Stowe whisks her off to a fashionable Boston marriage with a successful merchant, after which the author makes a final survey of the Poganuc people going about their business under the immemorial elms of the village.

Stowe seldom brought her psychological insights to bear on the development of her main characters, with the result that the less important ones invariably seem more convincing. Whether because her most productive years antedated the time of the realistic novel and particularly the psychological novel, or because she felt too strongly the nineteenth century prohibition against a woman exploring the conflicts and repressions of her own life, Stowe left unwritten what might have constituted her richest vein of realism. She never wrote a novel expressing what it felt like to be a vocationless Harriet Beecher approaching womanhood or the second Mrs. Calvin Stowe struggling with sickness, poverty, and the multitudinous demands of husband and children. The woman who wrote of domesticity in her time avoided calling attention to its tensions, exactions, and restrictions. Whatever else family life meant to Stowe, it helped prepare her to do what no American novelist had done before: write powerfully and feelingly about slavery.

Robert P. Ellis

Other major works

SHORT FICTION: *The Mayflower: Or, Sketches of Scenes and Characters of the Descendants of the Pilgrims*, 1843; *Sam Lawson's Oldtown Fireside Stories*, 1872.
POETRY: *Religious Poems*, 1867.

NONFICTION: *A Key to Uncle Tom's Cabin,* 1853; *Sunny Memories of Foreign Lands,* 1854; *Lady Byron Vindicated,* 1870; *Palmetto Leaves,* 1873.

CHILDREN'S LITERATURE: *First Geography for Children,* 1833 (as Catharine Stowe).

Bibliography

Boydston, Jeanne, Mary Kelley, and Anne Margolis. *The Limits of Sisterhood: The Beecher Sisters on Women's Rights and Woman's Sphere.* Chapel Hill: University of North Carolina Press, 1988. A superb study of Stowe and her sisters, Catharine and Isabella. Brief but insightful essays address each woman as an individual and as a sister. Primary documents are appended to each chapter, providing excellent resources. Illustrations, careful documentation, and a detailed index make this an invaluable text.

Donovan, Josephine. *Uncle Tom's Cabin: Evil, Affliction, and Redemptive Love.* Boston: Twayne, 1991. Part of the Twayne Masterworks Series, Donovan's book follows the series format by first placing *Uncle Tom's Cabin* in literary and historical context, then delivering a particular reading of the work. As her subtitle suggests, Donovan views Stowe's masterpiece as a book about evil and its redemption, taking it more or less at face value and reading it with the approach she believes Stowe intended—which has a decidedly feminist bent.

Hedrick, Joan D. *Harriet Beecher Stowe: A Life.* New York: Oxford University Press, 1994. Stowe's family kept a tight reign on her literary remains, and the only previous attempt at a full-scale independent biography, Forrest Wilson's *Crusader in Crinoline* (1941) is now very much out of date. Hedrick's book makes use of new materials, including letters and diaries, and takes fresh approaches to Stowe occasioned by the Civil Rights and women's movements.

Lang, Amy Schrager. *Prophetic Woman: Anne Hutchinson and the Problem of Dissent in the Literature of New England.* Berkeley: University of California Press, 1987. An excellent feminist study, focusing on *Uncle Tom's Cabin* and Stowe's role in the history of Puritan suppression of women who achieve public notice. Stowe's novel constitutes a culmination in this process and presents a model of women as moral superiors who represent the possibility of a future without slavery.

Stowe, Charles Edward. *Life of Harriet Beecher Stowe.* Boston: Houghton Mifflin, 1889. Written by her seventh child, this is the first full-length biography of Stowe, drawn from her letters and her journal. Though not critical, it offers extensive excerpts of her personal writings and of correspondence from other renowned writers. An annotated primary bibliography and a detailed index are included.

Sundquist, Eric J., ed. *New Essays on "Uncle Tom's Cabin."* Cambridge, England: Cambridge University Press, 1986. An excellent collection of essays on Stowe's most famous novel. The insightful introduction discusses changing literary theories as they relate to *Uncle Tom's Cabin.* The six diverse contributions by notable scholars include analyses of genre and gender issues. A selected bibliography also notes additional criticism.

Tompkins, Jane. *Sensational Designs: The Cultural Work of American Fiction, 1790-1860.* New York: Oxford University Press, 1985. Tompkins addresses *Uncle Tom's Cabin* from the perspective of "the politics of literary history." Nineteenth century popular domestic novels represent attempts to reorganize culture from a woman's perspective, and Stowe's novel is representative of "America's religion of domesticity" as empowerment of women. An excellent and influential study.

THEODORE STURGEON

Edward Hamilton Waldo

Born: Staten Island, New York; February 26, 1918
Died: Eugene, Oregon; May 8, 1985

Principal long fiction · *The Dreaming Jewels*, 1950 (also known as *The Synthetic Man*, 1957); *More Than Human*, 1953; *I, Libertine*, 1956 (as Frederick R. Ewing, with Jean Shepherd); *The Cosmic Rape*, 1958; *Venus Plus X*, 1960; *Some of Your Blood*, 1961; *Voyage to the Bottom of the Sea*, 1961; *Alien Cargo*, 1984; *Godbody*, 1986.

Other literary forms · While Theodore Sturgeon was not as prolific as some of the science-fiction fraternity, he wrote more than 190 short stories, 130 articles, and a number of radio and television scripts. His short fiction was assembled in many collections, ranging from *Without Sorcery* (1948) to *The Golden Helix* (1980).

Achievements · Theodore Sturgeon's work was once called "the single most important body of science fiction by an American to date." A founder of modern American science fiction, he contributed to the genre's transition from underground to mainstream literature. He was the recipient of Argosy (1947), International Fantasy (1954), Nebula (1970), and Hugo (1971) awards.

Biography · Theodore Sturgeon was born Edward Hamilton Waldo, on February 26, 1918, on Staten Island, New York. His parents were divorced, and, after his mother remarried in 1929, his name was legally changed when he was adopted by his stepfather. After he was graduated from high school, where his career as a gymnast was ended by rheumatic fever, he finished a term at Penn State Nautical School and then spent three years at sea. During that time he began to write, producing some forty conventional short stories for McClure's Syndicate before turning to science fiction, which he began to publish in John W. Campbell, Jr.'s *Astounding Science Fiction* in 1939.

Sturgeon recalled that science fiction was "the pornography of its day" and recounted how his stepfather discovered and destroyed his 1935 issues of *Amazing*. When he took up science fiction, Sturgeon was making a commitment to a literary form which promised little prestige and very modest financial returns. He married in the same year he launched his science-fiction career and contributed regularly to *Unknown* and *Astounding Science Fiction* in order to support his family. Although he produced highly regarded stories, such as "It" (1940) and "Microcosmic God" (1941), he had to seek employment outside of writing to earn a living.

After operating a hotel in the British West Indies in 1940, Sturgeon worked as a door-to-door salesman, as assistant chief steward at Fort Simonds, and as a bulldozer operator. In 1942, he pursued the latter occupation in Puerto Rico. Except for *Killdozer*, a novelette about a machine possessed by a malignant force, his literary output declined sharply between 1942 and 1944, when he returned to the United States and became a copy editor. These were difficult years for Sturgeon, financially and emotionally. Not until 1946, after his marriage ended in divorce, did he fully resume his career under the encouragement of John Campbell.

While continuing to write, Sturgeon tried his hand at running a literary agency and producing advertising copy. The first substantial public recognition for his work came in 1947 when he won a thousand-dollar prize for "Bianca's Hands." (The runner-up in the contest, sponsored by the British magazine *Argosy*, was Graham Greene.) "Bianca's Hands" had been written on Sturgeon's honeymoon years earlier but had found no market because of its bizarre treatment of a "passionate human attachment." Its acceptance marked a turning point for Sturgeon, which was closely followed by the publication of the first of his many anthologies, *Without Sorcery*, with an introduction by Ray Bradbury.

As he entered the period of his greatest creativity, Sturgeon's personal life again underwent change, with a second marriage in 1949 and a third in 1951. His output of fiction was unabated, however, with *The Dreaming Jewels*, his first novel, appearing in 1950, and *More Than Human*, published in 1953, winning the 1954 International Fantasy Award, a confirmation of his rank as one of America's foremost writers of science fiction. His stories continued to be anthologized in his own collections and those of others, and he engaged in a broad range of literary activity, from a hoax with Jean Shepherd, *I, Libertine*, published under the name Frederick R. Ewing, to a fictional case history of vampirism, *Some of Your Blood*, and a novel depicting an androgynous utopia, *Venus Plus X*.

As a major author of speculative fiction, he helped to create a climate of acceptance for the genre among the general public. In his book reviews for the *National Review* (1961-1973), for example, he explained and defended his art while introducing some of contemporary science fiction's finest authors to an audience who might otherwise not have learned of them. He was involved in science fiction's growth in other media also, in 1966 moving to Los Angeles to write for the television series *Star Trek*. Late in his life, he published little new fiction, but he continued to compile anthologies of his previous work for new audiences. He married for the fourth time in 1969. Sturgeon was living in Eugene, Oregon, at the time of his death in 1985.

Though Sturgeon deplored the "inexcusable invasions into . . . authors' most intimate motivations" by academic critics, there are nevertheless certain definite biographical influences on his work. Beverly Friend called him "a highly personal writer drawing from his own suffering for his craft." She cites his parents' divorce, his estrangement from his stepfather, his illness in adolescence, and his marital and professional problems as sources for his art.

Analysis · Theodore Sturgeon once said, "All great literature is great because it is fable—because it creates typical and archetypical characters and situations which can be applied outside the work to illuminate the human condition." He repeatedly insisted that he did not undervalue the science of science fiction, but he clearly inclined toward minimizing technology as a focus for his work; rather, he concentrated upon fable, often premising his work on occult matters upon which science has had little to say. He said that "in teaching, reviewing, and enjoying science fiction, my emphasis is always on the fiction." This is, he explained, "because I like writers to be read and remembered and (when they can) to move people and shake them; to ignite, to increase their ability to share their visions and their joy and their terror, as well as their knowledge." Sturgeon's criteria for art were more affective than cognitive, and he generally concentrated upon rites of passage rather than technological extrapolation.

Whatever Sturgeon's premise for a story, scientific, psychological, or occult, he wished the work to reflect essential human experiences: "love, and pain, and greed, and laughter, and hope, and above all loneliness." Loneliness is most significant, since he asserted that "what I have been trying to do all these years is to investigate this matter of love, sexual and asexual," and his major fictions are fables of growth toward community and maturity.

The four science-fiction novels which are the heart of Sturgeon's work (*The Dreaming Jewels, More Than Human, The Cosmic Rape,* and *Venus Plus X*) develop the idea that "our strange species has two prime motivating forces: sex, of course, and worship." Throughout his writing, the latter is the more important, and Sturgeon was unwilling to see the highest self-sacrificial and altruistic acts as having any foundation in sexuality. Sturgeon's center of worship, however, is not to be found outside man but in humanity.

Sturgeon's first novel, *The Dreaming Jewels*, is an exploration of what it means to be human. Its premise is the creation of a "synthetic man" by the action of alien crystals which have a deep collective life of their own, apparently unrelated to the affairs of people. These crystals, seemingly without purpose, "dream" objects into existence, sometimes imperfectly, creating freaks and monsters, and sometimes—when they are mating—perfectly, creating creatures with the power of self-transformation. Such materials are better suited to psychological symbolism than scientific discussion. This is precisely the direction of Sturgeon's art; since he found "more room in inner space than in outer space," his fables are essentially paradigms of psychological growth which begin with the frustrations and alienation of youth and end in maturation and integration. On a number of occasions, he defined science fiction in terms of the derivation of the word "science" from the Latin "to know." "Science fiction is knowledge fiction," he wrote, adding that "by far most of the knowledge is psychological."

In *More Than Human*, Sturgeon makes significant use of syzygy, a concept of nonreproductive union signified by a strange word. A collective identity is formed by a group of persons who retain their individuality while contributing to a gestalt which has the ultimate promise of a god. The collective person remains distinctly human, however, and the worship due it is finally worship of humanity. Here the components of the human being, conscience being the highest, are integrated and raised to the highest power. So, too, in a novel which deals directly with sexuality, *Venus Plus X*, the integration of the human personality and worship become paramount, with Sturgeon using androgyny as a symbol of wholeness and providing his utopia's inhabitants with a religion which worships the promise of man.

The form of Sturgeon's novels can present the critical reader with problems. Sturgeon is perhaps most at home as a writer of short stories, and his techniques of composition reflect at times an incomplete transition to the novel's demands. He seemingly pieces together sections which finally form the whole. This is not to say that the structuring of his books is unskillful, for he does finally bring to focus elements which run through them in parallel directions. Also, such a method can be seen as organic to Sturgeon's themes of integration, with loosely related parts finally encompassed in a total vision. Whatever a reader's verdict on form, however, his principal response will probably be to Sturgeon's handling of theme.

Sturgeon's work takes seriously his claim that "the best of science fiction is as good as the best of any modern literature—articulate, poetic, philosophical, provocative, searching, courageous, insightful." He once complained that though the finest science-fiction writers "open their veins into their typewriters, taking their craft and their readers seriously, they seem to be categorically disqualified from the serious attention of mainstream critics and readers." Fortunately, this is no longer the case, in part because of Sturgeon's fables of human nature.

The Dreaming Jewels · The reprinted title of *The Dreaming Jewels* is *The Synthetic Man,* a title which more clearly reflects the subject matter of Sturgeon's first novel but which loses some of the symbolic suggestiveness of the original. Paul Williams has commented that the work is in part based on Sturgeon's resentment of his stepfather and has pointed out the significance of the dream to the creative act of writing science fiction. To this might be added the importance of jewel symbolism in the light of Sturgeon's view of science fiction as "knowledge fiction."

Jewels often symbolize arcane knowledge and spiritual transformation; here they are connected with an unconscious dream-power that can be brought to light for good or ill, and in which reside keys to transformation and regeneration. Contesting for this power are Horty, the "synthetic man"—created by alien crystals that can bring objects, or people, into existence—and Pierre Monetre, a most thoroughgoing misanthrope who would delight in the destruction of humankind. Horty's victory over Monetre (called "maneater" by his subordinates) comes about through his capacity to tap the power of the unconscious, and through the willing sacrifice of Zena, whose education of Horty to human values keeps him from becoming like the alienated Monetre.

Horty's potential alienation comes from abuse by a cruel stepfather, Armand Bluett, a figure Sturgeon has himself identified with "a lot of bitterness and hostility that I wanted to get out." Bluett's viciousness results in the accidental loss of three of Horty's fingers, and the young boy flees after bidding farewell to Kay Hallowell, a girl whose love balances Bluett's hatred. In his flight, Horty is befriended by carnival people, especially Zena, a midget, who notices the boy's sympathetic connection with his only possession, a jack-in-the-box with strange jewels for eyes. These gems prove to have had their effect on the child, gradually transforming him into a creature capable both of communicating with the inner life of the jewels and of transforming himself at will.

Horty's identity is hidden from Monetre, who owns the carnival. Zena disguises him as a girl and warns him never to reveal that he has regenerated his three lost fingers, which Monetre had treated upon his arrival. During his years with the carnival, Horty fails to grow and is only forced to leave when the owner discloses some curiosity about his hand. After leaving, he discovers his gift of transformation, which is useful when he encounters Armand Bluett, now a judge, victimizing Kay Hallowell. Horty cools off the sexually aggressive Bluett by taking Kay's place and slicing off his regenerated fingers, at which sight Bluett passes out. Horty thus becomes the woman who represents love for him so that he might perform a sacrificial mutilation which is both saving and vengeful.

In a series of improbable events, Kay comes under the power of Bluett and Monetre, who is clearly contrasted with Horty. While both are brilliantly gifted, Horty's mind, under Zena's guidance, has been shaped by "humanity and the extensions of humanity," as against Monetre's, which has been twisted by hatred and desire for power. In the confrontation between Horty and Monetre in a psychic duel, Zena sacrifices herself, instructing Horty to use his power to destroy jewel-created creatures. Since Monetre's character is so inhuman, he is assumed to be one. Ironically, Monetre is biologically human, without possessing any spirit of humanity, while Zena, a synthetic creature, sacrifices herself. In the end, however, Horty kills his adversary, resurrects Zena, who becomes his wife, and assumes Monetre's identity while traveling about trying to undo some of the harm he has done.

Sturgeon has assessed *The Dreaming Jewels* as "a rotten novel." Its chief faults are a contrived plot and a style which lacks the energy of the best of his stories of the 1940's. The use of psychological materials is compelling, however, making it one of Sturgeon's most popular works. Horty's series of transformations are representative of his possession of the secret of the unconscious, the capacity to convert revenge into sacrificial love, whose highest exemplar is Zena. The novel moves from mutilation to regeneration, from revenge to love, with Horty progressing toward wholeness by overcoming alienation and linking the transforming power of the unconscious to positive human values.

More Than Human · *More Than Human*, Sturgeon's second and best novel, has at the center of its three-part structure a section entitled "Baby Is Three," which was published separately a year before the novel appeared. According to Sam Moskowitz, Sturgeon wrote a prologue and epilogue to this section to compose the novel. Like *The Dreaming Jewels*, "Baby Is Three" is about an alienated superman, fifteen-year-old Gerry Thompson, who in a strong first-person narration relates his visit to a psychiatrist, to whom he reveals his murder of his guardian, Miss Alicia Kew. Gerry also explains that he is part of a composite being, *homo gestalt*, a uniting of persons with extraordinary telepathic and telekinetic powers. Gerry has the capacity to probe the minds of others–he does this with the psychiatrist to make sure that he will not remember his visit–but he lacks human sympathy and moral awareness.

Sturgeon once said that "you cannot write stories about ideas–which is why so much hard-core, nuts-and-bolts science fiction fails as literature." In *More Than Human*, however, he is fortunate in combining a powerful idea with a sure grasp of style and an effective structure. The first section of the novel, "The Fabulous Idiot," focuses on Lone (a shortened form of *alone*), who is an idiot in the root sense of the word. He is aware of himself alone. He gradually becomes aware of others, first through Miss Kew's sister, Evelyn, who along with Alicia had been the victim of a demonically sexually repressive father, and then through the Prodds, a pathetic couple who take him in, and whose retarded child, "Baby," becomes the center of the gestalt being.

Lone becomes aware of a human community to which he has at least rudimentary obligations and of a more specialized group, composed of abandoned or runaway children, to which Gerry belongs, and which is destined to become a new being. By the end of the novel, this group has become a potential god, "not an exterior force, not an awesome Watcher in the sky, but a laughing thing with a human heart and reverence for its origins." In the book's last section, "Morality," Hip Barrows, the being's final component, its conscience, confronts and converts the ruthless Gerry; Hip sees himself as "an atom and his gestalt as a molecule. He saw these others as cells among cells, and he saw the whole design of what, with joy, humanity would become." His response is a "sense of worship." He participates in a vision not unlike that shared by many Romantic writers of the nineteenth century, what Walt Whitman's follower R. M. Bucke called "Cosmic Consciousness." Sturgeon said that the willingness of science-fiction writers to treat religious themes, "to invent and extrapolate and regroup ideas and concepts in this as in all other areas of human growth and change delights me and is a source of my true love for the mad breed." *More Than Human* is Sturgeon's best illustration that such themes can be explored profitably.

More Than Human, like *The Dreaming Jewels*, traces the progress of the growth and integration of the person. In each novel, characters move from alienation to wholeness, but in *More Than Human*, the key conflict between misanthropy and humanity is handled with greater dramatic skill. In general a more sophisticated work in conception and structure, *More Than Human* manages to present the idea of a collective entity without losing sight of individual characters or the dynamics of personality. As a speculative fiction, it deserves the praise and popularity it has enjoyed.

The Cosmic Rape · *The Cosmic Rape* also employs the gestalt theme of *More Than Human*, extending the union to all of humankind, which in turn is joined to Medusa, an intergalactic composite creature. While the underlying theme of the book is essentially the same as that of *More Than Human*, it is by no means as successful. Its premises are extrapolated in far less believable fashion, and its structure is not dramatically engaging. Intercut scenes, which range from the United States to Rome to Africa, are skillfully coordinated, but character development suffers in the effort to show individuals becoming a part of the whole.

In *The Cosmic Rape*, Sturgeon attempts to put love into the largest terms, but, ironically, he employs a character most unlikely to initiate cosmic harmony. One Dan Gurlick, a loathsome bum, has become an atom in Medusa by ingesting a sort of seed concealed in a fragment of hamburger. Through him, Medusa seeks to take over the earth telepathically. Medusa is at first thwarted, having dealt only with collective minds elsewhere in the universe. This lack in humanity is repaired, however, as psychic unity among people appears as they cooperate in the destruction of invading machines created by Medusa. In the course of attaining collective consciousness, a variety of characters emerge from sexual repression and exploitation or social alienation to sacrifice themselves. Notable is the metamorphosis of Guido, a misfit who has turned to anarchism because his musical genius has been suppressed by a wicked stepfather.

Ultimately, Medusa is joined to the human collective mind. This connection occurs when Gurlick, himself excluded from the universal intelligence, is permitted to act out the sexual fantasies which Medusa has used to control him. What Gurlick intends as rape is welcomed by a woman now sexually liberated as a part of a larger design; likewise, the joining of humanity to Medusa is transformed from rape to consent. Medusa is in fact possessed by humanity rather than possessing it.

The Cosmic Rape extends the ideas of *More Than Human* as far as they can go. Unfortunately, the extrapolation is ultimately too fanciful and the dramatic power of Sturgeon's myth of human integration is diffused. There is a sense of his recognition of this in his next book, which he calls "a tract"; the social criticism of *Venus Plus X* gives ballast to an imagination which had overextended itself.

Venus Plus X · Sturgeon responded to the charge that "science fiction is characteristically asexual and unaware of love in its larger and largest senses." He believed that this impression had sometimes arisen because writers of science fiction often "work in geological or astronomical time rather than in biographical or historical perspective." Sturgeon had dealt with themes of love in both cosmic and personal perspectives in his earlier novels, but in *Venus Plus X* he turned to utopian fiction to keep the action on a more human scale.

Though Sturgeon had written stories on sex before–"The World Well Lost" (1953) deals with homosexuality, for example–*Venus Plus X* is his most extended statement on sexism and sexual taboos. While the book has been praised for its pioneering study of sex roles, preceding Ursula K. Le Guin's much discussed *The Left Hand of Darkness* (1969) by nine years, *Venus Plus X* is also notable for its skillfuly ironic employment of science-fiction conventions and for its handling of the symbolism of androgyny.

The novel is structured in alternating chapters of action which are connected only by theme. The first set of chapters deals with suburban life and the questions of sexual identity posed to America in the 1950's. Along with standard problems of sex-role definition for children and general sexism, there are hints of change; Herb Raile comes to realize how Western culture has degraded women and catches glimpses of the significance of androgyny in the style of a rock singer. Contrasted with suburban America is Ledom (*model* inverted), a utopia founded upon the fact that its inhabitants are biologically hermaphrodites. Here, sex-role definition is no problem, and the wholeness of the human being in assuming all social duties is stressed. Against the predatory capitalism and commercialized worship of the suburbs are posed charitable religion and universal sharing.

Androgyny is used by Sturgeon as a symbol of wholeness. Like the universal man of *More Than Human*, androgyny can be found in mystical thought as signifying the primordial unity of humankind. In order to stress this aspect of his work, Sturgeon provides the Ledomites with a religion that is an ecstatic celebration of the child. "We keep before us," says the guide to this utopia, "the image of that which is malleable and growing–of that which we have the power to improve. We worship that very power in ourselves, and the sense of responsibility which lives with it." Here again is Sturgeon's drive toward totality, a worship of human potential, yet in order to present this theme, he undercuts a number of science-fiction conventions to make his readers more aware of the symbolic nature of his statement.

The reader discovers that the book's nominal hero, Charlie Johns, is not a time-traveler as he first believes. Ledom does not exist in the distant future as it first appears; rather, it is a society hidden from the eyes of men. The Ledomites wish to test the reaction of the outside world to their culture, and they use Charlie Johns's responses as a gauge. After overcoming his initial bewilderment, Charlie embarks on a course of education, learning that Ledom's technical superiority consists in a machine that can inscribe thought patterns and has revolutionized learning, and a power supply that makes the community self-sufficient. Charlie's approval of technology comes to a screeching halt, however, when he discovers that the hermaphroditism of Ledomites is biologically engineered. His reaction convinces utopian planners that the world is not ready for the revelation of Ledom.

Charlie now regards Ledom as a den of perversion and indicates that it ought to be destroyed. His education, however, has been limited: He has not detected the hints throughout that the whole culture is symbolic, that its essence is "transition." It has been designed to preserve human values while the outside world destroys itself. The novel's disquisition on religion, in fact, suggests that if one human generation could adopt the religion of Ledom, it would be saved. No hermaphroditism would be necessary for a sense of human wholeness.

The final emphasis given Ledom's symbolic nature is the revelation that Charlie Johns is not actually Charlie Johns at all, but merely a collection of his memories, obtained when he was dying after a plane crash and inscribed on the previously blank mind of a biological control. The plot, however, first permits Johns to attempt the standard escape from a dystopia. He finds the one girl who has not been biologically altered, and he tries to leave in what he thinks is a time machine. When he does so, the Ledomites are forced to tell him the truth. He and his girl therefore take up life somewhere between the two worlds, trying to sort out their identities, presumably overcoming the sexism of the man Charlie was, and learning from the wisdom of Ledom. At the same time, on the other side, Herb Raile is working his way slowly and painfully to gain some of Ledom's values.

In spite of some dated writing in the sections on suburbia in the 1950's, this is a book which powerfully anticipates many of the themes taken up by feminists in the 1960's and 1970's. Sturgeon also made fine use of the conventions of utopian fiction only to undercut them, which is most appropriate to his major points about the nature of dynamic evolutionary change throughout his fiction. Utopia, he wrote, "must be life-oriented and recognize that life is change, which is why utopias, be they by Plato or Sir Thomas More, or Joanna Russ, have hidden in them the characteristics of the necropolis." He avoided this by permitting his own utopia to self-destruct, leaving behind the impact of its symbols, and providing in *Venus Plus X* what Sturgeon saw in William Golding's *Lord of the Flies* (1954), "a fable of cultural structures, with a meaning—a 'moral' if you like—far greater than the narrative itself."

Henry J. Lindborg

Other major works

SHORT FICTION: *Without Sorcery*, 1948; *E Pluribus Unicorn*, 1953; *A Way Home*, 1955; *Caviar*, 1955; *A Touch of Strange*, 1958; *Aliens 4*, 1959; *Beyond*, 1960; *Sturgeon in Orbit*, 1964; . . . *And My Fear Is Great/Baby Is Three*, 1965; *The Joyous Invasions*, 1965; *Starshine*, 1966; *Sturgeon Is Alive and Well*, 1971; *The Worlds of Theodore Sturgeon*, 1972; *To Here and the Easel*, 1973; *Sturgeon's West*, 1973 (with Don Ward); *Case and the Dreamer*, 1974; *Visions and Venturers*, 1978; *The Stars Are the Styx*, 1979; *The Golden Helix*, 1980.

Bibliography

Friend, Beverly. "The Sturgeon Connection." In *Voices for the Future: Essays on Major Science Fiction Writers*, edited by Thomas D. Clareson. Vol. 1. Bowling Green, Ohio: Bowling Green University Popular Press, 1977. A stimulating discussion of the themes and formal structures of Sturgeon's fiction.

Gordon, Joan, and Veronica Hollinger, eds. *Blood Read: The Vampire as Metaphor in Contemporary Culture*. Philadelphia: University of Pennsylvania Press, 1997. Treats *Some of Your Blood* as a harbinger of the more recent sympathetic vampire novels. Includes a bibliography.

Hassler, Donald M. "Images for an Ethos, Images for Change and Style." *Extrapolation* 20 (Summer, 1979): 176-188. An analysis of Sturgeon's themes of love, loneliness, newness, and the nature of change in relation to his ethics and versatile technique. The works discussed include "Microcosmic God," "Slow Sculpture," *More Than Human*, and *The Cosmic Rape*.

Lawler, Donald L. "Theodore Sturgeon." In *Twentieth-Century American Science Fiction Writers*, edited by David Cowart and Thomas L. Wymer. Vol. 8 in *Dictionary of Literary Biography*. Detroit: Gale Research, 1981. An interesting and informative biography and critical analysis of Sturgeon's fiction. Includes photographs and selected primary and secondary bibliographies.

Moskowitz, Sam. "Theodore Sturgeon." In *Seekers of Tomorrow: Masters of Modern*

Science Fiction. New York: Harper & Row, 1966. A discussion of Sturgeon's early fiction through *More Than Human*, with emphasis on his virtuoso style and inventiveness. Includes brief summaries of many Sturgeon plots.

Sackmary, Regina. "An Ideal of Three: The Art of Theodore Sturgeon." In *Critical Encounters: Writers and Themes in Science Fiction*, edited by Dick Riley. New York: Frederick Ungar, 1978. A discussion of Sturgeon's frequent use in his fiction of groupings of threes to develop his themes of isolation, loneliness, love, wholeness, and unity. Includes notes for the essay.

WILLIAM STYRON

Born: Newport News, Virginia; June 11, 1925

Principal long fiction · *Lie Down in Darkness*, 1951; *The Long March*, 1952 (serial), 1956 (book); *Set This House on Fire*, 1960; *The Confessions of Nat Turner*, 1967; *Sophie's Choice*, 1979.

Other literary forms · Until 1990, William Styron was among the few major modern literary figures who bear discussion in only a single genre–in his case, the novel. Except for a slight and rather odd play, *In the Clap Shack* (1972), and a collection of essays, *This Quiet Dust* (1982), Styron mainly concentrated on novels. In 1990, however, the publication of *Darkness Visible: A Memoir of Madness* was widely hailed. A candid and insightful recounting of Styron's personal battle with severe clinical depression, *Darkness Visible* was an immediate popular success. *A Tidewater Morning: Three Tales from Youth* is a collection of short stories published in 1993.

Achievements · Until the publication of *The Confessions of Nat Turner* in 1967, Styron was well known in literary circles as a young novelist of great talent but largely unrealized potential. *The Confessions of Nat Turner*, riding the crest of a wave of social activism in the late 1960's and capitalizing on a national interest in black literature and history, gave Styron a major popular reputation as well as making him the center of a vitriolic controversy between academic and literary critics on one side, who tended to see the novel as an honest attempt to come to terms with history, and a small group of strident black critics on the other hand, who questioned, often abusively, the ability of any white writer to deal with the black experience, and who called Styron's portrait of Nat Turner unflattering and inaccurate. The book and the debate it engendered made Styron a major voice in twentieth century fiction, as well as a rich man.

Despite the twelve-year hiatus between the publication of *The Confessions of Nat Turner* and that of *Sophie's Choice*, Styron's reputation grew, particularly in terms of his role as an interpreter of the South. *Lie Down in Darkness* was recognized as one of the finest presentations in fiction of the modern southern family, haunted by memory, guilt, and time, and *The Confessions of Nat Turner* came to be seen as representative of the concern of southern writers with the burden of history. *The Confessions of Nat Turner* was accepted as a rhetorically beautiful evocation of the past, whatever its historical inaccuracies.

The publication of *Sophie's Choice* in 1979 cemented Styron's position as one of the major figures of contemporary literature. Although several major critics had reservations about the novel, its ambitious confrontation of a moral theme of enormous implication–the Holocaust–and Styron's compelling, lyrical prose made the novel the literary event of the year. With *Sophie's Choice*, some of Styron's lifelong concerns as a novelist become clearer: the unanswerable problem of pain and suffering, the elusive nature of memory, and the ambiguous legacy of history.

Biography · William Styron was born June 11, 1925, in Newport News, Virginia, which he later called "a very Southern part of the world." His mother, Pauline

Peter Simon

Margaret Abraham Styron, was from the North, but his father, William Clark Styron, a shipyard engineer, came from an old, if not aristocratic, land-poor Virginia family, and Styron remembers his grandmother telling him as a little boy of the days when the family owned slaves, a memory he was to incorporate years later into *Sophie's Choice.* Styron's father was a "Jeffersonian gentleman," liberal in his views for a southerner, who implanted in his son much of the philosophical curiosity which characterized the young Styron's novels. His mother, a gentling influence, died when Styron was twelve after a long, painful siege with cancer, an experience which was also to leave a mark on his fiction in the form of an almost obsessive concern with physical pain and suffering and the vulnerability of the flesh. After his mother's death, Styron began "going wild," and his father sent him to an Episcopal boys' school in Middlesex County, where he was an indifferent student but a voracious reader.

Graduating, he enrolled in Davidson College during World War II but soon dropped out to enlist in the marines.

Styron's stint in Officers Candidate School marked the beginning of his writing career, for while there, he enrolled in a creative writing course at Duke University under William Blackburn, whom Styron acknowledges as the most powerful formative influence on his work. One of his stories, about a Southern lynching, similar in tone and execution to William Faulkner's "Dry September," appeared in a student anthology, Styron's first published fiction. At the tail end of the war, Styron was commissioned and was stationed on a troop ship in the San Francisco Bay, but the Japanese surrendered before he ever left port. Styron was to speak later of his sense of guilt at not having seen action, as well as his feeling of horror at the waste and destruction of the war and the terrible, almost casual way in which life could be lost. Styron condemned the absurdity of Marine Corps life, but he praised the tough training that transformed him physically and mentally. Styron resumed his program at Duke and was graduated in 1947. He took a job in New York as an associate editor in the book division at McGraw-Hill. His senior editor and immediate superior was Edward C. Aswell, the august second editor of Thomas Wolfe and an *éminence grise* to rival editor Maxwell Perkins; Aswell was to appear grotesquely as "The Weasel" in an autobiographical passage in *Sophie's Choice* nearly thirty years later. The callow young Styron found McGraw-Hill humorless and confining, and after six months he was fired.

Living in a Brooklyn boardinghouse on a tiny legacy from his grandmother, Styron took another creative writing course, this time from Hiram Haydn at the New School for Social Research. He began work on his first novel, *Lie Down in Darkness*, the story of a star-crossed upper-middle-class southern family whose failure to find love and meaning in life drives the sensitive daughter, Peyton Loftis, to insanity and suicide. The complex treatment of time in the novel and its high Southern rhetoric showed the influence of William Faulkner, whom Styron had been reading intensely, but *Lie Down in Darkness* was manifestly the work of a powerful and original talent. At first, Styron found the writing of the book slow and difficult. Two years after leaving McGraw-Hill, he had written only a few pages that were usable. After Styron made drastic changes to the novel, dropping the original title ("Inheritance of Night"), eliminating the character Marcus Bonner, shifting the point of view to an omniscient narrator, and withholding the reader's knowledge of Peyton Loftis, Styron found the writing went surprisingly fast—he finished the book and saw it accepted for publication by Bobbs-Merrill before he was recalled by the Marine Corps for service in the Korean War. The novel was published in 1951. Styron was then on active reserve duty, from which he was eventually discharged for an eye problem, but which became the basis for his second novel, *The Long March*.

Lie Down in Darkness was an immediate critical success and a moderate popular one, winning the prestigious Prix de Rome in 1952. At that time, Styron had decamped to Paris and fallen in with a young crowd of American expatriate intellectuals, many of whom would later make names for themselves in literature. George Plimpton and Peter Matthiessen were at the center of a moiling, motley, talented crowd that included Harold Humes, John P. C. Train, Donald Hall, and, on the fringe, writers such as James Baldwin, James Jones, and Irwin Shaw. In 1952 and 1953, the group began compiling a literary magazine, *The Paris Review*, which was to become one of the most influential literary periodicals of the postwar period. Plimpton became the first editor and Matthiessen the fiction editor, and Styron wrote the statement of purpose for the first issue. He also gave the periodical one of the first of its famous "Writers at Work" interviews. It was recorded by Matthiessen and Plimpton at Patrick's, the *Paris Review* crowd's favorite bar, and in it Styron claimed that "this generation . . . will produce literature equal to that of any other generation" and that "a great writer . . . will give substance to and perhaps even explain all the problems of the world." From the start, his ambitions were large.

Although he later said he drank enough brandy in bistros to develop a *crise de foie*, and spent months in the summer of 1952 on a sybaritic "Ovidian idyll" on the Riviera with Humes, Styron was also writing at top speed during this period. In just six weeks, he wrote a novella based on his Marine Corps training-camp experience, *The Long March*, and it was accepted for publication in the fall by *discovery*, a literary magazine (Knopf would publish it as a book four years later). In 1953, he used the money from his Prix de Rome to travel in Italy, an experience that laid the groundwork for his 1960 novel of expatriates, *Set This House on Fire*, and during this time he met Rose Burgunder, a Jewish poet with some family money from Baltimore, whom he soon married. They returned to America, to Roxbury, Connecticut, which would remain Styron's home, and where he began work on the "big novel" that he planned to follow up the success of *Lie Down in Darkness*.

This was *Set This House on Fire*, a sprawling account of American intellectuals living a life of self-indulgence and self-destruction in postwar Italy. The book contained fine lyrical passages of description, particularly of the physical beauty of Italy and the horrifying squalor and suffering of its people, but as Styron later admitted, the novel was seriously flawed—undisciplined and melodramatic. The reviews were very mixed, and some of them savage. Styron's former friend Norman Mailer called *Set This House on Fire* "a bad, maggoty novel," suggesting that Styron could "write like an angel about landscape, but like an adolescent about people." The novel was better received by Styron's European critics—it is still highly regarded in France—but Styron was wounded by his first really bad press, and he retreated to Roxbury to work on his next book, a novel he resolved to make so thoroughly a work of craftsmanship as to defy criticism.

The Confessions of Nat Turner took years to research and write, and true to Styron's expectations, it was immediately acclaimed as a masterpiece. For years, Styron had had his mind on Nat Turner's 1831 slave rebellion as a subject for fiction. It had taken place close to his own Tidewater Virginia home, and Styron saw the suffering, the violence, and the misunderstanding of the revolt as emblematic both of the South's guilt and pain and of his personal concerns as a writer. Styron claimed that reading Albert Camus's *L'Étranger* (1942; *The Stranger*, 1946) furnished him with the technique he was to use in presenting Nat Turner's story—the narrative persona reflecting from jail—and there is no doubt that much of the novel's perspective on black people and black problems was derived from Styron's friend, the black writer James Baldwin, who was a guest of Styron for months while he was writing *Another Country* (1962), Baldwin's first major novel about black/white relations. Styron called *The Confessions of Nat Turner* "less a 'historical novel' than a meditation on history," but despite critical accolades, including the praise of Baldwin, who suggested that the novel might be considered the beginning of a black/white "mutual history," Styron became the target of a group of critics who protested vehemently Styron's depiction of Nat Turner. These critics assaulted Styron in print, accused him of racism and of attempting to demean the reputation of a great hero of black history, and hounded him at meetings, readings, and lectures. Ironically, Nat Turner, as Styron presented him, was a strong and sensitive character, unquestionably the hero of the novel, but so volatile was the political climate of America in the late 1960's that for some critics, any black character who was not a warrior saint was unacceptable as a fictional creation.

The critical assaults provoked by *The Confessions of Nat Turner* left Styron bruised, but he was encouraged by the praise for the novel's powerful rhetoric and masterly structure, not to mention its enormous financial success. Of the controversy, he said, "It really had very little effect on me . . . largely because of the fact that I knew that it was politically motivated and hysterical, and that I had not violated any truth that a novelist is capable of doing." He turned to new work, first to a lengthy projected novel, tentatively titled "The Way of the Warrior," a novel that explored the psyche of a career army officer, then to *Sophie's Choice*. While on Martha's Vineyard, Styron dreamed of Sophie, a Polish Catholic survivor of Auschwitz whom he had met in Brooklyn in 1949. He woke with a vision, seeing her name on a door; he decided that the book would focus on a mother who is forced to send her child to death. The book began as an autobiographical reminiscence of his aimless days as a junior editor at McGraw-Hill, when he found himself frustrated artistically, philosophically, and sexually. As he worked through his memories in the character of his narrator, Stingo, whose fictional background is almost identical to Styron's own, he found his real theme: the life and eventual death by suicide of a woman who survived the Nazi concentration camps but emerged terribly scarred emotionally. This woman, the Sophie of the title, becomes the vehicle through which Stingo confronts the potential horror of life, and through her he matures.

Sophie's Choice was five years in the writing, but Styron was richly rewarded when it was finally published in 1979. A few critics, notably John Gardner, raised questions about its structure, and about the sometimes jejune intrusions of the shallow Stingo, but for the most part the novel was accepted as a fine and satisfying offering by a major writer. "It has the feel of permanence," Peter Prescott wrote. The gratifyingly large sales were capped by a spectacular sale of the film rights. In 1983, Meryl Streep won an Academy Award for Best Actress for her portrayal of Sophie in that film.

In 1985, Styron was hospitalized with acute clinical depression. His struggle to overcome his suicidal feelings and to return to health are recounted in his memoir *Darkness Visible*, published five years later. Styron credited the peaceful seclusion of his hospital stay and the loving patience of his wife and grown children (three daughters and a son) as the principal factors in his recovery. After his hospitalization, Styron immediately wrote "A Tidewater Morning," a long short story that fictionalized the death of his mother. After writing *Darkness Visible*, he returned to his work on a novel set during World War II.

Analysis · The informing patterns of William Styron's fiction are by no means self-evident, and they may not yield themselves readily to the casual critic. Unlike William Faulkner, whom he often resembles in style and technique, his subjects are radically diverse—a doomed Southern family, the intellectual jet set of American expatriates, a historical slave revolt, the horror of the Holocaust. He can shift stylistically from the direct "plain style" of *The Long March* to the purple rhetoric of sections in *Set This House on Fire*, and he moves easily from romantic abstraction to concrete objectivity.

Styron is preeminently, almost self-consciously, a writer of "big" novels of weighty moral significance—a fictional *homme sérieux*, as the French say (which may account for some of Styron's great popularity with French critics). The eternal verities embody themselves relentlessly in Styron's writing. Death, suffering, the silence of God–grave truths lumber ponderously and insistently at the reader in each novel, mercifully relieved by flashes of humor and lyrical passages of poetic beauty, which spare Styron the gray fate of being a sort of American Thomas Mann. Still, the metaphysical predominates in Styron's books.

Strongly underlying all of his novels is a concern with the past, not so much in the form of the passage of time, but rather an awareness that it is either lost or potentially reclaimable. Each of the major novels moves from the present to the past in an attempt to explain or understand how things came to be as they are. *Lie Down in Darkness*, with its relentless burrowing in the Loftis family past, looks backward to explain Peyton's death. In *Set This House on Fire*, Peter Leverett moves very deliberately into the past in pursuit of a piece of himself that is missing, and his whole purpose in dredging up the Italian incidents that form the body of the novel is to reveal the past so that he may deal with the present. Both *The Confessions of Nat Turner* and *Sophie's Choice* are historical novels concerned with the actual past and with what Robert Penn Warren has called "the awful burden of history."

Styron's fiction is historical, but in an intensely personal and psychological way. Each exploration of the past is filtered through the consciousness of a protagonist–Milton Loftis, Cass Kinsolving, Nat Turner, Sophie–and strongly colored by the neuroses of those characters. The alcoholism of Milton and Cass, Nat's brooding rage, and Sophie's aching guilt over her murdered child–at the core of each novel is psychological exploration rather than historical exposition. Historical process is only the context within which individual psychologies grope for resolution. Each of Styron's characters lives on the verge of apocalyptic catastrophe, always on the edge of mental breakdown. Each of his protagonists is close to outright insanity. Two actually commit suicide (Peyton and Sophie); Nat Turner essentially does; and Cass Kinsolving of *Set This House on Fire* is only saved from it by the thinnest of margins. His people may be constantly close to madness, yet Styron makes the reader feel that the madness is legitimate, for his characters search for meaning in a mad world, and only when they fail to find it do they become deranged. Peyton Loftis's loveless family, Nat Turner's unjust world, and the horrors of the concentration camp for Sophie are atmospheres in which genuine sanity is difficult, if not impossible. Perhaps the most representative Styron "hero," though, is Cass Kinsolving of *Set This House on Fire*, the only protagonist who is a philosopher as well as a sufferer. Cass's madness derives from his contemplation of the horror of human life and misery, and he staggers drunkenly around postwar Italy demanding a teleological answer for the chaos of existence in which God is silent; "you can shake the whole universe and just get a snicker up there."

Perhaps it is this tendency to project the struggles of his characters beyond the ordinary world and to magnify them to the borders of melodrama that gives all of Styron's novels powerful religious overtones. Some of this tendency derives from Styron's own Episcopalian background, which is strongly echoed in the style of *Lie Down in Darkness* and *Set This House on Fire* and is particularly evident in the rhetoric of Nat Turner, who is stylistically more Anglican than Baptist. The central problem in these novels is the conspicuous absence of God from human life. Styron's world is one in which, as Cass says in *Set This House on Fire*, "God has locked the door and gone away to leave us to write letters to Him." They are unanswered. By the time Styron comes to reflecting on the horror of the Holocaust in his last book, it seems no answer is possible.

This is Styron's theme—the absence of God and the meaninglessness of life. Consistently, he approaches it through a single technique, the presentation and contemplation of pain and suffering. Styron's novels are a catalog of the slings and arrows of outrageous fortune, some physical, some mental, and some simply the result of an empathic identification with the suffering state of humankind.

On its most elemental level, Styron's depiction of suffering is as pure physical pain. Peyton Loftis is tortured by the ache in her womb, the soldiers of *The Long March* by the agony of their exhausted bodies, Nat Turner by the cold of his cell and the torments of his imprisonment, and Sophie by the tortures of the concentration camp. In *Set This House on Fire*, physical suffering is Styron's primary metaphor for the pain of humankind's empty relationship with the universe, and the novel is shot through with characters in various stages of suffering from "abuse of the carnal envelope."

Vivid as the physical suffering of Styron's characters is, it is nothing compared to their mental and emotional anguish. Often, this mental anguish derives from their acute sense of alienation—from one another and from God. Milton Loftis, Peyton, Cass Kinsolving, Nat Turner, and Sophie writhe painfully and actively, aware of a pervasive emptiness in their lives.

Lie Down in Darkness · The structural complexities of *Lie Down in Darkness*, combined with the florid rhetoric of the novel, obscure for many readers the essentially simple causality which underlies the book. It is the story of how and why Peyton Loftis becomes insane and kills herself, tracing the roots of her tortured madness to her father's weakness and her mother's inability to love. Peyton's father, Milton, showers her with an excessive adoration that is one facet of his alcoholic self-indulgence; he smothers his daughter with a sloppy, undemanding adulation that counterpoints his wife Helen's psychotic frigidity. Helen is only able to show love in terms of compulsive formal discharge of parental obligations, bitterly resentful of the martyr role she has chosen to play. Eventually, Peyton instinctively rejects both her father's almost unnatural affection and her mother's unnatural lack of it. By the time Peyton cuts herself loose, however, she has been emotionally crippled, unable to accept any genuine love from a series of lovers, including the Jewish artist she marries and who might have brought her peace. She retreats deeper and deeper inside herself, watching first other people and finally the real world recede before her disintegrating mind. The last major section of the novel is her tormented, insane monologue, a brilliant tour de force reminiscent of the Benjy sections of Faulkner's *The Sound and the Fury* (1929).

When *Lie Down in Darkness* was published in 1951, it was widely hailed as a significant addition to the "southern" school of writing led by Faulkner, Ellen Glasgow, Flannery O'Connor, and Thomas Wolfe. Thematically, *Lie Down in Darkness* is not a markedly "southern" novel. Although the Loftis family is from Tidewater, Virginia, and there are mannerisms described in the book that are definitively southern, Milton Loftis's weakness, his wife's cold rage, and their daughter's breakdown are in no way regional. The story could as easily be that of a New England family, such as Eugene O'Neill's Manions. What is actually distinctive about the tragedy of the Loftises is how much it is exclusively their own, rather than a product of the dictates of fate or society. In this respect, the novel differs from Styron's later works, in which he increasingly attributes humanity's sufferings to forces beyond the individual. While the novel is a tragedy of a single family, Styron is condemning an entire generation that lost its children. In describing her parents' generation as lost,

Peyton Loftis says, "They thought they were lost. They were crazy. They weren't lost. What they were doing was losing us."

If Styron traces a source of the Loftis family's deterioration, it is perhaps in their lifestyle. On one level, *Lie Down in Darkness* is almost a novel of manners, for in keeping with the Loftises' "country club" lives, much of the novel delineates social activity—parties, dances, dinners. Emblematic of this are three scenes in which Milton, Helen, and Peyton go through the motions of conventional social rituals while they are torn by violent emotions lying beneath the facade of meaningless behavior. The first of these is a dance at the country club at which Peyton tries to play the role of belle-of-the-ball while her father makes drunken love to his mistress in a cloakroom and Helen seethes at both father and daughter in a jealous rage. Later, a Christmas dinner turns into a grotesque, painful fiasco, as Helen screams insults at her daughter while Milton slobbers drunkenly. Finally, Peyton's wedding becomes a nightmare when Milton again gets drunk and sloppy, and Helen, as always thinly concealing a bitter resentment of Peyton, finally cracks, screaming "Whore!" at her daughter. In a rage, Peyton claws her mother's face with her nails and flees the family forever.

The loss of love, or rather the failure to find it, informs the entire book. The three Loftises grope at one another in despair, reaching out to one another in their separate, psychologically crippled ways for an understanding and affection that will bring them some sort of emotional peace. That peace, though, is impossible because their psychic natures are flawed beyond redemption. Sigmund Freud spins the plot: Milton loves Peyton not wisely, but too well, as she uncomfortably senses, so his love of her must always seem unrequited, and he is destined to be deserted by her at the last; Helen suffers a patent jealous hatred for Peyton, who has a capacity for love that Helen lacks, and who is stranded between the two poles of her parents' emotional inadequacy. The result is endless pain and ultimately annihilation. As Milton wails, "It was awful not to be able to love. It was hell."

It is not hell, though, but obliteration—nothingness—that truly underlies this novel. In the opening scene, Milton meets the train that brings Peyton's body home for burial. The final scene is her throwing herself to her death from a New York City rooftop. Everything between, the whole body of the novel, is an explanation of that death, and the knowledge of Peyton's unavoidable extinction hangs heavily during the entire book. The title is taken from Sir Thomas Browne's gloomy *Hydriotaphia: Or, Urn Burial* (1658), a seventeenth century meditation on the inevitability of death, and the "darkness" of the title is that of the grave. Images of death haunt the dreams of the tortured characters, and the reader is never allowed to forget the ultimate negation implicit in the agony of life.

The Long March · The agony of life, more than the nullity of death, became the focus of Styron's fiction following *Lie Down in Darkness*. His short novel *The Long March* serves almost as a précis for the motif of pain that came to dominate Styron's writing. Not much longer than a substantial short story, *The Long March* stands between the turgid psychological weight of *Lie Down in Darkness* and the ponderous solemnity of *Set This House on Fire* like a breath of fresh air. Short, clean, concise, and plotted without a wasted word, this unpretentious novella contains some of Styron's most disciplined and readable prose. He trimmed away all the heavy rhetorical and philosophical baggage of his "big" novels, leaving before the reader only his lean and awful central subject—pain and suffering. Appropriately, the pain here is of the most basic and primitive sort—pure physical agony. Stylistically, Styron's writing of the book in 1952 was anomalous in the development of his career, for it was at this period that he was gearing up to write *Set This House on Fire*, and the stylistic and structural complexities of *Lie Down in Darkness* were being inflated to match the ambitious range of the novel to come.

Like the best of Ernest Hemingway, *The Long March* is deceptively simple—a step-by-step account of a thirty-six-mile forced march inflicted on some Marine reserves by their mindless officers and endured by the men with varying degrees of courage or cowardice, acceptance or rejection, but mainly endured with pain. The march itself is relentlessly real for the reader on page after page, the physical pain of the characters becoming a kind of rhythmic pattern in the book. If the novel has a "message," it is embodied in the final lines, in which Captain Mannix, who has undergone the march protesting its sadistic insanity, swollen and aching, confronts a sympathetic barracks maid who asks if it hurts: "His words [were] uttered . . . not with self-pity, but only with the tone of a man who, having endured and lasted, was too weary to tell her anything but what was true. 'Deed it does,' he said."

Set This House on Fire · After the critical success of *Lie Down in Darkness* and the artistic success of *The Long March*, there followed the better part of a decade before the 1960 publication of *Set This House on Fire*. Comfortably ensconced in Roxbury, Connecticut, prosperous, rearing a family, and moving into the center of the New York literary world, Styron's reputation grew steadily, although his literary output did not. His house, along with George Plimpton's New York City apartment, became one of the new camping grounds for the old *Paris Review* crowd, and Peter Matthiessen, James Jones, and James Baldwin were frequent visitors. Throughout the late 1950's, word of his forthcoming "big" novel spread as Styron gave private readings from it, and the publication of *Set This House on Fire* was eagerly awaited.

The novel was indeed big; actually, it sprawled embarrassingly. In place of the personal, family tragedy of *Lie Down in Darkness*, Styron broadened his scope by giving the suffering in this novel a universal dimension and by exploring the metaphysical bases of it. It is not a family that suffers, but the world. The reader sees this world through the eyes of Peter Leverett, a Styron surrogate, but the real protagonist is Cass Kinsolving, a sensitive, drunken American artist in Italy in the 1950's who is aghast by the suffering of humanity. Much of the story is told to Leverett (and the reader) by Cass, who looks for the ultimate implications of every grain of sand. Looking back, he tells Leverett that he remembers Italy as "an infinity of remembered pain," and he finds divine aspects even in his drunkenness: "God surely had clever ways of tormenting a man, putting in his way a substance whereby He might briefly be reached, but which in the end . . . sent Him packing over the horizon trailing clouds of terror." To achieve this broadened projection, Styron enlarges his cast of characters, heightens his rhetoric, and throws the whole show on an enormous stage. A vast parade of people moves through *Set This House on Fire*, many of them poor, sick, or abused, the rest venal and contemptible. The action is lifted from the commonplace to the melodramatic; rape, murder, and mystery dominate. The characters, except for Leverett and Cass's wife, Poppy, are exotic. Mason Flagg is a monstrous idiot typifying Victor Hugo's Quasimodo of *The Hunchback of Notre Dame* (1831). He is the "super bastard" aesthete rich boy, whose cultivated corruption is nauseating but still rich and strange. Cass deteriorates theatrically, staggering about and raving lines from Greek tragedy, a far cry from the humdrum drunkard Milton Loftis.

Heightened rhetoric is Styron's principal method of extending the scope of *Set This House on Fire*. Much of the novel reads like gothic Thomas Wolfe, from Mason's mother's description of "the horror" of her son's expulsion from prep school to Leverett's account of one of the book's several nightmares: "an abomination made of the interlocking black wings of ravens crawling and loathsome with parasites . . . a country in cataclysm and upheaval." Cass spends much of the book in deliberate blasphemy, "raving at that black, baleful, and depraved Deity who seemed coolly-minded to annihilate His creatures," when he is not suffering from delirium tremens and seeing visions of a boiling sea, or giant spiders on Mt. Vesuvius.

This rhetoric not only complements, but makes possible, the projection of much of the novel on a dream level. Styron had done this before, in a Freudian fantasy of Helen Loftis's, in one of Peyton's lover's dreams of babies burning in hell, and in Peyton's entire closing soliloquy. In *Set This House on Fire*, though, the use of dream, vision, and hallucination is so pervasive that much of the novel approaches phantasmagoria. Leverett dreams of a malevolent fiend for several pages, and has recurrent, elaborately described nightmares; Cass is repeatedly haunted, and his drunken ordeal ends with an extended vision of disaster, a passage drawing heavily on Dante and the Book of Revelation. So extensive is Styron's use of dramatic and fantastic imagery that it is often difficult to tell whether he is presenting the reader with a metaphor or a dream, and at one point, when Cass describes himself first making love to a beautiful girl, then suddenly "groping for an answer on some foul black shore," it is impossible to tell whether he is just thinking or hallucinating again. Cass himself probably does not know.

Although they differ in scope and ambition, *Lie Down in Darkness* and *Set This House on Fire* are essentially the same kind of novel. Both are studies in personal alienation and deterioration. Both work through an elevated rhetoric and through psychological revelation. Although *Set This House on Fire* reaches self-consciously for transcendence and philosophical universality, the novel centers on the psychological aberrations of two characters, Cass Kinsolving and Mason Flagg. Similar to the tragedy of the Loftis family in *Lie Down in Darkness*, theirs are individual, not universal, tragedies. In *Lie Down in Darkness*, the tragedies are individual, but they represent the failings of a self-indulgent generation. In *Set This House on Fire*, the tragedies are also individual, yet they represent the tragedies of a hedonistic generation, a generation that was decadent and destructive.

The Confessions of Nat Turner · Styron called *The Confessions of Nat Turner* "a meditation on history." Its subject is not only the character of Nat, but also the meaning of slavery itself—what it does to people, and to society. Like Styron's previous novels, the book is a contemplation of horror, with a protagonist who becomes a victim of that horror, but in this case, the horror is not a purely personal one. Significantly, unlike the Loftises and Cass Kinsolving, Nat does not deteriorate, but grows through the course of the book as his comprehension of society and life grows. Nat Turner is the richest and most psychologically complex of Styron's characters, and the historical subject matter of the work is filtered through his sensitive consciousness to produce a visionary "meditation" on the world of slavery, dreamlike in quality and poetic in execution. Southern Virginia of the 1830's, the novel's world, is very much a projection of Nat's mind—a mind produced by that world, and savaged by it.

To develop the subtlety of Nat's mind, Styron drew on all his technical and rhetorical resources. His mastery of time-shifts and dream sequences, already amply demonstrated, was enhanced in this novel, and he explored a variety of rhetorical styles, varying from rural black dialect to a high Anglican style echoing Joan Didion's *A Book of Common Prayer* (1977) for Nat's more poetic utterances. Nat's mind ranges with astonishing virtuosity over his universe–the natural world, the complexities of human relations, the elusive mysteries of God, and the bitterness of mortality. An enormously sophisticated narrative persona, Nat moves fluidly across time, contemplating the painful mystery of the past, represented by his long-dead African grandmother, and of the future, represented by his own forthcoming death. Nat tells the entire novel in flashback, remembering his abortive slave rebellion and the personal and historical events leading up to it, constantly trying to cipher out the meaning of those events. The novel is a study of the growth of knowledge and of the growth of Nat's mind. In the introspective isolation of his anguished imprisonment, he reconstructs his lifelong struggle to understand the meaning of existence. He recalls his progression from childhood, when he had no comprehension of what slavery meant, to an early adult period when he accepted his condition either bitterly or philosophically, to a final understanding of slavery in personal, societal, and moral terms. Ironically, as Nat becomes more morally and aesthetically sensitive, he becomes more insensitive in human terms, gravitating toward an acceptance of the violence that finally characterizes his revolt. Only a sudden, visionary conversion to a God of love at the end of the novel saves him from closing the book as an unrepentant apostle of retributory cruelty.

In the process of expanding his knowledge and developing his terrible vision of deliverance from slavery by violence, Nat becomes the spokesman for two familiar Styron themes–the complexity of human psychology and the mystery of human suffering. The most self-searching of Styron's characters, Nat exhaustively explores the ambivalence and ambiguity of his feelings about race, sex, religion, and violence. Although he casts himself convincingly as a Christian prophet, Nat is no simplistic fundamentalist, for he recognizes in his own emotional turmoil personal depths that he can plumb with only partial understanding. His psychology is the battleground of conflicting feelings, symbolized by his powerful attraction to his master's gentle daughter and his vitriolic hatred for all she represents. When he eventually kills her, neither he nor the reader can discriminate his motives. She dies imploring, "Oh, Nat, it hurts so!" and his realization of her pain is the climax of his apprehension of the myriad pains of all humankind, particularly those of his own people. In this concern, he is representative of all Styron's protagonists.

It is almost impossible to deal with *The Confessions of Nat Turner* without mentioning the storm of controversy that followed its publication and success. A number of critics maintained that the novel was historically inaccurate (for example, it portrayed Nat as having homosexual tendencies, but never mentioned that there are records indicating that the real Nat Turner had a wife). Styron was also accused of demeaning a black hero, in that his Nat has reservations about his mission and is squeamish about wholesale slaughter. The real complaint against Styron, though, most thoroughly summarized in a casebook edited by John Henrik Clarke, *William Styron's Nat Turner: Ten Black Writers Respond* (1968), was that he was a white man attempting a theme that should be the province of black writers. In answer to the historical criticism, Styron and his defenders point out that *The Confessions of Nat Turner* is a work of fiction which does not pretend to be straight history, and that it violates no factual information known to Styron at the time of writing. The second complaint, that it degrades a black hero, is more difficult to understand. Unquestionably, Styron, like any true artist, presents his hero with his neuroses, self-doubts, and weaknesses. In the main, how-ever, Nat is without doubt a positive and even heroic character, arguably the most admirable in all Styron's fiction. Only a critic in search of a black plaster saint *sans peur et sans reproche* could consider the creation of as rich and sensitive a character as Nat a slur. While Styron was researching *The Confessions of Nat Turner*, James Baldwin lived in Styron's cottage, and Baldwin encouraged Styron to write the book. Although Styron never acknowledged Baldwin as the model for his Nat Turner, there are similarities in thinking and speech, and Turner's sexual ambivalence may be based on Baldwin. In any case, Styron's Turner is as much a modern intellectual who ponders the effects of slavery as a historical figure.

Sophie's Choice · Styron's novel *Sophie's Choice* was some twelve years in the works, if somewhat less in the writing, and is in every way as ambitious a novel as *The Confessions of Nat Turner*, although its rank in the Styron canon is still in question. Having dealt in earlier novels with suicide, physical agony, existential despair, and slavery, Styron chose the Holocaust as the logical next state of human misery suitable for artistic contemplation. For a long time, Styron had been moving his narrative personae closer toward the subjects of his novels, introducing clearly autobiographi-cal narrators in *The Long March* and *Set This House on Fire*, and making *The Confessions of Nat Turner* an intensely personal first-person narrative. For *Sophie's Choice*, Styron turned to the confessional form plied by novelists as various as Saul Bellow and Norman Mailer and poets such as Robert Lowell. The narrator of *Sophie's Choice*, a young southerner named Stingo, is, for all intents and purposes, indistinguishable from the young Styron. A young artist *manqué* in New York, Stingo meets and is fascinated by a beautiful survivor of a Nazi concentration camp, Sophie, who is permanently psychologically scarred by the horror she has undergone, the most ghastly aspect of which was being forced to decide which of her two children would live and which would die. Stingo is the ultimate naïf: sexually, emotionally, morally, and artistically immature. As he comes to know Sophie, he comes to know himself. Stingo is an artist in search of a subject, as Styron evidently felt that he himself had been. Styron's problems with finding subject matter commensurate with his talents as a technician have been pointed out by William Van O'Conner in "John Updike and William Styron: The Burden of Talent" (1964) and by other critics. Styron himself acknowledged his concern with finding a fit subject for his early fiction, but he also felt that a concern with pain had been central to his earlier work. In 1970, he said, "Consciousness of pain and suffering has informed my work. . . . I hope my present work will not be so preoccupied." At that time, he was working on his military novel "The Way of the Warrior," which he eventually abandoned to write a book that returned to the pain motif with a vengeance, along with the other leitmotif of *Sophie's Choice*, that of the artist's finding of himself.

The emotional pain of Peyton Loftis is alienation from family and love. Cass Kinsolving suffers from guilt brought on by self-hatred and contemplation of human suffering. Nat Turner's ultimate pain derives from his isolation from all humankind and God. Sophie and Stingo suffer the pain of guilt. Stingo, the apotheosis of Styron's autobiographical WASP characters, feels he has not "paid his dues," suffered as others have suffered, and he learns of Sophie's anguished life with a guilty voyeurism. Sophie's guilt has a specific origin in her hideous choice to doom one of her children. She also feels ashamed that in Auschwitz she somehow "suffered less" since she was the commandant's mistress and finally survived when others died. Constantly and compulsively her mind plays over the fates of those dead—her little girl, her tortured friends, and the gassed millions whom she never knew. Even memories of her murdered husband and of her father, both of whom she despised, bring her reproach and grief. The knowledge that she did what she had to gives no relief. She says, "I see that it was—beyond my control, but it is still so terrible to wake up these many mornings with the memory of that, having to live with it . . . it makes everything unbearable. Just unbearable." Soon, she will kill herself to stop the pain.

After Sophie's death, the shattered Stingo, who had just become her lover, walks on the beach trying to find some sort of personal resolution and acceptance of a world in which horror and anguish such as Sophie's exist. Her message, though, has been clear: There is no resolution. Madness and suffering of the magnitude represented by the Holocaust can be neither accepted nor understood. Sophie, like Herman Melville's Ishmael, realizes that "there is a wisdom that is woe, and there is a woe that is madness." Stingo has come to know it, too.

With the death of Sophie, Styron seems to have come full circle in his exploration of human suffering and his search for meaning in a flawed and painful world. Both Sophie and Peyton Loftis find death to be the only release from lives so agonizing and painful as to be unbearable. In both his first novel and this one, Styron leads the reader to the edge of the grave and points to it as the goal of life—"therefore it cannot be long before we lie down in darkness, and have our light in ashes." The crucial difference between *Sophie's Choice* and *Lie Down in Darkness*, however, is the character of Stingo, who like Ishmael escapes to tell the tale. The earlier novel leaves the reader in desolation, but the latter, through Stingo, holds forth the possibility of an alternative existence, one not horribly haunted by the knowledge of pain. Stingo's life is hardly one of euphoria, but it is a tenable existence compared to Sophie's untenable one. To some degree, Stingo has paid his dues through her; he has come to know pain and evil through her sacrifice, and therefore he is sadder and wiser, but not destroyed as she is. His survival counterpoints her destruction; the novel that Stingo will write grows out of her ashes and becomes her immortality.

Sophie's Choice is not a cheerful novel, or even an affirmative one, but it is not nihilistic. Perhaps Stingo's optimism at the close is unjustified. A number of critics feel that when Stingo walks on the beach after Sophie's death and finds the morning "excellent and fair," anticipating his own promising career, Styron is simply tacking on an upbeat ending hardly defensible in view of the horror explored by the novel. Similarly, Cass Kinsolving in *Set This House on Fire* never satisfies his thirst for metaphysical answers to terrible questions, but simply decides to stop thirsting and take up fishing. In each of Styron's novels, characters suffer, and some suffer unto death. These tragedies reveal an unjust world, not a nihilistic one—Styron's tragedies are moral pronouncements. As moral pronouncements, the novels point to the possibility of a better way.

John L. Cobbs, updated by Roark Mulligan

Other major works

SHORT FICTION: *A Tidewater Morning: Three Tales from Youth,* 1993.

PLAY: *In the Clap Shack,* pr. 1972.

NONFICTION: *This Quiet Dust,* 1982; *Darkness Visible: A Memoir of Madness,* 1990.

Bibliography

Casciato, Arthur D., and James L. W. West III, eds. *Critical Essays on William Styron.* Boston: G. K. Hall, 1982. A collection of critical essays that covers all of Styron's major novels and that includes bibliographical references.

Coale, Samuel. *William Styron Revisited.* Boston: Twayne, 1991. A brief biography and an analysis of Styron's novels. Coale devotes a chapter to each major work, including a selected bibliography.

Cologne-Brookes, Gavin. *The Novels of William Styron: From Harmony to History.* Baton Rouge: Louisiana State University Press, 1995. This work traces the influence of the modernist movement on Styron, explores Styron's psychological themes, and analyzes his shifting patterns of discourse. Includes analysis of Styron's later work.

Hadaller, David. *Gynicide: Women in the Novels of William Styron.* Madison, N.J.: Fairleigh Dickinson University Press, 1996. Explores women in Styron's fiction. In particular, Hadaller examines the deaths of women and the meaning of these deaths, arguing that Styron's depictions force the reader to question a society that victimizes women.

Morris, Robert K., and Irving Malin, eds. *The Achievement of William Styron.* Athens: University of Georgia Press, 1975. Provides essays by various critics on Styron's fiction up to *Sophie's Choice.* The essay by Morris and Malin on Styron's career as a visionary novelist is a good introduction to his work.

West, James L. W., III, ed. *Conversations with William Styron.* Jackson: University Press of Mississippi, 1985. A collection of interviews with William Styron in which Styron attempts to "restore a little balance," giving his side to the many controversies that his books have caused.

_____. *William Styron: A Life.* New York: Random House, 1998. The first comprehensive biography of Styron, West's extraordinary work lucidly and cogently connects events in Styron's life to his fiction. This is an essential work for anyone who wishes to understand Styron and his writing.

AMY TAN

Born: Oakland, California; February 19, 1952

Principal long fiction · *The Joy Luck Club*, 1989; *The Kitchen God's Wife*, 1991; *The Hundred Secret Senses*, 1995.

Other literary forms · She is best known for her novels, but Amy Tan's work also includes short essays, short stories, and two children's books—*The Moon Lady* (1992) and *The Chinese Siamese Cat* (1994). In addition, Tan wrote the screenplay for the 1993 film version of *The Joy Luck Club*.

Achievements · Amy Tan is one of the best-known and most popular Asian American writers and, like Maxine Hong Kingston, is considered a guide to the landscape of the Asian American experience. Gracing the best-seller lists, Tan's novels have earned critical and popular acclaim, and *The Joy Luck Club* was made into a major motion picture. Tan won the Commonwealth Gold Award and the Bay Area Book Reviewers Award for *The Joy Luck Club*, which was also nominated for the National Book Award and the National Book Critics Circle Award.

Tan's novels contribute to the dialogue about the meanings of "Asian" and "American" by portraying the intercultural conflict threatening many Asian American immigrant families. Her strong storytelling ability ensures the accessibility of her fiction to general readers; moreover, her work appeals to feminist readers and critics because, as Sau-ling Cynthia Wong points out, Tan's novels belong to significant "discursive traditions" including "mainstream feminist writing; Asian American matrilineal literature; quasi ethnography about the Orient; Chinese American 'tour-guiding' works."

Biography · Amy Tan was born to Daisy and John Tan, both of whom had immigrated from China; they met and married in the United States. As a child, Tan was acutely conscious that she was different from her classmates. She remembers wearing a clothespin on her nose in an effort to reshape that appendage to look more Caucasian. Like most Asian American young people, Tan was American at school and Chinese at home. Although her mother spoke to her in Chinese, Tan answered in English. The tensions in her dual heritage eventually found their way into her novels in her portrayal of the generational conflicts in immigrant families.

At fifteen, Tan lost both her father and her older brother: They died of brain tumors within months of each other. Her mother reacted by leaving California with the remaining children, moving first to the East Coast and then to Europe, where Tan finished high school in Switzerland.

Tan attended three colleges before earning her degree in English and linguistics from San Jose State University. Marrying Louis DeMattei, a tax lawyer, after graduation, Tan began work toward a doctorate in linguistics, but she abandoned her studies for a career before earning her degree. After years as a business writer, Tan realized that, despite a lucrative career, she was unsatisfied, and she decided to attempt a different kind of writing. When she was eight years old, she had won an essay contest, and she cherished dreams of someday writing fiction. Tan set out to fulfill those dreams. Joining a writer's group led by author Molly Giles, she commenced work on the short stories that became the nucleus of her first book.

Tan's first novel, *The Joy Luck Club*, published in 1989, was a critical and popular success, catapulting the author into the ranks of significant American novelists. *The Kitchen God's Wife* followed two years later, garnering high praise and another berth on the best-seller lists. In 1995, Tan published her third novel, *The Hundred Secret Senses*, an exploration of the nature of memory and love.

Analysis · Like the works of many late twentieth century writers, Amy Tan's books are difficult to classify into a single fictional genre. Although Tan's works are indisputably novels, readers and critics agree that her fiction fuses several narrative genres: memoir and autobiography, mythology and folktale, history and biography. Moreover, like Maxine Hong Kingston, Tan appropriates Chinese talk story—a combination of narrative genres from Chinese oral tradition expressed in a local vernacular—to give shape and a distinctive voice to her novels.

Tan's fictional landscape is both geographically vast and spatially confined. The American spaces embrace San Francisco and the Bay Area, while the Chinese locations include a large territory from Guilin to Shanghai and encompass time from feudal China to the twentieth century. Between her protagonists' ancestral homeland and their adopted country lies the Pacific Ocean, symbolically crossed by the woman and the swan in the tale that begins *The Joy Luck Club*. Nonetheless, the crucial events in Tan's novels are contained within definitive boundaries: a circumscribed Chinatown neighborhood, the tiny village of Changmian, one-room accommodations for Chinese pilots and their wives, a stuffy apartment crammed with elderly mah-jongg enthusiasts.

Enclosed by framing narratives set in the late twentieth century, the embedded stories in Tan's novels are set in earlier eras, transporting readers to nineteenth century rural China, war-ravaged Nanking during World War II, or cosmopolitan Shanghai between the wars. Juxtaposing events separated by decades, Tan parallels the dislocations experienced by immigrants from a familiar culture into an alien one with their daughters' painful journeys from cultural confusion to acceptance of their dual heritage.

Tan's protagonists—members of that diaspora community called Asian Americans—represent two groups: Chinese-born immigrants, imperfectly acculturated despite decades of life in America, and American-born women of Chinese ancestry, uncomfortably straddling the border between their ethnic heritage and the American milieu that is their home. Enmeshed by their shared histories in California's ethnic neighborhoods, the women in Tan's novels struggle to create personal identities that reflect their lives, needs, and desires.

Through her fiction, Tan examines identity—its construction, boundaries, and contexts. Indelibly branded by their visible ethnicity, Tan's characters daily negotiate the minefields of cultural disjunction and tensions between Chinese tradition and Americanization, family connections and individual desires. These tensions inevitably surface, causing intergenerational conflict and the disintegration of family relationships as members of the older generation look back to China while their daughters remain firmly connected to California.

The Joy Luck Club · *The Joy Luck Club* tells the stories of four mother-daughter pairs: Suyuan and Jing-mei Woo, An-Mei and Rose Hsu Jordan, Lindo and Waverly Jong, and Ying-ying and Lena St. Clair. Implicit in the generational conflicts that erupt between the women is the bicultural angst separating the Chinese-born mothers from their American-born, assimilated daughters. Initially unable to discover common ground, the two groups of women speak different languages, embrace different values, aspire to different ambitions, and lead divergent lives.

The social club of the title binds together the lives of these eight women. As the novel opens, Jing-mei Woo prepares to take her dead mother's place at the mah-jongg table that anchors the club's activities. During Jing-mei's first game, the older women beg her to go to China on her mother's behalf, and their pleas trigger in Jing-mei painful memories of her Chinatown childhood. Jing-mei's first narrative introduces the other narrators, and except for Suyuan, whose story emerges through Jing-mei's, each woman tells her own story.

Representing the immigrant generation that fled China after World War II, the mothers have had difficult early lives: Suyuan Woo is driven to abandon twins to give them a chance to survive, An-Mei Hsu's mother commits suicide to force her husband to acknowledge An-Mei as his child; Lindo Jong endures an arranged marriage at twelve to an even younger child; and Ying-ying St. Clair, deserted by her first husband, experiences a decade of poverty. In the United States, the mothers must negotiate the traumas of leaving a war-ravaged homeland, starting over in an alien country, and trying to learn a strange language. Through their vicissitudes, they cling to memories of China and to fading traces of their ancestral culture, and they eventually establish stable new lives for themselves.

In contrast with their mothers, the daughters have had good lives—with plenty to eat, comfortable homes, intact families, music lessons, and college educations. Nevertheless, the daughters are discontented and unhappy: Jing-mei is single and aimless, Rose is separated from her husband, Waverly is already divorced, and Lena has summoned up the courage to examine her dysfunctional marriage. Each daughter feels detached from herself, her family, and her community; none of them knows how to reconnect.

The novel traces the evolution of understanding between the mothers and daughters, who are, at the end, finally able to articulate the depth of their caring for each other. The novel concludes when Jing-mei travels to China to meet her two half sisters—the women who were the infants that Suyuan lost in wartime China.

The Kitchen God's Wife · *The Kitchen God's Wife* also explores dynamics of the mother-daughter relationship in the context of cultural and ethnic disjunctions, albeit in less detail than does *The Joy Luck Club*. Instead, *The Kitchen God's Wife* focuses on a woman's journey to wholeness after an eventful life that replicates the Chinese immigrant experience in microcosm. The novel's title refers to Winnie Louie's version of the story of the Kitchen God who achieves deity status when he proves to be capable of shame upon discovering that the wife he has mistreated still cares about his welfare. Unfortunately, according to Winnie, the Kitchen God's wife is denied membership in the Chinese pantheon of deities despite her fidelity.

The novel tells two stories: the sketchy framing narrative that involves the widening rift between Winnie and her daughter, Pearl; and the fully developed chronicle of Winnie's life in China. Through her story, Pearl contextualizes Winnie's reminiscences, describing a series of events and revelations that ultimately changes their relationship. Required by family obligations to attend the funeral of an ancient "aunt" and the engagement party of a "cousin," Pearl spends more time with Winnie than she has in many months, and the enforced companionship prompts the younger woman to examine the roots of their estrangement. Winnie, goaded to action by a letter from China that closes a painful chapter in her past, decides to tell Pearl about her life in China.

Save for the early chapters in which Pearl speaks, and the epilogue in which Winnie and Pearl deify the Kitchen God's wife as Lady Sorrowfree, the novel chronicles the eventful life of Jiang Weili–Winnie's Chinese name–as she negotiates the difficult journey from a privileged childhood through an abusive marriage and the tragedy of war, and ultimately to a secure life in the United States.

The daughter of a wealthy Shanghai merchant, Jiang Weili marries the dashing Wen Fu, only to discover after the wedding that he has misrepresented his family's wealth and status. Worse yet, he turns out to be an adulterer, abuser, and pathological liar. Forced to follow her pilot husband as he is posted to different cities during the war, Weili tries to be a good wife and mother, laboring to establish a home wherever they happen to be assigned. She must spend her dowry for family expenses when Wen Fu gambles away his pay or squanders it on a mistress. After silently enduring her miserable existence and the deaths of her two children, Winnie finally escapes to America and a new life with Jimmy Louie.

The Hundred Secret Senses · Unlike Tan's first two novels, which examine the dynamics of the mother-daughter dyad, *The Hundred Secret Senses* explores the psychological and emotional bonds between sisters. Still, the novel displays several characteristics common to Tan's fiction: conflict between generations in immigrant families; multiple points of view; a strong grounding in Chinese culture and history; and compelling narratives.

Although *The Hundred Secret Senses* is Olivia's story, Kwan is central to every narrative in the novel. One of Tan's most stunningly original creations, Kwan is an energetic woman who is Chinese at the core despite having adopted Western dress and American slang. Kwan claims to have *yin* eyes, which she describes as an ability to see and converse with the dead, whom she calls "*yin* people."

Central to the novel is the uncomfortable relationship between American-born Olivia and her Chinese sister, Kwan, who arrived in San Francisco at eighteen. Although sharing a father, the two women are markedly different: Olivia, whose mother is American, is completely Westernized; Kwan, born to a Chinese first wife, never completely assimilates, remaining predominantly Chinese. Embarrassed by Kwan's exuberant Chineseness, Olivia resists her sister's attempts to form a close relationship. She declines invitations, evades contact, and refuses all overtures of friendship. Despite Olivia's coolness, Kwan continues her friendly attempts to be a real sister to Olivia, whose unhappiness is palpable. Maneuvering Olivia and Olivia's estranged husband, Simon, into a trip to the hills beyond Guilin in China, Kwan engineers a situation that forces Olivia and Simon to reassess their relationship and take tentative steps toward reconciliation.

Paralleling Olivia's story and embedded in the novel are Kwan's narratives about a previous life when she was Nunumu, a Chinese servant to a group of missionaries. In that household, Nunumu was befriended by Nelly Banner, a young American woman whose passion for a deceitful adventurer imperils the group, and whose love for a half-breed leads to death for herself and Nunumu. The story of Nunumu and Nelly Banner is set against the backdrop of the nineteenth century Taiping Rebellion, led by a charismatic leader who claimed to be Jesus's younger brother.

As in her first two novels, Amy Tan establishes clear parallels between past and present, between historical events and contemporary problems. Constantly relaying messages from her *yin* friends, who seem inordinately interested in Olivia's marital problems, Kwan brings Olivia to the brink of believing that she, Olivia, has somehow participated in Nunumu's life, has experienced fear of approaching rebel soldiers, has faced death on a rainy hillside. Whether Olivia truly once was Nelly Banner is never certain—what is certain at the end of the novel is Olivia's understanding of the unbreakable ties of love that exist between sisters, friends, and lovers.

E. D. Huntley

Other major works

NONFICTION: "The Language of Discretion," 1990 (in *The State of the Language,* Christopher Ricks and Leonard Michaels, editors).

CHILDREN'S LITERATURE: *The Moon Lady,* 1992; *The Chinese Siamese Cat,* 1994.

Bibliography

Cheung, King-Kok. *An Interethnic Companion to Asian American Literature.* Cambridge, England: Cambridge University Press, 1997. An essay collection with a critical overview of Asian American literary studies. Most interesting to readers of Tan's novels are essays by Sau-ling Cynthia Wong, Shirley Geok-lin Lim, Jinqi Ling, and Donald Geollnicht.

Huntley, E. D. *Amy Tan: A Critical Companion.* Westport, Conn.: Greenwood Press, 1998. Writing for general readers and students, Huntley introduces and discusses Tan's novels in the context of Asian American fiction. A feature of the book is the incorporation of a several critical approaches to the novels.

Lim, Elaine. *Asian American Literature: An Introduction to the Writings and Their Social Context.* Philadelphia: Temple University Press, 1982. The first critical guide to Asian American literature, Lim's book is an essential introduction to the historical and literary contexts of Tan's work.

Ling, Amy. *Between Worlds: Women Writers of Chinese Ancestry.* New York: Pergamon, 1990. A chronological and thematic introduction to prose narratives in English by American women of Chinese or partial Chinese ancestry. Includes an extensive annotated bibliography of prose by Chinese American women.

Pearlman, Mickey, and Katherine Usher Henderson. "Amy Tan." *Inter/View: Talks with America's Writing Women.* Lexington: University Press of Kentucky, 1990. Provides biographical information on Tan, revealing the sources of some of the stories in *The Joy Luck Club.*

Somogyi, Barbara, and David Stanton. "Amy Tan." *Poets & Writers* 19, no. 5 (September 1, 1991): 24-32. One of the best interviews with Tan. Tan speaks about her childhood and her early career as a business writer, her decision to write fiction, and her success with *The Joy Luck Club.*

PAUL THEROUX

Born: Medford, Massachusetts; April 10, 1941

Principal long fiction · *Waldo,* 1967; *Fong and the Indians,* 1968; *Murder in Mount Holly,* 1969; *Girls at Play,* 1969; *Jungle Lovers,* 1971; *Saint Jack,* 1973; *The Black House,* 1974; *The Family Arsenal,* 1976; *Picture Palace,* 1978; *The Mosquito Coast,* 1981; *Half Moon Street: Two Short Novels,* 1984; *O-Zone,* 1986; *My Secret History,* 1989; *Chicago Loop,* 1990; *Millroy the Magician,* 1994; *My Other Life,* 1996; *Kowloon Tong,* 1997.

Other literary forms · In addition to a steady stream of novels, Paul Theroux published collections of short stories, *Sinning with Annie and Other Stories* (1972), *The Consul's File* (1977), *World's End* (1980), and *The Collected Stories* (1997); a volume of criticism, *V. S. Naipaul: An Introduction to His Work* (1972); a memoir, *Sir Vidia's Shadow: A Friendship Across Five Continents* (1998); travel books, *The Great Railway Bazaar: By Train Through Asia* (1975) and *The Old Patagonian Express: By Train Through the Americas* (1979); and collections of children's stories, *A Christmas Card* (1978) and *London Snow: A Christmas Story* (1979). In addition to his books, Theroux wrote numerous reviews and articles, many of them based on his perceptions of events in the non-Western world; these are to be found in newspapers and periodicals such as *The New York Times Magazine,* the *Sunday Times* (of London), *Harper's,* and *Encounter.*

Achievements · It is in the quirky nature of fame that Theroux, a prolific writer of novels, should be better known for his travel writing than for his fiction. *The Great Railway Bazaar* became a best-seller in 1975, gaining for Theroux both popular and commercial success. A second travel book, *The Old Patagonian Express,* published four years later, firmly established his popular reputation. Both offer the reader elegant and humane examples of a genre widely practiced between the world wars but not commonly seen today.

In the long run, however, Theroux's achievements will rest upon his fiction. He won a small share of awards for his work, including four Playboy Editorial Awards for fiction (1972, 1976, 1977, and 1979), the Literature Award from the American Academy of Arts and Letters (1977), and the Whitbread Prize for Fiction (for *Picture Palace,* 1978). In 1982, he won the James Tait Black Memorial Prize and the *Yorkshire Post* Best Novel of the Year Award for *The Mosquito Coast.* In 1984, Theroux was inducted into the American Academy and Institute of Arts and Letters. *The Mosquito Coast* was released as a motion picture, starring Harrison Ford, in 1986; *Half Moon Street* was also turned into a film in 1986, starring Sigourney Weaver and Michael Caine.

Theroux writes in the best tradition of English literature, demonstrating a mastery of fictional conventions as well as a willingness to grapple with some of the thornier issues of modern life. Critics have compared him to, among others, Charles Dickens, Joseph Conrad, W. Somerset Maugham, Graham Greene, and Evelyn Waugh. Interested in neither the splashy innovations of a Donald Barthelme nor the lurid headline material of a Norman Mailer, Theroux is nevertheless a novelist to follow.

Biography · Paul Edward Theroux was born of French Canadian and Italian parentage in Medford, Massachusetts, in 1941, the third of the seven children of Albert and Anne Theroux. Literature and writing were important aspects of his early life. Albert Theroux, a leather salesman, read daily to the family from the classics and encouraged the publication of family newspapers. For his efforts, he was rewarded with two novelists: Paul, and his brother Alexander.

After conventional public schooling and a B.A. in English from the University of Massachusetts, Theroux volunteered for the Peace Corps in 1963 to escape the draft. He taught English in Malawi for two years until he was expelled for his unwitting involvement in the convolutions of African politics. From Malawi, Theroux went to Makerere University in Kampala, Uganda, where he lectured on seventeenth century English literature and maintained a careful political stance during the beginnings of Idi Amin's rise to power. At Makerere, Theroux met V. S. Naipaul, who became for a time his literary mentor. Theroux left Uganda in 1968 after being trapped in a street riot and went to Singapore, where he spent the next three years lecturing at the university.

Throughout this period, Theroux was writing prodigiously, both fiction and reportage, which he published in a variety of journals, both African and European. In 1967, he married Anne Castle, then also a teacher, and fathered two sons, Louis and Marcel. In 1972, judging himself able to earn his living by his pen alone, Theroux gave up teaching and moved his family to London. After he and his wife divorced, he returned to the United States, making his home in Massachusetts.

©1996 Newsday

The Catholic background, the leftish political interests, the ten years in Africa and Asia, the friendship with V. S. Naipaul—these heterogeneous influences all left their mark on Theroux's fiction. At the same time, one notes how Theroux secularizes, liberalizes, and makes contemporary the Catholic ethic, turns the African experience into a metaphor for all social experience, and absorbs and makes his own the lessons of Naipaul.

Analysis · Paul Theroux approaches his major theme—the ethical behavior of people in society—by way of postcolonial Africa and Southeast Asia, in stories that explore cultural interaction and the meaning of civilization. The three early African novels, *Fong and the Indians, Girls at Play,* and *Jungle Lovers,* set the scene, as it were, and suggest the terms for nearly all of his later fiction. These African novels offer not only a fictional portrait of the Third World struggling toward independence, but also a metaphor for all modern society and social ethics. In the apparently simpler world of East Africa, where white ex-patriot confronts black African, where Chinese meets Indian meets German meets American meets Australian, Theroux explores the ways individuals interact to form a social unit and the results, often absurd, of attempts to impose foreign values and ideas of civilization upon the primitive life of the jungle.

Although the later novels leave behind the specifically African setting, they continue to explore the theme of civilization versus jungle, expanding in particular upon the moral and ethical implications of certain kinds of social behavior. *The Family Arsenal* and *Saint Jack* provide instructive examples. In the former, Valentine Hood, and American ex-diplomat from Vietnam living in London, is struck by the domesticity displayed by the members of the terrorist band with which he lives: It is like a family. From this insight develop both the central theme of that novel and its plot structure. In *Saint Jack,* Jack Flowers creates a secular religion out of "giving people what they want." In *The Black House* and *The Mosquito Coast,* Theroux separates his protagonists from society to explore the meaning of exile, foreignness, and individualism. Yet underlying all of these fictions will be found the basic assumption that every human experience, from death to redemption, from fear to loneliness, from love to murder, must be understood in a social context.

Fong and the Indians · *Fong and the Indians,* the first of Theroux's African novels, is the witty tale of the business partnership between Sam Fong, a Chinese grocer, and Hassanali Fakhru, the Indian entrepreneur who rents him the store, supplies his goods, and, when business is poor, even becomes his customer. Fakhru dominates Fong's economic life, manipulating it for his own benefit by taking advantage of Fong's innocent incompetence as a businessman. Yet as the plot unfolds, it becomes clear the the relationship between Fong and Fakhru is far from one-sided. Moreover, it also becomes clear that this relationship is representative of all social and economic relationships. Each individual in a society suffers limitations of understanding that arise both from his own prejudices and from his cultural heritage. When two people meet to do business, they may well be speaking different languages, either literally or metaphorically. Misunderstandings are unavoidable, and the outcome of any action is unpredictable: Good intentions may or may not result in good consequences; the same is true of bad intentions. Chaos and absurdity reign when no one quite understands what anyone else is doing.

The plot of *Fong and the Indians* is an intricate comedy of errors involving Fong, the unwilling grocer; Fakhru, the capitalist swindler; and two CIA agents on a mission to convert suspected Communists. The fiction works as both a satirical portrait of African society today and an allegory in which the grocery business, the swindles, and the "good will" mission–artifices of civilization–are, in the context of African reality, revealed to be absurd. In *Fong and the Indians*, Theroux explores "civilization"; in later books, *Jungle Lovers, Girls at Play, The Black House,* and *The Mosquito Coast*, he explores the meaning of "Africa"–the reality of the jungle. At no time does Theroux become an apologist for the Third World, elevating primitive civilization over modern. Rather, he turns "jungle" into a metaphor for humanity's natural environment: The jungle is both dangerous and nurturing; it demands that its inhabitants concentrate upon basic human needs. Although the metaphor is most easily understood when Theroux sets his story in the literal jungle of Africa or Central America, there is "jungle" too in South London, in an English village, even in Florida.

In *Fong and the Indians*, Fakhru swindles Sam Fong by convincing him that canned milk represents a victory of civilization. In Africa, however, canned milk makes no sense. Africans do not need it; Europeans prefer the fresh milk from Nairobi. Fong's only hope of becoming rich rests upon the wild improbability that the milk train will one day be wrecked. Aware of the absurdity, Fong accepts both the hope and the improbability of its fulfillment. Fong triumphs because he learns to love what he does not understand. He has the patience to submit, to accommodate his life to the requirements of survival. His change of diet, from the traditional Chinese cuisine he has maintained for all his thirty-seven years in Africa to a free, native one based on bananas and fried locusts, is at once a measure of his economic decline and an assurance of his ultimate triumph.

Saint Jack · Theroux's ethic, then, appears to be based upon the virtue of inaction. Because human understanding is limited, all events appear ambiguous. Even innocently motivated attempts to improve the lot of humanity may prove unexpectedly destructive, such as Marais's attempt to bring revolutionary ideals to Malawi in *Jungle Lovers*, Valentine Hood's murder to rid the world of Ron Weech in *The Family Arsenal*, or even Maud Coffin Pratt's photographs of the pig feast and of her brother and sister in the mill in *Picture Palace*. Because all events are ambiguous, it is impossible to predict which actions will prove evil and which actions will prove good. Therefore, the only possible moral strategy is to take no action at all, to be patient and accommodate oneself to the unknowable mystery of the jungle.

Inaction, however, should not be confused with selfish laziness; rather it is an active, morally motivated inaction akin to the traditional Christian virtue of patience. Patience redeems the absurdity of the modern world, protecting humankind from despair and leading ultimately to a triumph of innocence and virtue that will in turn redeem society. This is the lesson of *Saint Jack*.

A middle-aged, balding, American ex-patriot, full of muddle, fear, and loneliness, Jack Flowers jumps ship in Singapore. A stranger and a misfit, Jack sees no hope of rescue; he does not believe in miracles. He is a modern man making a realistic appraisal of his chances in an unfriendly and dangerous world. Yet Jack wrests from this vision of despair an ad-lib ethic based upon fulfilling the desires of others. He becomes what others would have him be. Condemning no one, pardoning all, Jack participates in each person's unique fantasy. In the public world, he is called a pimp–he may even be a spy–but in his own private world, Jack is a saint: thoroughly reliable and incapable of cultural misunderstanding. He gives to each what everyone needs–pleasure, security, and forgiveness–and stands ready with whatever is needed to meet even an unexpected desire—be it pornographic pictures, the kind attentions of a good girl, or a game of squash. Jack shapes his own needs to match his companion's: He is the perfect friend and protector.

Jack's tattooed arms, emblazoned with Chinese obscenities and curses disguised as flowers, symbolize the way he eases the pain of human loneliness and fear by providing an illusion of hope and friendship and the reality of a temporary pleasure taken in safety. Pity, compassion, and a stubbornly innocent vision of human needs save Jack himself from doing evil and redeem the actions of all those he takes care of, even General Maddox himself.

The terms of this novel are coyly religious—Saint Jack, the manager of Paradise Gardens—but God is not really present in Singapore. What might in a Christian fiction be termed grace, is here good luck, and even Jack's redeeming power itself results, in the end, from his own fantasy. The effect is, on the one hand, tongue in cheek, and on the other, quite serious. Theroux appears to be walking the delicate line between a modern recognition that, in this absurd world, good and evil are meaningless categories and a commonsense realization that people need moral categories and at least an illusion of meaning in order to survive relatively sane.

The Family Arsenal · The search for meaning and moral categories provides both the theme and the structure of *The Family Arsenal*. When the story opens, Valentine Hood has come to live with a group of unrelated people in South London. Their domesticity makes them a parody of the typical middle-class family: Mayo, the mother, a thief; Valentine, the father, a murderer; and Murf and Brodie, the teenage children, terrorist bombers. Early in the novel, many odd characters are introduced: Ralph Gawber, an accountant with a fondness for puzzles and a doomsday foreboding; Araba Nightwing, a radical actress who plays Peter Pan; Ron Weech, the hoodlum whom Hood chases and murders; Lorna Weech, his wife; Rutter, a gunrunner; and Lady Arrow. Initially, the relationships among these characters appear obscure if not irrelevant; yet as the plot develops, groupings take shape until the reader discovers, with Valentine Hood, that all are inextricably bound together by all sorts of dirty secrets, making them, in the words of one character, like one big family no one can quit.

The puzzlelike structure of this novel parodies the conventional thriller plot. Its purpose is, however, not action-packed adventure, but rather the slow revelation that, as Hood has suspected all along, inaction is best because all events (be they murder, theft, or bombing) are morally ambiguous. Thus, Hood changes from social avenger to listener. He develops an innocent vision of pity and love akin to Jack Flowers's that not only reveals the human bonds among all members and classes of society but also redeems his own guilt and saves at least some from the dangers and death that threaten them. By the end of the story, all is discovered and characters are regrouped into more pleasing families based on love rather than convenience.

Paralleling the revelation of relationships in the plot of *The Family Arsenal* is Hood's changing perception of the artistic organization of the stolen Van der Weyden that hangs in Mayo's closet. Mayo stole the painting believing that its theft would signal the beginning of social revolution. It does not: The world cares little about stolen artworks except as an interesting excuse for a headline. Yet, in an unexpected and very personal way, the painting does, in the end, play a revolutionary role in the story: It becomes the symbolic focus for the way art can organize seemingly disparate shapes and colors into a single beautiful whole. The Van der Weyden, like the tattoos on Jack's arms, suggests the resemblance between the personal vision of innocence that can redeem through pity and love and the vision of the artist that can change brutal reality into beauty.

Picture Palace · The most extensive development of this theme occurs in *Picture Palace*, which becomes less a song of triumph for the artist's vision than a warning of the danger that arises when that vision becomes separated (as it necessarily must) from its real social context. Civilization versus the jungle, art versus reality—in Theroux's fiction these themes become almost versions of each other. The ethical effects of efforts by either art or civilization to improve human society are always unclear, dependent as much upon luck as fantasy. Instinctively, Maud Coffin Pratt seems to realize this tenet and locks away her photograph of Phoebe and Orlando in an incestuous embrace: To her, the picture represented love and innocent fulfillment, but when her brother and sister find it, they see only their own guilt and death. Unlike Jack Flowers (who can grab back his photographs of General Maddox) or Valentine Hood (whose revelations of family secrets save them in the end), Maud's personal vision of innocence redeems no one; indeed, it backfires completely, and she is left alone at the end of her life, famous but anonymous.

The Mosquito Coast · In *The Mosquito Coast*, Theroux returns to the jungle milieu to explore further the consequences of extreme individualism, the separation of self from society and environment. With his perpetual motion ice machine, Allie Fox expends a mad energy trying to produce icebergs in order to impress the Indians with the superiority of his civilized genius. Needless to say, whether he floats the ice downstream to a native village or carries it by sledge across the mountains, the ice melts: The impressiveness of civilization disappears in the heat of the sun. Relying completely upon his own creativity, Fox, the Yankee inventor, may be seen as a type of the artist. His attempt to impose his personal vision of utopia upon the brutal reality of the jungle fails utterly; his story reads as a warning of the danger of art without social context.

Like Sam Fong's canned milk in *Fong and the Indians*, Fox's ice machine in *The Mosquito Coast* represents an absurd attempt to civilize the jungle; yet Fong is rewarded with riches (the milk train does wreck), while Fox dies mad and beaten on the beach of Central America. Both may be seen as emblems of the modern world, alone in a strange land, possessing nothing, trying to shape a life out of events that are mysterious, ambiguous, possibly dangerous, and probably absurd. Their differing responses to the jungle environment determine their different ends and provide the reader with the key to Theroux's view of social ethics.

Allie Fox rejects patience and accommodation; he rejects the mystery and the ambiguity of the jungle. He will build a bugless outpost of civilization; he would rather starve than eat a banana. In Theroux's world, it is poetic justice that Fox should misinterpret events and bring about the ruin of all that he has built. With true tragic irony, Fox learns from his failure not the value of accommodation, but only the need for an increased purity, an increased separation from the jungle, a separation doomed to failure. If Fong is the comic face of humanity, then Fox must be the tragic face.

O-Zone · With *O-Zone*, Theroux fashions a future in which major American cities are sealed off from one another and aliens stalk the now-deserted outside. Despite Theroux's descriptive skills, however, critics disliked *O-Zone*—mainly because it had very little plot, which they believed had been sacrificed for Theroux's love of narrative (turned to better use in his travel writing).

My Secret History · About *My Secret History*, on the other hand, critics complained because the narrative takes the first third of the book to really begin. A long novel that is really six novellas grouped together, it follows a young man from Massachusetts who moves to Africa and, from there, to England. Andrew Parent (who changes his first name to "Andre" while in college) starts out as an altar boy in Boston, becoming first a Peace Corps volunteer in one African country, then a teacher in another African country, before finally deciding to become a writer, ultimately moving to London.

Ultimately, Andre becomes an international womanizer, as well as a successful writer, and the last chapter/novella concentrates on his facing the consequences of what he has done to his life. Theroux's cosmopolitan experiences are what fuel his characters, and that he draws from his own life is only natural for a writer. Some critics have believed that his work is too self-referential—that it is thinly disguised autobiography. Pointing to his mentor V. S. Naipaul's 1987 autobiographical novel *The Enigma of Arrival*, they have wondered whether *My Secret History* is a midlife crisis *roman à clef*.

Theroux's work, however, cannot be so easily categorized or dismissed. The progression of Theroux's novels demonstrates a marked coherence of interest and an increasing complexity of thematic and structural development. Although Theroux draws freely from the modern storehouse of pornography, violence, and antiheroism, he displays at the same time a real if not profound interest in some of the classic themes of Western literature—the source of good and evil, the use of pity and love in society, art, and reality. Technically, his work shows a similar melding of popular fiction (the gothic horror story, the thriller) with the structure and conventions of the classic novelists.

My Other Life · Just as he resists any preconceived notions of a foreign culture he is about to enter, Theroux expects the same of readers who immerse themselves in his writings. "My secret is safe," he states in his introduction to *The Collected Stories*. The secret is his identity as a writer. To assign him to a category is to overlook the sense of separation that drives him in all directions in life. He is the consummate explorer who not only delights in discovery but also observes and records in imaginative detail. Yet as Theroux asks readers not to label him, he also reminds them that "My stories are the rest of me," and "I inhabit every sentence I write," statements that could be directed to his novel *My Other Life*. Written as a companion piece to *My Secret History*, the novel reflects what the author considers his "need to invent." In this case it is an "imaginary memoir" designed to portray his life as a series of short stories, a device that led one critic to refer to the work as another example of a Theroux novel being better for its parts than its whole.

Later novels · The "other life" is a common theme throughout Theroux's works. He utilizes it to reveal the darker side of human nature, as exemplified in *Chicago Loop*, the story of Parker Jagoda, a respected Chicago businessman with a wife and children. Jagoda's sexual obsessions compel him to explore the baser instincts of like-minded people who inhabit other worlds within his city. Such obsessions often are at the core of his stories, as in *Millroy the Magician*, the satirical tale of a vagabond magician and his teenage sidekick who set out to rid a bloated America of its culture of consumption by advocating a biblical diet, in addition to other inventive schemes.

In *Kowloon Tong* Theroux resurrects the sense of separation and belonging that permeates earlier works such as *The Mosquito Coast.* He also returns to the Far East for his setting, specifically Hong Kong at the time Britain's rule over the colony was coming to a close. The central figure, Neville "Bunt" Mullard, symbolizes the internal conflicts and contradictions that invariably arise between colonists and the colonized. Among the latter is Mr. Hung, a mysterious Chinese figure whose efforts to take over Mullard's business expose the less appealing aspects of the two competing cultures.

Linda Howe, updated by William Hoffman

Other major works

SHORT FICTION: *Sinning with Annie and Other Stories,* 1972; *The Consul's File,* 1977; *World's End,* 1980; *The London Embassy,* 1982; *The Collected Stories,* 1997.

PLAY: *The Autumn Dog,* pr. 1981.

SCREENPLAY: *Saint Jack,* 1979 (with Peter Bogdanovich and Howard Sackler).

NONFICTION: *V. S. Naipaul: An Introduction to His Work,* 1972; *The Great Railway Bazaar: By Train Through Asia,* 1975; *The Old Patagonian Express: By Train Through the Americas,* 1979; *The Kingdom by the Sea: A Journey Around Great Britain,* 1983; *Sailing Through China,* 1983; *The Imperial Way,* 1985 (with Steve McCurry); *Sunrise with Seamonsters: Travels and Discoveries, 1964-1984,* 1985; *Patagonia Revisited,* 1985 (with Bruce Chatwin); *Riding the Iron Rooster: By Train Through China,* 1988; *To the Ends of the Earth: The Selected Travels of Paul Theroux,* 1990; *The Happy Isles of Oceania: Paddling the Pacific,* 1992; *The Pillars of Hercules: A Grand Tour of the Mediterranean,* 1995; *Sir Vidia's Shadow: A Friendship Across Five Continents,* 1998.

CHILDREN'S LITERATURE: *A Christmas Card,* 1978; *London Snow: A Christmas Story,* 1979.

Bibliography

Barth, Ilene. "A Rake's Progress on Four Continents." *Newsday* June 1, 1989. This review of *My Secret History* gives a detailed plot summary of this lengthy novel. Barth compares it to Theroux's "prickly travelogues," noting the similarities between his fiction and his life.

Baumgold, Julie. "Fellow Traveler." *Esquire* 126 (September, 1996): 184. This informal conversation with Theroux provides some insight into the author's method of blending fact and fiction as part of his creative process.

Burns, Jim. "The Travels of Theroux: Seventeen Books Pay for a Lot of Train Tickets." *Herald Examiner* (Los Angeles), May, 1988. This interview with Theroux provides a good sketch of what motivates him to write, to travel, and to write about traveling. Some biographical information is also included.

Coale, Samuel. *Paul Theroux.* Boston: Twayne, 1987. Part of Twayne's United States Authors series, this book provides a comprehensive look at Theroux's work as well as providing a chronology of events in the author's life. Includes references for each chapter and a bibliography of both primary and secondary sources and an index.

Glaser, E. "The Self-Reflexive Traveler: Paul Theroux on the Art of Travel and Travel Writing." *Centennial Review* 33 (Summer, 1989): 193-206. This article provides more insight into what motivates Theroux's writing and traveling. This in-depth profile and interview of Theroux is invaluable in the light of the scarcity of book-length works about him; includes some references.

MARK TWAIN

Samuel Langhorne Clemens

Born: Florida, Missouri; November 30, 1835
Died: Redding, Connecticut; April 21, 1910

Principal long fiction · *The Gilded Age*, 1873 (with Charles Dudley Warner); *The Adventures of Tom Sawyer*, 1876; *The Prince and the Pauper*, 1881; *Adventures of Huckleberry Finn*, 1884; *A Connecticut Yankee in King Arthur's Court*, 1889; *The American Claimant*, 1892; *Tom Sawyer Abroad*, 1894; *The Tragedy of Pudd'nhead Wilson*, 1894; *Personal Recollections of Joan of Arc*, 1896; *Tom Sawyer, Detective*, 1896; *Simon Wheeler, Detective*, 1963; *Mark Twain's Mysterious Stranger Manuscripts*, 1969 (William M. Gibson, editor).

Other literary forms · In addition to his novels, Mark Twain wrote a great deal of short fiction, which can be divided, although often only very arbitrarily, into short stories, tales, and humorous sketches. One of the best examples of his short stories is "The Man That Corrupted Hadleyburg," and one of the best examples of his humorous sketches is the jumping frog story. Somewhere between the story and the sketch are tales such as "Captain Stormfield's Visit to Heaven." Twain also wrote speeches and essays, both humorous and critical. Representative of his best satiric essays, which range from the very funny to the very sober, are "Fenimore Cooper's Literary Offenses" and "To the Person Sitting in Darkness." The first of these is a hilarious broadside against Cooper's style and invention in which Twain is obviously enjoying himself while at the same time continuing his ongoing war against the romanticizing of the past. "To the Person Sitting in Darkness," considered by some to be his finest piece of invective, is his attack upon what he saw as the exploitation of the Philippines following the Spanish-American War by, in his words, "The Blessings-of-Civilization Trust." Early in his career, he wrote the travel sketches and impressions, *The Innocents Abroad* (1869), *Roughing It* (1872), and *A Tramp Abroad* (1880), and later, *Following the Equator* (1897). Two of his most important books are autobiographical, *Life on the Mississippi* (1883) and *Mark Twain's Autobiography*, published after his death in various editions in 1924.

Achievements · The coincidental appearance of Halley's comet in the years of Twain's birth and death, 1835 and 1910, has been much remarked. A historical event, however, in contrast to the cosmic one, occurring very near the midpoint of his life, provides a better symbol for his career and his achievement than does the mysterious, fiery comet. In 1869, at Promontory Point, Utah, a golden spike was driven to complete the first North American transcontinental railroad. The subsequent settling of the great midwestern center of the continent and the resulting transformation of a frontier society into a civilized one, a process people thought would take hundreds of years, was to be effected in several decades. Twain's life spanned the two Americas, the frontier America that produced so much of the national mythology and the emerging urban, industrial giant of the twentieth century. At the heart of Twain's achievement is his creation of Tom Sawyer and Huck Finn, who embody that mythic America, midway between the wilderness and the modern super-state.

Tom and Huck, two of the nation's most enduring characters, give particular focus to Twain's turbulent, sprawling, complex career as journalist, humorist, entrepreneur, and novelist. The focus is dramatic because the two characters have made their way into the popular imagination with the abiding vitality of legend or folklore. They have been kept before generations of Americans in motion pictures, television, cartoons, and other popular art forms as well as in their original form in the novels. The focus is also symbolic because of the fundamental dualism which the two characters can be seen to represent on the personal, the literary, and the cultural planes.

On the personal plane, Tom and Huck represent aspirations so fundamental to Twain's life as to make them seem rather the two halves of his psyche. Like good and bad angels, they have been taken to represent the contending desires in his life: a strong desire for the security and status of material success on the one hand, set against the deeply ingrained desire for freedom from conventional social and moral restraints on the other. It has been conjectured that steamboat piloting was perhaps the most satisfying of Twain's occupations because it offered him high degrees of both respect-ability and freedom. Although the character of Tom, the symbol of perennial boy-hood, can be easily overburdened by this perspective, there is in him the clear outline of the successful, settled, influential man-of-affairs-to-be. If Tom had grown up, he–like Twain himself–might well have made and lost a fortune in the publishing business and through investments in the Paige typesetter. He almost certainly would have been a successful professional or businessman. He would likely have traveled abroad and would have been eager to associate with nobility at every opportunity. It is relatively easy to imagine Tom growing up. It is instructive to realize that it is almost impossible to imagine Huck's doing so.

On the literary plane, the two may also be seen as representing contending forces, those of the two principal literary schools of the period, the Romantic and the realistic. Surely, Twain's pervasive attacks upon Romantic literature are somewhat compulsive, reminiscent of Nathaniel Hawthorne's preoccupation with the Puritans. Both protest too much. Twain is one of America's foremost Romantics, even if he did see himself as a realist, and even if he did engage much of his time in puncturing the sentimental balloons of the disciples of Sir Walter Scott, Cooper, and the graveyard poets. He was both Romantic and realist, and Tom and Huck emerge almost allegorically as symbols of the two major literary schools of the late nineteenth century.

Tom as the embodiment of socially conforming respectability and as a disciple of Romantic literature contrasts illustratively with Huck as the embodiment of the naturally free spirit, who is "realistic" in part because of his adolescent honesty about such things as art, royalty, and the efficacy of prayer. It is the symbolic dualism on the historical plane, however, that brings into sharpest focus the nature of Twain's central and most enduring achievement. On the historical plane, his two central characters reflect most clearly Twain's principal legacy to posterity: the embodiment in fiction of that moment in time, a moment both real and imaginary, given some historical particularity by the driving of the golden spike at Promontory Point in 1869, when America was poised between the wilderness and the modern, technological state. In this context, Tom represents the settlements that were to become the towns and cities of the new century, and Huck represents the human spirit, freer, at least in the imagination, in the wilderness out of which the settlements were springing. At the end of *Adventures of Huckleberry Finn*, Twain sends Huck on that impossible mission that has been central to the American experience for centuries, when he has him decide to "light out for the territory" before Aunt Sally can "adopt" and "civilize" him.

Twain the humorist and satirist, Twain the silvermining, Paige-typesetting entrepreneur, Twain the journalist, the family man, the anguished, skeptical seeker after religious faith—all must be taken into consideration in accounts of the nature of his achievements. Without Tom Sawyer and Huck Finn, he would have made his mark as a man of his time, a man of various and rich talents. Most likely, his reputation would rest today largely upon his talents as a humorist and satirist, and that reputation still figures largely in assessment of his overall achievement. With Tom and Huck, however, his achievement is given the depth and dramatic focus of a central contribution to the national mythology. Huck's "voice" is frequently compared to the voice of Walt Whitman's "Song of Myself" (1855). Such comparisons rest in part upon rhetorical similarities between the two voices, similarities in what has been called the "vernacular mode." More significantly, they derive from the similarities of the achievements of the poet and the novelist in the establishing of historically and culturally distinctive American "voices" in poetry and fiction. Tom Sawyer and Huck Finn loom large on the nineteenth century literary horizon. They stand, along with

Library of Congress

Cooper's Natty Bumppo and Chingachgook, Hawthorne's Hester Prynne and Arthur Dimmesdale, and Whitman's persona in "Song of Myself," as the principal characters of the emerging national literature. Twain's contribution to that body of literature is at the deepest center of his achievement as a major American writer.

Biography · Mark Twain was born Samuel Langhorne Clemens in Florida, Missouri, in 1835. He first used the pen name "Mark Twain," taken from the leadsman's cry for two fathoms of water, in 1862.

Twain's father was a Virginia lawyer, and the family was of poor but respectable southern stock. In 1839, the family moved to Hannibal, Missouri, the Mississippi River town that provided the source material and background of some of Twain's best-known fiction. After his father died in 1847, Twain left school to become an apprentice in the printing shop of his brother Orion. From 1853 to 1856, Twain worked as a journeyman printer in St. Louis, New York, Philadelphia, Keokuk, and Cincinnati. Between 1857 and 1860, he acquired much of his knowledge of the Mississippi River as a pilot, beginning that short though richly productive career under the tutelage of a senior pilot, Horace Bixby. He was a Confederate volunteer for several weeks after the Civil War began. In 1861, he left for the Nevada Territory with his brother Orion, where he drifted into prospecting and journalism, beginning his career as a reporter with the *Virginia City Territorial Enterprise*, and continuing it with the San Francisco *Morning Call.*

Twain's literary career and the beginning of his fame might be said to have begun in 1865 with the publication in the New York *Saturday Press* of "Jim Smiley and His Jumping Frog" (later known as "The Celebrated Jumping Frog of Calaveras County"). As a journalist, he went to the Sandwich Islands in 1866 and to Europe and the Holy Land in 1867. The latter of the two provided him with the experiences which he shaped into his first book, *The Innocents Abroad. Roughing It*, his narrative of pioneers striving to establish civilization on the frontier, appeared in 1872, and his first novel-length fiction, written with Charles Dudley Warner, *The Gilded Age*, came in 1873.

In 1870, Twain married Olivia Langdon. After beginning their married life in Buffalo, New York, they resettled in Hartford, Connecticut, in 1871. Their infant son Langdon died in 1872, the year Susy, their first daughter, was born. Her sisters, Clara and Jean, were born in 1874 and 1880. Twain's most productive years as a novelist came in this middle period when his daughters were young and he was prospering. *The Adventures of Tom Sawyer, The Prince and the Pauper, Adventures of Huckleberry Finn,* and *A Connecticut Yankee in King Arthur's Court*, were all written during this highly productive period.

By 1890, Twain's financial fortunes were crumbling, mostly owing to bad investment in his own publishing firm and in the Paige typesetter. In 1891, Twain closed the Hartford mansion, sold the furniture, and went to Europe to economize. In 1896, after he completed a round-the-world lecture tour, his daughter Susy died, and his wife, Livy, shortly afterward suffered a nervous collapse from which she never recovered. Twain blamed himself for bringing on his beloved family the circumstances that led to both tragedies. His abiding skepticism about human nature deepened to cynicism and found expression in those dark stories of his last years, such as "The Man That Corrupted Hadleyburg," "The Mysterious Stranger," and the essay "What Is Man?" He died in 1910 at the age of seventy-four in Redding, Connecticut.

Analysis · It is instructive to note that the most pervasive structural characteristic of Mark Twain's work, of his nonfiction as well as his fiction, is dualistic. That observation is not worth much without detailed application to specific aspects of particular works, but even before turning to particulars, it is useful to consider how many "pairs" of contending, conflicting, complementary, or contrasting characters, situations, states of being, ideas and values run through Twain's work. One thinks immediately of Tom and Huck, of Huck and Jim, of Huck and Pap, of Aunt Sally and Miss Watson, of the prince and the pauper, of the two sets of twins in *The Tragedy of Pudd'nhead Wilson.* One thinks of boys testing themselves against adults, of youth and adulthood, of the free life on the river contrasted with the settled life of the river towns, of the wilderness and civilization, of the promises of industrial progress against the backdrop of the humbler, traditional rural setting, of Eden and everything east of Eden, and, finally, of good and evil.

The tonal quality of Twain's works is also dualistic. The jumping frog story is almost pure fun. "The Mysterious Stranger," first published in bowdlerized form after Twain's death, is almost pure gloom. Most of Twain's fiction comes between the two, both chronologically and thematically. Except for *The Gilded Age*, which he wrote with Charles Dudley Warner, the novels, from *The Adventures of Tom Sawyer* to the final two, *The Tragedy of Pudd'nhead Wilson* and *Personal Recollections of Joan of Arc*, fall within the thematic and tonal extremes established by the short fiction. That is, Tom's adventures take place in the hallowed light of innocence and virtue beyond the reach of any truly effective evil forces, while Roxy's adventures in *The Tragedy of Pudd'nhead Wilson*, are of almost unrelieved gloom. *Adventures of Huckleberry Finn* is midway between the extremes, with its blending of the light and affirmation that shine so brightly in Twain's childhood idyll with the darkened vision of the later years.

The Adventures of Tom Sawyer · Nearly everyone agrees that *The Adventures of Tom Sawyer*, Twain's second novel, is an American classic, and nearly everyone agrees that there is no accounting for its success. It is at the same time a novel of the utmost simplicity and of deep complexity. The novel is a marvelous boy's adventure story, a fact given perspective by Twain's observation that "it will be read only by adults." That is, the essence of childhood can be savored only after the fact, only after one has passed through it and can look back upon it. Popularizations of Tom's adventures are produced for children, but the continuing vitality of the novel depends upon the adult sensibility and its capacity and need for nostalgic recollection. Twain plays on all the strings of that sensibility as he guides the reader through Tom's encounters with the adult world, represented by Aunt Polly and Judge Thatcher, through Tom's romance with Becky, and finally to the adventurous triumph over evil in the person of Injun Joe.

Aunt Polly is the perfect adult foil for a perfect boyhood. Not only does she provide the emotional security that comes from being loved in one's place, but she also serves as an adult Tom can challenge through his wits, thereby deepening his self-confidence about his place in the adult world. The fence whitewashing episode is surely one of the best known in American literature. In it, Tom not only outwits his friends, whom he persuades to whitewash the fence for him, but also successfully challenges the adult world which, through Aunt Polly, assigned the "boy's chore" to him in the first place. The episode also provides Twain an opportunity to exercise his irony, which, in contrast to much that was to come in the later fiction, is serenely gentle here. Judge Thatcher represents the secure, if somewhat pompous, authority of the adult world beyond the domestic circle. The much desired recognition of that authority is achieved with decisive pomp when the Judge makes the treasure found in the cave legally Tom's and Huck's.

The romance with Becky is almost pure idyll, although the young lovers' descent into the cave inevitably raises speculations about deeper implications. While Injun Joe as evil incarnate is believable enough to raise the hair along the back of the necks of adults as well as children, especially when the last candle burns out in the cave, there is never any doubt that Tom and Becky will be saved, that good will triumph—never any doubt, that is, for the adult sensibility, secure beyond the trials and tribulations of adolescent infatuation and terror.

The book as childhood idyll is really a simple matter, but that does not diminish the significance of that dimension of the work. Rather, it affirms an understanding of the book's success on that level. There is more to be considered, however, especially in terms of the companion piece to come, *Adventures of Huckleberry Finn*. The poignance of *The Adventures of Tom Sawyer* is attributable in part to the fact that it is an imaginative reconstruction of youthful experience from the perspective of early middle age. The actual historical frame of the re-creation adds its own deeply poignant dimension to the book. The American national experience was clearly in the transitional state between frontier and modern society when the novel was published in 1876. Twain's idyll of boyhood is set in a time and place in history calculated to deepen the significance of the adult's backward recollection of a time of innocence and joy. The American wilderness was never Eden, but that image has haunted the American imagination from at least the time of James Fenimore Cooper's creation of his frontiersman, Natty Bumppo, down to at least the time of Robert Frost's creation of his travelers through the dark, lonely woods.

Finally, in part because it is one of those many pairings of characters so pervasive in Twain's work, Tom's relationship with his half-brother, Sid, should be noted. The relationship is instructive in that it foreshadows that of the later Tom-Huck relationship. Sid is the "model" boy who serves as Twain's foil for Tom's adventuresome independence. While Tom is never good in the subservient, lap-dog sense that Sid is, there is a kind of lateral movement of his character from the early to the later novel; in *The Adventures of Tom Sawyer*, Tom plays off the foil of Sid's pious "respectability," while in *Adventures of Huckleberry Finn*, Tom, himself, has moved over to provide a similar foil for Huck's freedom.

The Prince and the Pauper · Unlike its predecessor, *The Prince and the Pauper* is a "children's book" which has remained simply that, a book for children. Twain professed to have taken great joy in the writing of it, probably in part because of the relief he felt upon completing the troublesome *A Tramp Abroad*. His wife and children admired the book, as did William Dean Howells and the reviewers for the New York *Herald*, the Boston *Transcript*, *The Atlantic Monthly*, and the *Century*. Nevertheless, the novel holds little interest for the mature reader except in terms of its relationship to the two superior novels which preceded and followed it.

Its plot hinges upon one of Twain's most explicit pairings, that of Prince Edward with the pauper Tom Cantry. The switching of these look-alike adolescents in the England of Henry VIII allows the Prince to learn what poverty and hardship are like in the alleyways of his kingdom and the pauper to satirize, through his innocence, the foibles of royalty and court life. Neither the satire nor the compassion, however, ring true. It is almost as if Twain were finding his way from his first classic to his second through this experiment, set in a time and place far removed from his native Mississippi River valley.

With that contrast in mind, it is perhaps reasonable to see the prince and the pauper as another Sid and Tom, another Tom and Huck, all of the sets representing at various removes those two basic drives of Twain's nature for respectability and freedom. Huck and Tom Cantry, the pauper, are "freer" than are Tom and Prince Edward, although the relationships are not that simple, since the members of each pair are attracted like magnetic opposites to their mates. This attraction is made most explicit in *The Prince and the Pauper*, where the two actually exchange places. Later in his career, in *The Tragedy of Pudd'nhead Wilson*, Twain made a comparably explicit exchange with wholly tragic consequences. In *The Prince and the Pauper*, it is all play with little consequence at all except for the exigencies of a contrived, melodramatic plot. Twain's truest pairing, that of Huck and Jim, was yet ahead of him.

Adventures of Huckleberry Finn · *Adventures of Huckleberry Finn* is almost universally hailed as Twain's best book, as well as one of the half dozen or so American classics of the nineteenth century. This is not to say that the novel is without defects. The ending, in particular, presents some very real problems, structurally, thematically, and rhetorically. The very high place of the novel, however, is generally conceded. This success depends upon several considerations. In the first place, the novel continues the mythic idyll of American boyhood begun with *The Adventures of Tom Sawyer*. That connection and that continuation by itself would have insured the book a place in the national archives if not the national heart. Most agree, however, that its success derives from even deeper currents. *Adventures of Huckleberry Finn* is Twain's best book because, for whatever reasons, he brought together in it, with the highest degree of artistic balance, those most fundamental dualities running through his work and life from start to finish. The potentially destructive dualities of youth and age, of the need for both security and freedom, of the wilderness and civilization, of innocence and corruption, all are reconciled by means of an aesthetic transformation. Historical, realistic dualities as well as psychological and moral dualities are brought into an artistic synthesis, into a novel, the most distinctive feature of which, finally, is its own modal duality, played out in the terms of a delicate balance between lyricism and satire.

Huck's relationship with Jim, the runaway slave, is central to the novel's narrative, to its structure, and to its theme. Escaping "down" the river, a cruel irony in itself, provides the episodic structure, which is the narrative thread that holds together the developing relationship between the two runaways on the raft. The escape, the quest for freedom, is literal for both Huck and Jim as they flee from Pap and Jim's owner, Miss Watson. It may also be seen as symbolic on several planes: historical, philosophical, and moral. The historical setting of the novel is that pivotal era in American history when the new nation was being carved out of the wilderness. The flight down the river is a flight from the complexities of the ever-expanding, westward-moving settlements of the new civilization. The continuing vitality of the novel depends in part upon the survival in the twentieth century of the need for that imaginative escape. Like Henry David Thoreau's Waldon Pond, Huck's Mississippi River, originally an escape from what may now seem some of the simpler strictures of society, continues to serve the American psyche as an imaginative alternative to modern civilization.

The philosophical dimensions of the rapidly disappearing frontier are those of nineteenth century Romanticism. Celebrating their freedom on the raft from the legal and social strictures of the town along the river, Huck and Jim are at the same time affirming the central Romantic thesis concerning people's need to return to nature and to the natural self. There are two kinds of Romanticism in the novel: that which Tom espouses in his adolescent preoccupation with adventure, and that which Huck practices on the river under the stars and, most significantly, in the final resolution of the problem of Jim as a runaway slave. Twain holds up Tom's bookish Romanticism as childish at best and, for the most part, as silly. This attack on Romanticism–a secondary theme in *Adventures of Huckleberry Finn*, where Twain sends the derelict steamer, the *Walter Scott*, to its destruction on a rock–was one of Twain's lifelong preoccupations. It was continued with a vehemence later in *A Connecticut Yankee in King Arthur's Court*, but its deep-running, destructive potential for Twain is harnessed in *Adventures of Huckleberry Finn*. The satire is there, but it is in the largely playful terms of the antics of the King and the Duke, their mangling of Shakespeare, and the graveyard art and poetry of Emmeline Grangerford. This playful treatment of one of his serious themes results in part from the fact that Twain is here working a deeper vein of Romanticism in the person of his supreme fictional creation, Huck.

The moral climax of the novel comes in chapter 31, when Huck decides that he will "go to hell" rather than turn in Jim. The difficulties with the ending of the book derive largely from that relatively early resolution of its central theme. Shortly thereafter, Huck is reunited with Tom, who is responsible for all the preposterous plans to save Jim, who, ironically, no longer needs to be saved. There are real problems here with the plot, with motivation, and with the prose itself, which is no longer sustained by the lyricism of Huck's accounts of life on the raft. The artistic achievement of the climax, however, makes such problems pale into relative insignificance. Twain embodies in Huck and dramatizes in his decision a principal line of American political and moral thought which has its roots in Thomas Jefferson and Thomas Paine, its "philosophical" development in Ralph Waldo Emerson and Thoreau, and its aesthetic transformation at the hands of Twain and Whitman. Huck is the embodiment of both the political and the Romantic ideals of common humanity, with no past or roots, whose principal guide is experience rather than tradition. He is one of the principal literary symbols of that fundamental American mythical dream of moral rejuvenation in the Edenic wilderness of the "new" continent. He stands at the center of nineteenth century American literature and at the center of Twain's achievements.

In *Adventures of Huckleberry Finn*, Twain's attack upon the Romantic glorification of the past is a peripheral theme. In *A Connecticut Yankee in King Arthur's Court*, it is central and devastating, both in the novel itself and in its signaling of the direction in which Twain's thought and creative energies were heading. Although this too is a boy's book of a kind, there is about it none of the idyllic radiance of *The Adventures of Tom Sawyer* nor the harmonious balancing of opposites of *Adventures of Huckleberry Finn*. Rather, there is finally outright war between the forces of the feudal past and those of the progressive present, with considerable ambiguity about which is to be considered the good and which the evil.

There is no doubt that the reader's sympathies at the outset are with the Yankee mechanic, Hank Morgan, who, after a blow on the head, wakes up in King Arthur's England of 528 C.E. After saving himself from execution as a witch by "prophesying" a total eclipse of the sun, he vies successfully with Merlin for power and prestige at court. He is like Huck in his commonsense responses to life in general, and in particular to the romantic claims of the feudal society in which he finds himself. He

is unlike Huck in his vigorous progressivism, in his determination to bring the fruits of nineteenth century democracy and technology to feudal England. He introduces explosives, sets up schools to train workmen in the mechanical arts, gives instruction in journalism to his page with an eye to a national press, and stretches telephone lines haphazardly across the countryside. His talents, taken for magic for the most part, earn for him the title "the Boss," and the abiding enmity of Merlin, whom he replaces at court. He plans to declare a republic after Arthur's death, and the sixth century kingdom enjoys all the fruits of progress: schools, trains, factories, newspapers, the telephone and telegraph. The end of the story, however, just before Hank returns to his own century, pictures anything but the envisioned utopia. Arthur dies in a battle with Lancelot, Camelot is reduced to shambles, and Hank fortifies himself in a castle against the surviving chivalry of England. One of his final concerns is with the pollution caused by the dead bodies piled in the trenches around his fortress. The repressive, superstitious nightmare of feudal society has been compounded by the fearful efficiency of nineteenth century technology.

The ambiguity of the ending of the novel is symptomatic. The artistic balance of *Adventures of Huckleberry Finn* is no longer in evidence. Twain, always something of an allegorist, was by 1889 becoming more and more a polemicist, increasingly more interested in conflicts between abstract ideas and values than in the development and portrayal of human characters in all their complexities. Hank can be identified with Huck in terms of their common sense and their human values, but the big difference between them is that Huck's chief concern is with another human being while Hank's is with an abstraction called feudalism.

The Tragedy of Pudd'nhead Wilson · Twain was to do some of his most important writing in the last two decades of his life, including short fiction and social and moral criticism. His best novels, however, were completed in 1876 and in the 1880's. Of those coming after 1889, *The Tragedy of Pudd'nhead Wilson* is the most readable and the most consistent with the principal direction of his deepening cynicism about the "damned human race." The novel's only really interesting character is Roxy, a slave woman who switches her son with that of her owner Percy Driscoll to save her child from eventually being sold "down river." The whole of the dark tale that follows indicates, in Maxwell Geismar's words, how much "irony and tragedy have taken over the center stage in [Twain's] comic proscenium of life."

Lloyd N. Dendinger

Other major works

SHORT FICTION: *The Celebrated Jumping Frog of Calaveras County, and Other Sketches*, 1867; *Mark Twain's Sketches: New and Old*, 1875; *The Stolen White Elephant and Other Stories*, 1882; *The £1,000,000 Bank-Note and Other New Stories*, 1893; *The Man That Corrupted Hadleyburg and Other Stories and Essays*, 1900; *A Double-Barrelled Detective Story*, 1902; *Extracts from Adam's Diary*, 1904; *King Leopold's Soliloquy: A Defense of His Congo Rule*, 1905; *Eve's Diary*, 1906; *The $30,000 Bequest and Other Stories*, 1906; *A Horse's Tale*, 1906; *Extract from Captain Stormfield's Visit to Heaven*, 1909; *The Curious Republic of Gondour and Other Whimsical Sketches*, 1919; *Letters from the Earth*, 1962; *Mark Twain's Fables of Man*, 1972 (John S. Tuckey, editor); *Life as I Find It*, 1977 (Charles Neider, editor).

PLAYS: *Colonel Sellers*, 1874; *Ah, Sin, the Heathen Chinee*, 1877 (with Bret Harte).

NONFICTION: *The Innocents Abroad*, 1869; *Roughing It*, 1872; *A Tramp Abroad*, 1880; *Life on the Mississippi*, 1883; *Following the Equator*, 1897; *How to Tell a Story and Other Essays*, 1897; *My Début as a Literary Person*, 1903; *What Is Man?*, 1906; *Christian Science*, 1907; *Is Shakespeare Dead?*, 1909; *Mark Twain's Speeches*, 1910 (Albert Bigelow Paine, editor); *Mark Twain's Letters*, 1917 (2 volumes; Paine, editor); *Europe and Elsewhere*, 1923 (Paine, editor); *Mark Twain's Autobiography*, 1924 (2 volumes; Paine, editor); *Sketches of the Sixties*, 1926 (with Bret Harte); *The Adventures of Thomas Jefferson Snodgrass*, 1926; *Mark Twain's Notebook*, 1935 (Paine, editor); *Letters from the Sandwich Islands, Written for the Sacramento Union*, 1937; *Letters from Honolulu, Written for the Sacramento Union*, 1939; *Mark Twain in Eruption*, 1940 (Bernard De Voto, editor); *Washington in 1868*, 1943; *The Love Letters of Mark Twain*, 1949 (Dixon Wecter, editor); *Mark Twain to Mrs. Fairbanks*, 1949 (Dixon Wecter, editor); *Mark Twain of the Enterprise: Newspaper Articles and Other Documents, 1862-1864*, 1957 (Henry Nash Smith and Frederick Anderson, editors); *Traveling with the Innocents Abroad: Mark Twain's Original Reports from Europe and the Holy Land*, 1958 (Daniel Morley McKeithan, editor); *Mark Twain-Howells Letters: The Correspondence of Samuel L. Clemens and William D. Howells, 1872-1910*, 1960 (Henry Nash Smith and William M. Gibson, editors); *Mark Twain's Letters to Mary*, 1961; *Mark Twain's Letters to His Publishers, 1867-1894*, 1967 (Hamlin Hill, editor); *Clemens of the Call: Mark Twain in San Francisco*, 1969 (Edgar M. Branch, editor); *Mark Twain's Correspondence with Henry Huttleston Rogers, 1893-1909*, 1969 (Lewis Leary, editor); *Mark Twain Speaking*, 1976 (Paul Fatout, editor).

MISCELLANEOUS: *The Portable Mark Twain*, 1961 (Bernard De Voto, editor); *The Writings of Mark Twain*, 1968 (25 volumes); *Collected Tales, Sketches, Speeches, and Essays, 1891-1910*, 1992 (Louis J. Budd, editor).

Bibliography

Giddings, Robert, ed. *Mark Twain: A Sumptuous Variety*. Totowa, N.J.: Barnes & Noble Books, 1985. A useful collection of critical essays about Twain and his works.

Lauber, John. *The Inventions of Mark Twain*. New York: Hill & Wang, 1990. Very well-written and often humorous, this biography reveals Twain as an extremely complex, self-contradictory individual. Includes an annotated bibliography.

Long, E. Hudson, and J. R. LeMaster. *The New Mark Twain Handbook*. New York: Garland, 1985. A very useful work which discusses Twain's career, his development as a mythic figure, and the literature on his life and writings. Each section contains an extensive bibliography.

Miller, Robert Keith. *Mark Twain*. New York: Frederick Ungar, 1983. Links events in Twain's life to critical analyses of his major works and summarizes viewpoints of Twain scholars. Miller also offers his own conclusions about Twain's attitudes. Includes a helpful chronological table.

Paine, Albert Bigelow. *Mark Twain: A Biography*. 3 vols. New York: Harper and Brothers, 1912. Though long out of print, this remains the standard, and best, biography of Twain.

Rasmussen, R. Kent. *Mark Twain A-Z*. New York: Facts on File, 1995. The most impressive reference tool available. Virtually every character, theme, place, and biographical fact can be researched in this compendious volume. Contains the most complete chronology ever compiled.

ANNE TYLER

Born: Minneapolis, Minnesota; October 25, 1941

Principal long fiction · *If Morning Ever Comes*, 1964; *The Tin Can Tree*, 1965; *A Slipping-Down Life*, 1970; *The Clock Winder*, 1972; *Celestial Navigation*, 1974; *Searching for Caleb*, 1976; *Earthly Possessions*, 1977; *Morgan's Passing*, 1980; *Dinner at the Homesick Restaurant*, 1982; *The Accidental Tourist*, 1985; *Breathing Lessons*, 1988; *Saint Maybe*, 1991; *Ladder of Years*, 1995; *A Patchwork Planet*, 1998.

Other literary forms · In addition to her novels, Anne Tyler published more than forty short stories, including several in *Harper's, Mademoiselle, The New Yorker, Seventeen*, and the *Southern Review*. There is no collection to date, although two stories appeared in the O. Henry Prize volumes for 1969 and 1972 and others in the first edition of the Pushcart Prize anthology (1976), *Best American Short Stories* (1977), *Stories of the Modern South* (1978, 1981), *The Editor's Choice: New American Stories* (1985), *New Women and New Fiction* (1986), *Louder than Words* (1989), and several anthologies of American literature published by major publishing houses for use in college and university courses. Tyler also wrote several autobiographical and personal essays, one for *The Washington Post* in 1976 and another for *The Writer on Her Work* (1980), edited by Janet Sternburg. In 1975 her reviews of current fiction, criticism, and biography began appearing in major newspapers and magazines, including the *Boston Globe*, the *Chicago Sun-Times* and the *Chicago Tribune*, the *Detroit News, The New Republic, The New York Times Book Review, USA Today*, and *The Washington Post*.

Achievements · Despite praise for the truth of her characterizations and her eye for details, Tyler did not receive much national recognition for her fiction until the publication of her sixth novel, *Searching for Caleb*. Prior to 1976, the largest segment of her audience was in the South, although her short stories appeared in prestigious national magazines throughout the 1960's and 1970's. All of her novels except *A Slipping-Down Life* have been published abroad. Besides English editions, translations into Danish, French, German, Italian, and Swedish have appeared. Still, the American academic and critical communities were slow to appreciate Tyler's work. Her strong supporters include John Updike, who favorably reviewed her novels for *The New Yorker*, beginning with *Searching for Caleb*, and Reynolds Price, Tyler's professor at Duke University, who also reviewed her work.

In 1976 Tyler began to receive increasing recognition. In 1977, the American Academy and Institute of Arts and Letters cited her as a novelist of excellence and promise. *Earthly Possessions* and *Morgan's Passing* also received largely favorable national reviews. While a few critics, including Updike, expressed some disappointment in *Morgan's Passing*, the Writers Workshop of the University of Rochester awarded it the sixth annual Janet Heidinger Kafka prize for fiction by an American woman.

With the publication of *Dinner at the Homesick Restaurant*, her first novel to make the best-seller list, Tyler at last acquired full national stature. Benjamin DeMott's front-page notice in *The New York Times Book Review* pointed to the novel's wit and the depth of Tyler's psychological insight and characterizations. DeMott saw the book as clear evidence of Tyler's having joined the ranks of major novelists. Updike reiterated this praise, citing *Dinner at the Homesick Restaurant* as a work of considerable power. As a result of this increasing recognition and praise, scholarly studies of Tyler's work, including her early novels, began to appear. Tyler's reputation as a major contemporary American novelist was fixed with the publication of *The Accidental Tourist,* which won the 1985/1986 National Book Critics Circle Award for fiction. The successful film version of the novel increased Tyler's popularity with the reading public. *Breathing Lessons* was nominated for the National Book Award and won the 1989 Pulitzer Prize for fiction.

©Diana Walker

Biography · Anne Tyler was born in Minneapolis, Minnesota, on October 25, 1941, to Phyllis Mahon, a social worker, and Lloyd Parry Tyler, an industrial chemist. She was the oldest of four children, the only girl. Both parents were Quakers dedicated to finding an ideal community, a quest that produced the theme of frustrated idealism in Tyler's fiction. As a consequence of her parents' idealism, Tyler spent most of her early years, from infancy until age eleven, in various rural Quaker communes scattered throughout the midwestern and southern United States. When she was six, the family was settled in Celo, North Carolina–a large, isolated valley commune virtually independent of the outside world and unquestionably the setting for Tyler's short story "Outside," which appeared in the *Southern Review* in 1971.

Tyler later wrote of the impact of her early years on her fiction. Unable to sleep at night and needing to amuse herself, she began telling herself stories at age three. Her isolation in the rural communes in which she lived as a child contributed to the themes of isolation and community dominant in her novels. Additionally, growing up in North Carolina, where she spent summers tying tobacco, she listened carefully to the stories of the tobacco handlers and tenant farmers. Later, she was able to capture the cadences of everyday speech in her fiction, realizing that the stories these workers told could form the basis for literature. She was also to rely heavily on the North Carolina tobacco country as the setting for her early novels, especially *The Tin Can Tree* and *A Slipping-Down Life.*

When Tyler was eleven, she and her family moved to Raleigh, where they finally settled into an "ordinary" middle-class existence. There, Tyler attended Broughton High School and received encouragement in her writing. She also discovered the work of Eudora Welty, which was to have great influence on Tyler's own fiction.

In September, 1958, Tyler entered Duke University as an Angier Duke Scholar majoring in Russian. She was encouraged by Reynolds Price, who taught her freshman composition and later introduced her to his agent. At Duke, Tyler helped edit the *Archive* (the student literary magazine), published three early stories there, acted in several productions of the Wesley Players, and learned a great deal about the craft of fiction from reading Leo Tolstoy and the other major Russian novelists. She twice received the Anne Flexner award for creative writing at Duke and was graduated Phi Beta Kappa, just three years after entering, in 1961.

In September, 1961, Tyler began work on a master's degree in Russian at Columbia University, an experience that provides some of the background for *If Morning Ever Comes.* She completed the coursework for the degree but quit before writing her thesis. The following summer she spent in Maine, supporting herself by working on a schooner and proofreading for a local newspaper.

In 1962, Tyler returned to Duke University as the library's Russian bibliographer. That fall, she met her future husband, Taghi Modarressi, an Iranian child psychiatry student at the Duke Medical Center. The couple married in May, 1963, three months after the publication of Tyler's first short story in a national magazine. They moved to Montreal, Canada, that spring; during their four years there, Tyler wrote her first novel, taught herself Persian in anticipation of living in Iran, and worked as a librarian at the McGill University law library. In September, 1965, she gave birth to her first child, Tezh, a girl. The publication of *The Tin Can Tree* followed the next month.

In June, 1967, the Modarressis moved to Baltimore, Maryland. While Tyler's short stories continued to appear frequently in national publications between 1965 and 1970, her third novel was not published until January, 1970, first in condensed form in *Redbook* and later that same year in its entirety by Alfred A. Knopf. Between *The Tin Can Tree* and *A Slipping-Down Life* came one other book—*Winter Birds, Winter Apples*—which was not published. A second daughter, Mitra, was born in November, 1967, in Baltimore. A dedicated mother and a productive, organized writer, Tyler managed her dual careers for years by writing in the mornings while her children were at school. Although Tezh moved to New York and Mitra to San Francisco, Tyler and her husband continued to live in Baltimore. Taghi Modarressi died there of lymphoma in April, 1997, at age sixty-five. Tyler continued to reside in, and set her fiction in, Baltimore.

Analysis · In *The Writer on Her Work*, Anne Tyler discusses the importance of her having lived as a child in "an experimental Quaker community in the wilderness." For her, this early experience of isolation and her later effort "to fit into the outside world" provided the "kind of setting-apart situation" the writer requires for aesthetic distancing. Tyler's early isolation and struggle to belong also provided both the style and material for her fiction: the ironic distance characteristic of her prose as well as the subject of the individual's relationship to the community, particularly to other members of one's own household and family. Most of Tyler's short fiction and all of her novels published to date, from *If Morning Ever Comes* to *A Patchwork Planet*, concern the intricacies of family relationships and the isolation of the individual within the family. For Tyler, families clearly provided not only her major source for learning about the world as a child, but also fertile ground for studying how people endure the pain of loss and disappointment of life, adjust to living with others, and yet continue to love. All of the major conflicts and central themes of her novels evolve from this concern with the family and the individual's relationship to the community.

In this regard, Tyler falls clearly within the southern literary tradition with its emphasis on family life and history. As Paul Binding points out in *Separate Country: A Literary Journey Through the American South* (1979), Tyler, like her mentor Reynolds Price, relies on interaction and "badinage between members of a family or between people who know one another well in order to illuminate personality." Tyler does not, however, evoke or write of a regional past. She focuses on the present, narrating the past to provide a personal or familial, not a regional, history. Nor are her characters and families symbolic figures. They are, instead, idiosyncratic personalities, truthfully depicted, memorable yet atypical. In all but her first three novels and, to an extent, *Ladder of Years*, Tyler's setting is not the small towns and rural landscapes so often considered synonymous with southern life. Rather, her terrain is the border city of Baltimore and the decay and transience of modern urban life. Price, in fact, has said that she is the closest thing the South has to an urban novelist, indicating Tyler's somewhat unusual position among late twentieth century American writers: a southerner with a traditional interest in family, community, and the past; a modern woman fascinated with change and drawn to urban life; a writer with faith in humankind's ability to love and endure yet keenly aware of the difficulties of contemporary life, particularly the failure of communication within the family.

In her concern for familial relationships, Tyler's novels raise the existential issues of freedom and commitment. Significantly, hers is a compassionate art without explicit moral judgment–an absence of judgment for which some critics have faulted her. The effect of this gentle portrayal of serious themes is ironic: The disturbing failure of Tyler's characters to understand fully and to be understood by those they love is counterbalanced by a witty, carefully detailed style. Violence is usually absent from her work as well, and so are the grotesques found in the fiction of Flannery O'Connor and Carson McCullers. The most disfigured character in Tyler's work–Evie Decker, the fat teenager in *A Slipping-Down Life* who carves a local rock singer's name in her forehead–is compassionately portrayed. Like Eudora Welty, Tyler populates her novels with ordinary people, all of whom, she comments in *The Writer on Her Work*, are mildly eccentric in some way and "have something unusual" at their centers, something "funny and strange" and "touching in unexpected ways." From Ben Joe Hawkes in *If Morning Ever Comes*, who reads upside down to relieve boredom, to the elusive and difficult black sheep of her fictional families–Caleb and Duncan Peck,

Morgan Gower, Cody Tull, and Barnaby Gaitlin–Tyler warmly and humorously portrays a wide spectrum of fascinating yet ordinary human beings.

Tyler's view of human nature, her talent for realistically capturing generations of squabbling families, her keen ear for dialogue, and her interest in character and the isolation of the individual within the family derive from various sources. Her own "setting apart" experience in the North Carolina wilderness, her early childhood habit of telling herself bedtime stories for rest and amusement, and her long periods listening to tenant farmers' stories contributed substantially to her art. Shy, quiet, and keenly observant, she listened carefully to the stories the workers told. Later, she could call up the words of her own characters. "Having those voices in my ears all day," she has written, "helped me to summon up my own characters' voices." Additionally, with Reynolds Price as her teacher and Eudora Welty as a model, Tyler saw early in her career the rich source of literary materials offered by commonplace experience. Paul Binding also cites the influence of Tyler's study of the Russian masters, particularly Ivan Turgenev and Anton Chekhov, as a basis for her tolerant and warm portrayal of multiple generations of entangled and eccentric families. Finally, perhaps most prominent is Tyler's own witness to her parents' idealism, their quest for a perfect community throughout her youth, and later their apparently easy adjustment to an ordinary existence in a middle-sized southern city. Like her own father, whom she describes in *The Writer on Her Work*, the heroes of Tyler's novels are those who are "infinitely adapting" and always "looking around . . . with a smile to say, 'Oh! So this is where I am!'" They are complex people, enriched and deepened by experience–Elizabeth Abbott in *The Clock Winder*, Justine Peck in *Searching for Caleb*, Charlotte Emory in *Earthly Possessions*, Jenny Tull in *Dinner at the Homesick Restaurant*, Maggie Moran in *Breathing Lessons*, and Delia Grinstead in *Ladder of Years* best represent the type–able to enjoy life because they view themselves and others with tolerance and wit.

In an interview with Clifford Ridley for the *National Observer*, Tyler commented that she did not particularly "like either" of her "first two books" because "they seem so bland." Ben Joe Hawkes, the hero of *If Morning Ever Comes*, is "a likable guy; that's all you can say about him." While it is true that Ben Joe lacks the zaniness and interest which some of Tyler's later characters exhibit, his struggle to deal with his family, to recognize both his own independence and theirs, and to come to terms with the past and the psychological distance that isolates people even within an intimate group, provides a basis for understanding Tyler's later work and her place within the southern literary tradition. *If Morning Ever Comes* had its origins in two short stories: "I Never Saw Morning," which appeared in the April, 1961, *Archive* and was later collected in *Under Twenty-five: Duke Narrative and Verse, 1945-1962* (1963), edited by William Blackburn; and "Nobody Answers the Door," which appeared in the fall, 1964, issue of the *Antioch Review*. Both involve incidents suggested by the novel but occurring prior to the time of its opening. With the novel, they indicate Tyler's strong sense of the continuity of her characters' lives.

If Morning Ever Comes · As in later novels, the plot and subject of *If Morning Ever Comes*, Ben Joe's five-day journey home to Sandhill, North Carolina, from Columbia University, where he is a law student, evolve from family conflict. The family of women Ben Joe has left behind–six strikingly independent sisters, a proud mother, and a spry, seventy-eight-year-old grandmother, the first of Tyler's zanies–fail to tell him what is happening at home. Jenny, the family letter-writer, is all business. No one mentions the illegitimate son whom Ben Joe's father left behind with a mistress when he died, nor the support payments Ben Joe personally delivered for years before he left for New York. The family treats lightly even the fact that Ben Joe's oldest sister, Joanne, has taken her child, left her husband, and returned home after seven years. Their behavior and their failure to understand Ben Joe's concern and worry point clearly to the theme of the individual's isolation within the family, here a male in an entire family of women.

On the surface, *If Morning Ever Comes* is a simply structured novel covering less than a week in the life of its hero. As one critic has observed, however, going home is "only partly a spatial relocation." Ben Joe, like other southern literary heroes, "from Quentin Compson to Jack Burden," must return home "to embrace the spiritual crisis" created by an unsettled past and attempt to forge a future shaped by that very past. In this regard, *If Morning Ever Comes* is clearly a southern novel. That it draws on a sharp contrast between the peaceful North Carolina setting and the briskness of New York, as well as the hero's discomfort and sense of dislocation in the North, is also suggestive of Tyler's southern literary roots.

The Tin Can Tree · Although not widely reviewed nor acclaimed, *The Tin Can Tree* is a moving novel which expands and deepens Tyler's treatment of family relationships and the individual's struggle to remain committed in the face of significant loss and change. Just as Ben Joe Hawkes in *If Morning Ever Comes* remained committed to his family despite their pride and reticence, and to his father's memory despite the elder Hawkes's unfaithfulness, so also the characters in *The Tin Can Tree*, the members of three separate families sharing one house—the Pikes, the Greens, and the Potters—must deal with the commonly experienced grief at the death of the Pikes's six-year-old daughter, Janie Rose, adjust, and resume the task of living. Tyler's achievement here is that she captures eight different characters' varying responses to grief while avoiding the sentimental and maudlin. She opens the novel with the close of the funeral service, thus deliberately focusing on life, rather than death, and the resumption of the tasks of everyday living.

In addition to this theme of grief, *The Tin Can Tree* explores the background and interactions of James and Ansel Green and Joan Pike, Janie Rose's cousin. The study of James's commitment to his ailing brother Ansel, the two brothers' alienation from their family, and Joan's distance from her own elderly parents as well as her unresolved romantic involvement with James, give the novel a depth lacking in *If Morning Ever Comes*, with its heavy focus on one central character. As one reviewer noted, *The Tin Can Tree* illustrates Tyler's talent for bringing "into focus a remarkable range of human traits and emotions." Lou Pike's depressive withdrawal and immobility after her daughter's death, her husband's worried yet practical concern, their son Simon's sense of rejection and neglect, Joan's uncertainty and anger at James and his brother Ansel—all acquire full portraiture. A love of detail permeates the book, from the Potter sisters' eccentric way of wearing hats and gloves even when visiting only at the other end of the porch to the details of Janie Rose's behavior, her "tin can tree" made in honor of God during a religious period and her wearing layer upon layer of underwear on "her bad days." Such details make the characters real and Janie Rose's death more immediate and painful.

The Tin Can Tree is also the first Tyler novel to draw explicitly on the author's tobacco-field experience. Joan Pike, a school secretary, spends part of her summers handling tobacco in the warehouses, as Tyler herself did as a teenager. Besides providing elements of plot and characterization, the Tobacco Road landscape mirrors the sterility of the characters' lives following Janie Rose's death and provides a spokesman for the novel's theme. "Bravest thing about people, Miss Joan," one of the tobacco tiers says, "is how they go on loving mortal beings after finding out there's such a thing as dying." Unlike Erskine Caldwell, whose stereotypical white trash characters are often farcical grotesques, Tyler deepens the Tobacco Road landscape by a compassionate, detailed account of the grief of several families at the death of a child. Hers is a fiction of psychological insight, not a document for social change. *The Tin Can Tree*, as one critic observed, is "a novel rich in incident that details the closing of a family wound and the resumption of life among people stunned by the proof of mortality."

A Slipping-Down Life · In her third novel, *A Slipping-Down Life*, Tyler returned to the existential themes of the individual's isolation, his struggle for identity, and the lack of understanding and meaningful communication among people living closely together. Set in the fictional towns of Pulqua and Farinia, North Carolina–suspiciously similar to the actual town of Fuquay-Varina near Raleigh–it was the last of the Tyler's books set entirely in North Carolina but also the first to portray the barrenness of familial relationships in a clearly modern setting. While most of *If Morning Ever Comes* and all of *The Tin Can Tree* are set in peaceful, remote areas where family life, though troubled, seems unaffected by distinctly modern problems, *A Slipping-Down Life* draws heavily on the impact of modern American culture and media on family life. Also, where Tyler's first two novels covered only a few days in the lives of the principal characters, *A Slipping-Down Life* chronicles one full year in the life of its heroine–a fat, dowdy, teenage girl named Evie Decker–indicating a development in Tyler's ability to handle character over an extended period of time.

Originating in a "newspaper story about a fifteen-year-old girl in Texas who'd slashed 'Elvis' in her forehead," the novel traces Evie's barren interaction with her father, her only living relative, as well as the development and dissolution of a relationship with a local rock singer named Bertram "Drumstrings" Casey, the first of Tyler's unadmirable yet likable antiheroes–exploitative and selfish yet touchingly shy and dependent on his parents and Evie. Evie's entanglement with Drum, leading eventually to their marriage, is tragically initiated by her carving the name "Casey" in her forehead with a pair of nail scissors, and ends, equally as tragically, with the couple's separation, the death of Evie's family, and her discovery of Casey in bed with another woman. Throughout, Evie thinks of herself as though she were acting on a stage set, taking her cues from the soap operas she watches daily with Clotelia, the Deckers' sullen maid and Evie's sometime childing surrogate mother. Like Joan Pike in *The Tin Can Tree* and later Tyler heroines–Justine Peck in *Searching for Caleb* and Charlotte Emory in *Earthly Possessions*–Evie is an only child faced with growing up alone in a dark, stifling household and creating an identity without the companionship and aid of siblings or understanding parents.

Besides its characterizations, *A Slipping-Down Life* is also noteworthy for capturing at least part of the American experience in the 1960's: the lonely world of teenagers, the generation gap, the high school student's unending quest for popularity and romance, as well as a small town's tawdry local rock scene, featuring the chilled air in a roadside house, painfully loud music, necking couples, and the smell of stale beer. As one reviewer observed, *A Slipping-Down Life* captures "a *way* of life, a way that is tacked upon teenage bulletin boards, sewn to dresses 'decorated with poodles on loops of real chain,' enclosed in high-school notebooks containing *Silver Screen* magazine."

The Clock Winder · Tyler's first three novels all involve some type of journey home during which a central character confronts both the distance between himself and his family and the difficulties of unresolved past conflicts. Ben Joe's journey from New York to Sandhill in *If Morning Ever Comes* fits this pattern, as do James Green's trip to Caraway, North Carolina, in *The Tin Can Tree* and, in *A Slipping-Down Life*, Evie Decker's return to her father's house following his death. A similar trip occurs in *The Clock Winder*. A novel characterized by Sarah Blackburn as having all the "virtues" of southern writing—"an easy, almost confidential directness, fine skill at quick characterization, a sure eye for atmosphere, and a special nostalgic humor"—*The Clock Winder* was at the time of its publication Tyler's most ambitious work, tracing the intricate relationships of a large cast of characters over an entire decade. It was also her first novel set in Baltimore.

The diverse, eccentric, eight-member Emerson family of Baltimore and their one adopted member, Elizabeth Abbott, clearly form one of those "huge," "loving-bickering" southern families Tyler told Clifford Ridley she hoped to create in writing *If Morning Ever Comes*. Mrs. Emerson—a skinny, fragile widow—is unrelenting in nagging her children about their neglected duties to her. She is, consequently, estranged from all but one: Timothy, a pressured medical student who, with his twin Andrew, is one of the most neurotic and disturbed characters in Tyler's novels. Into this entangled, crisis-prone family, Elizabeth Abbott brings the very skills she is unable to practice with her own family in Ellington, North Carolina. Tolerant, practical, dextrous, and witty—the first of Tyler's "infinitely adapting" heroines based on her own father—Elizabeth is a handyman and a godsend for the nervous Mrs. Emerson. In Ellington, she is a bumbler, a rebellious college dropout, and a painful reminder of failure to her minister father. Her life at home is bleak, ordinary, and restricted. Commitment to the Emersons, despite their family feuds, offers interest and freedom from the Abbott family's dicta, an opportunity to form a new identity and life free of reminders of past mistakes.

Besides expanding character, setting, and timeframe, *The Clock Winder* is unusual among Tyler's first four works for its use of violence and its experimentation with point of view. Timothy Emerson commits suicide by shooting himself in Elizabeth's presence, sending her home to her family for several years. Later, after her return to Baltimore, his twin shoots her, though he causes only a flesh wound. Also, where earlier Tyler novels used omniscient point of view focusing largely on one major character—the exception is *The Tin Can Tree*, in which Joan Pike and James Green serve alternately as centers of consciousness—*The Clock Winder* shifts perspective among many characters, some of them minor. In one chapter, the reader witnesses the succession of disconnected thoughts, the confusion of physical sensations, and the temporal disorientation accompanying Mrs. Emerson's stroke. Another presents the views of the youngest Emerson, Peter, who appears only in the final chapter of the novel. These shifts in point of view result in an intimate portrait not only of the novel's central character, Elizabeth, but also of the Emersons—a varied, contrasting family of idiosyncratic individuals.

Celestial Navigation · With *Celestial Navigation*, Tyler moved her novels to a totally urban landscape. Eight months after the novel's publication, she told a Duke University audience that she "could no longer write a southern novel" since she had lived away from the South too long to capture realistically the "voices" and behavior of the people who live there. Set almost exclusively in a seedy Baltimore boardinghouse "smack in the middle" of a deteriorating inner-city neighborhood, *Celestial Navigation* is Tyler's portrait of the artist. It covers thirteen years in the central character's life, expanding the study of character development found in earlier novels and illustrating her increasing skill in handling point of view. The various boarders narrate firsthand their experiences and relationships to other residents. Additionally, since it focuses largely on boarders rather than kin, somewhat like *The Tin Can Tree* with its three families unrelated by blood, and since it includes the common-law marriage of its hero, *Celestial Navigation* redefines the meaning of family ties as characterized in Tyler's novels. It also intensifies the isolation of the protagonist. Jeremy Pauling, the artist-hero of the novel and the owner of the rooming house, is so reclusive that for years he has not left the city block where he lives. His principal ties are not with his two sisters in Richmond, neither very understanding of his peculiar artistic temperament, but with the boarders with whom he lives.

The caring family of boarders the novel studies, however, are essentially isolated strangers living in private rooms. They are mostly older people with severed family connections or no remaining kin. Ironically, they exhibit more tolerance and unquestioning respect for the peculiarities and privacy of one another than do many blood-related members. Mrs. Vinton, an aged spinster who works in a bookstore, stays on to care for Jeremy years after the others move or die, yet she never interrupts his trancelike states or work. With the other boarders—the elegant widow Mrs. Jarrett, the nubile Mary Tell, the young Olivia, and the fractious old Mrs. Somerset shuffling about in slippers—Mrs. Vinton is a testament to Tyler's talent for realistically capturing a gallery of idiosyncratic yet identifiably ordinary people.

The real achievement of *Celestial Navigation*, though, is Jeremy Pauling. He is one of Tyler's minor grotesques. A pale, pudgy sculptor, he rarely speaks and withdraws for days at a time to his secluded bedroom-studio. The novel works as Jeremy's story, however, partly because Tyler gives him a full range of emotions—including sexual attraction to several female boarders and a love for the children he has by his common-law marriage. She also views him with both compassion and humor and lets the reader see him from several points of view. Tyler shifts to third-person point of view to narrate Jeremy's chapters, since Jeremy himself is incapable of communicating his impressions in the coherent manner of the other characters. Tyler has said that the character of Jeremy is based in part on a shy, easily flustered little man she helped one day in the library where she worked, but she added several of her own traits to the character: a dread of telephones and doorbells (something retained from her isolated childhood) and, most important, her own artistic vision, an eye for the "smallest and most unnoticed scenes on earth," very much like those details Tyler captures in *Celestial Navigation*.

Searching for Caleb · *Searching for Caleb* marked a turning point in Tyler's career. It was her first novel to receive national recognition, at a time when Tyler's own reviews began to appear in national publications. As Walter Sullivan commented in 1977 when reviewing *Searching for Caleb* for the *Sewanee Review*, Tyler "retained" in her work "a kind of innocence . . . a sense of wonder at all the crazy things in the world and an abiding affection for her own flaky characters." *Searching for Caleb* was also evidence that Tyler had retained her southern literary roots and her delight in huge families and the range of human characters those families produce. Something of a combined family history and detective story, the novel is one of Tyler's most ambitious works, tracing five generations of one large, dichotomous, and extremely long-lived clan, the Pecks of Baltimore, from the 1880's through 1973. As in *The Clock Winder* and *Celestial Navigation,* Tyler shows her strong fascination with urban life, a result perhaps of her own early life in remote areas. She also returns to Roland Park, one of Baltimore's oldest residential neighborhoods and the main setting of *The Clock Winder.*

As the title suggests, *Searching for Caleb* involves a quest for the vanished Caleb, the great uncle of the novel's protagonists, Duncan and Justine Peck, and the half-brother of their grandfather, Daniel Peck. Representing one side of the family, Caleb, Justine, and Duncan are outcasts of a sort: spirited, talented, imaginative, and free individuals unable or unwilling to live as family rules dictate. Caleb becomes a musician, Justine a fortune-teller. Duncan, her husband and first cousin, leads an unsettled life as a mechanic and jack-of-all-trades, foreshadowing Morgan Gower, the hero of *Morgan's Passing.* Like Morgan and, later, Barnaby Gaitlin of *A Patchwork Planet,* Duncan dismays his family.

The other side of the family, the Pecks of Roland Park, headed by Daniel, are uniformly humorless and restricted. The women, though educated, are unthreatening; the men, all attorneys educated at Johns Hopkins, drive black Fords and dress in Brooks Brothers suits. They are, above all, clannish, living side by side in similar Roland Park houses. For them, family tradition and training—in effect, the past—are inescapable. Even Daniel's late-life quest for his half-brother evolves from his ties to family and an unsettled conflict. It represents a delayed response to the question frequently asked in his childhood: "Daniel, have you seen Caleb?"

Searching for Caleb, like Tyler's earlier novels, also illustrates the author's belief in the need for human adaptability, tolerance, and love. Justine epitomizes the philosophy. She weathers a dark and uncertain childhood with a depressive mother, frequent moves with her restless husband, the death of both parents and her grandfather, and the loss of her one daughter in marriage to a Milquetoast minister. Yet, she remains spirited and continues to love her family. She insists on visiting Roland Park, a longing Duncan cannot understand, and she is committed to finding Caleb, not only out of a love of travel and adventure but also to share the experiences with her grandfather and to find her own roots. With its focus on community and family and its delineation of the unsettled conflicts of the past impacting on the present, *Searching for Caleb* indicates Tyler's own roots in the family of southern literature.

Earthly Possessions · When it appeared in 1977, *Earthly Possessions* was Tyler's most unfavorably received novel. Among disapproving reviewers, Roger Sale in *The New York Times Review of Books* saw the book as "a cartoon" of sorts, with the life of Charlotte Emory, the protagonist, "reduced . . . by her own hand" until all "possible anguish is . . . lost." The reason for this response is no doubt the sardonic nature of Charlotte herself, an entrapped housewife who sets out to leave her husband but gets kidnapped instead in a bungled bank robbery. Such reversals characterize Charlotte's life and have led her to "loosen" her hold so that she sees everything from an ironic distance. Charlotte, moreover, is the novel's only narrator, and she tells her life-story in chapters alternating perfectly with those narrating her experiences with Jake Simms, her kidnapper, on their trip south from Clarion, Maryland, Charlotte's hometown. Along the way, Tyler captures the fragmentation and transience of modern life, reflected in a string of drive-in restaurants, banks, and films. The triumph of the novel is not, as in earlier Tyler works, characterization, but the panorama of contemporary American life that the book captures during this journey of hostage and kidnapper.

With its contrapuntal chapters, *Earthly Possessions* is Tyler's most highly structured novel, the first to be told entirely in the first person by one narrator. The result is an artificial temporal arrangement and a restricted focus, one lifetime as compared with those of eight or nine Emersons, five generations of Pecks. Also, the reader is always in the presence of two somewhat unsavory characters: a nail-biting, minor league criminal and a stoical, cynical woman. All might have come from the pen of Flannery O'Connor but for the touchingly human flaws Tyler draws. Neither Jake nor Charlotte, despite their failings, is morally culpable. What they share is a common, impractical desire for freedom from the entanglements of life: for Charlotte, marriage complete with a house full of relatives and in-laws, rooms of furniture (earthly possessions), even sinners from the mourner's bench at her husband's church; for Jake, jail for a petty crime and a pregnant girl friend. Heading south to rescue Mindy Callendar, Jake's Kewpie-doll girl friend, from a home for unwed mothers, Jake, Charlotte realizes, is like herself "criss-crossed by strings of love and need and worry." Even Charlotte and Jake's relationship grows into a type of commitment. Eventually the two share the driving as well as their troubles. Any "relationship," Tyler told Marguerite Michaels in an interview for *The New York Times Book Review*, even one "as bizarre as" that of "a bank robber and hostage could become . . . bickering [and] familiar. . . . Anything done gradually enough becomes ordinary."

Earthly Possessions, despite its problems, shares with *The Tin Can Tree* and *Celestial Navigation* a redefinition of family ties. With Tyler's other novels, it also illuminates the problems and conflicts of the individual within a close relationship, whether familial or not, and focuses on the eccentric nature of ordinary lives, the ordinariness of the bizarre.

In her eighth novel, Tyler returned to the heart of Baltimore for her setting and to a central character, Morgan Gower, who is strikingly eccentric. Reviewers compared him with Saul Bellow's Henderson and Joseph Heller's Major Major. He also resembles Duncan Peck as well as other Tyler protagonists. Like those heroes, Morgan is in conflict with his family: seven daughters who find him embarrassing, a slovenly though good-natured wife, a senile mother, and a depressed, inert sister. Like Ben Joe Hawkes, Morgan feels trapped and misunderstood in a house cluttered with "the particles of related people's unrelated worlds" and full of women with whom he is unable to communicate satisfactorily. While his family insists on going about life unconsciously, Morgan, spirited and highly inventive, faces a mid-life crisis that calls for a change. He must also come to terms with his past, the consequences of marrying Bonny for her money as well as his father's inexplicable suicide when Morgan was a teenager. Like Duncan Peck, Morgan is a kind of mechanical genius who takes up various projects, then drops them—"a tinkering, puttering, hardware sort of man." Like the renegade Pecks, he eventually abandons his Baltimore family to take up a new life and identity with a traveling amusement company.

Despite these resemblances to other Tyler heroes, Morgan is a unique creation, the product of Tyler's maturing vision of life. Her understanding of his sexual attraction to a young puppeteer and her portrayal of his frustration with his wife suggest a depth of insight into the problems of marriage, a depth lacking in the early *If Morning Ever Comes*. Morgan is also a complex character, a genuine impostor who tries on identities complete with appropriately matching costumes. At times he is "Father Morgan, the street priest of Baltimore"; at other times, he is an immigrant with family still abroad, a doctor who delivers a baby in the backseat of a car—any role in which people will accept him. Though most of this role-playing is harmless, Morgan is an antihero lacking a firm identity, a modern eccentric who revels in the anonymity and emptiness of decaying city neighborhoods and a man who assumes a false identity to take up life with another man's wife without benefit of divorce. Not surprisingly, reviewers found it difficult to like Morgan, but few found him unbelievable.

Tyler's increasing skill in capturing and making believable such a character testifies to her maturation as a writer. As John Leonard commented in *The New York Times* when reviewing the novel, readers "are obliged to care" about Tyler's "odd people" "because their oddities are what we see at an angle in the mirror in the middle of a bad night." Drawing from selected everyday scenes covering twelve years in Morgan's life, Tyler roots her novel firmly in the here and now. Morgan becomes believable because he is not always posing. He reads the morning paper over coffee, affectionately slaps his wife on her rear end, smokes too much, attends a daughter's wedding, despairs over a quarrel-filled family vacation, works in a hardware store, and comes down with a terrible cold. Tyler's is a realistic art illuminating family conflict and solidly based in the ordinary details of life.

Dinner at the Homesick Restaurant · Of all Tyler's novels, *Dinner at the Homesick Restaurant* most inspires comparison with the work of Flannery O'Connor. The title is reminiscent of O'Connor's wit and irony, and the mood of the novel, as one reviewer noted, is that of "O'Connor's Gothic South" with its "sullen, psychic menace." At her best, as in *Celestial Navigation*, Tyler captures the pain, anxiety, and isolation beneath the surface of ordinary lives. At times, however, particularly in *Earthly Possessions* but also *Morgan's Passing*, she treats this pain lightly, thus denying a sense of genuine struggle. In *Earthly Possessions*, Charlotte is flippant and ironic; in *Morgan's Passing*, Morgan is a zany, the mood quick and light. *Dinner at the Homesick Restaurant*, representing what John Updike called a "darkening" of Tyler's art, presents the other side of the coin from *Morgan's Passing*, not only in mood but also in story line. Its focus is not the husband who abandons his family to find a new life, but the family he left behind. It is a stunning psychological portrait of the Tulls, Pearl and her three children, and the anger, guilt, hurt, and anxiety they feel growing up in an uncertain world without a father. All carry their pain through life, illustrating more profoundly than any of Tyler's earlier books the past's haunting influence on the present.

Covering thirty-five years, three generations of Tulls, the novel opens with Pearl on her deathbed. This first chapter, reminiscent of Katherine Anne Porter's short story, "The Jilting of Granny Weatherall," depicts Pearl as a stoical, frightened woman who has weathered a youth filled with dread of being an old maid, a quick marriage, and a lonely struggle to rear three "flawed" children: Cody, the oldest boy, a troublemaker from childhood, "prone to unreasonable rages"; Jenny, the only girl, "flippant" and "opaque"; Ezra, his mother's favorite, a gentle man who has not "lived up to his potential," but instead has become the ambitionless owner of the Homesick Restaurant. Not one of Pearl's children has turned out as she wished. Consequently, she like other Tyler characters, feels "closed off" from her family, the very children to whom she has devoted her life. Later chapters reveal why, focusing on each of the children in turn and tracing the evolution of their lives as well as their fear of their mother's rages. All, like their mother, end up in some way "destroyed by love."

Tyler's compassionate portrayal of her characters and her characteristic humor do mitigate the darkness of this novel. Although Pearl, her forehead permanently creased from worry, verbally and physically abuses her children, Tyler lets the reader understand the reasons for Pearl's behavior, even though he may not forgive her, and shows a far mellower Pearl in old age. Jenny, after struggling through medical school, two marriages, and a nervous breakdown, is nursed back to health by her mother. Cody spares no expense in caring for his family, even though he is unable to forgive Pearl for mistreating him as a child. The teenager Cody plays cruel but funny tricks on his brother Ezra—partly out of resentment of Ezra's being the favorite, but also from Cody's own pain and sense of rejection. Taking slats from Ezra's bed, Cody strews the floor with pornographic magazines so Pearl will think Ezra the kind of disappointment she finds Cody to be. Later, after stealing Ezra's sweetheart, he recognizes not only his guilt but also his love for his brother. These tales fill out the dark psychological portrait Tyler draws, making *Dinner at the Homesick Restaurant*, like many of Tyler's earlier books, a confirmation of life's difficulty as well as of the value of love.

The Accidental Tourist · A mood of dark comedy pervades *The Accidental Tourist*. It is the only Tyler work in which a murder occurs, and a sense of the inexplicable, tragic nature of reality moves the plot and forms a backdrop for the novel. The book opens with Macon and Sarah Leary returning from a truncated beach vacation and the sudden announcement by Sarah that she wants a divorce. Macon, the central character, is a forty-four-year-old writer of guidebooks for businessmen who find themselves in foreign places but prefer the familiarity of home. The logo for the series, entitled Accidental Tourist, is a winged armchair, a motif suggesting Macon's attitude toward the disruptions of travel. In the opening pages of *The Accidental Tourist*, the reader learns of the death of Macon and Sarah's twelve-year-old son, Ethan, who was killed in a robbery at a burger stand. Besides their grief at the death of their son, Macon and Sarah must confront the permanent jarring of their world by the random nature of the crime: The robber shot Ethan as an afterthought; Ethan and his friend had impulsively stolen away from a summer camp. With Sarah's leaving, Macon's life tailspins, yet he strives desperately to maintain control, to reduce life to its simplest terms. He sleeps in one sheet sewn together like a body bag and showers in his shirt to save on laundry. In a spirit of fun, Tyler gives Macon an alter ego, a Welsh corgi, Edward, who becomes increasingly surly as Macon's life disintegrates. Through Edward, Tyler introduces the unpredictable Muriel Pritchett, a dog trainer set on finding a father for her sickly son, Alexander.

Told from a limited third-person point of view, *The Accidental Tourist* displays Tyler's art at its best: her eye for idiosyncratic behavior and the accidental quality of reality, her focus on family as the center of life's triumphs and tragedies. The family here is not only Macon and Sarah but also Macon's siblings: his sister Rose, whose romance with Julian Edge, Macon's publisher, forms a dual plot to Macon's romance with Muriel, and his two brothers, Charles and Porter. For part of the novel, Tyler centers on the Leary siblings, all marred by their mother's carefree abandonment of them. Both Charles and Porter are divorced, and Rose now maintains her grandparents' home for her brothers. What is striking about the house is its orderliness—every item in the kitchen is shelved in alphabetical order—and its changelessness. When Macon breaks a leg in a freak accident, he returns to his siblings and resumes life just as if he had never been married, had a child, and lived away for years. The characteristics of families, Tyler suggests, are permanently etched. It is the occurrences of life that constantly shift.

Breathing Lessons · In *The Accidental Tourist*, Anne Tyler depicted the dissolution of a twenty-year marriage following the violent death of the Learys' son. In *Breathing Lessons*, she presents the opposite: the duration of Ira and Maggie Moran's marriage for twenty-eight years. Told primarily through flashbacks as the couple journeys to the funeral of a friend, the novel covers nearly thirty years in one September day and contrasts the Morans' courtship and marriage with the relationship of their son, Jesse, and his former wife, Fiona. From its beginning, *Breathing Lessons* concerns not only Ira and Maggie's bickering, love, and tolerance for each other but also Maggie's struggle to reconcile Jesse and Fiona.

Set in Pennsylvania and Baltimore, the novel has three principal divisions, each told from a restricted third-person point of view. The first and third sections focus on Maggie's consciousness, while the middle section, which constitutes something of an interlude, centers on Ira's thoughts. Somewhat reminiscent of the film *The Big Chill* (1983), the first section wittily depicts the music and mores of the 1950's. The second part depicts a side trip in which Ira and Maggie temporarily become involved with an elderly black man who has separated from his wife of more than fifty years. This section also provides Ira's family history and his response to his wife and children. Tyler reveals here a masterful handling of exposition through internal thought sequences and flashbacks. The novel's third section, which introduces the characters of Fiona and Leroy, her daughter, returns to Maggie's thoughts and her memories of Jesse and Fiona's relationship. A return to Baltimore with Fiona and Leroy completes the section, suggesting the cyclical nature of experience, a central theme in the novel.

In *Breathing Lessons*, Tyler continues to balance a lighthearted view of human nature with a depth of insight into the darker side of marriage. Maggie and Ira's marriage, while offering a sound balance of two contrasting personality types who can bicker and then reconcile, has its dark side also: a "helpless, angry, confined feeling" which Maggie experiences "from time to time." Ira, too, realizes that marriage involves "the same old arguments, . . . the same old resentments dragged up year after year." The joyful side of Tyler's fiction is her fondness for zany characters, her keen eye for the bizarre in human behavior, which she observes with amused detachment, and her finely tuned ear for human speech. *Breathing Lessons* offers many examples, beginning with the zesty, lowerclass names of her characters: Serena, Fiona, Duluth. Maggie herself belongs to a long line of lively, unpredictable Tyler heroines—most expert caretakers—beginning with Granny Hawkes in *If Morning Ever Comes*, Tyler's first novel. In fact, in both her acute observations of others and her repeated attempts "to alter people's lives," Maggie resembles her creator, the fiction writer who manipulates the lives of her characters to fill her plot.

Saint Maybe · The "darkening" of Tyler's work continues in *Saint Maybe* despite its lovably offbeat characters and unambiguously happy ending. Possible marital infidelity, child neglect, and suicide set the novel moving. The Bedloes are an "ideal, apple-pie" family, determined to be happy and "normal." Trouble invades their Eden in the form of Lucy, a sexy single mother who marries the elder son Danny, bringing along two young children and, most likely, another she is carrying when she meets her new groom. She also brings an insatiable restlessness. The Bedloes welcome the addition to the fold, proclaiming their son fortunate to have found "a ready-made

family." It is the seventeen-year-old protagonist Ian, Danny's younger brother, who questions Lucy's virtue, a query with lethal consequences: Danny's suicide when he sees himself a cuckold and Lucy's when she forfeits a bleak future with an overdose of pills.

Guilt over the tragedy he believes he has caused drives Ian to join the Church of the Second Chance, a congregation of born-again Christians who pursue active atonement for their failings. Obsessively seeking forgiveness, Ian drops out of college at nineteen to raise his brother's orphaned stepchildren. Christlike, he forswears sexual activity and pursues carpentry. He leads a martyred though by no means solitary existence over the next twenty-three years. As with many Tyler heroes, Ian lacks self-awareness: He cannot recognize his own goodness, does not understand that he has paid any debt in full. Yet when at forty-two he marries Rita diCarlo, a character reminiscent of Muriel Pritchett, Macon Leary's freewheeling lifeline in *The Accidental Tourist*, Ian is delightfully surprised to realize that he has not spent his years paying a penance but leading a rich—if unorthodox—life.

Ladder of Years · *Ladder of Years* tells the story of forty-year-old Cordelia Grinstead's circular flight from her upper-middle-class life in Baltimore. Until she simply walks away from her husband and teenage children during their vacation, Delia has never left home. Having passively married her father's assistant, who chose her as a helpmate in assuming the family medical practice, Delia lives her married life in her girlhood home, where she suffocates under the weight of domesticity. Her presence is defined by the demands of the family she nurtures, yet her children's increasing self-sufficiency threatens her with obsolescence. Fleeing home, Delia embarks on a journey toward self-discovery, a quest reminiscent of Charlotte Emory's in *Earthly Possessions*. She initially revels in her spare new existence in a small Maryland town, but as with other of Tyler's would-be renegades from the hearth, the caregiver's habits of heart and mind reassert themselves. Realizing that she has re-created the very role she believed she had shed, Delia embraces her identity as a nurturer and returns home, aware finally of her family's genuine yet unvoiced appreciation.

A Patchwork Planet · *A Patchwork Planet* revisits *Saint Maybe*'s theme of debt and repayment. Black sheep Barnaby Gaitlin is a former juvenile delinquent who, to the shame of his affluent parents, was arrested in his youth for breaking into the homes of their wealthy Guilford neighbors. To keep her son out of jail, Margot Gaitlin (born Margo Kazmerow, "just a Polish girl from Canton") swallowed her pride to beg and buy her neighbors' silence. Barnaby's freedom cost $8,700, a sum his embittered mother continually holds over him. Though Barnaby eventually repays this debt, he learns that self-respect cannot be purchased.

A handyman who performs odd jobs for an assortment of crotchety yet colorful senior citizens, Barnaby stumbles across a client's "Twinform" while tidying her attic. The mannequin—shaped and painted to resemble the owner—was invented by his great-grandfather as an aid to foolproof dressing: By first modeling an outfit on a "double," one could gauge and adjust the effect of the intended apparel. Barnaby is intrigued by this premise of the trial run, and he imputes his many mistakes to his failure to hold metaphoric dress rehearsals for his life. He is convinced that he lacks necessary information for successful living, a need which prompted the boyhood burglaries during which he would examine his victims' photographs and diaries for clues to how they managed their lives. He remains rudderless at thirty, wavering between intentionally disappointing his parents through exaggerated irresponsibility and straining to please them, nearly marrying the unsuitably staid Sophia Maynard because she lends him the respectability he lacks.

Barnaby sinks to an emotional low when he is wrongly accused of theft, a crime Sophia believes him guilty of and a charge that he feels he vicariously deserves. However, in the homemade blanket alluded to in the novel's title, Barnaby finds the expansive perspective from which to accept the love and faith that his clients rightly place in him. On an elderly woman's quilt he sees that Earth is "makeshift and haphazard, clumsily cobbled together, overlapping and crowded and likely to fall into pieces at any moment." He is moved to accept and forgive his own failings as a universal condition of his humanity. The novel ends with his resolute goodbye to the girlfriend who doubted his goodness: "Sophia, you never did realize. I am a man you can trust."

Stella A. Nesanovich, updated by Theresa M. Kanoza

Bibliography

Gullette, Margaret M. *Safe at Last in the Middle Years—The Invention of the Midlife Progress Novel: Saul Bellow, Margaret Drabble, Anne Tyler, and John Updike.* Berkeley: University of California Press, 1988. Devotes a chapter, originally published as a separate essay in the *New England Review*, to Tyler's presentation of the conflicts of adulthood in her novels.

Petry, Alice Hall. "Bright Books of Life: The Black Norm in Anne Tyler's Novels." *The Southern Quarterly* 31, no. 1 (Fall, 1992): 7-13. A study of Tyler's favorable portrayals of African Americans as wise and knowing characters.

Robertson, Mary F. "Anne Tyler: Medusa Points and Contact Points." In *Contemporary American Women Writers: Narrative Strategies*, edited by Catherine Rainwater and William J. Scheick. Lexington: University Press of Kentucky, 1985. A discussion of the narrative form of Tyler's novels, focusing on her disruption of the conventional expectations of family novels.

Salwak, Dale, ed. *Anne Tyler as Novelist.* Iowa City: University of Iowa Press, 1994. A collection of essays addressing Tyler's development, attainments, and literary reputation. Contributors include John Updike and Linda Wagner-Martin. Novels discussed range from *If Morning Ever Comes*, Tyler's first published novel, to her twelfth, *Saint Maybe*.

Stephens, C. Ralph, ed. *The Fiction of Anne Tyler.* Jackson: University Press of Mississippi, 1990. A collection of essays selected from papers given in 1989 at the Anne Tyler Symposium in Baltimore and representing a range of interests and approaches.

Voelker, Joseph C. *Art and the Accidental in Anne Tyler.* Columbia: University of Missouri Press, 1989. The first book-length study of Anne Tyler's fiction, this volume focuses on the development of Tyler's aesthetics and her treatment of character, particularly her view of selfhood as mystery and of experience as accidental.

JOHN UPDIKE

Born: Shillington, Pennsylvania; March 18, 1932

Principal long fiction · *The Poorhouse Fair*, 1959; *Rabbit, Run*, 1960; *The Centaur*, 1963; *Of the Farm*, 1965; *Couples*, 1968; *Bech: A Book*, 1970; *Rabbit Redux*, 1971; *A Month of Sundays*, 1975; *Marry Me: A Romance*, 1976; *The Coup*, 1978; *Rabbit Is Rich*, 1981; *Bech Is Back*, 1982; *The Witches of Eastwick*, 1984; *Roger's Version*, 1986; *S.*, 1988; *Rabbit at Rest*, 1990; *Memories of the Ford Administration*, 1992; *Brazil*, 1994; *In the Beauty of the Lilies*, 1996; *Toward the End of Time*, 1997; *Bech at Bay: A Quasi-Novel*, 1998.

Other literary forms · Since publishing his first story in *The New Yorker* in 1954, Updike has truly become a man of letters, publishing in virtually every literary genre— poetry, short fiction, novel, essay, drama, art criticism, and autobiography. His first short-story collection, *The Same Door*, appeared in 1959; many more followed, including *The Afterlife and Other Stories* in 1994. Updike's play *Buchanan Dying* was published in 1974. His poetry has appeared in many volumes of his own, beginning with *The Carpentered Hen, and Other Tame Creatures* (1958), as well as in anthologies. Updike published his first nonfiction prose collection in 1965; most of his nonfiction works are collections of essays and criticism, but the autobiographical *Self-Consciousness: Memoirs* appeared in 1989 and the single-themed *Golf Dreams: Writings on Golf* was published in 1996.

Achievements · One of the major figures to emerge in American fiction after World War II, John Updike is widely acclaimed as one of the most accomplished stylists and prolific writers of his generation. Showing remarkable versatility and range, his fiction represents a penetrating chronicle in the realist mode of the changing morals and manners of American society. Updike's work has met with both critical and popular success. His first novel, *The Poorhouse Fair*, was awarded the Rosenthal Award of the National Institute of Arts and Letters in 1960. In 1964, he received the National Book Award for *The Centaur*. He was elected in the same year to the National Institute of Arts and Letters. A number of his short stories have won the O. Henry Prize for best short story of the year and have been included in the yearly volumes of *Best American Short Stories*. In 1977, he was elected to the prestigious American Academy of Arts and Letters. In 1981, his novel *Rabbit Is Rich* won the Pulitzer Prize for Fiction and the American Book Award. In that same year, he was awarded the Edward MacDowell Medal for literature. While Updike's novels continue the long national debate on the American civilization and its discontents, perhaps what is most significant about them is their depiction of restless and aspiring spirits struggling within the constraints of flesh, of time and gravity—lovers and battlers all. For Updike (writing about the novel in an essay), "Not to be in love, the capital N novel whispers to capital W western man, is to be dying."

Biography · The only child of Wesley and Linda Grace (née Hoyer) Updike, John Updike spent the first thirteen years of his life living with his parents and grandparents in his maternal grandparents' home in Shillington, Pennsylvania, in rather strained

©Davis Freeman

economic conditions. In 1945, the Updikes had to move to the family farm in Plainville, ten miles away from Shillington. Updike's father supported the family on his meager salary as a mathematics teacher at the high school. His mother had literary aspirations of her own and later became a freelance writer. A number of short stories, such as "Flight," and the novels *The Centaur* and *Of the Farm* drew upon this experience. As a youth, Updike dreamed of drawing cartoons and writing for *The New Yorker*, an ambition he fulfilled in 1955. Updike went to Harvard University in 1950 on a full scholarship, majoring in English. He was editor of the Harvard *Lampoon* and graduated in 1954 with highest honors. In 1953, he married Radcliffe student Mary Pennington, the daughter of a Unitarian minister; they were to have four children.

After a year in Oxford, England, where Updike studied at the Ruskin School of Drawing and Fine Art, he returned to the United States to a job offered him by E. B. White as a staff writer with *The New Yorker*, for which he wrote the "Talk of the Town" column. In April of 1957, fearing the city scene would disturb his development as a writer, Updike and his family left New York for Ipswich, Massachusetts, where he would live for the next seventeen years and which would serve for the model for the settings of a number of stories and novels. During this time, Updike was active in

Ipswich community life and regularly attended the Congregational Church. In 1974, the Updikes were divorced. In 1977, Updike remarried, and he and his new wife, Martha Bernhard, settled in Georgetown, Massachusetts.

During the late 1950's and early 1960's, Updike faced a crisis of faith prompted by his acute consciousness of death's inevitability. The works of such writers as Søren Kierkegaard and, especially, Karl Barth, the Swiss orthodox theologian, helped Updike come to grips with this fear and to find a basis for faith. Religious and theological concerns pervade Updike's fiction. In a real sense, like Nathaniel Haw-thorne's writing more than one hundred years earlier, Updike's fiction explores for his time the great issues of sin, guilt, and grace–of spiritual yearnings amid the entanglements of the flesh.

Updike's success as a writer enabled him to travel under government auspices. In 1964-1965, Updike traveled to Russia, Romania, Bulgaria, and Czechoslovakia as part of the U.S.S.R.-U.S. Cultural Exchange Program. In 1973, he traveled and lectured as a Fulbright lecturer in Ghana, Nigeria, Tanzania, Kenya, and Ethiopia. Updike's Bech novels and *The Coup* reflect those journeys.

Analysis · A writer with John Updike's versatility and range, whose fiction reveals a virtual symphonic richness and complexity, offers readers a variety of keys or themes with which to explore his work. The growing and already substantial body of criticism Updike's work has engendered, therefore, reflects a variety of approaches. Alice and Kenneth Hamilton were among the first critics to give extensive treatment to the religious and theological elements in Updike's fiction. Rachel Burchard explores Updike's fiction in terms of its presentations of authentic quests for meaning in our time, for answers to age-old questions about humanity and God, and of its affirmation of human worth and hope despite the social and natural forces threatening defeat of the human enterprise. Considering technique as well as theme, Larry Taylor treats the function of the pastoral and antipastoral in Updike's fiction and places that treatment within a long tradition in American literature. The British critic Tony Tanner discusses Updike's fiction as depicting the "compromised environment" of New England suburbia–the fear and dread of decay, of death and nothingness, and the dream of escaping from the complications of such a world. Edward Vargo focuses upon the recurrence of ritualistic patterns in Updike's fiction, the struggle to wrest something social from an increasingly secularized culture. Joyce Markle's thematic study of Updike's fiction sees a conflict between "Lovers," or Life-givers, and the embodied forces of convention, dehumanizing belief, and death.

In a 1962 memoir entitled "The Dogwood Tree: A Boyhood," Updike discusses his boyhood fascination with what he called the "Three Great Secret Things: Sex, Religion, and Art." The critic George W. Hunt contends that "these three secret things also characterize the predominant subject matter, thematic concerns, and central questions found throughout his adult fiction." Detailing Updike's reliance upon the ideas of Søren Kierkegaard and Karl Barth, Hunt's study is interested in the religious implications of Updike's work. A more sociological interest informs Philip Vaughan's study of Updike's fiction, which, to Vaughan, provides readers with valid depictions of the social conditions–loneliness, isolation, aging, and morality–of our time. David Galloway sees Updike's fiction in existential terms, seeing Updike's protagonists as "absurd heroes" seeking meaning in an inhospitable universe. More impressionistic but quite suggestive is Elizabeth Tallant's short study of the fate of Eros in several of Updike's novels. Believing that a thesis or thematic approach does not do full justice

1062 Notable American Novelists

to Updike's work, Donald J. Greiner examines Updike's novels more formalistically in order to "discuss the qualities that make Updike a great writer."

Using a comparative approach, George Searles discusses Philip Roth and Updike as important social realists whose work gives a true sense of life in the last half of the twentieth century. To Searles, Updike's overriding theme is cultural disintegration—questing but alienated protagonists confronting crises caused by a breakdown of the established order. Jeff Campbell uses Updike's long poem *Midpoint* (1969) as a key to an analysis of Updike's fiction. Seeing Updike as an "ironist of the spiritual life," Ralph C. Wood discusses Updike's fiction—along with the fiction of Flannery O'Connor, Walker Percy, and Peter De Vries—as depicting the "comedy of redemption," a study deeply indebted to the theology of Karl Barth.

In a compendious study of American fiction since 1940, Frederick R. Karl offers a useful overview of Updike: "Updike's fiction is founded on a vision of a compromised, tentative, teetering American, living in suburban New England or in rural Pennsylvania; an American who has broken with his more disciplined forebears and drifted free, seeking self-fulfillment but uncertain what it is and how to obtain it." While this rather global description fairly represents the recurring condition in most of Updike's novels, it does not do justice to the complex particularities of each work. Nevertheless, it does point to the basic predicament of nearly all of Updike's protagonists—that sense of doubleness, of the ironic discrepancy of the fallen creature who yet senses, or yearns for, something transcendent. Updike's people are spiritual amphibians—creatures in concert with two realms, yet not fully at home in either. Updike employs an analogous image in his novel *The Centaur*—here is a creature that embodies the godly with the bestial, a fitting image of the human predicament in Updike's fiction. His fiction depicts the ambiguity of the "yes-but" stance toward the world, similar to the paradox of the "already and the not-yet." In his fine story "The Bulgarian Poetess" (1966), Updike writes: "Actuality is a running impoverishment of possibility." Again there is a sense of duplicity, of incompleteness. In such a world, problems are not always solved; they are more often endured if not fully understood. Yet even the curtains of actuality occasionally part, unexpectedly, to offer gifts, as Updike avers in his preface to *Olinger Stories: A Selection* (1964)—such gifts as keep alive a vision of wholeness in an often lost and fragmented world.

The Poorhouse Fair · Updike's first novel, *The Poorhouse Fair*, may seem anomalous in comparison with the rest of his work. In fact, the novel depicts a collision of values that runs throughout Updike's work. As in so much of Updike's fiction, the novel is concerned with decay, disintegration, a loss or abandonment of vital traditions, of values, of connection to a nurturing past. This opposition is embodied in the two principal characters: ninety-four-year-old John Hook, former teacher and resident of the poorhouse, and Stephen Conner, the poorhouse's prefect. The novel is set in the future, sometime in the late 1970's, where want and misery have virtually been eliminated by a kind of humanistic socialism. Such progress has been made at a price: sterility, dehumanization, spiritual emptiness, regimentation. In a world totally run by the head, the heart dies. Hook tells Conner, in response to the prefect's avowed atheism: "There is no goodness, without belief." Conner's earthly paradise is a false one, destroying what it would save. The former prefect, Mendelssohn, sought, as his name would suggest, to fulfill the old people's spiritual needs in rituals and hymn singing.

Out of frustration with Conner's soulless administration, the old people break into a spontaneous "stoning" of Conner in the novel's climax. In effect, Conner is a corrupt or preverted martyr to the new "religion" of godless rationalism. The incident symbolizes the inherent desire and need for self-assertion and individualism. Conner's rationalized system is ultimately entropic. The annual fair is symbolic of an antientropic spirit in its celebration of the fruits of individual self-expression—patchwork quilts and peach-pit sculptures. In its depiction of an older America—its values of individuality, personal dignity, and pride—being swallowed up by material progress and bureaucratic efficiency, the novel is an "old" and somber book for a young author to write. In effect, Updike depicts an America become a spiritual "poorhouse," though materially rich. It is Hook, one of the last links to that lost America, who struggles at the end for some word to leave with Conner as a kind of testament, but he cannot find it.

The Centaur · In a number of stories and the novels *The Centaur* and *Of the Farm*, Updike draws heavily upon his experiences growing up in Shillington, Pennsylvania. Both novels—though very different from each other—concern the reckoning of a son with a parent, in the case of *The Centaur* with his father and in *Of the Farm* with his mother, before he can proceed with his life. This is emotional and spiritual "homework" necessary for the son's passage to maturity, to freedom from the past, yet also to a new sense of responsibility. As in all Updike's fiction, this passage is difficult, complex, and ambiguous in its resolution.

The Centaur is arguably Updike's most complex novel, involving as it does the complicated interweaving of the myth of Chiron the centaur with the story of an adolescent boy and his father one winter in 1947. While the novel won the National Book Award, its reception was quite mixed. A number of reviewers thought the use of myth to be pretentious and not fully realized, while others praised the author's achievement. The novel is part *Bildungsroman*, a novel of moral education, and part *Künstlerroman*, a novel of an artist seeking his identity in conflict with society and/or his past. Operating on different levels, temporally and spatially, the nine chapters of the novel are a virtual collage, quite appropriate for the painter-narrator, nearly thirty, self-described as a "second-rate abstract expressionist," who is trying to recover from his past some understanding that might clarify and motivate his artistic vocation. Peter Caldwell, the narrator, reminisces to his black mistress in a Manhattan loft about a three-day period in the winter of 1947, fourteen years earlier. On the realistic level, Peter tells the story of his self-conscious adolescence growing up an only child, living on a farm with his parents and Pop Kramer, his grandfather. His father is the high school biology teacher and swim coach, whose acts of compassion and charity embarrass the boy. On the mythic level, the father is depicted as Chiron the centaur, part man and part stallion, who serves as mentor to the youthful Greek heroes. As such, he suffers for his charges. By moving back and forth between the mythic and the realistic levels, Peter is able to move to an understanding of his father's life and death and to a clarification of his own vocation.

Just as Chiron sacrifices his immortality—he accepts death—so that Prometheus may be free to live, so too does George give his life for his son. While George is obsessed with death, it is doubtful that his sacrifice takes the form of death. Rather, his sacrifice is his willingness to go on fulfilling his obligations to his family. In reflecting upon this sacrifice by his father, Peter, feeling a failure in his art, asks: *"Was it for this that my father gave up his life?"* In the harsh reappraisal his memory provides, Peter is learning what he could not know as an adolescent. Love, guilt, and sacrifice are somehow inherent in the very structure of life. It is this that his mythicized father reveals to him in the very act of his narrating the story. For many critics, George Caldwell's sacrificial act frees the son to resume his artistic vocation with courage. For others, the novel is a mock epic showing in Peter the artist, the son of a scientist father and the grandson of a preacher, a loss of the metaphoric realm that makes great art possible and that leaves Peter diminished by his confinement to the earth alone. However the end is taken, the mythic element of the narrative richly captures the doubleness of human existence so pervasive in Updike's fictions.

Of the Farm · A short novel, *Of the Farm* is another tale of the intricacy of love, guilt, sacrifice, and betrayal. In *The Centaur*, Peter Caldwell, stalled and failing in his artistic vocation, goes home through a creative act of the memory and imagination to recover his lost vision, a basis to continue his work. Peter can fulfill his Promethean charge because his father was Chiron. In contrast, *Of the Farm*'s Joey Robinson goes home to get his mother's blessing on his recent remarriage. Joey seeks forgiveness of the guilt he bears for the acts of betrayal that have constituted his life. He betrays his poetic aspirations by becoming an advertising executive and betrays his marriage to Joan and his three children through adultery and divorce. Bringing home for his domineering mother's approval his sensuous new wife, Peggy, sets the stage for more betrayals and recriminations. As the weekend progresses, Peggy and Joey's mother vie for Joey's soul. Joey cannot please both women or heal the wounds of his past betrayals. For Joey, Peggy is the "farm" he wishes to husband. At the end, failing to win his mother's blessing, Joey and Peggy return to their lives in the city, leaving Joey's mother to die amid the memorials of her own unrealized dreams. If the novel is an exploration of human freedom, as the epigraph from Jean-Paul Sartre would suggest, the reader sees that freedom escapes all the characters, bound as they are by conflicting desires, guilt, and obligation.

Rabbit, Run · When Updike published *Rabbit, Run* in 1960, a story of an ex-basketball player and his floundering marriage set in the late 1950's, he had no intention of writing a sequel. Yet, Updike returned to Harry "Rabbit" Angstrom once every ten years for four novels–*Rabbit Redux* (1971), *Rabbit Is Rich* (1981), and *Rabbit at Rest* (1990)–as a kind of gauge of the changes occuring in American culture. This series of novels is among the most popular of his work.

For *Rabbit, Run*, Updike uses a quote from Pascal for an epigraph: "The motions of Grace, the hardness of heart; external circumstances." Updike has commented that those three things describe our lives. In a real sense, those things also describe the basic movements and conflicts in the Rabbit novels. From *Rabbit, Run* to *Rabbit at Rest*, as the titles themselves suggest, Rabbit's life has been characterized by a series of zigzag movements and resistances and yearnings, colliding, often ineffectually, with the external circumstances of a fast-paced and changing world. *Rabbit, Run* takes place in the late 1950's, when Harry Angstrom, a former high school basketball great nicknamed Rabbit, at twenty-six finds himself in a dead-end life: with a job selling items in a dime store and a marriage to a careless and boozie woman. Wounded by the stifling boredom of everyday life and the cloying pressures of conforming and adapting to his environment, so characteristic of the 1950's, Harry wonders, confusingly, what has happened to his life. The disgust he feels about his present life is aggravated by his memories of when he was "first-rate at something" as a high school basketball great. Out of frustration, Rabbit bolts from his life-stifling existence, feeling that something out there wants him to find it. The novel is the study of this nonhero's quest for a nonexistent grail. Rabbit's zigzagging or boomeranging movements from wife Janice to mistress Ruth, the part-time prostitute, wreaks havoc: Janice accidentally drowns the baby; Ruth is impregnated and seeks an abortion. Pursued by the weak-faithed, do-gooder minister Eccles and failed by his old coach Tothero, Rabbit has no one to whom he can turn for help. Rabbit, like so many of Updike's protagonists, is enmeshed in the highly compromised environment of America, locked in the horizontal dimension yet yearning for something transcendent, the recovery of the vertical dimension. For Rabbit, the closest he can come to that missing feeling is sex, the deep mysteries of the woman's body replacing the old revelations of religion. Rabbit, though irresponsible, registers his refusal to succumb to such a world through movement, his running replacing the lost territories of innocent escape.

Rabbit Redux · Ten years later, in *Rabbit Redux*, Rabbit has stopped running. He is back home with Janice and works as a typesetter. It is the end of the 1960's, and Rabbit watches the Moon landing on television as well as the upheavals of civil rights, campus demonstrations, and the Vietnam War. Rabbit feels that the whole country is doing what he did ten years earlier. As Janice moves out to live with her lover Stavros, Rabbit and his son Nelson end up as hosts to Jill, a runaway flower-child, and a bail-jumping Vietnam veteran and black radical named Skeeter. This unlikely combination allows Updike to explore the major cultural and political clashes of the 1960's. This time Rabbit is more a passive listener-observer than an activist searcher. Skeeter's charismatic critiques of the American way of life challenge Rabbit's unquestioning patriotism and mesmerize him. As a result, Rabbit is helpless when disaster comes—his house is set on fire and Jill dies inside. Rabbit helps Skeeter escape. Fearing for her lover's heart, Janice returns to Rabbit. Unlike the restless figure of the first novel, Rabbit now seems to have capitulated or resigned himself to those powerful "external circumstances" from which he once sought escape. Rabbit bears witness, numbingly, to a disintegrating America, even as it puts a man on the Moon. America's spiritual landscape is as barren as that on the Moon. The novel ends with Rabbit and Janice asleep together. Perhaps they can awake to a new maturity and sense of responsibility for what they do in the world.

Rabbit Is Rich and **Rabbit at Rest** · In the first two Rabbit novels, Rabbit was out of step with the times—running in the placid 1950's, sitting in the frenetic 1960's. In *Rabbit Is Rich*, he is running again, but this time in tune with the rhythms of the 1970's. Rabbit now jogs, which is in keeping with the fitness craze that began in the 1970's. He and Janice are prospering during the decade of inflation and energy crises. They own a Toyota agency and are members of a country club. Rabbit plays golf and goes to Rotary Club lunches. Instead of newspapers, as in *Rabbit Redux*, he reads *Consumer Reports*, the bible of his new status. The ghosts of his past haunt him, however: the drowned baby, the child he did or did not have with Ruth, memories of Jill and Skeeter. The chief reminder of the sins of his past is his son Nelson, returning home, like something repressed, to wreak havoc on the family's new affluent complacency. Like his father of old but lacking Rabbit's conscience and vision, Nelson's quest for attention practically wrecks everything that he touches: his father's cars, his relationships. Rabbit can see himself in Nelson's behavior and tries to help him avoid recapitulating Rabbit's mistakes, but communication is difficult between them. With Skylab falling and America held hostage by Iranians, the present is uneasy and anxious, the future uncertain. Characteristically, Rabbit turns to sex to fill the spiritual void. He and Janice make love on top of their gold Krugerrands. Rabbit lusts for the lovely Cindy, but in the wife-swapping escapade during their Caribbean holiday, Rabbit gets Thelma Harrison instead and is introduced to anal sex–a fitting image of the sense of nothingness pervading American culture at the end of the "Me Decade." Updike does not end there. He leaves Rabbit holding his granddaughter, "another nail in his coffin," but also another chance for renewal, perhaps even a motion of grace, a richness unearned.

The sense of exhaustion–of a world "running out of gas" in so many ways–that pervades *Rabbit Is Rich* becomes more serious, even terminal, in *Rabbit at Rest.* The fuzzy emptiness and mindlessness of the 1980's pervade the novel, even as so much is described in such vivid detail. Rabbit and Janice now winter in Florida and Nelson runs the car dealership. Rabbit sustains himself on junk food and endless television viewing, images of the emptiness of American life under Ronald Reagan. He suffers a heart attack and undergoes an angioplasty procedure. His son's cocaine addiction and embezzlement of $200,000 from the business shock the family. Yet this often coarse and unsympathetic man continues to compel the reader's interest. He wonders about the Dalai Lama then in the news. As the Cold War dissipates, Rabbit asks: "If there's no Cold War, what's the point of being an American?" The man called "Mr. Death" in *Rabbit, Run* now must face death in his own overblown body and contemplate it in relation to a world he has always known but that now is no more. Can such a man find peace, an acceptance and understanding of a life lived in such struggle and perplexity? In *Rabbit Is Rich*, Harry confesses to Janice the paradox of their lives: "Too much of it and not enough. The fear that it will end some day, and the fear that tomorrow will be the same as yesterday." In intensive care in Florida, at the end of *Rabbit at Rest*, Rabbit says, "Enough." Is this the realization and acceptance of life's sufficiency or its surplus? A confession of his own excesses and indulgences, or a command of sorts that he has had enough? These are only a few of the questions raised by the Rabbit novels.

Marry Me · Many critics praise Updike for being the premier American novelist of marriage. Nearly all of his fiction displays the mysterious as well as common-place but ineluctable complexities and conflicts of marriage. It is one of Updike's major concerns to explore the conditions of love in our time. His fiction is his updating and reworking of the Tristan and Isolde myth, about which Updike had commented in his review of Denis de Rougement's book *Love in the Western World* (1956)–lovers whose passion is enhanced by the obstacles needed to be overcome to fulfill it; the quest for an ideal lover who will assuage the fear of death and the longing for the infinite; the confusions of *eros* and the death wish. Many of Updike's male protagonists are aspects of both Tristan and Don Juan in their quest for a life-enhancing or death-denying passion. Such are the ingredients in the novels *Couples, Marry Me: A Romance,* and *The Witches of Eastwick.* All the novels are set in the 1960's–the spring of 1962 to the spring of 1963 in *Marry Me,* the spring of 1963 to the spring of 1964 in *Couples,* and probably 1969 for *The Witches of Eastwick.* In their various ways, each novel tries to answer the question, "After Christianity, what?" Human sexuality is liturgy and sacrament of the new religion emerging in America in the 1960's–a new end of innocence in a "post-pill paradise." The three novels make an interesting grouping because all deal with marriages in various states of deterioration, and all explore the implications of "sex as the emergent religion, as the only thing left," Updike says. While not published until 1976, *Marry Me* was actually written before *Couples.* In fact, one story seems to lead right into the other. *The Witches of Eastwick* explores the theme from a woman's perspective.

Both Jerry Conant of *Marry Me* and Piet Hanema of *Couples* are educated professionals, married with children, and live in upper-middle-class suburbs of great cities. They are both suffering spiritually, longing for an affirmation from outside their selves, for some sort of blessing and certainty. As Jerry says, "Maybe our trouble is that we live in the twilight of the old morality, and there's just enough to torment us, and not enough to hold us in." The mortal fear that such an insight inspires leads both men to desperate quests for a love that will mend or heal their spiritual brokenness or emptiness. *Marry Me* takes place during the second year of the Kennedy administration, when the charm of the Camelot myth still captivated the country. Significantly, Updike calls *Marry Me* a "romance" rather than a novel, in order to suggest an attempt to use the freer form to explore the ambiguities of love, marriage, and adultery. The novel ends in ambiguity, with no clear resolution. In fact, there are three possible endings: Jerry with his lover Sally in Wyoming, Jerry with his wife Ruth in France, and Jerry in the Virgin Islands alone, on the island of St. Croix, symbolizing perhaps Jerry's self-immolation.

Couples · *Couples* takes place during the last year of the Kennedy presidency, including his assassination, and is thus a much more cynical book, harsher and darker than *Marry Me*. A certain light has gone out in the land; death and decay haunt the imagination. In contrast to *Marry Me*, choices are made and lives reconstitute themselves in a kind of cyclical way at the end of *Couples*. These two rather weak men fail at their quest to find in the flesh what they have lost in the spirit. Both men are believers and churchgoers, and both face a crisis in their faith. The church, committed to secularity and worldliness, fails them. Their respective wives are naturalistic and feel at home on earth and offer them little surcease to their anxiety. In *Marry Me*, Jerry must contend with Sally's husband Richard, an atheist with one blind eye, who insists on clear-cut decisions. For Jerry, however, every choice involves a loss that he cannot tolerate. In *Couples*, Piet is pitted against Freddy Thorne, the self-proclaimed priest of the new religion of sensuality. To Freddy, it is their fate to be "suspended in . . . one of those dark ages that visits mankind between millennia, between the death and rebirth of gods, when there is nothing to steer by but sex and stoicism and the stars." The many adulteries among the ten couples of *Couples* lead finally to divorce and disintegration of the secular paradise of Tarbox, the fictional suburb of the novel. Piet leaves his unattainable but earthbound wife, fittingly named Angela, for the sensuous Foxy Whitman, whose abortion of Piet's child Freddy arranges. When his church is destroyed by fire, Piet is freed from his old morality and guilt and the tension inherent in his sense of fallenness. Yet the satisfaction obtained with Foxy is a foreclosure of the vertical hope, and is a kind of death. Both novels depict the failure of sex as a religion as well as the profound disappointments with love in its romantic or secular forms. Such may be Updike's answer to the question he posed: "After Christianity, what?"

The Witches of Eastwick · The setting of *The Witches of Eastwick* is a small town in Rhode Island during the first year or so of Richard Nixon's presidency, an era of protest and discontent. Three divorcees, Alexander Spofford, Jane Smart, and Sukie Rougemont, discover the power of sisterhood and femininity and become witchlike in their powers. The delicate balance of their friendship is upset by the entrance of the apparently demoniac Darryl Van Horne, who takes them all as his lovers. The novel's three parts, "The Coven," "Malefica," and "Guilt," suggest a progression from their newfound power and independence through an encounter with the demoniac to a rediscovery of responsibility through an awareness of guilt. Like Updike's many male protagonists, the three women must come to grips with death before they can reconstitute a meaningful life. Van Horne is a satanic figure whose machinations lead to a dissipation of the women's powers. When he chooses the young Jennifer Gabriel for his wife, the women employ their powers to create a curse to bring about Jennifer's death. When she does die, the women feel guilt, even though it is not clear that their curse caused the girl's cancer. Van Horne preaches a sermon on the evilness of a creation saturated with disease and leaves town with Jennifer's brother, Christopher. The three women disband and find their way into suitable marriages. Such use of witchcraft allows Updike to explore the nature of evil and its connections with nature, history, and technology. The ambiguities of feminism are examined in the context of the moral and social confusions of the late 1960's in an effort to break down the destructive and outmoded polarities of the patriarchical tradition.

Bech and *The Coup* · The first two Bech books—*Bech: A Book* and *Bech Is Back*—and *The Coup* are novels and stories resulting from Updike's travels to Eastern Europe and to Africa. Each work offers the author an opportunity to develop a very different persona from those of his domestic novels, as well as the chance to explore another aspect of "otherness" and "difference." *Bech: A Book* is a collection of seven stories about a middle-aged and very successful Jewish novelist, Henry Bech, and his various experiences both abroad and in America. The collection is framed by the fiction of Updike writing about an actual person contemporary with him. The book has a foreword by the putative author as well as two appendices. Such devices afford Updike an opportunity for humorous satire of the literary life in America. Bech emerges as a strong and believable character struggling with the failure of his success as a writer in a success-plagued culture. In *Bech Is Back*, Updike creates seven more stories about Bech's travels and his wrestling with the ambiguities of fame, fortune, and human worth, the protagonist's success with women an index of his success and worth as a writer. He must struggle with the question of whether he has sold out his talent for the marketplace, defiling both. Felix Ellellou, the protagonist of *The Coup*, is a bold creation for Updike, a black Islamic Marxist whose memoirs constitute the novel. Now in exile, the former president of the fictional sub-Saharan nation of Kush recounts the story of his rise and fall and of his perpetual struggle to avoid the ambiguous gifts of American aid. He fears not only the junk food but also the forces of secularity and materialism that will ultimately make his beloved Kush a spiritual wasteland. He virtually stands alone in his resistance to the so-called benefits of American civilization, toward which he admits ambivalence. In Ellellou, one can see an African version of Updike's body-spirit conflict so prevalent in his fiction. For Ellellou, freedom must be freedom from material possessions, yet he anguishes over his people's poverty-stricken plight. He believes that it is better to die in poverty than from spiritual loss. In privation, he believes, the spirit will soar. Despite Ellellou's stoicism, his faith is plagued by doubts. He suspects that the new world religion will be godless and entropic. Updike's African novel is a replay of the author's critical interrogation of the moral and spiritual failures of the West.

A Month of Sundays, Roger's Version,* and *S. · Updike's concern with love, marriage, and adultery in so much of his fiction links him to Nathaniel Hawthorne's great novel

The Scarlet Letter (1850), America's first great treatment of the complex social and religious consequences of adulterous love. Three novels in particular treat different dimensions of that adulterous triangle of Hawthorne's novel–*A Month of Sundays*, *Roger's Version*, and *S.* Hawthorne's Dimmesdale is updated in the figure of the Reverend Tom Marshfield, the exiled protagonist of *A Month of Sundays*. Roger Lambert of *Roger's Version*, the professor of theology specializing in heresies, is Updike's treatment of Hawthorne's Roger Chillingworth. Sarah Worth of *S.* is a contemporary depiction of Hawthorne's Hester, the truly noble and strong character of *The Scarlet Letter*. Hawthorne's Dimmesdale is crushed by his inability to integrate the body-and-soul division. So, too, does Updike's Marshfield suffer from this split in a novel with many allusions to *The Scarlet Letter*. Marshfield marries the former Jane Chillingworth, whose father was Marshfield's ethics instructor. The retreat center is managed by Ms. Prynne, who reads the diary entries of Marshfield and his fellow clerical exiles. The novel traces Marshfield's integration of body and spirit, a mending of Marshfield's fragmented self, enabling him to return to his ministry as a true helper to the faithful. Roger Chillingworth in *The Scarlet Letter* was the cockolded husband seeking revenge for his wife's adultery. In *Roger's Version*, Roger Lambert imagines that his wife Esther is having an affair with Dale, the computer science graduate student trying to prove God's existence by computer. Dale is a kind of innocent, a fundamentalist seeking technological support for his faith. By the end, Dale's project has failed, as Roger believed it would, and Dale returns to Ohio, his faith demolished. Yet, Dale's project provoked Roger to revivify his own faith and to engage his world more responsibly than he has. Updike's Sarah Worth of *S.* is certainly one possible version of a late twentieth century Hester Prynne. Sarah is a woman who has taken her life fully into her own hands without shame or illusion. After bolting from her faithless but wealthy physician husband, Sarah goes to an ashram in Arizona for spiritual renewal. That proves to be a false endeavor, but Sarah survives intact (and with much of the cult's money). Loving and compassionate yet willful and worldly, Sarah Worth dares to follow her own path.

Toward the End of Time · Ever the chronicler of societal obsessions, Updike in 1997 provided his readers with a millennial book, *Toward the End of Time*. In this, his twentieth novel, the year is 2020, and the Sino-American nuclear war has recently destroyed the North American infrastructure and the U.S. government. In a universe of two moons and new life-forms, the "metallobioforms" that rose up out of the nuclear slime, the normal order of things seems to have come undone. Updike's protagonist, Ben Turnbull, seems at times to assume the identities of such disparate entities as an ancient Egyptian tomb robber and a medieval monk, and he is having an affair with a dark-eyed young woman whom he suspects is also a doe. Updike spends considerable time mulling over the mysteries of quantum mechanics and string theory, implying that such abstractions may contain the key to the enigma of time. In the end, though, the drama of Ben's post-millennial existence seems an elaboration of the sublunary obsessions of other Updike protagonists. The story of this sixty-six-year-old retired financial adviser could almost serve as a coda to the *Rabbit* books.

Bech at Bay · With *Bech at Bay: A Quasi-Novel*, Updike ended the saga of another of his favorite alter-egos, the now septuagenarian Henry Bech. Like its predecessors, this "quasi-novel" consists of a series of linked stories concerning the crabbed but accomplished—and now superannuated—Jewish novelist. *Bech at Bay* finds Bech at the heart of late twentieth century American literary life; however, that life, like Bech himself, seems to have lost nearly all its vitality. The mood is set in the book's opening section, "Bech in Czech," in which Bech finds himself on a book tour in the gloom of Prague, haunted by the uneasy feeling that he is no more than a character in someone else's book. In another episode, Bech is tapped to head an elite artistic organization called "The Forty"—a group not unlike the American Academy of Art and Letters, which Updike served as chancellor—but finds himself presiding over its demise when the elderly existing members refuse to admit any new blood.

Nonetheless, Bech has not lost all his imaginative powers. In "Bech Noir," he fantasizes the murders of critics who have abused him. Then, in the volume's finale, Bech is awarded the Nobel Prize. Delivering his acceptance speech before the Swedish Academy, Bech asserts his vitality by holding aloft his newborn daughter for the audience's edification. The gesture is, if nothing else, life affirming. Exactly how Bech—a "semi-obscure" writer with a slim body of work—arrived at this pinnacle of literary recognition is no clearer than the import of Bech's entire literary saga. Updike may be saying that for his fictional counterpart, this jaded urban Jew with writer's block, life and sex trump art. As the title of the book tells the reader, this last installment of the Bech series is a quasi-novel, and Henry Bech seems often to be merely a mask for his creator. The epigraph, "Something of the unreal is necessary to fecundate the real," which Updike borrows from Wallace Stevens, points to the correspondence between creator and creation.

With the astonishing variety and richness of his narratives, John Updike's fiction constitutes a serious exploration and probing of the spiritual conditions of American culture in the late twentieth century. The fate of American civilization is seen in the condition of love—its risks and dangers as well as its possibility for gracious transformation.

John G. Parks, updated by Lisa Paddock

Other major works

SHORT FICTION: *The Same Door*, 1959; *Pigeon Feathers and Other Stories*, 1962; *Olinger Stories: A Selection*, 1964; *The Music School*, 1966; *Museums and Women and Other Stories*, 1972; *Problems and Other Stories*, 1979; *Too Far to Go: The Maples Stories*, 1979; *Trust Me*, 1987; *Brother Grasshopper*, 1990 (limited edition); *The Afterlife and Other Stories*, 1994.

PLAYS: *Three Texts from Early Ipswich: A Pageant*, pb. 1968; *Buchanan Dying*, pb. 1974.

POETRY: *The Carpentered Hen, and Other Tame Creatures*, 1958; *Telephone Poles and Other Poems*, 1963; *Midpoint and Other Poems*, 1969; *Tossing and Turning*, 1977; *Facing Nature*, 1985; *Mites and Other Poems in Miniature*, 1990; *A Helpful Alphabet of Friendly Objects*, 1995.

NONFICTION: *Assorted Prose*, 1965; *Picked-Up Pieces*, 1975; *Hugging the Shore: Essays and Criticism*, 1983; *Just Looking: Essays on Art*, 1989; *Self-Consciousness: Memoirs*, 1989; *Odd Jobs: Essays and Criticism*, 1991; *Golf Dreams: Writings on Golf*, 1996; *More Matter: Essays and Criticism*, 1999.

Bibliography

Detweiler, Robert. *John Updike*. Boston: Twayne, 1984. This is an expanded and revised edition of Detweiler's 1972 study of Updike's fiction. It is an excellent introductory survey of Updike's work through 1983. It contains a chronology, biographical sketch, analysis of the fiction and its sources, a select bibliography, and an index. It provides a good discussion of religious and theological themes in the fiction.

O'Connell, Mary. *Updike and the Patriarchal Dilemma: Masculinity in the Rabbit Novels.* Carbondale: Southern Illinois University Press, 1996. Examines the themes of men, masculinity, and patriarchy in Updike's Rabbit series. Includes an index and bibliography.

Rogers, Michael. "The Gospel of the Book: *LJ* Talks to John Updike." *Library Journal* 124, no. 3 (February 15, 1999): 114-116. Updike expounds on books, contemporary writers, and the state of publishing at the end of the twentieth century.

Schiff, James A. *Updike's Version: Rewriting "The Scarlet Letter."* Columbia: University of Missouri Press, 1992. Schiff explores the influence of Hawthorne's novel on Updike's oeuvre. Contains an index and bibliography.

Trachtenberg, Stanley, ed. *New Essays on "Rabbit, Run."* Cambridge, England: Cambridge University Press, 1993. Essays in this collection address Updike's notable novel and such themes as middle-class men in literature. With bibliographical references.

Uphaus, Suzanne Henning. *John Updike.* New York: Frederick Ungar, 1980. An introductory analysis of Updike's fiction through 1979. Biographical information, a chronology, notes, bibliography, and an index.

Wood, Ralph C. *The Comedy of Redemption: Christian Faith and Comic Vision in Four American Novelists.* Notre Dame, Ind.: University of Notre Dame Press, 1988. A sophisticated theological analysis of Updike's Rabbit novels as well as *The Centaur* and *Couples,* along with a treatment of the fiction of Flannery O'Connor, Walker Percy, and Peter De Vries. The book contains notes and an index.

GORE VIDAL

Edgar Box

Born: West Point, New York; October 3, 1925

Principal long fiction · *Williwaw*, 1946; *In a Yellow Wood*, 1947; *The City and the Pillar*, 1948, revised 1965; *The Season of Comfort*, 1949; *A Search for the King: A Twelfth Century Legend*, 1950; *Dark Green, Bright Red*, 1950; *The Judgment of Paris*, 1952, revised 1965; *Death in the Fifth Position*, 1952 (as Edgar Box); *Death Before Bedtime*, 1953 (as Box); *Death Likes It Hot*, 1954 (as Box); *Messiah*, 1954, revised 1965; *Julian*, 1964; *Washington, D.C.*, 1967; *Myra Breckinridge*, 1968; *Two Sisters: A Memoir in the Form of a Novel*, 1970; *Burr*, 1973; *Myron*, 1974; *1876*, 1976; *Kalki*, 1978; *Creation*, 1981; *Duluth*, 1983; *Lincoln*, 1984; *Empire*, 1987; *Hollywood: A Novel of America in the 1920's*, 1990; *Live from Golgotha*, 1992; *The Smithsonian Institution*, 1998.

Other literary forms · Gore Vidal wrote short stories as well as novels, and he is considered a master essayist, having regularly published collections of essays. Vidal also wrote or adapted plays during the so-called golden age of television, and he wrote screenplays during the last days of the Hollywood studio system.

Achievements · Gore Vidal is considered a leading American literary figure. While primarily a novelist, he has mastered almost every genre, except poetry. He won success in films, in television, and on Broadway. Many readers consider him a better essayist than novelist, though Vidal emphatically rejects that judgment.

While many of his contemporaries focused their writings on mundane details of everyday life, Vidal continued to write the novel of ideas. He maintained his focus on the largest questions: What is the nature of Western civilization? What flaws have prevented the United States from achieving its democratic promise? How does a free individual live an intellectually fulfilling and ethically proper life in a corrupt society? These concerns are reflected not only in his writing but also in his political activities, including a bid for the U.S. Senate in 1982. Vidal won a National Book Award in 1993 for his collection of essays *United States: Essays, 1952-1992*, and his books are routinely included in "best" lists and course syllabi.

Biography · Eugene Luther Vidal was born on October 3, 1925 (he took the name Gore when he was fourteen). He was born at West Point, where his father, Eugene, taught aeronautics at the military academy. Eugene Vidal helped establish civil aviation in the United States and later became the director of air commerce in the administration of Franklin D. Roosevelt. Gore's mother, Nina, was a beautiful socialite, the daughter of powerful Oklahoma senator Thomas P. Gore. Soon after Gore's birth, the family moved to Senator Gore's mansion in Washington, D.C. Gore Vidal, one of the most learned of contemporary writers, never went to college. His education began at the home of Senator Gore: The senator, who was blind, used his grandson as a reader and in return gave him free run of his huge library. In 1935, the Vidals were divorced, and Nina married Hugh D. Auchincloss, a member of a prominent

family of bankers and lawyers.
Gore Vidal then moved to the
Auchincloss estate on the Po-
tomac River in Virginia. Here
his education included rub-
bing shoulders with the nation's political, economic, and
journalistic elite.

Vidal was brought up re-
moved from real life, he says,
protected from such unpleasant realities as the effects of the
Great Depression. He joined
other patrician sons at St. Al-
bans School, after which he
toured Europe in 1939, then
spent one year at Los Alamos
School in New Mexico, before
finishing his formal education
with three years at Phillips Ex-
eter Academy in New Hamp-
shire.

©Jane Bown

In 1943, Vidal joined the
army and served on a transport ship in the Aleutian Islands. His military service gave
him subject matter and time to write his first novel, *Williwaw*. He finished his second
book, *In a Yellow Wood*, before he left the army. In 1946, he went to work as an editor
for E. P. Dutton and soon published *The City and the Pillar*. Good critical and popular
response brought him recognition as one of the nation's best young authors. He used
Guatemala as his home base from 1947 to 1949 and then bought an old estate,
Edgewater, on the Hudson River in New York. He wrote five more novels before he
was thirty years old.

Meanwhile, a controversy engulfed him and shifted his life and career. *The City and
the Pillar* had dealt with homosexuality; because of this, the literary establishment
removed him from its list of "approved" writers, and critics largely ignored his next
few novels. To earn money in the 1950's, he wrote mysteries under the name Edgar
Box and wrote scripts for the major live television dramatic series. He also became a
successful screenwriter, with such films as *The Catered Affair* (1956) and *Suddenly Last
Summer* (1959, with Tennessee Williams). In addition, he wrote plays. He achieved
major Broadway successes with *Visit to a Small Planet: A Comedy Akin to a Vaudeville*
(1957) and *The Best Man: A Play About Politics* (1960).

These were his years of "piracy," Vidal says, aimed at gaining enough financial
security to allow him to return to his first love, novels. His years in Hollywood and
on Broadway established Vidal's public reputation for sophisticated wit and intelligence. He ran for Congress in 1960, supported by such famous friends as Eleanor
Roosevelt, Joanne Woodward, and Paul Newman. Although he was defeated, he ran
better in his district than did the Democratic presidential candidate, John F. Kennedy.
Vidal shared a stepfather with Jacqueline Kennedy and had become friends with the
Kennedy family; this connection pulled him further into public affairs.

In 1964, Vidal published *Julian*, his first novel in ten years. It was a major critical and public success. Many best-sellers followed, including *Myra Breckinridge, Burr, Creation,* and *Lincoln.*

Conflict over civil rights, the Vietnam War, and the Watergate scandal made the 1960's and 1970's one of the most tumultuous periods in American political history. Vidal's essays, published in major journals, established his reputation as an astute and hard-hitting social critic. His acid-tongued social commentary brought him to many television guest shows, where he made many friends and enemies. He had spectacular public feuds with members of the Kennedy family and with such fellow celebrities and authors as William F. Buckley, Jr., Norman Mailer, and Truman Capote. In 1968 he was a cofounder of the New Party, and in 1970-1972 he was cochair of the People's Party. In 1982, he ran for the U.S. Senate in California, and, out of a field of eleven in the Democratic primary, came in second, behind Governor Jerry Brown.

The range and breadth of Vidal's interests showed in *United States,* a thousand-page collection of his essays which won the National Book Award for 1993. Here one finds literary discussions ranging from readings of Henry James and William Dean Howells to attacks on those of his contemporaries (John Barth, Thomas Pynchon) whom he calls "the academic hacks," novelists writing only for an audience of literature professors. He also attacks what he calls the "heterosexual dictatorship" and the United States' increasingly grandiose and imperial self-image.

Palimpsest: A Memoir (1995) was a book that Vidal said he had sworn never to write, a personal memoir. He revealed his family background and told of his struggles with establishments literary and political, concluding with his view of his quarrel with the Kennedy family. In a lyrical passage, he spoke of the great love of his teenage years, a classmate named Jimmie Trimble who died in World War II. In the 1990's Vidal added a new aspect to his public persona by appearing as a character actor in several films, including *Bob Roberts* (1992), *With Honors* (1994), *The Shadow Conspiracy* (1996), and *Gattaca* (1997).

In 1998 Vidal was embroiled in further public debate as a member of the committee that selected the Modern Library's one hundred best twentieth century English-language novels. One of many controversial aspects of the list was the absence of those writers he called academic hacks. Vidal insisted that his role was only to make recommendations and that he bore no responsibility for the final selections.

Analysis · In an age and country that have little room for the traditional man of letters, Gore Vidal has established that role for himself by the force of his writing and intelligence and by his public prominence. He is a classicist in writing style, emphasizing plot, clarity, and order. Iconoclastic wit and cool, detached intelligence characterize his elegant style.

Since Vidal knows most contemporary public figures—including jet-setters, Wall Street insiders, and Washington wheeler-dealers—many readers comb his writing to glean intriguing bits of gossip. *Two Sisters: A Memoir in the Form of a Novel,* for example, is often read as an account of the lives and loves of Jacqueline Kennedy Onassis and her sister, Lee Bouvier. Some people search Vidal's writing for clues to his own life and sexuality.

Vidal draws from his own rich experience as he creates his fictional world. Yet he is a very private person, and he resists people's urge to reduce everyone to a known quantity. Vidal refracts real people and events through his delightfully perverse imagination. The unwary gossipmonger can easily fall into Vidal's many traps.

If one can with certainty learn little from Vidal's fiction about such famous people as the Kennedys, readers can learn much about his major concern, the nature of Western civilization and the individual's role within it. He is interested in politics–how people make society work–and religion, the proper perspective on life as one faces death. In his early novels, one can see Vidal's interest in ideas. Vidal's young male protagonists find themselves entering a relativistic world in which all gods are dead. A "heterosexual dictatorship" and a life-numbing Christian establishment try to impose false moral absolutes. Society tempts the unwary by offering comfort and security and then removes the life-sustaining freedom of those who succumb to the temptation.

The City and the Pillar · In writing his third novel, Vidal probed the boundaries of society's sexual tolerance. The result, *The City and the Pillar*, affected the rest of his career. To Vidal, the book is a study of obsession; to many guardians of moral purity, it seems to glorify homosexuality. In American fiction, either homosexuality had been barely implied or the homosexual characters had been presented as bizarre or doomed figures. In contrast, Vidal's protagonist is an average young American man, confused by his homosexual proclivities and obsessed with the memory of a weekend encounter with another young man, Bob Ford. While Bob regards the weekend as a diversion to be enjoyed and forgotten, Jim enters the homosexual world. If he is doomed, it is not because he prefers men to women, but because he is obsessed with the past. When he finally meets Bob again and tries to revive the affair, Bob rejects him. Enraged and humiliated, Jim kills Bob. Vidal later issued a revised edition in which Jim forces Bob to submit sexually; in the emotional backwash from the confrontation, Jim realizes the sterility of his obsession.

Vidal later said that he could have been president had it not been for the homosexual label applied to him. Readers assumed that Vidal must be the character he invented. Vidal is a sexual libertarian who believes that sex in any form between consenting adults is a gift to be enjoyed. He believes, furthermore, that a "heterosexual dictatorship" has distorted human sexuality. "There is no such thing as a homosexual or a heterosexual person," Vidal says. "There are only homo- or heterosexual acts. Most people are a mixture of impulses if not practices, and what anyone does with a willing partner is of no social or cosmic significance." In 1948, people were not ready for that message. Although the book was a best-seller, such powerful establishment journals as *The New York Times* eliminated him from the list of "approved" writers. His next few books were failures, critically and financially.

The Judgment of Paris · Two of the books ignored after *The City and the Pillar*, *The Judgment of Paris* and *Messiah*, later found admirers. In these novels Vidal began to develop the style that is so recognizably his own. Moreover, it is in these two books that Vidal fully expresses his philosophy of life: "I have put nearly everything that I feel into *The Judgment of Paris*, a comedic version, and *Messiah*, a tragic version of my sense of man's curious estate."

In *The Judgment of Paris*, Vidal retells the ancient myth of Paris, who was asked by Zeus to choose the most beautiful of three goddesses: Hera (power), Athena (knowledge), and Aphrodite (love). In Vidal's novel, Philip Warren, an American innocent, meets Regina Durham (Hera) in Rome, Sophia Oliver (Athena) in Egypt, and Anna Morris (Aphrodite) in Paris. Regina and Sophia offer him, respectively, political power and life of the intellect. To Philip, political power rests on manipulation of people, and intellectual life requires the seclusion of the scholar from humanity. He chooses love, but he also leaves Anna Morris. His choice implies that one must accept no absolutes; nothing is permanent, not even love. One must open oneself to love and friendship and prepare to accept change as one moves through life.

Messiah · Many readers consider *Messiah* an undiscovered masterpiece. Religion, the human response to death and nothingness, has been a major concern in Vidal's fiction, especially in *Messiah, Kalki,* and *Creation. Messiah* is narrated by Eugene Luther, an old man secluded in Egypt. He is a founding member of a new religion that has displaced Christianity and is spreading over the world. Luther, who has broken with the church he helped build, scribbles his memoirs as he awaits death. The movement was built around John Cave, but Cave was killed by his disciples and Cave's word was spread by an organization using modern advertising techniques. One can readily find in *Messiah* characters representing Jesus Christ, Saint Paul, Mother Mary, and Martin Luther. The process by which religious movements are formed interests Vidal. *Messiah* shows, by analogy, how the early church fathers manipulated the Gospels and the Christ figure for their own selfish needs.

Julian · With *Julian*, Vidal again examines the formation of a religious movement, this time looking directly at Christianity. Julian the Apostate, Roman emperor from 361 to 363 C.E., had long been the object of hatred in the West, because he had tried to reverse the Christianization of the empire. In the nineteenth and twentieth centuries, Julian began to attract admirers who saw him as a symbol of wisdom and of religious toleration.

Julian, reared as a Christian, lived in an age when the modern Christian church was taking shape. Warring prelates conducted abstract debates that robbed religion of its mystery and engaged in persecutions that ignored Jesus' message of love and peace. Julian was trained as a philosopher. His study of ancient wisdom awakened in him love and respect for the gods of the ancient world and for the Eastern mystery religions then being suppressed by Christianity. When he became emperor, Julian proclaimed religious toleration and tried to revive "paganism."

Like Paris before him and Philip Warren after, Julian was offered the worlds of intellect, love, and power. Julian chose power, but he tempered the absolute authority of emperor with love and wisdom. He was also a military genius, who like Alexander the Great was tempted by the dream of world conquest. He was killed during an invasion of Persia.

Vidal bases his novel on a fictive memoir written by Julian and presenting Julian's own view of himself and his world. The novel opens in 380 C.E., seventeen years after Julian's death. Two friends of Julian, the philosophers Libanius of Antioch and Priscus of Athens, correspond as they prepare Julian's memoirs for publication. Their letters and comments on the manuscript provide two other views of the events described by Julian. Since they are writing as the Emperor Theodosius is moving to destroy the ancient religions, Julian's life takes on a special poignancy. Vidal's major point, says biographer Ray Lewis White, is that modern people of the West are the descendants of the barbarians who destroyed the classical world, and that the modern world has yet to be civilized. If Julian had lived, Vidal believes, Christianity might well have remained only one of several Western religions, and Western civilization might now be healthier and more tolerant than it is.

Creation · In 1981 Vidal took readers even further back into history in *Creation*. In 445 B.C.E., Cyrus Spitama, an elderly Persian diplomat to Athens and grandson of the Persian prophet Zoroaster, begins to dictate his memoirs to his nephew, the philosopher Democritus. Cyrus is angry after hearing the historian Herodotus give his account of the Persian-Greek war, and he decides to set down the truth.

Here Vidal traces the earliest foundations of Western civilization and the formation of major world religions. Cyrus, a diplomatic troubleshooter for the Persian court, takes the reader on a tour of the ancient world. He knows Persian emperors Darius and Xerxes; as a traveler to China and India, he meets the Buddha and Confucius, and he remembers his own grandfather, Zoroaster. In Athens he talks with such famous figures as Anaxagoras and Pericles and hires Socrates to repair his wall. In *Creation*, Vidal shows the global interaction of cultures that goes back to the ancient world. He rejects the provincialism that has allowed historians to wall Western civilization off from its Asian and African sources.

Burr · Next this master of historical fiction turned his attention to the United States. Starting with *Washington, D.C.*, Vidal began a sequence of novels covering United States history from its beginning to the post-World War II era. In chronological sequence, the novels are *Burr, Lincoln, 1876, Empire, Hollywood,* and *Washington, D.C.* Vidal's iconoclastic view of the past may have shocked some readers, but in the turmoil of the Vietnam and Watergate era, many people were ready to reexamine United States history. At a time when many Americans held that the old truths had failed, Vidal said that those truths had been hollow from the start.

Burr is one of the most widely admired of Vidal's novels. Aaron Burr, the preeminent American maverick, appealed to Vidal personally. *Burr* is narrated by Charlie Schuyler, who in 1833 is a twenty-five-year-old clerk in Burr's law office. He is an aspiring author who writes for William Leggett and William Cullen Bryant, editors of the *New York Evening Post*. Disliking Martin Van Buren, President Andrew Jackson's heir apparent, Leggett and Bryant set Charlie to work running down the rumor that Van Buren is the illegitimate son of Burr; if the rumor is true, they can use the information to destroy Van Buren. The seventy-seven-year-old Burr responds warmly to Charlie's overtures to write about his life. In the next few years, Burr gives the young writer copies of his journal and dictates to him his memories of the past.

Although Vidal's portrait of the Founding Fathers shocks some readers, his interpretation is in line with that of many of the nation's best historians. Vidal reminds the reader that Burr was one of the most able and intelligent of the Founding Fathers. Vidal allows Burr, from an insider's viewpoint, to demystify the founders of the republic. George Washington, Alexander Hamilton, Thomas Jefferson, and the other Founding Fathers created the republic, Burr says, because it satisfied their personal economic and political interests to do so.

Burr admires some of his contemporaries, especially James Madison and Andrew Jackson, but he detests Thomas Jefferson. Jefferson is a ruthless man who wants to create a nation "dominated by independent farmers each living on his own rich land, supported by slaves." What Burr cannot excuse is Jefferson's cant and hypocrisy:

> Had Jefferson not been a hypocrite I might have admired him. After all, he was the most successful empire-builder of our century, succeeding where Bonaparte failed. But then Bonaparte was always candid when it came to motive and Jefferson was always dishonest.

What are the motives of the Founding Fathers? Burr tells Alexander Hamilton: "I sense nothing more than the ordinary busy-ness of men wanting to make a place for themselves. . . . But it is no different here from what it is in London or what it was in Caesar's Rome." The Founding Fathers write the Constitution because it suits their purposes, and they subvert it when it suits their purposes.

Burr makes no secret of his opportunism, although he does regret his mistakes. He should have realized that the world is big enough for both Hamilton and himself, he says. Instead, Vice President Burr kills Hamilton in a duel and is then accused by Jefferson of heading a plot to break up the United States and establish himself as the king in a new Western empire.

Charlie does find evidence that Van Buren is Burr's son, but Charlie, having come to love the old man, refuses to use it. Van Buren rewards him with a government position overseas.

Lincoln* and *1876 · With *Lincoln*, Vidal surprised those who expected him to subject the Great Emancipator to the same ridicule he had directed at Washington and Jefferson. Vidal's Lincoln is a cold, remote, intelligent man who creates a unified, centralized republic that is far different from the one envisioned by the Founding Fathers. In *1876*, Charlie Schuyler returns to the United States from Europe, where he has lived since 1837. He left in the age of Jackson and returns in the age of Ulysses S. Grant to a booming industrializing, urbanizing nation. He watches, in the American centennial year, as the politicians steal the presidential election from Democrat Samuel J. Tilden. He sees members of the ruling class using the rhetoric of democracy but practicing it as little as they had in the days of Washington and Jefferson.

Empire · In *Empire*, Vidal creates wonderful portraits of Henry Adams, Henry James, William Randolph Hearst, John Hay, and Theodore Roosevelt, along with the fictional characters of newspaper publishers Caroline and Blaise Sanford and Congressman James Burden Day. The creation of the internal empire, begun by Jefferson's Louisiana Purchase, had already made shambles of the American democratic promise. Now Roosevelt and other American leaders begin to look overseas for new areas to dominate. Their creation of the overseas empire lays the groundwork for the increasingly militarized republic that emerges in the twentieth century.

Hollywood · Many of these same figures appear in *Hollywood*, set a few years later, in the administrations of Woodrow Wilson and Warren Harding. While the forging of the American empire continues, Vidal turns his gaze on a new force that is corrupting the democratic promise, the mass media. Newspaper publisher Hearst and the Sanfords have long understood the power of the press, but Hearst and Caroline Sanford see that the new medium of film has potential power beyond the printed page. Instead of reporting events, film could create a new reality, within which newspapers and politicians would have to work.

Washington, D.C. · In *Washington, D.C.*, Blaise Sanford, his son Peter, Senator James Burden Day, and his assistant, Clay Overbury, are locked in a political and moral drama. Senator Day, a southern conservative, much like Senator Gore, opposes the new republic being created by Franklin Delano Roosevelt, Harry Truman, and Dwight D. Eisenhower. He has a chance to be president but lacks money. Burden Day gives in to temptation and takes a bribe; his presidential bid fails, and later Clay

Overbury, using his knowledge of the bribe, forces Day out of the Senate and takes his seat. Overbury is a young man who cares nothing for friends or ideas or issues. Winning personal power is the only thing that interests this politician, who is modeled on John F. Kennedy.

As Day is dying, he says to the spirit of his unreconstructed southern father: "You were right. . . . It has all gone wrong." Aaron Burr would have understood what he meant.

Myra Breckinridge · If most scholars approved of Vidal's well-researched historical fiction, many staid readers were shocked at *Myra Breckinridge*. Myra opens her book with the proud proclamation: "I am Myra Breckinridge whom no man will ever possess." She maintains her verve as she takes readers on a romp through popular culture. Since the novel is dead, she says, there is no point in writing made-up stories; the film of the 1940's is the high point of Western artistic creation, although it is being superseded by a higher art form, the television commercial. Myra has arrived in Hollywood to fulfill her destiny of reconstructing the sexes. She has a lesson to teach young would-be stars such as Rusty Godowsky and old cowboy stars such as Buck Loner:

> To be a man in a society of machines is to be an expendable, soft auxiliary to what is useful and hard. Today there is nothing left for the old-fashioned male to do, . . . no physical struggle to survive or mate. . . . [O]nly in travesty can he act out the classic hero who was a law unto himself, moving at ease through a landscape filled with admiring women. Mercifully, that age is finished. . . . [W]e now live at the dawn of the age of Women Triumphant, of Myra Breckinridge!

Beneath the gaiety of Myra's campy narrative, a serious purpose emerges. Her dead homosexual husband, Myron, had been abused and humiliated by many males. Myra carries out her plan to avenge Myron, and to revive the Female Principle, by forcing Buck Loner to submit to her demands to take over his acting studio, and by raping with a dildo the macho, all-American stud Rusty.

Myra is brought down by an automobile accident, which upsets her hormonal balance. Her breasts vanish, and she sprouts a beard; she is, in fact, Myron, after a sex-change operation. As the book ends, Rusty is a homosexual, and Myron/Myra is married and living happily with Rusty's former girlfriend. In a sequel, *Myron*, Myron and Myra struggle for domination of the single body and again have much to say about popular culture, the mass media, and human sexuality.

Perhaps as respites from the scrupulous historicity of the American history novels, Vidal interspersed them with fantasies in which reality was plastic and ever-changing. In *Myron*, characters were likely to find themselves in the midst of the old films they were watching. *Duluth* represented a deliberately postmodernist interpenetration of an actual Duluth with a serial television show also called *Duluth*.

Live from Golgotha · *Live from Golgotha* continued the motif of a reality subject to random change. It is set in 96 C.E., but the first century is being manipulated by forces from the twentieth, operating through psychic channelers and the Hacker, whose computer manipulations apparently can destroy not only records of the past but even memories of those records. Indeed, there is a plan afoot to return to the Crucifixion, televise it live, and perhaps even change the events.

Timothy, the narrator, is the biblical Timothy to whom St. Paul wrote epistles. He has been chosen to preserve the Gospel story in the face of these computerized depredations, though his knowledge of the event is at best second-hand, coming from Paul, who knows it only through a vision. The story departs radically from the standard biblical story. Timothy and Paul are actively bisexual, as are most of the first-century people depicted. Jesus is thought to have been morbidly obese. Anachronistic terms such as "Mossad" and "intifada" abound. Future figures such as Mary Baker Eddy and Shirley MacLaine make appearances.

Timothy eventually learns that the actual Jesus was a Zealot, a political revolutionary. With electronic assistance, Jesus framed Judas, the fat man Paul saw in the vision, and fled to the twentieth century. There he became the Hacker in order to clear out images of "gentle Jesus meek and mild." He plans to start Armageddon through a nuclear attack on Arab capitals. Timothy uses more advanced technology to prevent Jesus's escape from arrest. The Crucifixion takes place, with the real Jesus, but Japanese technicians add to the image a rising sun and the mother goddess Amaterasu. *Live from Golgotha* was condemned for its irreverence and blasphemy, as well as for the outlandishness of its central conceit, but many readers nevertheless enjoyed its wit and its lusty portrayal of the first-century Roman world.

The Smithsonian Institution · Vidal's next novel, *The Smithsonian Institution*, also dealt with retroactive time change, but of a political rather than a theological sort. T., a thirteen-year-old mathematics prodigy in 1939, is summoned to the Smithsonian Institution to take part in a secret scientific experiment. He soon learns that the apparent wax dummies that are part of the project are actually living people. Indeed, T. is seduced by Mrs. Grover Cleveland. T. has an Einstein-like ability to visualize equations dealing with time. Anxious to ward off the coming of World War II because it would lead to the development of terrifying new weapons, the scientists secretly in charge of the Smithsonian (with the assistance of the supposed wax dummies of political leaders) plan to use T.'s ideas to construct a time machine and change the past so that the war will not occur. After one trip that only makes things worse, T. returns to a war in which he saves an alternate version of himself and enables the war to be concluded more quickly, without the weapons development.

Some commentators said that the audience Vidal created for himself with his highly regarded historical novels was destroyed by *Myra Breckinridge* and *Myron* and by his later campy fantasies *Kalki* and *Duluth.* Yet Vidal continued to write one best-seller after another, and his books have steadily gained critical admirers. Vidal's books, essays, and television appearances stimulated, intrigued, and angered a large part of his audience. Yet his appeal as a writer and public figure remained compelling. As long ago as 1948, with *The City and the Pillar*, Vidal made a decision to live his life and conduct his artistic career in his own way. To many admirers, he is a symbol of freedom. The turmoil of the modern age makes his civilized voice of reason seem more necessary than ever before. Often accused of cynicism, Vidal responded that he is a pessimist and a realist who also believes that people can, or must act as if they can, take action to make the world better.

William E. Pemberton, updated by Arthur D. Hlavaty

Other major works
SHORT FICTION: *A Thirsty Evil: Seven Short Stories*, 1956.
PLAYS: *Visit to a Small Planet: A Comedy Akin to a Vaudeville*, pr. 1957; *The Best Man:*

A Play About Politics, pr. 1960; *Romulus: A New Comedy*, pr., pb. 1962; *An Evening with Richard Nixon*, pr. 1972.

SCREENPLAYS: *The Catered Affair*, 1956; *Suddenly Last Summer*, 1959 (with Tennessee Williams); *The Best Man*, 1964.

NONFICTION: *Rocking the Boat*, 1962; *Reflections upon a Sinking Ship*, 1969; *Homage to Daniel Shays: Collected Essays, 1952-1972*, 1972; *Matters of Fact and of Fiction: Essays, 1973-1976*, 1977; *The Second American Revolution and Other Essays, 1976-1982*, 1982; *At Home: Essays, 1982-1988*, 1988; *The Decline and Fall of the American Empire*, 1992; *Screening History*, 1992; *United States: Essays, 1952-1992*, 1993; *Palimpsest: A Memoir*, 1995; *Gore Vidal, Sexually Speaking: Collected Sex Writings*, 1999.

MISCELLANEOUS: *The Essential Vidal*, 1999.

Bibliography

Baker, Susan, and Curtis S. Gibson. *Gore Vidal: A Critical Companion.* Westport, Conn.: Greenwood Press, 1997. A helpful book of criticism and interpretation of Vidal's work. Includes bibliographical references and index.

Dick, Bernard F. *The Apostate Angel: A Critical Study of Gore Vidal.* New York: Random House, 1974. An entertaining and perceptive study, based on interviews with Vidal and on use of his papers at the University of Wisconsin at Madison. Dick focuses on Vidal's work rather than on his biography. The book contains footnotes and a bibliography.

Kiernan, Robert F. *Gore Vidal.* New York: Frederick Ungar, 1982. This study of Vidal's major writings tries to assess his place in American literature and gives astute descriptions of the Vidalian style and manner. The book, which uses Vidal's manuscript collection, contains a brief note and bibliography section.

Parini, Jay, ed. *Gore Vidal: Writer Against the Grain.* New York: Columbia University Press, 1992. Vidal's distaste for much of the academic study of contemporary fiction has been mirrored in a lack of academic study of his work. Jay Parini sought to redress the balance by compiling this work, which deals with both Vidal's fiction and nonfiction. The book reprints chapters from the Dick, Kiernan, and White studies referenced here, as well as encomia and reviews by such writers and critics as Louis Auchincloss, Italo Calvino, and Harold Bloom. In addition, there are eight newly commissioned essays, including essays by James Tatum and Donald E. Pease.

Stanton, Robert J., and Gore Vidal, eds. *Views from a Window: Conversations with Gore Vidal.* Secaucus, N.J.: Lyle Stuart, 1980. A compilation of interviews excerpted and arranged along themes. Vidal comments on his and other authors' works, on sexuality, and on politics. Vidal edited the manuscript and made corrections, with changes noted in the text.

KURT VONNEGUT, JR.

Born: Indianapolis, Indiana; November 11, 1922

Principal long fiction · *Player Piano*, 1952; *The Sirens of Titan*, 1959; *Mother Night*, 1961; *Cat's Cradle*, 1963; *God Bless You, Mr. Rosewater: Or, Pearls Before Swine*, 1965; *Slaughterhouse-Five: Or, The Children's Crusade, a Duty-Dance with Death*, 1969; *Breakfast of Champions: Or, Goodbye Blue Monday*, 1973; *Slapstick: Or, Lonesome No More!*, 1976; *Jailbird*, 1979; *Deadeye Dick*, 1982; *Galápagos*, 1985; *Bluebeard*, 1987; *Hocus Pocus*, 1990; *Timequake*, 1997.

Other literary forms · Although known primarily for his novels, Kurt Vonnegut, Jr., also wrote for Broadway and television and published a children's book and several books of essays.

Achievements · Critical acclaim eluded Vonnegut until *Slaughterhouse-Five* was published in 1969. An immediate best-seller, it earned for Vonnegut respect from critics who had previously dismissed him as a mediocre science-fiction writer. Vonnegut has been honored as the Briggs-Copeland Lecturer at Harvard University, as a member of the National Institute of Arts and Letters, and as the Distinguished Professor of English Prose at the City University of New York. Through his insightful and sympathetic treatment of the psychologically and morally crippled victims of the modern world, Vonnegut earned his reputation as one of the greatest humanist writers of his time.

Biography · Kurt Vonnegut, Jr., was born in Indianapolis, Indiana, in 1922. Both the location and the era of his birth helped shape his distinctive worldview, which informs all of his works. Growing up in the American heartland in the calm interval between the world wars, Vonnegut had a brief vision of a middle-class world that embraced the values of honesty, decency, and human dignity. For Vonnegut, this was the world as it should be, a world unravaged by violence and war, a world untouched by technology. This period of childhood happiness was, however, merely the calm before the storm in this life that would be rocked by a series of personal and national disasters: the death of his mother by suicide on Mother's Day; his prisoner-of-war experience in World War II; the deaths of his sister and brother-in-law; the dissolution of his first marriage; the bombings of Dresden and Hiroshima; the assassinations of President John F. Kennedy and civil rights activist Martin Luther King, Jr.; the Vietnam War; the death of his first wife, with whom he had maintained a close friendship; and the death of his brother Bernard. All the heartaches of his family and his nation reverberate through Vonnegut's work, while the artist, through his fiction, stands as advocate for a saner, calmer world.

During the Depression years, Vonnegut's family suffered emotional and financial setbacks. When Vonnegut entered Cornell University in 1940, his father forbade him to study the arts and chose instead for his son a career in science, a career with guaranteed job security. In 1943 Vonnegut left Cornell to enlist in the army, despite his own public opposition to the war. Less than one year later, he was captured by the

Germans and, in 1945, survived one of the greatest massacres of the war, the Allied firebombing of Dresden. This horror pursued Vonnegut for twenty-three years, until he worked through the pain by writing *Slaughterhouse-Five.*

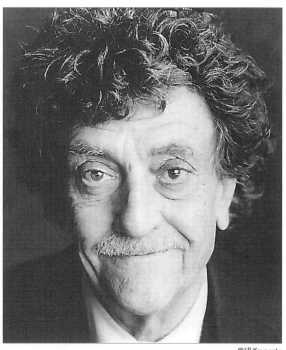

©Jill Krementz

After the war, Vonnegut married and began studies in anthropology at the University of Chicago. After three years, he left college and took a job as a publicist with General Electric (GE), where his brother worked as a physicist. Vonnegut's background in science and his disillusionment at GE influenced his first two novels, *Player Piano* and *The Sirens of Titan,* both parables of dehumanization in a technological society.

Between 1952 and 1998, Vonnegut wrote more than a dozen novels, numerous essays, a Broadway play, and a musical work, *Requiem,* which was performed by the Buffalo Symphony. He and Joe Petro III had a showing of twenty-six of their silk-screen prints in Denver in 1996. Despite his varied artistic talents, however, Vonnegut has always been known for his fiction. Vonnegut remarried in 1978; he and his wife, Jill Krementz, settled in New York.

Analysis · In his novels, Kurt Vonnegut, Jr., coaxes the reader toward greater sympathy for humanity and deeper understanding of the human condition. His genre is satire—sometimes biting, sometimes tender, always funny. His arena is as expansive as the whole universe and as tiny as a single human soul. Part philosopher, part poet, Vonnegut, in his fictive world, tackles the core problem of modern life: How can the individual maintain his dignity and exercise his free will in a world overrun by death and destruction, a world in which both science and religion are powerless to provide a solution? The reader will find no ready answers in Vonnegut, only a friendly guide along the questioning path.

Vonnegut has, himself, behaved with a commendable sense of responsibility, dignity, and decency: He has labored long to show humankind its ailments and to wake it to the work it has to do. He admits to his and his family's having lived comfortably while so many of the world's population suffered, but in quoting the words of American socialist Eugene Debs in his dedication to *Hocus Pocus* he seems to define the position that he himself has taken as human being and as author and public figure for half of the twentieth century: "While there is a lower class I am in it. While there is a criminal element I am of it. While there is a soul in prison I am not free."

He has spoken out in many forums for many causes and for all of humankind, and his has been a wide audience.

Player Piano · Ilium, New York, sometime in the near future, provides the setting for Vonnegut's first dystopian novel, *Player Piano*. Ilium is a divided city. On one side of the river live the important people, the engineers and managers who program and run the computers and machines that run people's lives. On the other side of the river, Homestead, live the downtrodden inhabitants of the city, those locked into menial, dehumanizing jobs assigned to them by the central computer.

Paul Proteus, the protagonist, is the brilliant young manager of the Ilium Works, a man being groomed for even greater success. Yet just as Ilium is a divided city, so is Paul divided about his life and his future. Paul suffers a growing discontent with his job at the Ilium Works, where people have been replaced by machines and machines are supervised by computers. Outwardly, Paul has no reason for worry or doubt. He has the best job and the most beautiful wife in Ilium; he is being considered for the highest post in his company; he is climbing the ladder of success. Nevertheless, Paul's uneasiness increases. At first he seeks escape, settling on a farm in an attempt to get back to nature and free himself from his automatic life. He finds, however, that he has become an automaton, completely out of touch with the natural world, and his attempt at escape fails.

Finally, Paul is drawn to the other side of the river. His sympathy for the dehumanized masses and his acknowledgment of complicity in their plight drive Paul to join the masses in armed revolution. The fighters take to the streets, frantically and indiscriminately destroying all machines. Yet the revolution fails, leaving Paul disillusioned and defeated, realizing that he has been manipulated by leaders on both sides of the conflict. Now he must surrender and face execution.

Paul's manipulation, first by those who would replace person with machine and then by those who would destroy the machines, is symbolized by the "player piano" of the title. The simplest of machines, the player piano creates its music without the aid of human beings, neatly rendering the skilled musician obsolete. Paul is entranced by the music of the player piano, in his fascination manipulated by the machine just as it manipulates its ivory keys.

The most striking symbol of the story, however, is the small black cat befriended by Paul as it wanders aimlessly through the Ilium Works. The cat, symbol of all that is natural and pure, despises the monstrous factory machines. The doomed animal is helplessly sucked into an automated sweeper, which spits it down a chute and ejects it outside the factory. Miraculously, it survives, but as Paul races to its rescue, the cat is roasted on the factory's electric fence, symbolizing humanity's destruction by the forces of technology. With characteristic Vonnegut irony, however, *Player Piano* ends on an affirmative note. Although the price of escape is its life, the cat does escape the Ilium Works. Near the end of the novel, Paul sees beautiful flowers growing outside the factory–flowers rooted in cat excrement, signifying ultimate rebirth and a glimmer of hope for Paul and his world.

Mother Night · In his third novel, *Mother Night*, Vonnegut peers even more deeply into the human soul, exploring the roots of human alienation, probing the individual's search for his "real" identity, and uncovering the thin veil that separates reality from illusion. The story is told as the memoirs of Howard W. Campbell, Jr., a self-proclaimed "citizen of nowhere." A successful writer and producer of medieval romance plays,

Campbell sees himself as a sensitive *artiste*. Nevertheless, he allows himself to be recruited by Major Frank Wirtanen to be an American double agent posing as a Nazi radio propagandist in Germany. Secretly, Campbell sends coded American messages in his propaganda broadcasts, but he does not understand the code and never comprehends the messages he transmits. Still unaware, he even transmits the news of his beloved wife's death.

Publicly, Campbell is reviled as a traitorous Nazi hatemonger, but he does not mind, because he enjoys being on the radio. Eventually, though, he begins to lose touch with his "real" self. Is he the sensitive artist, the cruel Nazi, or the American patriot? Like Paul Proteus, Campbell allows himself to be manipulated by those around him. With no will or identity of his own, Campbell is easy prey for those who would use him for their own ends.

Two of Campbell's manipulators are his postwar friend George Kraft and his sister-in-law Resi, who poses as Campbell's long-lost wife, Helga. George and Resi are actually Russian spies plotting to capture Campbell and transport him to Russia. They abandon this plan, however, when they realize their love for Campbell, and they finally attempt to escape to freedom with him. Before the three can flee together, however, the Russians are arrested by American agents. Campbell is arrested as well but is soon freed by his friend Frank Wirtanen.

Gripped by existential fear at finding himself a free man, Campbell appeals to a Jewish couple in his apartment building, a doctor and his mother, both survivors of Auschwitz. Campbell begs to be tried for his crimes against the Jews and soon finds himself awaiting trial in a Jerusalem prison. Before Campbell goes to trial, Frank Wirtanen sends a letter on his behalf, explaining how he had recruited Campbell and honoring him as an American patriot. Yet Campbell can never be a truly free man until he purges his conscience. Upon his release from prison, he is nauseated by the prospect of his freedom, knowing that he is one of the many people "who served evil too openly and good too secretly." In his failure to resist evil and his openness to manipulation by others, Campbell had given up his free will and lost his ability to choose. Coming to this realization, he finally asserts his will to choose and ironically chooses to die, vowing to hang himself "for crimes against himself."

Cat's Cradle · Equally dark is Vonnegut's fourth novel, *Cat's Cradle*. In addition to its broad parody of science and religion, *Cat's Cradle* expands on Vonnegut's earlier themes of the dangerous misuse of science and technology, humans' moral responsibility in an immoral world, and the importance of distinguishing reality from illusion. The parodic tone is set in the very first line, "Call me Jonah," bringing to mind the Old Testament Book of Jonah. Like that Jonah, this protagonist (really named John) faithfully pursues God's directives but never truly comprehends the order behind God's plan. Continuing the parody, John encounters the Bokononist religion, whose bible, The Books of Bokonon, proclaims in its first line, "All of the true things I am about to tell you are shameless lies," an obvious inversion of the Johannine maxim "You will know the truth, and the truth will make you free" (John 8:32). In the world John inhabits, the only real freedom is the ultimate freedom–death.

John is writing a book, "The Day the World Ended," an account of the bombing of Hiroshima. His obsession with the destruction of Hiroshima foreshadows his involvement in the eventual destruction of the world by "ice-nine," a substance that converts liquid into frozen crystals. In *Cat's Cradle*, the atomic bomb and ice-nine are both the doomsday toys of an amoral scientist, Dr. Felix Hoenikker. Hoenikker pursues his work so intensely that he has little time for his three children, who grow up to be emotionally warped and twisted Products of Science. Hoenikker's only legacy to his children is the ice-nine he was brewing in the kitchen before his sudden death on Christmas Eve. After their father's death, the three children—Angela, Frank, and Newt—divide the ice-nine among themselves, knowing that it is their ticket to a better future. Newt, a midget, barters his ice-nine for an affair with a Russian ballerina. The homely Angela uses her portion to buy herself a husband. Frank gives his to Miguel "Papa" Monzano, dictator of the Caribbean Republic of San Lorenzo, in exchange for the title of general and the hand of Monzano's beautiful adopted daughter, Mona.

Pursuing information on the Hoenikker family, John finds himself in San Lorenzo, where he is introduced to Bokononism. The people of San Lorenzo are desperately poor, for the soil of the island is as unproductive as the Sahara. The island's teeming, malnourished masses find their only comfort in Bokononism, which urges them to love and console one another. John finds that, ironically, the religion started as a game by the island's founders. Knowing no way to lift the country from its destitution, they decided to give the people hope by inventing a religion based on *foma*, or comforting lies. The religion encouraged people to find strength in their *karass*, groups of people with whom they are joined to do God's mysterious will. To strengthen the faith of the people, Bokononism was outlawed, its founder banished on pain of death. As the people's faith grew, so did their happiness and their dependence on *foma*, until all the inhabitants of the island were "employed full time as actors in a play." For the inhabitants of San Lorenzo, illusion had become reality.

Soon after his arrival on the island, John finds that Papa Monzano is critically ill; it is expected that "General" Frank Hoenikker will succeed Papa and take the beautiful Mona as his bride. Secretly, though, Frank has no desire to rule the island or marry Mona. He is a simpering mass of insecurities, hiding behind his fake title. Frank's life, like everything around him, has been a lie: He has bought a false sense of dignity, which he wears like a military uniform, but inside he is gripped with fear, the same fear that pulses through the veins of the dying dictator. Papa and Frank become symbols for all people, running scared and grasping at false comforts as they confront brutal reality. Faced with the horror of an agonizing death, Papa clutches his vial of ice-nine, his last illusion of security and power. Uttering the desperate cry, "Now I will destroy the whole world," he swallows the poison and turns himself into an ice-blue popsicle. Papa's power proves illusory, however, as John and the Hoenikker children clean up the mess and seal off Papa's bedroom.

John, Frank, Angela, and Newt inform the staff that Papa is "feeling much better" and go downstairs to watch a military celebration. Yet, despite their success at covering up Papa's death and hiding their secret, they sense impending doom. As all the islanders watch the military air show, a bomber careens out of control and bursts into flame, setting off a massive explosion and landslide. As his castle disintegrates, Papa's body is propelled from the bedroom closet, plunging into the waiting sea, infecting all with ice-nine.

As the story ends, only John, Newt, and Bokonon remain, awaiting their imminent death. John recalls Angela's heroic end, remembering how she had clutched her clarinet bravely and played in the face of death, music mocking terror. John dreams of climbing the highest mountain and planting some magnificent symbol. Yet as John's heart swells with the vision of being the last man on the highest mountain, Newt mocks him and brings him back to earth. The story concludes with the last verse of

The Books of Bokonon, in which Bokonon mourns human stupidity, thumbs his nose at God, and kills himself with ice-nine.

Like many of Vonnegut's satirical writings, *Cat's Cradle* functions as humanity's wake-up call. For Vonnegut, heroism is not a dream; dignity is not an illusion. Still, he understands all too well the fear that grips a man on the brink of action, the torpor that invades the soul. In his frustration, all the artist can do is plod on, calling out his warnings as he goes.

Slaughterhouse-Five · Vonnegut's efforts to touch the soul of humanity are most fully realized in his sixth novel, *Slaughterhouse-Five*, his most touching and brilliant work. Incorporating all Vonnegut's common themes—the nature of reality and illusion, the question of free will and determinism, the horror of humankind's cruelty to itself, the vision of life as an ironic construct—*Slaughterhouse-Five* produces "an image of life that is beautiful and surprising and deep." This often-misunderstood novel leads the reader on a time-warped journey, as popular films say, "to hell and back." Emotionally suffocated by his experience in World War II, Vonnegut waited twenty-three years to tell the story of his capture by the Germans and his survival of the Allied firebombing of Dresden, the calculated annihilation of a quarter of a million refugees and civilians in an unguarded city.

As befits a tale of such distorted experience, *Slaughterhouse-Five* breaks all novelistic conventions. The story is divided into ten sections, spanning the years from 1944 to 1968. Opening with a simple, first-person narrative, Vonnegut describes his return to Dresden in 1967. He recounts his life after the war, discusses his wife and children, and relives a conversation with his old war buddy Bernard V. O'Hare, in which he reveals why *Slaughterhouse-Five* is subtitled *The Children's Crusade*. In the original Children's Crusade of 1213, Catholic monks raised a volunteer army of thirty thousand children who were intent on traveling to Palestine but instead were sent to North Africa to be sold as slaves. In the end, half the children drowned en route and the others were sold. For Vonnegut, this incident provides the perfect metaphor for all wars: hopeless ventures fought by deluded children. Thus Vonnegut prepares the reader for this personal statement about the tragedy of war. Nevertheless, the reader finds himself unprepared for the narrative shape of the tale.

Breaking from his reverie, Vonnegut reads from a Gideon Bible the story of Lot's wife, turned to a pillar of salt for looking back on Sodom and Gomorrah. To Vonnegut, her reaction was tender, instinctively human, looking back on all those lives that had touched hers, and he adopts Lot's wife as a metaphor for his narrative stance. *Slaughterhouse-Five* will be a tale told by a "pillar of salt." Vonnegut assumes the role of a masked narrator, a disinterested party, allowing himself the aesthetic distance he needs to continue his painful journey. Yet, when the reader turns to chapter 2, he finds another surprise, as chapter 2 begins, "Listen: Billy Pilgrim has come unstuck in time."

To increase his emotional distance from the story, Vonnegut, the masked narrator, tells not his own story but the story of pathetic Billy Pilgrim, Vonnegut's mythical fellow soldier. Through time travel over which he has no control, Billy is forced to relive the chapters of his life, in seemingly random order. For Billy, as for Vonnegut, his war chronology is too unsettling to confront head on. Instead of assimilating his life experiences, Billy unconsciously tries to escape the memory of them by bouncing back and forth in time from one experience to another. Not until the end of the tale can he face the crucial moment, the horror of Dresden.

The reader first sees Billy as a forty-six-year-old retired optometrist living in Ilium,

New York. Billy's daughter, Barbara, thinks that he has lost his mind. Billy has given up interest in business and devotes all of his energies to telling the world about his travels to the planet Tralfamadore. Two years earlier, Billy had been captured by aliens from Tralfamadore and had spent six months on their planet. Billy's belief in Tralfamadorian philosophy is the great comfort of his life, and he is eager to share this philosophy with the world. The aliens taught Billy, the optometrist, a better way to "see." On Tralfamadore, time is not linear; all moments are structured and permanent; death is merely one moment out of many moments in a person's life. The Tralfamadorians do not mourn the dead, for even though one may be dead in one moment, he is alive and happy in many others. The Tralfamadorians respond to life's temporary bad moments with a verbal shrug, "So it goes." Their world is a world without free will, without human responsibility, without human sorrow. On an intellectual level, Billy hungrily embraces their philosophy. Yet deep inside him (as inside Vonnegut) stirs the need to reconstruct his life, to reconcile his past. So, armed with Tralfamadorian detachment, Billy steps back in time to where it all began.

It is 1944, and Billy, a night student at the Ilium School of Optometry, is drafted into action in World War II. No soldier is more unsuited to war than is Billy. Timid and friendless, he is a chaplain's assistant, a hapless soul with a "meek faith in a loving Jesus which most soldiers found putrid." Billy's marching companion is Roland Weary, a savage young man, even by military standards. Weary's father collects ancient instruments of torture, and Weary regales Billy with gruesome tales of cruelty, giving the gentle boy an unwanted view of a monstrous world. Weary, a callous, stupid killing machine, is the natural result of humanity's barbarity. Although physically robust, he is morally depleted, a symbol of the spiritually bankrupt world into which poor Billy has been thrust. Billy–kind, sensitive, tenderhearted–has no natural defenses against the barbarity which surrounds him. So he becomes unstuck in time.

After a brief respite of time travel, Billy returns to the war. He and Weary have been captured behind German lines, taken prisoner by two toothless old men and two young boys. The Germans are accompanied by a guard dog, a female German shepherd named Princess who had been stolen from a farmer. Princess and Billy are confused and shivering from the cold. Of the whole motley group, only the barbarous Weary belongs at war. Billy, Princess, the old men, and the young boys symbolize helpless humanity in the grip of military madness.

Billy and his fellow prisoners, including Vonnegut and Bernard V. O'Hare, are taken to a prisoner-of-war camp before their transport to Dresden. As Billy recalls these moments of his life, he is moved to time travel many times. He flashes forward to 1948, when, emotionally shattered by his war experience, he checks himself into a veterans' hospital for mental patients. Here the reader is introduced to Valencia Merble, Billy's unlovely fiancée, and Eliot Rosewater, his fellow mental patient. In the hospital, Eliot and Billy devour the science-fiction novels of Kilgore Trout. They are drawn to Trout's work for the same reason Billy is drawn to the philosophy of Tralfamadore: Human experience on earth has been too disturbing; life seems meaningless. Escaping to the world of science fiction relieves the pressure, enabling Eliot and Billy to "reinvent" themselves in a kinder universe.

Before Billy returns to his war story, he again relives his adventures on the planet Tralfamadore, where he spends six months in the Tralfamadore Zoo, displayed in a glass cage. Here Billy learns of his own death in 1976. He will be murdered by Paul Lazarro, a former inmate in Billy's prisoner-of-war camp. The maniacal Lazarro, incorrectly blaming Billy for the death of Roland Weary, has plotted revenge since

1944. Naturally, Billy's innocence makes his meaningless death doubly absurd. At this time, Billy also learns of the eventual destruction of the world by the Tralfamadorians. While testing a new rocket fuel for their spacecraft, they accidentally blow up the universe. "So it goes."

When Billy returns to his war story, he and his fellow American soldiers are in Dresden, working in a factory producing vitamin syrup for pregnant women. Yet soon there will be no pregnant women in Dresden. The American soldiers are quartered underground in a former pig butchery—slaughterhouse number five. On the night of February 13, 1945, Billy (and Vonnegut) nestles safely in the shelter while the city is flattened by British and American firebombs. The next morning, the prisoners go aboveground, finding the city as lifeless as the surface of the moon. Only the one hundred American prisoners and their guards had survived.

In chapter 10, Vonnegut himself returns as narrator. It is 1968. In the intervening years, Billy has survived an airplane crash in which all of his fellow passengers have died. Valencia, frantically hurrying to see Billy in the hospital, has died of accidental carbon-monoxide poisoning. Robert Kennedy and Martin Luther King, Jr., have been assassinated. The Vietnam War is raging.

Finally, Vonnegut takes the reader back to Dresden. He and Billy are there, where the prisoners of war are digging for bodies, mining for corpses. Billy's digging companion dies of the dry heaves, unable to face the slaughter. Billy's friend Edgar Derby is executed for stealing a teapot. When the corpse mines are closed down, Billy, Vonnegut, and their companions are locked up in the suburbs to await the end of the war. When the war is over, the freed soldiers wander out into the street. The trees are blooming, and the birds are singing; springtime has finally arrived for Kurt Vonnegut.

Looking back on the novel, the reader realizes that Billy's time travels have been more than simply a coping device; they provide a learning tool as well. The jumble of events to which Vonnegut subjects Billy are not random and meaningless. Even if Billy remains blankly ignorant of the connections between events in his life, both the reader and the author learn about emotional survival in the modern world. For Vonnegut, who has called himself "the canary in the coal mine," Billy's story is a parable and a warning to all humankind: a warning that men and women must resist the temptation to abandon their free will, as Billy had, and an exhortation to keep one's dignity in the face of modern dehumanization.

That *Slaughterhouse-Five* is a story of survival may seem contradictory, ironic, but that is always Vonnegut's approach. It would be hard for the reader to imagine more death than he witnesses here—the slaughter in Dresden and the deaths of Billy, his wife, his father, and assorted soldiers, all culminating in the foretelling of the destruction of the universe by the Tralfamadorians. Yet the reader comes to understand that everything about Vonnegut's tale is ironic. Edgar Derby is executed, amid the Dresden corpse mines, for stealing a teapot; Billy, sitting in a slaughterhouse, is saved from destruction. No wonder Billy sees himself as the plaything of uncontrollable forces. Yet Vonnegut knows better. Billy, comfortably numbed by Tralfamadorian philosophy, never reinvents himself—but Vonnegut does. Writing this book enabled the author to face his past, his present, and his future. In fact, after writing *Slaughterhouse-Five*, Vonnegut proclaimed that he would never need to write another book. *Slaughterhouse-Five* embodied for Vonnegut the spirit of the phoenix: his soul, through his art, rising from the ashes.

After the spiritual and psychological rejuvenation wrought by *Slaughterhouse-Five*, Vonnegut became a totally unfettered artist in his next two books, *Breakfast of*

Champions and *Slapstick*. In *Breakfast of Champions*, he sets all of his characters free, disdaining his role as puppeteer. Admitting that, in English poet John Keats's words, he had been "half in love with easeful Death," he asserts that he has rid himself of this dangerous fascination. In *Slapstick*, he becomes frankly autobiographical, abandoning his aesthetic distance, eschewing all masks, facing his uncertain future and painful past with calm equanimity.

Galápagos · In *Galápagos*, called by Vonnegut himself his best novel, the ghost of Leon Trotsky Trout, son of Kilgore Trout, calmly tells the story of humankind from 1986 to a point one million years in the future. He tells of the end of humankind as known by its "big-brained" twentieth century readers and of the new Adam and Eves and their new Eden. Satirist and atheist that he is, Vonnegut idealizes no part of or party to his story. Knowledge is still the poisoned apple, but naturalist Charles Darwin, not God, is the featured figure of this final record of human life as known to its recorder.

Leon Trout died in the construction of the luxury liner the *Bahia de Darwin*, the launching of which is advertised as "the nature cruise of the century." Worldwide crises, however, cause all but a paltry few to withdraw their names from the list of passengers and crew. The cruise itself is begun by accident, and Mary Hepburn, not the figurehead captain, Adolf von Kleist, guides it to its destination. This unaware Adam and sterile-but-godlike Eve, with six Kanka-bono girls "from the Stone Age," begin the new race according to Darwin's (and God's?) dictum: Having eaten of the rotten apple, humankind, with its big, self-destructive brain, is no longer fit to survive; it is a matter of shrink and swim or die. Humankind thus becomes small-brained fisherkind as witnessed by the curious ghost of Leon Trout—who can now, having so witnessed, travel through the blue tunnel into the Afterlife.

Satirist, moralist, and spokesperson for humankind that he is, Vonnegut, as Jonathan Swift before him, has offered in *Galápagos* his modest proposal to a human-kind bent on its own destruction. He has also offered as epigraph to his tome the words of Anne Frank: "In spite of everything, I still believe people are really good at heart."

Timequake · In *Timequake* Vonnegut has humankind, because of a glitch in time, replay years 1991 to 2001 "on automatic pilot." He speaks as failed author of a ten-year project, *Timequake One*. Kilgore Trout, whom he personally identifies as his alter ego and as look-alike to his father, plays a crucial role in this novel. Vonnegut reprises his authorial roles as science-fiction writer, fiction writer, autobiographer, and spokes-man for humankind.

Vonnegut's fictional story shows characters living and dying, living and dying again, and then waking and reeling from the reintroduction of free will. When humanity is roused from its ten years on automatic pilot, Trout becomes its hero. Because people have had no free will for ten years, they have forgotten how to use it, and Trout shows them the path to readjustment. Trout's words, for which he is celebrated, are: "You were sick, but now you're well again, and there's work to do."

Vonnegut's epilogue honoring his "big brother Bernie," who died toward the end of *Timequake*'s composition, calls to mind his prior references to saints he has known who, in an indecent society, behave decently. His references throughout *Timequake* and this final tribute to Bernard Vonnegut seem a recommendation of that gentle man to the status of saint.

Karen Priest, updated by Judith K. Taylor

Other major works

SHORT FICTION: *Canary in a Cat House,* 1961; *Welcome to the Monkey House,* 1968.
PLAY: *Happy Birthday, Wanda June,* pb. 1970.
TELEPLAY: *Between Time and Timbuktu: Or, Prometheus-5, a Space Fantasy,* 1972.
NONFICTION: *Wampeters, Foma, and Granfalloons (Opinions),* 1974; *Palm Sunday: An Autobiographical Collage,* 1981; *Fates Worse than Death: An Autobiographical Collage of the 1980's,* 1991.
CHILDREN'S LITERATURE: *Sun Moon Star,* 1980 (with Ivan Chermayeff).

Bibliography

Allen, William Rodney. *Understanding Kurt Vonnegut.* Columbia: University of South Carolina Press, 1991. Allen's study, part of the Understanding Contemporary American Literature series, places Vonnegut, and especially *Slaughterhouse-Five,* in the literary canon. Contains an annotated bibliography and an index.

Broer, Lawrence R. *Sanity Plea: Schizophrenia in the Novels of Kurt Vonnegut.* Ann Arbor: University of Michigan Press, 1989. The comprehensive work covers all Vonnegut's major fiction from the perspective of psychology, viewing Vonnegut's characters as psychologically damaged by the traumas of the modern world. The book lacks a chronology, but has an excellent introduction, an index, and a thorough bibliography.

Giannone, Richard. *Vonnegut: A Preface to His Novels.* Port Washington, N.Y.: Kennikat Press, 1977. This comprehensive work covers all Vonnegut's major fiction up to 1977. Giving special treatment to the unity of Vonnegut's themes, this book has an outstanding introduction, a brief chronology, a brief bibliography, and a brief index.

Klinkowitz, Jerome. *"Slaughterhouse-Five": Reforming the Novel and the World.* Boston: Twayne, 1990. This book contains the most thorough and most modern treatment available of *Slaughterhouse-Five.* With care and insight, Klinkowitz debunks earlier, fatalistic interpretations of the novel. Features a comprehensive chronology, a thorough bibliography, and an index.

_____. *Vonnegut in Fact: The Public Spokesmanship of Personal Fiction.* Columbia: University of South Carolina Press, 1998. Klinkowitz makes a case for Vonnegut as a sort of redeemer of the novelistic form, after writers such as Philip Roth declared the novel dead. He traces Vonnegut's successful integration of autobiography and fiction in his body of work. Provides an extensive bibliography and an index.

Merrill, Robert, ed. *Critical Essays on Kurt Vonnegut.* Boston: G. K. Hall, 1990. Merrill claims to have compiled "the most comprehensive collection of criticism on this author yet assembled." An index is provided.

Mustazza, Leonard, ed. *The Critical Response to Kurt Vonnegut.* Westport, Conn.: Greenwood Press, 1994. Presents a brief history of the critical response to Vonnegut and critical reviews. A selected bibliography and an index are provided.

Schatt, Stanley. *Kurt Vonnegut, Jr.* Boston: Twayne, 1976. This volume is notable for its discussion of Vonnegut's plays and short stories, as well as its retrospective of Vonnegut's life, entitled "The Public Man." It also offers a comprehensive treatment of the fiction, a brief chronology, a bibliography, and an index.

ALICE WALKER

Born: Eatonton, Georgia; February 9, 1944

Principal long fiction · *The Third Life of Grange Copeland*, 1970; *Meridian*, 1976; *The Color Purple*, 1982; *The Temple of My Familiar*, 1989; *Possessing the Secret of Joy*, 1992; *By the Light of My Father's Smile*, 1998.

Other literary forms · Alice Walker published several volumes of short fiction, poetry, and essays in addition to her novels. Walker was an early editor at *Ms.* magazine, in which many of her essays first appeared. Her interest in the then little-known writer Zora Neale Hurston led to her pilgrimage to Florida to place a tombstone on Hurston's unmarked grave, to Walker's editing of *I Love Myself When I Am Laughing . . . And Then Again When I Am Looking Mean and Impressive: A Zora Neale Hurston Reader* (1979), and to her introduction to Robert Hemenway's *Zora Neale Hurston: A Literary Biography* (1977).

Achievements · Walker's literary reputation is based primarily on her fiction, although her second book of poetry, *Revolutionary Petunias and Other Poems* (1973), received the Lillian Smith Award and a nomination for a National Book Award. Her first short-story collection, *In Love and Trouble: Stories of Black Women* (1973), won the Rosenthal Award of the National Institute of Arts and Letters. In addition, she received a Charles Merrill writing fellowship, an award for fiction from the National Endowment for the Arts, and a Guggenheim Fellowship. She was also a Bread Loaf Scholar and a fellow at the Radcliffe Institute. *The Third Life of Grange Copeland* was widely and enthusiastically reviewed in publications as varied as *The New Yorker, The New Republic,* and *The New York Times Book Review,* although journals aimed primarily at a black readership were often silent or critical of the violence and graphic depiction of rural black life. With the publication of *Meridian,* Walker's second novel, her work as a poet, novelist, essayist, editor, teacher, scholar, and political activist came together. *Meridian* was universally praised in scholarly journals, literary magazines, popular magazines, and black-oriented journals. Some critics, mainly black male reviewers, objected again to the honest, straightforward portrayals of black life in the South and to Walker's growing feminism, which they saw in conflict with her commitment to her race. Walker's third novel, *The Color Purple,* was widely acclaimed; feminist and *Ms.* editor Gloria Steinem wrote that this novel "could be the kind of popular and literary event that transforms an intense reputation into a national one," and Peter Prescott's review in *Newsweek* began by saying "I want to say at once that *The Color Purple* is an American novel of permanent importance." These accolades were substantiated when Walker received both the American Book Award and the 1983 Pulitzer Prize for fiction.

Biography · Alice Walker was born in Eatonton, Georgia, on February 9, 1944, the last of eight children of Willie Lee and Minnie Lou Grant Walker, sharecroppers in rural Georgia. Her relationship with her father, at first strong and valuable, became strained as she became involved in the civil rights and feminist movements. A moving depiction of her estrangement from her father occurs in her essay "My Father's

Country Is the Poor," which appeared in *The New York Times* in 1977. For Walker, a loving and healthy mother-daughter relationship has endured over the years. An account of that relationship is central to her essays "In Search of Our Mothers' Gardens" and "Lulls–A Native Daughter Returns to the Black South" and in Mary Helen Washington's article "Her Mother's Gifts," in which Walker acknowledges that she often writes with her mother's voice– "Just as you have certain physical characteristics of your mother . . . when you're compelled to write her stories, it's because you recognize and prize those qualities of her in yourself."

One of the central events in Walker's childhood was a BB gun accident which left her, at age eight, blind in one eye. Scar tissue from that wound, both physical and psychological, seems to have left her with a compensating acuteness of vision, despite the conviction that she was permanently disfigured. Walker was affected enough by the accident to say in a 1974 interview with John O'Brien, "I have always been a solitary person, and since I was eight years old (and the recipient of a disfiguring scar, since corrected, somewhat), I have daydreamed–not of fairytales–but of falling on swords, of putting guns to my heart or head, and of slashing my wrists with a razor."

Jeff Reinking/Picture Group

Walker's partial blindness allowed her to attend Spelman College in Atlanta on a scholarship for the handicapped, following her graduation from Butler-Baker High School in 1961. She left Spelman after two years—which included summer trips to the Soviet Union and to Africa as part of a group called Experiment in International Living—for Sarah Lawrence College, from which she graduated in 1965.

Walker's political activity governed her movements during the years immediately following her college graduation: She spent the summer of 1965 in the Soviet Union and also worked for civil rights in Liberty County, Georgia. The next year she was a case worker for New York City's Department of Social Services, and then a voter-registration worker in Mississippi. In 1967, she married Melvyn Leventhal, a civil rights lawyer, and moved to Jackson, Mississippi, where she continued her civil rights work, lived in the heart of the South as part of an interracial couple, and taught at Jackson State University, while continuing to write stories, poems, and essays. She taught at Tougaloo College in Mississippi for a year before returning to the East, where she was a lecturer in writing and literature at Wellesley College, an editor at *Ms.* magazine, and an instructor at the University of Massachusetts at Boston. By 1977, she had divorced her husband, accepted a position as associate professor of English at Yale University, and written six books.

After *The Color Purple* won critical acclaim in 1986, Walker and her family shared the success with Eatonton. Walker's sister established The Color Purple Educational Scholarship Fund, and Walker adopted three elementary schools to help provide needed supplies for students who maintained above-average grades. Walker continued her activities in political forums as well, working for civil rights and protesting against nuclear weapons. She also became an avid objector to female genital mutilation ("female circumcision") in Africa through public speaking and through her novel *Possessing the Secret of Joy* and her nonfiction book *Warrior Marks: Female Genital Mutilation and the Sexual Blinding of Women* (1993), which focus on the horrors and scars of this practice.

Walker also used her success to help other women writers. She advocated women's literature classes and helped promote neglected women and black writers. In 1984, Walker began her own publishing company, Wild Trees Press. Throughout the 1980's and 1990's she lived in Northern California, where she continued to write stories, essays, poems, and novels.

Analysis · The story of Alice Walker's childhood scar provides the most basic metaphor of her novels: the idea that radical change is possible even under the worst conditions. Although she was never able to regain the sight in one eye, Walker's disfigurement was considerably lessened:

> I used to pray every night that I would wake up and somehow it would be gone. I couldn't look at people directly because I thought I was ugly. . . . Then when I was fourteen, I visited my brother Bill [who] took me to a hospital where they removed most of the scar tissue—and I was a *changed person*. I promptly went home, scooped up the best-looking guy, and by the time I graduated from high school, I was valedictorian, voted 'Most Popular,' and crowned queen!

The idea that change and personal triumph is possible despite the odds is central to all of Walker's writing. Her work focuses directly or indirectly on the ways of survival adopted by black women, usually in the South, and is presented in a prose style characterized by a distinctive combination of lyricism and unflinching realism.

Walker's women attempt not merely to survive, but to survive completely with some sense of stability, despite the constant thread of family violence, physical and mental abuse, and a lack of responsibility on the part of the men in their lives. Walker is simultaneously a feminist and a supporter of civil rights, not only for black Americans, but also for minorities everywhere.

Walker's vision was shaped in part by a work from the first flowering of black writing in America: Jean Toomer's *Cane* (1923). She said in 1974 about Toomer's book that "it has been reverberating in me to an astonishing degree. *I love it passionately*; could not possibly exist without it." Like *Cane*, the first part of which centers mainly on women in the South, Walker's novels are made up of nearly equal parts of poetry, portraiture, and drama, broken up into a series of sections and subsections. Other important literary influences on Walker include Zora Neale Hurston, from whom she inherited a love of black folklore; Flannery O'Connor, who wrote of southern violence and grotesqueries from her home in Milledgeville, Georgia, less than ten miles from Walker's childhood home; and Albert Camus, whose existentialism speaks to the struggle for survival and dignity in which Walker's characters are engaged. Walker herself defined her "preoccupations" as a novelist: "The survival, the survival *whole* of my people. But beyond that I am committed to exploring the oppressions, the insanities, the loyalties, and the triumphs of black women." *The Third Life of Grange Copeland*, on the surface a novel about the cycle of rage and violence torturing the lives of a father and his son, is as much about the recipients of that rage–the women and children whose lives are directly affected. Although the novel is unremitting in its picture of desperate poverty's legacy of hatred, hopelessness, and cruelty, it concludes optimistically with Ruth Copeland's hope for a release from sorrow through the redemption promised by the early days of the civil rights movement and by the knowledge and love inherited at the sacrifical death of her grandfather.

The Third Life of Grange Copeland · Writing in 1973, Walker observed that her first novel, *The Third Life of Grange Copeland*, "though sometimes humorous and celebrative of life, is a grave book in which the characters see the world as almost entirely menacing." This dark view of life is common to Grange Copeland, the patriarch of a family farming on shares in rural Georgia, his son Brownfield, and the wives and daughters of both men. For all these characters, the world is menacing because of the socioeconomic position they occupy at the bottom of the scale of the sharecropping system. Father and son menace each other in this novel because they are in turn menaced by rage born out of the frustration of the system. Although the white people of the book are nearly always vague, nameless, and impersonal, they and the system they represent have the ability to render both Grange and Brownfield powerless.

It is not accidental that these characters' names have agricultural connotations. "Grange" suggests a late nineteenth century association of farmers, a feudal farm and grain storage building, and a combination of graze and range, while "Brownfield" and "Cope*land*" are self-explanatory–for the inability to cope with the land is what leads both male characters along virtually parallel paths. For the father, the mere appearance of the white farm boss's truck is enough to turn his face "into a unnaturally bland mask, curious and unsettling to see." The appearance of the truck causes the son to be "filled with terror of this man who could, by his presence alone, turn his father into something that might as well have been a pebble or a post or a piece of dirt." Although Grange is, in this same image, literally a piece of land, he eventually returns to the South and learns to live self-sufficiently, farming a section of soil he tricked his second wife into giving to him. Brownfield, in contrast, is never able to escape from the sharecropping system, although he sees that, like his father, he is "destined to be no more than overseer, on the white man's plantation, of his own children." Brownfield is able to live obliviously on a farm in Georgia, content to blame all of his problems on others. The poor rural black workers of this novel are themselves little more than a crop, rotated from farm to farm, and producing a harvest of shame and hunger, cruelty and violence.

Unlike the men of the novel, the women are menaced by both blacks and whites, by both the agricultural system and the "strange fruit" it produces. Margaret, Grange's first wife, is both physically and mentally degraded by her husband and then sexually exploited by a white truck driver, resulting in her second pregnancy. Unable to cope with this situation, Grange deserts his family, after which his wife poisons both her child and herself. Following his father's pattern, Brownfield marries and begins to work the land, but after "a year when endless sunup to sundown work on fifty rich bottom acres of cotton land and a good crop brought them two diseased shoats for winter meat" he too begins to abuse his wife. Although Brownfield's wife, Mem, is a schoolteacher intelligent enough to try to break the cycle of raising others people's crops, her brief rebellion against her husband's malevolent beatings and mental tortures is a failure: He is able to subjugate her through repeated pregnancies that sap her rebellion as they turn her once rich and strong body into a virtual wasteland of emaciation. Because her body, which represents the land of the South, is still able to produce children despite its depleted condition, Brownfield is enraged enough to murder her in retaliation for her physical shape: "he had murdered his wife because she had become skinny and had not, with much irritation to him, reverted, even when well-fed, to her former plumpness. . . . Plumpness and freedom from the land, from cows and skinniness, went all together in his mind." Despite his irrational abuse of her, Mem is not ashamed "of being black though, no matter what he said. . . . Color was something the ground did to the flowers, and that was an end to it."

What the ground did to these generations of southern black people is the subject of Walker's novel—the whole lurid history of violence, hatred, and guilt that she chronicles in this story of one family's griefs. By the book's end, Brownfield Copeland has murdered his wife and an unnamed albino baby, while Grange Copeland has murdered his son Brownfield—first spiritually, then physically—and indirectly has killed his first wife and her infant.

Walker's characters are allegorical representations of the classic modes of survival historically adopted by black Americans in dealing with their oppression. Brownfield identifies with whites by daydreaming of himself on a southern plantation, sipping mint juleps, and then by bargaining for his freedom with the sexual favors of black women. Both of Grange's wives attempt to live up to the white stereotype of black women as promiscuous sexual beings, free of any moral restraints. Brownfield's wife, Mem, attempts the passive resistance advocated by Martin Luther King, but she is destroyed by what her husband calls "her weakness . . . forgiveness, a stupid belief that kindness can convert the enemy." Brownfield's daughter, Daphne, who calls herself the Copeland Family Secret Keeper, tries the strategy of inventing a falsely romantic history of the past, of the good old days when her father was kind, echoing those historical revisionists who try to argue that slavery was not that bad. Brownfield's other daughters try to stay away from their father altogether, regarding him "as a human devil" of whom they were afraid "in a more distant, impersonal way. He was like bad weather, a toothache, daily bad news."

Each of the title character's three lives (at home in the South as a sharecropper married to Margaret; in the North as a hustler of alcohol, drugs, and women; and finally back in the South as a farmer married to Josie and rearing his granddaughter Ruth) parallels a traditional survival strategy, which Grange summarizes as follows, "The white folks hated me and I hated myself until I started hating them in return and loving myself. Then I tried just loving me, and then you, and *ignoring* them much as I could." To put it another way, Grange tries at first to adapt to the system by believing what whites say about blacks; then he turns to the classic escape of the runaway slave–heading North to freedom; finally, he tries the technique of praising black life while ignoring whites altogether. A large part of the novel's devastation is caused by the repeated use of these techniques, not against whites, but against other members of the Copeland family. Only Ruth, the granddaughter through whom Grange seeks redemption, is able to deal with whites in an intelligent, balanced, nondestructive yet independent way. She has learned from her grandfather, and from her family history, that pure hatred becomes self-hatred, violence begets self-violence, and she therefore becomes the novel's symbol of the new black woman, ready to assume her place in black history as a courageous worker in the Civil Rights movement which the rest of her family has been groping to discover.

Meridian · Walker's second novel, *Meridian*, picks up chronologically and thematically at the point where her first novel ended. *Meridian* describes the struggles of a young black woman, Meridian Hill, about the same age as Ruth Copeland, who comes to an awareness of power and feminism during the Civil Rights movement, and whose whole life's meaning is centered in the cycles of guilt, violence, hope, and change characteristic of that dramatic time. Thematically, *Meridian* picks up the first novel's theme of self-sacrificial murder as a way out of desperate political oppression in the form of the constant question that drives Meridian Hill–"Will you kill for the Revolution?" Meridian's lifelong attempt to answer that question affirmatively (as her college friends so easily do) while remaining true to her sense of responsibility to the past, her sense of ethics, and her sense of guilt of having given to her mother the child of her teenage pregnancy, constitutes the section of the novel entitled "Meridian." The second third of the novel, "Truman Held," is named for the major male character in the narrative. The third major section of the novel, "Ending," looks back at the turmoil of the Civil Rights movement from the perspective of the 1970's. Long after others have given up intellectual arguments about the morality of killing for revolution, Meridian is still debating the question, still actively involved in voter registration, political activism, and civil rights organization, as though the movement had never lost momentum. Worrying that her actions, now seen as eccentric rather than revolutionary, will cause her "to be left, listening to the old music, beside the highway," Meridian achieves release and atonement through the realization that her role will be to "come forward and sing from memory songs they will need once more to hear. For it is the song of the people, transformed by the experiences of each generation, that holds them together."

In 1978, Walker described *Meridian* as "a book 'about' the Civil Rights movement, feminism, socialism, the shakiness of revolutionaries and the radicalization of saints." Her word "about" is exact, for all of these topics revolve not chronologically but thematically around a central point–the protagonist, Meridian Hill. In some ways, Meridian *is* a saint; by the book's end she has sustained her belief in the Civil Rights movement without losing faith in feminism and socialism, despite family pressures, guilt, literally paralyzing self-doubts, the history of the movement, and the sexism of many of its leaders. In contrast, Truman Held represents those males who were reported to have said that "the only position for a woman in the movement is prone." Although Truman Held is Meridian's initial teacher in the movement, she eventually leaves him behind because of his inability to sustain his initial revolutionary fervor, and because of his misogyny. Unlike Brownfield Copeland, Truman argues that women are of less value than they should be, not because of skinniness, but because "Black women let themselves go . . . they are so fat." Later in the novel, Truman marries a white civil rights worker, whose rape by another black man produces disgust in him, as much at his wife as at his friend. When Truman seeks Meridian out in a series of small southern hamlets where she continues to persuade black people to register to vote and to struggle for civil rights, he tells her that the movement is ended and that he grieves in a different way than she. Meridian answers, "I know how you grieve by running away. By pretending you were never there." Like Grange Copeland, Truman Held refuses to take responsibility for his own problems, preferring to run away to the North.

Meridian's sacrificial dedication to the movement becomes a model for atonement and release, words that once formed the working title of the book. *Meridian* could also have been called "The Third Life of Meridian Hill" because of similarities between Meridian's life and Grange Copeland's. Meridian leads three lives: as an uneducated child in rural Georgia who follows the traditional pattern of early pregnancy and aimless marriage; as a college student actively participating in political demonstrations; and as an eccentric agitator–a performer, she calls herself–unaware that the movement is ended. Like Grange Copeland in another sense, Meridian Hill is solid proof of the ability of any human to change dramatically by sheer will and desire.

Meridian is always different from her friends, who, filled with angry rhetoric, ask her repeatedly if she is willing to kill for the revolution, the same question that Grange asked himself when he lived in the North. This question haunts Meridian, because she does not know if she can or if she should kill, and because it reminds her of a similar request, posed in a similar way by her mother: "Say it now, Meridian, and be saved. All He asks is that we acknowledge Him as our Master. Say you believe in Him . . . don't go against your heart." In neither case is Meridian able to answer yes without going against her heart. Unlike her college friends and Truman Held, who see the movement only in terms of future gains for themselves, Meridian is involved with militancy because of her past: "But what none of them seemed to understand was that she felt herself to be, not holding on to something from the past, but *held* by something in the past."

Part of the past's hold on her is the sense of guilt she feels about her relationships with her parents. Although her father taught her the nature of the oppression of minorities through his knowledge of American Indians, her strongest source of guilt comes from her mother, who argues, like Brownfield Copeland, that the responsibility for *all* problems stems from outside oneself: "The answer to everything," said Meridian's mother, "is we live in America and we're not rich." Meridian's strongest sense of past guilt comes from the knowledge she gains when she becomes pregnant: "it was for stealing her mother's serenity, for shattering her mother's emerging self, that Meridian felt guilty from the very first, though she was unable to understand how this could possibly be her fault."

Meridian takes the form of a series of nonchronological sections, some consisting of only a paragraph, some four or five pages long, that circle around the events of

Meridian's life. The writing is clear, powerful, violent, lyrical, and often symbolic. Spelman College, for example, is here called Saxon College. The large magnolia tree in the center of the campus, described with specific folkloric detail, is destroyed by angry students during a demonstration: "Though Meridian begged them to dismantle the president's house instead, in a fury of confusion and frustration they worked all night, and chopped and sawed down, level to the ground, that mighty, ancient, sheltering music tree." This tree (named The Sojourner, perhaps for Sojourner Truth) expands symbolically to suggest both the senseless destruction of black ghettos by blacks during the turmoil of the 1960's, and also Meridian Hill herself, who receives a photograph years later of The Sojourner, now "a gigantic tree stump" with "a tiny branch, no larger than a finger, growing out of one side." That picture, suggesting as it does the rebirth of hope despite despair, also evokes the last vision of Meridian expressed by the now-shamed Truman Held: "He would never see 'his' Meridian again. The new part had grown out of the old, though, and that was reassuring. This part of her, new, sure and ready, even eager, for the world, he knew he must meet again and recognize for its true value at some future time."

The Color Purple · Like her first two novels, *The Color Purple* has an unusual form. *The Color Purple* presents the author's familiar and yet fresh themes—survival and redemption—in epistolary form. Most of the novel's letters are written by Celie, an uneducated, unloved, black woman living in rural Georgia in the 1920's; Celie's letters are written in what Walker calls "black folk English," a language of wit, strength, and natural humor. Ashamed of having been raped by her stepfather, a man whom Celie thinks at the time is her father, she begins to send letters to God, in the way that children send letters to Santa Claus, because her rapist told her to tell nobody but God. Although her early letters tell of rape, degradation, and pain, of her stepfather's getting rid of the two children born of his cruelty, the tone is nevertheless captivating, ironic, and even humorous. Soon the despair turns into acceptance, then into understanding, anger, rebellion, and finally triumph and loving forgiveness as the fourteen-year-old Celie continues to write until she reaches an audience, some thirty years later. Like the author, who began writing at the age of eight, and who has turned her childhood experience in rural Georgia into three novels of violence, hatred, understanding, love, and profound hope for the future, Celie is a writer, a listener, a thinker, and a promoter of Walker's constant theme: "Love redeems, meanness kills."

Like Meridian Hill, Celie compares herself to a tree. After her stepfather's repeated rapes, Celie is sold into a virtual state of slavery to a man who beats her, a man she neither knows, loves, nor talks to, a man she can never call anything but Mr. —, an ironic throwback to the eighteenth century English epistolary novel. Celie tries to endure by withholding all emotion: "I make myself wood. I say to myself, Celie, you a tree. That's how come I know trees fear man." Like The Sojourner, or like the kudzu vine of the deep South that thrives despite repeated attempts to beat it back, Celie continues to express her fears and hopes in a series of letters written in a form of black English that is anything but wooden. The contrast between the richly eccentric prose of Celie's letters and the educated yet often lifeless sentences of her sister Nettie's return letters supports Walker's statement that "writing *The Color Purple* was writing in my first language." The language of the letters is at first awkward, but never difficult to follow. As Celie grows in experience, in contact with the outside world, and in confidence, her writing gradually becomes more sophisticated and more like standard written English, but it never loses its originality of rhythm and phrase.

Based on Walker's great grandmother, a slave who was raped at twelve by her owner, Celie works her way from ignorance about her body and her living situation all the way through to an awakening of her self-worth, as well as to an understanding of the existence of God, the relations between men and women, and the power of forgiveness in uniting family and friends. Much of this transformation is brought about through the magic of a blues singer named Shug Avery, who guides Celie in understanding sexuality, men, and religion without causing her to lose her own fresh insights, naïve though they are.

The letters that make up the novel are something like the missives that the protagonist of Saul Bellow's novel *Herzog* (1964) writes but never sends, in that they are often addressed to God and written in an ironic but not selfconscious manner. Because of the combination of dark humor and despair, the letters also evoke memories of the desperate letters from the physically and spiritually maimed addressed to the hero of Nathanael West's *Miss Lonelyhearts* (1933). Although Celie is unlettered in a traditional sense, her ability to carry the complicated plot forward and to continue to write—first without an earthly audience, and then to her sister, whom she has not seen for more than twenty years—testify to the human potential for self-transformation.

Discussing Celie's attempts to confirm her existence by writing to someone she is not certain exists, Gloria Steinem says, "Clearly, the author is telling us something about the origin of Gods: about when we need to invent them and when we don't." In a sense, Shug Avery becomes a god for Celie because of her ability to control the evil in the world and her power to change the sordid conditions of Celie's life. Early in the book, when Celie is worrying about survival, about rape, incest, beatings, and the murder of her children, her only source of hope is the name "Shug Avery," a name with a magical power to control her husband. Not even aware that Shug is a person, Celie writes "I ast our new mammy bout Shug Avery. What it is?" Finding a picture of Shug, Celie transfers her prayers to what is at that point only an image: "I see her there in furs. Her face rouge. Her hair like somethin tail. She grinning with her foot up on somebody motocar. Her eyes serious tho. Sad some. . . . An all night long I stare at it. An now when I dream, I dream of Shug Avery. She be dress to kill, whirling an laughing." Shug Avery becomes a god to Celie not only because she is pictured in the first photograph Celie has ever seen, but also because she is dressed in a style that shows a sense of pride and freedom.

Once Celie's sister's letters begin to appear, mailed from Africa, where Nettie is a missionary, the ironic connection between the primitive animism of the Africans and Celie's equally primitive reaction to Shug's picture becomes clear. Although Nettie has crossed the ocean to minister to a tribe of primitive people, her own sister is living in inhuman conditions in Georgia: ignorance, disease, sexism, lack of control of the environment, and the ever-increasing march of white people. When Shug explains her own animistic religious beliefs—which include the notion that God is not a he or a she, but an it (just as Celie once thought Shug Avery was an it)—Celie is converted to a pantheistic worship that makes her early identification with trees seem less naïve.

When the narrator of Herman Melville's "Bartleby the Scrivener" tries to explain Bartleby's withdrawal from life, he thinks of the dead letter office in which the scrivener was rumored to have worked, and says, "On errands of life, these letters speed to death." In contrast, Celie's and Nettie's letters, ostensibly written to people long thought to be dead, speed across the ocean on errands of life, where they grow to sustain, not merely the sisters in the book, but all those lucky enough to read them. As the author says of *The Color Purple*, "It's my happiest book . . . I had to do all the other writing to get to this point." For the reader who has gotten to this point in Walker's career by reading all of her other books, there is no question that Alice Walker's name could be substituted for Celie's in the author's statement about her most recent novel: "Let's hope people can hear Celie's voice. There are so many people like Celie who make it, who come out of nothing. People who triumph."

Possessing the Secret of Joy · The novels *By the Light of My Father's Smile* and *Possessing the Secret of Joy* share strong characters whose sexual identities suffer in order to conform to the society in which they live. Only through death can Tashi and Mad Dog become complete and escape the male-dominated world and its restrictions.

Walker combines fact and fiction in *Possessing the Secret of Joy* to illustrate the effects that female genital mutilation has on the women who are subjected to the procedure. The main character, Tashi, an African tribal woman, willingly undergoes the tribal ritual of genital mutilation in a desire to conform to her culture and feel complete. This procedure leaves her physically and mentally scarred. Tashi realizes that the procedure destroyed her emotionally and made her feel as if she were something other than her true self. After her mutilation, she marries Adam Johnson and moves to America. She is renamed Evelyn Johnson, and her chapter headings shift from "Tashi" to "Evelyn" in order to demonstrate the conflict within her as she struggles to find her true identity. The conflict leads her to madness.

Tashi strives to understand her insanity and to interpret her recurring nightmares of a tower. With the help of her therapists, Mzee and Raye, and the members of her family, Tashi realizes the reasons for her insanity and gradually becomes stronger and able to face her nightmares and what they represent. The chapters are told through the eyes of all the main characters, a technique that provides insight into the effect that Tashi has on those around her. Through its main characters, Tashi, Olivia, and Adam, *Possessing the Secret of Joy* is connected to, but is not a sequel, to Walker's previous novels *The Color Purple* and *The Temple of My Familiar*.

By the Light of My Father's Smile · Walker's sixth novel, *By the Light of My Father's Smile*, follows the Johnson family on a journey through life, and to rebirth through death. Magdalena, referred to as Mad Dog, discovers her sensuality and its connection with her spirituality while living with her parents in Mexico. Her parents are pretending to be missionaries in order to do an anthropological study of the Mundo people. Magdalena is acutely aware of her emotions and sensuality, but she is severely beaten by her father when he discovers her sexual activity.

Magdalena's sister Susannah, shadowed by Magdalena's anger and frustration, is awakened to her true desires by her friend Irene, who is able to survive and accept life on her own terms despite the restrictions placed on her by her society. Susannah realizes that her unhappiness is the result of having been "sucked into the black cloth" and hypocrisy of the world. Each member of the Johnson family suffers through life searching for true love and happiness, which they find only in death. The story moves between the spiritual world and physical world as the father watches his two daughters come to terms with their anger and their true spirits. As characters pass into the spiritual world, they are enlightened to their failings in the physical world and make amends with those they have injured. Only when acceptance of each soul is obtained can the four family members cross the river and live in eternity.

Timothy Dow Adams, updated by Mary A. Blackmon

Other major works

SHORT FICTION: *In Love and Trouble: Stories of Black Women*, 1973; *You Can't Keep a Good Woman Down*, 1981; *The Complete Stories*, 1994.

POETRY: *Once: Poems*, 1968; *Five Poems*, 1972; *Revolutionary Petunias and Other Poems*, 1973; *Goodnight, Willie Lee, I'll See You in the Morning: Poems*, 1979; *Horses Make a Landscape Look More Beautiful*, 1984; *Her Blue Body Everything We Know: Earthling Poems, 1965-1990*, 1991.

NONFICTION: *In Search of Our Mothers' Gardens: Womanist Prose*, 1983; *Living by the Word: Selected Writings, 1973-1987*, 1988; *Warrior Marks: Female Genital Mutilation and the Sexual Blinding of Women*, 1993; *The Same River Twice: Honoring the Difficult*, 1996; *Anything We Love Can Be Saved: A Writer's Activism*, 1997.

CHILDREN'S LITERATURE: *Langston Hughes: American Poet*, 1974; *To Hell with Dying*, 1988; *Finding the Green Stone*, 1991.

EDITED TEXT: *I Love Myself When I Am Laughing . . . And Then Again When I Am Looking Mean and Impressive: A Zora Neale Hurston Reader*, 1979.

Bibliography

Bloom, Harold, ed. *Alice Walker: Modern Critical Views*. New York: Chelsea House, 1989. A book-length compilation of the best of criticism on Walker. Authors Diane F. Dadoff and Deborah E. McDowell explore the resonant Zora Neale Hurston/Alice Walker relationship. Naturally radical feminism is addressed in this study, and Bloom discusses the mother/daughter motif in Walker's works.

Christian, Barbara. *Black Feminist Criticism*. New York: Pergamon Press, 1985. Throughout the book there are references to the characters in Alice Walker's novels. Chapters 2 and 6 focus entirely on Walker's women characters and the motifs in her work, in particular growth through pain. Chapter 17 discusses her novel *Meridian*, and chapter 15 her novel *The Color Purple*. The book is a valuable resource for black literature as well as for insights into Walker's characterization.

Gates, Henry Louis, Jr., and K. A. Appiah, eds. *Alice Walker: Critical Perspectives Past and Present*. New York: Amistad, 1993. Contains reviews of Walker's first five novels and critical analyses of several of her works of short and long fiction. Also includes two interviews with Walker, a chronology of her works, and an extensive bibliography of essays and texts.

Gentry, Tony. *Alice Walker*. New York: Chelsea House, 1993. This biography is geared toward the high school student. The text is simple to read but thorough in providing biographical information about Walker and discussing her writing. A chronology and brief bibliography are also included.

Montelaro, Janet J. *Producing a Womanist Text: The Maternal as Signifier in Alice Walker's "The Color Purple."* Victoria, B.C.: English Literary Studies, University of Victoria, 1996. Examines themes of feminism, motherhood, and African American women in literature.

Winchell, Donna Haisty. *Alice Walker*. New York: Twayne, 1992. Provides a comprehensive analysis of Walker's short and long fiction. A brief biography and chronology precede the main text of the book. Each chapter refers to specific ideas and themes within Walker's works and focuses on how Walker's own experiences define her characters and themes. Following the narrative is a useful annotated bibliography.

EUDORA WELTY

Born: Jackson, Mississippi; April 13, 1909

Principal long fiction · *The Robber Bridegroom*, 1942; *Delta Wedding*, 1946; *The Ponder Heart*, 1954; *Losing Battles*, 1970; *The Optimist's Daughter*, 1972.

Other literary forms · In spite of her success and acclaim as a novelist, Eudora Welty always regarded herself as essentially a writer of short stories. In an interview that appeared in the fall, 1972, issue of the *Paris Review*, she says, "I'm a short-story writer who writes novels the hard way, and by accident." In 1980, all of her previously collected short fiction and two uncollected stories were published in one volume, *The Collected Stories of Eudora Welty*. Another new collection, *Moon Lake and Other Stories*, was published in the same year, and *Retreat* was released in 1981. Prior to that, some had appeared in *Short Stories* (1950) and in *Selected Stories of Eudora Welty* (1954). Other early short-story collections are *A Curtain of Green and Other Stories* (1941); *The Wide Net and Other Stories* (1943); *The Golden Apples* (1949), regarded by some as a loosely structured novel, but considered by Welty to be a group of interconnected stories; and *The Bride of the Innisfallen, and Other Stories* (1955). Welty also published numerous essays and reviews, some of which were collected in *The Eye of the Story: Selected Essays and Reviews* (1978). In addition, she published a book for children, *The Shoe Bird* (1964), and books of her own photographs, *One Time, One Place* (1971) and *Eudora Welty: Photographs* (1989). A memoir, *One Writer's Beginnings*, appeared in 1984.

Achievements · Although it was not until she wrote *Losing Battles* and *The Optimist's Daughter* that Welty's name began to appear on the best-seller lists, her work had long been recognized and appreciated by discerning readers. In five decades of writing and publishing, she received nearly every major award for fiction offered in the United States. Among them are the prestigious William Dean Howells Medal of the Academy of Arts and Letters for "the most distinguished work of American fiction" for the years 1950 through 1955, the National Institute of Arts and Letters Gold Medal for the Novel in 1972, the Pulitzer Prize for Fiction in 1973, and the National Medal for Literature at the American Book Awards ceremony in 1980. In addition, she was awarded several honorary doctorates, Guggenheim Fellowships, special professorships, and membership in the National Institute of Arts and Letters.

Disinterested in either fame or fortune, Welty simply wanted the opportunity to write and the assurance that there are readers who enjoy her work. She repeatedly expressed gratitude to such writers and editors as Robert Penn Warren, Cleanth Brooks, Albert Erskine, Ford Madox Ford, and Katherine Anne Porter, who were among the first persons of influence to recognize her ability and to promote interest in her early stories. Warren, Brooks, and Erskine accepted some of her first stories for The Southern Review and thus opened the door for subsequent publication in such magazines as The Atlantic Monthly, Harper's Bazaar, and The New Yorker. This exposure to a national audience also facilitated the publication of her first volume of stories.

Richard O. Moore

Biography · Eudora Alice Welty was born in Jackson, Mississippi, on April 13, 1909. She would spend most of her life in Jackson. She was the only daughter of Christian Webb Welty and Mary Chestina Andrews Welty; she had two younger brothers. Soon after their marriage in 1904, Welty's parents moved to Jackson. Her father, who came from Ohio, where his father owned a farm, was president of the well-established Lamar Life Insurance Company. Her mother, a West Virginian, was descended from pre-Revolutionary War Virginia stock, engendered by country preachers, teachers, and lawyers. Welty, who claimed that she would feel "shy, and discouraged at the very thought" of a biography about her, felt that a "private life should be kept private." Still, though she insisted that it is the writer's work, not his or her life, that is important, she did finally write a memoir of her family history and her early years, *One Writer's Beginnings*, which was published in 1984 and received positive critical comment.

Perhaps one reason she suggested that her own biography would not "particularly interest anybody" is that she lived for the most part in the mainstream of American society. As Katherine Anne Porter aptly observes in her introduction to *A Curtain of Green*, Welty is not the "spiritual and intellectual exile" that typifies the modern artist. She attended Central High School in Jackson, then went for two years to Mississippi State College for Women, in Columbus, before transferring to the University of Wisconsin in 1927. After graduating with a bachelor of arts degree in English in 1929, she enrolled in the School of Business at Columbia University, where she studied advertising for a year. By then, the country was in the throes of the Depression, and she returned to Jackson to seek work. During the next several years, she held a variety of jobs in advertising, radio scriptwriting, and part-time newspaper work. She also began writing stories. Possibly the most important of those early jobs was the position of "Junior Publicity Agent" with the Works Progress Administration from 1933 to 1936. In this position, Welty was required to travel extensively through Mississippi doing newspaper stories on various WPA projects. Her work involved taking photographs, talking with a great variety of people, and, perhaps most important, listening to them. As Welty herself confessed, she had a "good ear" and a visual imagination, qualities that enabled her to hear and observe things and people during those three years that she would use in her fiction throughout her life.

A number of the photographs she took while on her WPA assignment were displayed for a month in the Lugene Gallery in New York, a small camera shop. Later, some of them appeared in her published collection of photographs *One Time, One Place*. Only after several years of discouraging rejection slips did Welty finally publish a story, "Death of a Traveling Salesman," in a small magazine called *Manuscript* in 1936. Soon after that, her talent was discovered by Robert Penn Warren, Albert Erskine, and Cleanth Brooks. Then, John Woodburn of Doubleday, Doran, and Company became interested in her work, and with his support, her first collection of short stories, *A Curtain of Green and Other Stories*, was published in 1941. The next year, her first novel, *The Robber Bridegroom*, appeared. Two of her books have been success-fully adapted for the stage, *The Ponder Heart* as a New York stage play in 1956 and *The Robber Bridegroom* as a Broadway musical in 1974.

Humane, thoughtful, and generous, Welty modestly accepted the many honors that came to her. Scarcely a year would pass after 1940 in which she would not received a major award of some kind. She also gave abundantly of her time to schoolchildren, scholars, interviewers, and aspiring writers. She was active in community causes in Jackson, gave scores of lectures and readings, assisted numerous charities, and even provided recipes for cookbooks.

Welty asserted in a famous article, "Place in Fiction" in *The South Atlantic Quarterly* (1956), that a deep sense of place is vital to a writer's development. She herself spent her entire adult life in the neo-Tudor house her father built in 1926 across the street from the campus of Belhaven College in Jackson. In fact, as a young woman she would listen, through the open window of her bedroom, to the melodious sounds emanating from the music building on the Belhaven campus. Music, as well as the visual arts, became an important motif in her fiction. Welty said that aspects of two women characters in her fiction most greatly illustrate qualities of her own life—the high regard for art held by Miss Eckhart, the piano teacher in "June Recital" (in *Golden Apples*), and the great concern of Laurel McKelva Hand (*The Optimist's Daughter*) with her family's past. However, Laurel, unlike Miss Eckhart, is able to deal with her conflicts and achieves "a separate peace."

During the years of severe unrest over civil rights issues, Welty's critics attacked her for not actively taking up that cause in her fiction. She answered those critics eloquently in a 1965 *Atlantic Monthly* essay entitled "Must the Novelist Crusade?" However, in *The New Yorker* the next year, Welty published a short story, "Where Is the Voice Coming From?," attacking the ugly racism of the South that resulted in the murder of a black civil rights leader.

In her introduction to *The Collected Stories of Eudora Welty*, Welty expresses charac-teristic gratitude for the help and encouragement she received during her career. In her memoir she speaks of her good fortune in being reared in a family that encouraged the reading of books. She had a particular love for myths, fairy tales, and legends, and she believed it her good fortune to have grown up in a region where, as she said, people love talking and delight in a good yarn. Even though she was teased as a child for having a "Yankee" father, her work is deeply rooted, like its creator, in the South as a place. Still, neither she nor her fiction could be called "regional" in any narrow sense of the term. In fact, she balked at the regionalist title. Her work, for all its down-home southern flavor, attests the universality of her vision and the capacity of her art to elude easy labels. Her subject is not the South, but humanity.

Analysis · Paramount in Eudora Welty's work is the sense of what "community," or group membership, means in the South and how it is expressed through manners, attitudes, and dialogue. Clearly, it provides a special way of seeing and responding. In Welty's published essays and interviews, certain concerns keep surfacing–the relationship between time and place and the artistic endeavor; the importance of human relationships in a work of fiction; the necessity for the artist to be grounded in real life and yet be aware of life's "mystery"; the value of the imagination; and the function of memory. These concerns find expression in her work principally in the tension between what is actual, what is seen and heard in a specific time and place, and what is felt or known intuitively. Welty uses the sometimes conflicting demands of the community and the self, the surface life and the interior life, to describe this tension in her novels. On the one hand is the need for community and order; on the other is the need for the separate individual life which often works against community and order.

Typically, a Welty novel swings between overt action, including dialogue, and individual contemplation. This is especially evident in *Delta Wedding*, where Welty almost rhythmically alternates dialogue and action with the inner musings of her principal female characters. In *The Optimist's Daughter*, only Laurel Hand's thoughts are set against the exterior action, but it becomes apparent that her father, as he lies unmoving on his hospital bed, is silently contemplating the mystery of life and human relationships for perhaps the first time in his life. Her mother, too, near the end of her life, had begun speaking out the painful things she must have harbored for many years in her dark soul. Even Edna Earle Ponder in *The Ponder Heart* seems to talk incessantly to keep the inner life from raising itself into consciousness. In *Losing Battles*, where Welty says she consciously tried to tell everything through speech and action–she had been accused of obscurantism in previous works–the pattern still emerges. Instead of swinging between action and cerebration, however, this novel swings between action and description. Still, the effect is surprisingly similar, though the pages of action and dialogue far outnumber the pages of description, and the transitions between the two modes of narration are very abrupt. Even so, the young schoolteacher who chooses love and marriage against her mentor's advice slips occasionally into Welty's meditative mode. The alternation of thought and action is also the basic structural pattern of the stories in *The Golden Apples*.

Thus, in Welty's novels, external order is established through speech and action that sustain community, either the social or family group. In fact, the novels are often structured around community rituals that reinforce the group entity against outside intrusions and shore up its defenses against its most insidious foe, the impulse to separateness in its individual members. *Delta Wedding* is set entirely in the framework of one of these community-perpetuating rituals. For the moment, the wedding is everything, and members of the group pay it homage by gathering, giving gifts, feasting, and burying their individual lives in its demands. *Losing Battles* is also framed by a community ritual, the family reunion. The threat from individual outsiders is felt constantly, and the family takes sometimes extreme measures to ward off influences that might undermine its solidarity. There are at least two rituals that provide structure for *The Ponder Heart*, the funeral and the courtroom trial. The first of these is conducted in enemy territory, outside the acceptable group domain; the second is conducted in home territory, and acquittal for the accused member of the group is a foregone conclusion. A funeral is also the major external event of *The Optimist's Daughter* and becomes the battleground in a contest for supremacy between two opposing groups or communities. Several of the stories or chapters in *The Golden Apples* are also structured around community rituals, including the June piano recital, the girls' summer camp, and the funeral.

In addition to these large, highly structured observances, there are the multitude of unwritten laws that govern the group. Welty's community members attach great importance to certain objects and practices: a treasured lamp given to the bride, a hand-crafted breadboard made for a mother-in-law, the establishment of family pedigrees, the selection of one male member of the community for special reverence and heroic expectation, the protection of the past from intrusion or reassessment, and, perhaps most important of all, the telling of stories as an attestation of the vitality and endurance of the group.

Underlying all of this attention to ritual and group expectation, however, is the unspoken acknowledgment that much of it is a game the participants have agreed to play, for their own sake and for the sake of the community. Some of the participants may be fooled, but many are not. Aware but fearful, they go through the motions of fulfilling community requirements in an effort to hold back the dark, to avoid facing the mystery, to keep their individual selves from emerging and crying for existence. They sense themselves to be at what Welty calls "the jumping off place," and are afraid to make the leap in the dark. They agree to pretend to be fooled. They tell stories instead of rehearsing their fears and uncertainties. The bolder ones defy the group and either leave it or live on its periphery. In every book, there are moments when a character confronts or consciously evades the dark underside of human personality and experience, and memory becomes a device for dealing with the effects of that confrontation or for evading it.

Paradoxically, storytelling, an important ritual for securing the past and bolstering community against passion, disorder, the intimations of mystery, and the erosive effects of individual impulses and yearnings, assists in the breakdown of the very group it was intended to support. The risk of indulging in rituals is that they sometimes set people to thinking and reevaluating their own individual lives and the lives of others close to them. The ritual is performed by the group, but it may stir the solitary inner being to life and to the kind of probing contemplation that jeopardizes the group's authority. Such a countereffect may be triggered by the storytelling ritual even though that ritual is meant to seal up the past for ready reference whenever the group needs reinforcement. Because storytelling relies on memory, it can become an exercise of the individual imagination. It tends to lapse, as one commentator observes, "into the memory of a memory" and thus shifts sides from the group's activities into the realm of mystery. The community's habit of setting up straw men for heroes can similarly erode community solidarity because it too relies upon imagination and memory. It glorifies the individual rather than the group spirit.

As Welty presents this conflict, then, between the self and the group, and between the intuitive and the actual, she writes into her work a sense of foreboding. The community, especially the traditional southern community, is doomed. It cannot forever maintain itself on the old terms, for it is dependent upon the acquiescence of separate individuals who seem increasingly impervious to the efforts of the group to contain them. Welty's work also suggests that some of the things the community prizes and perpetuates are merely gestures and artifacts with little intrinsic value or meaning.

When the meanings behind what a community treasures have been lost or forgotten, that community cannot long endure. In actively laboring to exclude others, the group works against its own best nature, its capacity for loving and caring. Threats to order and community may indeed come from the outside, but Welty insists that the more serious threats come from the inside, from that part of the human heart and mind that seeks to go its own way.

The Robber Bridegroom · Welty's first novel, *The Robber Bridegroom*, is quite unlike her others. Its most noticeable differences are its setting in a much older South, on the old Natchez Trace in the days of bandits and Native Americans, and its fairy-tale style and manner. Even with these differences, Welty establishes what becomes her basic fictional stance. She achieves tension between the actual and the imaginary by freighting this very real setting with fabulous characters and events. The legendary characters are transformed by Welty's imagination and deftly made to share the territory with figures from the Brothers Grimm. Welty indicated the double nature of her novel, or novella, when in an address to the Mississippi Historical Society she called it a "Fairy Tale of the Natchez Trace." A favorite of William Faulkner, the book is a masterpiece, a delightful blend of legend, myth, folklore, and fairy tale that swings from rollicking surface comedy and lyrical style to painful, soul-searching explorations of the ambiguities of human experience. Although it deals with love and separateness—Robert Penn Warren's terms for the conflicting needs of communities and individuals in Welty's work—it does not deal with them in the same way that the later novels do. Clement Musgrove, a planter whose innocence leads him into marriage with the greedy Salome and an excursion into humanity's heart of darkness, learns what it is like to face the cold, dark nights of despair comfortless and alone. His daughter, Rosamond, is beautiful and loving, but she is also an inveterate liar who betrays her husband's trust in order to learn his "real" identity. Jamie Lockhart, who leads a double life as both bandit and gentleman, keeps his true identity hidden even from her whom he loves. Thus, like so many Welty characters, the principal actors in *The Robber Bridegroom* have interior lives that threaten the equilibrium of their exterior worlds.

In another sense, too, *The Robber Bridegroom* is closely linked with Welty's other novels. In writing the book, Welty testifies to the value of stories and the storytelling ritual that buttresses community, a theme that reappears in all her novels. She finds common ground with her readers in this novel by spinning a yarn full of their favorite childhood fairy tales. Then, too, fairy-tale worlds, imaginative though they are, sustain surface order, for they are worlds of sure answers, of clear good and evil, of one-dimensional characters, and of predictable rewards and punishments. As such, they confirm what the community collectively believes and perpetuates. Just as imagination, intuition, and the ponderings of the individual human soul jeopardize the codes a community lives by in other Welty novels, so do they undercut the basic assumptions of the fairy tale in this novel. Here, answers are sometimes permanently withheld, people are complex and unpredictable, the richest prize is found in human relationships rather than in kingdoms and gold, appearances are deceiving, and evil may lie in unexpected places. It is worthy of note that Welty began her novel-writing career with a book that delights in the fairy tale at the same time that it questions community assumptions about fairy-tale morality.

Delta Wedding · The tension between community expectations and individual yearnings and apprehensions is central to *Delta Wedding*. The narrative takes place in the

Mississippi delta country, during the week of Dabney Fairchild's wedding. The Fairchild family, after whom the nearby town is named, is of the social elite and has moderate wealth, mostly in property. The wedding provides an occasion for the family to gather and exercise the rituals and traditions that bind them together and strengthen their sense of community. The wedding itself is the principal ritual, of course, with its attendant food preparation, dressmaking, rehearsal, and home and yard decorating. Welty's eye for manners and ear for speech are flawless as the Fairchilds deliberate over the consequences of George Fairchild's having married beneath him and Dabney's seemingly unfortunate repetition of her father's mistake. The Fairchilds still claim George, however, even though they have little use for his wife, Robbie Reid, and they will continue to embrace Dabney in spite of her choosing to marry an outsider, Troy Flavin. It is the habit of community to maintain order by defining and placing people and things in relation to itself. A person either does or does not have legitimate ties to the group.

The Fairchilds also repeat family stories in order to keep the past secure and give stability to the present. Their current favorite story is also one that makes a hero out of the male heir-apparent. George's dead brother was apparently more remarkable than he, but George is the one survivor, and the family's hopes rest with him. At least a dozen times in the book, some version is told of George's staying on the railroad track with his mentally retarded niece whose foot was caught in the rails. Instead of leaping to safety with the others, he stayed to face the oncoming train. Luckily, the engineer of the Yellow Dog was able to stop the train in time. By choosing to stay with Maureen instead of answering his wife's plea to save himself, George made a reflexive choice for honor and blood over marital obligation. Later, he again chooses family over wife when he comes for the prewedding activities instead of looking for his absent, heartbroken wife.

Running counter to the speech and actions that affirm order and community, however, is an undercurrent of threat to that order. Welty intersperses the overt actions and attitudes of the family, especially of the aunts, whose sole desire is to perpetuate the clan structure, with individual ruminations of other female characters who are part of that structure and yet somewhat peripheral to it. Ellen, who married into the Fairchilds and has never dared resist them, has moments of personal doubt that would be regarded as treasonous were they known by her aunts. Dabney also wonders, in a brief honest moment, about the homage paid to the wedding ritual for its own sake. Further, she accidentally breaks a treasured lamp, a family heirloom given her by the aunts as a wedding present. Little Laura, having lost her mother, has also lost her basic tie to the family. From her position on the edge of the Fairchild clan, she questions the community tenets that exclude her. Even George seems ready to violate community expectations by his apparent willingness to deprive two of the aunts of their home.

The novel's essential statement, then, is that the community is losing its hold. In an interview published in 1972 by The Southern Review, Welty is asked the question: "Is Shellmound [the home of the Fairchilds] with its way of life and its values doomed?" She replies, "Oh, yes. I think that was implicit in the novel: that this was all such a fragile, temporary thing. At least I hope it was." She adds, "Well, you're living in a very precarious world without knowing it, always." The community's position is inexorably altered in the face of individual yearning and independent action.

The Ponder Heart · There are two large community rituals in *The Ponder Heart*: the funeral of Bonnie Dee Peacock and the trial of Uncle Daniel Ponder for her murder.

Such narrative matter sounds ominous enough to one unfamiliar with Welty's capacity for comedy, but to the initiated, it promises a hilarious display of southern talk and manners. Still, *The Ponder Heart* is troubled, as Welty's other novels are, by an ominous current running beneath its surface action. Like the Fairchilds of *Delta Wedding*, the Ponders have social position and wealth—perhaps greater than that of the Fairchilds. They are on the decline, however, in spite of the efforts of Edna Earle Ponder, Welty's first-person narrator, to maintain the family and its image. Symbolic of the failing family or community image that Edna Earle seeks to perpetuate and protect are two buildings which the family owns, the Beulah Hotel, run by Edna Earle, and the Ponder home a few miles out of town. In the end, both buildings are virtually empty. The family has shrunk to two members, and the future holds no promise.

The storyline tells of middle-aged Uncle Daniel's taking to wife young Bonnie Dee Peacock, losing her, regaining her, losing her again, reclaiming her, and then finally losing her by tickling her to death in the aftermath of an electric storm. Uncle Daniel's mental age is considerably lower than his chronological age, but he is blessed with a generous nature. He gives away everything he can get his hands on, and has to be watched continually. Not that Edna Earle cares to restrain him very much, for he is the revered scion, like George in *Delta Wedding*, without whose approbation and presence the community would totter. Her duty is to protect and sustain Daniel, and she will not even permit herself private doubts over what that duty requires. The entire novel is the report of her conversation about Uncle Daniel with a visitor who is stranded at the Beulah. Clearly, Edna Earle's talk and actions are designed to maintain order and community as she has known them all her life. She believes that if she relaxes her vigil, the structure will collapse.

The ritual of the Peacock funeral is important because it is grossly inferior to the Ponder notion of what constitutes a funeral. The Peacocks are what the Ponders (except Daniel, who in his innocence would not know the difference) would call "country"; in other words, they are regarded as comically inferior beings who have no business marrying into the Ponder family. The trial is more to Edna Earle's liking, though it is threatened by the presence of the low-bred Peacocks and a prosecuting shyster lawyer who is an outsider. Edna Earle gets caught in a lie designed to protect Daniel, but the day is saved when Daniel begins passing out greenbacks in the courtroom. The jury votes for acquittal in record time, and Daniel cheerily dispenses the whole family fortune. He discovers to his sorrow afterward, however, that people who have taken his money can no longer face him. Thus, in the end, Daniel, who wanted nothing more than company and an audience for his stories, is left lonely and friendless. Though Edna Earle tries to inject new hope through the promise of a new audience—her captive guest at the Beulah—doom is on the horizon for the Ponders even more surely than it was for the Fairchilds. The collapse of community structure in this novel, as in *Delta Wedding*, can be laid partly to the failure of the community's rather artificial system of supports—rituals, traditions, family stories, pedigrees, and a family "hero." It must also be laid, however, to the fact that Uncle Daniel, in his innocence, breaks away and acts as an individual. He is not capable of the contemplation that undermines community in *Delta Wedding*, but neither can he be restrained to act as a member of the group instead of as himself.

Losing Battles · In *Losing Battles*, Welty partially turns the tables on what she had done with the conflict between community and self in her previous two novels and in *The Golden Apples*. Here, she shows that community, though mildly ruffled by individual needs and doubts, can prevail when it is sustained by strong individuals who are also loyal group members. Welty indicates in a *Southern Review* interview that she deliberately chose as her setting the poorest section of Mississippi during the time of the Depression, so that her characters would be shown on a bare stage with themselves as their only resource, without "props to their lives." Thus, the artificial structures built of money and status that support community in *Delta Wedding* and *The Ponder Heart* are not available to the Vaughn-Beecham-Renfro clan in *Losing Battles.* Perhaps that is one reason for their greater durability.

The story is told almost entirely through dialogue and action, interlaced with occasional lyrical descriptions of setting and even less frequent ruminations of the story's principal outsider, Gloria Renfro, the hero's wife. The action takes place entirely in one day and the following morning, with details of the past filled in through family storytelling. Jack Renfro, the young grandson who has been exalted by family hope and expectations, bears some resemblance to George Fairchild and Daniel Ponder. On him lies the chief burden of sustaining the family, of guaranteeing its survival as a unit. He returns home from the state penitentiary to the waiting family reunion that is celebrating old Granny Vaughn's birthday. He finds there not only his bride, but a baby daughter he has never seen. The family has believed, has had to believe, that things will be better once Jack has returned home. Jack himself believes it and, as Welty indicates, the others take their faith from his. Through a series of wild, funny episodes–and more than a few tender moments–the family prevails. Welty says that in this comic novel she intended to portray the indomitability, the unquenchable spirit of human beings. Folks such as these may be losing the battles, but they are still fighting them, and that is what counts.

Welty describes "the solidity of the family" as "the strongest thing in the book." She also recognizes that, in a clan such as this, a character sometimes has to be himself before he can reinforce the unity of the group. Welty says that such a "sticking together" as is seen in *Losing Battles* "involves both a submerging and a triumph of the individual, because you can't really conceive of the whole unless you *are* an identity." The extended family of *Losing Battles* engages in rituals to maintain itself just as the Fairchild family does in *Delta Wedding.* It acknowledges milestones reached by its members, milestones such as weddings and ninetieth birthdays; it tells stories; it creates a hero; and it works painstakingly to establish and affirm blood relationships with any who might seek entrance into the group. All is done with the honor of the clan–or the individual as member of the clan–in mind, whether it is going to jail or rescuing a car from a cliff on Banner Top.

In spite of the prevailing unity and the optimistic conclusion to the novel's events, there are small rumblings of individual assertion against community. Gloria loves Jack, but she does not want to be a member of his family. She envisions a smaller community, made up of just her, Jack, and their baby, Lady May. The group, however, will not allow her to build a community of her own. Against her will, it tries to reconstruct a parentage for her that would make her a blood relation. The relatives perform a rather cruel ritual of pouncing on her and forcing her to eat watermelon, but she remains adamant. She also remains steadfast in her admiration for Miss Julia Mortimer, the schoolteacher who picked Gloria as her successor and who fought a losing battle all her life against the joyful ignorance of the likes of Jack's family.

Thus, there are several influences in the book that threaten, though not seriously, the sense of community. Gloria and her child, and Miss Julia, are the most obvious ones. It becomes apparent, though, in the very style of the narration, which repeatedly turns from family action and talk to brief imaginative description, that the ordering of the actual and the real according to community necessity does not entirely carry the day. There is another side to experience, the imaginative, the intuitive–a part of the individual soul that resists allegiance.

The Optimist's Daughter · In *The Optimist's Daughter*, Welty returns to a more balanced combination of action and contemplation. The book's perceiving eye is Laurel Hand, daughter of Becky and Judge McKelva. The abiding question for Laurel is why, after the death of the intelligent, sensitive Becky, the Judge took for a wife a crass, tasteless woman half his age. Laurel helplessly watches her father's still form as he silently reviews his life in a hospital room, ironically set against the backdrop of the Mardi Gras festival. She repeats her helpless watch as he lies in his coffin at Mount Salus while his wife, Wanda Fay Chisom, performs her gnashing, wailing ritual of bereavement and his old friends perform their ritual of eulogy. The Chisom family, who nod appreciatively as Fay grossly mourns, are the same breed as the Peacocks in *The Ponder Heart*, entirely out of context in the McKelva home. Laurel, however, is equally uncomfortable with her own group's rites of community preservation–telling stories about the Judge that make a hero of him, despising the intrusive outsider, urging Laurel to stay and bolster the old relationship. Laurel's husband Phil was killed in military service many years ago and Laurel herself is working in Chicago, but the women who were bridesmaids at her wedding have kept that group intact and still refer to themselves as "the bridesmaids."

Laurel's last night at home is spent in anguish. Trapped by an invading chimney swift in rooms full of memories, she is caught hopelessly in the past. In the course of the night, she is forced to examine the protective structure she had built around her parents' marriage and her own. In doing so, she must allow memory and imagination to reinterpret the past which she had wanted to keep sealed away in the perfection of her own making, and she must relinquish her old idea of what constitutes group unity and loyalty. The Wanda Fays of the world will always claim their space, will always intrude. The secret for surviving their intrusion, Laurel discovers, is to withdraw one's protective walls so that the Fays have nothing to knock down. Laurel at last allows truth to dismantle the edifice of community as she had conceived it, and she finds, through the imagination and the heart, a new source of strength in watching the artificial construct tumble. Thus, the foreboding and pessimism arising from the impending doom of community in *Delta Wedding* and *The Ponder Heart*, diverted for a time in the paradoxical optimism of *Losing Battles*, are to some extent reversed in Laurel's final acceptance in *The Optimist's Daughter*. *The Golden Apples* had foretold such an outcome, for a number of its characters must also deal with the relationship between their individual lives and the group life.

The miracle of Welty's work is the skill with which her imagination bears on the actual and makes a reconciliation out of the conflicting demands of the community and the private life, out of that which can be perceived by the senses and that which can be known only intuitively. For Welty, the actual is mainly the realities of Mississippi life. In her work, however, the reality of Mississippi becomes a springboard rich with possibilities for an imagination that knows how to use time and place as doorways to the human heart.

Marilyn Arnold, updated by Philip A. Tapley

Other major works

SHORT FICTION: *A Curtain of Green and Other Stories*, 1941; *The Wide Net and Other Stories*, 1943; *The Golden Apples*, 1949; *Short Stories*, 1950; *Selected Stories of Eudora Welty*, 1954; *The Bride of the Innisfallen, and Other Stories*, 1955; *The Collected Stories of Eudora Welty*, 1980; *Moon Lake and Other Stories*, 1980; *Retreat*, 1981.

NONFICTION: *Music from Spain*, 1948; *The Reading and Writing of Short Stories*, 1949; *Place in Fiction*, 1957; *Three Papers on Fiction*, 1962; *One Time, One Place: Mississippi in the Depression, a Snapshot Album*, 1971; *A Pageant of Birds*, 1974; *The Eye of the Story: Selected Essays and Reviews*, 1978; *Ida M'Toy*, 1979; *Miracles of Perception: The Art of Willa Cather*, 1980 (with Alfred Knopf and Yehudi Menuhin); *One Writer's Beginnings*, 1984; *Eudora Welty: Photographs*, 1989; *A Writer's Eye: Collected Book Reviews*, 1994 (Pearl Amelia McHaney, editor).

CHILDREN'S LITERATURE: *The Shoe Bird*, 1964.

Bibliography

Devlin, Albert J. *Eudora Welty's Chronicle: A Story of Mississippi Life.* Jackson: University Press of Mississippi, 1983. Devlin analyzes certain works, such as *Delta Wedding*, in great detail. He offers insightful criticism and suggests that Welty's writing contains a historical structure, spanning from the territorial era to modern times.

Evans, Elizabeth. *Eudora Welty.* New York: Frederick Ungar, 1981. Presents a reliable but not comprehensive overview of Welty's life and work.

Manning, Carol S. *With Ears Opening Like Morning Glories: Eudora Welty and the Love of Storytelling.* Westport, Conn.: Greenwood Press, 1985. An advanced book offering a critical interpretation of Welty's writing. Manning believes that the root of Welty's creativity is the southern love of storytelling. Offers a select bibliography.

Mortimer, Gail L. *Daughter of the Swan: Love and Knowledge in Eudora Welty's Fiction.* Athens: University of Georgia Press, 1994. Concentrates primarily on the short stories and discusses one novel, *The Optimist's Daughter*, in detail.

Vande Kieft, Ruth M. *Eudora Welty.* Rev. ed. Boston: Twayne, 1987. Vande Kieft offers an excellent critical analysis of Welty's major works, an overview of Welty's career, and an annotated secondary bibliography. A well written, useful study for all students.

Waldron, Ann. *Eudora: A Writer's Life.* New York: Doubleday, 1998. The first complete but unauthorized biography of Welty. Offers a balanced study of her life as well as sensitive and sensible analyses of her short stories and novels.

Westling, Louise Hutchings. *Sacred Groves and Ravaged Gardens: The Fiction of Eudora Welty, Carson McCullers, and Flannery O'Connor.* Athens: University of Georgia Press, 1985. Westling examines the lives and works of Welty and the other authors in terms of their common concerns as women, such as their relationships with men and with their mothers. Offers a provocative and original viewpoint.

Weston, Ruth D. *Gothic Traditions and Narrative Techniques in the Fiction of Eudora Welty.* Baton Rouge: Louisiana State University Press, 1994. Examines Welty's fiction, especially the novels *Losing Battles* and *Delta Wedding*, in terms of their relation to "myth, . . . 'mystery and magic,'" inspired by Welty's acquaintance with the literary gothic tradition.

NATHANAEL WEST

Nathan Weinstein

Born: New York, New York; October 17, 1903
Died: El Centro, California; December 22, 1940

Principal long fiction · *The Dream Life of Balso Snell,* 1931; *Miss Lonelyhearts,* 1933; *A Cool Million: The Dismantling of Lemuel Pitkin,* 1934; *The Day of the Locust,* 1939.

Other literary forms · Nathanael West often used the short-story form for preliminary sketches of characters and themes that later appeared in his novels. Between 1930 and 1933 especially, he wrote stories with a broader focus and in a more sophisticated style than his first work, *The Dream Life of Balso Snell.* The stories include "The Adventurer," "Mr. Potts of Pottstown," "Tibetan Night," and "The Sun, the Lady, and the Gas Station," all unpublished. After the publication of *Miss Lonelyhearts* in 1933, West also worked as a scriptwriter in Hollywood for several years.

Achievements · Since West's death in a automobile accident in 1940, his work has steadily gained critical attention. His characters' hysterical pitch of loneliness, their frustration, and their inability to find a source of relief have gradually interested a wide audience, especially since World War II. Stripped of their professional masks, the people in West's novels reveal a talent for cruelty. They tease, exploit, or murder to ensure their own survival in a world reminiscent of T. S. Eliot's *The Waste Land* (1922), but their world is without Eliot's hint of redemption or spirituality. In *Miss Lonelyhearts,* the world is dead; in *The Day of the Locust,* it is corrupt and jaded, a modern Sodom which West symbolically destroys. This last novel was made into a film in the 1970's; although it never became a box-office hit, West would have approved of its powerful treatment of dreamers and misfits.

Biography · Nathanael West was born Nathan Weinstein in New York City on October 17, 1903. His father's and mother's families had known one another before they emigrated to the United States from Russia. His father's side used construction skills learned in the old world to become successful contractors in the new country, taking advantage of the building boom of the turn of the century. His mother's side was well educated, and Anna Wallenstein Weinstein wanted her son Nathan and her two daughters to have all the perquisites of an upwardly mobile, middle-class life. Soon after settling in New York City, the Weinsteins learned to enjoy their comforts and to value them highly. They also assumed that their son would receive the finest possible education, pursue a professional career, or at least join the family business. West was an avid reader but a much less ambitious student. He attended a variety of grammer schools before his parents placed him in DeWitt Clinton High School. West, however, preferred exploring Central Park during the day and the theater district in the evenings. He was particularly attracted to the vaudeville shows, his first exposure to techniques such as slapstick and stereotypes which he later used in his fiction.

West was not very disciplined, but his clever and adventurous nature helped to get

New Directions

him into Tufts University without a high school diploma. After one unsuccessful year there, he attended Brown University. West's biographer attributes Brown's acceptance of West to a complicated mismatching of transcripts with another student whose name was also Weinstein, though whether this was planned or accidental is not absolutely certain. Whatever the case, West was graduated from Brown in 1924 with a degree in philosophy, which he earned in only two and a half years.

Neither West nor his parents had much nostalgia for their Jewish Lithuanian roots; instead, they concentrated on rapid assimilation. In 1926, he legally changed his name to Nathanael West. Even so, the subject of roots still appears in most of his work. The degree of corruption in Lemuel Pitkin's hometown in *A Cool Million* is nothing compared to what he finds elsewhere in the country. The protagonist in *Miss Lonelyhearts* suffers from acute isolation despite his efforts to communicate, and this seems to stem from his earliest memories of childhood; he is estranged from his Baptist upbringing and has only a single comforting memory of his youth. Tod Hackett in *The Day of the Locust* leaves the East Coast, where he was an undergraduate at the Yale School of Fine Arts, for Hollywood. He observes other new arrivals and decides that they have come to California to die in one way or another. Although he does not include himself in this category, it is clear that he too succumbs to the superficial glitter and wastefulness.

West convinced his parents to send him to Paris in 1926. He enjoyed the artistic and literary circles there, but signs of the coming Depression were being felt in the construction industry and West had to return to New York after three months. Relatives managed to find him a job as a night manager of a midtown hotel, providing

West with an income, a place to write, and a steady flow of guests to watch. West found these people fascinating, and so it is not surprising that seedy hotels and their transient occupants find their way into *The Day of the Locust.* Working as a night manager also gave West time to revise *The Dream Life of Balso Snell,* which he had begun while in college. William Carlos Williams liked the manuscript and recommended that Moss and Kamin publish it; five hundred copies were printed in 1931.

S. J. Perelman, also a student at Brown, married West's sister Laura. Through Perelman, who worked at *The New Yorker,* West met other writers and artists. It was also through his brother-in-law that West conceived of the controlling idea for *Miss Lonelyhearts.* Perelman knew a writer named Susan Chester who gave advice to readers of *The Brooklyn Eagle.* The three of them met one evening in 1939, and she read samples of the letters. West was moved by them and eventually used an advice-to-the-lovelorn column and a tormented newspaper columnist for what is probably his most famous novel. *Miss Lonelyhearts* was published by Liveright in 1933.

West soon went to Southern California to work on film scripts. His experience with the less glamorous aspects of Hollywood and the film industry, with the masses of aspiring actors and actresses, with people who had little talent to begin with, but compensated for that with their dreams, helped provide the themes, landscapes, and characters of West's final novel, *The Day of the Locust.* In 1940, West married Eileen McKenney, the sister of Ruth McKenney, who worked with Perelman at *The New Yorker.* West's careless driving was known to all his friends, and a few months after his marriage, he and his wife were killed in an automobile crash.

Analysis · Although all of Nathanael West's fiction is concerned with certain recurring themes, it gradually matures in tone, style, and subject. *The Dream Life of Balso Snell,* his first novel, has a clever but sarcastic and ugly adolescent tone. *The Day of the Locust,* his last novel, is also satirical and sarcastic, but its greater maturity and empathetic tone make it both disturbing and profoundly moving.

West's Miss Lonelyhearts dreams that he is a magician who does tricks with doorknobs: He is able to make them speak, bleed, and flower. In a sense, this conceit explains all of West's work. His protagonists travel across dead landscapes which they try to revivify. In *The Dream Life of Balso Snell,* the landscape is mechanical, wooden, purely farcical; in *A Cool Million,* West shows one American town after another, all equally corrupt. *Miss Lonelyhearts* is set in the dirt and concrete of New York City, and *The Day of the Locust* is set in the sordid but irresistible Southern California landscape. West's typical protagonist is a quester, intent on bringing life wherever he travels; Miss Lonelyhearts especially is obsessed with the challenges of a savior. The task of making a dead world bloom, however, seems hopeless. Life may surface in a moment of communication or lovemaking, but something is likely to go awry, as the moment reverses itself into an unnatural distortion. For example, as Miss Lonelyhearts tries to comfort an old man he meets in Central Park, he suddenly has the urge to crush and destroy him. Shrike, his employer at the newspaper office, compares making love to his wife with sleeping with a knife in his groin. This dichotomy is at the heart of West's vision. Characters driven by benevolent ambitions are thwarted—by themselves, by those in need of their help, by cosmic and divine indifference—until they become grotesque parodies of their original selves. Innocence and success can be recalled only through dreams. At best, the world is passively dead; at worst, it is aggressively violent.

The Dream Life of Balso Snell · The quester of *The Dream Life of Balso Snell* does not take himself seriously, and the novel itself seems to be an extended literary joke. Balso Snell describes a dream in which he encounters the famous wooden horse of the Greeks in ancient Troy. A brash and distinctly modern tour guide leads him through the interiors of the horse, which quickly become the subject of numerous adolescent witticisms. The inside of the horse expands to a landscape that Balso explores for the rest of his dream. West's purpose is humor and parody, which he accomplishes mercilessly although unpleasantly, beginning even with the title of this first book. Following his "path," Balso meets a Catholic mystic, and West has the opportunity to mock the literary lives of saints. Then Balso meets a schoolboy who has just hidden his journal in the trunk of a nearby tree. Balso reads its entries, which serve as a parody of the nineteenth century Russian novel. Balso then meets the boy's teacher, Miss McGeeny, who has been busily writing a biography of a biographer's biographer; West parodies another literary genre.

The Dream Life of Balso Snell is not a significant work of fiction, but it is useful for readers to appreciate how quickly West's style and perspective deepened. His later novels have the same piercing quality, and West never lost his tendency to satirize, but the later novels are finely and precisely directed. West's later fiction also has the same motifs—quester, mechanical or obsessive journeys, dreams, and suffering humanity—but West examines them much more seriously in the later novels.

Miss Lonelyhearts · West is in superb control of his material in *Miss Lonelyhearts*, published only two years after *The Dream Life of Balso Snell*. The vituperative tone of the earlier work is balanced by greater development of plot and diversity of character. Following his preference for fast action and exaggeration, West uses comic-strip stereotypes: the meek husband and the bullying wife, Mr. and Mrs. Doyle; the bullish employer, Shrike, and his castrating wife Mary; and Miss Lonelyhearts's innocent but dumb girl friend Betty. Miss Lonelyhearts himself is only somewhat more developed, primarily because he is in almost every episode and because the third-person voice sardonically presents his private thoughts.

As in *The Dream Life of Balso Snell*, a central quester travels a barren landscape. Between the newspaper office and the local speakeasy is Central Park. As Miss Lonelyhearts walks across it, he realizes that there should be signs of spring but, in fact, there are none to be seen. Then he recalls that last year, new life seemed wrenched from the soil only in July. Miss Lonelyhearts's job as a newspaper columnist thrusts him into the position of a quester, and he makes a highly unlikely candidate. Simultaneously attracted to and repelled by his mission to assuage the grief of his readers, he makes attempts to get close to some of them, such as Mr. and Mrs. Doyle, but he then suddenly feels a need to keep separate from them. This dichotomy keeps him reeling like a puppet from one person's apartment to another, building a pressure that is released only when Miss Lonelyhearts has a final breakdown.

In each new location, the newspaperman tries to make a meaningful connection with another human being. Strict chronology becomes vague as the protagonist's state of mind becomes increasingly disturbed. He reaches toward Betty when they are sitting on the couch in her apartment but suddenly has no interest in her. He does remain sexually interested in Mary Shrike, but she refuses his advances as long as they stay in her apartment, and in the restaurant she teases him sadistically. He telephones Mrs. Doyle, a letterwriter, saying he will advise her in person. He exploits her unhappiness to satisfy his own need but, not surprisingly, is disappointed in the results.

Rather than help others, the quester of this novel uses them as targets for venting his own anger. As he is increasingly frustrated in his task of bringing beauty and gentleness into the world, Miss Lonelyhearts takes to the isolation of his own room.

Here a second quest occurs that parodies the earlier quest. Rather than embark on further quests from one location to another in New York City, Miss Lonelyhearts hallucinates a journey; his bed serves as his mode of transportation. It appears to him a perfect world and a perfect journey, sanctioned by God, who finally communicates to him that he has chosen the right conclusion to his quest. Miss Lonelyhearts feels that he has become a rock, perfect in its design not because God has helped to create it, but because it is impenetrable to all but its own existence. It is ironic that the driven quester actually drives himself into a blissful delusion of isolation.

Reality intrudes. Mr. Doyle, incensed at being cuckolded, rushes up the stairs to the apartment. Miss Lonelyhearts rushes down the stairs, hoping to meet him and welcome what he assumes is Doyle's conversion. Instead, there is a scuffle and Doyle's gun fires. Only in dreams do doorknobs blossom and human beings turn into gentle and compassionate creatures—at least in West's novels. Miss Lonelyhearts dies, a victim of his own miscalculation.

A Cool Million: The Dismantling of Lemuel Pitkin · The protagonist of *A Cool Million: The Dismantling of Lemuel Pitkin*, is another miscalculating quester. Pitkin is an idealistic young man who leaves his hometown to seek his fortune. The fact that the immediate cause of his departure from Ottsville, Vermont, is the dishonest foreclosing of his mother's mortgage does not dampen his enthusiastic belief that his nation is the land of limitless possibilities. He has faith in himself and in those who insist they are using him for his own good.

Mr. Shagpole Whipple, ex-president of the United States and now director of the Rat River National Bank in Ottsville, becomes Lemuel's earliest supporter. He advises his young friend that America "is the land of opportunity," a land that "takes care of the honest and the industrious." Lemuel is inspired and sets out in what becomes a parody of the Horatio Alger myth. On the train to New York City, he enjoys a conversation with a Mr. Mape, who was left "a cool million" by his father. Lemuel is impressed, especially since, he explains, he must make his fortune starting with only the thirty dollars in his pocket. By the end of the trip, he has been divested of that thirty dollars. Lemuel is the fall guy for another scheme, so that he, and not the thief, is apprehended by the police, brought to trial, and declared guilty. Being sent to prison is only the first of a long series of misfortunes. Lemuel is always someone's dupe or prey, but he bounces back to try again, although he repeatedly gets nothing out of his adventures. In fact, the more he travels, the less he has. Lemuel loses his teeth, his scalp, his eye, part of a hand, one leg; each time there is someone close by who can benefit from his new loss. Lemuel is used by entrepreneurs and thieves of all varieties.

A Cool Million is fast-paced and episodic. Its characters are pure stereo-types—the ingenuous dupe, the patriot, the innocent young girl, the deceitful villain. Everyone and everything is satirized: midwesterners, Jews, southerners, capitalists, and socialists. *A Cool Million* shows how West was beginning to use his material for clearly defined purposes and to control his sharpedged humor and black comedy in order to make a point. This novel, however, remains a minor work in comparison to *Miss Lonelyhearts* and *The Day of the Locust*. In these works, pathos emerges from West's stereotypes and seems all the more powerful because of its sources. *A Cool Million* is clever and biting but not poignant or profound.

The Day of the Locust · West is at his best in *The Day of the Locust.* Tod Hackett, the central quester, comes to Hollywood from the East to learn set and costume designing. The people he gets to know are desperately in need of beauty, romance, and renewal, but, as in *Miss Lonelyhearts*, the harder they struggle to achieve these goals, the farther away they are. The story is about dreamers who have traveled to what they believe is the dream capital of America, which West portrays as the wasteland of America. In addition to Tod, there is Faye Greener, beautiful but exploitative, making up in vanity what she lacks in intelligence. Homer Simpson is a thickheaded but sincere middle-aged bachelor from the Midwest. He has run from his one attempt to break through his dull-witted loneliness because the memory of failure is too painful. Characters such as Faye and Homer are particularly successful; though they are stereotypes, they have something unpredictable about them. This quality usually manifests itself invol-untarily by a spasm or quirk. For example, Faye is obviously a second-rate actress, but Tod sees through her tawdry facade to a deep archetypal beauty. Faye is unaware of any such quality; even if she knew, she would not appreciate it, because it has almost nothing in common with the self she has created. Homer Simpson has difficulty controlling parts of his body. He does not fall asleep easily because waking up is so arduous. His hands seem disassociated from his psyche; he has to put them under cold running water to rouse them, after which his fingers seem to follow their own rhythms. Like Faye, he has a structural purity without means to express it. Like Miss Lonelyhearts, his emotions swell in intensity, causing pressure that eventually must find release.

Faye becomes Tod's obsession. If he is a quester, she is his grail, and a most difficult challenge. Tod can neither support her nor further her acting career. Instead, he becomes a voyeur, watching her tease Earle Shoop, the cowboy from Arizona, and Miguel, the Mexican. He settles for simply painting Faye in a mural he calls "The Burning of Los Angeles." Tod observes that people come to California to die, despite their ambitions, and the mural reflects their disappointments. In the mural, a mob chases Faye, who seems oblivious to imminent danger and maintains a calm, detached expression. Those who realize they have failed need to express their anger, and those who think they have succeeded exist in a state of happy but dangerous ignorance. As in all of West's fiction, the challenge is as impossible as turning doorknobs into flowers. As the dreamers recognize the gap between their desires and accomplish-ments, thwarted ambition leads to frustration, and frustration to violence. The power of *The Day of the Locust* derives from the last few chapters, which describe the mindless and destructive product of such frustrated dreams.

It is the evening of a motion-picture premiere; violet lights run across the sky, and crowds of fans are kept under control by police barricades. The premiere provides the opportunity for fans to see face-to-face the "stars," the ones who have made it. The tension is too great, however, and the control too tenuous. The crowd begins to charge toward the theater, and Tod is caught in the pressure. *The Day of the Locust* is a tight, "pressured" novel, but all gives way at the end. As the crowd surges, it builds up strength from the people whose lives are filled with boredom and mistakes. There is mass pandemonium. Homer, moving like a robot, mechanically and swiftly murders a child who has been teasing him. Tod, submerged in the crowd, is hurt, but steadies himself at the base of a rail. In agony, he begins to think about his mural, "The Burning of Los Angeles," until reality and his thoughts merge. He thinks of the burning city, of mobs of people running into the foreground with baseball bats, and he and his friends fleeing from the mob. He actually believes he is painting the flames when policemen grab him from the rail and lift him into a police car. When the siren begins, Tod is not sure whether he or the siren has been making the noise. In effect, he succumbs to the chaos around him.

The Day of the Locust is a bleak novel, reflecting West's belief that recognizing limitations is difficult for humanity, which prefers to think that all things are possible. West shows limitations to be everywhere: within the masses; within the questers trying to save them; within the arid landscape itself. As the limitations prove insurmountable, natural ambitions and desires for harmony are inverted. Love becomes pantomime and compassion a veil for selfish and sadistic purposes. West's characters and settings desperately need to be renewed, but the job of salvation is difficult, one that West's protagonists fail to achieve.

Miriam Fuchs

Other major works

SCREENPLAYS: *Follow Your Heart*, 1936 (with Lester Cole and Samuel Ornitz); *The President's Mystery*, 1936 (with Cole); *Ticket to Paradise*, 1936 (with Jack Natteford); *It Could Happen to You*, 1937 (with Ornitz); *Born to Be Wild*, 1938; *I Stole a Million*, 1939; *Five Came Back*, 1939 (with Jerry Cady and Dalton Trumbo); *Men Against the Sky*, 1940.

Bibliography

Bloom, Harold, ed. *Nathanael West.* New York: Chelsea House, 1986. This useful collection includes essays on all of West's work in what Bloom hopes is a representative selection. S. E. Hyman's essay is a valuable introduction to West. Contains a bibliography.

_____, ed. *Nathanael West's "Miss Lonelyhearts."* New York: Chelsea House, 1987. This valuable collection offers nine essays from a variety of viewpoints on *Miss Lonelyhearts*. Includes a chronology and a bibliography.

Martin, Jay, ed. *Nathanael West: A Collection of Critical Essays.* Englewood Cliffs, N.J.: Prentice-Hall, 1971. This collection contains some brief critical commentaries by West himself as well as analyses by others. Martin's introductory essay is a useful summary; some of the others presuppose a fairly sophisticated reader. Includes a selected bibliography.

Siegel, Ben, ed. *Critical Essays on Nathanael West.* New York: G. K. Hall, 1994. Divided into two sections—reviews and essays. In addition to the comprehensive introduction surveying West's life and career, the essay section provides studies of individual novels and of West's work as a whole. Notes and index but no bibliography.

Veitch, Jonathan. *American Superrealism: Nathanael West and the Politics of Representation in the 1930's.* Madison: University of Wisconsin Press, 1997. Contains separate chapters on each novel as well as an introduction discussing of the "crisis of representation in the 1930's." Includes very detailed notes but no bibliography.

Widmer, Kingsley. *Nathanael West.* Boston: Twayne, 1982. Widmer's general introduction concentrates on "West as the prophet of modern masquerading, role-playing, and its significance" while offering useful analyses of West's work. Lengthy notes and an annotated bibliography are provided.

Wisker, Alistair. *The Writing of Nathanael West.* New York: St. Martin's Press, 1990. Chapters on each novel and a series of appendices on various aspects of West's work, including his handling of violence, his unpublished fiction, and revisions of his work. Includes notes and bibliography.

EDITH WHARTON

Born: New York, New York; January 24, 1862
Died: St.-Brice-sous-Forêt, France; August 11, 1937

Principal long fiction · *The Touchstone,* 1900; *The Valley of Decision,* 1902; *Sanctuary,* 1903; *The House of Mirth,* 1905; *Madame de Treymes,* 1907; *The Fruit of the Tree,* 1907; *Ethan Frome,* 1911; *The Reef,* 1912; *The Custom of the Country,* 1913; *Summer,* 1917; *The Marne,* 1918; *The Age of Innocence,* 1920; *The Glimpses of the Moon,* 1922; *A Son at the Front,* 1923; *Old New York,* 1924; *The Mother's Recompense,* 1925; *Twilight Sleep,* 1927; *The Children,* 1928; *Hudson River Bracketed,* 1929; *The Gods Arrive,* 1932; *The Buccaneers,* 1938.

Other literary forms · In addition to her novels, of which several had appeared serially in *Scribners, The Delineator,* and *The Pictorial Review,* Edith Wharton published eleven collections of short stories and three volumes of poetry as well as a variety of nonfiction works. She wrote an early and influential book on interior decorating, *The Decoration of Houses* (1897, in collaboration with architect Ogden Codman, Jr.), a short book on the art of narrative, *The Writing of Fiction* (1925) published originally in *Scribner's Magazine,* and a delightful if highly selective autobiography, *A Backward Glance* (1934), which includes among other things an amusing account of Henry James's circumlocutory manner of speech. Wharton, an indefatigable traveler, recorded accounts of her travels in *Italian Villas and Their Gardens* (1904), *Italian Backgrounds* (1905), *A Motor-Flight Through France* (1908), and *In Morocco* (1920). During World War I, she wrote numerous pamphlets and letters to inform Americans about French and Belgian suffering and to enlist sympathy and support. Articles she wrote to explain the French people to American soldiers were later collected in the volume *French Ways and Their Meaning* (1919), and accounts of her five tours of the front lines were published under the title *Fighting France from Dunkerque to Belfort* (1915). Wharton also published a great many short stories, articles, and reviews that have never been collected. A number of her stories and novels have been adapted for the stage, motion pictures, and television, and have also been translated into French, Italian, Spanish, German, Danish, Finnish, and Japanese.

Achievements · Unlike Henry James, whose readership was small and intensely discriminating, Wharton managed to attract a large audience of general readers and at the same time command the interest of critics and fellow writers as well. Among her admirers were Sinclair Lewis and F. Scott Fitzgerald; Bernard Berenson, the art critic; and Percy Lubbock. Wharton's popularity remained high almost to the end of her career in the 1930's, but critical enthusiasm began to diminish after 1920, when the quality of her fiction declined. Even in the early years, 1905 to 1920, when Wharton's best fiction was being published, there were reservations expressed or implied by those who thought her a follower of and to some extent a lesser James, a charge easier to disprove than to eradicate. The truth is, that, though Warton learned from James—and a few of her novels, particularly *Madame de Treymes* reflect Jamesian themes as well as techniques—Wharton had her own manner as well as her own subject, and as she grew older, she continued to discover differences between her fiction and James's. It should also be pointed out (whether in praise or blame will depend on the critic) that James was a more dedicated artist than Wharton; his fiction had a finish and a coherence to be found in only a half-dozen of her novels; moreover, Wharton sometimes skated on the thin ice of superficiality, and in one novel, *The Glimpses of the Moon*, plunged through. Toward the end of her career, she also grew increasingly out of touch with life in the postwar world, much of which offended her. Her long residence in France, moreover, not only cut her off from the life of her fellow countrymen, but also–since she spoke French or Italian almost exclusively–loosened her grasp of English, so much so that a critic such as the young Edmund Wilson could complain that there were awkward phrases even in her masterpiece *The Age of Innocence*.

Wharton's major talent was for social observation. Unlike James, whose interest was ultimately metaphysical and whose novels were often invented from the slightest hints and employed few details, she filled her novels with precise accounts of the decoration of houses, of dress and of dinner parties, describing them often down to the cut of a waistcoat and the contents of the soup tureen. This is not to say that such details were signs of superficiality, but rather that Wharton's fiction depended heavily on the notation of manners and were the result of direct observation. Wharton tended to write–again, unlike James–out of her own direct experience. Even novels such as *Ethan Frome* and *Summer*–both set in provincial New England, and so different from the world she inhabited in New York and Paris–were created with remarkable attention to surface details, of which the famous cut glass, red pickle dish of Zeena's in *Ethan Frome* is a familiar example.

Wharton's fiction, it now appears, was (again, unlike James's) significantly autobiographical. Even the novels of provincial life, so different on the surface, treated issues that came out of the tensions of her own restricted upbringing and her unhappy marriage. Marriage was one of Wharton's principal subjects and provided her with a way of exploring and dramatizing her two main themes: the entrapment of an individual, as R. W. B. Lewis puts it in his *Edith Wharton: A Biography* (1975), and the attempt by an outsider, often a vulgar lower-class individual, to break into an old, aristocratic society. There is a sense in which these two themes are contradictory; the first one implies a point of view that identifies with the individual rather than with society; the second one judges from the point of view of society. The apparent contradiction, however, merely points up the range and boundaries of the author's sensibility. In some novels, *Ethan Frome* and *The House of Mirth*, for example, Wharton writes with sympathy of the trapped individual; in others, *The Custom of the Country*, and *The Children*, she writes from the standpoint of a traditional society. In her best novels, there is both sympathy for the trapped individual and the invocation of an outside claim–marriage vows, moral code, traditional manners–with the balance of sympathy tipped to the individual.

Wharton's major work was written between 1905, the year *The House of Mirth* was published, and 1920, when *The Age of Innocence* appeared. Interesting novels were still to come: *The Mother's Recompense, The Children*, and *The Buccaneers*, which has the best qualities of her earlier fiction; but the major works of the late 1920's and early 1930's, *Hudson River Bracketed* and *The Gods Arrive*, betray a serious falling off of energy and of talent. In these novels, Wharton was attempting to judge the contemporary world by the values of the past, but was so out of sympathy with the life around her and so out of touch with its manners that her representation of it in these later books can hardly be taken seriously.

Despite this later decline, however, and despite the undeniable influence of James on some of her early work, Wharton produced a considerable body of original fiction, high in quality and superior to most of what was being published at the time. Her fiction also influenced other, younger American writers, notably Sinclair Lewis and F. Scott Fitzgerald. After a long decline in readership and a period of critical indifference, there now appears to be a renewal of interest in her writing, both by critics and scholars of the American novel and by feminist scholars interested in extraliterary issues.

Library of Congress

Biography · Edith Wharton was born Edith Newbold Jones on January 24, 1862, in New York City. Her parents, George Frederic and Lucretia Rhinelander Jones, were descendants of early English and Dutch settlers and belonged to the pre-Civil War New York aristocracy, families whose wealth consisted largely of Manhattan real estate and who constituted in their common ancestry, landed wealth, and traditional manners a tightly knit, closed society. With the industrial expansion that occurred during and immediately after the Civil War, the old society was "invaded" by a new class of self-made rich men such as John Jacob Astor and Cornelius Vanderbilt. Whereas the old society had lived unostentatiously, observing, outwardly at least, a strict code of manners–the women presiding over a well-regulated social life and the men making perfunctory gestures at pursuing a profession–the new rich spent lavishly, built expensive, vulgar houses, and behaved in ways the old order found shockingly reprehensible. With its energy, its money, and its easier morality, the new order inevitably triumphed over the old, and this displacement of New York society constituted one of the chief subjects of Wharton's fiction, particularly in *The House of Mirth* and *The Custom of the Country*.

Wharton was educated at home by governesses, and later, tutors, and it was expected that she would assume the role young women of her class were educated to play, that of wife, mother, a gracious hostess. From an early age, however, Wharton showed intellectual and literary talents which, along with an acute shyness, kept her at the edge of conventional social life and later threatened to consign her at the age of twenty-three to a life of spinsterhood—the worst fate, so it was thought, that could befall a young woman of her class. After one engagement had been called off (because the young man's mother opposed it), and a promising relationship with a young lawyer, Walter Berry (who later became a close friend), had failed to develop romantically, Wharton married a man twelve years her senior, Edward ("Teddy") Robbins Wharton, a friend of her favorite brother.

Teddy Wharton was a socially prominent Bostonian without a profession or money of his own; Henry James and other friends in England were later incredulous that Wharton could marry a man so obviously her intellectual inferior and so incompatible in his interests; nevertheless, the marriage in the beginning must have been a liberation, both from the social pressure to marry and from her mother's domination. Wharton was close to her father, but there was a coolness between her and her mother that is frequently reflected in her fiction in the portrayal of mother-daughter relationships. By marrying Teddy, she was at last free to come and go as she pleased, to establish her own residence, which she did on a grand scale at Lenox, Massachusetts, and to travel abroad as often as she liked, In time, however, the marriage to Teddy became irksome, partly from lack of deep affection for him, but also because of his increasing bouts of depression and, later, his financial and sexual irresponsibilities. After revelations of his mismanagement of her estate and his adulterous affairs, she divorced Teddy in 1913. In his research for the biography of Wharton, Lewis uncovered the fact that she herself had had a brief but intense affair in 1908 with an American journalist named Morton Fullerton, and that that relationship had a profound influence on her fiction.

Wharton had lived and traveled in Europe as a child with her parents and after her marriage had visited abroad as often as possible, alternating the seasons between her house at Lenox and an apartment in Paris, with shorter visits to England and rural France. In 1903, when she met James in England, there began an important friendship, with frequent visits and exchanges of letters and motor trips in Wharton's powerful automobile. The Whartons always traveled in luxury, and their style and Edith's energy quite overwhelmed James at the same time he delighted in them. Like James, and for somewhat the same reasons, Wharton became in time an expatriate, giving up the newer, rawer life of America for the rich, deeply rooted culture of Europe. She felt at home in the salons and drawing rooms of Paris and London, where art and literature and ideas were discussed freely, where women were treated by men as equals, and where life itself was more pleasing to the senses and to the contemplative mind. Wharton also felt that in Europe, respect for the family, for manners, for learning, and for culture, even among the poorer classes, was very much alive.

Even before the final break with Teddy, Wharton had lengthened her frequent stays abroad and, finally, in 1911, allowed the house at Lenox to be sold. When World War I broke out, she remained in Paris and devoted her time, energy, and money to the relief of French and Belgian refugees; in 1916, she was officially recognized for her services to her adopted country by being made a Chevalier of the Legion of Honor. After the war, she bought a house just north of Paris and, later, another in the south of France. She made only one more trip home, in 1923, to receive an honorary degree at Yale. The remainder of her life was spent abroad.

According to those who knew her well, Wharton was a highly intelligent, well-read, brilliant conversationalist, somewhat remote at first, though the grand manner that many complained of was apparently a way of covering up her deep shyness. She read and spoke Italian and French fluently, and her salons in both Paris and Saint Claire were gathering places for literary, artistic, and social luminaries of the time, including such well-known figures as F. Scott Fitzgerald, Bernard Berenson, Jean Cocteau, Aldous Huxley, and Kenneth Clark. Despite the hectic pace of her social life and her frequent travels, Wharton continued to write regularly, turning out novels and short stories and articles, most of which sold well and brought her a great deal of money. She suffered a slight stroke in 1935, which for a time curtailed her activities; two years later, she was fatally stricken. After a short illness, she died at her home in St.-Brice-sous-Forêt, August 11, 1937. Her body was buried in a cemetery at Versailles, beside the grave where the ashes of her old friend Walter Berry had been buried earlier.

Analysis · On a surface level, there is a surprising variety in the kinds of characters and the aspects of life with which Edith Wharton was familiar. In *The House of Mirth*, for example, one of her best novels, she was able to create characters such as the Trenors and the Van Osburghs, who belong to opposite ends of the upper level of old New York society, as well as Nettie Struther, the poor working-class girl who befriends Lily Bart when she has sunk from the glittering world of Fifth Avenue social life to a seedy, boardinghouse existence. In *The Fruit of the Tree*, she created not only the world of the fashionable Westmores, but also the factory milieu in which the foreman John Amherst attempts to bring industrial reform. In *The Reef*, she could treat life in a French chateau, as well as in a sordid hotel in Paris, and in her two brilliant short novels, *Ethan Frome* and *Summer*, she managed to depict a life in rural Massachusetts that she could only have known by observation, rather than by direct experience.

It must be admitted, however, that Wharton is at times less than convincing. Some critics consider her attempt to deal with factory life in *The Fruit of the Tree* inept, even ludicrous, though others believe it entirely adequate; and certainly the life of impoverished Nettie Struther is delineated with nothing like the thoroughness of Lily Bart's, whose upper-class milieu Wharton knew at firsthand. Still, the extent of Wharton's social range and her ability to create realistic characters from a background quite different from her own is impressive, unrivaled in American fiction of the time.

As for variety of character types, one might cite in particular those to be found in *The House of Mirth*, in the range of male characters–from the fastidious Selden to the rapacious Gus Trenor and the socially ambiguous and vulgar Simon Rosedale, all of them suitors for Lily's attention. Both *Ethan Frome* and *Summer* present a more limited range, but both contain sharply realized and distinctly differentiated characters, including the powerful Ethan, the pretty young Mattie, and Zeena, the neurasthenic wife of Ethan. In *Summer*, Charity Royall, the mountain girl, is vividly created, as is her feckless young lover and her elderly guardian and attempted seducer, Lawyer Royall.

Despite this surface breadth, this impressive range of social observation, Wharton's novels have a rather narrow thematic focus. It has been said that Edith Wharton's chief theme is entrapment. Blake Nevious, in *Edith Wharton: A Study of Her Fiction*

(1953), points out how this theme is implicit in the principal relationships among characters in many of the novels, in which a superior nature is caught in a wasteful and baffling submission to an inferior nature. It was a situation that Wharton herself must have experienced, not only with a mother who was obsessed with fashion and propriety, but also in a society narrowly given up to the pursuit of pleasure. It was a situation in which she later found herself in her marriage to Teddy, who disliked and resented her interest in social and intellectual life. In novel after novel, one sees this same situation treated—superior individuals trapped in relationships with their inferiors and prevented from extricating themselves by a finer sensibility.

The House of Mirth · In *The House of Mirth*, Lily Bart is impoverished by the bankruptcy and later the death of her father and is obliged to recoup her fortune in the only way open to her, by attempting to marry a rich man. Lily's situation was not Wharton's, but the social pressures on her must have been similar: to make a suitable marriage, with social position certainly, and, if possible, money as well. In the novel, Lily is given a choice that Wharton apparently did not have: an offer of marriage from an emancipated young lawyer of her own class (though Walter Berry, a lawyer, was thought at one time to have been Wharton's suitor). Wharton chose a passionless marriage with Teddy; Lily was not allowed that solution. Selden deserts her at the crucial moment, and she dies of an overdose of sleeping medicine.

In her autobiography *A Backward Glance*, Wharton stated that her subject in *The House of Mirth* was to be the tragic power of New York society in "debasing people and ideas," and Lily Bart was created in order to give that power dramatic scope. Lily's entrapment by society and her eventual destruction are not the final story. Lily overcomes the limitations of her upbringing and aspirations and acts on principle. She has in her possession a packet of letters which could be used to regain her social position, but the letters would involve the reputation of Selden. She also has a ten-thousand-dollar inheritance which could be used to establish herself in a profitable business, but she burns the letters and uses the money to repay a debt of honor. Lily dies, but in choosing death rather than dishonor, she has escaped entrapment.

The Age of Innocence · In *The Age of Innocence*, published fifteen years after *The House of Mirth*, the underlying conflict is the same, though the tone of the novel and the nature of the entrapment are somewhat different. Here, the trapped individual is a man, Newland Archer, a young lawyer who is engaged to marry May Welland, a pretty and shallow young woman of respectable old New York society of the 1870's and 1890's. This is the world of Wharton's young womanhood, a society that is narrow and rigid and socially proper. Into this limited and self-contained world, she brings Ellen Olenska, a cousin of May, who belongs to this world by birth but left it years before and has since married a Polish count. Ellen has now separated from her husband, who has been notoriously unfaithful, and has returned to the bosom of her family for support and comfort. Archer is engaged by the family to help her in her quest for a divorce settlement. The inevitable happens. Archer and Ellen fall in love. Archer is attracted by Ellen's European sophistication, her freedom of thought and manners, and her refusal to take seriously the small taboos of New York society. Archer considers breaking with May and marrying Ellen. The family, sensing his defection, contrive with other members of the society to separate the lovers and reunite Archer with May, his conventional fiancée. Social pressure forces Ellen to return to Europe, and Archer is again thinking of pursuing Ellen; then May announces that she is expecting a baby. Archer is finally and permanently trapped.

As though to drive home the extent to which Archer has been defeated, Wharton takes him to Paris years later. His son is grown, his wife dead, and Ellen Olenska is now a widow living alone. Archer makes an appointment to see Ellen but gets only as far as a park bench near her apartment. At the last minute, he decides to send his son to see her, while he remains seated on the bench, telling himself that it would be more real for him to remain there than to go himself to see Ellen. The trap has done its work.

While one can see resemblances between Ellen and Wharton—the expatriation, the charm, the liberated views, perhaps even the slight French accent with which Ellen speaks—Archer is also Wharton, or that side of her that could never entirely escape the past. *The Age of Innocence* was thought by some reviewers to be a glorification of the past, which it clearly is not. Wharton does evoke with some nostalgia the old New York of her youth, but she also sets forth with delicate but cutting irony that society's limitations and its destructive narrowness. Archer has led an exemplary life, one is led to believe, but the happiness he might have had was gently but firmly denied him. Whereas a more popular novelist might have allowed Archer to be reunited with Ellen at the end of the novel, Wharton insists that that would be unreal; for her, personal happiness in the real world is the exception rather than the rule.

Ethan Frome · Two of Wharton's best novels, also two of her shortest, both deal with protagonists trapped by passionless marriages. The earliest of these, *Ethan Frome*, is about a Massachusetts farmer married to an older, neurasthenic wife, whose pretty young cousin has come to work for her. The inevitable again happens. Ethan falls in love with Mattie and dreams about running away with her. Ethan's jealous wife, however, arranges for Mattie to be sent away, and Ethan is obliged to escort her to the train station. It is winter, and the lovers stop for a brief time together. They embrace, realize the inevitability of separation, and decide to kill themselves by coasting down a steep hill into a great elm tree. During the ride down the steep hill, Ethan accidentally swerves the sled; a crash occurs, in which the lovers are seriously injured but survive. Mattie becomes a whining invalid, while Zeena, the neurotic wife, takes over the running of the household, and Ethan, who is severely disfigured, feels himself like a handcuffed convict, a prisoner for life.

As Lewis has pointed out, the situation in *Ethan Frome* is very much like the situation in Wharton's own life at the time. If one shifts the sexes, Frome is Wharton trapped in a loveless marriage with the neurasthenic Teddy and passionately in love with a younger man who shared her interests and feelings, Morton Fullerton. The violent ending, of course, may be seen as Wharton's passionate statement about her own desperate situation. The success of *Ethan Frome*, however, does not depend on making such biographical connections; the book is a brilliantly realized work of realistic fiction that owes its power not to some abstractly conceived pessimistic philosophy of life, but to Wharton's successful transposition of her own emotional life into the language of fiction.

Summer · *Summer* was published six years after *Ethan Frome* and was called by Wharton and her friends the "hot Ethan." As in *Ethan Frome*, there is a triangle: Lawyer Royall, elderly guardian of Charity, a pretty young mountain girl, and a visiting architecture student, Lucius Harney. During the idyllic summer months, an intense and passionate affair takes place between Charity and Harney. Harney returns to Boston, and Charity is left to face her guardian, who is also in love with her, and the prospect of an illegal abortion. The novel concludes with a reconciliation between Charity and her guardian and a secure if passionless marriage with him. While it would be a mistake to overemphasize biographical parallels, they are unmistakable. The affair of Charity and Harney suggests Wharton's earlier affair with Fullerton, while the intrusive presence of the fatherly Lawyer Royall suggests Teddy's irksome claims on Wharton's loyalties. An interesting alteration of chronology is in making the marriage with the older man follow the affair rather than precede it, as it had in Wharton's own life. *Summer* was written four years after the Whartons were divorced, and by then, she may have had time to view her marriage to Teddy more dispassionately, as the practical solution it must originally have been. Like Lily's death, the surrender to marriage is a defeat as well as a moral triumph.

  Summer is one of Wharton's finest novels, written according to her own testimony, in a state of "creative joy" and reflecting in its characters, scenes, and symbolic structures, the deep well of the unconscious that seems to nourish the most powerful works of American fiction.

The Reef · *The Reef,* published the year before the Whartons' divorce, and commonly acknowledged to be Wharton's most Jamesian novel, again deals with conflicts between the individual and society and the problems of marriage. In this novel, however, the society is remote; the inheritor of the society's standards, Anna Leath, an American widow of a French nobleman, is reunited with an old friend, George Darrow, also an American, a lawyer, living in Europe. Anna and Darrow become engaged and are about to be married when Anna discovers that Darrow has had an affair with Sophy Viner, her daughter's governess, a girl of a lower class, and that Sophy, who is also her stepson's fiancée, is still in love with Darrow. For Darrow, the situation is a matter of diplomatic maneuvering, of steering his way between the two women and the stepson, but for Anna, it presents a moral dilemma involving, on the one hand, an inherited code of conduct, which tells her that Darrow must be abandoned, and a personal one, which tells her not to give him up. The moral complexities of the novel are a good deal more complicated than summary can indicate—indeed, are so ambiguous that one is hard pressed to decide where the author stands. It is possible, however, to see in this novel situations parallel to Wharton's earlier involvement with Fullerton, and a possible moral dilemma over her own infidelity. In a sense, Wharton is Sophy Viner, but Sophy (and Wharton's affair with Fullerton) seen in the light of a later moral judgment; Wharton is also Anna, attempting to accept the break with conventional morality that led to Darrow's affair with Sophy. The trap in which Anna finds herself is doubly baited, and no matter which way she turns, she must fall, either morally or emotionally. The fact that Anna chooses Darrow after all suggests the same kind of compromise other Wharton protagonists have made, Justine of *The Fruit of the Tree* and Charity Royall of *Summer* especially, both of whom were betrayed by the weakness of the men they loved but settled for what was finally available.

The Custom of the Country · *The Custom of the Country* is a different sort of work, influenced by the French realist Honoré de Balzac rather than by Henry James; it attempts to deal, as did Balzac, with the destruction of an aristocracy by the invasion of uncivilized materialists. The protagonist of the novel, Undine Spragg, is a handsome young woman from Apex, a city in the American Middle West. Undine's father made a great deal of money in Apex and now has come East to try his hand in New York City. The Spraggs move into an expensive, vulgar hotel, and the parents would be content to exist on the fringes of New York society, but Undine, who is as ambitious as she is vulgar, manages to meet and then marry Ralph Marvel, an ineffectual member of old New York society. When life with Marvel grows boring, Undine becomes the mistress of a richer and more aggressive New York aristocrat, Peter Van Degen; when Van Degen drops her, she manages to snare the son of an old aristocratic French family, the Marquis de Chelles. Undine marries de Chelles, but she has learned nothing, being without taste, manners, or ideas; her sole interest is in amusing and gratifying herself. As soon as she gets what she thinks she wants, she becomes dissatisfied with it and wants something she decides is better. She grows tired of having to fit herself into the demands of the feudal aristocracy into which she has married; when she attempts to sell family heirlooms, whose value she does not understand, her husband divorces her. Her third husband is a perfect match, a hard-driving vulgar materialist from Apex, Elmer Moffat, whose chief interest is in buying up European art. Moffat also aspires to an ambassadorial post, but is barred because he is married to Undine, a divorced woman.

The Custom of the Country is regarded by some critics as among Wharton's best fiction, but, as Blake Nevius has observed, during the course of the novel, Undine ceases to be a credible character and becomes an "inhuman abstraction." Clearly, she came to represent everything that Wharton detested in the America of 1912, and, at a deeper and vaguer level, perhaps also expressed Wharton's fear and resentment at the displacement of her own class by more energetic and less cultivated outsiders. The fact that such fears were real enough and the implicit social criticisms valid, does nothing to alter the fact that, measured against books such as *The House of Mirth, Ethan Frome, Summer,* and *The Reef, The Custom of the Country* is crude and unconvincing. James had been right years earlier in advising Wharton to write about that part of the world she knew best, for in attempting to deal with the Middle West in *The Custom of the Country,* and later, in *Hudson River Bracketed* and *The Gods Arrive,* with bohemian circles about which she knew very little, she condemned herself to superficiality and caricature. It is difficult to take seriously Undine Spragg of *The Custom of the Country* or Advance Weston, the protagonist of *Hudson River Bracketed* and *The Gods Arrive,* who is said to be from Pruneville, Nebraska, and later Hallelujah, Missouri, and Euphoria, Illinois. Caricature is an expression of outrage, not understanding.

The Buccaneers · Fortunately, the last of Wharton's novels, *The Buccaneers,* published the year after her death, was a return to the territory of her earlier fiction, old New York of the 1870's. The novel was unfinished at her death and lacks the coherence of her best early work, but she could still write with the sharpness and scenic fullness that had characterized *The House of Mirth* and *The Age of Innocence.*

Wharton was a novelist of manners, then, not a chronicler of large social movements, and her real subject was the entrapment of superior individuals who keenly feel the pull of moral responsibility. Her talents for social observation, for noting subtleties of dress and decoration, for nuance of voice and phrase, and for language—precise and yet expressive—were essential instruments in the creation of her novels. Wharton has been unduly charged with pessimism; her characteristic tone is ironic, the product of a sensibility able to see and feel the claims on both sides of a human dilemma. If her voice faltered in her later years and she conceded too much to the popular taste for which she increasingly wrote, she nevertheless produced some of the finest American fiction published in the first two decades of the century, and her name deserves to stand with those of James and F. Scott Fitzgerald, who outrank her only at their best.

W. J. Stuckey

Other major works

SHORT FICTION: *The Greater Inclination,* 1899; *Crucial Instances,* 1901; *The Descent of Man,* 1904; *The Hermit and the Wild Woman,* 1908; *Tales of Men and Ghosts,* 1910; *Xingu and Other Stories,* 1916; *Here and Beyond,* 1926; *Certain People,* 1930; *Human Nature,* 1933; *The World Over,* 1936; *Ghosts,* 1937; *The Collected Short Stories of Edith Wharton,* 1968.

POETRY: *Verses,* 1878; *Artemis to Actæon,* 1909; *Twelve Poems,* 1926.

NONFICTION: *The Decoration of Houses,* 1897 (with Ogden Codman, Jr.); *Italian Villas and Their Gardens,* 1904; *Italian Backgrounds,* 1905; *A Motor-Flight Through France,* 1908; *Fighting France from Dunkerque to Belfort,* 1915; *French Ways and Their Meaning,* 1919; *In Morocco,* 1920; *The Writing of Fiction,* 1925; *A Backward Glance,* 1934; *The Letters of Edith Wharton,* 1988; *The Uncollected Critical Writings,* 1997 (Frederick Wegener, editor).

Bibliography

Ammons, Elizabeth. *Edith Wharton's Argument with America.* Athens: University of Georgia Press, 1980. Ammons proposes that Wharton's "argument with America" concerns the freedom of women, an argument in which she had a key role during three decades of significant upheaval and change. This engaging book examines the evolution of Wharton's point of view in her novels and discusses the effect of World War I on Wharton. Contains a notes section.

Bell, Millicent, ed. *The Cambridge Companion to Edith Wharton.* Cambridge, England: Cambridge University Press, 1995. Essays on *The Age of Innocence, Summer, The House of Mirth, The Fruit of the Tree,* and *The Valley of Decision,* as well as on Wharton's handling of manners and race. Bell gives a critical history of Wharton's fiction in her introduction. Includes a chronology of Wharton's life and publications and a bibliography.

Bendixen, Alfred, and Annette Zilversmit, eds. *Edith Wharton: New Critical Essays.* New York: Garland, 1992. Studies of *The House of Mirth, The Fruit of the Tree, Summer, The Age of Innocence, Hudson River Bracketed,* and *The Gods Arrive,* as well as on Wharton's treatment of female sexuality, modernism, language, and gothic borrowings. There is an introduction and concluding essay on future directions for criticism. No bibliography.

Benstock, Shari. *No Gifts from Chance: A Biography of Edith Wharton.* New York: Scribner's, 1994. A valuable work by a noted Wharton scholar, this supplements but does not supplant Lewis's biography. Divided into sections on "The Old Order," "Choices," and "Rewards." Includes a chronology of works by Wharton, a bibliography, notes, and index.

Dwight, Eleanor. *Edith Wharton: An Extraordinary Life.* New York: Abrams, 1994. A lively succinct biography, copiously illustrated. Includes detailed notes, chronology, and bibliography.

Gimbel, Wendy. *Edith Wharton: Orphancy and Survival.* New York: Praeger, 1984. Drawing upon psychoanalytic theories and feminist perspectives, Gimbel analyzes the four works that she sees as key to understanding Wharton: *The House of Mirth, Ethan Frome, Summer,* and *The Age of Innocence.* The analyses of these works, with their deeply psychological overtones, are well worth reading.

Lewis, R. W. B. *Edith Wharton: A Biography.* 2 vols. New York: Harper & Row, 1975. An extensive study on Wharton, who Lewis calls "the most renowned writer of fiction in America." Notes that Wharton thoughtfully left extensive records, made available through the Beinecke Library at Yale, on which this biography is based. Essential reading for serious scholars of Wharton or for those interested in her life and how it shaped her writing.

Lindberg, Gary H. *Edith Wharton and the Novel of Manners.* Charlottesville: University Press of Virginia, 1975. Presents Wharton's style with a keen understanding of the ritualism of the social scenes in her work. Strong analytical criticism with a good grasp of Wharton's use of irony.

THORNTON WILDER

Born: Madison, Wisconsin; April 17, 1897
Died: Hamden, Connecticut; December 7, 1975

Principal long fiction · *The Cabala*, 1926; *The Bridge of San Luis Rey*, 1927; *The Woman of Andros*, 1930; *Heaven's My Destination*, 1934; *The Ides of March*, 1948; *The Eighth Day*, 1967; *Theophilus North*, 1973.

Other literary forms · Thornton Wilder is as well known for his plays as for his fiction. *Our Town* (1938), *The Merchant of Yonkers* (1938, revised as *The Matchmaker*, 1954), and *The Skin of Our Teeth* (1942) are some of his best known. Collections of his short plays were published in *The Angel That Troubled the Waters and Other Plays* (1928) and *The Long Christmas Dinner and Other Plays in One Act* (1931). *A Life in the Sun*, commonly known as *The Alcestiad*, was published in 1955, and a collection of his essays, *American Characteristics and Other Essays*, were published in 1979. A set of cullings from his diaries, *The Journals of Thornton Wilder, 1939-1961*, was released in 1985.

Achievements · Wilder began his career as a teacher and in a sense never gave up the practice of that profession. He attempted to persuade generations of readers of the power of love, the need for individual integrity, the importance of maintaining faith in people's essential goodness. His clear style and straight-forward narrative earned for him a broad readership, transcending categories of age, class, or education. Though detractors have labeled him middle class and middlebrow, he received enthusiastic praise throughout his career from such critics as Edmund Wilson, Malcolm Cowley, Edmund Fuller, Henry Seidel Canby, and John Updike. Wilder has been less a subject of scholarly research than some of his contemporaries—F. Scott Fitzgerald and Ernest Hemingway, for example—yet he has remained widely read since his first novel was published in 1926, and his versatility as a writer—of two Pulitzer-Prize-winning full-length plays and dozens of short plays—has brought him worldwide recognition.

Wilder won a Pulitzer Prize for fiction in 1928, a National Book Award in 1967, and the first National Medal for Literature in 1964, besides being the recipient of several honorary doctorates.

Biography · Thornton Niven Wilder was born in Madison, Wisconsin, on April 17, 1897, the son of Amos Parker Wilder and Isabella Thornton Niven Wilder. His father, a newspaper editor, moved the family to Hong Kong in 1906 when he was assigned a diplomatic post there. The young Wilder attended the Kaiser Wilhelm School, then the China Inland Mission Boys' School, where he harbored a brief desire to become a missionary himself. When his family returned to the United States, settling in California, he continued his education at the Thacher School in Ojai, then Berkeley High School, where he first began to write plays and act in class productions. In 1915, he entered Oberlin, a school his father chose because it was less socially elite than his own alma mater, Yale. At Oberlin, Wilder continued his involvement in theatrical productions and contributed prolifically to the college's literary magazine. After two years there, Wilder was allowed by his father to enroll at Yale, where, after a period of homesickness for Oberlin, he again proved himself, in the words of professor and literary critic William Lyon Phelps, to be "a star of the first magnitude . . . unusually versatile, original, and clever." Wilder was graduated with no specific career goals in mind. His father, believing a European experience would be broadening, sent him to study at the American Academy in Rome for a summer. Meanwhile, he searched for a suitable job for his son and found one at Lawrenceville, a preparatory school in New Jersey. There, when his French classes were over, Wilder began a novel with the working title *Memoirs of a Roman Student*, to be published as *The Cabala* in 1926. In the same year, Wilder took advantage of Lawrenceville's proximity to Princeton to earn his master of arts degree. He took a year's leave of absence from teaching and began work on a new novel, *The Bridge of San Luis Rey*, published to enormous acclaim in 1927, and earning Wilder his first Pulitzer Prize.

In 1929, Wilder was invited to teach at the University of Chicago by an Oberlin classmate, Robert Hutchins, who had just been named president of the prestigious Illinois university. Wilder was writing intensely: *The Woman of Andros* was published in 1930, a collection of short plays in 1931, and *Heaven's My Destination* in 1934. He remained at the University of Chicago until the mid-1930's, teaching one semester and writing during the next. More and more, he was drawn to the theater. He completed *The Merchant of Yonkers*, later revised as *The Matchmaker* (and still later transformed into the Broadway musical *Hello, Dolly!*) in 1937 and then turned to a more serious play, *Our Village*, soon retitled *Our Town*. This play was met with great enthusiasm when it opened in New York in 1938 and earned Wilder his second Pulitzer Prize.

The political upheaval in Europe, soon to involve America, found its way into Wilder's next play, *The Skin of Our Teeth*, which evoked a deep response in audiences both in the United States and abroad; the play was awarded a Pulitzer Prize in 1942. Wilder served in the army during World War II, and emerged with his optimism intact and his faith in humanity unshaken.

In the late 1940's, Wilder again turned to fiction, dealing with the problem of authority and dictatorship in *The Ides of March*. This novel reflected his talks with Gertrude Stein, whom Wilder had met in 1934 when Stein was lecturing at the University of Chicago. They shared ideas on the problem of identity and the creation of a believable reality for readers. Stein attempted to deal with these problems in her own book, *Ida, a Novel* (1941); Wilder took as his subject Julius Caesar.

In 1950, Wilder delivered the Charles Eliot Norton lectures at Harvard, then traveled–always a stimulation and joy for him–and worked on *The Alcestiad*, his retelling of the Greek legend of Alcestis. In the early 1960's, he retreated to Arizona to write *The Eighth Day*. By the end of the decade, his pace had slowed. He worked on short plays and completed his quasi-autobiographical *Theophilus North*. He died in his sleep on December 7, 1975.

Analysis · Thornton Wilder's seven novels, written over nearly fifty years, show a remarkable consistency in theme and tone. His early books, contemporaneous with Theodore Dreiser's *An American Tragedy* (1925) and Sinclair Lewis's *Arrowsmith* (1925), are far from the realism and naturalism which dominated American literature in the 1920's and 1930's. Though he joined groups active in civil rights and social justice, these themes did not find their way into his works in the manner of John Dos Passos or John Steinbeck. His later works, similarly, show none of the interest in psychoanalysis which may be found in the works of Sherwood Anderson, for example, none of the angry intensity of a Norman Mailer.

Wilder chose not to comment on contemporary politics, social problems, psychological angst, or cultural changes, preferring instead to mine those themes he considered of utmost importance: love, brotherhood, tolerance, and faith. His faith was expressed not in strictly Judeo-Christian terms, but in humanistic convictions which incorporated diverse religious beliefs. Without being didactic, Wilder wished to educate, to inspire, to allow his readers to move beyond an obsession with the individual case to a consideration of humankind and its history. His second novel, *The Bridge of San Luis Rey*, is representative of the themes which recur throughout his works, and his final statement in that book well expresses his one abiding conviction: "There is a land of the living and a land of the dead and the bridge is love, the only survival, the only meaning."

The Cabala · Though Wilder drew on his memories of Rome for his first novel, *The Cabala*, the book is a fantasy, only incidentally autobiographical. The "Cabala" is an aristocratic social circle in which two Americans find themselves involved. These two, Samuele and James Blair, represent Wilder's interest in duality of personality which recurs in later works and results in part from his having been born a twin (his sibling was stillborn). Samuele is a typical Wilder character: innocent, sensitive, stable, with a deep strain of common sense. Blair is the dry intellectual so obsessed by books that he fears real life.

Samuele is the vehicle by which a number of episodes are linked, since he is asked by various members of the Cabala to intervene in the lives of others. First, he is called in to restrain the impetuous and licentious Marcantonio, but fails: The young man engages in incest and then kills himself. Then, Samuele must console the lovely young Alix, unfortunate enough to fall in love with James Blair. Finally, he must deal with the royalist Astrée-Luce in her plot to "prop up" and empower cynical Cardinal Vaini. Samuele is baffled by these obsessed and decadent characters, and is hardly satisfied by an explanation offered to him that the group is possessed by ancient gods who have passed on their power to unsuspecting mortals. Finally, on advice from Vergil's ghost, Samuele returns to America. For Wilder, Europe, for all its richness of culture, was too deeply mired in the past to allow the spirit to grow. Samuele could thrive only in America, a country of youth and intellectual freedom.

The Bridge of San Luis Rey · In his second novel, *The Bridge of San Luis Rey*, Wilder again uses a structure of separate episodes linked by one thread, this time the collapse of an ancient bridge over a chasm in Peru. Again, he offers a religious figure, but instead of the jaded Cardinal, there is the sympathetic brother Juniper, who searches for meaning in the deaths of those who perished: the Marquesa de Montemayor; Pepita, her maid; Esteban, a young Indian; Uncle Pio, an aging actor, and his ward Jaime. Brother Juniper finds that the five were victims of love, and those who survive are forced to a change of consciousness by the deaths of those they spurned or misjudged.

As in *The Cabala*, Wilder explores twinness in the tale of Esteban and his twin brother Manuel. The two are extraordinarily close, and when Manuel falls in love with a woman, Esteban becomes despondent. Yet he nurses his brother faithfully after Manuel is injured, suffering his delirious ravings until Manuel dies. Nearly mad with grief, Esteban first assumes his dead brother's identity, then attempts suicide, only to die when the bridge collapses. A sea captain, Alvarado, had offered to sign him on his crew, and tried to console him by reminding him, "We do what we can. We push on, Esteban, as best we can. It isn't for long, you know. Time keeps going by. You'll be surprised at the way time passes." Wilder was always conscious of the brevity of life and the need, therefore, to cling to love where one finds it. In *The Bridge of San Luis Rey*, he urges the celebration and fulfillment of love as the only meaning in the world.

The Woman of Andros · From eighteenth century Peru, Wilder moved to pre-Christian Greece in his third novel, *The Woman of Andros*, again dealing with love; its theme, as in *The Bridge of San Luis Rey*, is "How does one live? . . . What does one do first?" Society on the island of Brynos was not essentially different, according to Wilder, from that of his own America. When Chrysis, the central character, says "Lift every roof, and you will find seven puzzled hearts," she speaks of people's bewilderment in the face of the unknown, their search for communion, their need for love—basic human struggles which are not rooted in any particular time or place.

In 1930, however, a number of critics were disappointed with this message. In a time of economic and social crisis, Wilder seemed to retreat into yet another esoteric setting, far removed from the urgencies of the day. One critic writing in *The New Republic* dubbed Wilder a "Prophet of the Genteel Christ" who wrote for a wealthy elite not interested in social problems. The article touched off a month of debate, with letters supporting or attacking Wilder appearing in each issue of the journal. At the end of December, Wilder finally received his greatest support when Sinclair Lewis, accepting the Nobel Prize for Literature, praised his fellow writer "who in an age of realism dreams the old and lovely dreams of the eternal romantic."

Heaven's My Destination · Throughout the controversy, Wilder remained silent. He was sensitive to the criticism, however, and in his next novel attempted to find a setting and characters which would appear relevant to his own time. *Heaven's My Destination* concerns the misadventures of George Marvin Brush, a salesman of religious textbooks, who travels across Depression-ridden America preaching, moralizing, and interfering in the lives of ordinary citizens. Converted to Bible Belt Christianity by a woman evangelist at Shiloh Baptist College, he has proceeded to spread his own fundamentalist version of the Gospel wherever he goes. Wilder returned to the episodic structure of his first two novels in presenting George's adventures in picaresque form. Unlike Don Quixote, however, with whom George has been compared, Wilder's protagonist is rarely endearing, more often exasperating.

George is different from the "normal" Americans with whom he interacts, yet Wilder is satirizing not only his earnest hero, but also those who spurn him. George, after a while, becomes depressed by his society and exclaims, "It's the world that's crazy. Everybody's crazy except me; that's what's the matter. The whole world's nuts." Why, asks this ardent believer, is God "so slow" in changing things?

For all his misconceptions, George does act upon truly humanistic beliefs. He takes a vow of poverty and occasionally of silence, refuses his interest from the bank and dislikes raises in pay. "I think everybody ought to be hit by the depression equally," he says, as he gives away his money. Like Samuele, George maintains his integrity in an environment which threatens to corrupt him and is selfless in his efforts to aid those who need him—even if they protest against his interference.

George Brush was Wilder's answer to the critics who dismissed his previous works, and in a sense, he gave them what he thought they deserved—a priggish, monomaniacal American overreacting to mundane occurrences. Even with such a cartoon-strip character, however, Wilder could not help but imbue him with gentleness and humility, and for Edmund Wilson, George Brush emerged as a "type of saint . . . and therefore a universal character."

In part, it was George's earnestness, his reluctance to see evil and his determination to do good, that caused Wilder to exclaim, "I'm George Brush." Certainly his persistent faith in humanity unites him with his character, but there is further correspondence in Brush's essential isolation, the loneliness which causes him to reach out for companionship. For Wilder, such isolation was characteristically American: Solitude was to be treasured, but loneliness was threatening. He once noted an adage which he thought well expressed the American spirit: "If you can see the smoke from your neighbor's chimney, you're too near." In his next novel, thirteen years later, he created yet another lonely, questing character, but this time Wilder eschewed satire and humor to deal seriously with people powerful before the world, yet powerless before death.

The Ides of March · *The Ides of March,* written just after World War II, deals with an archetypal dictator, Julius Caesar. Here, Wilder aimed to revive the spirit of the man from a palimpsest of historical and fictional treatments. The novel, therefore, becomes a study in identity and a technical challenge in creating for readers a believable reality. In structure, *The Ides of March* differs sharply from Wilder's previous work. He assembles fictionalized letters, diary entries, messages, and documents in an effort to offer a vibrant picture of Roman life. Caesar himself is a man obsessed not only with power but also with death, and he must learn how to celebrate life faced with a dark world and an uncaring universe.

Wilder contrasts Caesar with his friend and counselor Lucius Turrinus, who offers a philosophy which was by then familiar to Wilder's readers: "The universe is not aware that we are here," Lucius tells Caesar. "Hope has never changed tomorrow's weather." Yet love could change the world, and Caesar comes to exclaim, "I wish to cry out to all the living and all the dead that there is not part of the universe that is untouched by bliss."

Caesar's urge to seize life and live it to the fullest causes his companions to label him rash and irreverent; but he feels himself to be above them because he has clearly envisioned his own death, and in so doing believes himself "capable of praising the sunlight." Wilder transfers to the Roman dictator much of the sentiment expressed in his play *Our Town,* where Emily Webb dies and is allowed to return to Earth for one day. Only then does she realize how wonderful life is, how desperately she wants to live, and how foolish most people are in squandering their brief existence. Caesar refuses to be foolish; perhaps he will be ruthless, impetuous, temperamental, passionate—but he will live each moment.

The Ides of March had two major inspirations: the war itself, with its focus on the use and misuse of power, the character of a dictator, and the death of innocents; and a personal confrontation with death—first that of Wilder's friend and mentor Edward Sheldon, a playwright whose character informs Lucius Turrinus, and upon whose wisdom Wilder often relied; then, and most important, the death of his mother, his most ardent supporter and admirer.

The Eighth Day · After *The Ides of March* was published, Wilder devoted nearly two decades to his plays; not until 1967 would he write another novel. In *The Eighth Day*, Wilder returned to an American setting, the turn-of-the-century Midwest, and to traditional narrative. He carefully unfolds the tale of John Barrington Ashley, tried for the murder of his neighbor, Breckenridge Lansing, and found guilty. Five days after being sentenced to death, he escapes with the help of an unknown accomplice. Five years later, Ashley is found innocent on the basis of new evidence. Ashley's flight, which takes him to Chile, is contrasted with the life of his wife and children in a small town which barely tolerates the outlaw's family.

Wilder's concern, however, is not with one family's history, but with the archetypal family, and Ashley represents not one wronged citizen, but the man of the Eighth Day, a new man with faith in humanity and a strong commitment to working toward a better future. Wilder tells his readers that faith and action can bring about a better life. Throughout the novel, he assigns several characters to speak for him, most notably Dr. Gillies, a country physician, who observes:

> Nature never sleeps. The process of life never stands still. The creation has not come to an end. The Bible says that God created people on the sixth day and rested, but each of those days was many millions of years long. That day of rest must have been a short one. Man is not an end but a beginning. We are at the beginning of the second week. We are children of the eighth day.

On the eighth day, people must begin to forge their own futures, and though Dr. Gillies knows that there will be "no Golden Ages and no Dark Ages," still he believes in the power of each individual to work toward the collective fate of humankind.

Because the novel is concerned essentially with imparting a message, the characters—as in *The Cabala* and *Heaven's My Destination*—are not fully realized individuals, but instead are one-dimensional representations of predictable types. The Ashley family, ignored and rebuffed by their neighbors, never lose their aristocratic elegance. They persist in their nightly reading of William Shakespeare even when economic problems would seem severe enough to lower their morale. Here, Wilder pleads for art as the true salvation of humankind, its highest achievement, "the only satisfactory products of civilization."

Through Dr. Gillies, who echoes the sentiments of Chrysis in *The Woman of Andros* and *Lucius* in *The Ides of March*, Wilder reminds his readers that they occupy only a brief span of time when contrasted with eternity and so must exhibit proper humility. They are small specks in a vast universe, and their duty is not to enhance their own egos, but to work together toward a higher good. "We keep saying that 'we live our lives,'" Dr. Gillies exclaims. "Shucks! Life lives us." Wilder had sent this message for forty years; he insisted again, in the turbulent, self-conscious, self-indulgent late 1960's, on attempting to awaken his readers to his own values.

Theophilus North · Wilder was seventy when *The Eighth Day* was published, the time of a writer's life when he might consider writing his autobiography or memoirs. Wilder, however, chose not to reveal his memories or bare his soul: Instead, he wrote a last novel, *Theophilus North*, with a protagonist, he once told an interviewer, who was what his twin brother might have been if he had lived.

Theophilus may be Wilder's imaginary brother, but his life bears striking similarities to that of Wilder himself. He has lived in China, attended Yale, and spent a summer in Rome; after teaching at a boys' preparatory school in New Jersey, he leaves his job to explore life and goes to Newport, Rhode Island—a town where Wilder often vacationed—to set his new course. Like Samuele, Theophilus is gentle, well mannered, polite, helpful. These traits endear him to the Newport natives, and he is asked to intervene in several lives. The structure here, as in many previous Wilder novels, is one of loosely linked episodes.

Theophilus succeeds in such tasks as separating mismatched lovers, liberating an aging man from the manipulation of his daughter, allowing a shrewish wife to mend her ways, extricating one man from his unwitting involvement with criminals, bringing home a wayward husband, finding a lover for a maimed young man, and impregnating a woman whose husband is sterile. Throughout, Theophilus is a typical Wilder hero—a man of good will, of faith, of sincerity.

Theophilus North is Wilder's only novel in which sexuality is of central importance. The sexual episodes are conducted offstage and seem unbelievable and strained. Theophilus, in his seductions and in his everyday relationships with his neighbors, is curiously unaffected and uninvolved. Though he displays emotion, he seems to lack passion.

Wilder's characters, from Samuele to John Ashley, from the circle of Roman aristocrats to Newport society, remain thin and superficial, emblems rather than specific, rounded human beings. Such characterization was in keeping with Wilder's conviction that each individual was, in the long history of the human race, of but little importance. His trials, anguish, suffering, and joy were not significant when placed in the context of all human suffering and all human joy. Rather than writing about individual human beings, Wilder chose to write about humanity; rather than dealing with the intricacies of individual lives, he chose to compress those lives into brief episodes to demonstrate the multiplicity of life.

Wilder, deeply philosophical and reflective, was always the teacher, the educator, with an abiding concern for the future of humanity. "Hope," he wrote in *Theophilus North*, "is a projection of the imagination; so is despair. Despair all too readily embraces the ills it foresees; hope is an energy and arouses the mind to explore every possibility to combat them." In all his works, he exuded hope and, even in dark times, urged his readers to work together in faith and in love.

Linda Simon

Other major works

PLAYS: *The Trumpet Shall Sound*, pb. 1920; *The Angel That Troubled the Waters and Other Plays*, pb. 1928 (includes 16 plays); *The Happy Journey to Trenton and Camden*, pr., pb. 1931 (one act); *The Long Christmas Dinner*, pr., pb. 1931 (one act; as libretto in German, 1961; translation and music by Paul Hindemith); *The Long Christmas Dinner and Other Plays in One Act*, pb. 1931 (includes *Queens of France, Pullman Car Hiawatha, Love and How to Cure It, Such Things Only Happen in Books*, and *The Happy Journey to Trenton and Camden*); *Lucrece*, pr. 1932 (adaptation of André Obey's *Le Viol de Lucrèce*); *A Doll's House*, pr. 1937 (adaptation of Henrik Ibsen's play); *The Merchant of Yonkers*, pr. 1938 (adaptation of Johann Nestroy's *Einen Jux will er sich machen*); *Our Town*, pr., pb. 1938; *The Skin of Our Teeth*, pr., pb. 1942; *The Matchmaker*, pr. 1954 (revision of *The Merchant of Yonkers*); *A Life in the Sun*, pr. 1955 (commonly known as *The Alcestiad*; act four pb. as *The Drunken Sisters*); *Plays for Bleecker Street*, pr. 1962 (3 one-acts: *Someone from Assisi; Infancy*, pb. 1961; and *Childhood*, pb. 1960).

SCREENPLAYS: *Our Town,* 1940 (with Frank Craven and Harry Chantlee); *Shadow of a Doubt,* 1943 (with Sally Benson and Alma Revelle).

NONFICTION: *The Intent of the Artist,* 1941; *American Characteristics and Other Essays,* 1979; *The Journals of Thornton Wilder, 1939-1961,* 1985.

TRANSLATION: *The Victors,* 1948 (of Jean-Paul Sartre's play *Morts sans sépulture*).

Bibliography

Castronovo, David. *Thornton Wilder.* New York: Ungar, 1986. Two chapters on Wilder's early and later novels. A useful introductory study, including chronology, notes, and bibliography.

Goldstein, Malcolm. *The Art of Thornton Wilder.* Lincoln: University of Nebraska Press, 1965. An early and still useful introduction to Wilder's novels and plays. A short biographical sketch is followed by an in-depth look at his work through the one-act play *Childhood* (1962). Includes bibliographical notes and an index.

Goldstone, Richard H. *Thornton Wilder: An Intimate Portrait.* New York: Saturday Review Press, 1975. An intimate portrait of Wilder by a close friend who had written previous studies on the subject, had access to personal documents, and interviewed family and friends. Includes notes, a selected bibliography, and an index.

Harrison, Gilbert A. *The Enthusiast: A Life of Thornton Wilder.* New York: Ticknor & Fields, 1983. A chatty biographical study of Wilder by a biographer who was provided access to Wilder's notes, letters, and photographs. Harrison successfully re-creates Wilder's life and the influences, both good and bad, that shaped him.

Simon, Linda. *Thornton Wilder: His World.* Garden City, N.Y.: Doubleday, 1979. A solid biographical study of Wilder that includes examinations of his published works and photographs, notes, a bibliography, and an index.

Wilder, Amos Niven. *Thornton Wilder and His Public.* Philadelphia: Fortress Press, 1980. A short critical study of Wilder by his older brother, who offers an inside family look at the writer. A supplement includes Wilder's "Culture in a Democracy" address and a selected German bibliography.

LARRY WOIWODE

Born: Carrington, North Dakota; October 30, 1941

Principal long fiction · *What I'm Going to Do, I Think,* 1969; *Beyond the Bedroom Wall: A Family Album,* 1975; *Poppa John,* 1981; *Born Brothers,* 1988; *Indian Affairs,* 1992.

Other literary forms · Larry Woiwode is known primarily for his longer fiction, but he also frequently published short stories in such prominent literary periodicals as *The Atlantic Monthly* and *The New Yorker;* several of his stories were chosen for anthologies of the year's best. He wrote book reviews and essays for many newspapers, including *The New York Times. The Neumiller Stories* (1989), a collection of thirteen previously uncollected stories, including three penned in the 1980's, expands the "family album" of narratives about the Neumiller clan that Woiwode began in his novels *Beyond the Bedroom Wall* and *Born Brothers.* He also published a well-received book of poetry, *Even Tide* (1977).

Achievements · Woiwode's first novel, *What I'm Going to Do, I Think,* won for him the prestigious William Faulkner Foundation Award for the "most notable first novel" of 1969 and the American Library Association Notable Book award in 1970 and brought him immediate critical attention. It was a best-seller and has been translated into several foreign languages. His second novel, *Beyond the Bedroom Wall,* actually begun before *What I'm Going to Do, I Think,* was nominated for both the National Book Award and the National Book Critics Circle Award, and it won the American Library Association Notable Book award in 1976. It became an even bigger commercial and critical success than his first novel. Woiwode's third novel, *Poppa John,* however, was much less successful commercially and critically. The novel's premise and protagonist indeed represented a departure from the regional narrative Woiwode had successfully employed in his previous fiction, but it did earn the Cornerstone Best Book of the Year Award in 1982.

Poppa John notwithstanding, critics are quick to credit Woiwode's idiosyncratic, family-centered narratives with helping indirectly to rehabilitate the family chronicle, a genre long considered out of fashion. After a decade of relative publishing silence, Woiwode returned to this narrative genre in *Born Brothers* and *The Neumiller Stories.* Woiwode's evolving canon of Neumiller narratives depicts prodigal sons and daughters who, no matter where they tread, fulfill their destiny in rediscovering their roots and the family relationships which nurtured them early in their lives. Woiwode unabashedly admires the traditional nuclear family, and his fiction underscores the value of finding one's way by retracing one's steps. His narrative strength is thus seen in the fact that, even among readers accustomed to despondent, "lost" protagonists preoccupied with discovering the mysteries of life in the squalor of the city or some illicit relationship, Woiwode can make such old-fashioned premises seem startlingly fresh and appealing.

In the ebb and flow of many a writer's career, an acclaimed "first novel" often permanently overshadows subsequent efforts, and the disappointment with–and apparent dearth of fresh ideas that followed after–the publication of *Poppa John* provoked many critics and readers to wonder if Woiwode had lost his narrative vision. Such concerns were answered with the publication of *Born Brothers* and *The Neumiller Stories.*

Biography · Larry Alfred Woiwode (pronounced "why-wood-ee") was born in Carrington, North Dakota, October 30, 1941, and spent his early years in nearby Sykeston, a predominantly German settlement amid the rugged, often forbidding north-midwestern terrain. No doubt the beauty as well as the stark loneliness of this landscape heightened the author's appreciation for the effect of nature upon individual character. At the age of ten, he moved with his family to Manito, Illinois, another evocatively Midwestern environment capable of nurturing the descriptive powers of a budding fiction writer.

He attended the University of Illinois for five years but failed to complete a bachelor's degree, leaving

©1988 Nancy Crampton

the university in 1964 with an associate of arts in rhetoric. He met his future wife, Carol Ann Patterson, during this period and married her on May 21, 1965. After leaving Illinois, Woiwode moved to New York City and supported his family with freelance writing, publishing in *The New Yorker* and other prestigious periodicals while working on two novels.

He was a writer-in-residence at the University of Wisconsin, Madison, and had extended teaching posts at Wheaton College (Illinois) and at the State University of New York at Binghamton, where he served as a faculty member (intermittently) beginning in 1983. In 1977, he was awarded the Doctor of Letters degree from North Dakota State University. He and his family returned to North Dakota in 1978 to maintain an organic farm.

Analysis · To understand Larry Woiwode's craft and achievement, one must finally recognize the essentially religious character of his narratives and their thematic structure. He is an advocate for restoring a moral, even religious voice to modern letters. While believing that the most important human questions are, in fact, religious ones, Woiwode rejects the notion that there can be legitimate, compelling "novels of ideas"; for him, such fiction connotes mere propagandizing. Woiwode handles such questions not by placing philosophical soliloquies in the mouths of sophisticated, worldly protagonists, but by creating authentically ordinary characters, and settling them comfortably into the concrete and utterly mundane world of daily life.

In achieving this effective depiction of what might be called heightened normality, Woiwode's prose is consistently active, alive, and unassuming, approaching at times the crisp clarity of Ernest Hemingway but touched with a finely tuned lyricism. While Woiwode has sometimes been criticized for lapsing too easily into didacticism or marring an otherwise evocative scene with excessive detail, his keen eye for the extraordinary ordinariness of life makes his narrative vision compelling and believable.

As a novelist, Woiwode stands apart from most of his contemporaries in refusing to drown his characters in the angst-ridden excesses that have become so conventional in the modern American novel. His characters are not helpless victims of their times but participants in them; they are accountable not so much for what has happened to them but for what they do in response to their circumstances. Their conflicts, from Chris Van Eenanam's enigmatic search for manhood in *What I'm Going to Do, I Think* to Poppa John's drive to recover his self-identity, are not merely contrived psychological dramas played out inside their own consciousness, but compelling confrontations with the very concrete world of everyday life. This is a world which registers as authentic to the reader precisely because of Woiwode's gift for realism.

Woiwode's characters eventually recognize that the answer to their dilemmas is only partly in themselves. In the reestablishment of personal trust in friendships and the nostalgia of forgotten familial relationships, they recover a sense of balance and worth in themselves. However obliquely, each major Woiwode character finds himself in a quest for a transcendent moral order, a renewed trust in God and humanity that would give him a reference point for his life. This quest animates their rejection of narcissism and a search for a love and security that only marital and familial relationships can foster.

Woiwode's willingness to affirm that these relationships are central to self-fulfillment and to the stability of American culture makes him unique among a generation of writers whose thematic concerns tend to focus on their characters' dehumanization in society and alienation from family life and marital fidelity. Woiwode thus belongs in the company of self-consciously moralistic writers such as Walker Percy and Saul Bellow, who are more interested in the ways human beings survive and thrive in a fallen world than in the ways they capitulate to it.

When compared with other writers of his caliber, Woiwode cannot be considered a particularly prolific author. Yet two of his novels were critically acclaimed, national best-sellers, and they are among the best American novels written after 1960. The publication in consecutive years of *Born Brothers* and *The Neumiller Stories* seems to have redeemed Woiwode from the ambivalent response to *Poppa John*, and Woiwode's reputation as an important American writer in the second half of the twentieth century seems secure.

What I'm Going to Do, I Think · Woiwode's first novel, *What I'm Going to Do, I Think*, is an absorbing character study of two newlyweds, each of whom is originally drawn to the other as opposites proverbially attract. Chris Van Eenanam, the protagonist, is a listless mathematics graduate student, an unhappy agnostic unsure of his calling in life. The novel's title accentuates his self-doubt and indecision, echoing something Chris's father once said in observing his accident-prone son, "What I'm going to do,

I think, is get a new kid." Ellen Strohe, his pregnant bride, is a tortured young woman, dominated by the overbearing grandparents who reared her after her parents' accidental death. Neither she nor Chris can abide their interference and meddling.

Despite the fact that little action takes place "live" before the reader, the psychological realism in Woiwode's use of compacted action and flashbacks and the patterned repetition of certain incidents carry the reader along as effortlessly as might a conventionally chronological narrative. The reader learns "what happens" primarily as events filter through the conversations and consciousness of Chris and Ellen Van Eenanam during their extended honeymoon at her grandparents' cabin near the northwestern shore of Lake Michigan.

In this retreat from the decisions Chris elects not to face, the couple, now intimate, now isolated, confront a grim modern world, which has lost its faith in a supreme being fully in control of his created universe. This loss is exemplified most dramatically in the lives of Chris and Ellen as they try to sort out the meaning of affection and fidelity in their new relationship as husband and wife and as potential parents. Ellen's pregnancy is at first a sign of a beneficent nature's approval of their union, but later, as each has a premonition of their unborn child's death, it becomes a symbol of an ambivalent world's indifference to their marriage and its apparent fruitlessness.

In the absence of a compensatory faith even in humankind itself, a secondary faith arguably derived from faith in God, Chris and Ellen come to realize that they have lost their ability to navigate a hostile world with lasting, meaningful relationships. Neither mathematics nor nature can fill the vacuum left by an impotent faith whose incessant call is to fidelity and perseverance without passion or understanding. In a suspenseful epilogue which closes the novel with an explanation of what has happened to them in the seven years following their marriage, Chris and Ellen return to their honeymoon cabin. Chris retrieves the rifle he has not touched in many years, and, as the action builds toward what will apparently be his suicide, he repeats to himself the beginning of a letter (suicide note?) that he could not complete: *"Dear El, my wife. You're the only person I've ever been able to talk to and this is something I can't say. . . ."*

As he makes his way to the lake, he fires a round of ammunition into a plastic bleach container half-buried in the sand. In the novel's enigmatic final lines, Chris fires "the last round from his waist, sending the bullet out over the open lake." This curious ending seems intended by Woiwode to announce Chris's end of indecision–a recognition that his life can have transcendent meaning only in embracing fully his marriage commitment to Ellen.

Beyond the Bedroom Wall · The expansiveness and comic vitality of Woiwode's second novel, *Beyond the Bedroom Wall,* offer a marked contrast to *What I'm Going to Do, I Think.* In *Beyond the Bedroom Wall,* Woiwode parades sixty-three characters before the reader by the beginning of chapter 3. True to its subtitle, *A Family Album, Beyond the Bedroom Wall* is a sprawling, gangly work of loosely connected snapshots of the Neumiller family. An engaging homage to the seemingly evaporating family unit at the end of the twentieth century, the novel's "plot" is nearly impossible to paraphrase, consisting as it does of some narrative, some diary entries, and even its protagonist Martin Neumiller's job application for a teaching position. Since Woiwode published nearly a third of the forty-four chapters of *Beyond the Bedroom Wall* as self-contained short stories in *The New Yorker,* it is no surprise that the book reads as a discontinuous montage of events, images, and personalities.

The novel opens in part 1 with the funeral of Charles Neumiller, a German immigrant farmer who had brought his family to America before the war, and it continues, to part 5, closing with stories of the third generation of Neumillers in 1970, bringing the Neumiller family full circle from birth to life to death. Yet it is Martin Neumiller, Charles's son, a god-fearing, devoutly Catholic man and proud son of North Dakota, whose adventures and misadventures give the novel any unity it possesses. "My life is like a book," he says at one point. "There is one chapter, there is one story after another." The eccentric folks he encounters in and out of his extended family form a burlesque troupe of characters who boisterously sample both the joys and the sorrows of life on Earth. In the Neumiller "family album," Woiwode lends concreteness to his notion that reality is a fragile construction, one that sometimes cannot bear scrutiny "beyond the bedroom wall," that is, beyond the dreamy world of sleep, of its visions of what might be. Woiwode intimates that whatever hope there may be for fulfilling one's dreams, it is anchored in "walking by faith, and not by sight," by trusting in and actively nurturing family intimacy.

The rather sentimental, "old-fashioned" quality Woiwode achieves in this family chronicle, his evocation of once-embraced, now-lamented values, prompted critic and novelist John Gardner to place Woiwode in the company of literature's greatest epic novelists: "When self-doubt, alienation, and fashionable pessimism become a bore and, what's worse, a patent delusion, how does one get back to the big emotions, the large and fairly confident life affirmations of an Arnold Bennett, a Dickens, a Dostoevski? *Beyond the Bedroom Wall* is a brilliant solution."

Woiwode's eye for the rich details of daily life enables him to move through vast stretches of time and space in executing the episodic structure in this novel. His appreciation for the cadences of midwestern speech and his understanding of the distinctiveness of prairie life and landscape and its impact on the worldviews of its inhabitants recall other regional writers such as Rudy Wiebe and Garrison Keillor at their best.

Poppa John · *Poppa John* is shockingly short when compared with the massive *Beyond the Bedroom Wall*, and is more a novella than a novel. The book takes its title from the character Ned Daley played for many years on a popular television soap opera. His immense popularity beginning to overshadow the show itself, he is abruptly written out of the show in a dramatic "death." Ned thus finds himself suddenly unable to recover a sense of purpose, so long has he lived within the disguise of Poppa John, the fiery father figure, who often quoted Scripture to his television family. Now close to seventy, outspoken and Falstaffian in appearance and behavior, he seeks his deeply lost identity. Ned to his wife, but Poppa John to everyone else, he is lost in the malevolent nostalgia of growing old without self, or self-respect.

The novel opens two days before Christmas, a few months after Poppa John's television "death." Facing the Christmas season with wife, Celia, broke, broken, and without prospects for the future, the couple wander New York City, squandering their savings on gifts they had always wanted to buy for each other. Forced to "be himself," he finds he has leaned too heavily on the preacherlike Poppa John character, and his life begins to unravel. He is finally forced to face his own inconsistencies, his doubts, and even his sins, as Ned, an "elderly boy," is incapable of trusting in a life beyond the present. Speeding to a climax in its closing pages, the novel depicts Poppa John "coming to himself" on Christmas Day, realizing that he, after all these years, does believe in God, and therefore can come to believe in himself.

Poppa John perhaps deserved a better critical reception than it received; as a more than interesting attempt to portray an elderly actor's disintegrating life, it contains some of Woiwode's most lyrical scenes. In the end, however, it remains an unsatisfying chronicle—in part because the complexity apparent in Poppa John's character is never fully realized, presented as it is in a very compressed time frame. While Poppa John emerges as a potentially authentic character in the early parts of the novella, Woiwode gives the reader little insight into the motivations which would prompt his sudden conversion experience at the climax of the story.

Born Brothers · In *Born Brothers*, Woiwode returns to the characters, setting, and moral center that brought him his greatest and most uniformly favorable critical attention. Woiwode begins what he calls not a sequel but a "companion volume" to *Beyond the Bedroom Wall* in the middle of the twentieth century, the narration filtered through the consciousness of Charles Neumiller, a lost soul searching his memories for a meaning to life and a purpose for living it. He finds both in exploring his relationship with his brother Jerome. Charles's fragmentary childhood memories in fact become the narrative building blocks for the often elliptical and multiperspective chronicle that unravels before the reader in an even more challenging sequence than that of *Beyond the Bedroom Wall*. *Born Brothers* contains less a plot than a chain of remembrances; as family members and their ahistorical interactions with Charles are paraded before the reader in a kind of visual patchwork, one is compelled to enter Charles's consciousness and see the world through his convoluted epistemology.

Despite his outward sophistication and sense of being, Charles is obsessed with suicide; he seems incapable of conceiving of a meaningful order outside the family structure that had shaped his life and has now dissipated with the death of his mother and the collapse of his marriage. In part, it is Woiwode's intent to explain American society's apparent moral disintegration—rampant promiscuity, unwanted pregnancy, and divorce—by reference to the absence of strong family ties. Charles longs for the bond of brotherhood he once shared—or thinks he shared—with elder brother Jerome. That idyllic childhood in North Dakota, free from the cares and stresses modern, industrial life, impinges without provocation upon Charles's consciousness. Charles's strange career as a "radio personality" who is both the interviewer and the interviewee is somehow emblematic of his need for conversion, for freedom from self. He needs an "outside," a reference point, which, Woiwode hints, will come only from faith in the transcendent God whose eternal family Charles is invited to join.

Woiwode makes few compromises for the reader unwilling to attend to—or, perhaps eavesdrop upon—Charles Neumiller's open-ended musings. To refer to his ramblings as stream-of-consciousness narration is to give too precise a labeling, for not merely a consciousness is under consideration here but the history of a mind and a life as well. The journey to and through that history is not one that the casual reader will be inclined to take, which underscores the main criticism of Woiwode's prose shared even by critics sympathetic to his family chronicle: his apparent inattention to the toll his often exhaustive detail takes on both his characters and his readers. Jonathan Yardley's judgment seems most apt: "It's a pity to see a writer of Woiwode's talent and humanity stuck, at mid-career, in the endless exploration and reexploration of material that has yielded its last fresh insight if not its last lovely sentence."

Indian Affairs · With its broken sequence of scenes and lack of exposition or resolution of conflicts, *Indian Affairs* has elements of a postmodern novel. Woiwode uses this style to reflect the inner turmoil of Chris Van Eenanam, the main character of *What I'm Going to Do, I Think*. Chris and his wife Ellen return to an isolated cabin in the Michigan woods so that he can write his Ph.D. dissertation on American poet Theodore Roethke's natural philosophy and poetry. Mundane interruptions such as cutting firewood, installing a water pump, shopping, and tavern hopping distract him. A gang of drunken Native American teenagers threatens him when he does not supply them with beer, and a mysterious stalker forces him keep a loaded gun. On a deeper level, Chris undergoes an identity crisis—a need to affirm his masculinity, to cope with religious and moral dilemmas, and to resolve the conflict of whether his roots are Caucasian or American Indian.

Chris and Ellen's childless seven-year marriage has brought them no sense of permanence or hope for the future. Although they are thirty years old, Chris is still a graduate student, and they are dependent upon Ellen's wealthy grandparents for use of the cabin. Ellen's previous miscarriage and her ensuing barrenness symbolize the status of their marriage. Ellen resolves her unhappiness by recording her thoughts in a journal. Meanwhile, she joins a feminist discussion group, goes to a bar without an escort, and tries the hallucinogen peyote to ease her feelings of emptiness. Her conflicts disappear when she becomes pregnant again.

Chris spends much time with his bachelor friend Beau Nagoosa, a Chippewa Indian who has dropped out of white culture to build his own cabin. He supports himself as a woodcutter and justifies stealing wood on absentee landowners' property by telling himself it was once Native American land. Beau resents the invasion of white real-estate promoters, who claim to represent Volunteers in Service to America (VISTA), yet he accommodates them and compromises his ideals.

Chris and Beau discuss humanity's role within in the spiritual harmony of the natural world. For Chris, Roethke's claim that objects in nature are sentient is synonymous with Native American beliefs. Beau introduces Chris to peyote, which stimulates vivid sensory perceptions and fantasies but renders both Chris and Beau unable to cope with their real problems. Frustrated by chaotic events in his life and dissatisfied with the prospect of returning to academe in New York, Chris is overcome with depression. Feeling that nothing can guide him now except his own instincts, Chris decides to adhere to a line from one of Roethke's poems, "I'll be an Indian." Chris's future role as a teacher or leader is ambiguous.

As Chris begins to identify more strongly with his own Blackfoot Indian heritage and feel reverence for the natural world, conflicts escalate between the segregated white and Native American communities. The natural environment shrinks as urban development expands. Tribal leadership does not extend beyond exhibition dancing at powwows. American Indian families disintegrate, alcoholism and drug use destroy lives, and teenage youths engage in threat-making and violence. Woiwode's realistic and tragic portrayal of Native American life offers no solution to the problems.

To fully appreciate Woiwode's book, readers should have read *What I'm Going to Do, I Think* and have more than a passing acquaintance with the philosophies and writings of Theodore Roethke and Vine Deloria, an American Indian cultural nationalist. Woiwode's underlying theme is that modern Native Americans lack effective leaders to guide them.

Bruce L. Edwards, Jr., updated by Martha E. Rhynes

Other major works

SHORT FICTION: *The Neumiller Stories*, 1989; *Silent Passengers: Stories*, 1993.
POETRY: *Even Tide*, 1977.
NONFICTION: *Acts*, 1993.

Bibliography

Connaughton, Michael E. "Larry Woiwode." In *American Novelists Since World War II*, edited by James E. Kibler, Jr. 2d series. Detroit: Gale Research, 1980. An assessment of Woiwode's gift for regional fiction that explores the themes and narrative style of his first two novels.

Gardner, John. Review of *Beyond the Bedroom Wall*, by Larry Woiwode. *The New York Times Book Review* 125 (September 28, 1975): 1-2. An enthusiastic review of what most critics believe is Woiwode's best novel; Gardner's plaudits won a wide audience for Woiwode beyond the small circle of intellectuals who had hailed his first novel.

Jones, Timothy. "The Reforming of a Novelist." *Christianity Today*, October 26, 1992, 86-89. In this interview, Woiwode discusses his view of the nonreligious, humanistic approach of the East Coast literary establishment and the fact that his most recent writing includes greater emphasis on a religious view of such issues as belief and doubt.

Nelson, Shirley. "Stewards of the Imagination: Ron Hanson, Larry Woiwode, and Sue Miller." *Christian Century*, January 25, 1995, 82-86. An interview with three novelists in which they discuss their works and careers as well as the role of religion in their lives and writing. Includes an excerpt from Woiwode's *Poppa John*.

Pesetsky, Bette. Review of *Born Brothers* by Larry Woiwode. *The New York Times Book Review* 93 (August 4, 1988): 13-14. An affirmative evaluation of Woiwode's narrative mode and a defense of the novel's difficult thematic structure.

Woiwode, Larry. "An Interview with Larry Woiwode." *Christianity and Literature* 29 (1979): 11-18. An early, revealing interview in which Woiwode discusses those influences which shaped his narrative vision. Notable is his discussion of the centrality of family to his characterizations.

THOMAS WOLFE

Born: Asheville, North Carolina; October 3, 1900
Died: Baltimore, Maryland; September 15, 1938

Principal long fiction · *Look Homeward, Angel,* 1929; *Of Time and the River,* 1935; *The Web and the Rock,* 1939; *You Can't Go Home Again,* 1940; *The Short Novels of Thomas Wolfe,* 1961 (C. Hugh Holman, editor).

Other literary forms · During his lifetime Thomas Wolfe published four major works: two novels, *Look Homeward, Angel* and *Of Time and the River;* a collection of short stories, *From Death to Morning* (1935); and his description of his life as a creative artist, *The Story of a Novel* (1936). In addition to his major works, he also sold a few lengthy stories to magazines; *Scribner's Magazine* published "A Portrait of Bascom Hawke" (April, 1932) and "The Web of Earth" (July, 1939). Both of these have since been republished as short novels in *The Short Novels of Thomas Wolfe* (1961), a collection edited by C. Hugh Holman. Because Wolfe viewed each piece of his writing as only a part of some larger design, he frequently adapted past material to meet a present need. For example, he modified "A Portrait of Bascom Hawke" for later inclusion in *Of Time and the River,* and "The Child by Tiger" (1937), a short story he published in the *Saturday Evening Post,* appeared two years later with changes in point of view in *The Web and the Rock.* After his death, Wolfe's editor at Harper's, Edward Aswell, put together three posthumous books from two large packing cases of unfinished manuscript that Wolfe left behind. Two of these books—*The Web and the Rock* and *You Can't Go Home Again*—are novels; the third is a volume of stories, entitled *The Hills Beyond* (1941). Wolfe began his career (unsuccessfully) as a playwright with *The Mountains,* which he wrote in 1920 but which was not published until 1940 by the University of North Carolina at Chapel Hill, Wolfe's alma mater. Wolfe's letters and notebooks have also been published, allowing for firsthand insight into his personal and creative life.

Achievements · Wolfe captured the essence of what it meant to be young in his time with the publication of *Look Homeward, Angel.* He further influenced readers of the Depression-plagued 1930's with stories he published in magazines such as *The New Yorker, Harper's Bazaar, Redbook, Scribner's Magazine,* and the *Saturday Evening Post.* Widely read in America and abroad, Wolfe was a well-respected author during his lifetime, a man who in a very real sense lived the part of the driven artist. Wolfe is still read, even if not to the extent of his more significant contemporaries, Ernest Hemingway, William Faulkner, and F. Scott Fitzgerald. In retrospect, Wolfe's achievement is especially remarkable when one considers that his literary life spanned little more than a decade. In 1957, Faulkner ranked Wolfe above all of his contemporaries: "My admiration for Wolfe is that he tried the best to get it all said; he was willing to throw away style, coherence, all the rules of preciseness to try to put all the experience of the human heart on the head of a pin." Wolfe's weaknesses are now recognized, but he is still praised for his strengths. A balanced view of his work has emerged, and his reputation as an important figure in twentieth century American literature is secure.

Biography · Born on October 3, 1900, in Asheville, North Carolina, Thomas Wolfe was the youngest of the seven surviving children of Julia Elizabeth Westall and William Oliver Wolfe. Of Pennsylvania Dutch-German stock, Wolfe's father was a man of intense vitality, a stonecutter who instilled in Wolfe a love of language, whether it be the high rhetoric of Elizabethan poetry or the low vernacular of the mountain people surrounding Asheville. Wolfe's mother was more attuned to the values of commerce than her husband (she was forever speculating in real estate). In fact, one biographer has termed the match an "epic misalliance." Domestic rela-

Library of Congress

tions in the Wolfe household were often strained; young Wolfe grew up a witness to his father's drunken rampages and his mother's ensuing resentment. From this family cauldron came much of the autobiographical material Wolfe poured forth in *Look Homeward, Angel.*

In September of 1912, Wolfe entered the North State Fitting School, where he came under the influence of his teacher, Margaret Roberts (Margaret Leonard in *Look Homeward, Angel*). Roberts encouranged Wolfe's voracious appetite for reading by introducing him to the best of English literature. In 1916, at the precocious age of fifteen, Wolfe entered the University of North Carolina at Chapel Hill. Six feet tall and still growing (he would eventually reach six feet six inches), Wolfe was a skinny, long-legged youth, sensitive to the criticism of his older classmates. Wolfe's first year at Chapel Hill was unremarkable, but he eventually made a name for himself as an excellent student and a campus literary figure. In March of 1919, *The Return of Buck Garvin*, a play Wolfe had written in a dramatic writing course, was performed by the Carolina Playmakers, with Wolfe performing in the title role.

After graduating in 1920, Wolfe entered Harvard University to pursue his interests as a playwright. He was especially attracted by the famous workshop given by playwright George Pierce Baker (whom he would later depict as Professor Hatcher in *Of Time and the River*). Wolfe hoped to make a literary name for himself, but after a series of setbacks, he accepted an appointment as an instructor in English at the Washington Square College of New York University and began teaching in February of 1924, continuing to do so intermittently until 1930.

In October of 1924, Wolfe made his first trip to Europe. Many of his experiences there he later incorporated into *Of Time and the River*. Returning to New York in August of 1925, Wolfe met Aline Bernstein, a wealthy married woman who was involved in the theater world of New York. For the next seven years, Wolfe participated in a stormy on-and-off again affair with Bernstein, who was seventeen years his elder. She was the mother-mistress Wolfe seemed to need; certainly, she inspired *Look Homeward, Angel,* which he commenced while abroad with Bernstein in July of 1926.

The popular image of Wolfe as a literary lion is in part caused by the critical success he achieved with *Look Homeward, Angel* but is based mostly on his personal appearance and habits. Often dressed in shabby clothes, he was known to prowl the streets of Brooklyn, where he had settled after another trip abroad in 1931. One night while wandering the streets he was overheard to say, "I wrote ten thousand words today! I wrote ten thousand words today!" Although Wolfe resented efforts to publicize his eccentricities, it was inevitable that his behavior and fame would make him a legendary figure.

In December of 1933, Wolfe began work on what was to become *Of Time and the River.* It was also during this period that Maxwell Perkins, Wolfe's editor at Scribner's, worked closely with the author on the formation of the novel. Wolfe incorporated his experiences at Harvard, in Europe, and with Bernstein into *Of Time and the River,* which picks up the Eugene Gant story where *Look Homeward, Angel* concludes. In 1937, after critics had raised questions concerning Perkins's influence on his work, Wolfe left Scribner's for Harper and Brothers. His editor at Harper's was Edward C. Aswell, and Wolfe left two large crates containing nearly a million words of manuscript with him before leaving on a tour of the West in May of 1938. In July, Wolfe fell ill with pneumonia and was hospitalized near Seattle. In September, having been transferred to The Johns Hopkins Hospital in Baltimore, he underwent brain surgery for complications he suffered from tuberculosis. He died on September 15, 1938.

Analysis · Throughout Thomas Wolfe's fiction there is evidence of a powerful but sometimes uncontrolled mind at work. Few would argue Wolfe's genius, but many have questioned how well he directed it. Part of the difficulty may have come from his self-professed intention to create an American mythology. The result would be the record of an individual, lonely and lost in the flux of time, forever exploring the diversity of American life. Partly because of his early death and partly because of his own difficulties in giving form to ideas, Wolfe never managed to unify the vast body of his work. Add to this the considerable amount of influence his editors exerted upon his manuscripts, and there still remain some intriguing questions about the interrelationship of segments in the writings and the final form of his novels.

Wolfe wrote with passionate intensity, producing vast quantities of manuscript. His central themes focus on a lonely individual, the isolated artist, in search of self-discovery and the true meaning of the American experience. In *Look Homeward, Angel,* the first of these themes is most pronounced, for this is autobiography very thinly veiled. The story of Eugene Gant is in many ways the story of Thomas Wolfe. After the publication of *Look Homeward, Angel,* which was generally well received, some critics began to raise questions concerning the novel's weaknesses, especially the obvious attempt by Wolfe to capture experience at the expense of artistic control. It was not until 1936, however, that the landmark case against Wolfe would be launched with the publication in the *Saturday Review* of "Genius Is Not Enough," Bernard De Voto's indictment of Wolfe and his fiction.

De Voto was responding to *The Story of a Novel,* Wolfe's extremely frank account of his own life as a writer and the work that went into *Of Time and the River.* For Wolfe, writing was a chaotic experience, something done with great pain and toil. De Voto acknowledged that Wolfe was a genius "of the good old-fashioned, romantic kind, possessed by a demon, driven by the gales of his own fury, helpless before the lava-flood of his own passion"; he further argued, however, that such genius was in and of itself not enough. Today the legacy of De Voto's remarks remains manifest in a series of stereotypes: By some readers (especially academics), Wolfe is still thought of as one who never controlled his rhetoric, as one who was unable to organize his work, and as one who sometimes pushed autobiography to the limits of reporting.

To illustrate Wolfe's lack of rhetorical restraint, De Voto pointed to *Of Time and the River*, commenting that Wolfe invested each experience he described with so much raw emotion that a midnight snack took on the same importance as the death of Oliver Gant. As De Voto stated, "If the death of one's father comes out emotionally even with ham-on-rye, then the art of fiction is cockeyed." As for the charge that Wolfe was a writer who never exerted sufficient control over his material, De Voto and others have cited the sprawling sections of his mammoth novels where there is supportive evidence that episodes stand by themselves rather than in relation to others. The extent of Wolfe's involvement with his editors (Maxwell Perkins at Scribners from 1928 to 1937; Edward Aswell at Harper's from 1937 to 1938) also raises questions about his own ability to revise and organize his novels.

Perhaps the most revealing example of editorial influence on Wolfe's fiction concerns *Of Time and the River*. While Wolfe was working on the novel, Perkins met with him day and night for more than a year in an attempt to help him gain control over the voluminous amount of material he had written. Often Perkins would ask Wolfe to go home and cut a section, only to find that he would return with an episode thousands of words longer. In one of the most dramatic decisions any editor has made with a figure as significant as Wolfe, Perkins, without Wolfe's final approval, sent the manuscript of *Of Time and the River* to the printer in September of 1934. Perkins made the decision because he felt the novel was as complete as Wolfe could make it and that Wolfe needed to get on with other work. Whatever the reasons, the ultimate responsibility for the publication of any book rests squarely upon the writer. Because Wolfe was so deferential to his editor and because he was unable or unwilling to see his novel through to the end, he opened himself to questions concerning his craftsmanship, questions which are still being asked today.

Finally, there remains the issue of autobiography in Wolfe's novels. Wolfe himself claimed that autobiography was a part of any serious creative work, but there are in his novels, especially *Look Homeward, Angel*, sections that read like a mere diary. There is also a great deal of artistic invention in his novels, and certainly almost all writers use material based on their own experiences; nevertheless, many of Wolfe's depictions were so thinly fictionalized that individuals were easily recognized, and many were hurt and embarrassed by what they thought were the unflattering portraits Wolfe rendered of them. Wolfe's use of autobiography pushed to journalistic limits raises more questions about his fictional method.

Although Wolfe's rhetoric, his conception of structure, and the autobiographical element within his work have been discussed as weaknesses, these three elements can also be cited as the strengths of his writing. For example, it is true there is ample evidence to support De Voto's claim that Wolfe's rhetoric is often artificially heightened, but at the same time, one of his most compelling attributes is his ability to depict something as insignificant as a "ham-on-rye" so clearly that readers may suddenly find themselves hungry. More to the point, however, are passages such as the Laura James sections of *Look Homeward, Angel*, where Wolfe manages to capture as well as any writer what it means to be young and in love. There are also numerous passages within his other novels that stand as some of the most poetic set pieces to be found in prose. In large measure, Wolfe is still read today because of the magnificence of his style, however extravagant it may be at times.

Wolfe held to an organic theory of art, one in which content dictates form. He was constantly searching for new ways to communicate experience; in this sense, the criticism directed at him for being a "formless" writer may in some ways be unfair. Certainly there is no doubt that in his attempts to depart from traditional formats he sometimes lost control of his material–*Of Time and the River*, for example, is marred by this flaw. On the other hand, he did manage to find an effective structure in "The Web of Earth," his lengthy story written under the influence of James Joyce. The entire work is filtered through the consciousness of an old woman engaged in reminiscence, and it is the finest example of artistic unity in Wolfe's work. In *Look Homeward, Angel*, Wolfe modified a traditional novelistic form, the *Bildungsroman* (the story of a youth initiated by experience into maturity), organizing the novel not around a unified sequence of events but instead around a series of sense impressions. In this way, the loose structure serves to complement the rhapsodic style. The result is a powerful rendering of the book's central theme–that of an artistic youth lost and in search of self-knowledge and self-definition.

As for the contention that Wolfe is too highly autobiographical, that his writing too often approaches mere reportage, there can be no denying that on occasion, he is guilty as charged. In most instances, however, he was by no means a mere reporter of events. His fiction is memorable because he was such an apt interpreter of human beings and everyday experiences. He was able to synthesize experience into art; he himself claimed that everything in a work of art is changed, that nothing is a literal representation of actual experience. Whether he always achieved this transmutation, it can safely be said that Wolfe is still read today because his novels stand as a testimony to human experience artistically rendered from a unique and personal vision.

Look Homeward, Angel · *Look Homeward, Angel*, Wolfe's first and most significant novel, made use of extensive autobiographical material. In many ways, it is the story of his own life, the life of his family, his neighbors, and the region in which he lived. For those who know something of Wolfe's background, there are unmistakable connections between the fictional characters in *Look Homeward, Angel* and the real people among whom Wolfe grew up in Asheville, North Carolina. After the novel's publication, many from his hometown–and indeed many in his own family–were angered by what they took to be unflattering depictions of themselves in the novel. Wolfe's own account of the reaction to his novel can be found in *The Story of a Novel*, wherein he describes the uproar in Asheville and provides his own defense of his fictional method. Essentially, Wolfe believed that the people he described, whatever their faults, were magnificent. As magnificent as he thought his characters were, however, he often described them (no doubt truthfully) with all their faults made highly visible.

The ethics of his method can be questioned when one considers how it must have been to have lived in Asheville at the time the novel was published, to have opened its pages and to have found the characters so thinly fictionalized that their real counterparts could be easily identified. The ethical issue is not so much whether Wolfe was accurate in his depictions of the whole range of humanity he described, but rather how one would feel if he were identified as the model for the town drunk or as the counterpart of the unscrupulous businessman. It did not take long for the people of Asheville to start pointing fingers at one another after figuring out who was who in the novel. Perhaps with some justification, all fingers eventually pointed toward Wolfe himself; the controversy over what he had done to his town and the people in it was so pronounced that he was unable to return to Asheville until seven years after the publication of *Look Homeward, Angel.*

Wolfe departed from the development of a traditional plot in *Look Homeward, Angel* and instead made use of impressionistic realism to tie events and characters together. The narrator moves in and out of the consciousness of the principal characters, giving readers impressions of their inner feelings and motivations. As much as anything else, *Look Homeward, Angel* is the story of a quest, a search for self-knowledge and for lasting human interaction. The subtitle of the novel is *A Story of the Buried Life*, and much of what Wolfe depicts concerns itself with the inner lives of the characters in the novel—what they really think and feel as well as how isolated and alienated they are from one another. In this sense, the novel explores the relationship of time, change, and death as elements which will always frustrate the human desire for happiness and fulfillment.

Look Homeward, Angel was initially entitled *O Lost* and then *Alone, Alone.* The title on which Wolfe finally settled comes from "Lycidas," John Milton's poem in which the archangel Michael is asked to look back toward England to mourn a young man's death and all the unfulfilled potential it signifies. Eugene Gant, is, like most of Wolfe's protagonists, the isolated and sensitive artist in search of meaning and companionship in a hostile world. Given this theme, it is ironic that some of Wolfe's least effective passages are the results of his attempts to describe Eugene's feelings of loneliness and despair. In such segments (which recur in almost all of Wolfe's works), he often lapses into contrived language; rather than arising from natural consequences or from the interplay between one character and another, feelings seem forced by authorial intervention. On the other hand, the novel does contain some of his finest writing, especially when he describes people, places, and things with visionary intensity.

Look Homeward, Angel covers the first twenty years of Eugene Gant's life—his adolescence, his four years at the private school of Margaret Leonard, and his four years at the university. A pattern of potential fulfillment destroyed by frustration is personified in Eugene's parents, Eliza and Oliver, who are modeled after Wolfe's own mother and father. Oliver Gant is a stonecutter who passionately desires to create something beautiful, to carve an angel's head. He is an unfulfilled artist, a man of intense vitality who desires a full and sensuous life. His intensity, his capacity for life, is checked by his wife, Eliza, who is his antithesis: parsimonious, cold, and material-istic. This pattern of frustrated potential recurs throughout the novel. In one example, after spending his first year at the university and losing his innocence in a brothel, Eugene returns home to spend the summer at Dixieland, his mother's boardinghouse. There he meets and falls in love with Laura James (based on his own first love, Clara Paul). In his descriptions of the young, passionate love that develops between them, Wolfe's prose becomes a lyrical celebration that turns to tragic frustration as Eugene learns that Laura is engaged to marry another young man back home, that she will never be a part of his life again. Thus, potential (in this example, physical and spiritual union between Eugene and Laura) is checked by reality (separation and isolation). This pattern manifests itself in varying ways throughout the novel. The story of a youth coming of age by initiation into experience, *Look Homeward, Angel* is a compre-hensive account of the inner life of a sensitive and artistic youth.

With the publication of *Look Homeward, Angel*, Wolfe was thrust (not unwillingly) into the limelight as a legend, a novelist who demonstrated enormous potential. His success was spectacular, but because he was a driven artist (much like his fictional counterpart, Eugene Gant), his initial success created a good many subsequent problems. He immediately felt the burden to surpass his first effort with an even better second novel. At the same time, he ran into difficulty giving form to his expansive ideas (a problem with which he would grapple for the remainder of his life). During this same period, he also began leading a turbulent private life. He was involved with Aline Bernstein (the "A. B." to whom *Look Homeward, Angel* is dedicated), and their relationship—as tempestuous as any could conceivably be—would figure heavily in the remainder of his life and work.

Of Time and the River · Composed of eight sections, each of which is named after some epic or mythic figure, *Of Time and the River* exceeds nine hundred pages in length and spans two continents, continuing the story of Thomas Wolfe as personified in the character of Eugene Gant. Wolfe continues the story with Eugene's departure from Altamont for study at Harvard. He stated his ambitious theme for *Of Time and the River* in *The Story of a Novel*; his central idea was to depict the search for a father, not only in a literal but also in a figurative sense. While trying to exemplify his theme, Wolfe also struggled to form *Of Time and the River* out of the vast amount of manuscript he had written (a detailed discussion of that struggle is related in *The Story of a Novel*). The struggle reached its peak when his editor, Maxwell Perkins, sent the novel to press without Wolfe's knowledge. In one of his letters to Perkins, Wolfe claimed that another six months' work would have allowed him to complete the necessary revisions that would have made the book less episodic. There can be no doubt that had Wolfe written *Of Time and the River* without Perkins's influence, it would have been a very different novel—perhaps a better one than it is. As it stands, it is, as Wolfe himself noted, episodic; its parts are not always aligned to form a unified plot. Even so, there are fine passages throughout that more than compensate for its ponderous pace and meandering plot. In *The Story of a Novel*, Wolfe describes how he wrote one scene that ran to eighty thousand words (about two hundred pages). He was attempting to capture "the full flood and fabric" of four people simply talking to one another for four continuous hours. This scene, as good as he thought it was, eventually was cut, but it illustrates the massive amount of writing he did for the novel as well as the extensive amount of cutting he did to get it into publishable form.

Perhaps the novel's most magnificent scene is that which describes the death of Eugene's father, who has been slowly dying of cancer. Gant, the paternal figure whose presence was so unforgettable in *Look Homeward, Angel*, is now old and enfeebled. His death, which comes in a final moment of tranquillity, stands in stark contrast to his life, which was lived with violent gestures and howling protests. Often drunk, sometimes violent, he was a hard man to live with, but his death comes as a reminder that life lived intensely—however excessively—is life worth living. The death of his wife, Eliza, would not begin to elicit the intensity of emotion aroused by his final moments, for she stands as a testimony to all that opposes the force and fury of his life.

Other memorable scenes in the novel include those that take place in Boston with Eugene's uncle, Bascom Pentland. Uncle Bascom and his demented wife are two of the more finely drawn eccentrics in the novel. These segments as well as others involving Eugene's dreams to become a playwright, his time spent as an English instructor at a city university in New York, and his eventual travel to Europe, all contribute to Wolfe's attempt to describe the vast array of people, places, and things unique to the American experience.

While working out his central theme of a search for a father, Wolfe developed a three-part vision of time: time present, time past, and time eternal. The first, time present, is the time in which the actual events in the novel take place, the time of reality. The second, time past, represents all of the accumulated experience that affects time present. The third, time eternal, stands for the lasting time of oceans, forests, and rivers, of things that form the permanent backdrop for people's experiences. These three levels of time allow Wolfe to contrast, in a vast and symbolic scale, the relationship of past, present, and eternal experience with the experience of Eugene Gant. The result is an intensely personal search for meaning, an attempt to reconcile opposites, to find something lasting and meaningful.

Throughout the novel, a scene that takes place in the present may be linked with past scenes and eternal scenes. In this way, all three levels of time are united. For example, a train ride taking place in present time provides Eugene with the opportunity to recall the travelers of earlier days, their epic searching, their longing for discovery, for movement. During the same segment, Eugene speculates that other people in the future (eternal time) will also travel the earth in search of one another. The novel frequently develops itself in this way, and it is these segments which give the novel its mysterious, almost haunting, quality. At the same time, however, these same passages become repetitious (if not tedious), and illustrate once again the lack of restraint so evident throughout Wolfe's work. In contrast to these overwritten segments are a good many specific characterizations as well as a variety of satiric passages aimed at mediocre people, middle-class values, and intellectual pretenders. This is a vast and comprehensive book that ends when Eugene sets sail back to America. Aboard ship he meets Esther Jack (Aline Bernstein), who, although certainly not the father for whom he is searching, is nevertheless someone who can help him transcend the tormented youth he has endured to this point in his life.

Both *The Web and the Rock* and *You Can't Go Home Again* were put together by Edward Aswell, Wolfe's editor at Harper's, and published posthumously as novels. It was not until 1962, when Richard S. Kennedy published *The Window of Memory: The Literary Career of Thomas Wolfe*, that the extent of Aswell's influence on the two novels became fully known. Just before his death, Wolfe left a large packing crate of manuscript with Aswell. From that collection of manuscript, it was generally assumed that Aswell found two separate narratives, which he then published as the two posthumous novels. Surprisingly, however, Professor Kennedy discovered, after an extensive study of Wolfe's papers and manuscripts at Harvard University, that Aswell constructed *The Web and the Rock* and *You Can't Go Home Again* from what was a massive—but fragmentary—amount of manuscript that Wolfe apparently intended to condense into a single narrative. Had Wolfe lived, he most certainly would not have published the two novels as Aswell published them. In a very real way, they are as much the product of Aswell's editorializing as they are a product of Wolfe's imagination. Even so, the two novels represent a significant part of Wolfe's creative output, and analysis of them can help put his entire achievement into a clearer perspective.

The Web and the Rock · Wolfe claimed that he was turning away from the books he had previously written, that *The Web and the Rock* would be his most "objective" work to date. It should be noted that at that time, Wolfe had become particularly sensitive about the criticism he had received from De Voto and others concerning his alleged inability to exert artistic control over his material. As a result, not only did he claim his new novel to be objective, but also he abandoned his previous protagonist, Eugene Gant, in favor of a new one, George "Monk" Webber. The change was more in name than in substance, however, for Webber, like Eugene Gant, bears a close resemblance to Wolfe himself. Indeed, *The Web and the Rock* is quite similar to Wolfe's earlier works: Its first half parallels *Look Homeward, Angel,* while its second half stands as a sequel to *Of Time and the River.*

One of the strongest chapters in the novel is enlightening insofar as it illustrates how Wolfe continually reshaped past material. "The Child by Tiger" was first published in 1937 as a short story, but in the eighth chapter of *The Web and the Rock,* Wolfe reworks the story with changes in character and point of view. It is a moving story about the nature of good and evil, innocence and experience. Dick Prosser, a black man of ability and potential, is the object of the racial prejudice that was so pronounced in the South during the early part of the twentieth century. He is a man who befriends several young white boys; he teaches them how to throw a football, how to box, and how to make a fire. In short, he becomes a kindly father-figure who initiates them into experience. There is, however, another side to Prosser. Driven to the point of madness by prejudicial treatment, by his own apocalyptic brand of religion, and by his involvement with a woman, he goes on a shooting spree one night, killing blacks and whites alike. Eventually shot by the mob formed to hunt him down, his bullet-riddled body is hung up for display in the window of the undertaker's parlor. In the course of these events, the young men who were Prosser's friends are initiated into a world full of violence and death. For the first time in their lives, they experience profound loss, and they witness evil as it is personified in the bloodthirsty mob. Woven within the story are stanzas from William Blake's poem "The Tyger," from which the chapter title is derived.

In what makes up the second half of the novel, Wolfe deals with his own experiences in New York City. He explores his relationship with Bernstein, depicting her as a sophisticated mistress and himself as a brilliant but egocentric genius. Their relationship is described in detail—from their love-making and eating to their quarrels and reconciliations. These segments are remarkable for their candor and intriguing because of the insight they provide into the tempestuous relationship between the two. Webber's past experiences, the environment in which he was reared, and his ancestry symbolically form the web in which he is snared, and, as Esther Jack becomes a part of that web, he escapes to Germany. His search for the rock, the strength and beauty of vision that is represented by the father-figure for whom he longs, is interrupted by his realization at the end of the novel that "you can't go home again." In short, he knows that he must look to the future to escape the past.

You Can't Go Home Again · Continuing the chronicle of George Webber's life and artistic development, *You Can't Go Home Again* metaphorically develops the theme that Webber cannot go "home," cannot return to past places, old ideas, and former experiences because time and change have corrupted them. In this sense, "home" is an idealized vision of America as it appeared to George in his youth. These youthful visions come into abrupt contact with reality, and the resulting clash allows Wolfe to explore the very fabric of American society.

The novel begins approximately six months after *The Web and the Rock* ends. Webber has returned home to America, and, against his better judgment, he decides to resume his relationship with Esther Jack. He also resumes work on his novel *Home* to *Our Mountains (Look Homeward, Angel)* and finds a publisher, James Rodney & Co. (Scribner's), as well as a sympathetic editor and father-figure, Foxhall Edwards (Maxwell Perkins). Before his book is published, however, he returns home for the first time in years to attend the funeral of his Aunt Maw. Home in this novel is Libya Hill (like the Altamont of *Look Homeward, Angel*, the locale still represents Asheville, North Carolina). On the train trip home, he meets his childhood friend Nebraska Crane, a one-time big-league baseball star. Crane, a Cherokee Indian, is now satisfied to lead the simple life of a family man and part-time tobacco farmer, standing in contrast to Webber, whose intellectual drive and literary ambition make him a driven "city" man.

Also on the train is Judge Rumford Bland, a blind syphilitic whose corruption serves to symbolize the corruption in Libya Hill toward which Webber is traveling. Upon his arrival, Webber finds that his quiet boyhood town has become crazed from a land-boom mentality that has everyone making huge paper fortunes in real estate (these events parallel those immediately preceding the Depression). Thus, his idealized expectations of home are shattered by the corruption and madness running rampant throughout Libya Hill.

After the publication of his novel, Webber receives abusive letters from the residents of Libya Hill. Typically, Wolfe incorporated his own experiences into his fiction. In this instance, he drew upon his unpleasant memories of what happened after he published *Look Homeward, Angel*. An entire book in the novel ("The World That Jack Built") is devoted to the wealthy lives of Esther and Frederick Jack (the Bernsteins). Writing about his own breakup with Aline Bernstein, Wolfe describes Webber's move to Brooklyn and the end of his relationship with Esther Jack. In Brooklyn, Webber learns to love the low-life characters who inhabit the streets–the prostitutes, the derelicts, and the petty criminals–for they are very much a part of the American experience. To ignore them–or worse yet, to explain them away somehow–would be to deny the underbelly of America that Webber (and Wolfe) found so compelling.

After his years in Brooklyn (with scenes devoted to his relationship with Foxhall Edwards, his editor), Webber tires of New York and sails for Europe. In Germany, he is welcomed with the fame and notoriety he has sought for so long, but he also witnesses the darker side of Nazi Germany. The novel is the story of one man's pilgrimage, a search for a faith that will endure within a society so corrupt that each individual is destroyed by it. *You Can't Go Home Again* is not an entirely cynical book, however, for it concludes with a sense of hope and faith in the future.

Throughout his novels, Wolfe explored isolation, death, and the changes wrought by time–themes that exemplify his interest in the darker elements of life. In his attempts to capture the essence of a moment, he often overlooked the artistic demands that the novel imposes upon any writer. He was not a craftsman of the novel because he often sacrificed form, unity, and coherence to capture experience. His reputation is linked directly to his ambitious attempts to say it all, and *Look Homeward, Angel*, although only the beginning of the story Wolfe desired to tell, stands as his most satisfying and fully realized work.

Philip A. Luther

Other major works

SHORT FICTION: *From Death to Morning*, 1935; *The Hills Beyond*, 1941; *The Complete Short Stories of Thomas Wolfe*, 1987.

PLAYS: *Welcome to Our City*, pr. 1923 (published only in Germany as *Willkommen in Altamont*); *The Mountains*, pb. 1940; *Mannerhouse*, pb. 1948.

POETRY: *The Face of a Nation: Poetical Passages from the Writings of Thomas Wolfe*, 1939; *A Stone, a Leaf, a Door: Poems by Thomas Wolfe*, 1945.

NONFICTION: *The Story of a Novel*, 1936; *Thomas Wolfe's Letters to His Mother*, 1943; *The Portable Thomas Wolfe*, 1946; *The Letters of Thomas Wolfe*, 1956; *The Notebooks of Thomas Wolfe*, 1970; *The Thomas Wolfe Reader*, 1982; *Beyond Love and Loyalty: The Letters of Thomas Wolfe and Elizabeth Nowell*, 1983; *My Other Loneliness: Letters of Thomas Wolfe and Aline Bernstein*, 1983.

Bibliography

Bloom, Harold, ed. *Thomas Wolfe*. New York: Chelsea House, 1987. Several essays are devoted to *Look Homeward, Angel*, but Wolfe's other novels are covered as well, with an introduction, chronology, and bibliography.

Donald, David Herbert. *Look Homeward*. Boston: Little, Brown, 1987. Donald's fine late biography stresses Wolfe's accomplishment as a social historian and his novels as "a barometer of American culture." Like others, Donald admits the presence of much bad writing but confesses to responding enthusiastically to the good. Makes full use of Wolfe's letters to his mistress, Aline Bernstein.

Evans, Elizabeth. *Thomas Wolfe*. New York: Frederick Ungar, 1984. This quarto volume provides an excellent shorter introduction to Wolfe for both the beginning and the advanced student. Economical and accurate, it is keyed clearly to Wolfe scholarship and is rich in unpretentious literary allusion. Though Evans is cautious in her admiration of Wolfe's fiction, she is appreciative of it as well. Contains a chronology and a good short bibliography.

Holman, C. Hugh. *The World of Thomas Wolfe*. New York: Charles Scribner's Sons, 1962. An older text, an example of the "controlled research" concept popular in the 1960's, this book is specifically designed for high school and college students. A good cross section of Wolfe criticism is offered, with practical information for further study. Topics for library research and term papers are suggested.

Idol, John Lane. *A Thomas Wolfe Companion*. New York: Greenwood Press, 1987. Chapters on Wolfe's ideas, major themes, editors, and critics. Also a glossary of characters and places, a genealogical chart, collections of Wolfe material, and various organizations devoted to his study. An annotated bibliography and chronology make this a highly useful resource.

Kennedy, Richard S. *The Window of Memory*. Chapel Hill: University of North Carolina Press, 1962. Remains indispensable to the study of Wolfe; objective, scholarly, and analytic, it melds the work and the man into an artistic synthesis. Particularly valuable as a study of the creative process.

Phillipson, John S., ed. *Critical Essays on Thomas Wolfe*. Boston: G. K. Hall, 1986. Essays on each of Wolfe's major novels, stories, and plays as well as overviews of his career. Includes an introduction but no bibliography.

Rubin, Louis D., Jr., ed. *Thomas Wolfe: A Collection of Critical Essays*. Englewood Cliffs, N.J.: Prentice-Hall, 1973. A collection, with an introduction by Rubin, of a dozen stimulating essays by a variety of critics, scholars, and writers ranging from the impressionistic—a mode Wolfe inevitably inspires—to the scholarly. Contains the notorious Bernard De Voto review (1936) of *The Story of a Novel* entitled "Genius Is Not Enough."

HERMAN WOUK

Born: New York, New York; May 27, 1915

Principal long fiction · *Aurora Dawn*, 1947; *The City Boy*, 1948; *The Caine Mutiny*, 1951; *Marjorie Morningstar*, 1955; *Slattery's Hurricane*, 1956; *Youngblood Hawke*, 1962; *Don't Stop the Carnival*, 1965; *The Lomokome Papers*, 1968; *The Winds of War*, 1971; *War and Remembrance*, 1978; *Inside, Outside*, 1985; *The Hope*, 1993; *The Glory*, 1994.

Other literary forms · Herman Wouk wrote several plays; the first, *The Traitor*, was produced on Broadway in 1949 and was published by Samuel French the same year. His most successful theatrical work, *The Caine Mutiny Court-Martial* (based upon the novel published in 1951), appeared on Broadway in 1954 and was published by Doubleday the same year. *Nature's Way* was produced on Broadway in 1957 and was published by Doubleday the following year. Eric Bentley, speaking of *The Caine Mutiny Court-Martial*, said that Wouk showed a gift for crisp dialogue that no other regular writer for the American theater could rival. The musical *Don't Stop the Carnival*, a collaboration with pop musician Jimmy Buffett, was produced in 1998. Wouk collaborated with Richard Murphy in writing the screenplay for *Slattery's Hurricane* (1949). Wouk also wrote teleplays, for *The Winds of War* (1983) and *War and Remembrance* (1988). *This Is My God*, which Wouk first published in 1959 and followed with a revised edition in 1973, is a description and explanation of Orthodox Judaism, especially as it is practiced in America. The volume was a Reader's Digest Condensed Book Club selection and an alternate selection for the Book-of-the-Month Club in 1959.

Achievements · It is a peculiarity of American criticism to denigrate popular success in literature. Almost from the outset of his career, Wouk was a very popular writer; putting aside prejudicial presuppositions, this can be acknowledged as a genuine achievement, for Wouk did not attain his popular status by catering to the baser tastes of his readers. Beginning with *The Caine Mutiny*, his books appeared regularly on best-seller lists. Several of his titles were selections of major book clubs. Wouk was awarded the Pulitzer Prize for Fiction in 1952 for *The Caine Mutiny*. That same year, Columbia University presented him the Medal of Excellence, an honor extended to distinguished alumni. Several universities awarded him honorary doctoral degrees.

Wouk might be described as a traditional novelist, in that his writing does not reflect the experimental qualities that are to be found in so much twentieth century American fiction. Like John Updike, he gives primacy of place to the narrative element in fiction; he brings to the novel his own peculiar brand of rough-hewn vigor. At a time when the conventional wisdom judged it bad form for a novelist to take a clear stand on moral issues—as if ambiguity itself were a virtue—Wouk consistently declared his moral position in his writings. This was not always to the benefit of his fiction, but by and large, his novels are stronger for his conviction that literary art does not subsist in a vacuum but is part of a larger moral universe.

Biography · Herman Wouk was born in New York City on May 27, 1915, the son of Abraham Isaac and Esther (Levine) Wouk. Wouk's father, an industrialist in the power laundry field, started out as an immigrant laundry worker earning three dollars a week. Wouk was educated at Townsend Harris Hall and at Columbia University, where he graduated with honors in 1934. While at Columbia, he studied philosophy and comparative literature and was editor of the *Columbia Jester*. From 1934 to 1935 he worked as a gag writer for radio comedians, and from 1936 to 1941, he was a scriptwriter for Fred Allen. In 1941, Wouk moved to Washington, D.C., following his appointment to the United States Treasury Department as a dollar-a-year man; his job was to write and produce radio shows to sell war bonds. He left this work to join the Navy. After completing Officer Candidate School, he was commissioned an ensign and assigned to mine sweeper duty in the Pacific fleet. He served in the Navy from 1942 to 1945, first aboard the U.S.S. *Zane* and then aboard the destroyer-minesweeper U.S.S. *Southard*; eventually he was to be promoted to the position of Executive Officer of that ship. He was decorated with four campaign stars during the war, and received a Unit Citation as well. When Wouk was processed out of the Navy in 1945, he held the rank of lieutenant. Wouk married Betty Sarah Brown in December, 1945. They had three sons, Abraham Isaac (who died before reaching his fifth birthday), Nathaniel, and Joseph.

Wouk began his career as a serious writer while he was in the Navy; before his release from the service, he had completed a good portion of his first novel. That novel, *Aurora Dawn*, was published by Simon and Schuster in 1947. The following year, his second novel, *The City Boy*, was published. Neither of these works gained a great deal of attention for Wouk, but with the publication of *The Caine Mutiny* in 1951 (awarded the Pulitzer Prize the following year), he was quickly established as a writer of consequence. His play, *The Caine Mutiny Court-Martial*, began its successful run on Broadway in 1954. *Marjorie Morningstar* appeared in 1955 and his nonfiction work on Jewish culture and religion, *This Is My God*, in 1959. The 1960's saw the publication of *Youngblood Hawke* and *Don't Stop the Carnival*. Wouk's sprawling two-volume fictional account of World War II, which he began writing in 1962, was published in the 1970's; the first volume, *The Winds of War*, appeared in 1971, and the second, *War and Rememberance*, in 1978. Wouk wrote the teleplay for the eighteen-hour television film based on *The Winds of War*, which was broadcast during the week of February 6-13, 1983. He was coauthor of the teleplay for the television adaptation of *War and Remembrance*, which appeared in 1988.

Unlike many contemporary popular novelists, Wouk shunned the public spotlight throughout his career. Though the Wouks spent more than a decade after they were married in New York, they moved to the Virgin Islands in 1958, partly so that Wouk could find a place to write free of interruptions. In 1964, the family moved to Georgetown, a Washington, D.C., suburb, so that he could be closer to archival materials he needed to consult in order to write *The Winds of War* and *War and Remembrance*. During the next three decades, Wouk divided his time between his home in the nation's capital and one in Palm Springs, California, occasionally appearing at public events to accept awards or participate in fund-raising or religious events. In 1995, Wouk entered into an agreement with popular singer Jimmy Buffett to write the book for a musical based on *Don't Stop the Carnival*. Featuring a number of Caribbean songs composed by Buffett, the musical opened in Florida in 1997 and moved to Broadway in 1998.

Wouk's great popular success enabled him to devote his full time to his craft, but on occasion he took academic or semiacademic positions. From 1953 to 1957, he was a visiting professor of English at Yeshiva University, and during 1973-1974, he was scholar-in-residence at the Aspen Institute for Humanistic Studies. He has served on the board of directors for institutions and organizations such as the College of the Virgin Islands, the Washington National Symphony, and Kennedy Center Productions.

Analysis · Herman Wouk is a novelist in the tradition of the great English novelists of the nineteenth century; he is also a spiritual descendant of such American writers as James Fenimore Cooper, William Dean Howells, Theodore Dreiser, and James T. Farrell. What he has in common with these writers is narrative prowess, a commitment to realism, and a lively moral consciousness. Furthermore, like these writers, Wouk addresses himself to the population at large. Since World War II, there has been detectable in American fiction a distinction between writers who seem to be inclined to write primarily for other writers or for academic critics, and those inclined to write for a general audience. That Wouk is numbered among the latter would appear to be traceable to a definite decision on his part. His first novel, *Aurora Dawn*, has the flavor of the experimental fiction that began to proliferate in the postwar period. If one were to have speculated in 1946 upon the course that Wouk's literary career was going to take, it would have been a safe guess to say that he would probably continue down the road of experimentation, that he would become more and more concerned with language as an end in itself, and that eventually, he would be writing books destined to be read only in upper-division English courses in universities. This was not what happened, however; in his second novel, *The City Boy*, Wouk followed a conventional narrative pattern and told his story in language which was not constantly calling attention to itself.

In *Aurora Dawn* and *The City Boy*, Wouk was still stretching his muscles and attempting to find his proper level as a writer. He came into his own with *The Caine Mutiny*. In that novel, and in every novel that followed for the next four decades, there is the presence of a central theme, treated in various ways and from varying perspectives. The theme is the conflict between traditional values and a modern consciousness which is either indifferent to those values or flatly antipathetic toward them. The conflict is not treated in abstract terms, but in terms of individuals who are caught up in it, and how the individual fares is in great part determined by the side with which he chooses to ally himself.

Aurora Dawn · Wouk's first novel, *Aurora Dawn*, which he began while serving as an officer in the Navy, is an effort at satire. The butt of the satire is the advertising industry and, more generally, the foolishness of anyone in business whose ethical consciousness is dimmed by avarice. The moral of the story is explicit: Greed is the root of all evil. Andrew Reale, the novel's young protagonist, is bright, energetic, and imaginative, but until he undergoes a conversion at novel's end, his primary concern is getting ahead. He wants to be successful above all else, and to him, success means money. In his scramble to get to the top as quickly as possible, his myopia becomes acute and his values are severely twisted. He is willing to make compromises where compromises should not be made. A connection is intimated between Reale's moral weakness and his failure to continue to adhere to the religious principles according to which he was reared, a recurring theme in Wouk's fiction.

Reale's obsessive pursuit of success leads him to jilt his fiancée, the beautiful and innocent Laura Beaton, so that he can take up with the beautiful but frivolous Carol Marquis, daughter of the despicable but very rich Talmadge Marquis. It leads him to be crassly manipulative in his dealings with the Reverend Calvin Stanfield, who is simple, straightforward, and a good man. Finally, it leads him, in a move of pure expediency, to quit an employer who has been generous with him so that he can join forces with Talmadge Marquis. All Reale's machinations, however, are to no avail. The hastily courted Carol Marquis runs off with an eccentric painter, and Laura Beaton, brokenhearted at Reale's rejection of her, marries an older man. In the end, Reale gets better than he deserves. His thwarted attempt to blackmail Father Stanfield proves to be the occasion of a conversion experience for him. He suddenly sees the wickedness of his ways and decides to alter his course. Laura Beaton is miraculously released from her unconsummated marriage, so that Reale is able to get the woman of his dreams after all. Fleeing the wicked city, the bride and groom go off to live together in New Mexico.

The novel is not realistic and cannot be judged according to the criterion of verisimilitude. It is a light, playful work in which humor plays an important part. Despite several brilliant passages, however, the novel does not come across as successful satire, and that would seem to be attributable to the fact that Wouk is vacillating and hesitant in what he wants to say. What he takes with one hand, he gives back with the other. The novel is clever, in both good and bad senses. While its language is often lively, it can as well be pretentious and self-conscious at times. The anachronistic devices of addressing the reader directly, inserting explicit authorial commentary on the action, and interspersing the narrative with short philosophical asides do not always work to maximize the effect. The humor of the novel is capable of being right on the mark, but for the most part it is a bit forced; Wouk, the radio gagman, is too much in evidence. The flaws to be found in *Aurora Dawn* are flaws which are not uncommon in a first novel. Despite its weaknesses, however, already in evidence in this work are the two traits that have subsequently become the chief strengths of Wouk's fiction: a vigorous talent for narrative and a lively sensitivity to moral issues.

The City Boy · Perhaps the most striking thing about Wouk's second novel, *The City Boy*, is that, stylistically, it represents a marked departure from the standards he had established in his first novel. The language of the work does not call attention to itself; it is clear, straightforward, and unpretentious. The novel is humorous in tone, and its plot structure is loose. It revolves around the adventures—most of which take place in an upstate summer camp—of a New York City boy, Herbie Bookbinder. John P. Marquand's comparison of this novel with Mark Twain's *The Adventures of Tom Sawyer* (1876) is well-founded. In many respects, Herbie is an urban version of the scamp from the Midwestern frontier. He is a bright and enterprising lad, and if he is mischievous at times, it is seldom with malice. Much of what he does is calculated to impress Lucille Glass, the object of his single-minded puppy love. Herbie is unlike Tom Sawyer in that he is an outsider as far as other boys are concerned, largely because of his poor athletic skills and his penchant for things intellectual. A goodly amount of Herbie's efforts in the novel are given over to his attempts to gain the status of a regular guy. He succeeds, finally, and as a result is welcomed into the full fellowship of his peers. *The City Boy* is a light novel—in some respects a boy's book—but in it, Wouk's moral consciousness is manifested by his underscoring the difference between good and evil in the actions of the characters.

The Caine Mutiny · *The Caine Mutiny* is Wouk's best novel, the work on which his reputation rests. The novel takes place against the backdrop of war, but it cannot be regarded as a "war story" in any simplistic sense. It is a story about the subtle and complicated relationships that exist among men who are part of the enclosed world that constitutes the military establishment. One of its central themes concerns the matter of authority—how it is exercised within a military context, and how it is abused. The novel explores the manner in which various personality types act and react within a hierarchical, authoritarian structure. In addition, it examines the ways in which the lives of those caught up in the trauma of war are altered, sometimes profoundly. Other themes which the novel treats are loyalty and disloyalty, patriotism, doers versus sayers, personal integrity, and the process by which young men are tested in stressful situations.

The Caine Mutiny can easily be misread. One might conclude that its chief concern is the everlasting battle between despotism and democracy, that Captain Queeg therefore is clearly the villain of the piece, and that its heroes are Lieutenant Maryk, Willie Keith, Tom Keefer, and the others who were involved in the mutiny. It is not that simple. If it were, *The Caine Mutiny* would be little more than a melodrama. Captain Queeg is not a hero, but neither is he a diabolical type. He is a sorry human being; he has serious personal problems (his eccentricity is not amusing—he is, in fact, a sick man); and, perhaps most serious, given his status as a commanding officer, he is incompetent professionally. For all that, he is consistent in trying to do his job to the best of his ability. Queeg's problem is that he is a man who is in over his head; he can at times scarcely cope with situations which are his duty to control. The circumstances surrounding the event which lead to the mutiny are sufficiently ambiguous as to render doubtful the claim of the mutineers that, had they not relieved Queeg of command when they did, the ship would have been lost.

Wouk's assessment of the situation seems to be communicated most directly through the character of Lieutenant Greenwald, the young aviator-lawyer who defends Maryk at the court-martial. Greenwald is not sympathetic with the mutineers, but he decides to defend Maryk because he respects the Executive Officer's personal integrity and because he is convinced that Maryk, in assuming command of the *Caine* during the typhoon, was acting in good faith. Greenwald succeeds in having Maryk acquitted of the charge of mutiny, mainly by drawing out of Queeg in the courtroom telltale signs of his emotional instability, but he takes no joy in his victory. After the trial, he puts the damper on the victory celebration being staged by the *Caine*'s officers when he gives them a stinging tonguelashing. His ire is directed particularly at Tom Keefer, whom he perceives correctly as being the chief instigator of the mutiny, but one who refused, when the matter came to a head, to put himself on the line. Greenwald's position seems to be that, while the *Caine*'s officers are legally innocent, they are morally guilty. However sophisticated a rationale they might provide for their actions, what was at the bottom of those actions, in his view, was disloyalty, and disloyalty, for a military officer, is an unforgivable sin. One might say that the trial does not prove either clear-cut guilt or innocence. If anything, it demonstrates the complexity and ambiguity of all human situations. Greenwald's position is that, given the ambiguity, it is always better not to second-guess legitimately constituted authority. It is the chief responsibility of the naval officer to do his duty through thick and thin.

If there is a clear villain in *The Caine Mutiny*, Tom Keefer would appear to be the most likely candidate for the role. Keefer is, in many respects, a preeminently modern man. He is committed to what he presumably regards as the absolute truths of Freudian psychology, which he employs in a reductionist way, as weapons against those who do not share his worldview. He is in the Navy, but not of it, and, in fact, he rather enjoys and exploits his position as an iconoclastic outsider. He maintains an attitude of supercilious superiority toward people such as Queeg, and toward everything that the Navy represents. His view is narrow, restricted by the dictates of his overriding egotism. Keefer is a carping critic of the Navy, but he does not hesitate to take selfish advantage of what the Navy can offer him at every turn. His hypocrisy allows him to talk a big game, but when the pressure is on and when circumstances call for words to be translated into action, he invariably backs off. Perhaps the most damning thing that could be said of Keefer is that he is a coward, as he demonstrates when he is captain of the *Caine* and precipitously abandons ship. By the novel's end, however, Keefer seem to have arrived at a degree of self-awareness which hitherto had eluded him; he confesses to Willie Keith, who succeeds him as commanding officer, that Keith is a better man than he. He is right.

Willie Keith is the central character of the novel; his moral education is the real subject of *The Caine Mutiny*. Willie is an aristocratic rich kid from New York who comes to learn, among other things, the value of democracy. His relationship with Maria Minotti, alias May Wynn, can be interpreted in this way. The bulk of Keith's education, however, takes place in the Navy. When he first comes aboard the *Caine*, he is very much under the influence of Tom Keefer, and he accepts Keefer's cynical interpretation of things as the correct one. Eventually, Keith realizes that the Navy, though imperfect, is not a bad organization. What is more, given the realities of the modern world, it is a necessary organization. Unlike Keefer, Keith is prepared to acknowledge that the Navy in World War II is contributing toward the preservation of the way of life into which both men have been born and to which they are devoted, and that, excepting a total transformation of human nature, navies will probably always be needed to ensure the protection of people's freedom. Keith is not changed into a mindless patriot and militarist, but his criticism of the Navy and its personnel becomes more discriminate, more intelligent, more responsible. He learns to judge matters according to criteria which are not self-centered, and develops an appreciation for the larger scheme of things. He takes pride in his work, and as he rises in rank, his conscientiousness increases; he tries to be the best officer he can.

The world of the Navy, in *The Caine Mutiny*, is in certain respects a microcosm of the world at large. It is beset by all sorts of problems, but there is no perfect alternative somewhere to which one might flee. A person's maturity is measured by his or her ability to establish standards of excellence and to work assiduously to achieve them in spite of various limitations, sometimes severe—limitations in him- or herself, in others, and in the situation.

Marjorie Morningstar · On the surface, Wouk's fourth novel, *Marjorie Morningstar*, would seem to lead nowhere. It is the story of a young Jewish woman, the daughter of immigrants established comfortably in the middle class of New York, who has been sufficiently Americanized as to have for her chief ambition the desire to become a famous actress, a star. Marjorie Morningstar (née Morgenstern) is a beautiful woman whose theatrical talent, while not scintillating, is probably sufficient to underwrite the realization of her dream, given a lucky break here and there. She is willing to make the sacrifices, within certain bounds, and to invest the hard work which the ascent to stardom inevitably entails. If Marjorie is determined about anything, it is that she is not going to allow herself to lapse into the staid, conventional life that is the destiny of the vast majority of nice, middle-class Jewish girls. She is going to be different; she is going to break out of the mold. After several fruitless efforts to break into the theater and to make it big, after a sequence of adventures with an assortment of men, chiefly with Noel Airman, she ends up doing what she vowed she would never do. She marries a Jew, a successful lawyer by the name of Milton Schwartz, and she retires to a plush suburb to live the most conventional of conventional lives. The novel, then, would seem to end on an almost laughably anticlimactic note, but only if one fails to perceive the kind of statement that it is attempting to make.

If *The Caine Mutiny* delineates the education of Willie Keith, the education of Marjorie Morningstar is the primary concern of the novel that bears her name. If Marjorie comes full circle, as it were, and ends by embracing the conventional, it is because she discovers that the conventional is worthy of being embraced, the conventional not only as representing middle-class morality, but also, and much more important, as embodying traditional cultural and religious values. The glamorous life to which Marjorie aspired, whether or not she was always fully conscious of the fact, was a life that repudiated traditional values. As a teenager and young woman, she fought her own tradition, particularly as manifested in the Jewish religion; she looked upon it as crude and superstitious, a carry-over from humankind's primitive past. This tradition, however, was more deeply embedded in her, was more integral a part of her identity than she was willing to admit, and throughout her various experiences it guided her actions more than she knew.

Marjorie's failure to realize her dream of becoming a star actually represents the triumph of her better, truer self. Her concern shifts from thin, superficial values to those with substance and depth. The drama of her quest for self-realization is played out principally around her long and erratic affair with Noel Airman. When she first meets Airman, who is some ten years her senior, she is scarcely more than a girl, and she is completely enamored of him. He is handsome, intelligent, urbane, and witty, a talented composer of popular songs who shows promise of becoming a success in the theater. Noel represents much of what she wants to become, and all of what she has decided is most valuable in life, which is emphasized by the fact that she throws decorum to the winds and pursues him actively. When she finally catches him, however, she realizes that she does not really want him. The man who was once her ideal, her hero, the man whom she wanted to marry more than anyone else, is at last perceived, albeit faintly, as a god with clay feet.

Who is this Noel Airman? He is Saul Ehrmann, a man who has actively repudiated his Jewish identity and its associated traditions, but who has failed to come up with a viable substitute for either. He is a rootless vagabond, a shameless Casanova, a man who eschews commitment as a matter of principle, and who tries hard to make a profession of cynicism. It would be wrong, however, to think of him entirely in negative terms. He is not a character lacking in complexity, and he is not devoid of critical self-knowledge, which at times can be acute and penetrating. Still, this self-awareness serves only to accentuate the pathetic quality of the man, for in the final analysis, he is impotent to act upon his better impulses. He does not have the moral stamina to follow through, and this is so, Wouk implies, precisely because he has cut himself off from his tradition.

The fact that Marjorie arrives at a new state of consciousness which allows her to see Airman for what he is, and accordingly to reject him, is attributable in part to her brief but fateful acquaintance with Michael Eden. Eden, like Airman, is a Jew, but, unlike Airman, he is not in flight from the fact. He is a strong, taciturn man whose personal sufferings have led him to dedicate himself to a melancholy but determined altruism. He is involved in the very risky business of rescuing Jews from Nazi Germany. Here is a man who is every bit as bright and talented as Airman but who has what Airman lacks–integrity and a sense of purpose in life. Although it is not Marjorie's destiny to marry Eden, meeting him has the effect of altering her perception of Airman. Milton Schwartz, the man she marries, has in common with Eden a fundamental decency.

Youngblood Hawke · Wouk's sixth novel, *Youngblood Hawke*, based to some extent on the life of Thomas Wolfe, could be the story of many a young American writer of the twentieth century, and for that reason, the novel, besides its intrinsic worth as a work of fiction, has considerable value as a historical document. The story of Arthur Youngblood Hawke is a success story, but it is a story of failure as well. Indeed, Hawke's case is in many respects a tragic one. Hawke is a lanky, down-home Kentuckian who, after being released from the Navy at the end of World War II, moves to New York to conquer the city and the country, by his pen. He comes to his task with a spotty education, with an explosive imagination, and with a seemingly boundless store of energy. Writing is his life, and his engagement in it is passionate. There is much about Hawke which smacks of the all-American boy. He is crude and unpolished, but straightforward and gentle in his dealings with people–except with those who deserve otherwise. He is an honest man, in his way, and an assiduous worker. He wants to be a success as a writer. He wants to become a millionaire, not so that he can give up writing but so that, freed from financial worries, he can devote himself to it without distractions. Hawke is in the mold of the rustic innocent who has long played a part in American literature.

His early success works against him in the long run. His first novel, though receiving rough treatment at the hands of the critics, gains a large popular audience; his second novel wins the Pulitzer Prize and increasing respect from the critics. He is associated with a solid, respectable publishing house whose head values his work, has faith in his future, and is willing to be very generous in making contractual arrangements with him. Hawke's obsessional longing for financial independence, however, prompts him to break ties with his publisher and begin publishing his own books; he also makes some risky investments. His luck turns, and in a matter of months he finds himself on the threshold of bankruptcy. He determines that he is going to write his way out of his debts; leaving behind the plush life that he enjoyed only too briefly in New York, he returns to Kentucky, and there, living in a cabin in the woods, he works furiously to complete what proves to be his final novel. In fact, he overworks, devoting himself not only to the novel but also, earlier, to a theatrical production which he hopes will strike it rich. The strain brought about by his frenetic activities exacerbates an old head injury, and, after a wild chase to South America made in a state of delirium, he ends up back in New York. He is hospitalized there and dies at the age of thirty-three.

As Youngblood Hawke lies dying, his vaguely addressed prayer is that he might be given more time so that he can work. Everything that he has done he considers as only preparatory exercises to his great multivolume *Comedy*. That his magnum opus was never written is not simply attributable to the fact that Hawke showed poor business sense or that he was careless of his health. There is evidence in the novel to warrant the conclusion that Hawke's failure to fulfill his chief artistic ambition amounts to an exacting payment he has had to make for his sins. There have been two principal women in his life, but, by his own admission, there should have been only one. In the beginning of the novel, before he bursts upon the American literary scene, he meets a young editor, Jeanne Green, who subsequently becomes for him what Maxwell Perkins was for Thomas Wolfe. Jeanne, besides being a very talented editor, is, like Hawke, essentially a small-town person. She is simple, unpretentious, genuine. Hawke falls in love with Jeanne almost immediately–his better self tells him that this is the woman in his life, the woman he should marry–but he becomes involved in a torrid affair with a wealthy, sophisticated, fundamentally selfish New Yorker, Frieda Winters. Frieda is older than he; she is married, has three children, and is no stranger to adulterous affairs. Hawke is honest enough with himself to admit that he is involved in adultery; the reader is told that he hates both the word and the fact. He does not have the moral courage, however, to extricate himself from the affair–not until, as it turns out, it is too late. His relationship with Frieda proves to be an enervating experience; if it does not exactly destroy him, it contributes substantially toward his destruction.

What allowed Hawke to become involved in an affair which he knew to be wrong? One explanation is that he failed to be true to the basic religious principles which he had been taught as a boy but which in his impetuous youth he attempted to reject. Unlike Marjorie Morningstar, whose roots in a religious tradition were sufficiently deep and tenacious to carry her through the hard times, Hawke succumbs to the facile moral standards of a secularized society.

Don't Stop the Carnival · Wouk's next novel, *Don't Stop the Carnival,* is the weakest of his entire corpus. It is a comic novel and it would seem to have some kind of satiric intent, but the humor, instead of carrying the moral import of the tale, more often than not obstructs it. The work's humor is hampered by obtrusive, heavy-handed moralizing, and its seriousness is trivialized by a humor which too often degenerates into tedious slapstick. Most damaging for the novel is the fact that Wouk's narrative talent, which is his forte, serves him poorly here. The plot is too often based upon contrivance, and in some instances blatant authorial manipulation is very much in evidence. Add to this fact that characterization is unconvincing, and the sum total is a generally undistinguished piece of fiction that holds the reader's attention only by an adamant act of will. It is not that the novel is completely lacking in substance, but the detectably substantive elements are not allowed to emerge fully. There is, for example, a statement being made about the haplessness of "liberal" types who are awash in a world that in many respects is the result of their own brand of thinking, but the message is befuddled by static of various kinds and one must strain to detect it.

The Winds of War **and** ***War and Remembrance*** · Wouk's impressive companion novels, *The Winds of War* and *War and Remembrance*, published in 1971 and 1978, respectively, are in effect a single, sustained work of fiction, and therefore can be discussed together. Wouk spent sixteen years in completing the work, and it seems likely that he regards it as his magnum opus. *The Winds of War* is focused primarily on the European theater, beginning with the German invasion of Czechoslovakia and Poland, putting special emphasis upon the latter. The Battle of Britain is also treated at close range. The book ends with the bombing of Pearl Harbor, the point at which *War and Remembrance* takes up the story. This book, while continuing to trace the course of events in Europe, especially those events having to do with the systematic extermination of the Jews by the Nazis, shifts attention to the Pacific theater and provides poignant descriptions of the major naval battles fought there. The book ends with the dropping of the atomic bombs and the Japanese acceptance of unconditional surrender. In these two massive volumes which constitute a single work, an ambitious fictional history of World War II, Wouk once again shows himself to be a master of narrative. This is not a mere chronicle of events; rather, major events of the war are given dramatic immediacy by the tactic of having one of the many key characters in the narrative involved in those events. One is even provided access to the Axis point of view through excerpts from the analytic histories of the German General Armin von Roon, interspersed throughout the work.

The key character in the work is Victor "Pug" Henry, a naval officer who has given thirty years of his life to military service. He is a staid, conservative man, a patriot but not a jingoist, dedicated to professional excellence and quietly guided by deeply embedded religious principles. Following his various adventures in Europe and in the Pacific, one is not only brought into direct contact with important historical personages but treated to his thoughtful reactions to them as well. Wouk is the type of artist who likes to paint on a large canvas, but the canvas he is covering in this work is of mammoth proportions. All the more remarkable, then, is the control he exercises here; nothing gets away from him. There is about this wide-ranging tour de force a satisfying unity and completeness. It is thickly peopled with a vast array of characters, and their attitudes toward the war run the full gamut from self-sacrificing heroism to cold-blooded murderousness.

One of the most interesting characters in the work is Aaron Jastrow, a Jewish-American, world-renowned scholar and former Yale professor who at the outbreak of the war is living in active retirement in Italy. In tracing the story of Aaron Jastrow, and that of his Polish cousin Berel, Wouk recounts in moving fashion the sickening circumstances of the infamous "final solution." Aaron himself was born in Poland and reared in a strict Orthodox tradition. As he reached young manhood, he put aside his religion and settled into a benevolent agnosticism. Accompanied by his niece Natalie, he is hounded by the Nazis throughout Europe for years, until he finally ends up in the land of his birth, in a death camp. His life is choked out in the gas chambers. He speaks to the reader directly through *A Jew's Journey.* What one learns from this document is that the most significant journey in the waning months of Jastrow's life is a spiritual one. His personal confrontation with the horrors of Nazism has the effect of returning him to the religion of his birth. When he comes to die, he is possessed of an inner peace his murderers could never know, and he represents a basic human dignity which they have chosen to abandon for themselves and to attempt to destroy in others.

The Winds of War and *War and Remembrance* are about a specific war, but they are about war in general as well. Wouk does not romanticize World War II, but he suggests that it was absolutely essential that the Allied forces emerged as victorious. It was an unspeakably grim yet nevertheless necessary struggle. The bombs that ended the war, however, changed the nature of war forever. If humankind were capable before Hiroshima and Nagasaki of arguing that all-out war, however cruel and crude, was a workable solution to human problems, that argument proved no longer tenable. World War II was perhaps the most gruesome war that human beings have ever inflicted upon themselves. Wouk's thesis is that wars in the future will not be avoided simply by proclaiming them to be unthinkable. One must think about them; one must think especially about the most gruesome of wars. Through memory, perhaps a pathway to peace can be found.

Inside, Outside · Herman Wouk's *Inside, Outside* appeared in 1985. *The Caine Mutiny* is by consensus Wouk's single best work of fiction, but *Inside, Outside* could arguably be offered as a legitimate contender for that honor. Here one finds all Wouk's considerable skill in operation: his commanding ability to create characters that live and breathe and convince, telling their interesting and interlocking stories within the context of a fictional world which, while complex, never degenerates into incoherence. Wouk's characters move and make their marks in a world that can be as confused and disorienting as that created by any other modern fictionist, but the core, the center, of Wouk's world, although subjected to great strain, always manages to hold; that is, although Wouk's characters live in an extremely difficult and demanding world, that world preserves its essential meaningfulness. Wouk does not burden himself with the absurd task of attempting to populate an absurd universe.

It is difficult to specify what makes for the peculiar success of this novel, but certainly at work is Wouk's uncanny ability–which is singularly devoid of self-advertising and therefore easy to overlook–to create what one might call fictional immediacy. Wouk can effect the magic of bringing into being a fictional world which more than half persuades the reader that it is not fictional at all. In other words, he is a maker of art.

Inside, Outside revolves around the life and times of one Israel David Goodkind. It is principally his story, and he tells it with verve. The novel is interestingly structured. The time frame of the narration is 1973. In that year, Goodkind, a successful New York lawyer, finds himself in the rather unusual position–given the fact that he has been a lifelong Democrat–of serving in Washington as a special assistant to President Richard M. Nixon. The job, though flattering in its way, is anything but exacting, and Goodkind begins to expend his considerable free time in writing; however, this activity is not simply an idle exercise with which to fill the gaps in his undemanding day. He takes his writing quite seriously, and he intends to produce something of real literary worth. He endeavors to fulfill an ambition he has harbored since his youth, but which thus far he has not managed to accomplish. He writes about his own life, which takes him back to the turn of the century and the stories of his parents, two Jewish immigrants from Russia. They both arrive in New York; there they meet and marry, and there their children, Israel and Lee, are born. The reader follows the entire course of Goodkind's life as he recounts its developments, its delays, its assorted dramatic and melodramatic reversals, with meticulous and loving detail. The reader is brought into the very center of Goodkind's world and discovers it to be a world which is at once intensely provincial and intensely cosmopolitan–the kind of combination which is possible perhaps only in New York City. It is a wide world, thickly populated with a rich variety of relatives and friends. The reader is given the opportunity to meet them all, and, with differing degrees of completeness, to come to know their stories, too.

Such is the main strand of the novel's narrative. Its secondary strand is no less compelling. Goodkind is interrupted periodically in his recounting of his past by the pressing events that take place around him in 1973 as he continues his writing project. Two significant historical events mark that time period. One is the Israeli-Egyptian War; the other is the resignation of President Nixon in the wake of the Watergate scandal. The first event takes place within the time frame of the novel, and Goodkind reports on it as he writes. The second event draws closer and closer, but the novel ends without the president's resignation having yet taken place. The Israeli-Egyptian War plays an important symbolic role in the narrative because one of the central themes of the novel is the situation of the Jew in the modern world.

The "inside" of the novel's title refers to the somewhat self-enclosed, clearly identifiable, but far from homogeneous world of Jewish religion and culture, whereas the "outside" refers to the world at large. Herman Wouk is something of an oddity among contemporary American novelists because of his open and unapologetic commitment to his religious convictions. This fact largely explains the decided and persistent moral tone of his fiction. One can find expressions, more or less strong, more or less developed, of his commitment to Judaism throughout his fiction, but in no other novel, it seems, does his religious faith play so central and integral a part than in *Inside, Outside.*

What Wouk gives the reader in this novel, along with much else, is a dynamic and dramatic picture of the manifold consciousness that constitutes late twentieth century Judaism. The picture he presents is intricate, complicated, and in some respects even contradictory. Wouk deals with the rich reality that is Judaism in a manner which is—variously—intensely objective and intensely subjective. He seems to leave nothing out of the picture; negative elements are treated with as much thoroughness as are positive elements. Nevertheless, Wouk does not treat the heart of his subject matter, the essential identity of Judaism, with anything but respect and reverence.

If by novel's end one cannot identify its protagonist as a typical modern Jew, that is only because one has come to understand that there is no such thing. I. David Goodkind is a representative modern Jew, but so are many who are quite different from him, and Goodkind himself is far from simple. On the one hand, Goodkind reflects the "inside" component of his world, but a distinct "outside" dimension to his personality exists as well. Both together, "inside" and "outside," make up who he is. Goodkind is a religious Jew who faithfully practices his religion. He is also a political Jew who sympathizes with the Zionist tradition and takes great patriotic pride in the state of Israel. At the same time, Goodkind is a thorough American. In a larger sense, he is an eminently modern man, one who, even in spite of himself at times, reflects the consciousness of the contemporary Western intellectual, with all the limitations peculiar to it. His judgments on the major issues that impinge upon his life have to them a ring of confident cosmopolitanism, which disguises their lack of substantial metaphysical foundations. For example, although he is in many respects exemplary for his perspicacity and sensitivity, he is obtuse in response to some of the clear signs of decadence in modern culture.

Mention might be made of the unorthodox manner in which the novel deals with the character of President Nixon. Wouk goes beyond the crude journalistic stereotypes to discover in Nixon not merely a caricature but a real human being. Finally, *Inside, Outside* is simultaneously a serious and a humorous work, and both of these faces complement each other, helping to bring each into greater relief. In some of his other novels, Wouk has demonstrated his facility in handling humor, but that skill is especially in evidence in *Inside, Outside.*

The Hope* and *The Glory · Unfortunately, Wouk was not able to sustain in his next two novels the high level of artistry he achieved in *Inside, Outside.* In *The Hope* and *The Glory* he continues to exploit his interest in Judaic issues, using the techniques that proved successful in *The Winds of War* and *War and Remembrance.* Though published separately, *The Hope* and *The Glory* are much like Wouk's two-volume romance about World War II; collectively they provide a portrait of the early years of the state of Israel, depicting the struggles of the Jewish people to establish a new independent country in their ancestral homeland.

The Hope is set in the years immediately following World War II, when a small but determined group of Zionist freedom fighters ousted the British in Palestine and declared the foundation of the new state of Israel. As he did in *The Winds of War* and *War and Remembrance*, Wouk creates a number of fictional characters whose lives intersect with the real-life heroes and heroines of the new Jewish nation. Wouk offers a vivid account of the 1948 War of Independence, focusing on the struggles of leaders such as David Ben-Gurion and Moshe Dayan to unite the disparate political and paramilitary groups in the region. The climax of the novel is the stunning victory of the Israelis over their Arab enemies in the Six-Day War of 1967. *The Glory* is a sequel, containing many of the same characters. In recounting the tale of the Jewish nation from 1967 to the announcement of the Camp David Peace Accords, Wouk has his fictional characters support the likes of Golda Meir and Menachim Begin.

Though with less success than he realized in his World War II novels, Wouk gives his narrative a sense of immediacy by concentrating his attention on the effects of the Israelis' struggle on the lives of common men and women. To accomplish this, he creates four families whose fortunes are intertwined not only with historical personages of note but also with each other: the Baraks, the Blumenthals, the Pasternaks, and the Luries. Among them are fighters, local politicians, businessmen, and even ambassadors who represent Israel in the United States and at the United Nations. Political issues are paralleled by small acts of love and vengeance, bringing a certain degree of humanity to the large historical canvas on which Wouk depicts the nation he loves.

Like most novels published by Wouk since the appearance of *The Caine Mutiny*, both *The Hope* and *The Glory* attracted a large readership, but neither received praise from critics. The negative critical reaction seems justified. While the historical accounts are accurate and presented with a strong sense of control, at least one reviewer found this extremely complex political subject treated with "only slightly more subtlety than a grade-school Thanksgiving pageant." Knowing that he would be open to criticism because of his strong partisan views, Wouk was careful to offer a note in *The Hope* that he worked hard not to present a caricature of the Arabs. Unfortunately, there is a general laxity in dealing with both major and minor Jewish figures. Instead of striving for complexity, Wouk often resorts to stereotypes that create heroes and villains more commonly found in melodrama or popular romances. His men are almost all superhuman, his women submissive handmaids. What could have been a wonderful final performance in a distinguished career as a popular novelist seems to have emerged as little more than a drifting away into contemporary cliché.

Despite his broad popular appeal, Wouk has generally not found favor with the critics, especially academic critics. The common response of the latter has been simply to ignore him. It is difficult to explain precisely why this is so. Perhaps Wouk's very popularity militates against him, as if there existed a necessary relationship between popularity and artistic worth: The more popular a writer, the poorer the quality of what he writes. Perhaps Wouk's traditionalist worldview and forthright advocacy of Judeo-Christian moral principles, to which many critics today are hostile, account in part for the critical neglect of his work.

In any case, Wouk deserves more critical attention than he has received. He is not the greatest among the many fine novelists to appear in the United States since World War II, but neither is he an inconsequential figure. His prose is solid and vigorous, eschewing precosity and self-indulgence. Writing with intelligence and sensitivity, he appeals neither to a small clique of literary aesthetes nor to the lowest common denominator of a general audience. His attitude toward fiction is that shared by all the major novelists of literary history; his fiction is not concerned with itself but with the world at large. His fiction does not attempt the irrelevant task of creating a moral universe from scratch, but accepts and responds to the moral universe which is already in place.

Dennis Q. McInerny, updated by Laurence W. Mazzeno

Other major works

PLAYS: *The Traitor*, pr., pb. 1949; *The Caine Mutiny Court-Martial*, pr., pb. 1954; *Nature's Way*, pr. 1957; *Don't Stop the Carnival*, pr. 1998 (musical, with Jimmy Buffett).
SCREENPLAY: *Slattery's Hurricane*, 1949 (with Richard Murphy).
TELEPLAYS: *The Winds of War*, 1983; *War and Remembrance*, 1988.
NONFICTION: *This Is My God*, 1959, 1973.

Bibliography

Beichman, Arnold. *Herman Wouk: The Novelist as Social Historian*. New Brunswick, N.J.: Transaction Books, 1984. A lifelong friend of Wouk, Beichman offers a strident defense of the novelist against those who fault him for both his conservative political stance and his decision to stress narrative and action over complex characterization. Beichman attacks academic critics who demand that Wouk subscribe to the tenets of modernism. His critiques of individual novels are abbreviated and colored by his belief that Wouk is one of America's greatest novelists.
Mazzeno, Laurence W. *Herman Wouk*. New York: Twayne, 1994. Written for the U.S. Authors series, this volume offers a brief biographical sketch and analyses of the major novels through *Inside, Outside*. Mazzeno is generally sympathetic toward Wouk, finding his populism a strength in reaching a wide reading audience whom he wishes to influence on important social and moral issues. The book contains excerpts from hundreds of reviews of Wouk's fiction, thereby providing a sense of the contemporary reaction to each of Wouk's major works.
Shapiro, Edward S. "The Jew as Patriot: Herman Wouk and American Jewish Identity." *American Jewish History* 84 (December, 1996): 333-351. Shapiro provides a retrospective review of Wouk's career, arguing persuasively that Wouk is concerned principally with defining American Jewish identity. He offers sympathetic and perceptive readings of *The Caine Mutiny*, *The Winds of War*, *War and Remembrance*, *The Hope*, and *The Glory*. Shapiro claims that Wouk tries in all his novels to expose parallels between the United States and Israel, thereby making it palatable to claim that being a good Jew in America is equivalent to being a good American.

RICHARD WRIGHT

Born: Natchez, Mississippi; September 4, 1908
Died: Paris, France; November 28, 1960

Principal long fiction · *Native Son*, 1940; *The Outsider*, 1953; *Savage Holiday*, 1954; *The Long Dream*, 1958; *Lawd Today*, 1963.

Other literary forms · In addition to his five novels, Richard Wright published collections of essays and short stories and two autobiographical volumes. Two collections of short stories, the early *Uncle Tom's Children* (1938, 1940) and the posthumously collected *Eight Men* (1961), represent some of Wright's finest fiction. Wright himself felt that the characters in *Uncle Tom's Children* were too easily pitied and that they elicited from readers a sympathy that was unlike the tough intellectual judgment he desired. Wright later wrote that his creation of Bigger Thomas in *Native Son* was an attempt to stiffen that portrayal so that readers could not leniently dismiss his characters with simple compassion, but would have to accept them as free, fully human adults, whose actions required assessment. Nevertheless, the stories of *Uncle Tom's Children* are carefully written, and the characters, though sometimes defeated, embody the kind of independence and intractability that Wright valued in his fiction.

Two stories from *Eight Men* reveal the themes to which Wright gave sustained development in his novels. In "The Man Who Was Almos' a Man," the main character learns that power means freedom, and although he first bungles his attempt to shoot a gun, his symbol of power, he lies to his family, keeps the gun, and at the conclusion of the story leaves home to grow into manhood elsewhere. In "The Man Who Lived Underground," the main character, nameless at first, is accused of a crime he did not commit. Fleeing underground to the sewers of the city, he becomes a voyeur of life, seen now from a new perspective. The values that served him badly above ground do not serve him at all below. By the end of the story, he has come to understand that all men are guilty; his name is revealed, and with his new values, he ascends once more to accept responsibility for the crime. Since all men are guilty, it is less important to him that the crime is not his own than that he acknowledges freely that he shares in human guilt.

Even more important than these two collections is the first volume of Wright's autobiography, *Black Boy* (1945), which opens up a world of experience to the reader. It traces the first seventeen years of Wright's life—from his birth in Mississippi and the desertion of the family by his father, through years of displacement as he travels from one relative to another with his ill mother and religious grandmother. The early years find Wright, like his later protagonists, an outsider, cut off from family, from friends, from culture. He is as out of place among blacks as among whites, baffled by those blacks who play the roles whites expect of them, himself unable to dissimulate his feelings and thoughts.

Although the work is nonfiction, it is united by powerful metaphors: fire, hunger, and blindness. Wright's inner fire is mirrored throughout the work by actual fires; indeed, his first act is to set afire the curtains in his home. His physical hunger, a constant companion, is an image of his hunger for knowledge and connection, and his two jobs in optical factories suggest the blindness of society, a blindness given further representation in *Native Son.*

What Wright learns in *Black Boy* is the power of words. His early life is marked by physical violence: He witnesses murders and beatings, but it is the violence of words which offers liberation from his suffocating environment. Whether it is the profanity with which he shocks his grandmother, the literalness with which he takes his father's words, or the crude expressions with which he taunts Jewish shopkeepers, he discovers that words have a power which makes him an equal to those around him. When he feels unequal, as in his early school experiences, he is speechless. The culmination of this theme occurs when Wright acquires a library card and discovers through his readings in the American social critics of the early part of the twentieth century, such as H. L. Mencken and Sinclair Lewis, that he is not alone in his feelings and that there are others who share his alienation and discontent.

When Wright finally sees his father many years after his desertion, his hatred dissolves: He realizes that his father, trapped by his surroundings, with neither a cultural past nor an individual future, speaks a different language from his own, holds different thoughts, and is truly a victim and therefore not worthy even of his hatred. Wright's characters must never be victims, for as such they hold no interest. At the end of the book, he goes north, first to Memphis and, when that fails, north again to Chicago, pursuing the dream, having now the power of words to articulate it and to define himself.

The record of his years in Chicago is found in the posthumously published second autobiographical volume, *American Hunger* (written in 1944, published in 1977). Largely a record of his involvement and later disillusionment with the Communist Party, this book is interesting for its view of a later, mature Wright who is still struggling with institutions which would limit his freedom.

Achievements · In his best work, Wright gives American literature its strongest statement of the existential theme of alienated people defining themselves. Wright's use of the black American as archetypal outsider gives his work a double edge. On the one hand, no American writer so carefully illuminates the black experience in America: The ambivalence of black feeling, the hypocrisies of the dominant culture, and the tension between them find concrete and original manifestation in Wright's work, a manifestation at once revealing and terrifying.

It is not only in his revelation of black life, however, that Wright's power lies, for as much as his writing is social and political, it is also personal and philosophical. The story of alienated people is a universal one; because the concrete experiences of the outsider are so vividly rendered in Wright's fiction, his books have an immediate accessibility. Because they also reveal deeper patterns, they have further claims to attention. Much of Wright's later fiction seems self-conscious and studied, but it cannot diminish the greatness of his finest work.

Biography · Born in Mississippi of sharecropper parents, Richard Wright had a lonely and troubled childhood. His father deserted the family early, and after his mother suffered a stroke, Wright was forced at a young age to work to help support the family, which moved frequently from one relative to another. His portrayal of his mother is of a stern but loving parent, unable to contend with the stronger personality of his extremely religious grandmother. Wright's grandmother believed that all fiction was "the devil's lies"; her chief goal was to force Wright into a religious conversion, a goal in which she was singularly unsuccessful.

Wright moved from school to school, attempting to make friends and make his talents known. Though both tasks were difficult, he became valedictorian of his class. Even this accomplishment was spoiled when the principal insisted that Wright read a speech which the principal himself had written, and Wright refused. An uncle told Richard, "They're going to break you," and society, both black and white, seemed intent on doing so. Wright was determined to resist, not to be claimed by his environment as he felt so many blacks around him were.

Library of Congress

Wright left Mississippi for Memphis, Tennessee, had little luck there, and–with money stolen from the film theater where he worked–moved to Chicago. When others stole, Wright disapproved–not for moral reasons, but because he felt stealing did not change the fundamental relationship of a person to his environment. When it offered a chance to change that environment, Wright accepted it.

In Chicago, Wright became involved with others who viewed the country as he did, first in a federal theater project and then with the Communist John Reed Club, which supported his writing until Wright's goals differed from their own. In 1937, he moved to New York City to become the editor of the *Daily Worker*. A year later, he published his first important work, *Uncle Tom's Children*, after which he won a Guggenheim Fellowship, which provided him with the time and funds to write *Native Son*. The novel was published to great acclaim and was followed by a second major work, *Black Boy*. Although his writing career was a success, Wright was arguing more frequently with the Communist Party, with which he finally broke in 1944, and was becoming less optimistic about the hope of racial progress in America.

In 1946, Wright moved to France, where he spent the rest of his life. Although he wrote a great deal there, nothing in his later work, with the possible exception of *The Outsider*, approaches the strength of *Native Son* and *Black Boy*. The existentialism which was always implicit in his work became the dominant theme, but–displaced from his native environment–Wright never again found a convincing dramatic situation in which to work out his preoccupations.

Wright died in France of a heart attack on November 28, 1960. Since his death, three of his works, *Eight Men*, *Lawd Today*, and *American Hunger*, have been published.

Analysis · Richard Wright's best work is always the story of one man's struggle to define himself and by so doing make himself free and responsible, fully human, a character worthy not of pity but of admiration and horror simultaneously. Typically, the character is an outsider, and Wright uses blackness as a representation of that alienation, though his characters are never as interested in defining their blackness as in defining their humanity. Although many characters in Wright's works are outsiders without being aware of their condition, Wright is never interested in them except as foils. Many of them avoid confronting themselves by fleeing to dreams; religion and liquor are two avoidance-mechanisms for Wright's characters, narcotics that blind them to their surrounding world, to what they are and what they might be.

Even Wright's main characters must not think about that world too often: To let it touch them is to risk insanity or violence, and so his characters strive to keep the fire within in check, to keep the physical hunger satisfied. Thus, all of Wright's protagonists are initially trapped by desire and by fear—fear of what might happen to them, what they may do, if they risk venturing outside the confines of black life in America, and the desire to do so. The life outside may be glimpsed in films; Bigger Thomas, for example, goes to a film and watches contrasting and artificial views of black and white society. Yet as untruthful as both views are, they remind Bigger of a reality beyond his present situation. Desire is often symbolized by flight; Bigger, like other Wright characters, dreams of flying above the world, unchained from its limitations.

Most of Wright's stories and novels examine what happens when the protagonist's fear is mastered for a moment when desires are met. The manifestation of desire in Wright is almost always through violence (and it is here, perhaps, that he is most pessimistic, for other, more positive manifestations of desire, such as love, can come only later, after the protagonists have violently acted out their longings). Violence is central to Wright's fiction, for as important as sex may be to his characters, power is much more so, and power is often achieved through violence; in Wright's world, beatings and murders are frequent acts—central and occasionally creative.

Once the character has acted, he finds himself trapped again in a new set of oppositions, for in acting, he has left the old sureties behind, has made himself free, and has begun to define and create himself. With that new freedom comes a new awareness of responsibility. He is without excuses, and that awareness is as terrifying as—though more liberating than—the fears he has previously known. Although Wright does not always elaborate on what may follow, the characters open up new possibilities for themselves. If one may create one's self by violence, perhaps, Wright sometimes suggests, there are other, less destructive ways as well.

Some of Wright's novels end on this note of optimism, the characters tragically happy: tragic because they have committed violent and repulsive acts, but happy because for the first time they have *chosen* to commit them; they have freed themselves from their constraints, and the future, however short it may be, lies open. Others end simply with tragedy, the destruction achieving no purpose, the characters attaining no illumination.

Lawd Today · *Lawd Today*, written before *Native Son*, but not published until after Wright's death, tells the story of Jake Jackson from his awakening on the morning of February 12, 1936, to that day's violent conclusion. Jackson is Wright's most inarticulate protagonist: He has a banal life, undefined dreams, and a vague sense of discontent which he is unable to explain. Violent and prejudiced, he speaks in clichés, a language as meaningless as his life.

Technically, the book incorporates a montage of radio broadcasts, newspaper articles, and religious and political pamphlets into the narration of Jake's day. Divided into three sections, *Lawd Today* opens with Jake's dream of running up an endless staircase after a disappearing voice. That dream gives way to the reality of his life: hunger, anger, and recrimination. Tricked by Jake into an abortion for which Jake still owes five hundred dollars and now claiming to have a tumor which will cost another five hundred dollars to remove, Jake's wife represents his entrapment. In the first section, "Commonplace," Jake reveals his brutish and trivial character: his anger at his wife, a jealousy and resentment that lead him to bait her so he can hit her, a mockbattle straightening his hair, and a meeting with friends who work with him at the post office. As they play bridge to pass the time until work, Wright presents without comment their stupid, cliché-ridden conversation.

Section two, "Squirrel Cage," shows the men at work. They are all alienated in meaningless, routine jobs, but Jake's position is the most desperate, for his wife has been to see his boss, and he is now threatened with the loss of his job. Falling deeper into debt by borrowing more money and making mistakes on the job, Jake is trapped by his work—despite his own protestations, as a self-proclaimed Republican and capitalist, that work is liberating. This section, too, ends with a long, rambling, and banal conversation among the men at work.

In the concluding section, "Rat's Alley," the men go to a brothel for a good time on some of Jake's borrowed money. There, Jake is robbed and then beaten for his threats of revenge. Finally, Jake stumbles homeward, his day nearing an end. The February weather, pleasant when the book began, has turned bad. All of Jake's frustration and anger finally erupt; he beats his wife, whom he finds kneeling asleep by the bed in an attitude of prayer. As they struggle, he throws objects through the window. She grabs a shard of broken glass and slashes him three times. The book ends with Jake lying in a drunken stupor, bleeding, while his wife is on her knees, also bleeding, praying for death. Outside, the wind blows mercilessly.

Although some of the experimentalism of *Lawd Today* seems artificial, and although the protagonist is too limited to sustain the reader's interest, this early work is powerful and economical. The situation, if not the character, is typical of Wright's work, and the reader understands Jake's violent frustration. *Lawd Today* has its flaws, but it foreshadows the strengths of Wright's best work and in its own right is a daring and fascinating novel.

Native Son · Along with *Black Boy, Native Son* is one of Wright's finest achievements: a brilliant portrayal of, as Wright put it, the way the environment provides the instrumentalities through which one expresses himself and the way that self becomes whole despite the environment's conspiring to keep it divided.

The book parallels Theodore Dreiser's *An American Tragedy* (1925): Both are three-part novels in which there is a murder, in part accidental, in part willed; an attempted flight; and a long concluding trial, in both cases somewhat anticlimactic. Both novels are concerned with the interplay of environment and heredity, of fate and accident, and both have protagonists who rebel against the world which would hold them back.

In the first part of *Native Son*, Bigger Thomas is a black man cut off from family and peers. Superficially like his friends, he is in fact possessed of a different consciousness. To think about that consciousness is for him to risk insanity or violence, so Bigger endeavors to keep his fears and uncertainty at a preconscious level. On the day of the first section, however, he is required by the welfare agency to apply for a job as a menial at the home of the rich Dalton family. Mr. Dalton is a ghetto landlord who soothes his conscience by donating sums of money for recreational purposes. That it is a minuscule part of the money he is deriving from blacks is an irony he overlooks. Mrs. Dalton is blind, a fact that is necessary to the plot as well as being symbolic. Their daughter, Mary, is a member of the Communist Party, and from the moment she sees Bigger, who wants nothing more than to be left alone, she begins to enlist his support.

The first evening, Bigger is to drive Mary to a university class. In reality, she is going with Jan Erlone, her Communist boyfriend, to a party meeting. Afterward, they insist that Bigger take them to a bar in the black part of town. Jan and Mary are at this point satirized, for their attitudes toward blacks are as limited and stereotyped as any in the novel. Bigger does not want to be seen by his friends with whites, but that fact does not occur to Mary. After much drinking, Bigger must carry the drunken Mary to her bedroom. He puts her to bed, stands over her, attracted to the woman he sees. The door opens and Mrs. Dalton enters. When Mary makes drunken noises, Bigger becomes frightened that Mrs. Dalton will come close enough to discover him, so he puts a pillow over Mary's face to quiet her. By the time Mrs. Dalton leaves, Mary is dead.

Wright wanted to make Bigger a character it would be impossible to pity, and what follows is extremely grisly. Bigger tries to put Mary's body in the furnace and saws off her head to make her fit. However accidental Mary's death may appear to the reader, Bigger himself does not regard it as such. He has, he thinks, many times wanted to kill whites without ever having the opportunity to do so. This time there was the act without the desire, but rather than seeing himself as the victim of a chance occurrence, Bigger prefers to unite the earlier desire with the present act, to make himself whole by accepting responsibility for the killing. Indeed, he not only accepts the act but also determines to capitalize on it by sending a ransom note. Later, accused of raping Mary as well, an act he considered but did not commit, he reverses the process, accepting responsibility for this, too, even though here there was desire but no act. His only sign of conscience is that he cannot bring himself to shake the ashes in the furnace; this guilt is not redemptive, but his undoing, for, in an implausible scene in the Dalton basement, the room fills with smoke, the murder is revealed to newspaper reporters gathered there, and Bigger is forced to flee.

He runs with his girlfriend, Bessie Mears. She, like Bigger, has a hunger for sensation, which has initially attracted him to her. Now, however, as they flee together, she becomes a threat and a burden; huddled with her in an abandoned tenement, Bigger wants only to be rid of her. He picks up a brick and smashes her face, dumping her body down an airshaft. His only regret is not that he has killed her, but that he has forgotten to remove their money from her body.

The rest of the plot moves quickly: Bigger is soon arrested, the trial is turned into a political farce, and Bigger is convicted and sentenced to death. In the last part of the novel, after Bigger's arrest, the implications of the action are developed, largely through Bigger's relations to other characters. Some of the characters are worthy only of contempt, particularly the district attorney, who, in an attempt at reelection, is turning the trial into political capital. Bigger's mother relies on religion. In a scene in the jail cell, she falls on her knees in apology before Mrs. Dalton and urges Bigger to pray, but toughness is Bigger's code. He is embarrassed by his mother's self-abasement, and although he agrees to pray simply to end his discomfort, his attitude toward religion is shown when he throws away a cross a minister has given him and throws a cup of coffee in a priest's face. In his view, they want only to avoid the world and to force him to accept guilt without responsibility.

Bigger learns from two characters. The first is Boris Max, the lawyer the Communist Party provides. Max listens to Bigger, and for the first time in his life, Bigger exposes his ideas and feelings to another human. Max's plea to the court is that, just as Bigger must accept responsibility for what he has done, so must the society around him understand its responsibility for what Bigger has become and, if the court chooses to execute Bigger, understand the consequences that must flow from that action. He does not argue—nor does Wright believe—that Bigger is a victim of injustice. There is no injustice, because that would presume a world in which Bigger could hope for justice, and such a world does not exist; more important, Bigger is not a victim, for he has chosen his own fate. Max argues rather that all men are entitled to happiness. Like all of Wright's protagonists, Bigger has earlier been torn between the poles of dread and ecstasy. His ecstasy, his happiness comes from the meaningfulness he creates in his existence, a product of self-realization. Unhappily for Bigger, he realizes himself through murder: It was, he feels, his highest creative act.

If Max articulates the intellectual presentation of Wright's beliefs about Bigger, it is Jan, Mary's lover, who is its dramatic representation. He visits Bigger in his cell and, having at last understood the futility and paucity of his own stereotypes, admits to Bigger that he too shares in the responsibility for what has happened. He, too, addresses Bigger as a human being, but from the unique position of being the one who is alive to remind Bigger of the consequences of his actions, for Bigger learns that Jan has suffered loss through what he has done and that, while Bigger has created himself, he has also destroyed another.

Native Son ends with the failure of Max's appeals on Bigger's behalf. He comes to the cell to confront Bigger before his execution, and the novel closes with Bigger Thomas smiling at Max as the prison door clangs shut. He will die happy because he will die fulfilled, having, however terribly, created a self. *Native Son* is Wright's most powerful work, because his theme, universal in nature, is given its fullest and most evocative embodiment. In the characterization of Bigger, alienated man at his least abstract and most genuine, of Bigger's exactly rendered mind and milieu, and of Bigger's working out of his destiny, *Native Son* is Wright's masterpiece.

The Outsider · Wright's next novel, *The Outsider*, written in France and published thirteen years after *Native Son*, suffers from a surplus of internal explanation and a failure to provide a setting as rich as that of *Native Son*. Still, its portrayal of Cross Damon and his struggle to define himself, while too self-conscious, adds new dimensions to Wright's myth.

As the novel opens, Damon is trapped by his life. His post-office job is unfulfilling, his wife is threatening, and his underage mistress is pregnant. He "desires desire," but there is no way for that desire to be completed. "A man creates himself," he has told his wife, but the self Damon has created is a nightmare. He broods, his brooding as close as he comes to religion. Another underground man, Damon gets his chance for new life on the subway. Thought dead after his identification papers are found near the mangled body of another, Damon gets a chance to create himself anew. He must invent, he thinks, not only his future, but also a past to fit with his present; this new opportunity brings with it a different and more potent sense of dread.

From the beginning of this new life, Damon is remarkably successful at the mechanics of creating a past. He easily obtains a birth certificate and a draft card. At a deeper level, however, he traps himself as surely as he has been trapped in his old life, so that his new one becomes a continuous act of bad faith. Even before he leaves Chicago, he hides in a brothel where he encounters a co-worker who recognizes him. Damon murders the man and throws his body out a window. The pattern of violence, so typical of Wright's characters, begins in earnest for Damon.

Taking a train to New York, Cross meets two people who will influence his new life, a black waiter who introduces him to the world of Communist politics in New York City, and Ely Houston, the district attorney, who is the most articulate person in the novel and the only one fully to understand Damon. Houston asks Damon why, when all blacks are outsiders, so few seem conscious of this fact. Wright suggests that being human is too much to be borne by people, that the struggle to define oneself is too difficult; the novel is a testament to that suggestion.

The Communist Party members, too, are outsiders, and there is nothing unified about their company. Each one that Damon meets is playing god, hoping to protect and extend his personal power. Their awareness of their motives varies, but they are a threat to Damon, and the action of the book is propelled by a series of murders: Damon himself wants to act like a god. Near the end of the book, Houston comes to understand that Damon is the killer, but–rather than indicating and punishing him legally–Houston allows him to go free, alone with his knowledge of what he is. Damon is horrified by his fate, but he is robbed of even that when he is killed by two Communist Party members who fear him.

The Outsider is both an extension and a modification of Wright's earlier views; it is far more pessimistic than *Native Son*, and the influence of the French existentialists is more pervasive. Like earlier Wright heroes, Damon is engaged in defining the world and himself. "The moment we act 'as if' it's true, then it's true," he thinks, because each person, in the absence of a god, is able to create the world and its truth. From Fyodor Dostoevski, Wright again borrows the notion of underground man and the idea that without a god, all is permitted. Yet as each man plays god, as each becomes criminal, policeman, judge, and executioner, there are no longer limits. People desire everything, and desire is described as a floating demon. People are jealous gods here–the worlds they create are petty, their jealousy destructive. Cross Damon is loved in the novel, but that love, unlike the love in *Native Son*, which is held up as potentially meaningful, is here without promise. Although he creates himself and his world in *The Outsider*, all that is made is violent and brutal, a world without redemption even in the act of self-realization.

At the end of the novel, Cross Damon dies, not with Bigger Thomas's smile, but with the knowledge that alone, people are nothing. Searching in his last moments of freedom for a clean, well-lighted place in which to rest before he confronts the world again, Cross finds only death. Before he dies, he admits his final act of bad faith: He has thought that he could create a world and be different from other men, that he could remain innocent. Like Joseph Conrad's Kurtz in *Heart of Darkness* (1902), Damon dies realizing the futility of that hope; having looked into his own heart of darkness, he dies with the word *horror* on his lips.

It is Wright's bleakest conclusion; this book contains his most relentless examination of the consequences of his own philosophy. Though *The Outsider* may lack the narrative drive of *Native Son*, still it remains a strongly conceived and troubling piece of fiction.

The Long Dream · Wright's last novel, *The Long Dream*, despite some effective scenes, is one of his weakest. The story of Rex "Fishbelly" Tucker's growing up and coming to terms with his environment is a pale repetition of earlier themes. The first section describes Tucker's youth. His father, an undertaker, is the richest black man in town, but his money comes also from a brothel he runs on the side. Tucker admires his father's success while detesting his obsequiousness with whites. When, however, Fishbelly is arrested, he twice faints at the white world's threats. Having presented himself as a victim, he becomes one. Walking home after his father has arranged his freedom, Fishbelly sees an injured dog, which he puts out of its misery. Fishbelly then comes upon a white man, pinned to the ground with a car door on his body. When the white man calls out to Fishbelly, using the term "nigger," Fishbelly walks on, leaving the man to die.

In the second section, Fishbelly finds a woman, but she and forty-one others are burned to death in a fire at the bar. The rest of the novel is an unconvincing story of the police who want the return of the cancelled checks that Fishbelly's father has used to pay them off, the police's arranged murder of the father, the subsequent framing and imprisoning of Fishbelly for rape, and Fishbelly's keeping the checks for his future use. All of this is badly contrived. At the end, Fishbelly is on a plane leaving for France, where his childhood friends are stationed in the army, which they describe as exciting. He is talking to an Italian whose father has come to America and found a dream, where Fishbelly himself has known only a nightmare. France, he dreams, will offer him what America has not.

In Fishbelly's attempt to understand himself and his environment, he is a typical Wright protagonist. He is weaker than Wright's usual characters, however, and that shallowness, coupled with an implausible plot, prevents Wright's last work of long fiction from succeeding.

Unlike many highly acclaimed books of the 1940's, *Native Son* and *Black Boy* have not dated. They are a lacerating challenge to contemporary readers and writers—a challenge to share the relentless integrity of Richard Wright's vision.

Howard Faulkner

Other major works

SHORT FICTION: *Uncle Tom's Children*, 1938, 1940; *Eight Men*, 1961.

PLAY: *Native Son: The Biography of a Young American*, pr. 1941 (with Paul Green).

NONFICTION: *Twelve Million Black Voices*, 1941; *Black Boy*, 1945; *Black Power*, 1954; *The Color Curtain*, 1956; *Pagan Spain*, 1957; *White Man, Listen!*, 1957; *American Hunger*, 1977.

Bibliography

Baldwin, James. *The Price of the Ticket: Collected Nonfiction, 1948-1985*. New York: St. Martin's Press/Marek, 1985. The essays "Everybody's Protest Novel" and "Alas, Poor Richard" provide important and provocative insights into Wright and his art.

Bloom, Harold, ed. *Richard Wright*. New York: Chelsea House, 1987. Essays on various aspects of Wright's work and career, with an introduction by Bloom.

Fabre, Michel. *The Unfinished Quest of Richard Wright*. Translated by Isabel Barzun. New York: William Morrow, 1973. The most important and authoritative biography of Wright available.

_____. *The World of Richard Wright*. Jackson: University Press of Mississippi,

1985. A collection of Fabre's essays on Wright. A valuable but not sustained full-length study.

Hakutani, Yoshinobu. *Richard Wright and Racial Discourse*. Columbia: University of Missouri Press, 1996. Chapters on *Lawd Today, Uncle Tom's Children, Native Son, The Outsider*, and *Black Boy*, as well as discussions of later fiction, black power, and Wright's handling of sexuality. Includes introduction and bibliography.

Kinnamon, Keneth, ed. *Critical Essays on Richard Wright's "Native Son."* New York: Twayne, 1997. Divided into sections of reviews, reprinted essays, and new essays. Includes discussions of Wright's handling of race, voice, tone, novelistic structure, the city, and literary influences. Index but no bibliography.

_____. *The Emergence of Richard Wright*. Urbana: University of Illinois Press, 1972. A study of Wright's background and development as a writer, up to the publication of *Native Son* (1940).

Walker, Margaret. *Richard Wright: Daemonic Genius*. New York: Warner Books, 1988. A critically acclaimed study of Wright's life and work written by a respected novelist.

Webb, Constance. *Richard Wright: A Biography*. New York: Putnam, 1968. A well-written biography which remains useful.

TERMS AND TECHNIQUES

Allegory: A literary mode in which a second level of meaning, wherein characters, events, and settings represent abstractions, is encoded within the surface narrative. The allegorical mode may dominate the entire work, in which case the encoded message is the work's primary excuse for being, or it may be an element in a work otherwise interesting and meaningful for its surface story alone. Elements of allegory may be found in Jonathan Swift's *Gulliver's Travels* (1726) and Thomas Mann's *The Magic Mountain* (1924).

Anatomy: Literally the term means the "cutting up" or "dissection" of a subject into its constituent parts for closer examination. Northrop Frye, in his *Anatomy of Criticism* (1957), uses the term to refer to a narrative that deals with mental attitudes rather than people. As opposed to the novel, the anatomy features stylized figures who are mouthpieces for the ideas they represent.

Antagonist: The character in fiction who stands as a rival or opponent to the *protagonist*.

Antihero: Defined by Seán O'Faoláin as a fictional figure who, deprived of social sanctions and definitions, is always trying to define himself and to establish his own codes. Ahab may be seen as the antihero of Herman Melville's *Moby Dick* (1851).

Archetype: The term "archetype" entered literary criticism from the psychology of Carl G. Jung, who defined archetypes as "primordial images" from the "collective unconscious" of humankind. Jung believed that works of art derived much of their power from the unconscious appeal of these images to ancestral memories. In his extremely influential *Anatomy of Criticism* (1957), Northrop Frye gave another sense of the term wide currency, defining the archetype as "a symbol, usually an image, which recurs often enough in literature to be recognizable as an element of one's literary experience as a whole."

Atmosphere: The general mood or tone of a work; it is often associated with setting, but can also be established by action or dialogue. A classic example of atmosphere is the primitive, fatalistic tone created in the opening description of Egdon Heath in Thomas Hardy's *The Return of the Native* (1878).

Bildungsroman: Sometimes called the "novel of education," the *Bildungsroman* focuses on the growth of a young *protagonist* who is learning about the world and finding his place in life; typical examples are James Joyce's *A Portrait of the Artist as a Young Man* (1916) and Thomas Wolfe's *Look Homeward, Angel* (1929).

Biographical criticism: Criticism that attempts to determine how the events and experiences of an author's life influence his work.

Bourgeois novel: A novel in which the values, the preoccupations, and the accoutrements of middle-class or bourgeois life are given particular prominence. The heyday of the bourgeois novel was the nineteenth century, when novelists as varied as Jane Austen, Honoré de Balzac, and Anthony Trollope both criticized and unreflectingly transmitted the assumptions of the rising middle class.

Character: Characters in fiction can be presented as if they were real people or as stylized functions of the plot. Usually characters are a combination of both factors.

Classicism: A literary stance or value-system consciously based on the example of classical Greek and Roman literature. While the term is applied to an enormous diversity of artists in many different periods and in many different national literatures, "classicism" generally denotes a cluster of values including formal discipline, restrained expression, reverence for tradition, and an objective rather than a subjective orientation. As a literary tendency, classicism is often opposed to *Romanticism*, although many writers combine classical and romantic elements.

Climax/Crisis: Whereas climax refers to the moment of the reader's highest emotional response, crisis refers to a structural element of plot. Crisis refers to a turning point in fiction, a point when a resolution must take place.

Complication: The point in a novel when the conflict is developed or when the already existing conflict is further intensified.

Conflict: The struggle that develops as a result of the opposition between the *protagonist* and another person, the natural world, society, or some force within the self.

Contextualist criticism: A further extension of formalist criticism, which assumes that the language of art is constitutive. Rather than referring to preexistent values, the art work creates values only inchoately realized before. The most important advocates of this position are Eliseo Vivas, *The Artistic Transaction* (1963), and Murray Krieger, *The Play and Place of Criticism* (1967).

Conventions: All those devices of stylization, compression, and selection that constitute the necessary differences between art and life. According to the Russian formalists, these conventions constitute the "literariness" of literature and are the only proper concern of the literary critic.

Deconstruction: An extremely influential contemporary school of criticism based on the works of the French philosopher Jacques Derrida. Deconstruction treats literary works as unconscious reflections of the reigning myths of Western culture. The primary myth is that there is a meaningful world which language signifies or represents. The Deconstructionist critic is most often concerned with showing how a literary text tacitly subverts the very assumptions or myths on which it ostensibly rests.

Defamiliarization: Coined by Viktor Shklovsky in 1917, the term denotes a basic principle of Russian formalism. Poetic language (by which the formalists meant artful language, in prose as well as in poetry) defamiliarizes or "makes strange" familiar experiences. The technique of art, says Shklovsky, is to "make objects unfamiliar, to make forms difficult, to increase the difficulty and length of perception. . . . Art is a way of experiencing the artfulness of an object; the object is not important."

Detective story: The so-called "classic" detective story (or "mystery") is a highly formalized and logically structured mode of fiction in which the focus is on a crime solved by a detective through interpretation of evidence and ratiocination; the most famous detective in this mode is Arthur Conan Doyle's Sherlock Holmes. Many modern practitioners of the genre, however, such as Dashiell Hammett, Raymond Chandler, and Ross Macdonald, have deemphasized the puzzlelike qualities of the detective story, stressing instead characterization, theme, and other elements of mainstream fiction.

Determinism: The belief that an individual's actions are essentially determined by biological and environmental factors, with free will playing a negligible role. (See *Naturalism.*)

Dialogue: The similitude of conversation in fiction, dialogue serves to characterize, to further the plot, to establish conflict, and to express thematic ideas.

Displacement: Popularized in criticism by Northrop Frye, the term refers to the author's attempt to make his story psychologically motivated and realistic, even as the latent structure of the mythical motivation moves relentlessly forward.

Dominant: A term coined by Roman Jakobson to refer to that which "rules, determines, and transforms the remaining components in the work of a single artist, in a poetic canon, or in the work of an epoch." The shifting of the dominant in a *genre* accounts for the creation of new generic forms and new poetic epochs. For example, the rise of realism in the mid-nineteenth century indicates realistic conventions becoming dominant and romance or fantasy conventions becoming secondary.

Doppelgänger: A double or counterpart of a person, sometimes endowed with ghostly qualities. A fictional character's *Doppelgänger* often reflects a suppressed side of his personality. One of the classic examples of the *Doppelgänger* motif is found in Fyodor Dostoevski's novella *The Double* (1846); Isaac Bashevis Singer and Jorge Luis Borges, among others, offer striking modern treatments of the *Doppelgänger.*

Epic: Although this term usually refers to a long narrative poem which presents the exploits of a central figure of high position, the term is also used to designate a long novel that has the style or structure usually associated with an epic. In this sense, for example, Herman Melville's *Moby Dick* (1851) and James Joyce's *Ulysses* (1922) may be called epic.

Episodic narrative: A work that is held together primarily by a loose connection of self-sufficient episodes. *Picaresque novels* often have an episodic structure.

Epistolary novel: A novel made up of letters by one or more fictional characters. Samuel Richardson's *Pamela* (1740-1741) is a well-known eighteenth century example. A nineteenth century example, Bram Stoker's *Dracula* (1897) is largely epistolary. The technique allows for several different points of view to be presented.

Euphuism: A style of writing characterized by ornate language that is highly contrived, alliterative, and repetitious. Euphuism was developed by John Lyly in his *Euphues, an Anatomy of Wit* (1578) and was emulated frequently by writers of the Elizabethan Age.

Exposition: The part or parts of a fiction which provide necessary background information. Exposition not only provides the time and place of the action, but also introduces the reader to the fictive world of the story, acquainting him with the ground rules of the work.

Fantastic: In his study *The Fantastic* (1970), Tzvetan Todorov defines the fantastic as a *genre* that lies between the "uncanny" and the "marvelous." All three embody the familiar world, but present an event that cannot be explained by the laws of the familiar world. Todorov says that the fantastic occupies a twilight zone between the uncanny—when the reader knows that the peculiar event is merely the result of an illusion—and the marvelous—when the reader understands that the event is supposed to take place in a realm controlled by laws unknown to humankind. Thus, the fantastic is essentially unsettling, provocative, even subversive.

Flashback: A scene in a fiction that depicts an earlier event; it can be presented as a reminiscence by a character in the story or it can simply be inserted into the narrative.

Foreshadowing: A device to create suspense or dramatic irony by indicating through suggestion what will take place in the future.

Formalist criticism: There have been two particularly influential formalist schools of criticism in the twentieth century: the Russian formalists and the American New Critics. The Russian formalists were concerned with the conventional devices used in literature to defamiliarize that which habit has made familiar. The New Critics believed that literary criticism is a description and evaluation of its object and that the primary concern of the critic is with the work's unity. Both schools of criticism, at their most extreme, treated literary works as artifacts or constructs divorced from their biographical and social contexts.

Genre: In its most general sense, the term "genre" refers to a group of literary works defined by a common form, style, or purpose. In practice, the term is used in a wide variety of overlapping and, to a degree, contradictory senses. Thus, tragedy and comedy are described as distinct genres; the novel (a form which includes both tragic and comic works) is a genre; and various subspecies of the novel, such as the *gothic* and the *picaresque*, are themselves frequently treated as distinct genres. Finally, the term *genre fiction* refers to forms of popular fiction in which the writer is bound by more or less rigid conventions. Indeed, all these diverse usages have in common an emphasis on the manner in which individual literary works are shaped by the expectations and conventions of a particular genre: this is the subject of genre criticism.

Genre fiction: Categories of popular fiction such as the mystery, the romance, and the Western. Although the term can be used in a neutral sense, "genre fiction" is often pejorative, used dismissively to refer to fiction in which the writer is bound by more or less rigid conventions.

Gothic novel: A form of fiction developed in the eighteenth century which focuses on horror and the supernatural. In his Preface to *The Castle of Otranto* (1764), the first gothic novel in English, Horace Walpole claimed that he was trying to combine two kinds of fiction, with events and story typical of the medieval romance and character delineation typical of the realistic novel. Other examples of the form are Matthew Lewis's *The Monk* (1796) and Mary Shelley's *Frankenstein* (1818).

Grotesque: According to Wolfgang Kayser (*The Grotesque in Art and Literature,* 1963), the grotesque is an embodiment in literature of the estranged world. Characterized by a breakup of the everyday world by mysterious forces, the form differs from fantasy in that the reader is not sure whether to react with humor or with horror and in that the exaggeration manifested exists in the familiar world rather than in a purely imaginative world.

Hebraic/Homeric styles: Terms coined by Erich Auerbach in *Mimesis: The Representation of Reality in Western Literature* (1953), to designate two basic fictional styles: the Hebraic, which focuses only on the decisive points of narrative and leaves all else obscure, mysterious, and "fraught with background," and the Homeric, which places the narrative in a definite time and place and externalizes everything in a perpetual foreground.

Historical criticism: In contrast to *formalist criticism,* which treats literary works to a great extent as self-contained artifacts, historical criticism emphasizes the historical context of literature; these approaches, however, need not be mutually exclusive.

Ernst Robert Curtius's *European Literature and the Latin Middle Ages* (1940) is a prominent example of historical criticism.

Historical novel: A novel that depicts past historical events, usually public in nature, and that features real as well as fictional people. Sir Walter Scott's Waverley novels established the basic type, but the relationship between fiction and history in the form varies greatly depending on the practitioner.

Implied author: According to Wayne Booth (*The Rhetoric of Fiction*, 1961), the novel often creates a kind of second self who tells the story—a self who is wiser, more sensitive, and more perceptive than any real person could be.

Interior monologue: Defined by Édouard Dujardin as the speech of a character designed to introduce the reader directly to the character's internal life, the form differs from other monologues in that it attempts to reproduce thought before any logical organization is imposed upon it. See, for example, Molly Bloom's long interior monologue at the conclusion of James Joyce's *Ulysses* (1922).

Irrealism: A term often used to refer to modern or postmodern fiction that is presented self-consciously as a fiction or a fabulation rather than a mimesis of external reality. The best-known practitioners of irrealism are John Barth, Robert Coover, and Donald Barthelme.

Local colorists: A loose movement of late-nineteenth century American writers whose fiction emphasized the distinctive folkways, landscapes, and dialects of various regions. Important local colorists included Bret Harte, Mark Twain, George Washington Cable, Kate Chopin, and Sarah Orne Jewett. (See *Regional novel.*)

Metafiction: The term refers to fiction that manifests a reflexive tendency, such as Vladimir Nabokov's *Pale Fire* (1962) and John Fowles's *The French Lieutenant's Woman* (1969). The emphasis is on the loosening of the work's illusion of reality to expose the reality of its illusion. Such terms as *irrealism, postmodernist fiction,* "antifiction," and "surfiction" are also used to refer to this type of fiction.

Modernism: An international movement in the arts which began in the early years of the twentieth century. Although the term is used to describe artists of widely varying persuasions, modernism in general was characterized by its international idiom, by its interest in cultures distant in space or time, by its emphasis on formal experimentation, and by its sense of dislocation and radical change.

Motif: A conventional incident or situation in a fiction which may serve as the basis for the structure of the narrative itself. The Russian formalist critic Boris Tomashevsky uses the term to refer to the smallest particle of thematic material in a work.

Motivation: Although this term is usually used in reference to the convention of justifying the action of a character from his or her psychological makeup, the Russian formalists use the term to refer to the network of devices that justify the introduction of individual *motifs* or groups of *motifs* in a work. For example, compositional motivation refers to the principle that every single property in a work contributes to its overall effect; realistic motivation refers to the realistic devices used to make the work plausible and lifelike.

Myth: Anonymous traditional stories dealing with basic human concepts and antinomies. Claude Lévi-Strauss says that myth is that part of language where the

"formula *tradutore, tradittore* reaches its lowest truth value. . . . Its substance does
not lie in its style, its original music, or its syntax, but in the story which it tells."

Myth criticism: Northrop Frye says that in myth, "we see the structural principles of
literature isolated." Myth criticism is concerned with these basic principles of
literature; it is not to be confused with mythological criticism, which is primarily
concerned with finding mythological parallels in the surface action of the *narrative.*

Narrative: Robert Scholes and Robert Kellogg, in *The Nature of Narrative* (1966), say
that by narrative they mean literary works which include both a story and a
storyteller. Narrative usually implies a contrast to "enacted" fiction such as drama.

Narratology: The study of the form and functioning of narratives; it attempts to
examine what all *narratives* have in common and what makes individual *narratives*
different from one another.

Narrator: The character who recounts the *narrative,* or story. Wayne Booth describes
various dramatized narrators in *The Rhetoric of Fiction* (1961): unacknowledged
centers of consciousness, observers, narrator-agents, and self-conscious narrators.
Booth suggests that the important element to consider in narration is the relationship between the narrator, the author, the characters, and the reader.

Naturalism: As developed by Émile Zola in the late nineteenth century, naturalism is
the application of the principles of scientific *determinism* to fiction. Although it
usually refers more to the choice of subject matter than to technical conventions,
those conventions associated with the movement center on the author's attempt to
be precise and scientifically objective in description and detail, regardless of
whether the events described are sordid or shocking.

New Criticism. See *Formalist criticism.*

Novel: Perhaps the most difficult of all fictional forms to define because of its multiplicity of modes. Edouard, in André Gide's *The Counterfeiters* (1926), says the novel
is the freest and most lawless of all *genres:* he wonders if fear of that liberty is not
the reason the novel has so timidly clung to reality. Most critics seem to agree that
the novel's primary area of concern is the social world. Ian Watt (*The Rise of the
Novel,* 1957) says that the novel can be distinguished from other fictional forms by
the attention it pays to individual characterization and detailed presentation of the
environment. Moreover, says Watt, the novel, more than any other fictional form,
is interested in the "development of its characters in the course of time."

Novel of manners: The classic example of the form might be the novels of Jane Austen,
wherein the customs and conventions of a social group of a particular time and
place are realistically, and often satirically, portrayed.

Novella, novelle, nouvelle, novelette, novela: Although these terms sometimes refer to the
short European tale, especially the Renaissance form employed by Giovanni
Boccaccio, the terms often refer to that form of fiction which is said to be longer
than a short story and shorter than a novel. "Novelette" is the term usually
preferred by the British, whereas "novella" is the term usually used to refer to
American works in this *genre.* Henry James claimed that the main merit of the form
was the "effort to do the complicated thing with a strong brevity and lucidity."

Phenomenological criticism: Although best-known as a European school of criticism
practiced by Georges Poulet and others, this so-called "criticism of consciousness"
is also propounded in America by such critics as J. Hillis Miller. The focus is less
on individual works and *genres* than it is on literature as an act; the work is not seen

as an object, but rather as part of a strand of latent impulses in the work of a single author or an epoch.

Picaresque novel: A form of fiction that centers around a central rogue figure or picaro who usually tells his own story. The plot structure is normally *episodic,* and the episodes usually focus on how the picaro lives by his wits. Classic examples of the mode are Henry Fielding's *Tom Jones* (1749) and Mark Twain's *The Adventures of Huckleberry Finn* (1884).

Plot/Story: Story is a term referring to the full narrative of character and action, whereas plot generally refers to action with little reference to character. A more precise and helpful distinction is made by the Russian formalists, who suggest that plot refers to the events of a *narrative* as they have been artfully arranged in the literary work, subject to chronological displacement, ellipses, and other devices, while story refers to the sum of the same events arranged in simple, causal-chronological order. Thus, story is the raw material for plot. By comparing the two in a given work, the reader is encouraged to see the *narrative* as an artifact.

Point of view: The means by which the story is presented to the reader, or, as Percy Lubbock says in *The Craft of Fiction* (1921), "the relation in which the narrator stands to the story"–a relation which Lubbock claims governs the craft of fiction. Some of the questions the critical reader should ask concerning point of view are: Who talks to the reader? From what position does the narrator tell the story? At what distance does he place the reader from the story? What kind of person is he? How fully is he characterized? How reliable is he? For further discussion, see Wayne Booth, *The Rhetoric of Fiction* (1961).

Postmodernism: A ubiquitous but elusive term in contempory criticism, "postmod-ernism" is loosely applied to the various artistic movements which have followed the era of so-called "high modernism," represented by such giants as James Joyce and Pablo Picasso. In critical discussions of contemporary fiction, the term "post-modernism" is frequently applied to the works of writers such as Thomas Pynchon, John Barth, and Donald Barthelme, who exhibit a self-conscious awareness of their modernist predecessors as well as a reflexive treatment of fictional form.

Protagonist: The central character in a fiction, the character whose fortunes most concern the reader.

Psychological criticism: While much modern literary criticism reflects to some degree the impact of Sigmund Freud, Carl Jung, Jacques Lacan, and other psychological theorists, the term "psychological criticism" suggests a strong emphasis on a causal relation between the writer's psychological state, variously interpreted, and his works. A notable example of psychological criticism is Norman Fruman's *Coleridge, the Damaged Archangel* (1971).

Psychological novel: A form of fiction in which character, especially the inner life of characters, is the primary focus. The form has been of primary importance, at least since Henry James, and it characterizes much of the work of James Joyce, Virginia Woolf, and William Faulkner. For a detailed discussion, see *The Modern Psychological Novel* (1955) by Leon Edel.

Realism: A literary technique in which the primary convention is to render an illusion of fidelity to external reality. Realism is often identified as the primary method of the novel form: it focuses on surface details, maintains a fidelity to the everyday experiences of middle-class society, and strives for a one-to-one relationship between the fiction and the action imitated. The realist movement in the late nineteenth century coincides with the full development of the novel form.

Reception aesthetics: The best-known American practitioner of reception aesthetics is Stanley Fish. For the reception critic, meaning is an event or process; rather than being embedded in the work, it is created through particular acts of reading. The best-known European practitioner of this criticism, Wolfgang Iser, says indeterminacy is the basic characteristic of literary texts; the reader must "normalize" the text either by projecting his or her standards into it or by revising his or her standards to "fit" the text.

Regional novel: Any novel in which the character of a given geographical region plays a decisive role. Although regional differences persist in America, there has been a considerable leveling in speech, habit, and attitude, so that the sharp regional distinctions evident in nineteenth century American fiction no longer exist. Only in the South has a strong regional tradition persisted to the present. (See *Local colorists.*)

Rhetorical criticism: The rhetorical critic is concerned with the literary work as a means of the communication of ideas, the means by which the work affects or controls the reader. Such criticism seems best suited to didactic works such as satire.

Roman à clef: A fiction wherein actual persons, often celebrities of some sort, are thinly disguised.

Romance: The romance usually differs from the novel form in that the focus is on symbolic events and representational characters rather than on "as-if-real" characters and events. Richard Chase says that in the romance, character is depicted as highly stylized, a function of the plot rather than as someone complexly related to society. The romancer is more likely to be concerned with dreamworlds than with the familiar world, believing that reality cannot be grasped by the traditional novel.

Romanticism: A widespread cultural movement in the late-eighteenth and early-nineteenth centuries, the influence of which is still felt. As a general literary tendency, Romanticism is frequently contrasted with *classicism*. Although there were many varieties of Romanticism indigenous to various national literatures, the term generally suggests an assertion of the preeminence of the imagination. Other values associated with various schools of Romanticism include primitivism, an interest in folklore, a reverence for nature, and a fascination with the demoniac and the macabre.

Scene: The central element of narration; specific actions are narrated or depicted that make the reader feel he or she is participating directly in the action.

Science fiction: Fiction in which certain givens (physical laws, psychological principles, social conditions: any one or all of these) form the basis of an imaginative projection into the future or, less commonly, an extrapolation in the present or even into the past.

Semiotics: The science of signs and sign systems in communication. Roman Jakobson says that semiotics deals with the principles which underlie the structure of signs, their use in language of all kinds, and the specific nature of various sign systems.

Sentimental novel: A form of fiction popular in the eighteenth century in which emotionalism and optimism are the primary characteristics. The best-known examples are Samuel Richardson's *Pamela* (1740-1741) and Oliver Goldsmith's *The Vicar of Wakefield* (1766).

Setting: Setting refers to the circumstances and environment, both temporal and spatial, of a *narrative.*

Spatial form: An author's attempt to make the reader apprehend the work spatially in a moment of time rather than sequentially. To achieve this effect, the author breaks up the *narrative* into interspersed fragments. Beginning with James Joyce, Marcel Proust, and Djuna Barnes, the movement toward spatial form is concomitant with the modernist effort to supplant historical time in fiction with mythic time. For the seminal discussion of this technique, see Joseph Frank, *The Widening Gyre* (1963).

Stream of consciousness: The depiction of the thought-processes of a character, insofar as this is possible, without any mediating structures. The metaphor of consciousness as a "stream" suggests a rush of thoughts and images governed by free association rather than by strictly rational development. The term "stream of consciousness" is often used loosely as a synonym for *interior monologue.* The most celebrated example of stream of consciousness in fiction is the monologue of Molly Bloom in James Joyce's *Ulysses* (1922); other notable practitioners of the stream-of-consciousness technique include Dorothy Richardson, Virginia Woolf, and William Faulkner.

Structuralism: As a movement of thought, structuralism is based on the idea of intrinsic, self-sufficient structures which do not require reference to external elements. A structure is a system of transformations which involves the interplay of laws inherent in the system itself. The study of language is the primary model for contemporary structuralism. The structuralist literary critic attempts to define structural principles that operate intertextually throughout the whole of literature as well as principles that operate in *genres* and in individual works. The most accessible survey of structuralism and literature is Jonathan Culler, *Structuralist Poetics* (1975).

Summary: Those parts of a fiction which do not need to be detailed. In *Tom Jones* (1749), Henry Fielding says "If whole years should pass without producing anything worthy of . . . notice . . . we shall hasten on to matters of consequence."

Thematics: Northrup Frye says that when a work of fiction is written or interpreted thematically, it becomes an illustrative fable. Murray Krieger defines thematics as "the study of the experiential tensions which, dramatically entangled in the literary work, become an existential reflection of that work's aesthetic complexity." See Krieger's *The Tragic Vision* (1960).

Tone: Tone usually refers to the dominant mood of the work. (See *Atmosphere.*)

Unreliable narrator: A narrator whose account of the events of the story cannot be trusted, obliging the reader to reconstruct–if possible–the true state of affairs himself. Once an innovative technique, the use of the unreliable narrator has become commonplace among contemporary writers who wish to suggest the impossibility of a truly "reliable" account of any event. Notable examples of the unreliable narrator can be found in Ford Madox Ford's *The Good Soldier* (1915) and Vladimir Nabokov's *Lolita* (1958).

Victorian novel: Although the Victorian period extended from 1837 to 1901, the term "Victorian novel" does not include the later decades of Queen Victoria's reign. The term loosely refers to the sprawling works of novelists such as Charles Dickens and

William Makepeace Thackeray– works which frequently appeared first in serial form and which are characterized by a broad social canvas.

Vraisemblance/Verisimilitude: Tzvetan Todorov defines vraisemblance as "the mask which conceals the text's own laws, but which we are supposed to take for a relation to reality." When one speaks of vraisemblance, one refers to the work's attempts to make the reader believe that it conforms to reality rather than to its own laws.

Western novel: Like all varieties of *genre fiction,* the Western novel–generally known simply as the "Western"–is defined by a relatively predictable combination of conventions, *motifs,* and recurring themes. These predictable elements, familiar from the many Western series on television and in film, differentiate the Western from *historical novels* and idiosyncratic works such as Thomas Berger's *Little Big Man* (1964) which are also set in the Old West. Conversely, some novels set in the contemporary West are regarded as Westerns because they deal with modern cowboys and with the land itself in the manner characteristic of the *genre.*

Charles E. May

Time Line

Date and place of birth

Date and place of birth	Name
Sept. 15, 1789: Burlington, New Jersey	James Fenimore Cooper
July 4, 1804: Salem, Massachusetts	Nathaniel Hawthorne
June 14, 1811: Litchfield, Connecticut	Harriet Beecher Stowe
Aug. 1, 1819: New York, New York	Herman Melville
Nov. 29, 1832: Germantown, Pennsylvania	Louisa May Alcott
Nov. 30, 1835: Florida, Missouri	Mark Twain
Mar. 1, 1837: Martin's Ferry, Ohio	William Dean Howells
Apr. 15, 1843: New York, New York	Henry James
Oct. 12, 1844: New Orleans, Louisiana	George Washington Cable
Sept. 3, 1849: South Berwick, Maine	Sarah Orne Jewett
Feb. 8, 1851: St. Louis, Missouri	Kate Chopin
Jan. 24, 1862: New York, New York	Edith Wharton
Mar. 5, 1870: Chicago, Illinois	Frank Norris
Aug. 27, 1871: Terre Haute, Indiana	Theodore Dreiser
Nov. 1, 1871: Newark, New Jersey	Stephen Crane
Apr. 22, 1873: Richmond, Virginia	Ellen Glasgow
Dec. 7, 1873: Back Creek Valley	Willa Cather
Feb. 3, 1874: Allegheny, Pennsylvania	Gertrude Stein
Jan. 12, 1876: San Francisco, California	Jack London
Sept. 13, 1876: Camden, Ohio	Sherwood Anderson
Sept. 20, 1878: Baltimore, Maryland	Upton Sinclair
Feb. 7, 1885: Sauk Centre, Minnesota	Sinclair Lewis
July 23, 1888: Chicago, Illinois	Raymond Chandler
May 15, 1890: Indian Creek, Texas	Katherine Anne Porter
Jan. 7, 1891: Eatonville, Florida	Zora Neale Hurston
Dec. 26, 1891: New York, New York	Henry Miller
June 26, 1892: Hillsboro, West Virginia	Pearl S. Buck
May 27, 1894: St. Mary's County, Maryland	Dashiell Hammett
Jan. 14, 1896: Chicago, Illinois	John Dos Passos
Sept. 24, 1896: St. Paul, Minnesota	F. Scott Fitzgerald
Apr. 17, 1897: Madison, Wisconsin	Thornton Wilder
Sept. 25, 1897: New Albany, Mississippi	William Faulkner
Apr. 23, 1899: St. Petersburg, Russia	Vladimir Nabokov
July 21, 1899: Oak Park, Illinois	Ernest Hemingway
Oct. 3, 1900: Asheville, North Carolina	Thomas Wolfe

Date and place of birth	Name
Feb. 27, 1902: Salinas, California	John Steinbeck
Oct. 17, 1903: New York, New York	Nathanael West
Feburary 27, 1904: Chicago, Illinois	James T. Farrell
Jan. 31, 1905: Pottsville, Pennsylvania	John O'Hara
Feb. 2, 1905: St. Petersburg, Russia	Ayn Rand
Feb. 3, 1907(?): New York, New York(?)	James A. Michener
Aug. 31, 1908: Fresno, California	William Saroyan
Sept. 4, 1908: Natchez, Mississippi	Richard Wright
Feb. 18, 1909: Lake Mills, Iowa	Wallace Stegner
Apr. 13, 1909: Jackson, Mississippi	Eudora Welty
Jan. 6, 1910: Central City, Nebraska	Wright Morris
Dec. 30, 1910: New York	Paul Bowles
May 27, 1912: Quincy, Massachusetts	John Cheever
June 21, 1912: Seattle, Washington	Mary McCarthy
Feb. 5, 1914: St. Louis, Missouri	William S. Burroughs
Mar. 1, 1914: Oklahoma City, Oklahoma	Ralph Ellison
Apr. 26, 1914: Brooklyn, New York	Bernard Malamud
June 17, 1914: Tientsin, China	John Hersey
May 27, 1915: New York, New York	Herman Wouk
June 10, 1915: Lachine, Quebec, Canada	Saul Bellow
Dec. 13, 1915: Los Gatos, California	Ross Macdonald
May 28, 1916: Birmingham, Alabama	Walker Percy
Feb. 19, 1917: Columbus, Georgia	Carson McCullers
Sept. 27, 1917: Lawrence, New York	Louis Auchincloss
Feb. 26, 1918: Staten Island, New York	Theodore Sturgeon
Jan. 1, 1919: New York, New York	J. D. Salinger
Jan. 2, 1920: Petrovichi, Russia	Isaac Asimov
Aug. 22, 1920: Waukegan, Illinois	Ray Bradbury
Nov. 6, 1921: Robinson, Illinois	James Jones
Mar. 12, 1922: Lowell, Massachusetts	Jack Kerouac
Nov. 11, 1922: Indianapolis, Indiana	Kurt Vonnegut, Jr.
Dec. 29, 1922: New York, New York	William Gaddis
Jan. 31, 1923: Long Branch, New Jersey	Norman Mailer
Feb. 2, 1923: Atlanta, Georgia	James Dickey
May 1, 1923: Brooklyn, New York	Joseph Heller
Aug. 2, 1924: New York, New York	James Baldwin
Sept. 30, 1924: New Orleans, Louisiana	Truman Capote
Mar. 25, 1925: Savannah, Georgia	Flannery O'Connor
June 11, 1925: Newport News, Virginia	William Styron
Oct. 11, 1925: New Orleans, Louisiana	Elmore Leonard

Date and place of birth	Name
Oct. 3, 1925: West Point, New York	Gore Vidal
Apr. 23, 1926: Brooklyn, New York	J. P. Donleavy
Monroeville, Alabama: Apr. 28, 1926	Harper Lee
Sept. 3, 1926: Chicago, Illinois	Alison Lurie
Jan. 16, 1928: Albany, New York	William Kennedy
Dec. 16, 1928: Chicago, Illinois	Philip K. Dick
Feb. 17, 1929: New York, New York	Chaim Potok
Oct. 21, 1929: Berkeley, California	Ursula K. Le Guin
May 27, 1930: Cambridge, Maryland	John Barth
Jan. 6, 1931: New York, New York	E. L. Doctorow
Feb. 18, 1931: Lorain, Ohio	Toni Morrison
Feb. 4, 1932: Charles City, Iowa	Robert Coover
Mar. 18, 1932: Shillington, Pennsylvania	John Updike
Feb. 1, 1933: Macon, North Carolina	Reynolds Price
Mar. 19, 1933: Newark, New Jersey	Philip Roth
June 14, 1933: Lodz, Poland	Jerzy Kosinski
July 21, 1933: Batavia, New York	John Gardner
July 20, 1933: Providence, Rhode Island	Cormac McCarthy
Dec. 5, 1934: Sacramento, California	Joan Didion
Jan. 30, 1935: Tacoma, Washington	Richard Brautigan
Sept. 17, 1935: La Junta, Colorado	Ken Kesey
June 3, 1936: Wichita Falls, Texas	Larry McMurtry
Nov. 20, 1936: New York, New York	Don DeLillo
May 8, 1937: Glen Cove, New York	Thomas Pynchon
Oct. 30, 1937: Pastura, New Mexico	Rudolfo A. Anaya
Feb. 22, 1938: Chattanooga, Tennessee	Ishmael Reed
June 16, 1938: Lockport, New York	Joyce Carol Oates
Dec. 11, 1939: Wyandotte, Michigan	Thomas McGuane
Apr. 10, 1941: Medford, Massachusetts	Paul Theroux
Oct. 25, 1941: Minneapolis, Minnesota	Anne Tyler
Oct. 30, 1941: Carrington, North Dakota	Larry Woiwode
Oct. 4, 1941: New Orleans, Louisiana	Anne Rice
Mar. 2, 1942: Exeter, New Hampshire	John Irving
Apr. 1, 1942: New York, New York	Samuel R. Delany
Feb. 9, 1944: Eatonton, Georgia	Alice Walker
Oct. 1, 1946: Austin, Minnesota	Tim O'Brien
Sept. 8, 1947: Washington, D.C.	Ann Beattie
Sept. 21, 1947: Portland, Maine	Stephen King
1948: Peekskill, New York	T. Coraghessan Boyle
Mar. 5, 1948: Albuquerque, New Mexico	Leslie Marmon Silko

Date and place of birth	Name
May 25, 1949: St. Johns, Antigua	Jamaica Kincaid
Jan. 25, 1950: New York, New York	Gloria Naylor
Aug. 24, 1951: New York, New York	Oscar Hijuelos
Feb. 19, 1952: Oakland, California	Amy Tan
June 7, 1954: Little Falls, Minnesota	Louise Erdrich

NOTABLE AMERICAN NOVELISTS

INDEX

Abortion, The (Brautigan), 118
Absalom, Absalom! (Faulkner), 357
Accidental Tourist, The (Tyler), 1055
Active Service (Crane), 231
Actual, The (Bellow), 86
Adventures of Augie March, The (Bellow),
   77
Adventures of Huckleberry Finn, The
   (Twain), 1039
Adventures of Tom Sawyer, The (Twain),
   1037
Adventures of Wesley Jackson, The
   (Saroyan), 935
Aeneid (Vergil), 393
Age of Innocence, The (Wharton), 1126
Alcott, Louisa May, **1-7**
All My Friends Are Going to Be Strangers
   (McMurtry), 690
All the Pretty Horses. See Border trilogy
Almanac of the Dead (Silko), 942
Alnilam (Dickey), 266
Ambassadors, The (James), 512
American Dream, An (Mailer), 706
American Pastoral (Roth), 917
American Tragedy, An (Dreiser), 316, 1177
Americana (DeLillo), 248
Anatomy Lesson, The (Roth), 916
Anaya, Rudolfo A., **8-12**
Ancient Evenings (Mailer), 712
Anderson, Sherwood, **13-21**
Angle of Repose (Stegner), 958
Annie John (Kincaid), 566
Another Country (Baldwin), 46
Another You (Beattie), 72
Answered Prayers (Capote), 155
Antelope Wife, The (Erdrich), 336
Anything for Billy (McMurtry), 694
Appointment in Samarra (O'Hara), 829
Armies of the Night, The (Mailer), 709
Arrowsmith (Lewis), 622
As I Lay Dying (Faulkner), 352
Asimov, Isaac, **22-27**
Assistant, The (Malamud), 722

At Fault (Chopin), 196
Atlas Shrugged (Rand), 892
Auchincloss, Louis, **28-38**
Aurora Dawn (Wouk), 1161
Autobiography of My Mother, The
   (Kincaid), 567
Awakening, The (Chopin), 198

Babbitt (Lewis), 621
Bag of Bones (King), 579
Bailey's Café (Naylor), 790
Baldwin, James, **39-53**, 1009
Ballad of the Sad Café, The (McCullers),
   664
Barbary Shore (Mailer), 703
Barren Ground (Glasgow), 407
Barth, John, **54-67**
Beastly Beatitudes of Balthazar B, The
   (Donleavy), 295
Beat movement, 131, 543
Beattie, Ann, **68-73**
Beautiful and Damned, The (Fitzgerald),
   371
Bech (Updike), 1068
Bech at Bay (Updike), 1069
Beet Queen, The (Erdrich), 333
Being and Nothingness (Sartre), 393
Being There (Kosinski), 588
Bell for Adano, A (Hersey), 459
Bellarosa Connection, The (Bellow), 85
Bellefleur (Oates), 805
Bellow, Saul, **74-87**
Beloved (Morrison), 773
Bend Sinister (Nabokov), 781
Beowulf (Unknown), 393
Bernard Carr trilogy, The (Farrell), 343
Bernard Clare. *See* Bernard Carr
   trilogy, The
Beyond the Bedroom Wall (Woiwode),
   1143
Big Money, The (Dos Passos), 306
Big Rock Candy Mountain, The (Stegner),
   957

Big Sleep, The (Chandler), 173
"Big Two-Hearted River"
  (Hemingway), 446
Billy Bathgate (Doctorow), 287
Billy Budd, Foretopman (Melville), 733
Billy Phelan's Greatest Game (Kennedy),
  538
Bingo Palace, The (Erdrich), 335
Birds of America (McCarthy, M.), 655
Bless Me, Ultima (Anaya), 9
Blind Date (Kosinski), 589
Blithedale Romance, The (Hawthorne), 429
Blood Meridian (McCarthy, C.), 647
Blue Hammer, The (Macdonald), 674
Bluest Eye, The (Morrison), 766
Book of Common Prayer, A (Didion), 276
Book of Daniel, The (Doctorow), 284
Book of Lights, The (Potok), 863
Border trilogy (McCarthy, C.), 648
Born Brothers (Woiwode), 1145
Boston (Sinclair), 952
Bostonians, The (James), 510, 641
Bowles, Paul, **88-96**
Boyle, T. Coraghessan, **97-103**
Boys and Girls Together (Saroyan), 937
Bradbury, Ray, **104-114**
Brautigan, Richard, **115-120**
Brave New World (Huxley), 117
Breakfast at Tiffany's (Capote), 153
Breast, The (Roth), 914
Breathing Lessons (Tyler), 1056
Brewsie and Willie (Stein), 972
Bridge of San Luis Rey, The (Wilder),
  1134
Bridges at Toko-Ri, The (Michener), 739
Buccaneers, The (Wharton), 1129
Buck, Pearl S., **121-128**
Budding Prospects (Boyle), 99
Bullet Park (Cheever), 187
Burr (Vidal), 1077
Burroughs, William S., **129-138**
Bushwhacked Piano, The (McGuane), 679
By the Light of My Father's Smile
  (Walker), 1101

Cabala, The (Wilder), 1134
Cable, George Washington, **139-146**
Caine Mutiny, The (Wouk), 1162
Call of the Wild, The (London), 629

Cannibals and Missionaries
  (McCarthy, M.), 655
Capote, Truman, **147-156**
Caravans (Michener), 739
Carpenter's Gothic (Gaddis), 384
Carrie (King), 571
Catch-22 (Heller), 437
Catcher in the Rye, The (Salinger), 925
Cather, Willa, **157-167**
Cat's Cradle (Vonnegut), 1085
Caves of Steel, The (Asimov), 24
Celestial Navigation (Tyler), 1050
Centaur, The (Updike), 1063
Ceremony (Silko), 942
Ceremony in Lone Tree (Morris), 761
Chandler, Raymond, **168-179**, 411, 668
Charmed Life, A (McCarthy, M.), 653
Cheever, John, **180-192**
Chesapeake (Michener), 740
Chicago Loop (Theroux), 1031
Child of God (McCarthy, C.), 646
Childwold (Oates), 804
Chill, The (Macdonald), 672
Chilly Scenes of Winter (Beattie), 70
Chopin, Kate, **193-201**
Chosen, The (Potok), 860
Christine (King), 573
Christmas Carol, A (Dickens), 465
Cider House Rules, The (Irving), 495
Cities of the Plain. See Border trilogy
Cities of the Red Night (Burroughs), 135
City and the Pillar, The (Vidal), 1075
City Boy, The (Wouk), 1162
City of Illusions (Le Guin), 601
Clemens, Samuel Langhorne. *See*
  Twain, Mark
Clock Winder, The (Tyler), 1050
Clock Without Hands (McCullers), 666
Closing Time (Heller), 442
Color Purple, The (Walker), 1099
Comanche Moon (McMurtry), 694
Confederate General from Big Sur, A
  (Brautigan), 117
Confessions of Nat Turner, The (Styron),
  1015
*Cool Million: The Dismantling of Lemuel
  Pitkin, A* (West), 1118
Cooper, James Fenimore, **202-214**
Coover, Robert, **215-224**

Cosmic Rape, The (Sturgeon), 1002
Count of Monte-Cristo, The (Dumas), 189
Counterlife, The (Roth), 916
Country Doctor, A (Jewett), 519
Country of the Pointed Firs, The (Jewett), 521
Coup, The (Updike), 1068
Couples (Updike), 1067
Crane, Stephen, **225-233**
Creation (Vidal), 1077
Crossing, The. See Border trilogy
Crossing to Safety (Stegner), 960
Crying of Lot 49, The (Pynchon), 882
Cuba Libre (Leonard), 613
Custom of the Country, The (Wharton), 1128

Dain Curse, The (Hammett), 415
Daisy Miller (James), 507
Dandelion Wine (Bradbury), 111
Dangling Man (Bellow), 77
Dark Half, The (King), 577
Dark Laughter (Anderson), 20
Darwinism, 629
Davita's Harp (Potok), 863
Day of the Locust, The (West), 1119
Dead Man's Walk (McMurtry), 694
Dean's December, The (Bellow), 84
Death Comes for the Archbishop (Cather), 165
Death Is a Lonely Business (Bradbury), 112
Death of Ivan Ilyich, The (Tolstoy), 666
Deep Sleep, The (Morris), 759
Deephaven (Jewett), 518
Deer Park, The (Mailer), 704
Delany, Samuel R., **234-246**
DeLillo, Don, **247-255**
Deliverance (Dickey), 266
Delta Wedding (Welty), 1108
Democracy (Didion), 278
Destinies of Darcy Dancer, Gentleman, The (Donleavy), 296
Detective fiction, 411
Dhalgren (Delany), 240
Dharma Bums, The (Kerouac), 550
Dick, Philip K., **256-263**
Dickens, Charles, 348
Dickey, James, **264-269**

Didion, Joan, **270-281**
Dinner at the Homesick Restaurant (Tyler), 1054
Dispossessed, The (Le Guin), 243, 603
Do Androids Dream of Electric Sheep? (Dick), 260
Doctorow, E. L., **282-290**
Dodsworth (Lewis), 625
Dolores Claiborne (King), 578
Don Quixote de la Mancha (Cervantes), 723
Donleavy, J. P., **291-298**
Donleavy's Evolution in the 1980's (Donleavy), 296
Don't Stop the Carnival (Wouk), 1167
Doomsters, The (Macdonald), 670
Dos Passos, John, **299-307**
Dostoevski, Fyodor, 77
Dragon Seed (Buck), 127
Dream Life of Balso Snell, The (West), 1117
Dreaming Jewels, The (Sturgeon), 1000
Dred (Stowe), 991
Dreiser, Theodore, **308-318**
Duane's Depressed (McMurtry), 695
Dunne, John Gregory, 272

Earthly Possessions (Tyler), 1052
East and West (Cather), 161
East Is East (Boyle), 100
Education of Oscar Fairfax, The (Auchincloss), 37
Eight Cousins (Alcott), 5
1876 (Vidal), 1078
Eighth Day, The (Wilder), 1137
Electric Kool-Aid Acid Test, The (Wolfe), 553
Eliot, George, 988
Ellison, Ralph, **319-329**
Elmer Gantry (Lewis), 624
Embezzler, The (Auchincloss), 35
Empire (Vidal), 1078
Empire series (Asimov), 23
Empress of the Splendid Season (Hijuelos), 466
End of the Road, The (Barth), 59
End Zone (DeLillo), 248
Erdrich, Louise, **330-337**
Ethan Frome (Wharton), 1127

Executioner's Song, The (Mailer), 710
Existentialism, 88, 839
Expensive People (Oates), 803
Expressionism, 303
Eye in the Sky (Dick), 258

Face of Time, The. See
O'Neill-O'Flaherty series
Fahrenheit 451 (Bradbury), 110
Fairy Tale of New York, A (Donleavy), 295
Falconer (Cheever), 188
Falling in Place (Beattie), 70
Family Arsenal, The (Theroux), 1029
Fanshawe (Hawthorne), 425
Fantastic Voyage (Asimov), 25
Fantastic Voyage II (Asimov), 25
Farewell to Arms, A (Hemingway), 449
Farrell, James T., **338-344**
Father and Son. See O'Neill-O'Flaherty series
Faulkner, William, **345-364**, 559
Field of Vision, The (Morris), 761
Fifty-two Pickup (Leonard), 611
Financier, The (Dreiser), 314
Fitzgerald, F. Scott, **365-377**
Fitzgerald, Zelda, 367
Fixer, The (Malamud), 723
Flaming Corsage, The (Kennedy), 541
Flaubert, Gustave, 502
Flight to Canada (Reed), 900
Floating Opera, The (Barth), 57
Flow My Tears, the Policeman Said (Dick), 261
Fong and the Indians (Theroux), 1027
For Whom the Bell Tolls (Hemingway), 451
Foreign Affairs (Lurie), 637, 639
42nd Parallel, The (Dos Passos), 304
Foundation (Asimov), 24
Foundation and Empire (Asimov), 24
Foundation series (Asimov), 24
Fountainhead, The (Rand), 891
Four Ways to Forgiveness (Le Guin), 605
Fourteen Sisters of Emilio Montez O'Brien, The (Hijuelos), 465
Foxfire (Oates), 807
Freaky Deaky (Leonard), 612
Freddy's Book (Gardner), 398

Free-Lance Pallbearers, The (Reed), 898
Frolic of His Own, A (Gaddis), 385
From Here to Eternity (Jones), 530

Gaddis, William, **378-387**
Galápagos (Vonnegut), 1090
Galton Case, The (Macdonald), 670
Gardens in the Dunes (Silko), 943
Gardner, John, **388-402**
Generous Man, A (Price), 871
George's Mother (Crane), 228
Gerald's Game (King), 578
Gerald's Party (Coover), 222
Get Shorty (Leonard), 612
Ghost Town (Coover), 223
Ghost Writer, The (Roth), 915
Gift, The (Nabokov), 780
Gift of Asher Lev, The (Potok), 865
Giles Goat-Boy (Barth), 62
Ginger Man, The (Donleavy), 293
Glasgow, Ellen, **403-410**
Glass Key, The (Hammett), 416
Glory, The (Wouk), 1170
Go Down, Moses (Faulkner), 360
Go Tell It on the Mountain (Baldwin), 44
God Knows (Heller), 440
God's Grace (Malamud), 725
Gods Themselves, The (Asimov), 25
Going After Cacciato (O'Brien), 813
Good as Gold (Heller), 440
Good Earth, The (Buck), 125
Gospel According to the Son, The (Mailer), 714
Gothic novel, 904
Grandissimes, The (Cable), 143
Grapes of Wrath, The (Steinbeck), 262, 981
Grass Harp, The (Capote), 153
Graveyard for Lunatics, A (Bradbury), 112
Gravity's Rainbow (Pynchon), 883
Great Gatsby, The (Fitzgerald), 153, 373
Great Jones Street (DeLillo), 249
Green Shadows, White Whale (Bradbury), 112
Grendel (Gardner), 393
Group, The (McCarthy, M.), 654
Groves of Academe, The (McCarthy, M.), 653

Hammett, Dashiell, **411-419**, 668
Harlot's Ghost (Mailer), 713
Hawkline Monster, The (Brautigan), 118
Hawthorne, Nathaniel, **420-433**, 729
Hazard of New Fortunes, A (Howells), 474
Heart Is a Lonely Hunter, The (McCullers), 152, 662
Heart of Aztlán (Anaya), 10
Heart of Darkness (Conrad), 80
Heaven's My Destination (Wilder), 1135
Heller, Joseph, **434-443**
Hemingway, Ernest, 172, **444-454**, 610, 813
Henderson the Rain King (Bellow), 79
Hersey, John, **455-461**
Herzog (Bellow), 81
Hijuelos, Oscar, **462-466**
Hollywood (Vidal), 1078
Honorable Men (Auchincloss), 37
Hope, The (Wouk), 1170
Horror novel, 904
Horseman, Pass By (McMurtry), 688
Hotel New Hampshire, The (Irving), 494
House of Five Talents, The (Auchincloss), 31
House of Mirth, The (Wharton), 1126
House of the Prophet, The (Auchincloss), 36
House of the Seven Gables, The (Hawthorne), 427
Howells, William Dean, **467-476**
Huge Season, The (Morris), 760
Human Comedy, The (Saroyan), 934
Humboldt's Gift (Bellow), 83
Hundred Secret Senses, The (Tan), 1023
Hurston, Zora Neale, **477-484**, 1092

I Am the Clay (Potok), 865
I Married a Communist (Roth), 918
Ida, a Novel (Stein), 971
Ides of March, The (Wilder), 1136
If Morning Ever Comes (Tyler), 1047
Illustrated Man, The (Bradbury), 110
Imaginary Friends (Lurie), 642
In Cold Blood (Capote), 154
In Dubious Battle (Steinbeck), 979
In the Beginning (Potok), 862
In the Lake of the Woods (O'Brien), 813

In Watermelon Sugar (Brautigan), 117
Indian Affairs (Woiwode), 1145
Ink Truck, The (Kennedy), 536
Inside, Outside (Wouk), 1169
Interview with the Vampire. See Vampire Chronicles, The
Invisible Man (Ellison), 322
Iron Heel, The (London), 631
Ironweed (Kennedy), 539
Irving, John, **485-499**
It (King), 576

Jack and Jill (Alcott), 6
James, Henry, **500-514**
Japanese by Spring (Reed), 901
Jazz (Morrison), 773
Jennie Gerhardt (Dreiser), 313
Jewett, Sarah Orne, **515-525**
John's Wife (Coover), 223
Jonah's Gourd Vine (Hurston), 481
Jones, James, **526-534**
Jo's Boys (Alcott), 6
Joy Luck Club, The (Tan), 1021
Joyce, James, 292
JR (Gaddis), 383
Judgment Day. See Studs Lonigan: A Trilogy
Judgment of Paris, The (Vidal), 1075
Julian (Vidal), 1076
Jungle, The (Sinclair), 949
Just Above My Head (Baldwin), 48

Kate Vaiden (Price), 870
Keep the Change (McGuane), 683
Kendal-Mayfield saga (Price), 872
Kennedy, William, **535-542**
Kerouac, Jack, **543-552**
Kesey, Ken, **553-563**
Kierkegaard, Sören, 839
Killshot (Leonard), 612
Kincaid, Jamaica, **564-568**
King, Stephen, **569-582**
King Coal (Sinclair), 951
King, Queen, Knave (Nabokov), 779
Kitchen God's Wife, The (Tan), 1022
Kosinski, Jerzy, **583-591**
Kowloon Tong (Theroux), 1032
Kroeber, Theodora, 598

Ladder of Years (Tyler), 1057
Lancelot (Percy), 845
Lanny Budd series (Sinclair), 952
Lasher. See Mayfair Witches series
Last Days of Louisiana Red, The (Reed), 900
Last Gentleman, The (Percy), 843
Last Go Round (Kesey), 562
Last of the Mohicans, The (Cooper), 209
Last Picture Show, The (McMurtry), 688
Last Resort, The (Lurie), 638, 640
Last Thing He Wanted, The (Didion), 279
Last Voyage of Somebody the Sailor, The (Barth), 66
Laughing Matter, The (Saroyan), 936
Laughter in the Dark (Nabokov), 780
Lawd Today (Wright), 1176
Lee, Harper, **592-596**
Left Hand of Darkness, The (Le Guin), 602
Legs (Kennedy), 537
Le Guin, Ursula K., **597-607**
Leonard, Elmore, **608-614**
Let It Come Down (Bowles), 92
Letters (Barth), 64
Letting Go (Roth), 912
Lewis, Sinclair, **615-626**
Libra (DeLillo), 252
Lie Down in Darkness (Styron), 1012
Light in August (Faulkner), 354
Lincoln (Vidal), 1078
Linden Hills (Naylor), 788
Little Men (Alcott), 5
Little Women (Alcott), 3
Little Women, Part 2 (Alcott), 4
Live from Golgotha (Vidal), 1079
Local colorists, 515
Lockwood Concern, The (O'Hara), 834
Lolita (Nabokov), 782
London, Jack, **627-634**
Lonesome Dove (McMurtry), 691
Long and Happy Life, A (Price), 871
Long Dream, The (Wright), 1180
Long Goodbye, The (Chandler), 176
Long March, The (Styron), 1013
Look Homeward, Angel (Wolfe, Thomas), 1152
Loon Lake (Doctorow), 286
Losing Battles (Welty), 1110

Lost Lady, A (Cather), 164
Love Always (Beattie), 71
Love Among the Cannibals (Morris), 760
Love and Friendship (Lurie), 636, 638
Love and Work (Price), 870
Love in the Ruins (Percy), 844
Love Medicine (Erdrich), 332
Love's Pilgrimage (Sinclair), 950
Lucky Starr series (Asimov), 24
Lucy (Kincaid), 567
Lucy Church Amiably (Stein), 971
Lucy Gayheart (Cather), 163
Lurie, Alison, **635-643**

McCarthy, Cormac, **644-649**
McCarthy, Mary, **650-657**
McCullers, Carson, 152, **658-667**
Macdonald, Ross, **668-676**
McGuane, Thomas, **677-685**
McMurtry, Larry, **686-696**
McTeague (Norris), 797
Madame Bovary (Flaubert), 198
Madame Delphine (Cable), 144
Maggie (Crane), 227
Mailer, Norman, **697-715**
Main Street (Lewis), 619
Making of Americans, The (Stein), 970
Malamud, Bernard, **716-726**
Maltese Falcon, The (Hammett), 415
Mama Day (Naylor), 789
Mambo Kings Play Songs of Love, The (Hijuelos), 464
Man and Boy (Morris), 758
Man in the High Castle, The (Dick), 259
Man Who Was There, The (Morris), 758
Manassas (Sinclair), 948
Manhattan Transfer (Dos Passos), 303
Many Marriages (Anderson), 20
Mao II (DeLillo), 253
Marble Faun, The (Hawthorne), 430
Marching Men (Anderson), 17
Marilyn (Mailer), 710
Marjorie Morningstar (Wouk), 1164
Marquand, J. P., 30
Marry Me (Updike), 1066
Martian Chronicles, The (Bradbury), 109
Martian Time-Slip (Dick), 260
Martin Eden (London), 632
Mary (Nabokov), 779

Mason and Dixon (Pynchon), 885
Maximum Bob (Leonard), 613
Mayfair Witches series (Rice), 907
Melville, Herman, **727-735**
Member of the Wedding, The (McCullers), 665
Memnoch the Devil. See Vampire Chronicles, The
Men of Brewster Place, The (Naylor), 791
Meridian (Walker), 1097
Messiah (Vidal), 1076
Metafiction, 218
Metropolis, The (Sinclair), 950
Mexico (Michener), 742
Michener, James A., **736-744**
Mickelsson's Ghosts (Gardner), 399
Millar, Kenneth. *See* Macdonald, Ross
Miller, Henry, 293, **745-753**
Millroy the Magician (Theroux), 1031
Minister's Wooing, The (Stowe), 992
Miracle in Seville (Michener), 743
Misery (King), 577
Miss Lonelyhearts (West), 1117
Moby Dick (Melville), 731
Modern Instance, A (Howells), 471
Modern Mephistopheles, A (Alcott), 6
Modernism, 77, 967
Moneychangers, The (Sinclair), 950
Month of Sundays, A (Updike), 1068
Moods (Alcott), 2
Moran of the Lady Letty (Norris), 798
More Die of Heartbreak (Bellow), 85
More Than Human (Sturgeon), 1001
Morris, Wright, **754-764**
Morrison, Toni, **765-775**
Moses, Man of the Mountain (Hurston), 481
Mosquito Coast, The (Theroux), 1030
Mother, The (Buck), 126
Mother Night (Vonnegut), 1084
Moviegoer, The (Percy), 841
Mr. Ives' Christmas (Hijuelos), 465
Mr. Sammler's Planet (Bellow), 82
Mumbo Jumbo (Reed), 899
My Ántonia (Cather), 163
My Days of Anger. See O'Neill-O'Flaherty series
My Heart Laid Bare (Oates), 808

My Life, Starring Dara Falcon (Beattie), 72
My Name Is Aram (Saroyan), 934
My Name Is Asher Lev (Potok), 861
My Other Life (Theroux), 1031
My Secret History (Theroux), 1031
My Uncle Dudley (Morris), 757
My Wife and I (Stowe), 995
Myra Breckinridge (Vidal), 1079
Mysteries of Winterthurn (Oates), 806
Myth (Delany), 239

Nabokov, Vladimir, **776-784**
Naked and the Dead, The (Mailer), 700
Naked Lunch (Burroughs), 133
Naked Sun, The (Asimov), 24
Names, The (DeLillo), 251
Native Son (Wright), 1177
Natural, The (Malamud), 718, 720
Naturalism, 629, 793, 948
Naylor, Gloria, **785-792**
New Life, A (Malamud), 718
Nickel Mountain (Gardner), 395
"Nightfall" (Asimov), 25
1919 (Dos Passos), 305
Ninety-two in the Shade (McGuane), 679
No Star Is Lost. See O'Neill-O'Flaherty series
Nobody's Angel (McGuane), 680
Nonfiction novel, 311, 455
Noon Wine (Porter), 853
Norris, Frank, **793-800**
Notes from the Underground (Dostoevski), 550
Nothing but Blue Skies (McGuane), 683
Nova Express (Burroughs), 133-134
Nowhere City, The (Lurie), 637, 639

O Pioneers! (Cather), 162
O-Zone (Theroux), 1030
Oasis, The (McCarthy, M.), 652
Oates, Joyce Carol, **801-810**
O'Brien, Tim, **811-815**
O'Connor, Flannery, **816-823**, 1054
October Light (Gardner), 397
Octopus, The (Norris), 799
Of Mice and Men (Steinbeck), 980
Of the Farm (Updike), 1064
Of Time and the River (Wolfe), 1154

Oh What a Paradise It Seems (Cheever), 190
O'Hara, John, **824-836**
Oil! A Novel (Sinclair), 952
Old-Fashioned Girl, An (Alcott), 4
Old Man and the Sea, The (Hemingway), 452
Old Mortality (Porter), 852
Oldtown Folks (Stowe), 993
Omoo (Melville), 730
On the Road (Kerouac), 547
Once upon a Time (Barth), 67
One Flew over the Cuckoo's Nest (Kesey), 558
158-Pound Marriage, The (Irving), 491
One of Ours (Cather), 164
O'Neill-O'Flaherty series, 341
Onion Eaters, The (Donleavy), 295
Only Children (Lurie), 637
Optimist's Daughter, The (Welty), 1112
Orchard Keeper, The (McCarthy, C.), 646
Origin of the Brunists, The (Coover), 218
O'Ruddy, The (Crane), 232
Other Voices, Other Rooms (Capote), 151
Our House in the Last World (Hijuelos), 463
Outer Dark (McCarthy, C.), 646
Outsider, The (Wright), 1179

Painted Bird, The (Kosinski), 585
Pale Fire (Nabokov), 783
Pale Horse, Pale Rider (Porter), 854
Palimpsest and Web (Delany), 239
Panama (McGuane), 680
Paradise (Morrison), 774
Patchwork Planet, A (Tyler), 1057
Pearl, The (Steinbeck), 982
Pebble in the Sky (Asimov), 23
Penultimate Truth, The (Dick), 259
People, The (Malamud), 725
Percy, Walker, **837-849**
Persons, Truman Streckfus. *See* Capote, Truman
Pet Sematary (King), 575
Picaresque, 935
Picture Palace (Theroux), 1030
Picture This (Heller), 441
Picturing Will (Beattie), 71
Pioneers, The (Cooper), 206

Pit, The (Norris), 799
Place of Dead Roads, The (Burroughs), 135
Plains Song, for Female Voices (Morris), 762
Play It as It Lays (Didion), 275
Player Piano (Vonnegut), 1084
Poganuc People (Stowe), 995
Poland (Michener), 742
Ponder Heart, The (Welty), 1109
Poor White (Anderson), 19
Poorhouse Fair, The (Updike), 1062
Poppa John (Woiwode), 1144
Porter, Katherine Anne, **850-857**
Portrait in Brownstone (Auchincloss), 32
Portrait of a Lady, The (James), 508
Possessing the Secret of Joy (Walker), 1101
Postmodernism, 816
Potok, Chaim, **858-866**
Prague Orgy, The (Roth), 916
Prairie, The (Cooper), 211
Prayer for Owen Meany, A (Irving), 496
Price, Reynolds, **867-877**, 1043
Prince and the Pauper, The (Twain), 1038
Professor's House, The (Cather), 165
Promise, The (Potok), 860
Promise of Rest, The (Price), 875
Pronto (Leonard), 613
Psychological realism, 501, 727
Public Burning, The (Coover), 220
Pynchon, Thomas, 247, **878-888**

Queen of the Damned, The. See Vampire Chronicles, The
Quinn's Book (Kennedy), 540
Quod Erat Demonstrandum (Stein), 969

Rabbit at Rest (Updike), 1065
Rabbit Is Rich (Updike), 1065
Rabbit Redux (Updike), 1065
Rabbit, Run (Updike), 1064
Ragtime (Doctorow), 284
Rand, Ayn, **889-893**
Ratner's Star (DeLillo), 250
Real Life of Sebastian Knight, The (Nabokov), 781
Real People (Lurie), 637
Realism, 467, 985
Recapitulation (Stegner), 959

Reckless Eyeballing (Reed), 901
Recognitions, The (Gaddis), 381
Rector of Justin, The (Auchincloss), 33
Red Badge of Courage, The (Crane), 229
Red Harvest (Hammett), 414
Red Pony, The (Steinbeck), 980
Reed, Ishmael, **894-903**
Reef, The (Wharton), 1128
Reflections in a Golden Eye (McCullers),
  663
Resurrection, The (Gardner), 391
Rice, Anne, **904-908**
Rise of Silas Lapham, The (Howells), 472
Riven Rock (Boyle), 101
Road Between, The. See Bernard Carr
  trilogy
Road to Wellville, The (Boyle), 101
Robber Bridegroom, The (Welty), 1108
Robot series (Asimov), 24
Robots and Empire (Asimov), 24
Robots of Dawn, The (Asimov), 24
Rocannon's World (Le Guin), 600
Rock Wagram (Saroyan), 935
Roger's Version (Updike), 1068
Romantic Comedians, The (Glasgow), 408
Romanticism, 1039
Roth, Philip, **909-919**
Run River (Didion), 273

S. (Updike), 1068
Sabbath's Theater (Roth), 917
Sabbatical (Barth), 65
Saddest Summer of Samuel S, The
  (Donleavy), 294
Sailor Song (Kesey), 561
Saint Jack (Theroux), 1028
Saint Maybe (Tyler), 1056
'Salem's Lot (King), 572
Salinger, J. D., **920-928**
Sanctuary (Faulkner), 353
Saroyan, William, **929-939**
Scarlet Letter, The (Hawthorne), 426,
  1069
Schultz (Donleavy), 296
Science fiction, 234, 256
Sea-Wolf, The (London), 630
Searching for Caleb (Tyler), 1051
Second Coming, The (Percy), 846
Second Foundation (Asimov), 24

Sedges, John. *See* Buck, Pearl S.
Seize the Day (Bellow), 78
Seraph on the Suwanee (Hurston), 481
Sermons and Soda Water (O'Hara), 833
Set This House on Fire (Styron), 1014
Setting Free the Bears (Irving), 489
Shadows on the Rock (Cather), 166
Sheltered Life, The (Glasgow), 409
Sheltering Sky, The (Bowles), 91
Shining, The (King), 573
Ship of Fools (Porter), 855
Silko, Leslie Marmon, **940-944**
Sinclair, Upton, **945-954**
Singular Man, A (Donleavy), 294
Sirin, V. *See* Nabokov, Vladimir
Sister Carrie (Dreiser), 311
Slaughterhouse-Five (Vonnegut), 1087
Slipping-Down Life, A (Tyler), 1049
Smithsonian Institution, The (Vidal), 1080
So the Wind Won't Blow It All Away
  (Brautigan), 119
Soft Machine, The (Burroughs), 134
Solar Lottery (Dick), 258
Some Can Whistle (McMurtry), 691
Something Happened (Heller), 439
Something to Be Desired (McGuane), 681
Something Wicked This Way Comes
  (Bradbury), 111
Sometimes a Great Notion (Kesey), 559
Son of the Circus, A (Irving), 497
Song of Solomon (Morrison), 768
Song of the Lark, The (Cather), 162
Sophie's Choice (Styron), 1017
Sot-Weed Factor, The (Barth), 60
Sound and the Fury, The (Faulkner), 349
Source of Light, The (Price), 874
Space (Michener), 741
Spider's House, The (Bowles), 93
Sporting Club, The (McGuane), 678
Stars in My Pocket Like Grains of Sand
  (Delany), 243
Stegner, Wallace, **955-962**
Stein, Gertrude, 90, **963-974**
Steinbeck, John, **975-984**
Steps (Kosinski), 587
"Stillness" and "Shadows" (Gardner with
  Delbanco), 400
Stowe, Harriet Beecher, **985-996**
Streets of Laredo (McMurtry), 694

Studs Lonigan: A Trilogy (Farrell), 340
Sturgeon, Theodore, **997-1005**
Styron, William, **1006-1019**
Subterraneans, The (Kerouac), 549
Sula (Morrison), 767
Summer (Wharton), 1127
Sun Also Rises, The (Hemingway), 447
Sunlight Dialogues, The (Gardner), 394
Surface of Earth, The (Price), 873
Suttree (McCarthy, C.), 647
Swag (Leonard), 611
Swift, Jonathan, 129
Synthetic Man. See Dreaming Jewels, The

Tale of the Body Thief, The. See Vampire
    Chronicles, The
Tales of the South Pacific (Michener), 738
Taltos. See Mayfair Witches series
Tan, Amy, **1020-1024**
Taoism, 600
Tar Baby (Morrison), 771
Tehanu (Le Guin), 605
Ten North Frederick (O'Hara), 831
Tender Is the Night (Fitzgerald), 375
Terrible Threes, The (Reed), 901
Terrible Twos, The (Reed), 901
Texas (Michener), 742
Texasville (McMurtry), 689
Thanatos Syndrome, The (Percy), 847
That Darcy, That Dancer, That Gentleman
    (Donleavy), 297
Theft, A (Bellow), 85
Their Eyes Were Watching God (Hurston),
    483
Theophilus North (Wilder), 1137
Theroux, Paul, **1025-1032**
They Fly at Çiron (Delany), 244
Thin Man, The (Hammett), 417
Thin Red Line, The (Jones), 531
Third Life of Grange Copeland, The
    (Walker), 1095
Third Violet, The (Crane), 230
This Side of Paradise (Fitzgerald), 370
Three Lives (Stein), 969
Three Soldiers (Dos Passos), 302
Three Stigmata of Palmer Eldritch, The
    (Dick), 260
Ticket That Exploded, The (Burroughs),
    133-134

Tidewater Tales, The (Barth), 66
Time out of Joint (Dick), 259
Timequake (Vonnegut), 1090
Tin Can Tree, The (Tyler), 1048
To Kill a Mockingbird (Lee), 593
Tombs of Atuan, The (Le Guin), 605
Tomcat in Love (O'Brien), 814
Tongues of Angels, The (Price), 874
Tortuga (Anaya), 11
Tory Lover, The (Jewett), 523
Tough Guys Don't Dance (Mailer), 713
Toward the End of Time (Updike), 1069
Town and the City, The (Kerouac), 546
Tracks (Erdrich), 334
Tragedy of Pudd'nhead Wilson, The
    (Twain), 1041
Triton (Delany), 242
Tropic of Cancer (Miller), 749
Tropic of Capricorn (Miller), 750
Trout Fishing in America (Brautigan), 119
Truth About Lorin Jones, The (Lurie),
    638, 640
Twain, Mark, **1033-1042**
Tyler, Anne, **1043-1058**
Typee (Melville), 730

Ubik (Dick), 260
Uncle Tom's Cabin (Stowe), 989
Underground Man, The (Macdonald), 673
Underworld (DeLillo), 253
Universal Baseball Association, Inc.
    J. Henry Waugh, Prop., The (Coover),
    219
Up Above the World (Bowles), 93
Updike, John, **1059-1071**
U.S.A. (Dos Passos), 304

V. (Pynchon), 880
Valis (Dick), 262
Valley of the Moon, The (London), 633
Vampire Chronicles, The (Rice), 905
Vampire Lestat, The. See Vampire
    Chronicles, The
Vandover and the Brute (Norris), 796
Venus Plus X (Sturgeon), 1002
Very Old Bones (Kennedy), 540
Victim, The (Bellow), 77
Vidal, Gore, **1072-1081**
Vineland (Pynchon), 885

Violent Bear It Away, The (O'Connor), 820
Virginia (Glasgow), 406
Vonnegut, Kurt, Jr., **1082-1091**

Walker, Alice, **1092-1102**
Wall, The (Hersey), 460
Wapshot Chronicle, The (Cheever), 184
Wapshot Scandal, The (Cheever), 185
War and Remembrance (Wouk), 1167
War Between the Tates, The (Lurie), 637, 639
Washington, D.C. (Vidal), 1078
Water-Method Man, The (Irving), 490
Water Music (Boyle), 98
Waterworks, The (Doctorow), 289
We and Our Neighbors (Stowe), 995
Web and the Rock, The (Wolfe), 1155
Weinstein, Nathan. *See* West, Nathanael
Welcome to Hard Times (Doctorow), 283
Welty, Eudora, **1103-1113**
West, Nathanael, **1114-1120**
Western, 282, 957
Western Lands, The (Burroughs), 136
Wharton, Edith, **1121-1131**
What I Lived For (Oates), 807
What I'm Going to Do, I Think (Woiwode), 1142
Whistle (Jones), 532
White Fang (London), 631
White Noise (DeLillo), 251
Why Are We in Vietnam? (Mailer), 707
Widow for One Year, A (Irving), 498
Wild Boys, The (Burroughs), 135
Wilder, Thornton, **1132-1139**
Winds of War, The (Wouk), 1167
Windy McPherson's Son (Anderson), 16
Winesburg, Ohio (Anderson), 17
Wise Blood (O'Connor), 819

Witches of Eastwick, The (Updike), 1067
Witching Hour, The. See Mayfair Witches series
With Shuddering Fall (Oates), 803
Wizard of Earthsea, A (Le Guin), 604
Woiwode, Larry, **1140-1147**
Wolfe, Thomas, **1148-1158**
Woman of Andros, The (Wilder), 1135
Women of Brewster Place, The (Naylor), 787
Wonderland (Oates), 804
Work (Alcott), 5
Works of Love, The (Morris), 759
World According to Garp, The (Irving), 492
World I Never Made, A. See O'Neill-O'Flaherty series
World Is Round, The (Stein), 971
World's End (Boyle), 99
World's Fair (Doctorow), 286
Wouk, Herman, **1159-1172**
Wreckage of Agathon, The (Gardner), 392
Wright, Richard, 319, **1173-1182**
Wrong Information Is Being Given out at Princeton (Donleavy), 297

Yellow Back Radio Broke-Down (Reed), 899
Yet Other Waters. See Bernard Carr trilogy
You Can't Go Home Again (Wolfe), 1156
Young Lonigan. See Studs Lonigan: A Trilogy
Young Manhood of Studs Lonigan, The. See Studs Lonigan: A Trilogy
Youngblood Hawke (Wouk), 1166

Zebra-Striped Hearse, The (Macdonald), 671
Zuckerman Unbound (Roth), 915